FRENCH HISTORY SINCE NAPOLEON

Edited by

MARTIN S. ALEXANDER

Professor of Contemporary History and Politics,
University of Salford

A member of the Hodder Headline Group
LONDON • SYDNEY • AUCKLAND
Co-published in the United States of America by
Oxford University Press Inc., New York

To the memory of my father, David Harold Alexander
(1928–1993)

First published in Great Britain in 1999 by
Arnold, a member of the Hodder Headline Group
338 Euston Road, London NW1 3BH

http://www.arnoldpublishers.com

Co-published in the United States of America by
Oxford University Press Inc.,
198 Madison Avenue, New York, NY 10016

British Library Cataloguing in Publication Data
A catalogue record for this book is available from the British Library.

Library of Congress Cataloging-in-Publication Data
A Catalog record for this book is available from the Library of Congress

ISBN 0 340 67732 5 (hb)
ISBN 0 340 67731 7 (pb)

1 2 3 4 5 6 7 8 9 10

Production Editor: Wendy Rooke
Production Controller: Sarah Kett
Cover Design: Terry Griffiths

Typeset in 10/12 pt Sabon by York House Typographic Ltd, Ealing
Printed and bound in Great Britain by MPG Books Ltd, Bodmin, Cornwall

What do you think about this book? Or any other Arnold title?
Please send your comments to feedback.arnold@hodder.co.uk

Contents

Figures

Maps

Illustrations

Tables

Notes on contributors

Martin S. Alexander is Professor of Contemporary History and Politics in the European Studies Research Institute at the University of Salford and was a John M. Olin Fellow at Yale University in 1988–9. He has written *The Republic in Danger: General Maurice Gamelin and the Politics of French Defence, 1933–1939* (1993) and, with Helen Graham, has co-edited *The French and Spanish Popular Fronts* (1989).

Nicholas Atkin is Lecturer in History at the University of Reading. He is the author of *Church and Schools in Vichy France, 1940–1944* (1991) and *Pétain* (1998), and is joint editor, with Frank Tallett, of *Religion, Society and Politics in France since 1789* (1991), *Catholicism in Britain and France since 1789* (1995) and *The Right in France, 1789–1997* (1998).

Vicki Caron is Thomas and Diann Mann Professor of Modern Jewish Studies at Cornell University, Ithaca, New York. She formerly taught at Brown University and was a visiting fellow at the Oxford Centre for Postgraduate Hebrew Studies in 1997. She has published *Between France and Germany: The Jews of Alsace-Lorraine, 1871–1918* (1987) and *Uneasy Asylum: France and the Jewish Refugee Crisis, 1933–42* (1999).

Martin Evans is Lecturer in French and European Studies at the University of Portsmouth. He is author of *The Memory of Resistance: French Opposition to the Algerian War, 1954–62* and co-editor (with Ken Lunn) of *War and Memory in the Twentieth Century* (both published in 1997).

Alan Forrest studied with Richard Cobb at Oxford and has been Professor of Modern History at the University of York since 1989. His publications include: *Society and Politics in Revolutionary Bordeaux* (1975); *The French Revolution and the Poor* (1981); *Conscripts and Deserters: The Army and French Society during the Revolution and Empire* (1989); *The Soldiers of the French Revolution* (1990); *The French Revolution* (1995); and *The Revolution in Provincial France: Aquitaine, 1789–1799* (1996).

Colin Heywood is Senior Lecturer in Economic and Social History at the University of Nottingham. He has written *Childhood in Nineteenth-Century France* (1988), *The Development of the French Economy, 1750–1914* (1992) and various shorter works on nineteenth-century France and Europe. He is currently working on a history of childhood and a history of popular movements in the town of Troyes.

Julian Jackson is Reader in History at the University of Wales, Swansea. He is author of *The Popular Front in France: Defending Democracy* (1988) and *The Politics of Depression in France, 1932–1936* (1986). He is currently writing a book on Vichy France, 1940–4, and a history of France since 1914.

Jeremy Jennings is Professor of Political Theory in the Department of Political Science and International Studies, University of Birmingham. He has written *Syndicalism in France: A Study of Ideas* (1990) and *Georges Sorel: The Character and Development of His Thought* (1985) and has edited *Intellectuals in Twentieth-Century France* (1993).

J. F. V. Keiger is Professor of International History in the European Studies Research Institute, University of Salford. He is the author of *France and the Origins of the First World War* (1983); *Raymond Poincaré* (1997); and *France and the World since 1870* (2000).

Maurice Larkin was Richard Pares Professor of History at the University of Edinburgh and is the author of *France since the Popular Front, 1936–1996* (2nd edn. 1997), *Religion, Politics and Preferment in France since 1890: La Belle Epoque and its Legacy* (1995), and *Church and State after the Dreyfus Affair: The Separation Issue in France* (1974).

Roger Magraw is Senior Lecturer in the Department of History at the University of Warwick. He is author of *France, 1815–1914: The Bourgeois Century* (1983) and a two-volume *History of the French Working Class* (1992).

Susan Milner is Senior Lecturer in European Studies at the University of Bath. Her publications include *The Dilemmas of Internationalism: French Syndicalism and the International Labour Movement (1900–1914)* (1990) and several articles and book chapters on the French labour movement in the twentieth century. Current research interests include the role of the labour movement in economic and social policy-making and the regulation of working time.

Kenneth Mouré is Professor of History at the University of California, Santa Barbara and author of *Managing the Franc Poincaré. Economic Understanding and Political Constraint in French Monetary Policy, 1928–1936* (1991). He is co-editor, with Martin S. Alexander, of *France since the First World War: Crises and Renewal* (2000), and is completing a book on the gold standard between the two world wars.

Pamela Pilbeam is Professor of French History at Royal Holloway and Bedford New College, University of London. Her recent publications include *Republicanism in Nineteenth-Century France, 1814–1871* (1995) and *The 1830 Revolution in France* (1994). She is currently completing a book on the early socialists in France.

Charles Rearick is Professor of History at the University of Massachusetts, Amherst. He is the author of *Pleasures of the Belle Epoque: Entertainment and Festivity in Turn-of-the-Century France* and *The French in Love and War: Popular Culture in the Era of the World Wars* (1986 and 1997 respectively).

Siân Reynolds is Professor of French at the University of Stirling. She is the author of *France between the Wars: Gender and Politics* (1996), editor of *Women, State and Revolution: Essays on Power and Gender in Europe since 1789* (1986) and translator of Fernand Braudel's *The Identity of France* (1988).

Robert Tombs is a fellow of St John's College, Cambridge. He has written *The Paris Commune, 1871* (1999); *France, 1814–1914* (1996), *The War against Paris, 1871* (1981) and *Thiers, 1797–1877: A Political Life* (with J. P. T. Bury, 1986), and is editor of *Nationhood and Nationalism in France from Boulangism to the Great War, 1889–1918* (1991).

Acknowledgements

A book such as this is a collective endeavour – and not just in the obvious sense of being the work of a team of historians. To them, I am grateful for cooperation and patience in what has been a lengthy gestation. The enterprise was only completed, however, because of much hard work and dedication 'behind the scenes'. I wish especially to thank the European Studies Research Institute at the University of Salford for financial support, and to acknowledge the secretarial help provided by Wendy Pickles and Louise Graham of the Institute, by Kath Capper and Lesley Harris of the Department of Politics and Contemporary History, and by Tamsin Greaves and Ann-Marie Lowe. Each of them, more than once, also provided crucial 'emergency services' to pull me from the clutches of jammed photocopiers, recalcitrant computers and temperamental fax machines.

Anyone would be fortunate to have so supportive and tolerant a publisher as Christopher Wheeler, at Arnold. He, and his colleagues Elena Seymenliyska and Emma Heyworth-Dunn, have been unfailingly enthusiastic and forgiving of the delays that attended the manuscript's preparation.

I owe particular thanks to Joan Tumblety of the Department of History, University of Southampton. At short notice she gave time to share some of her own work with me and assist my grasp of recent trends in gender history and the study of constructions of identity. Several historians discussed the book's themes with me, offering ideas and insights. They may spot their suggestions in my introductory chapter. I hope none will feel traduced; any errors that may have crept in are my responsibility.

A great pleasure with this book was the opportunity it provided to write once again with my friend and colleague at Salford, John Keiger. It was, however, perhaps as well that 1998 was cursed with one of the rainiest Augusts on record – for if the sun had shone I think Vicky, Emma, Laura and Edward would have lynched me for making John pore over our computer screen rather than pour drinks in the garden. Partners, of course, are always the hidden heroes behind a book. My chief debt, again, is to Rosalie, my wife.

Save only for the writing, she lent a hand with every part of the project. Our telephone bills suggest she now probably knows many of the contributors better than I do.

Martin S. Alexander
Salford, January 1999

Introduction
Historians and the peculiarities of French history

MARTIN S. ALEXANDER

In an article in the late 1950s, early in the life of the journal of America's newly founded Society for French Historical Studies, David Pinkney doubted that 'Anglo-Saxon' historians could feasibly 'do' French history. At any rate, he questioned whether they could do 'oven-to-table' history, rich and satisfying, high on empirical calories and spiced with appetizing and novel interpretations, their books serving as hot platters to bring work straight from the archive to the reader. The physical distance from France of anglophone historians, most of them based in United States and Canadian universities, was, for Pinkney, an insuperable obstacle to the serving of such intellectual fare. This view was repeated in the 1980s, as if to confirm Pinkney's bleak prognostication, by Fernand Braudel, latter-day doyen of the French *Annales* school of historians of economy, society and mentalities. Braudel believed that historians could really work on an equal footing only with the history of their own country, deploying the instinctive or ingrained affinity that he felt everyone possessed for their land's past twists and turns, complexities, foibles and singularities. Never could the historian 'enjoy the same advantages, however great his learning, when he pitches his camp elsewhere'. The present book's authors have, however imprudently, forged ahead and disregarded this 'no doubt well-intentioned warning to would-be trespassers' (as Richard Cobb put it in a review of Braudel's *The Identity of France*).

It is true, of course, that scholars require a daunting amount of time with French sources to produce books based on detailed, extensive research. The practical obstacles to investigating the record of France's recent past can be large. French state bureaucracy, innately prone even in the nineteenth century to generating and maintaining files, found its opportunities – not to say paperwork – multiplying with the advent of the typewriter and the carbon copy in the twentieth. Lavish spending on archives never heads any party's electoral manifesto; unsurprisingly, therefore, repositories are often Aladdin's caves, stuffed to bursting with unsorted boxes.

Most time-constrained foreign historians have a tale to tell of a vital archival breakthrough achieved with help of an over-stretched French *conservateur*. But kindness cannot always make up for a want of inventories to permit holdings to be explored systematically. As one reviewer remarked sympathetically of a work on the rebuilding of northern France after 1918: 'the story of [...] French reconstruction [...] can only be incomplete. Many questions must remain unanswered due to the absence of ministerial records', departmental archives offering little recourse 'because floor-to-ceiling documents remain uncatalogued'.[1] A variation on this is recounted by Robert O. Paxton, the eminent American historian of the collaborationist Vichy regime of 1940–4, in his book on Henry Dorgères and French peasant fascism from 1929 to 1939. He tells how:

> My search for Dorgères and his movement in departmental archives across northern and western France was a frustrating one. I did not know when I began [...] how hard it would be to find material in French archives, public or private, concerning how previously inarticulate small farmers gathered and expressed their grievances in the 1930s [...] The Dorgérist movement itself left almost no documents, except its newspapers. The authentic farmers who ran it lived in an oral culture, in explicit rejection of the written culture of the French republican school system and bureaucracy [...] small farmers were indeed the disinherited of the Third Republic, neither listened to nor understood by public authorities.[2]

The lesson is instructive. It reminds us of the powerful urge to control and impose order that has suffused French regimes since the Jacobins, Robespierre and Danton, of the early 1790s – and how this has kept most central records cheek-by-jowl in Paris. This authoritarian, controlling instinct itself offers a rich theme for historical reflection. In the context of Paxton's frustrations, it underlines how the Revolution and Napoleon metaphorically and almost literally located Paris at the centre of the universe. This assisted research in French history – but also guaranteed that a disproportionate amount of that history would be written from the centre or 'from the inside out'. Problems for scholars increase immediately if they attempt bottom-up and 'outside-in' studies of regional, local and comparative history. Even the prefects, sub-prefects and police, local agents of the state and prime source for its records, had paid little heed to interwar grass-roots peasant organization. They had, on the other hand, maintained close surveillance of urban agitators. This says much, remarks Paxton, about mid-twentieth-century French republican bureaucrats. These had neither the training nor the temperament to monitor the protests of communities that possessed a voice, but lacked a literature. Given these difficulties, how much harder can be the task of the visiting scholar with limited time and money, attempting a book on regional religious observance in the 1790s or the 'subterranean' cultures of immigrant *bidonvilles* (shanty-towns) two centuries later.

Few non-French historians – except the unique Richard Cobb, almost an honorary Frenchman in the 1940s and 1950s before he secured a permanent university post in Britain – can match their Gallic counterparts' extended toil in the archives. The former have to produce doctoral theses in about 3 years or a book from a 12-month sabbatical. This, argued Pinkney, made for an insurmountable hurdle to Britons or Americans producing a convincingly grounded and thus persuasive treatment of any topic of French history. Pinkney's scepticism was reinforced by the factors that ordered the French history profession until the reforms of the late-1980s. Ordinarily a French academic 'apprenticeship' involved pursuing a gargantuan research project, of 10 or 15 years' duration. The outcome, typically, was a thesis submitted for the 'old-style' French doctorate of letters, in half-a-dozen volumes each as long as a whole British or North American Ph.D. dissertation. The French one was meant to be a complete, comprehensive, monumental treatment of its subject. Not surprisingly, the task could exhaust the author. Some French historians after giving birth to their academic equivalent of a baby elephant were too tired to produce any other significant work in the remainder of their careers.

Pinkney recommended that Britons and North Americans should not try to compete with this 'French model' of professional development, with its faith that one could produce 'definitive works' and write the 'last word' on a subject, and its daunting productionist ethic. They ought instead to quarry out the small nuggets glistening in the rich seams of French historical controversies. They might investigate unexamined but modest-sized documentary collections and shed new light on subjects not fully illuminated by the French. Anglo-Saxons were advised to practise the art of the possible – to be content with modest, creeping advances to an understanding of France that would mostly have to come from the French. For the rest, they should write works of synthesis, superior textbooks. This, interestingly, was almost the opposite to Braudel's view. It proposed not that foreigners could not comprehend the history and culture of other peoples, but that they might, thanks to their greater physical and imaginary distance or 'detachment', get to the essence of French theses and the only slightly abridged books they spawned.

French production of history, like French costume and clothing, was high art and craft. French creations might be the avant-garde; but Anglo-Saxons could play mass retailer. They could provide readers of history with a series of accessible off-the-peg versions of the Coco Chanels and Yves Saint-Laurents of the French academic masters – London and New York bringing *haute-couture* history, as it were, to the British and American high street. Anglo-Saxons could transform and commodify the inaccessible fabrications of French historians into elegant little numbers at a readable length and affordable price for a wider monolingual and/or student market. The role for Anglo-Americans was, then, to be not the creator of French history as such – but to be its importers, its agents of access and transmission. They would expand the understanding of France's past by synthesis and simplification. Doing this could enhance French colleagues' work, but not by vainly striving to write primary-documented items 'made in Britain' or 'made in the USA'.

What became of this supposed dichotomy between the Anglo-Saxon and Gallic approaches, and possibilities, for the writing of French history? From a late-1990s perspective, it appears that Pinkney was unduly pessimistic. Indeed, for some observers at the twentieth century's end, it was in France that the writing and reading of history was felt to be 'in crisis'. From about 1995, numerous symposia and books sought to 'establish an intellectual inventory of the profession' (in the words of Christophe Prochasson of the École des Hautes Études en Sciences Sociales in Paris). Great explanatory systems, drawn first from Marxism and then from structuralism, were out of favour – or at least had exhausted their capacity to convince. The crumbling, too, of the hegemony of the 'new history' of the 1960s and 1970s, which emphasized economic and social forces, quantification and pseudo-scientificism, encouraged a backlash by some conservative historians, especially historians of recent French politics. French historiography, at any rate in France itself, Prochasson lamented, had lost 'its former splendor'.[3]

The 'Anglo-Saxons', meanwhile, contrived to gainsay Pinkney (as he was pleased to acknowledge when he wrote a more optimistic codicil to his 'thesis' shortly before his death). Countless scholars from Canada, the USA, Britain and Australia contributed empirically based monographs, brightening the remotest corners of France's history. The respect shown by French historians for books in English (or indeed German or Italian) was noticeably higher in the 1990s than in the 1950s. Anglophones found invitations to French scholarly symposia easier to come by, and the coveted epithet 'serious' was more commonly applied to their works in French book-reviews and learned journals.

Credit for these changes should go, in part, to the organizations that promoted the study of French history – the Society for French Historical Studies which David Pinkney had founded with Shepard B. Clough and Evelyn M. Acomb, but also the Western Society for French History formed in 1974 and, in Britain, the Association for the Study of Modern and Contemporary France established in 1980 with its journal *Modern and Contemporary France*, and the Society for the Study of French History whose journal *French History* began in 1986.

Meanwhile, beside these learned bodies to support anglophone historians of France who wished to undertake primary research, Pinkney's challenge to write works of synthesis has not gone unanswered. The decades since 1960 have seen publication of respected, oft-reprinted textbooks: Gordon Wright's *France in Modern Times* and James F. McMillan's *Twentieth Century France, 1898–1991: Politics and Society* as well as Maurice Larkin's more chronologically restricted *France since the Popular Front: Government and People, 1936–1996* and Robert Gildea's *France since 1945*.[4] Another landmark was Cambridge University Press's laudable decision in the 1980s to translate all the volumes of a major series of research-led 'super textbooks' first published in France a decade before. This collection, *The Cambridge History of Modern France*, made the work of many distinguished French historians accessible in English.[5]

In another category, more substantial and more original than even a 'super textbook', but not quite a research monograph, was Theodore Zeldin's two-volume *France, 1848–1945*. This appeared during the 1970s in the Oxford History of Modern Europe. Breaking radically from the treatments of Russia and Spain in the same series, Zeldin was as revolutionary as many of the epochs enclosed within his often decidedly nominal chronological span. *France 1848–1945* is no ordinary journey through – still less 'story of' – the seismic shifts of French regimes and politics from the February and June revolutions of 1848 to the Liberation of 1945 (seen even 50 years later by a dwindling band of nostalgic resisters and by many communists as France's most recent revolutionary 'lost opportunity'). The books are explorations in French history pursued through sweeping themes. Zeldin is iconoclastic and innovative, blessed with a magpie-like eye for shiny gems to be plucked from a village schoolteacher's journal or a conscript soldier's letters to his mother.

Extremely rewarding (though perhaps more for the experienced student of France than the novice), Zeldin's work uniquely evokes the human emotions. What excites him are the prejudices and humours, moods and manners of the French, women and men, young and old, rich, poor and middling. Desire to exhume and reincarnate these passions of the past determined Zeldin's idiosyncratic organization of his material. Thus 'ambition', 'love' and (in a rare excursion into something approaching conventionality) 'politics' formed the thematic sub-divisions of one volume; 'intellect', 'taste' and 'anxiety' those of the other. Zeldin's distance from Whiggish or Marxist grand explanations, indeed from any 'master narrative', was marked more clearly still when the books appeared in French – one being entitled 'passions and hatreds'. In part paying homage to the *Annalistes*, Zeldin jettisoned conventional structure and played fast and loose with periodization. His history is painted on a broad canvas and resembles literary pointillism – closely juxtaposed local detail, colourful anecdotes and an evocation of mood and place deployed with dazzling results. The outcome, however, may seem anachronistic and disorientating to readers seeking from their history a chronology and explanation of change over time.

Here no claims are made to equal Zeldin's rich tapestry of local detail. This book nonetheless retains a sense of diversity befitting a people as heterogeneous as the French. It also seeks to overlay this diversity with a generally recognizable timescale. Authors have sought to connect themes and issues in French history since 1815 with dates that, one suspects, continue to resonate. The changes of regime, the revolutions, the wars, therefore receive a salience not present in Zeldin. The book endeavours to retain colour and texture – to be alive to the nuances of region and locality – yet at the same time situating the study of art and anarchism, humour and hatred, *théâtre comique* and the theatre of the guillotine, within a recognizable political context. This book respects social history and cultural history, the history of sport, crime, passion – but not such history treated anachronistically or disconnected from the national and international events swirling around an *histoire de tous les jours*, a 'history of the daily round'. This book does not present a dominant narrative or explanatory theory of what has happened to France since Napoleon. Yet each contributor might subscribe to a certain admiration for the cultivated 'historical consciousness', a cultural attunement to time and place, that seems particularly present in France. The French do seem more sensitive than the British to historical anniversaries and locations that resonate from the past ('sites of memory'), and to contests over their significance – or at least France's quality press does. If the French appear readier to visit what Pierre Nora terms *les lieux de mémoire* (sites or realms of memory), they do so with an anticipation that these sites, and French histories themselves, are properly and excitingly divisive and conflict-ridden – fluid, changing, disputed, ripe for revision by the next generation of historians.[6]

The chapters here suggest, in another sidelight on the Pinkney thesis after 40 years, that anglophone writing on modern and contemporary France enjoys encouragingly good health. The mentor and doctoral supervisor of many current British historians of modern France, Richard Cobb, wrote critically that Braudel's *Identity of France* 'wander[ed] too much both in time and in space' and unjustly ignored most of the work of historians who wrote in English. Braudel and his peers, reflected Cobb:

> were brought up as geographers as well as historians, no doubt much to their advantage. But a historian soon discovers his own geography [. . .] Even an English historian, by working on local records, can soon reconstruct the river network – Seine, Oise, Yonne, Marne – through which Paris was provisioned.

Like Cobb, the authors here have spent much time in France and are acknowledged specialists in their field. Each reflects the interdisciplinary approaches and eclecticism characteristic of current study of the French past. Naturally the choice of chapter topics – as well as the content of each – reflects the feelings of the editor and the authors as to the saliency of certain episodes, trends, individuals. No restrictive agenda or blueprint has been taken from Whig history, nor from Marxist history, post-modernist history, gender history. Authors have been left free to chart and explain the historiographical influence, the methodologies and interpretations, each regards as most important. One result is a recurrent echo, coming back at us from all French history since Napoleon, of James McMillan's remark about Annette Becker's work on religious faith from 1914 to 1930 that 'The historiography of the First World War exemplifies the general evolution of history as a discipline over the past thirty years', the war having 'now passed, by way of social historians preoccupied with social and economic change, into the province of cultural historians interested in mentalities, sensibilities and emotions'.[7]

Pamela Pilbeam opens by exploring some of the legacies of the French Revolution in terms of changes and continuities. She notes the rapid changes of regime in the first 15 years after the storming of the Bastille in 1789 – constitutional monarchy (1791–2), the First Republic (1792–1804), which included the rule by the three-man Consulate of 1799–1804, and then Napoleon Bonaparte's Empire until 1814–15. She questions whether the revolutionaries adopted any overarching political principles. Nineteenth-century republicans asserted that they did – but the Declaration of the Rights of Man and the Citizen along with the revolutionary–republican motto of 'liberty, equality, fraternity' were often abandoned. This certainly occurred when revolutionary and republican politicians were in a tight corner, as when the Consulate was faced by the *Chouan* unrest of 1799–1800, or when Prince-President Louis Napoleon Bonaparte staged a *coup d'état* on 2 December 1851 to transform the power he had held as president of the Second Republic of 1848 into the personal regime that would enable him to proclaim himself Emperor Napoleon III a year later (having meanwhile used the army of the Republic to crush opponents in the Allier and the Cher, in Languedoc, the Vaucluse and the Basses-Alpes). One of the most striking paradoxes of the 1789 Revolution – among many – was the way it left a 'tradition of cataclysmic political instability' yet also set in place nearly all 'the institutions of the modern, centralized French state'.

Socially and economically, too, there was paradox. Peasants and artisans, the less well-off, who had hoped for much from 1789, tended to do less well than middle-class or 'bourgeois' groups, state officials, doctors, lawyers and some businessmen. Subsequently more lawyers and journalists gravitated towards republicanism, cutting their political teeth in the 1830s and 1840s through involvement in the radical and socialist political clubs, in the production of tracts, pamphlets, underground newspapers. Later still this 'radical milieu' would be swollen, especially in the time of the Third Republic (1871–1940) by the burgeoning ranks of schoolteachers, whom some histor-ians see as the new 'republican notables' of provincial France of the 1880s and later. And the Revolution's legacies, notwithstanding Napoleon's papal concordat of 1801, included a prickly relationship between anti-clerical republicanism and the Church throughout the nineteenth century and into the twentieth, with pervasive political and social consequences (discussed below at more length). There is, admits Pamela Pilbeam, really no consensus on when the Revolution began and certainly not on when, if ever, it finished, or on what its significance has been. She points, also, to the lengthy absence of women from the history of 1789 and after, a perspective partially redressed by scholars including Olwen Hufton, Michelle Perrot, Arlette Farge and Mona Ozouf since about 1970.

The significance for the French historian Maurice Agulhon of the upheavals of 1789 to 1848 was that, 'The democratic Republic eventually

imposed itself as the normal political regime of contemporary France.[8] But
Robert Tombs shows the problems in accepting a neat notion that French
historical evolution progressed necessarily to a definitive, 'natural' end-state.
He is also critical of notions that the turbulence of 1792–1815 made for an
'exceptional' French destiny since Napoleon. He underlines the paradox of
modern French political history: that 'more than 150 years of passionate and
often bloody political struggle – often called the 'Franco-French war' –
produced an outcome little different from that of more peaceful [...]
neighbours'. He highlights the tendency, especially of celebrated nineteenth-
century historians such as Jules Michelet, to write the history of the nation as
a process of takeover by the history of the republic, presenting what tran-
spired as a tale of the gradual lessening of the grip of authoritarian forms of
rule, whether by royalists or Bonapartist dictatorships. As he has remarked
elsewhere, he finds a French version of Whig history 'too prevalent' in
modern scholarship. He challenges notions that the path followed by French
political development from 1789 to the 1990s was a predetermined route
walked by enlightened, rational people who understood all along that it was
logical, sensible, necessary for them to end their journey at the destination of
a secular, liberal, democratic and unitary republic.[9] Tombs denies that there
was a 'natural' trajectory culminating in what François Furet termed 'the
Revolution coming into port'.[10] He questions assumptions of a teleological
process of 'normalization', a making of a 'natural' and immutable republican
political form in France between *c.*1879 and 1889 – French élites and public
thereafter eternally part of a 'one and indivisible Republic' by dint of a
rational rejection of its monarchical and Bonapartist alternatives.

For Tombs the ship of state is not securely dry-docked – at least not in a
place with a specific, unalterable republican architecture. French history 'has
not ended'. It did not finish in 1879 with the capture of the institutions of the
Third Republic, the senate and the presidency, by republican politicians and
their embryonic political parties that went on to become the Radical Party of
1901, the SFIO Socialist Party (the Section Française de l'Internationale
Ouvrière) of 1905. Furet argues that the revolutionary impulse in France was
largely exhausted by the 1870s, victory conceded to 'the principles of 1789'
– civil equality and political liberty. But republicans from the nineteenth to
the mid-twentieth century offered a strictly circumscribed and gendered
concept of political liberties and civil equality. The so-called 'universal'
suffrage instituted in 1848 benefited adult males only. As J. F. McMillan,
Paul Smith, Siân Reynolds, Steven Hause and Anne Kenney, among others,
have shown, the Third Republic did not enfranchise women.[11] Indeed, it only
grudgingly and in piecemeal fashion improved women's rights before the
law, in education, in marriage and at the workplace. Nor was its record in
upholding political liberties unblemished. On the contrary: it displayed a
recurring propensity to unleash the repressive forces of the national police
and prison services, and even on occasion the army, upon strikers, trade
unionists, human-rights campaigners and political activists such as anarcho-

syndicalists and Communist Party members, notably in 1906–13, 1926–30 and 1939–40.

Regime changes in France did not in any case end in 1946, when a republic was re-established after the 'black years' of Marshal Philippe Pétain's Vichy state (*État Français*) from 1940 to 1944. Is it certain that the final change occurred with the establishment in 1958 of the Fifth Republic? Many commentators in 1995–8 noted that contemporary France and its people appeared neurotic and angst-ridden. There was continual talk of a 'crisis' – and not just an economic one of the post-industrial transition but an imagined worsening of what Alain Peyrefitte in the 1970s termed 'the French sickness' (*le mal français*). The French display self-doubt and divisions: disputing the proper role of their state, divided over what restrictions are acceptable on the sovereignty of their nation (especially *vis-à-vis* the European Union). Meanwhile the rights of citizens are widely debated, definitions of French identity and membership of the 'national community' the object of inflammatory polemic and sometimes violent agitation (Jean-Marie Le Pen's far-right National Front attracting some 13–15 per cent of the vote at parliamentary, presidential, regional and European elections since 1986 on a nationalistic/racially exclusionist ticket of 'France for the French'). France remains a country, Tombs pertinently reminds us, in which the unpredictable 'always seems possible'.

A society that was 'French' as a whole (and felt so) was also, arguably, the child of the post-Revolutionary state. Colin Heywod, however, notes the strength of scepticism as to the objective existence of the modernist notion of 'society'. An examination of the fluid, subjective and constructed nature of identity, the crucial roles played by language and by cultural icons, has been a strong feature of new approaches to historical study, borrowing conceptually and methodologically from literary criticism, sociology and cultural studies, since the 'new social history' of the 1970s. Heywood quotes Frederic Jameson's dismissal of the modernist conception of society as a 'fictive totalizing entity', contrasting this with scholarship published in the 1980s and 1990s. This work emphasizes diversity rather than unity, proposing that people move fluidly in and out of socially (and linguistically) constructed or 'imagined' communities or groupings – class, region, nation. Re-examining the long-dominant view of earlier historians that the nineteenth century was the 'age of the bourgeoisie', Heywood is inspired by the shift from writing 'social history' to a focus on 'history of society'. He observes that contemporary French commentators from about 1815 to 1852 were gripped by fear of social disintegration. They were terrified at the prospect of a return of anarchy and the decomposition of social bonds.

This phobia recurred intermittently. Indeed some political scientists see the last 200 years of French history as a continuous struggle between 'order' and 'movement'. Aristocrats such as the duc de Broglie, who rallied pragmatically to the conservative republic in the 1870s, proclaimed that their purpose was to rebuild a 'regime of moral order'. Seventy years later, after the defeat of 1940, Vichy, too, sought to effect a 'national renovation'. Pétain's discourse against the left, as well as his attacks on those defined as 'outsiders' such as immigrants, Jews and Freemasons, was steeped in a penitential language of chastisement and expiation. Meanwhile, the Resistance, looking to the bright dawn of Liberation, set its own very different visions of a renovated and 'cleansed' state at the centre of its 'plans for renewal'.[12] Later still, after de Gaulle's Fifth Republic came about in 1958, the state remained the lode-star, life-force and arbiter for how France should be governed, imagined, identified. The state was, and to a great extent remains, what holds the often mutually antagonistic and sometimes fratricidal French together. Heywood quotes Pierre Rosanvallon that it became 'the principal unifying agency for a society of atomized individuals'. De Gaulle despaired of organizing a people who could produce 365 different varieties of cheese.

Trying to present a thesis that the French had only belatedly become a national community with a shared identity, some 200 years after the geographical and territorial unifications of Louis XIV, the Sun King, and a century after the Revolution, the American historian Eugen Weber wrote in 1976 that the peasantry turned into 'Frenchmen' (and presumably women) between the 1860s and the 1890s. Only then, he asserted, did they meld together, acquiring a national consciousness if not a uniformity through an end to isolation and localism. The means for the transformation, affirmed Weber, was the flurry of canal, road and particularly railway construction initiated under Napoleon III and resumed between 1877 and 1885, complemented by the Third Republic's homogenizing policies – notably its mandating of universal military service and compulsory primary schooling.[13] Historians during the 1980s and 1990s have, however, grown sceptical of Weber's claims.[14] Alan Forrest's chapter here, on Paris versus the provinces, reminds us that a claim of attachment to the ancient provinces such as Gascony, the Midi, Languedoc, Lorraine, Franche-Comté and Brittany was often manufactured.

Professions of love for a province not uncommonly passed for the acceptable face of conservatism, anti-republicanism, even royalism. This was especially so during the passionate and frequently violent 1790s and 1800s. A self-serving 'invention of tradition' occurred a-plenty. At least six of the supposedly 'ancient' provinces had become part of France through post-war annexations as recently as the seventeenth and eighteenth centuries (Lorraine and Corsica as late as 1766 and 1768 respectively). Claims by champions of Occitanie for the region's cultural and linguistic unity were notoriously exaggerated. The Vendée scarcely possessed any regional self-consciousness before one was forced on its people, almost in spite of themselves, by state repression and military brutality in the 1790s. On the other hand, Forrest argues that an arrogant and facile Jacobin belief that a new French nationalism could be universally and equally created which would leave no place for local sentiment was crucial in revitalizing often moribund provincial identities. The Revolution, the Directory and the First Empire left an enduring image in many regions of an 'intolerant centralism'. Hence 'the memory of the Revolution that was passed on to the nineteenth century remained one dominated by the power of the state'.

Nor, think many who reflect on Weber's thesis, was there a closure on this matter, a definitive 'making of the nation', in the last third of the nineteenth century. As Herman Lebovics has shown, 'true France' remained a deeply contested concept from the Dreyfus affair to 1945, French 'culture wars' and struggles by left and right to establish a dominant paradigm of 'identity' and 'national community' causing heavy political and human casualties. The conflicts erupted anew with the French opposition to the Algerian war (1954–62), and some argue that they are barely under control as the twentieth century bids farewell. Centre versus periphery, nation versus region, authoritarianism versus democracy remain dichotomies. The tensions they express are not resolved. Studies of the force of political particularism in Brittany and Alsace, for example, suggest this.[15] These tensions permeate the pluralistic and competing visions that the French have formed of themselves as people, and as entity. They remain today, nearly 200 years after the institution of the Napoleonic legal code and the creation of the prefects to stamp a centralized unity on 'the Hexagon'.[16]

What might have been especially unpredictable 200 years ago is the slow pace of women's political, legal and economic emancipation. Yet there is evidence, as Siân Reynolds has argued elsewhere, that the republic was in practice constructed and ordered in a way which deliberately (rather than accidentally or inadvertently) excluded women from citizenship rights. She has reflected 'that the Republic was constructed as much against women as without them'.[17] Here she addresses the difficulty for the historian of hearing women's voices at all, during long stretches of French nineteenth and twentieth century political activity. Did this stem from an intrinsically gendered republicanism? The language of politics was a masculine discourse, and political culture was regulated by male behavioural and social norms. The words and conventions of politics, especially parliamentary politics, amounted to a male code and closed shop. This ensured that even when regimes were notionally 'of the left', when one might expect a 'progressive' politics, women remained excluded.[18]

The sexism of the left drew support from several factors. On the one hand was an institutional and attitudinal exclusionist impulse that was evidenced in male domination of leftist organizations. But in addition there was a pervasive fear on the left – particularly in the 1890s and early 1900s within Jules Guesde's POF (Parti Ouvrier Français) – of the threat to men's jobs and men's wage levels of a cheap and perhaps docile labour force. Why would the left ally itself with what was perceived as another enemy in economic terms, despite its notional subscription to 'equality'? Preconceptions of this sort were commonplace among male syndicalist leaders too.[19] Alongside women's conscious or unconscious connivance with men in sabotaging their own emancipation, this burden of suspicion and even humbug on the left helps explain – to use a phrase of Zeldin – 'Why Women's Liberation moves slowly'. Estimating women in France to be 'outsiders by birth', Siân Reynolds highlights a wider problem: that of researching and writing *political* history of French women. Whether because of the loud din of masculine discourses or because of what Michelle Perrot calls 'the silences of history', women's voices are left inaudible.[20] Along with other recent writers on French female experiences (Karen Adler, Hanna Diamond, Claire Duchen, Claire Gorrara and Corran Laurens among many), Reynolds scrutinizes formal and 'traditional' arenas of politics with a critical eye.[21] Conventional descriptors prove inadequate to imagine the varieties and modes of women's politics. The 'political' requires redefinition in a gendered way. A fresh meaning to where, how and why women 'did politics' is needed.

Reynolds and Perrot, among others, have emphasized that in spite of Marianne's feminine embodiment of the 'republican idea' on coins and stamps, narratives of women in French citizenship are largely a 'history of exclusion'. The celebrated 'universal suffrage' of 1848 was, we do well to remember, merely a universal *male* suffrage. Almost a century later a similar 'blind spot' afflicted the March 1944 programme of the National Council of the Resistance, the CNR (Conseil National de la Résistance), which referred to the need in post-Vichy France for the 'reestablishment of universal suffrage [*sic*]'.[22] What is striking is the continuity and automaticity of implicit, reflexive assumptions as to which sex normatively comprised (and hence constructed for itself) the 'proper' or legitimate political nation/political community. This serves to underline how women were mostly absent from the mainstream traditions of republicanism in France and from French history writing. It points up, also, that the organized Resistance's plans for renewal included a programme to liberate France but no programme to liberate women. As an example of what needs to be attempted by scholars seeking to recover a narrative of women who were excluded from politics at the time and excluded from much of the subsequent history, Patricia Prestwich – a Canadian working on the experiences of women activists in the Catholic party, the MRP (Mouvement Républicain Populaire), from 1944 to 1958 – suggests that:

> to discover what happened to feminists in the Fourth Republic, it is necessary to look once again to the world of alternative politics that was so important in the Third Republic [...] It is therefore important to study women's organisations, consumer advocacy groups, the civil service, and [...] groups that have traditionally been seen as conservative, such as Catholic family associations. As the history of women in the MRP demonstrates, you never know where you will find a feminist.[23]

Individual and group identity in France has also been derived to a significant extent from attitudes towards religion in general and Catholicism in particular. This is a point worth dwelling on at some length in this introduction – particularly because of the attenuation and in many cases complete disappearance from British-university history degrees of any component of religious history. Maurice Larkin acknowledges that the uninitiated Anglo-Saxon may experience understandable difficulty in fathoming why and in what ways religion and the Church mattered in French public and private life. He emphasizes that the twentieth century's early years saw the greatest upheaval in the existence of the Church in France since the 1790s. Indeed, in several regions religious observance was an 'affirmation of tribal identity'. The association of the Church hierarchy with the Restoration Monarchy of Louis XVIII and Charles X in 1815–30 and later with the Comte de Chambord, the Bourbon legitimist claimant to the throne in the 1860s and 1870s, ensured that battle-lines were drawn between Church and anti-clericalism. It also made these battle-lines identical to those between royalists and republicans. In the 1870s the Church had openly supported the monarchists, whom it viewed as a barrier against the secularizing policies of zealous republicans.

Education became the principal arena of conflict. The Church and the anti-clericals both strove for exclusive influence over the nation's impressionable young. In the 1880s the Church was dealt a serious blow by Jules Ferry's educational laws. These introduced free, compulsory and laic primary schooling. The Dreyfus affair (1894–1906) entrenched the opposing camps even more deeply. Under the so-called 'governments of republican defence' of René Waldeck-Rousseau (1899–1902) and Emile Combes (1902–1905) the Catholic orders, the Assumptionists and the Jesuits, were dissolved after allegations that they had undue influence among army officers (a body regarded as reactionary and one instinctively distrusted by republicans). Secularizers in parliament, who had grasped the baton of anti-clerical policies, subsequently ran more powerfully away with it than even Combes desired. The result was the separation law of 9 December 1905. This disestablished the Church and ended payment of state salaries to the bishops and parish clergy.

Arguing that separation was a missed opportunity for Catholicism in France, Maurice Larkin recounts the Church's struggle to adapt to changing socio-cultural *mores* in the twentieth century. Laic militancy had lost its mobilizing power after about 1924–5. Moreover, as Aline Coutrot's research has shown, Catholic youth movements and Catholic trade unionism (the CFTC or *Confédération française des Travailleurs Chrétiens* attracting some 400,000 members by 1936) presented two 'modernizing' and popular engagements with people's practical, everyday lives undertaken by the Church between c.1929 and 1940.[24]

Yet the 1940–4 occupation saw the French episcopate make a different kind of engagement: a highly damaging dalliance with Pétainism. Vichy found Church injunctions against divorce, abortion and contraception made a congenial underpinning to its ideology of pro-natalism and a role of compliant domesticity for women. This went hand in hand with Vichy's crusade for a 'return to the land' in which the regime vaunted supposed 'rural virtues' of community and deference to authority – notions that squared conveniently, and at least superficially, with Catholic Church teachings and hierarchical organization. Vichy made a series of only partly kept pledges to restore Church privileges. Meanwhile, however, and fortunately for the Church, rank-and-file clergy won respect as a result of courageous Resistance activity by some of their number.[25] Also counteracting the bishops' complaisance towards Vichy was the worker-priest movement of 1943 to 1954. The latter laboured to win back a Church foothold in the sprawling industrial suburbs which had been abandoned after 1914. Counter to the logic of past history, notes Larkin, the Church escaped any great reckoning after 1945, with the external and internal Resistance respectively being led by committed lay Catholics in Charles de Gaulle and Georges Bidault, a founder of France's most significant party of an avowedly confessional stamp, the MRP.

> By their splendid Resistance record the Christian Democrats proved that Catholics [...] could be loyal Republicans. By their support for nationalization, economic planning and the welfare state they showed that Catholics could be as interested as Socialists in economic and social justice.[26]

Yet the MRP flourished largely due to the atypical electoral situation in the late 1940s, the traditional right being in temporary disrepute after Vichy and the communists (founded in a split from the SFIO in 1920) appearing to pose a real danger from the left once they quit the government after 3 years, in May 1947, and adopted a Stalinist line of unparalleled strictness. With the founding in April 1947 of an alternative right-wing political force, the Gaullist Rassemblement du Peuple Français or RPF, many naturally conservative Catholic voters deserted the MRP. Moreover, from 1963 onwards the reassertion of conservative theological doctrine by Pope Paul VI and Pope John Paul II, occurring during decades of rising material prosperity, led to new disillusionment with the Church, especially among French 'progressive' Catholics. A sharp decline in the weekly attendance at mass set in. Religion decreased as a force in people's lives, in France as elsewhere in the west. In politics it ceased to be a defining factor. The MRP effectively folded in the mid-1960s, its survivors regrouping into a new party, the Centre Démocrate. Practising Catholicism ceased to be a key to making or unmaking careers in the civil service, armed forces or judiciary.

Division, intolerance and worse in the treatment of racial minorities inside French society is explored in greater detail by Vicki Caron. Taking the case of the Jews, she compares the anti-semitism during the Dreyfus affair with the second wave which arose in the later 1930s and culminated in Vichy's systematic promulgation of a French Holocaust between 1940 and 1944. Historians in France such as Pierre Birnbaum, Annette Wieviorka, Renée Poznanski, Henry Rousso, François Bédarida and Robert Frank have caught up with North American and British concern to expose the French state's part in the Holocaust and trace anti-semitism's past roots in France. Many have become politically active in the process.

Public engagement for French historians is not new, however. During the nineteenth century historians threw themselves self-consciously into political causes. They sought to write dominant narratives of national identity and establish normative political and cultural values. A key figure in this endeavour was Michelet, who gave a strong voice to the creed that France's interests and destiny were as one with those of humanity. The genius and specificity of France lay in its unique capacity to achieve unity from diversity and assimilate others, whether from Europe – or from, and in, the world beyond. Formulation of conceptions of 'the nation' by intellectuals is examined here by Jeremy Jennings. He traces ways in which the idea and ideal of 'motherland' (*patrie*) became imbued with a universalist quasi-religious meaning after 1789 and, at any rate for republicans, displaced religion in giving 'spiritual' or at least philosophical meaning to human lives. Later nineteenth-century analysis, as he shows, contested this model. Ernest Renan, lecturing at the Sorbonne after the Franco-Prussian war of 1870–1, affirmed that defeat and national crisis – including the temporary loss of Alsace-Lorraine to Germany – had occurred because France was weakened 'by democracy, demoralized by her prosperity' and rendered decadent through 'bourgeois materialism'. From the mid-1880s right-wing nationalists, such as Maurice Barrès and Edouard Drumont, poured out eloquent, hateful invective against people 'without roots' and against the Jews. Others offered a variant on this nihilism, refusing to ascribe any meaning to France. They included anti-patriot Gustave Hervé, who proclaimed at the outset of the twentieth century that 'Our country is our class'. Revolutionary syndicalism, at its most militant from 1900 to 1910, likewise 'combined its anti-capitalist and anti-militarist teachings with anti-patriotism'.

As Jennings shows, however, Michelet, Renan and others had another wider and enduring significance, for their public polemics and the explicitly political quality and purpose to their history ushered in a new form of political activism or commitment – that of the intellectual. Forged, many argue, in the fires of the Dreyfus controversy, the politically engaged intellectual became a key commentator and agenda-setter, a public figure uniquely characteristic of twentieth-century France. The pantheon stretches from Emile Zola, Charles Péguy, Barrès and Georges Sorel of the *fin-de-siècle* generation to the existentialists who dominated the 1940s and 1950s, Jean-Paul Sartre and Simone de Beauvoir. Later came ideological enemies such as Louis Aragon and Raymond Aron, who bitterly attacked each other's values and world-views from the pro- and anti-communist sides of the Cold-War barricades respectively, down to post-1968 protagonists such as André Glucksmann.

Many of these intellectuals reversed their political stance at some point in the mature years of their careers (some by a characteristically French *coup de théâtre* or public gesture involving a full-page manifesto in a newspaper such as *Le Monde* or *Libération* to advertise their 'conversion'). These intellectuals are frequently more famous now for their volte-face than for unwavering commitment to a cause. This appears to be the case with apostate philosophers of the left, such as Bernard-Henri Lévy and Alain Finkielkraut. It is true, too, of the communist historian Jean Elleinstein who, in the 1970s, condemned the Soviet Union's tyranny and tore up his membership card of the French Communist Party, the PCF, denouncing its slavish subservience to Moscow and the unbending Stalinism of its then general secretary, Georges Marchais. In the case of some, their political actions, as time went by, overshadowed and even superseded any 'pure' or 'philosophical' abstract achievements as intellectuals (Finkielkraut writing a book in 1987 entitled *The Defeat of Thinking*). On the other hand Pierre Vidal-Naquet continued and broadened his crusade against torture during the Algerian war (1954–62) into a ceaseless campaign of anti-racism and defence of human rights – a case of an intellectual's political mobilization over a particular issue mutating into lifelong work on behalf of a general principle.[27]

A deep national malaise or sense of national crisis was often agonized over by the intelligentsia. This foreboding eventually became – especially for the pessimistic, sometimes nihilistic intellectuals of the far right – a kind of self-fulfilling prophecy in face of the slaughter of French males in 1914–1918 and the bleak experiences of war and defeat in 1940–4. For Julian Jackson, such experiences are a key to much of the political behaviour of French people since 1815, and he pays special attention to the 'crisis of democracy' in the 1930s. The occupation of many cities and large swathes of French countryside by soldiers wearing *pickelhaube* or coal-scuttle helmets in 1870–1, 1914–18 and 1940–4 bred deep doubts about the ability of the French state to deliver the most elemental part of the contract between a regime and the people it governs – physical protection against external attack and conquest.

Nowhere was this more apparent than among those dwelling in what Richard Cobb termed 'the fragile northern and eastern frontiers'. The inhabitants of the Nord, Pas-de-Calais and Flanders, he found, brokered multiple autonomous relationships with the invader. They made their own arrangements, outwith the policies and prescriptions of the state, impelled by the stark choices and survivalist existentialism at the forefront of all lives in wartime. Individual, private accommodations occurred between *occupés* and *occupants*. In 1940–4 these could involve French homes hosting the sons of German soldiers who had been billeted with them in 1914–18 – half guards, half guests, quartered with the very families among whom their fathers and uncles had lived (and sometimes produced children) 25 years before.[28] Defeat in 1870 and 1940, the brush with disaster in 1914 and the German occupation of 10 northern and eastern *départements* until 1918 bred what Robert J. Young terms a profound 'ambivalence' among many French people about the fitness, the capacity, the very legitimacy of their nation-state.

The MRP, mentioned earlier for the relatively strong involvement of women in it, was one of several new political and social formations which sought, with very limited success, to make a 'clean break' at the end of the Second World War. For French people, the defeat of 1940 and subsequent 4 years of occupation by Nazi Germany, were, as Nicholas Atkin emphasizes, 'the most traumatic episode in contemporary French history'. Pétain's regime installed at Vichy in 1940 was, for almost 30 years after the Liberation, denounced as an un-French aberration, a German imposition. However, drawing on Robert Paxton's work as well as his own research, Atkin shows that Vichy took its cue from long-embedded and distinctively French traditions – traditions of counter-revolution, denial of political pluralism, repression of dissent, racial intolerance and misogyny. Nor were breaks in 1945 always, or even often, clean ones. In terms of 'purifying' the civil service, the prefectorial corps, the police and the armed forces, the purges of 1945–7 did not go deep.[29] Nor was the Liberation, for women, especially 'liberating'. Female writers and editors of the underground Resistance press of the occupation years, Joan Tumblety has shown, 'effectively reinforced rather than challenged prevailing notions of gender roles in France' and were more instrumental in 'creating a nationalist consciousness than an explicitly "feminist" one'.[30]

Turning to external aspects of post-Napoleonic French history, via the critique of the supposedly 'exceptionalist' 'trajectory' of France, a persuasive case may be made that the crucial political changes since 1792 have been precipitated not by internal but by external forces 'in a way that is true of no other European state – the radicalization of the Revolution; the rise and fall of Napoleon; the fall of Napoleon III and the installation of the Third Republic; the fall of the Third Republic and the final counter-revolutionary attempt of the Vichy regime; and the victory of de Gaulle'. Perhaps insufficient allowance has been made for the inflated expectations resulting from French success in continental war from 1792 to about 1812, in standard histories of post-Restoration France. In the Revolutionary and Napoleonic age the absence of a unified Germany, the myth of the nation-in-arms (the 'Bayonets of the Republic' in John Lynn's phrase) triumphing heroically over the enemies of French citizenry, and then Napoleon's astonishing feats against a combination of Prussia, Austria, Spain, Russia – these arguably gave the French an excessive faith in what the state, regardless of regime, could do in the name of France after 1815. Thus 1870 was a watershed. 'Defeat by Germany fundamentally altered French nationalism, making it more defensive and pessimistic, and unmistakeably changed perceptions of France's position in Europe.'[31]

Foreign and defence policy between the 1850s and 1990s is discussed by Martin Alexander and John Keiger. They identify three main themes: first, Franco-German rivalry, obviously enough; second, French competition with, and suspicions towards, 'the Anglo-Saxons'; and, third, France's global or 'blue-water' self-image as a great power with a maritime heritage and legitimate worldwide interests. Political leaders, along with organized commercial and religious groups, were constantly driven by a global and universalist ambition for French 'reach' or influence. As Alexis de Tocqueville in the mid-nineteenth century warned Adolphe Thiers (the consolidator of the Third Republic in the early 1870s), no government, indeed no dynasty could survive if the affairs of the world were decided without its participation. With land frontiers to the east as well as on the Alps and Pyrenees, but also possessing three major coastlines, France's geography ensured external policies commonly characterized by strategic schizophrenia. France was, since the mid-seventeenth century, both a maritime and a continental power – whether her leaders and population liked it or not.

Historians who have focused on Napoleonic France's military history, as well as writers on the post-1815 French army as an institution, have drawn an incomplete picture of the pattern of French external relations. They have exaggerated the question of metropolitan security and French relations with her continental neighbours. Whilst acknowledging Germany's central place in French foreign-policy planning since at least 1871, Alexander and Keiger contend that, in a long-term perspective, this obsession occurred quite late – a product of German unification (the latter itself completed through military triumph over France). In the long term, however, French competition with the 'Anglo-Saxons' seems the more dominant theme or 'governing passion'. This rivalry with the anglophone world possesses a greater power to explain the particular form that French external relations have assumed. It first manifested itself in the protracted struggle with Britain during the so-called Second Hundred Years' War of the 'long eighteenth century' (1689–1815), continuing right through the nineteenth century and even from 1919 to 1938; and then became transmuted into antagonism towards the USA, initially over President Woodrow Wilson's meddlesome activism (as many French contemporaries saw it) at the 1919 peace conference and accentuated after 1945. From a standpoint 200 years on, the Revolutionary and Napoleonic era does not look like a turning point for French foreign relations. It was, rather, an episode, albeit one of uncommon violence, in a protracted Franco/Anglo-Saxon struggle for worldwide linguistic, cultural, commercial and military ascendancy.

In cultural life, too, in the creative and performing arts, entertainment and popular taste, the state has assigned itself a central directing mission. Perhaps this is because culture has long been accorded a revered place, a depth of respect, rarely found outside France. Immense prestige accrues to French literature in general, to novelists such as Victor Hugo, Honoré de Balzac, Gustave Flaubert, Marcel Proust, André Gide and Marguerite Yourcenar (the first woman elected one of the forty 'immortals' of the Académie Française), playwrights such as Marcel Pagnol and Jean Anouilh, poets such as Paul Valéry and Louis Aragon (to name some major artists of post-Napoleonic vintage). Not far behind literature's esteem is the renown that the French media and state confers on French impressionist painters, on composers such as Hector Berlioz, Georges Bizet, Francis Poulenc, and, latterly, on dance choreographers such as George Balanchine and film directors (especially Alain Resnais, François Truffaut, Jean-Luc Godard, the 'New Wave' of the 1950s and 1960s).

Discussing the tensions between 'high' and 'low' culture since the first impressionist salons in the 1870s, Charles Rearick concludes that the state 'still assumes major responsibility for promoting French culture and provides support in ever-expanding forms' at the close of the twentieth century. Yet he also detects change. The French arts no longer occupy the prestigious primary place that was theirs historically. With globalization, he feels, 'those who cherish France's past glories in the arts alternate between an uneasy acceptance of new realities and defiant efforts of resistance' (perhaps most familiar in the lavish subsidies provided to French film-makers and in the official mandating of a guaranteed percentage of air time on French radio to francophone pop and rock music).

The strength of the state, with the related tendency of French people to look to it as provider and protector, partly explains the extreme difficulty for France since 1815 in reaching a peaceful accommodation with autonomous associations and groups. Repeatedly, the only recourse has been repression or co-option. Susan Milner, here scrutinizing the trade unions (*les syndicats*), argues that labour associations, too, have a history that has been written chiefly in terms of 'French exceptionalism'. The comparatively slow development of large-scale industrial capitalism in France (itself supposedly a key part in this 'exceptionalism') is widely adduced to explain why French trade unionists were not more numerous. Repression was severe under the Restoration monarchies, a law of 1834 tightening prohibitions on assembly and association. Often maintained clandestinely, at great personal risk to members, French workers' movements persisted under the Orléanist Monarchy and Second Empire and flourished during the Second Republic (1848–51) in between. The legal organization and representation of workers was another realm of post-Revolutionary history where there was no smooth Whiggish journey towards a utopia of social harmony and state benevolence. The Third Republic's advent, whether dated from the provisional government of 1871 or the constitution of 1875, did not bring immediate legalization of working people's organizations. Syndicates were approved only in 1884 (17 years after the foundation of the Trades Union Congress in Britain).

This ushered in what Susan Milner calls 'the decades – slightly less than a century – of the "heroic" working class'. But we should no more assume that legalization in 1884 marked a sheltered harbour for trade-union rights than we should accept that the Revolution had safely anchored in port in 1879. The full ferocity of state repression by a republic was felt by anarcho-syndicalist demonstrators in Paris, by striking miners in the Nord, and by militant vineyard workers in the Midi, notably between 1906 and 1913 (Georges Clemenceau, as prime minister from 1906–9, earning the sobriquet 'the first policeman of France').[32] Indeed the culmination of state hostility to self-defining groups organizing into autonomous associations occurred under Pétain. Having outlawed trade unions and dissolved political parties, Vichy decreed that the only permissible association for workers lay in membership of the official corporatist institutions authorized under the 1941 charter for labour (*charte du travail*).

However, in terms of how French social groups feel able to articulate their political feelings and aspirations legitimately, it is not clear that France has even now fully absorbed western liberal-democratic orthodoxies or embraced parliamentary forms of politics to the exclusion of all others. The political scientist Michel Winock has diagnosed a 'hexagonal fever' that periodically grips the French, inflaming political temperatures and provoking spasms of political violence and revolutions – or at any rate producing so-called 'revolutionary moments' – in 1830, 1848, 1871, 1934, 1936, 1944 and 1968. The politics of barricades, mass demonstrations and marches certainly did not end in the nineteenth century – even if Thiers' bloody repression of the Paris Commune in May 1871 may best be viewed as the last act in the 'passion play of the French Revolution'.

Long after what the government intended be a closure on the French penchant for politics-as-street-theatre, French people on the left retained a dynamic capacity to act out their politics as, in Henri Lefèbvre's phrase, a 'festival of the oppressed'. Twentieth-century examples of this abound: the communist and socialist counter-demonstration six days after the far right's riots in Paris on 6 February 1934, the wave of spontaneous strikes and factory occupations of May–June 1936, the carnivalesque enjoyment of the Liberation in much of France in August and September 1944, and the mass unrest of May 1968 – even the surge of a million protesters onto the streets of Paris in 1984 to oppose Alain Savery's bill to reduce the privileges of private schools (for all that this was more a case of middle-class people power).

Yet there seems something ephemeral, impermanent, about the pretensions of these 'revolutionary moments', particularly those of the twentieth century. Half a generation of the French middle class – and probably more than half a generation of admiring, impressionable, optimistic Anglo-Saxon francophiles – saw the May 1968 protests against de Gaulle as a watershed, the coming-of-age of a radical libertarian youth culture. But May 1968 no longer looks to have changed much in the heartland of student unrest, let alone to have redistributed governmental power and revolutionized the nature of the state. Many French retain a yearning to promote universalist ideals. In the abstract, in a philosophical sense, most still aspire to be champions of liberty, equality and fraternity. But bringing this about without risking plunging back into a nineteenth-century anarchy and violence that few would countenance remains, in Raymond Aron's phrase, 'the undiscoverable Revolution'. Even 30 years after May 1968, students at Nanterre University and the Sorbonne still face overcrowded lecture theatres in ill-maintained buildings, are still tutored by full professors only when they start work on a higher degree, and still lack a say in running university education. The fading paint of old slogans daubed on Nanterre's bleak concrete walls in the late-1960s and 1970s – 'Gaullists = hooligans', 'Shah: quit Iran' – were all that survived when I returned to the cradle of the student movement in 1981, ironically the year of the election of the Fifth Republic's first 'leftist' president, to work at Nanterre's International Library of Contemporary History.

These reflections connect with Theodore Zeldin's observation that 'the power of politicians is superficial and the important decisions are not made by them'.[33] In his chapter entitled 'Not backward but different?', Roger Magraw surveys how the historiography of the 1950s and 1960s damned French economic performance in the period 1789–1914 as 'at best, modest – hence France's inexorable decline from being *the* dominant power in 1700 to second-rank status'. He goes on to show that a major historiographical reassessment occurred in the 1970s, leading to the 'French model' or 'French path to modernization' being treated with more respect.

As Magraw notes, much criticism of France's performance, notably by the Sorbonne economic historian François Crouzet, had been by comparison with a 'British model' of assumed superiority. The latter was no longer clear, to say the least, in the Britain of mass industrial stoppages and three-day weeks of 1973–9. Indeed it could be questioned by any scrutiny of the faltering performance of the British economy after 1945. Perhaps July Monarchy *grands bourgeois* had the outlook of *rentiers* rather than industrialists; and firms in the period 1875–1936 may, as Alfred Sauvy alleged, have remained too long under cautious family ownership, denied capitalization and expansion through stockmarket listing. But as Correlli Barnett and others have noted, later-Victorian Britain had plenty of aristocrats and bourgeois, as well as a public-school and university system, whose cultural values were fundamentally anti-industrial.

The presumption of a British 'high road' to the modern world, to optimal economic productivity and social justice, began to look arrogant and implausible. The fixed ideas of liberals and Marxists alike about the inevitable, 'progressive' triumph of large-scale industry were re-evaluated. As a result 'France's socio-economic *sonderweg* came to be less harshly judged'. Recent research has shown, for instance, that Paris was among the world's great artisanal centres from the 1850s, with only 3 per cent of France's population producing 25 per cent of the value of French manufactured exports. A quarter of Parisian women were at this time in industry, often in outwork and finishing of specialist and luxury goods. Small-scale production was not a system waiting to die but one with its own logic.[34]

International comparisons undermined the credibility of the case for any single 'correct' path to the twentieth century. The phases in the historiography's view of French economic performance delineated by Roger Magraw indicate that the underlying trends mattered, but are as open to divergent explanations as is any other dimension of France's modern history. Without subscribing to economic determinism, the impact of *les forces profondes* beneath the surface of French societal and political evolution can be acknowledged. And the state, at different times, has been depicted as doing too little and too much. Magraw cites Richard Kuisel's analysis that 'the *real* problem in the period after 1880 was not *too much* governmental interference but *too little*'. He concludes that the Third Republic apparently lacked the will, the ideology, the data or the bureaucratic resources to respond positively to critics who pleaded for the state to act more directly through planning and macro-economic policy to address deficiencies in the French economy – such as sectoral shortages of capital, a dearth of apprentice schools to train skilled labour, or the automobile and aviation industry's economically rational but strategically unacceptable concentration around Paris.[35]

Vichy took action economically between 1940 and 1944, needless to say. But its ideologically driven schemes, though formulated by 'technocrats' such as Pierre Pucheu and François Lehideux, the successive ministers of industrial production and Yves Bouthillier, finance minister, either antagonized the workers, now stripped of union rights, or ran into the anti-industrial pull of Vichy's folkloric rural revivalists. Vichy's contradictory projects set back rather than advanced French 'modernization'. In any case, though not a puppet regime, Vichy was not fully sovereign either. German occupation imposed crippling exactions on French industry and agriculture. Labour service in Germany, compulsory for Frenchmen aged 16–60 after February 1943, exacerbated the economic and social disruption caused by the loss of 1.6 million Frenchmen taken prisoner in 1940. Widespread human misery resulted for the 790,000 wives (616,200 of them with children) left behind.[36]

Pondering these mid-twentieth century experiences, Kenneth Mouré nevertheless traces the intellectual roots of France's economic growth-spurt after the Liberation to the forcing-house of war, and finds some that antedate 1939. More imaginative economic planners broke free from the shackles of balanced budgets and defence of the franc at all costs. They instead pressed for a mixed economy and greater French exposure to global markets. This shift in principles was allied to nationalizations in banking, utilities, transport and aviation in 1945–6. Together it underpinned an impressive and rapid 'second industrial revolution' and a dramatic upturn in prosperity, infrastructural modernization and consumerism during France's '30 glorious years' (1945–74). Yet in economics, as in social identity and organization, in culture and the arts, the hand of the state seems ubiquitous – provident for enthusiasts of *dirigisme*, a throttling death-grip for critics. Strong 'public expectations that the state, rather than the marketplace, must solve the critical problems of unemployment and social exclusion', Mouré concludes, endured in France in the 1990s.

Social exclusion, particularly of immigrants from France's former empire and their descendants, has, for Martin Evans, ramifications far beyond questions of security, defence and the role of the state. The universalist ambitions of France's post-Revolutionary 'civilizing mission' formed a profoundly ambiguous, hypocritical and instrumental rationale for colonial domination down to the 1950s. They still provide mental structures, he reasons, for French post-colonial racism and racist-inspired civil discord. Strategies fostering subservience enabled France to control over 60 million non-metropolitan people in 1939. Imperialism disposed not just of a colonial administration, police and the army. Its instruments also included an enmeshing web of dominant cultural ties: the French language, the republican education system and its values, and paternalistic, racist assumptions about the relationship between colonial peoples and the metropolitan French. Echoing arguments that a 'Vichy syndrome' is the lasting legacy of the reactionary and collaborationist years of 1940–4 (a 'past that will not go away' in Henry Rousso and Eric Conan's expression), Evans concludes that France must face, into the twenty-first century, the challenge of living down a 'colonial syndrome'.[37]

Evidence in support of Evans's hypothesis has been accumulating since at least 1984 (when the National Front won 11 per cent of the vote and 10 members in the European parliamentary election). After that point Le Pen's rhetoric recommended 'putting the French first' (the title of his popular book, effectively his manifesto, of 1984, *Les Français d'abord*). This hoisted the National Front to electoral scores of between 10 and 15 per cent, as well as some highly contentious forays into local government as in Dreux.[38] Le Pen's success was constructed explicitly on a discourse of immigration, crime and taxation. But the National Front's novelty lay in its denial that immigrants could be assimilated into French society and in Le Pen's condemnation of the classic right with the gusto that conservatives normally reserved for the left. The Front drew on a long if tangled tradition stretching from nineteenth-century Bonapartism via the authoritarian, sometimes fascist, 'anti-party' formations of the interwar years to Pierre Poujade's movement of artisans and small shopkeepers of the 1950s (for which the young Le Pen had won a parliamentary seat). Above all, the National Front 'were populists who appealed to the people against the politicians'.[39]

In the early 1990s the Front made further inroads among an electorate dismayed at the apparent ineffectiveness of established conservatism, seen as presiding ineffectually over high unemployment, high taxes and frequent strikes during Edouard Balladur's and Alain Juppé's governments of 1993–7. The disrepute into which all 'mainstream' components of public life were sinking grew deeper because of political scandals that led to jail terms for former ministers Henri Emmanuelli and Bernard Tapie. Cover-ups and cronyism seemed to lurk in every corner of state administration.[40] Disconcerting details emerged in Mitterrand's last 2 years at the Elysée of his services to Vichy and use of his position to prevent the case against his friend René Bousquet, Vichy's secretary-general of the interior and right-hand man of collaborationist prime minister Pierre Laval, going to trial. This episode terminated without any national catharsis, Bousquet being conveniently assassinated in 1993 and Mitterrand dying in 1996. But it was followed by an outcry from human-rights groups and the newspaper *Libération* over the state's refusal to widen the trial in 1997 of Maurice Papon, for crimes against the Jews whilst Vichy sub-prefect at Bordeaux in 1942–4, to include the cover-up that, as Paris prefect of police, he afforded to police who in October 1961 murdered Algerians engaged in a peaceful protest against the Algerian war. The 'colonial syndrome' and its capacity to convulse French political life was plain in 1998, both in the schism that opened up between Le Pen and his aspiring successor as National Front leader, Bruno Mégret, and in the agitation as parliament and press engrossed themselves in debates about the status of illegal immigrants.

More widely, evidence from the 1997 parliamentary elections and municipal politics showed France increasingly afflicted by disillusion with politics and suffering, in Gildea's phrase, a 'crisis of representation'. France was not alone among western democracies at the end of the twentieth century in experiencing voter absenteeism and alienation. But it was a trend perhaps to give particular concern to the political class in a country where, more than in Britain and America, politics has been so emphatically, and in so many senses, a 'passion' since 1815. What to make of such contradictions as prohibiting late-twentieth-century France's most outrageous politician, Le Pen, from standing for public office after being found guilty of inciting racial hatred, whilst at the same time celebrating mid-twentieth-century France's most outrageous literary intellectuals to the extent of preparing a *Pléiade* edition of the long-proscribed works of the nihilistic anti-semite, Louis-Ferdinand Destouches (Céline)?

At the opening of the twenty-first century, then, French history still retains the capacity to deliver a shock. It declines any Whig interpretation, it eschews any incontrovertible pattern. In the end it confounds French national historians as much as it puzzles Anglo-Saxons. Two hundred years after Napoleon, French history and politics in many ways retains the 'laboratory status' assigned it by Karl Marx in his writings. But unlike Marx, who studied French history and politics in order to prove the inevitability of history in general, what emerges from this volume is the capacity of French history and politics even at the beginning of the twenty-first century to surprise.

National decadence and republican corruption seem obsessive themes for French people. Observers might be tempted to predict that France ends the 1990s teetering on the edge of a new abyss, crippled by political dysfunctionality and unravelling social cohesion. Yet they might hesitate in their forecast if they read the eerily similar warnings of a *fin-de-siècle* crisis that fill the British foreign office 'Confidential Print' files on France from 1896 to 1899 or the apocalyptic warnings in British diplomatic dispatches from Paris in the mid-1920s and mid-1930s. Conversely, those betting on French stability may ponder the swiftness of the Second Empire's demise in 1870, a year after embarking on a widely hailed programme of liberal reform, or the Fourth Republic's in 1958, a year after leading France into the new European Economic Community. In short, since the Revolution and Napoleon, Marianne has become practised at making a mockery of both the seasoned diplomatic observer and the imprudent historian-turned-soothsayer. Even after history's 'linguistic turn', the French archives, along with artistic representations and artefacts, remain a surer means for comprehending France's past than is a crystal ball for foretelling its future.

Acknowledgements

John Keiger and Joan Tumblety kindly criticized an earlier draft of this introduction and suggested a number of points that I have been pleased to add. Any remaining mistakes or misrepresentations are my responsibility.

Notes

1 Thomas W. Grabau, reviewing Hugh Clout, *After the Ruins: Restoring the Countryside of Northern France after the Great War*, in *American Historical Review*, 103:4 (Oct. 1998), p. 1261.
2 R. O. Paxton, *French Peasant Fascism: Henry Dorgères's Greenshirts and the Crises of French Agriculture, 1929–1939* (New York: Oxford University Press, 1997), pp. 6, 8.
3 Christophe Prochasson, 'Is there a "crisis" of history in France?', *Perspectives: The American Historical Association Newsletter*, 36:5 (May 1998), pp. 9–11.
4 McMillan's book first appeared as *Dreyfus to De Gaulle: French Politics and Society, 1898–1969* (London: Edward Arnold, 1985); M. J. M. Larkin, *France since the Popular Front: Government and People, 1936–1986* (Oxford: Oxford University Press, 1986, 2nd edn., 1997); R. Gildea, *France since 1945* (Oxford: Oxford University Press, 1996).
5 Maurice Agulhon, *The Republican Experiment, 1848–1852*; Alain Plessis, *The Rise and Fall of the Second Empire, 1852–1870*; Jean-Marie Mayeur and Madeleine Rebérioux, *The Third Republic from its Origins to the Great War, 1871–1914*; Philippe Bernard and Henri Dubief, *The Decline of the Third Republic, 1914–1938*; Jean-Pierre Azéma, *From Munich to the Liberation, 1938–1944*; Jean-Pierre Rioux, *The Fourth Republic, 1944–1958*; S. Berstein, *The Republic of de Gaulle, 1958–1969* (Cambridge: Cambridge University Press, 1983–93).
6 See R. Tombs's review (*Times Higher Education Supplement* 18 Apr. 1997, p. 31) of P. Nora, *Realms of Memory: The Construction of the French Past, Volume I: Conflicts and Divisions*, Ed. Lawrence D. Kritzman (New York: Columbia University Press, 1996).
7 Review in the *Times Literary Supplement* (1 Jan. 1999), p. 29, of A. Becker, *War and Faith: The Religious Imagination in France, 1914–1930* (Oxford: Berg, 1998). One research student saw this coming in 1978: his lament that months in the archives of the French army that occupied Germany in 1919–30 had turned up more on the men's wine rations and venereal diseases than on German breaches of the Versailles treaty led an eminent Oxford historian of France to retort: 'Marvellous: just the sort of history I want to see!'

8 Agulhon, *The Republican Experiment*, p. 187.

9 R. Tombs, 'Was there a French *Sonderweg?*', *European Identities – Identités Européennes* (1995), pp. 169–77.

10 F. Furet, *Revolutionary France, 1770–1880* (Oxford: Blackwell, 1992), p. 537. Cf. his *Interpreting the French Revolution* (Cambridge: Cambridge University Press, 1981).

11 S. C. Hause, *Hubertine Auclert, the French Suffragette* (New Haven and London: Yale University Press, 1988); S. C. Hause and A. R. Kenney, *Women's Suffrage and Social Politics in the French Third Republic* (Princeton: Princeton University Press, 1984); P. Smith, *Feminism and the Third Republic: Women's Political and Civil Rights in France, 1918–1945* (Oxford: Clarendon Press, 1996).

12 See A. W. H. Shennan, *Rethinking France: Plans for Renewal, 1940–1946* (Oxford, Oxford University Press, 1989).

13 E. Weber, *Peasants into Frenchmen: The Modernization of Rural France* (Stanford, CA: Stanford University Press, 1976).

14 See James R. Lehning, *Peasant and French: Cultural Contact in Rural France during the Nineteenth Century* (Cambridge: Cambridge University Press, 1995); Raymond A. Jonas, *Industry and Politics in Rural France: The Peasants of the Isère, 1870–1914* (Ithaca, NY: Cornell University Press, 1994). Weber reconsidered his thesis in 'Comment la politique vint aux paysans: a second look at peasant politicization', *American Historical Review*, 87 (Apr. 1982), pp. 357–89.

15 Suzanne Berger, *Peasants against Politics: Rural Organization in Brittany, 1911–1967* (Cambridge, MA: Harvard University Press, 1972); Philip C. F. Bankwitz, *Alsatian Autonomist Leaders, 1919–1947* (Lawrence: Regents' Press of Kansas, 1978).

16 See Vivien A. Schmidt, *Democratizing France: The Political and Administrative History of Decentralization* (Cambridge: Cambridge University Press, 1991); Howard Machin, *The Prefect in French Public Administration* (London: Croom Helm, 1977); J. E. S. Hayward, *The One and Indivisible French Republic* (London: Weidenfeld & Nicolson, 1973).

17 S. Reynolds, 'Marianne's citizens? Women, the Republic and universal suffrage in France', in idem (ed.), *Women, State and Revolution. Essays on Gender and Power in Europe since 1789* (Brighton: Harvester, 1986), p. 113.

18 See Andrée Michel, 'Socialism faces Feminism: The failure of synthesis in France, 1879–1914', in Marilyn J. Boxer and Jean Quataert (eds.), *Socialist women* (New York: Elsevier Press, 1978), pp. 75–111.

19 See Charles Sowerwine, *Sisters or Citizens? Women and Socialism in France since 1876* (Cambridge: Cambridge University Press, 1982).

20 T. Zeldin, *The French* (London: Collins Harvill, 1988), pp. 430–40. Cf. *France, 1848–1945*, I, pp. 343–64; M. Perrot, *Les Femmes ou les silences de l'histoire* (Paris: Flammarion, 1998).

21 See efforts to recover a women's history of the occupation and Liberation in the essays by these authors in H. R. Kedward and Nancy Wood (eds.), *The Liberation of France: Image and Event* (Oxford and Washington: Berg, 1995), chs. 5, 6, 9, 10, 11; also C. Duchen, *Women's Rights and Women's Lives in France, 1944–1968* (London Routledge, 1994); and *Modern & Contemporary France* 7:1 (Feb. 1999), a special issue entitled 'Gendering the occupation of France' (eds. H. Diamond and C. Gorrara).

22 'Programme of the CNR', Appendix B, in Peter Novick, *The Resistance versus Vichy: The Purge of Collaborators in Liberated France* (London: Chatto & Windus, 1968), p. 198.

23 P. Prestwich, 'Modernizing politics in the Fourth Republic: the case of women in the *Mouvement Républicain Populaire*, 1944–1958', in Martin S. Alexander and

Kenneth Mouré (eds.), *France Since the First World War: Crises and Renewal* (New York and Oxford: Berghahn, 2000).

24 A. Coutrot, 'Youth movements in France in the 1930s', *Journal of Contemporary History*, 5:1 (Jan. 1970), pp. 23–36.

25 Louis Allen, 'Resistance and the Catholic Church in France', in Stephen Hawes and Ralph White (eds.), *Resistance in Europe, 1939–1945* (London: Penguin, 1975), pp. 77–93; W. D. Halls, 'Church and State: prelates, theologians and the Vichy regime', in Nicholas Atkin and Frank Tallett (eds.), *Religion, Society and Politics in France since 1789* (London: Hambledon Press, 1991), pp. 167–86; 'Catholicism under Vichy: a study in diversity and ambiguity', in H. R. Kedward and Roger Austin (eds.), *Vichy France and the Resistance: Culture and Ideology* (Totowa, NJ: Croom Helm, 1985), pp. 133–46.

26 R. E. M. Irving, *Christian Democracy in France* (London: Allen & Unwin, 1973), p. 266.

27 See Tony Judt, *Past Imperfect: French Intellectuals, 1945–1956* (Berkeley: University of California Press, 1992); P. Vidal-Naquet, *Mémoires* (Paris: Seuil/La Découverte, 2 vols., 1995, 1998).

28 R. Cobb, *French and Germans, Germans and French: A Personal Interpretation of France under Two Occupations, 1914–18/1940–44* (Hanover, NH and London: University Press of New England, 1983). Cf. Philippe Burrin, *Living with Defeat: France under the German Occupation, 1940–1944* (London: Arnold, 1996).

29 See Herbert R. Lottman, *The People's Anger: Justice and Revenge in Post-Liberation France* (London: Hutchinson, 1986); Fred Kupferman, *Le Procès de Vichy: Pucheu, Pétain, Laval* (Brussels: Editions Complexe, 1980).

30 J. Tumblety, 'Obedient daughters of Marianne: discourses of patriotism and maternity in the French women's Resistance press during the Second World War', *Women's History Notebooks*, 4:2 (Summer 1997), pp. 1–6.

31 Quotations from Tombs, 'Was there a French *Sonderweg*?', pp. 170, 172.

32 See Leo A. Loubère, 'Left-wing Radicals, strikes and the military, 1880–1907', *French Historical Studies*, 3:1 (Spring 1963), pp. 93–105; Jean-Paul Brunet, *Saint Denis, la ville rouge. Socialisme et Communisme dans la banlieue ouvrière, 1890–1930* (Paris, 1980): Jacques Julliard, *Clemenceau, briseur de grèves: L'affaire de Draveil-Villeneuve-Saint-Georges* (Paris: Julliard, 1965).

33 Zeldin, *The French*, p. 440.

34 See Marilyn J. Boxer, 'Women in industrial home-work: the flowermakers of Paris in the Belle Epoque', *French Historical Studies*, 12:3 (Spring 1982), pp. 401–23; Theresa M. McBride, 'A women's world: department stores and the evolution of women's employment in France, 1870–1920', *French Historical Studies*, 10:4 (Fall 1978), pp. 664–83: Lenard R. Berlanstein, *The Working People of Paris, 1871–1914* (Baltimore: The John Hopkins University Press, 1984).

35 See Herrick E. Chapman. *State Capitalism and Working-Class Radicalism in the French Aircraft Industry* (Berkeley: University of California Press, 1991); Patrick Fridenson, *Histoire des Usines Renault, 1898–1939* (Paris: Seuil, 1972); Sylvie Schweitzer, *Des engrenages à la chaîne: les Usines Citroën, 1900–1935* (Paris: Publications de la Sorbonne, 1982).

36 See Alan S. Milward, *The New Order and the French Economy* (Oxford: Clarendon Press, 1970); Sarah Fishman, *We Will Wait: Wives of French Prisoners of War, 1940–1945* (New Haven: Yale University Press, 1991).

37 H. Rousso and E. Conan, *Vichy, un passé qui ne passe pas* (Paris: Fayard, 1994).

38 See Harvey G. Simmons, *The French National Front: The Extremist Challenge to Democracy* (Boulder, CO: Westview Press, 1996); Alec G. Hargreaves, *Immigration, 'Race' and Ethnicity in Contemporary France* (London: Routledge, 1995).

39 Gildea, *France since 1945*, pp. 190–1; Stanley Hoffmann, *Le mouvement Poujade* (Paris: Armand Colin, 1956).
40 Brian Jenkins and Peter Morris, 'Political scandal in France', *Modern and Contemporary France*, NS 1:2 (1993), pp. 127–37.

Further reading

Anderson, R. D. *France 1870–1914: Politics and Society* (London: Methuen, 1977).

Becker, J.-J. *The Great War and the French People* (Oxford: Berg, 1986).

Berstein, S. *Histoire du Parti Radical* (Paris: Presses de la FNSP, 2 vols., 1980–2).

Challener, R. D. *The French Theory of the Nation in Arms, 1866–1939* (Princeton: Princeton University Press, 1955).

Charle, C. *A Social History of France in the 19th Century* (Oxford: Berg, 1994).

Derfler, L. *President and Parliament: A Short History of the French Presidency* (Boca Raton, FL: University of Florida Press, 1983).

Fridenson, P. (ed.), *The French Home Front, 1914–1918* (Oxford: Berg, 1992).

Gibson, R. *A Social History of French Catholicism, 1789–1914* (London: Routledge, 1989).

Gildea, R. *The Past in French History* (New Haven: Yale University Press, 1994).

Girard, L. *Les Libéraux français, 1815–1875* (Paris: Aubier, 1985).

Gough, H. and Horne, J. (eds.), *De Gaulle and Twentieth Century France* (London: Edward Arnold, 1994).

Griffiths, R. *The Use of Abuse: The Polemics of the Dreyfus Affair and its Aftermath* (Oxford: Berg, 1991).

Ingram, N. *The Politics of Dissent: Pacifism in France, 1919–1939* (Oxford: Clarendon Press, 1991).

Irvine, W. D. *French Conservatism in Crisis: The Republican Federation in the 1930s* (Baton Rouge, LA: Louisiana State University Press, 1979).

——, *Boulangism Reconsidered* (Oxford: Oxford University Press, 1989).

Judt, T. *Socialism in Provence, 1871–1914: A Study in the Origins of the Modern French Left* (Cambridge: Cambridge University Press, 1979).

——, *Marxism and the French Left: Studies on Labour and Politics in France, 1830–1981* (Oxford: Clarendon Press, 1986).

Kedward, H. R. *Occupied France: Collaboration and Resistance, 1940–44* (Oxford: Blackwell, 1985).

——, *In Search of the Maquis: Rural Resistance in Southern France, 1942–44* (Oxford: Oxford University Press, 1993).

Kuisel, R. F. *Capitalism and the State in Modern France: Renovation and Economic Management in the Twentieth Century* (Cambridge: Cambridge University Press, 1981).

——, *Seducing the French: The Dilemma of Americanization* (Berkeley: University of California Press, 1993).

Larmour, P. *The French Radical Party in the 1930s* (Stanford, CA: Stanford University Press, 1962).

Lebovics, H. *True France: French Culture Wars and Identity, 1900–1945* (Berkeley: University of California Press, 1992).

Lynch, F. M. B. *A History of the French Economy: From Vichy to Rome, 1944–1958* (London: Routledge, 1996).

Magraw, R. *France 1815–1914: The Bourgeois Century* (London: Fontana, 1983).

Margadant, J. B. *Madame le Professeur: Women Educators in the Third Republic* (Princeton: Princeton University Press, 1990).

Marrus, M. R. 'Coming to terms with Vichy', *Holocaust and Genocide Studies*, 9:1 (Spring 1995), pp. 23–41.

McMillan, J. F. *Housewife or Harlot: The Place of Women in French Society, 1870–1940* (Brighton: Harvester, 1981).

——, *Napoleon III* (Harlow: Longman, 1994).

——, *Françaises: The Social Condition of Women and the Politics of Gender in France, 1789–1914* (London: UCL Press, 1997).

McPhee, P. *A Social History of France, 1780–1880* (London: Routledge, 1993).

Miller, M. B. *The Bon Marché: Bourgeois Culture and the Department Store, 1869–1920* (Berkeley: University of California Press, 1981).

Mortimer, E. *The Rise and Fall of the French Communist Party, 1920–1947* (London: Faber & Faber, 1984).

Nelms, B. F. *The Third Republic and the Centennial of 1789* (New York: Garland, 1987).

Nicolet, C. *L'Idée républicaine en France (1789–1914): essai d'histoire critique* (Paris: Presses de la FNSP, 1982).

Ory, P. *Une Nation pour mémoire, 1889–1939–1989: trois jubilés révolutionnaires* (Paris, 1992).

——, and Jean-François Sirinelli, *Les Intellectuels en France, de l'Affaire Dreyfus à nos jours* (Paris: Armand Colin 1986).

Paul, H. W. *The Second Ralliement: The Rapprochement between Church and State in France in the Twentieth Century* (Washington DC: Catholic University Press of America, 1967).

Paxton, R. O. *Vichy France: Old Guard and New Order, 1940–44* (New York: W. W. Norton, 1972).

Perrot, M. *Workers on Strike in France, 1871–1914* (Leamington Spa: Berg, 1986).

Prost, A. *In the Wake of War: 'Les Anciens Combattants' and French Society, 1914–1939* (Oxford: Berg, 1992).

Ralston, D. B. *The Army of the Republic: The Place of the Military in the Political Evolution of France, 1871–1914* (Cambridge, MA: Harvard University Press, 1967).

Rémond, R. (ed.), *Pour une histoire politique* (Paris: Seuil, 1988).

Reynolds, S. *France between the Wars: Gender and Politics* (London: Routledge, 1996).

Rothney, J. *Bonapartism after Sedan* (Ithaca, NY: Cornell University Press, 1970).

Rousso, H. 'L'Epuration en France: une histoire inachevée', *Vingtième Siècle*, 33 (Jan.–Mar. 1992), pp. 78–105.

Rubenstein, D. 'Publish and perish: the *épuration* of French intellectuals', *Journal of European Studies*, 23 (Mar.–Jun. 1993), pp. 71–91.

Schneider, W. H. *Quality and Quantity: The Quest for Biological Regeneration in Twentieth-Century France* (Cambridge: Cambridge University Press, 1991).

Serman, W. *Les Officiers français dans la nation, 1848–1914* (Paris: Aubier, 1982).

Shields, J. G. 'Antisemitism in France: The Spectre of Vichy', *Patterns of Prejudice*, 24:2–4 (1990), pp. 5–17.

Singer, B. 'The teacher as Notable in Brittany, 1880–1914', *French Historical Studies*, 9:4 (Fall 1976), pp. 635–59.

Shennan, A. W. H. *De Gaulle* (Harlow: Longman, 1993).

Stearns, P. N. *Revolutionary Syndicalism and French Labor: A Cause without Rebels* (New Brunswick: Rutgers University Press, 1971).

Tanenbaum, E. R. *The Action Française: Diehard Reactionaries in Twentieth-Century France* (New York: Columbia University Press, 1962).

Tombs, R. *The War against Paris, 1871* (Cambridge: Cambridge University Press, 1981).

Vinen, R. *The Politics of French Business, 1936–1945* (Cambridge: Cambridge University Press, 1991).

——, *Bourgeois Politics in France, 1945–1951* (Cambridge: Cambridge University Press, 1995).

Waites, N. (ed.), *Troubled Neighbours: Franco-British Relations in the Twentieth Century* (London: Weidenfeld & Nicolson, 1971).

Wall, I. M. *The French Communist Party in the Era of Stalin, 1945–1962* (Berkeley: University of California Press, 1983).

Watson, D. R. *Clemenceau* (London: Eyre Methuen, 1974).

Weber, E. *France: Fin-de-Siècle* (Cambridge, MA: Harvard University Press, 1986).

Zeldin, T. *France, 1848–1945 Vol. I: Ambition, Love and Politics; Vol. II: Intellect, Taste and Anxiety* (Oxford: Oxford University Press, 1973–7).

1

Revolution, Restoration(s) and beyond

Changes, continuities and the enduring legacies of 1789

PAMELA PILBEAM

Agreeing on an interpretation of the 1789 Revolution is akin to finding predictable patterns in a kaleidoscope. What other event is symbolized by two flags, the tricoloured representing the triumphant nation-state and the red flag of the international social revolution, both of which have continuing worldwide resonance? This chapter will begin with a brief outline of these legacies as a touchstone for an exploration of how successive generations defined and redefined them up to the present, with a particular focus on the years up to 1851.

The political legacy

The Revolution was the attempt of the wealthy élite (quickly refined to bourgeois) to modify the predominantly absolutist rule of the Bourbon king, Louis XVI with a written constitution inaugurating a parliamentary system in return for agreeing tax changes necessitated by the government's financial crisis. Peasants and artisans saw the opportunity to push their own demands with increasing violence. Bourgeois and popular revolution was followed by counter-revolution. In western France peasants and nobles fought against the Revolution in defence of the Church in a civil war that persisted throughout the 1790s. Some nobles emigrated with the king's two brothers and their opposition to the Revolution encouraged France's neighbours to invade. France was at war with one or more (mostly more) of her neighbours until 1815.

The French experimented with constitutional monarchy (1791–2) in which a small wealthy élite voted, declared a Republic (1792–1804), elected a Convention by almost universal suffrage (albeit indirect) and executed the king in 1793. The pressures of civil and foreign war and internecine political conflicts among the Revolutionaries led to power passing from the main assembly to a 12-man committee of public safety, controlled by the Jacobins. Led by a middle-class lawyer, Maximilien Robespierre, this committee pushed the French army from defence to conquest and persecuted opponents of all kinds in a campaign which came to be known as the Terror. The committee tried, dramatically, but ineffectually, to control prices and food supplies in the desperate economic crisis which resulted from Revolutionary legislation and war. In 1794 Robespierre's enemies in the Convention engineered his murder. In 1795 a new assembly, the Directory, replaced the democratic constitution which the Jacobins had voted but never implemented with a system where voting was again restricted to a small, rich, middle-class élite.

In 1799 quarrels among the Directors and fear of a monarchist counter-revolution encouraged them to offer a share in political power to the most successful of the generals, Napoleon, in a three-man Consulate. Any shadow of representative government was interred with this barely disguised military dictatorship. In 1804 it was transformed into an Empire and the Republic quietly forgotten. Thus in political terms the Revolution offered no agreed model for subsequent regimes, other than a tradition of rebellion and a cascade of contrasting experiments.

Can one say that the Revolutionaries adopted a set of overarching political principles? Nineteenth-century revolutionaries, in France and elsewhere, implied that they did, admiring the emphasis on individual liberty and equality, liberal constitutional and national ideals. The relevance of these will be assessed in what follows. Suffice it to say at this point that the often-quoted ideas of the eighteenth-century enlightened writers offered no simple template. Their advice on politics ranged from direct democracy and faith in the 'general will' (Rousseau) to representative institutions and separation of powers (Montesquieu). In the bi-centenary celebrations in 1989 the Declaration of the Rights of Man was honoured, but in the Revolutionary decades these rights were repeatedly ignored or revised. The Revolutionaries may have proclaimed liberty, equality and fraternity, but the three were frequently abandoned.

The institutional legacy

If the Revolution left a tradition of cataclysmic political instability, it was accompanied by the creation of all of the institutions of the modern, centralized French state (except political); council of state, departments, prefectures, judicial, fiscal and educational systems, which allowed the state to survive the repeated upheavals of the nineteenth century. Standardized codes of law were worked out. What is more, these institutions were

exported by the conquering French armies and remained in place in parts of
Italy and Germany through the nineteenth century.

The social legacy

At first the dismantling of traditional privileges was supported by a number
of influential clerics and nobles within the privileged orders of society. On 4
August 1789 the Assembly declared an end to feudal privileges, which had
constituted a hated extra rent from peasants to noble, and some bourgeois,
owners. However the escalation of the Revolution, and particularly the
attack on the Church, alienated many nobles, some of whom emigrated and
were accused of betraying France. Emigré property was confiscated and sold.
By 1814 the nobility owned about 20 per cent of France; their share had
dropped by 5 per cent since 1789. The amount confiscated varied between
regions and the nobility remained dominant in areas where, traditionally,
they had been the richest group. Nobles (real and imagined) were persecuted
during the Terror and nobles were denied political rights. The only tangible
aspect of 'fraternity' in the 1790s was the title 'citizen'. Napoleon re-
introduced titles and a Legion of Honour. From 1801 he encouraged noble
émigrés to return and gave them jobs on such a scale that one-third of his
officials had served the pre-Revolutionary monarchy.

Those who gained from the Revolution were the already prosperous,
traditional middle-class groups, state officials, lawyers, doctors, landowners
and some businessmen and industrialists. Those who had been employed by
the state before 1789 had bought their jobs, and the Revolutionaries, in
abolishing venal office as an aspect of privilege, compensated them. The
former office-holders often spent their gains on confiscated church and noble
property, and frequently were back as civil servants within a few years. The
less well off, peasants and artisans, who had hoped for much from 1789,
tended to do least well. Their gains from the abolition of feudal rights and the
tithe paid to the Church were often illusory. Leases were redrafted and rents
were increased. Common land was sometimes sold off, depriving poorer
peasants of timber and grazing rights which were vital to their survival. The
abolition of guilds and a ban on associations threatened to leave artisans
without the protection of their traditional trade corporations. The state
replaced the Church as the provider of rudimentary social services, poor
relief, hospitals and schools, but the cost of war left nothing with which to
build new institutions, beyond the promises of the Jacobins in the desperate
economic crisis of the mid-1790s. The social legacies of the Revolution for
the poor were fine sentiments of freedom and equality, in an economy which
swung between relative prosperity and crisis, not just in the war years, but
throughout the nineteenth century. The repeated popular disturbances with
which the century was punctuated, and which created the opportunity for

ambitious politicians to seize power, were the direct product of the combined destabilization of Revolutionary legislation and economic change.

Those who did worst of all in the 1790s were the 50 per cent of the population who were almost universally ignored by historians until the 1970s: women. Traditionally, the Catholic Church swung between reverence for Mary, virgin mother of Jesus, and contempt and fear for all women, mere products of Adam's rib, evil temptresses of men, dominated by their bodily function of procreation and permanently subordinate to men. Enlightened writers claimed, on the contrary, that women had an identity distinct from that of men. However they concluded, most emphatically Jean-Jacques Rousseau, that women's natures were essentially emotional, bereft of the male faculty of reason.

Before 1789 a few wealthy, educated women, such as Madame Necker, wife of one of Louis XVI's chief ministers, ran salons, through which they exercised an informal political influence. Female property-owners could delegate their vote when elections were held. Traditionally poorer women also had a voice, as a leading element in bread riots and demonstrations in times of dearth. This last role was reiterated during the Revolution, when women took a prominent role in marches. An educated minority of women asserted that rights demanded for all men should be accorded to women. Olympe de Gouges wrote a Declaration of the Rights of Women, Pauline Lacombe and Pauline Léon set up women's clubs and women attended those run by men, for instance the Jacobins. Others formed groups to help the war-effort, making bandages rather than fighting. Women represented the Revolution in the festivals of the 1790s. Some male Revolutionaries, such as J. A. Condorcet, were initially sympathetic to demands for decent education for girls. Divorce was made legal for the first time and between 1792 and its withdrawal in 1816 75 per cent of petitioners were deserted wives.

In all other respects the Revolution was hostile to women. The Jacobins stood by Rousseau's view and ejected women from the clubs. They insisted that virtuous female Revolutionaries would confine themselves to breast-feeding and rearing the next generation of republican soldiers. War and economic depression made the Revolutionary years disastrous for poorer women, who increasingly bore the brunt as lone parents, trying to feed and sustain families. They were often hostile to legislation, which took away from the Church the traditional ceremonies surrounding birth, marriage and death, which had legitimated the social fabric on which they depended to reinforce family loyalties. The civil code, completed in 1804, actually reduced the rights of women, depriving them of control over their dowries and their children and denying a woman's right to remonstrate with an unfaithful spouse unless he actually obliged her to share a bed with him and his mistress.

A few women had notable roles in the revolution. Marie-Antoinette seemed to reinforce 'old-Eve' prejudices, while Charlotte Corday's spectac-ular murder of Marat supported the notion that women were dominated by their emotions. Madame Roland had a substantial 'behind-scenes' influence on Revolutionary politics for a time, while Madame de Staël, daughter of Necker, expanded the traditional concept of the salon by her much-read commentaries on the Revolution.

The most contentious aspect of 1789, which provoked the escalation of Revolution and brought repeated conflict through the nineteenth century, was religion. At the outset the Church was the single richest landowner, in possession of 10 per cent of France. These estates were declared national property and sold, mostly to wealthy middle-class Revolutionaries. Clergy were paid a salary by the government. A civil constitution of the clergy was imposed in 1790, but many clerics refused to accept it. Church ceremonies for birth, marriage and death were outlawed for a number of years and the committee of public safety instituted a new religion of the Supreme Being. After the fall of Robespierre Catholicism was gradually restored and in 1801 Napoleon signed a concordat with the pope, which brought an uneasy peace. While some people shared the anti-clericalism of the Revolutionaries, many did not, for most clergy were not privileged fat cats, but sons of peasants.

The patriotic legacy

At the outset the Revolutionaries emphasized that the war on privilege would liberate the nation. France would become a nation of free individuals, not subjects, through legal and fiscal equality. At first talk of patriotism and the nation was not aggressive towards neighbouring states. When the government went to war in the spring of 1792 it was to liberate oppressed people. This fiction persisted in public discourse throughout the war years. Radicals continued to believe in it and nineteenth-century revolutionaries in Poland, Belgium and Italy, were inclined to look – fruitlessly – to France for help. Sadly war turned patriotism into the obligation of all young, male adults to be subject to military service and the obligation of everyone to pay for the war. As it turned out, the French armies conquered more of Europe than anyone since Charlemagne. The scale of France's empire became the measure of the patriotic legacy, which effectively meant that patriotism became rolled into reverence for the emperor himself.

Beginning and ending the Revolution

Historians have disagreed on the significance of all manifestations of the Revolutionary years, philosophical, ideological, institutional, socio-economic, cultural, even and especially on its time-span. There is no consensus on when the Revolution began and particularly on when, even if, it finished. To agree on a starting date involves a debate on the origins of the Revolution itself. The variety of answers depends, not on factual uncertainty, but on the respondent's political and social assumptions. The meeting of the Estates-General, France's formerly almost moribund elected assembly in May 1789, is normally considered the date to begin, but some historians have argued that the crisis which led to a quarter of a century of upheaval was set off by the refusal of the assembly of notables, 1787, to agree to taxation reform. Historians who select one of these dates are likely to consider that the Revolution was mainly precipitated by the short-term political and fiscal crisis, a view that was common in the early nineteenth century and is popular again at the end of the twentieth. Those who have favoured a more long-term perspective can be divided into those who thought 1789 was a revolution of the mind and those who thought it was one of the body. The first, including the doyen of present-day Revolutionary historians, François Furet, stressed the contribution of the theories of enlightened writers like Voltaire and Rousseau to the Revolution; the other, which has included all socialist and communist historians, who dominated thinking on the Revolution for the first 50 or so years of the twentieth century, believed that the Revolution was a class war, marking, quintessentially, the rise of the bourgeoisie and the aggravated impoverishment of the masses.

Dating the end of the Revolution is even more contentious. The fall of Robespierre and the demise of the Jacobins in 1794 is often preferred, although in recent years historians have realized that the new institutions and codes of law were prepared by the Directory. Subsequent upheavals in 1830–4, 1848–51 and 1870–1 may be considered as elements in a continuum of which 1789 was the auspicious or disastrous initiation. When did the Revolution end? Is it finished? The French still take to the streets: lorry-drivers, farmers, fishermen, even civil servants, tolerated by fellow citizens. The fundamental essence of all revolution, written into the Jacobin constitution of 1793, is surely the right to rebel. Is not the claim that the Revolution has 'come into port'[1] merely a denial of that right?

There have been three broad trends of political response to the Revolution: a royalist right-wing rejection; a very fluid liberal centre, which always claimed to deplore violence and favour moderate change; and a republican left, which honoured the radical Jacobin phase (1793–4). Over the last two centuries other factors, including economic change and successive revolutions in France and elsewhere, have caused the main outlines of each broad tendency to be adjusted, sometimes radically reshaped, while remaining intrinsically parallel, if not openly conflictual.

The Revolution has always been refashioned by succeeding generations to address contemporary concerns. To put themselves in a good light the Directory and Napoleon damned Robespierre and the Jacobins, whom they condemned for the violence of the Terror, hoping that their own denial of political liberties would thus be obscured. In 1815 France's enemies, the four major states of Europe, combined finally to defeat and exile Napoleon and to restore the Bourbons as constitutional rulers.

The Liberal Revolution and the Restoration liberals, 1814–1830

The retelling of the Revolution began during the Restoration, spurred on by the contemporary passionate interest in the past, but also catering to a market which hoped to read more titillating tales of the Terror. The Revolution was as good for the 'history business' as is Nazi Germany at the end of the twentieth century. One publisher planned a 12-volume edition of Revolutionary memoirs and found 53 eager contributors. When memorialists ran thin, Honoré de Balzac and Victor Hugo produced fictionalized autobiographies.

There were a large number of ambitious unemployed officials, dismissed particularly after Napoleon's escape and hundred-day return from exile in 1815, who were anxious to justify their past. At first interest focused on the early 1790s, but in Charles X's reign the more problematical Convention was addressed. The Terror was played down. Adolphe Thiers and François Mignet, representing a younger generation, wrote influential accounts, which gloried in the Revolution in order to circumnavigate the censor, display the inadequacies of the Restoration and prophesy a future in which they would have a political role. Thiers thought the initial Revolution was a mere accident, pushed forward by ambitious politicians, which could have been curtailed by modest conciliation by the king. Mignet's more probing, though fatalistic, analysis blamed the crisis on arbitrary and decadent royal government and the resistance of the notables. The Revolution had a progressive, national and liberatingly constitutional shape for liberals like Thiers and Mignet. They lauded the patriotism of the 1790s, the way in which the invading Prussians had been repulsed and territory acquired. This facilitated unflattering comparisons with the defeats and lack-lustre foreign policy of the restored Bourbons, as long as one forgot that it was actually Napoleon who was twice defeated in 1814 and 1815. Thiers and Mignet gloried in the fairy-tale triumph of the constitutional principles of the third estate over the absolute regime of Louis XVI at a time when Restoration liberals were doing battle with ultra-royalists in parliament. But could anyone forget that the Revolution had led to military dictatorship?

The politicians of the 1790s, all educated in the classical tradition, had looked back to the ancient world for precedents when they prepared their revolutionary alternative to the *ancien-régime* monarchy. The liberal historians/politicians of the 1820s emphasized more recent Revolutionary examples. The quarrel between the National Assembly and Louis XVI was compared with the English Revolution of 1642, which gave assiduous historical minds the opportunity to compare the restored Stuarts, Charles II and James II with the Bourbon brothers, Louis XVIII and Charles X. England's 'Glorious' Revolution of 1688 was presented by liberals as an exemplar for the French in the late 1820s – tailor-made history!

The liberals claimed that the institutional changes of the Revolution signified the transition from a feudal, aristocratic kingdom to an enlightened, rational society. The Revolution spelled the end of the privilege of birth, replacing it with the more egalitarian (it was claimed) privilege of acquired wealth, honoured in the limited franchise of the first constitution of 1791, which gave a vote to the 60000 most wealthy taxpayers. The new lay secondary schools and the extension of professional tertiary education, both sectors with competitive examinations, created the basis for careers open to talent (and cash). The new society that the liberals welcomed was essentially elitist; codified legal equality was partnered by liberty for the rich and the third icon of 1789, fraternity, was temporarily forgotten.

These structures were retained at the Restoration; the Constitutional Charter of 1814 tacked the Bourbon monarchy onto the new institutions of the revolutionary and imperial decades. Lacking an acceptable revolutionary model, the constitution-makers adopted a bi-cameral parliament not unlike that of England. The lower house or chamber of deputies was directly elected by up to 100000 wealthy taxpayers, the chamber of peers was nominated by the king. Liberals claimed this constitutional arrangement as a legacy of the Revolution and rolled together their admiration for a patriotic, liberal, state-building Revolution with their fondness for the 1814 Charter.

A more radical, and even more 'creative' interpretation of the Revolution was heard in 1828. P. Buonarroti, Gracchus Babeuf's former associate in the conspiracy of the equals of 1796, published his account of their abortive revolt, which had led to his own imprisonment and Babeuf's execution. Buonarroti produced a veritable *tour de force* of distortion in describing the Jacobinism of the Convention and Robespierre through a prism of Babouvist egalitarian communism. His prize piece of 'evidence', which he and subsequent neo-Jacobins reproduced at will, was the Jacobin constitution, passed by the Convention in 1793 and never implemented. The Convention would not have dreamt of attacking private ownership as Babeuf had envisaged.

The Restoration Right: Revolution as the overturning of society

The right, not unnaturally, took a very different view of 1789. In 1796 Joseph de Maistre saw the hand of a judgmental providence, not progress and human determination, in the Revolution. 'The very rascals who appear to lead the Revolution are involved only as simple instruments.'[2] J. de Maistre and, during the Restoration, Louis de Bonald, set the tone of right-wing condemnation of 1789 as a whirlwind of destruction, visited upon an errant people as expiation for their sins. In 1797 the influential Abbé Barruel set an ever-popular hare running with the view that the Revolution was a conspiracy of philosophers, such as Voltaire and d'Alembert, and Freemasons. At the Restoration right-wing ultra-royalists, ostensibly speaking for the purists who spent the Revolutionary decades as émigrés, toyed with a variety of forms of clericalist, aristocratic, royalist counter-revolution. The Constitutional Charter made no mention of the Revolutionary years, merely noting that divine providence had recalled Louis XVIII to the throne of his ancestors. School history lessons stopped at 1789. The realization that the defeat of Napoleon would not permit, and could not facilitate, a return to 1789, made the Restoration constitutional compromise potentially viable for a majority of royalist supporters – after all it provided a check on royal power which notables had sought, but failed to agree on in 1787. Thus although the Revolution was anti-Christ to the right, the new state institutions, including parliament, were not entirely disagreeable to the more moderate majority among them. Louis XVIII was determined to make the settlement work and in 1814 retained most of Napoleon's officials, despite the grumbles of émigrés.

In recent years historians have suggested that the Restoration was an 'impossible monarchy'.[3] At the outset, this did not appear to be so; serious difficulties were created by Napoleon's escape from Elba, the brief resurrection of the Empire under the same set of officials, and the consequent release of right-wing émigré ultra-royalist revenge once the allies had again defeated Napoleon. It cannot be denied that some ultra-royalists on the extreme right dreamt of a mythical alternative to the Revolution in which king, Church and nobility ruled a grateful people in a decentralizing anti-Revolution. What made the Restoration impossible was that the leader of the ultras became king in 1824.

During the Restoration, the 1789 Revolution was perceived as a social as well as a political phenomenon. Friends and enemies all acknowledged that the 1790s witnessed the access to power of 'the bourgeoisie'. To the right the unnatural and deplorable attack on the power of traditional élites within the Church and nobility was a consequence of the mistakes of royal ministers. It undermined spiritual and cultural values, as well as socio-economic status. Irreligion and materialism merged into social degeneration. The deeply pessimistic social perspective of the right was the mirror-image of the optimistic, sometimes triumphalist, presentation of the rise of the bourgeoisie offered by liberal friends of the Revolution in the early nineteenth century.

Ultra perceptions of a 'bourgeois Revolution' had some reverberations in contemporary politics. Charles X tried to reverse the perceived bourgeois ascent by preferring ancient lineage above professional training in appointments and promotions in civil administration, the judiciary, the army and the church. Not unnaturally his prefects reported the ubiquitous presence of 'bourgeois' liberal opponents, and were disastrously out of touch with local élites, ensuring that liberals strengthened their control of parliament in the 1830 elections.

The attack on the Church remained the worst aspect of 1789 for the right. The 1814 constitution attempted a compromise: Church land sales were not questioned, state salaries for clergy remained, but Catholicism was restored as the state religion. Religious differences were exacerbated by ultra ambitions after the Hundred Days. A vigorous evangelical campaign was launched, closely linked to ultra counter-revolutionary senior clerics, such as de Quelen, archbishop of Paris. Small groups of young priests toured the country, spending a week in a commune, ostensibly recalling the community to the faith. Book-burnings, figuring Voltaire and other writers honoured by the Revolutionaries, were a feature of their visit. Their final day was taken up with a service of penitence, not for individual transgressions, but for the Revolution. Missionary crosses were placed on civil land to mark their passage.

The Church made a determined effort to recover its former control over education. A senior cleric, Monseigneur de Frayssinous, became grand master of the university in 1822. Liberal academics, including Victor Cousin and François Guizot, were ousted from their posts and replaced by priests. In 1825 sacrilege was made a capital offence. From 1822 clergy were engaged as electoral agents, to preach in favour of ultra candidates. Charles X made a point of being crowned in a 'traditional' ceremony in Rheims cathedral, unlike his brother who had taken a simple oath at Notre-Dame. The religious differences of the Revolutionary years were thus rekindled by ultra intransigence and ineptitude in the 1820s and were a matter of politics, not history. It should be noted however that right-wing politicians were themselves divided over religious matters. In 1828 the Martignac government expelled the Jesuits. Liberal politicians voiced fears for the religious settlement, but only the most radical supported popular anti-clerical demonstrations against missionary crosses and so on in 1830. Most saw value in the social conservatism of the Church and many were religious, despite their anti-clericalism.

1830 and the Revolution that pretended it never happened

Why was there renewed revolution in 1830? At the level of national politics the July Days were the classic case of two stationary cars colliding. A political crisis developed after the 1827 election. Liberals, brought together in defence of the 1814 constitution, and especially up in arms at overt government cheating on electoral lists and elections themselves, gained 160–180 seats, equal with royalists, ultras controlling the remaining 60–80 seats. Liberals then won nearly all the 100 or so by-elections needed because of accusation of government corruption. Normal practice was for the king to select ministers who matched the predominant political trends in parliament, vital if legislation was to be passed. The king refused to countenance a set of liberal ministers, although he made one of their leading spokesmen, Pierre Royer-Collard, president of the chamber of deputies. Indeed when his centre-right government, led by the comte de Martignac, failed to persuade the conflicting parliament groups to pass any legislation, the king appointed an assortment of ultra-royalists, led by his friend, the prince de Polignac.

When parliament was recalled after several months' delay in March 1830, a liberal majority of 221 passed an unprecedented motion of no confidence in the government. The king called new elections, which he lost. Both sides invoked the 1814 constitution, both risked revolution. Using the excuse that liberals threatened revolution (after all in 1829 they had organized petitions to refuse taxes unless voted by the assembly) Charles hesitated, then invoked Article 14 of the Charter which allowed him to make decree laws in a national emergency. He issued four ordinances at the end of July 1830 which forced the liberal newspapers to close, dissolved the new assembly before it could meet and called new elections in which only the quarter richest voters, who had had a second vote since ultra legislation in 1820, would be able to vote.

This ultra counter-revolution came within an ace of success. The liberal journalists protested that the ordinances were not justified by the constitution, but the editors could not agree on open defiance. The liberal deputies talked, but were even further from active opposition. What brought barricades, the July Days and the overthrow of Charles, was the escalation of the long-standing incipient rebellion in artisan Paris, itself a product of the economic depression which had begun in 1827. Street demonstrations had been common since 1827, workers demanding government action against high food prices, short-time working and unemployment. The four ordinances added newspaper workers to the militants, and an overt political element to their protest.

Barricades were erected in the same central right-bank districts of the capital which had been the heart of revolution in the 1790s. Folk-memory/myth of earlier revolutions contributed to the symbols adopted by those who fought, including the tricolour flag, the resurrection of the National Guard, dissolved for insubordination by the king in 1827, and the decision to march on the *hôtel de ville*. Non-commissioned officers and men, many of whom had fought with Napoleon, deserted to the rebels. Recollected revolutionary *élan* may have been less significant however in creating a new insurrection than a shortage of troops in Paris: only 6000 could be mustered, a large section of the army being in Algeria. Equally significant was the dangerously volatile urban geography of central Paris, where artisan and governmental centres were cheek by jowl with newspaper offices in narrow streets in which barricades were easily erected.

A Revolutionary Monarchy? 1830–1848

The Restoration liberals gained control of this artisan movement and brought the revolt to an abrupt end, ostensibly to prevent civil war and possible foreign invasion. They invited Charles X's cousin, Louis-Philippe, duc d'Orléans, to be king and adopted the Revolutionary flag, the tricolour, as the national standard. They hastily revamped the 1814 constitution in an afternoon, claiming that few changes were needed. The electorate was increased to 166000 by the inclusion of 200-franc taxpayers. The electoral principle was later applied to local councils, which enfranchised about 2 million men. Article 14 was abolished. The principle of hereditary succession to the chamber of peers was abolished in favour of life-membership. The National Guard was revived, its officers elected by its members, and the Catholic Church was disestablished.

The decision to offer the throne, vacant when Charles X fled to England at the beginning of August, to his cousin, was opportunistic convenience. Thiers placarded Paris proclaiming Louis-Philippe's devotion to the Revolution, which as the liberal deputies explained in their proclamation making the duke lieutenant-general of France on 31 July, consisted of his fighting for the Revolutionary armies at Valmy and Jemappes. During the Revolution his father renamed himself Philippe-Egalité, was elected to the Convention and voted the death of his cousin in January 1793. Thus the Orléans family had a tradition of acrimonious waiting in the wings, but Louis-Philippe's Revolutionary connections had been a passing fancy. Subsequently he joined his cousins as an émigré and returned to France with them in 1814. He returned the richest landowner in the kingdom and in 1825 he and his sister were the largest beneficiaries of the state loan indemnifying former émigrés for lands they had lost during the Revolution. Louis-Philippe was no Revolutionary, but a prudent family man. His banker, the liberal Jacques Laffitte, surrounded himself with a small group of Orléanist hopefuls in the late 1820s, but Louis-Philippe kept clear. His cousin Charles X was not young, he was 79 when he died in 1836, and his heir, the posthumously born 'miracle-child' Henri, son of the duc de Berri, was 8 in 1830. Louis-Philippe was likely to be regent during Henri's minority.

Thus it required some sleight of hand to present a plausible image of Louis-Philippe as an element in the Revolutionary tradition, although the liberals and their new 'king of the French people' tried hard. He was called 'king of the barricades', a republican, even a bourgeois, king. He played the part. In all of his many official portraits he was the very model of a modern monarch, dressed in National Guard uniform, usually clutching a copy of the revised constitution, with no hint of the old-world splendour of Charles X's formal portraits. He maintained his father's tradition at the Palais-Royal. The grounds were open to the public, the tree-lined courts still lined with shops, small theatres, exhibitions and cafés. He was always approachable and could be seen with his rolled umbrella (a real sign of bourgeois stability) walking around the paths. His sons attended the local *lycée*. He contributed to a visual reworking of the Great Revolution, transforming the palace of Versailles into a museum to the Revolutionary years, filled with suitably heroic specially commissioned paintings.

Illustration 1.1 Jean-Victor Schnetz: The Fight for the Hôtel-de-Ville, 28 July 1830. The Hôtel-de-Ville in central Paris was the symbol of popular revolution. Note the tricolour flag and rosette on the top hat, the mixture of workers and middle-class activists, the flag carrying the declamation 'Long live the Charter'. (Paris, Musée du Petit Palais. Photo: AKG London, Erich Lessing.)

Republicans and the Revolution of the people, 1830–1848

The Restoration liberals had been held together less by a common affection for the Great Revolution and the 1814 settlement, than by their hostility to Polignac and their suspicions of Charles X. Once this negative bond was broken by the July Days, the liberal alliance fell apart. It was soon apparent that the former allies held contrasting views on what 1789 had meant and what 1830 ought to achieve. The new Orléanist or July Monarchy was the work of the most cautious liberals, such as Guizot and Casimir Périer, who became known as the resistance and who by March 1831 were in control. Their aim was to modify the 1814 settlement as little as possible. The limited nature of the changes made to the constitution did not suit more radical politicians, including Jacques Laffitte and Odilon Barrot, who had hoped that the July Days would bring wide-ranging political reform, but who were manoeuvred out of government in March 1831. They were dubbed the movement. The radicals who were most disappointed with the new regime quickly became overtly republican and organized themselves into neo-Jacobin clubs, notably Friends of the People, later the Rights of Man, names recalling the First Republic, whose sections had names like Robespierre and St Just. Influenced by Buonarroti, they talked vaguely of democracy and even less precisely of the need for social reform. Their rules usually included regulations about weapons and training, and the presence of artisan and peasant members alongside doctors, lawyers and other middle-class radicals caused Orléanist governments some concern. By the late 1830s a number of these were calling themselves socialists or communists.

The July Revolution of 1830 may have been a mere 'three glorious days', in contrast to the earlier decade of revolution, but popular unrest persisted sporadically until the Lyon rising of April 1834 and beyond. Artisan and peasant demonstrators were supported by the most radical of the former liberals, some of whom briefly held official posts after the Revolution. They used the traditional symbols of the Great Revolution, the tree of liberty, red bonnets and flags and sang Ça Ira and the Carmagnole. Their protests were habitually anti-clerical; Restoration missionary crosses were replaced with trees of liberty. This movement culminated in the sacking of the church of St Germain l'Auxerrois in central right-bank Paris, following a memorial service for the duc de Berri in February 1831. The less well-off had hoped that the new regime would reduce or abolish indirect taxes on wine, salt and tobacco and solve basic economic problems of high food prices and short-ages produced by harvest failure. When political uncertainty aggravated the economic crisis, tax collectors were attacked and their offices fired and bread riots were accompanied by the forced sale of grain. Peasants protested against the sale of common lands and the withdrawal of their rights to its use. Rebels were thus preoccupied with issues which had moved their predecessors in the 1790s, and were equally ineffectual. In the 1790s it was the comfortably-off property-owner, professional man and state servant who profited from revolution. 1830 was no different. A new factor had been added to unrest: the impact of economic change. From 1830 the popular movement was driven less by the past than by contemporary economic problems.

The social problems of proto-capitalism and the development of capitalist industry, with accompanying periodic economic crises and unemployment, were central to the 1830 Revolution and gave a new slant to how radicals perceived 1789. Radical journalists were quick to criticize the Orléanists' failure to deal with the problem of poverty in 1830, linking the issues to disappointed expectations in the 1790s. A number wrote influential accounts of both revolutions. One of the first was Etienne Cabet, soon to declare himself a republican socialist, who noted how little the new regime did for the poor and coined the phrase that 1830 was 'smuggled away' from the actual revolutionaries, the artisans. His subsequent history of 1789, written in the late 1830s when Orléanist persecution forced him into exile in London, was unusual for a republican account in its criticism of the Jacobins. He rejected revolution as a means to social reform and by 1840, when he returned to Paris, had settled for a utopian, communist, alternative, which he carefully distinguished from the revolutionary communism of Babeuf and Auguste Blanqui.

Louis Blanc, enthused by popular neo-Jacobinism, wrote his interpretation of the Great Revolution in the early 1840s after completing a multi-volume account of the first 10 years of the July Monarchy. The first volume of his history of 1789 appeared in 1847, the final in 1862, during his extended exile in London where he was the first to use the huge collection of revolutionary journals and pamphlets in the British Museum. Like his equally famous contemporary, Jules Michelet, Blanc saw 1789 as a Revolution of ideas, spirituality and destiny; he even found the masonic-plot theory credible. He argued that history was successively dominated by authority, individualism and fraternity and noted Voltaire as the prophet of the second and Rousseau of the third. Blanc was the first historian of the Revolution to differentiate between the contribution of the various enlightened philosophers to give weight to social and economic forces, a sign of his own commitment to socialism.

Preoccupied with the contemporary big issue of the 1830s and 1840s, the social question, Blanc linked 1789 with 1830 and, inspired by Buonarroti, portrayed the Jacobins as embryonic socialists. Referring to a theme which would have been familiar to his readers, Blanc noted that 1830 had been a revolution controlled by a bourgeoisie which had gained control in the 1790s. 1830 was a Bourgeois Revolution, not because it put the bourgeoisie into power, but because it left them there. The incompleteness of both revolutions made further social change to improve the status and security of the poor essential, although Blanc hoped that this could be achieved without violence.

Scornful of the Orléanists' failure to develop a more parliamentary system, commentators began to stress the parliamentary aspects of the 1790s. The radicals of the July Monarchy were profoundly religious, revering 'Christ of the barricades', and they stressed that religion had been important to the revolutionaries of the early 1790s, despite their anticlericalism. Philippe Buchez, a Christian socialist, was the joint author in 1837 of a history which stressed both the religious faith of the revolutionaries and the importance of the 1790s for the birth of a parliamentary tradition. In 1846 Edgar Quinet, a professor at the Collège de France, put the defence of Christianity at the heart of his version of what was still an anticlerical revolution.

Books on 1789 filled the shelves in the years just before the 1848 Revolution, just as they had in the late 1820s. The first volume of Jules Michelet's passionate and acclaimed description of the liberation of the 'people' appeared in 1847, the last in 1853, and it was translated into English in 1860. Alphonse de Lamartine, a poet, aristocratic landowner and radical member of the chamber of deputies, criticized the social inequities of the Orléanist regime and in 1847 brought out a romantic and inaccurate tale of the role of the Girondins in three volumes, which was also later translated into English. In the same year a parallel defence of the Jacobins was made by the radical Alphonse Esquiros. By 1848 the small number of avowed republicans in France had been taught by most histories to see the Great Revolution through a neo-Jacobin haze.

Bonapartism and the Revolution, 1814–1848

Reverence for Napoleon made progress during the July Monarchy, less as written history than as patriotic commemoration of past military glory. Painters of the Restoration and July Monarchy turned Napoleon into the sentimental hero on a white horse. Louis-Philippe tried to put himself at the head of Romantic Bonapartism, organizing the official installation of Napoleon's ashes in Les Invalides in 1840. The Orléanists regarded republicans as a threat, banning all mention in the press after 1835, but Bonapartism was seen as a patriotic sentiment lacking a current patron. Louis-Philippe failed to insert his own claim and merely earned a few scornful Daumier cartoons portraying a portly king perched on a horse – white, it is true, but a broken-down nag. There was no credible imperial heir after Napoleon's death in 1821. His son, 'the little eagle', died in Vienna in 1832. His great-nephew, Louis-Napoleon, did his best to make his name trying to seize power in Strasbourg in 1836 and Boulogne in 1840, his only reward being imprisonment. He wrote a brief summary of Napoleon's ideas, recalling the liberal parliamentary constitution of the Hundred Days and the implausible tale told in Napoleon's memoirs, that the emperor had not wanted to be a military dictator but had been forced to fight by European enemies. In 1848

Bonapartism seemed to be an inspiring harmless historic memory and myth with no future, sustained by the collusion of Orléanists, kept alive by former officers like Marshal Nicolas Soult, a vicar-of-Bray figure who, after a distinguished military career under Napoleon (statue in the Luxembourg Gardens), went on to serve every subsequent regime without too much trouble for his own (or their) conscience(s).

Illustration 1.2 Un héros de juillet, May 1831. Less than a year after the July revolution of 1830, an impoverished veteran of the fighting is ready to end his life in despair. Note the parliament building with tricolour flag.

Cloning 1789: the February Revolution 1848 and the Second Republic

There were two violent upheavals in 1848, February and June. February need never have happened and June should never have occurred. In February Louis-Philippe's constitutional monarchy was replaced by a democratic republic. The Guizot government, in office since 1840, had been constantly criticized in parliament and in newspapers like *Le National* and *La Réforme* for its unwillingness to extend the electorate from the 250 000 or so 200-franc taxpayers. From the previous summer 70 banquets, attended by 22 000 subscribers and addressed by 100 members of the chamber of deputies, had pressed the case for suffrage reform. It was the government's order demanding the cancellation of a banquet to be held in the Latin quarter of Paris on 22 February which set off the revolution. What made the government nervous about this banquet was the predominance of artisan banqueteers. In addition they planned to precede the banquet with a march protesting at the government's failure to tackle the problem of unemployment, endemic since the 1845 harvest failures and commercial and industrial recession. Socialists, including Etienne Cabet whose Icarian movement had amassed over 100 000 associates in 78 departments, also demanded radical socio-economic change to tackle poverty and unemployment.

The banquet campaign was less threatening than the government feared. The banqueteers had no agreed programme of reform. Every year reformers in parliament proposed revision of the electoral laws and every year they failed to attract majority support. Indeed the Guizot government strengthened its initially weak position in parliament in the elections of 1842 and 1846. Reformers pointed out that 40 per cent of deputies were salaried state servants and parliament did not represent the nation. The cancelled banquet should not have led to a change of regime. The organizers accepted the cancellation, but the march of workers and students went ahead. Scuffles broke out and troops fired on the marchers; barricades were erected, national guardsmen deserted. Louis-Philippe agreed to dismiss Guizot, but quickly lost control of Paris and fled. On 24 February republican journalists and a handful of deputies declared France a democratic republic. Urged by the socialist Louis Blanc, they added 'social' to the title.

The February Revolution, 1848, was to have a profound effect on attitudes to the Revolutionary years. The republican politicians of the 1848 Revolution and the Second Republic self-consciously copied the First Republic, taking the Jacobin constitution as their model, unsurprising given the emphasis which recent histories had placed on the Jacobins. The decision to adopt universal male suffrage, to call a constituent assembly to write a new constitution, the plethora of political clubs, the reversion to a uni-cameral assembly, even the preoccupation with the issue of work, were closely modelled on past republican experience. In reality the First Republic did not offer a coherent template, either in its politics or social policy. In addition in 1848 republicans were a tiny minority, and were split between those who wanted a democratic republic and no more, and those, like Louis Blanc, who hoped for social reform to address the problems of unemployment and poverty. Direct democratic elections had never been attempted in France, however often Buonarroti, Blanc and others reprinted the Jacobin constitution. Michelet's acclaimed history encouraged its readers to believe that 1789 was the Revolution of 'the people'. The 'people' were the heroes of 1848.

The republicans of 1848 seem to have believed that the often-quoted principles of liberty and equality were best translated into a mass vote. They were quickly disillusioned when the democratic electorate chose a constituent assembly stacked with monarchists. Louis-Napoleon was elected in an artisan constituency in Paris. Later in the year he received overwhelming acclaim in the presidential election. The massive majority he secured perhaps indicates that the most lasting memorial to the Revolution was not the pursuit of liberty, equality and fraternity, but military victory.

The republicans of 1848 remembered that the Great Revolution had also claimed to be one of fraternity, and held their own festival of fraternity in May. Fraternity was reworked into early socialism, embracing the right of association and the right to work. The wording for Victor Considérant's proposal that the right to work be formally written into the new constitution was lifted directly from the Jacobin constitution.

The voice of women

With fraternity came fleeting hints of sorority. In 1808 Charles Fourier had asserted that society would never improve until women were given the same rights to education and jobs as men. He demanded that the burden of women's family duties be lifted by reorganizing society into *phalanges*, profit-sharing communes with communal nurseries and dining facilities. He also argued that monogamous marriage was contrary to the nature of both sexes. From 1825 the Saint-Simonians took up the theme of the liberation of women, but contemporary society was so shocked by their 'trial' marriages that the leaders were themselves tried and imprisoned as immoral in 1832. In the late 1830s socialists and other social reformers drew attention to the low pay women endured and the consequent pressure on the poorest to supplement the family income by prostitution.

In 1848 a number of former Saint-Simonians, including Eugénie Niboyet, Pauline Roland and Jeanne Deroin, created a women's club and newspaper, *The Voice of Women*. They demanded the vote, better pay, crèches, women's worker associations and a divorce law. Deroin and Roland organized associations of working women. The former Saint-Simonian Hippolyte Carnot became education minister in 1848 and appointed the well-known feminist Ernest Legouvé to a newly created chair at the prestigious Collège de

France dedicated to finding ways of improving conditions for women. Legouvé had lectured on women's beneficial moral influence on society at the Collège in 1847. In 1848 he gave a course of Saturday lectures in which he urged better education and jobs for women, the creation of crèches and the introduction of divorce.

Conservative Catholic opinion revolted against the feminism of 1848, despite its strong emphasis on morality. Deroin and Roland's association was forced to close, along with others, and both were imprisoned. On her release Deroin left France and spent the rest of her life scraping a living as a teacher in England, caring for her mentally retarded son. Roland was deported to Algeria and died on her release. Niboyet continued to be involved in small-scale feminist ventures. The voice of women was attended to no more than in 1789. Why? Women activists based their claim for equality on woman's role in the family and on her spiritual, moral and pacific qualities. A few male radicals backed them, such as the Fourierist Victor Considérant and the former Saint-Simonian doctor, Ange Guépin, but feminists did not create a sense of urgency in their demands, neither among the male political élite, nor among the masses, male and female.

The June Days

More pressing issues were the first democratic (male-only) election in Europe and the economic crisis. Under the control of Louis Blanc, a parliament of industry was set up at the Luxembourg Palace, where the chamber of peers had previously met. This gathering of workers and employers was asked to investigate the causes of the economic downturn and suggest solutions to the new National Assembly. It was given no budget to put theory to action, but cooperative workshops were started to make uniforms for the national guard. The upheaval of revolution exacerbated the economic crisis and everyone expected the government to solve it. The industry minister, Marie, had no sympathy with Louis Blanc's hopes that the state should give loans to groups of artisans to found social workshops. Instead he organized traditional national workshops, similar to those of 1830 and the early 1790s. The aim was to provide temporary assistance to the unemployed, until the economy recovered. By June over 120000 had enrolled in the workshops. It was never possible to find work for more than 10 per cent. The 'workshops' were simply old-style charity and the dole payments had to be reduced as numbers increased. The new assembly had to deal with a huge mass of idle and discontented artisans. It was faced with massive financial problems; revolutions encouraged people to stop paying taxes and the temporary 45-per cent increase in the land tax decreed by the provisional government was resented by peasants who felt they were being fleeced to pay workers to do nothing. The workshop programme, in the provinces as well as the capital, vastly overran its initial budget. The new deputies, far more representative of the old élites than the new republican spirit of fraternity, debated the problem, decided that the workshops should be closed and unmarried members drafted into the army, but hesitated to make their decision public until 20 June. Two days later worker demonstrations and protests at the closures brought 20000 onto the streets, more barricades, a state of siege and a military campaign. After six days of bitter fighting, in which even the government admitted nearly 1500 rebels were killed and 15000 arrested, of whom 5000 were sent to Algeria, the future of the republic lay in ruins. Rebels fought to defend jobs and the 'social' republic; General Cavaignac, his troops and National Guardsmen believed that they were also fighting for the democratic republic.

Class war and Revolution: Tocqueville and Marx

The failure of the democratic Republic of 1848 and its translation into a new Empire in 1852 left those who were unhappy with this democratic dictatorship time to rewrite the first Revolution, to try to analyse what had gone wrong. The best known was Alexis de Tocqueville, a member of a Legitimist notable family, who made his name in the 1830s as a respected expert on politics with his study of American democracy. As a member of the chamber of deputies before 1848 he was always ready to upbraid the Orléanists for their selfish lack of concern about social problems. Elected to the constituent assembly in 1848, he was briefly jailed after Louis-Napoleon's *coup d'état* of December 1851 and devoted the last few years of his life to his writing. His memoirs focused on what had gone wrong in the Second Republic. His vivid description of the barbaric behaviour of the rebels in the June Days, which he dubbed a 'servile war', confirmed for his contemporaries that the neglected poor were a dangerous sub-species. His history of 1789 is probably the most reprinted and most influential liberal analysis of the Great Revolution ever produced. Tocqueville attributed the failures of 1848–51 to the mistakes of 1789. For him 1789 was 'the natural conclusion to the long-term evolution of the ancien régime'.[4] Tocqueville was unusual for his time in seeing 1789, and subsequent upheavals, as primarily social revolutions. Like earlier writers he recognized that anti-clericalism was fundamental in bringing and driving the Revolution, but he was the first to point to its political and economic roots. He coined the view that a regime is at its weakest when attempting to reform. He tried to explain why reform led, not to a liberal, but to a dictatorial, system. He was opposed to centralization and deplored the replacement of the despotic centralism of the *ancien régime* by the Napoleonic dictatorship. He was even more disillusioned when the democratic electorate voted in Louis-Napoleon in 1848 and acquiesced to his *coup d'état* in 1851.

An even greater influence on interpretations of 1789 and subsequent revolutions came from Karl Marx. His theoretical writings sought to prove that history was driven by socio-economic change and was destined to move from feudal aristocratic control to bourgeois capitalism and proletarian rule. The climax of his messianic view of social progress was a classless society. There was widespread conviction on all sides that 1789 had been a social revolution benefiting the bourgeoisie. Marx's accounts of the Second Republic took up Louis Blanc's dismissal of 1830 as another bourgeois revolution, but contradicting Blanc, Marx asserted that in 1830 the bourgeoisie definitively replaced the aristocracy. Marx included middle-class landowners in his bourgeoisie; it was not exclusively an entrepreneurial capitalist group. He explained February 1848 as a takeover by less well-off members of the middle class, who had been denied a share in the July Monarchy when Guizot refused to countenance electoral reform in the 1840s. The June Days heralded the proletarian revolution.

Parliamentary, democratic and Jacobin: the Third Republic and the centenary of 1789

The writers and politicians of the Third Republic found much to admire in Marx and the early socialists like Blanc. The republic was to survive longer than any previous post-1789 system (1870–1940), but it had a shaky start. Its partisans were committed to creating the myth that 1789 was bound to lead to a permanent democratic republic, i.e. their own. Georges Weill, whose history of nineteenth-century republicanism has been constantly reprinted since its first appearance in 1900, was so committed to inventing the fiction that a parliamentary republic was an inevitable development, that he left the 'inconvenient' Paris Commune of 1871 out of his story.

During the Third Republic the image of the Revolution also became increasingly socialist, as Radical Socialists, who represented the interests of peasants and small businessmen, and then the Socialist Party, which spoke for industrial and white-collar workers, became dominant in both government and academic life. The centenary commemoration of 1789 was carefully orchestrated to present a parliamentary and Jacobin interpretation. Alphonse Aulard was a dominant figure. In 1886 he gave a course on Revolutionary history at the Sorbonne and a year later founded a periodical devoted to its history. In 1891 came a Sorbonne Chair in the history of 1789. A government commission was financed to gather together and collate documents on the Revolution. The bound volumes present the researcher with the Revolution as primarily a centralized, benevolent, bureaucratic Jacobin state. In 1901 appeared Aulard's Radical-Socialist history of the Revolution, in which Georges Danton had an honoured place.

Jean Jaurès, the leader of the first united socialist party in the Third Republic, was Aulard's doctoral student, continuing a well-established convention that politicians were frequently historians. He was convinced that his socialist history of the Revolution, also published in 1901, complemented that of his tutor. For him 1789 was a revolt against privilege and saw the triumph of capitalists and financiers, rebelling against the hijacking of the state by king, Church and nobles.

In his socialist history Albert Mathiez put Robespierre firmly in the driving seat of a Revolution partly caused by the failure of royal attempts at reform, but mainly the consequence of an emergent bourgeoisie rebelling against the feudal reaction of the late eighteenth century. Workers and peasants, brought into the struggle by the economic crisis, figure prominently in his account. Mathiez expounded and developed what became republican dogma that all revolutions since 1789 were ideologically progressive, culminating in the Bolshevik Revolution of 1917.

Vichy and counter-revolution

Right-wing historians saw the German victory over France in 1940 as the direct consequence of 1789. The well-worn right-wing view had always been that 1789 was primarily a social revolution, replacing the legitimate aristocratic ruling élite with an upstart bourgeoisie. At the time of the Dreyfus affair at the end of the nineteenth century the anti-semitic journalist Edouard Drumont blamed wealthy bourgeois Jewish families in particular for sapping French vitality. The French had been left vulnerable by the establishment of the rule of the wealthy bourgeoisie during the Revolution and subsequently. The victory of the Germans in 1940 marked their third invasion since 1814. In 1943 a four-volume invective (reprinted in 1964) claimed to expose the responsibilities of wealthy bourgeois dynasties, which, under a mask of democratic revolution, had, since the Revolution, enriched themselves. The author, E. de Beau de Lomenie, went through the names of specific 'dynasties' which he claimed firmly established themselves in control of the French state under Napoleon and consolidated their power under Louis-Philippe. For him 1789 was thus an Orléanist revolution, representing Philippe-Egalité's betrayal of his cousin in 1793. Liberal democratic institutions were merely a smoke screen for rule by a few families. This type of partial analysis was not, of course, confined to the extreme right. In the mid-1920s the Radical-Socialist government led by Edouard Herriot launched a war against the '200 families' who, they claimed, ruled France through the bank and the bourse. In recent years the notion of a conspiratorial takeover by a tiny privileged minority has been focused on the so-called *énarques*, the graduates of the École Nationale d'Administration who dominate senior administrative posts, just as wealthy bourgeois dynasties had indeed operated in the nineteenth century.

The *Annales* school and 1789

In 1929 a periodical was founded, currently known as *Annales: économies, sociétés, civilisations*, which was to re-mould the Revolution and French academic life. The *Annalistes*, led by Lucien Febvre and Marc Bloch, launched a determined assault on the study of the past focused on a narrow, chronological, political prism. As 1789 was always written as a narrative, the first generation of *Annalistes* rewrote the early modern period from a perspective of geography, economics, psychology and anthropology for a tiny specialized audience. It was only after the Second World War that the *Annales* became establishment, Marxist and the centre of Revolutionary study. Its adherents came to dominate posts in élite educational institutions. A leading figure was Ernest Labrousse, who changed the shape of 1789 in a number of ways, none entirely new. He and his pupils stressed long-term factors in historical change, they shared a more structured Marxist approach, they emphasized regional differences instead of Jacobin centralism and finally they introduced more precision, both in the evidence they selected and the tools, adding machines, then computers, with which they assessed economic change.

The dimensions of the Revolution expanded in all directions. Looking at long-term origins statistically led to the detailed, and mind-numbing, tabulation of bread and other commodity prices in the decades before 1789 to expose the significance of economic causation, the poverty of the masses and the rise of the bourgeoisie. In this atmosphere the Revolution was seen primarily as a matter of economics; the ideas of the enlightened writers were left on the periphery. Labrousse contributed with his study, published in 1944, of the pre-Revolutionary economic crisis, in which he concluded that although 1789 marked the ascendancy of the bourgeoisie over the long term, it was born of the misery of peasants in the short-term collapse of agricultural prices, recession and unemployment after 1778.

The study of quantifiable collective mentalities became all-pervasive. In 1973 Michel Vovelle, a pupil of Labrousse and his heir as Mr Revolution, explored the origins of dechristianization through 30 000 wills, discovering that funerals became simpler in the decades before 1789 and concluding that the attack on religion was not the work of Voltaire and enlightened writers, but had grass-roots origins. Jacques Ozouf and François Furet, another of Labrousse's pupils, addressed the issue of the intellectual origins of 1789 in a study of literacy over two centuries (1977). Other tools brought in included psychology and particularly Sigmund Freud. New attitudes to time, space and number began to influence approaches to the Revolution.

Although the *Annalistes* discounted politics in their history, most were members of the Communist Party. The dominance of Marxist attitudes to 1789 was undermined by events in eastern Europe, 1956 and especially 1968. In the late 1970s number-crunching was also questioned, partly because of difficulties in assembling adequate statistical material. Where

detailed regional social analysis was attempted, the sweeping social classifi-
cations of the past, 'bourgeois', 'proletarian' etc., were found to be
inadequate. Georges Lefebvre, whose sparkling 1939 analysis of the causes
of the Revolution was translated into English in 1947, although broadly
following traditional dogma, noted that although 1789 was a bourgeois
revolution, the French bourgeoisie was tiny and did not universally gain from
the 1790s. However he concluded that the Revolution promoted capitalism
in the name of economic freedom.

Revisionists and 1789

Anglo-Saxon sceptics such as Alfred Cobban questioned whether 1789 could
have been a bourgeois capitalist revolution, given the modest pace of
economic change and the empirical evidence that the ascendant bourgeoisie
of the 1790s were predominantly landowners, professionals, especially lawyers, and state servants.[5] The class war evaporated. The Revolution began to
re-assume a narrative political format. François Furet's re-interpretation was
a seminal work. He quoted no bread prices: the enlightened writers of the
eighteenth century and the liberal historians of the nineteenth filled his text.
Tocqueville was his hero. The dimensions of the Revolution moved yet
again. Tsunamis were replaced by tidal ripples. Class struggle and collective
mentalities gave way to individuals: Mirabeau, Robespierre, Napoleon,
Louis XVI. The search for long-term origins was no rigorous statistical
calculation but a gentle stroll followed by an account of totally political
manoeuverings in the 1790s.

Committed Marxists, led by Albert Soboul, were appalled that 1789 was
being miniaturized. If the Revolution was not part of a universal class
struggle and its dynamic was purely local, it had no resonance in world
history. In an interpretative study published in 1981 Soboul condemned
Furet as an anti-patriotic traitor who left 1789 stranded as a small-scale
localized series of texts, often written by unknown historians. He accused
Furet of robbing the French of their heritage. This was a mere swan-song.
Soboul's own detailed research and that of other contemporary Marxists
revealed the ambiguities and complexities of class analysis.

The 'Atlantic' Revolution

The generation which rejected the Marxist Revolution replaced it in the
1950s and 1960s with a liberal-democratic world revolution. Jacques
Godechot (1956) and the American historian R. R. Palmer (1961–4) demonstrated that France was not alone in exploring radical new departures at the
end of the eighteenth century, that attitudes were shared through Europe and
across the Atlantic. This approach was facilitated as French historians

themselves began to exploit the advantages of lecture tours in America. The atmosphere of the Cold War encouraged the virtual reality of this 'Atlantic revolution', which offered a challenging and exhilarating world-view. Unfortunately it was not sustained by detailed investigation. The exploration of European radicalism, for instance T. C. W. Blanning's investigation of the Revolutionary Rhineland, revealed French dominance, not home-spun initiative. An amusing tail-piece to the Atlantic revolution were the original plans for the celebration of the bicentenary, sketched by Vovelle on a world tour in 1981 which included a meeting with 40 or so British historians of France in University College London. We were asked how we planned to celebrate the English response to 1789 and Vovelle was puzzled to be told that we would be focusing on the Revolution *in* France.

Ultimately 170 conferences celebrated in 1989. The official bicentenary was a Mitterrand 1789; the Declaration of the Rights of Man and democracy. The image of the Revolution was sanitized; there was little reference to peasants, workers, bread prices or even violence. The focus was on the development of French political culture, a fitting conceptualization of the Revolution for a Fifth Republic which included a shrinking proletariat and peasantry and a burgeoning bourgeoisie on which the Mitterrand regime depended for its survival. Ironically the biggest conference at the Sorbonne, complete with a blockbuster four volumes of almost 300 papers totalling 2709 pages, was financed by Robert Maxwell.

The Revolution is always with us

The torpedoing of class war by revisionists such as G. Chaussinand-Nogaret, Furet and others, was pushed to the point of asserting the presence of a consolidated group of notables in pre-Revolutionary France, that wealthy non-nobles were able to advance and intermarry with nobles and that nobles were as much involved in capitalist ventures as commoners. The deconstruction of class war among the better-off, taken to its extreme, makes nonsense of the social cleavages displayed at the time and subsequently. Class war may be out of fashion, but the investigation of social conflicts cannot be ruled out of history. The loosening of the Marxist straitjacket has not banished social conflict from history; it has made social tensions more nuanced and more credible. On the other hand revisionists have made a useful contribution to the study of the consequences of the Revolution by demonstrating that the nobility survived 1789 to remain the richest element in French society until the middle of the nineteenth century and beyond. Revisionists have also added to our understanding of the 1790s by their research on the counter-revolution. Recent historians, led in France by Maurice Agulhon, have fruitfully explored the regional and popular reverberations of 1789 in a broader chronological context, which has added to our understanding of the nineteenth century. Even the very tentative questioning of the all-pervasive republican myth allows a more realistic approach to attitudes to monarchy, Bonapartism and Gaullism.

Since around 1970 a generation of feminist historians, in France, America and Britain, has explored the absence of women from the history of 1789. Olwen Hufton, Michelle Perrot, Arlette Farge and Mona Ozouf, amongst many others, have created a new perspective on the formerly forgotten half of humanity. Perhaps appropriately in a television age, historians have also taken a new look at the way in which symbols, songs, plays, poetry, statuary and paintings contribute to a collective memory. An outstandingly comprehensive example of the dissection of what constitutes memory was the multi-volume compendium edited by Pierre Nora in which experts analysed a huge range of elements, tangible and intangible. The 1789 Revolution will continue to overshadow debates on France's subsequent history, just as the institutions it created are still extant. It is to be hoped, however, that rigid definitions of its legacies will continue to be as elusive as a rainbow.

Notes

1 F. Furet, *Revolutionary France 1770–1880*, trans. A. Nevill (Oxford: Blackwell, 1992).
2 R. Lebrun (ed. and trans.), *Joseph de Maistre: Considerations on France* (Cambridge: Cambridge University Press, 1992), p. 7.
3 R. Tombs, *France 1814–1914* (Harlow: Longman, 1996).
4 A. de Tocqueville, *The Old Regime and the French Revolution*, trans. S. Gilbert (New York, 1955).
5 A. Cobban, *The Social Interpretation of the French Revolution* (Cambridge: Cambridge University Press, 1964); the main thesis is summarized in his inaugural lecture, 'The myth of the French Revolution', at University College, London, 1955, repr. in his *Aspects of the French Revolution* (London, 1968).

Further reading

Agulhon, M. *1848, ou l'apprentissage de la république* (Paris: Plon, 1973). Trans. J. Lloyd, *The Republican Experiment* (Cambridge: Cambridge University Press, 1983).
——, *Marianne au combat: l'imagerie et la symbolique de 1789 à 1880*, (Paris 1979). Trans. J. Lloyd, *Marianne into Battle: Republican Imagery and Symbolism in France, 1789–1880* (Cambridge: Cambridge University Press, 1981).
Baker, K. *Inventing the French Revolution* (Cambridge: Cambridge University Press, 1990).
Blanning, T. C. W. *The Rise and Fall of the French Revolution* (Chicago: University of Chicago Press, 1996).
Forrest, A. *The French Revolution* (Oxford: Blackwell, Historical Association Studies, 1995).
Furet, F. *Interpreting the French Revolution*, trans. E. Forster (Cambridge: Cambridge University Press, 1981).

——, *Revolutionary France 1770–1880*, trans. A. Nevill (Oxford: Blackwell, 1992).

Gildea, R. *The Past in French History* (Oxford: Oxford University Press, 1994).

Hufton, O. *Women and the Limits of Citizenship in the French Revolution* (Toronto: University of Toronto Press, 1992).

Hunt, L. 'Engraving the Republic: print and propaganda in the French Revolution', *History Today*, 30 (Oct. 1980), pp. 11–17.

——, *Politics, Culture and Class in the French Revolution* (Berkeley: University of California Press, 1984).

—-, *The Family Romance of the French Revolution* (London: Routledge, 1992).

Lucas, C. (ed.), *Re-writing the French Revolution* (Oxford: Clarendon Press, 1991).

Mason, L. *Singing the French Revolution: Popular Culture and Politics, 1787–1799* (Ithaca, NY: Cornell University Press, 1996).

McPhee, P. *The Politics of Rural Life: Political Mobilization in the French Countryside, 1846–1852* (Oxford: Clarendon Press, 1992).

Nora, P. (ed.), *Lieux de mémoire* (Paris: Gallimard, 1984–93). 7 vols.

Ozouf, M. *La Fête révolutionnaire* (Paris: Gallimard, 1976). Trans. A. Sheridan, *Festivals and the French Revolution* (Cambridge, MA: Harvard University Press, 1988).

Palmer, R. R. *The Age of the Democratic Revolution*, 2 vols., (Princeton: Princeton University Press, 1959, 1964).

Parker, N. *Portrayals of Revolution: Images, Debates and Patterns of Thought on the French Revolution* (Brighton: Harvester Wheatsheaf, 1990).

Pilbeam, P. M. *The Constitutional Monarchy in France, 1814–1848* (Harlow: Longman, 1999).

Price, R. *The French Second Republic: A Social History* (London: Batsford, 1972).

Reynolds, S. (ed.) *Women, State and Revolution: Essays on Power and Gender in Europe since 1789* (Brighton: Harvester Wheatsheaf, 1986).

Sutherland, D. M. G. *France 1789–1815: Revolution and Counter-Revolution* (London: Fontana, 1985).

|2|

Inventing politics

From Bourbon Restoration to republican monarchy

ROBERT TOMBS

An obvious paradox of modern French political history is that more than 150 years of passionate and often bloody political struggle – often called the 'Franco-French war' – produced an outcome little different from that of more peaceful, even somnolent, neighbours. A casual observer today would notice little difference between political life in France and that in Holland or Denmark. A severe critic might even suggest that, if there is a significant difference, it is that the French republic, two centuries after the execution of Louis XVI, is effectively less democratic than any European monarchy.

This is not usually how French political history is told. The most influential 'grand narrative' of the Revolutionary and post-Revolutionary period is of a long struggle to establish a republic, seen as the embodiment of the universal democratic values of the 1789 Revolution. The subsequent narrative thereafter revolves round recurring threats to and, after 1879, the consolidation of the republic. Liberal and democratic institutions are widely presented as synonymous with revolutionary and republican tradition. Hence the bicentenary celebrations in 1989 took as their theme republican France as the home of the rights of man. This is the past as the great republican historian Jules Michelet (1798–1874) saw it, a mixture of patriotism and partisanship in which the history of the republic takes over the history of the nation. Politics became simplified into a choice of regimes: 'the form permanently dominated the content,' observes Pierre Rosanvallon, 'as if attachment to the Republic was all that mattered'.[1] Events, themes or periods that do not fit the overall framework have often been discounted as political dead-ends or parentheses. This was long the case of the Vichy period (1940–4) and tends still to be so for much of the early nineteenth century, and for the phenomenon of Bonapartism.

Recent changes in historiographic fashion in France do not necessarily subvert what has been called the 'master narrative of modernity'. Indeed, the eclipse of Marxist social history, which analysed history as class conflict, with politics and ideology as merely reflections of this deeper reality, has removed the main discordant voice. The decline of the *Annales* school's influence has permitted a revival of interest in personalities, events and ideas as opposed to deep impersonal structures and long-term trends. One sign of this is the self-confident appearance of a rejuvenated school of political history in France. Another self-conscious innovation, led by Pierre Nora, of presenting the past in terms of 'national memory', emphasizing the importance of beliefs, traditions and symbols, also tends to buttress a view of history centred on the clash of political 'representations' and ideologies. Indeed, Nora has even suggested that the 'feeling of identity' in contemporary France is 'sustained by an enduring sense of its own divisions'.[2]

The contrast between this stirring history of political struggle and the ordinariness of its outcome provides the starting point for this essay, which improvises freely on observations made by two of the most original of present-day French historians. Rosanvallon has commented that there are two diametrically opposed French political histories, a 'Jacobin' and an 'English'. Alain Corbin has suggested that the nineteenth century developed not by 'annulation' but by 'recapitulation, assembly and combination'.[3] While there was indeed a turbulent history of revolutions, ruptures and violent struggle for democracy – the 'Jacobin' history – there was also a simultaneous pragmatic process – the 'English' history – by which politicians adapted to change, invented or copied political rules, and built on the practices of their predecessors.

The 'Jacobin history': conflict and conquest

Legacy of the Revolution

The aspirations, victories, defeats and traumas of the Revolutionary years – the proclamation of the rights of the nation and the Rights of Man and the Citizen, the Terror, civil war, religious persecution, war, mass political and military mobilization, conquest, economic suffering, invasion and final defeat – left behind a mass of unresolved problems. How was France to be governed: who had the right, and who had the power? By what methods would they rule? On whose behalf and in whose interests? In the name of what creed?

The alarming awareness of division and the ever-present threat of conflict led many thinkers to call for unity of belief as the only way of creating a harmonious society. Hence the importance of religious and educational institutions, seen as ways of instilling approved values, and also of public symbols and ceremonies – statues, flags, parades, commemorations – used by all regimes and parties to try to establish a certain version of the nation, its past and by implication its future. But any such act was itself a bone of contention, for unity of belief clearly did not exist, and so any attempt to propagate one conception of unity created hostile and fearful reactions. This is why control of the school system, for example, has been one of the great recurring contests in French political history.

The two deepest, and overlapping, ideological divisions were between non-Catholics and Catholics, and between democrats and non-democrats. Catholics, such as the major counter-revolutionary thinkers Louis de Bonald (1754–1840) and Joseph de Maistre (1753–1821), wanted to restore an authoritarian Christian monarchy at the head of a hierarchical, paternalist society. Recognizably similar aspirations, even if diluted by circumstances, persisted well into the twentieth century, for example in the theories of Charles Maurras (1868–1952) and his Action Française movement in the 1920s and 1930s, and were reflected in the support of much of the Catholic clergy for the authoritarian regime of Marshal Pétain in 1940–4. At the other end of the spectrum, republicans and from the 1820s socialists saw themselves as creating a new political society based on fulfilment of the democratic, egalitarian and secular values of the Revolution. In between these poles stood a variety of liberal monarchists, moderate republicans and Bonapartists, who opposed reaction, accepted some consequences of the Revolution (national sovereignty, legal equality and religious liberty), but feared further upheaval and tried to make the best of the shifting status quo.

Divisions were far more than merely intellectual: they were also sociological and anthropological, in that they had become part of the cultural identity of families, communities and social groups. This made them all the more difficult to reconcile. In certain regions the Revolutionary years had created ineradicable antagonisms. Civil war in the west and Catholic versus Protestant violence in the south left deep communal hatreds that were kept alive throughout the nineteenth century. Grass-roots rivalry between individuals, clans and villages over rights to common pasture and woodland, over jobs and patronage, or over possession of *biens nationaux* (the property formerly belonging to the Church or to émigrés, nationalized by the Revolution and sold off), took on a political colouring which persisted for generations. Community loyalties and often violent antagonisms were kept alive by public ceremonies. These included the local saint's day, the carnival, the king's or emperor's birthday, the republican 14 July holiday (established in 1880), processions, planting trees, unveiling statues, and the recurring ritual of elections. Group solidarity could mean near unanimity in politics – for example, all the voters in a village going to the polls in a body to give public support to their favoured candidate. As a prefect reported of two rival villages in the 1860s, 'When St Jean votes black, St Paul votes white.'[4] Local and regional loyalties have proved very durable: maps showing support for or opposition to the Revolution are still recognizable in the political patterns of left and right in the mid-twentieth century. The rural Allier department, 'Jacobin' in the 1790s and which turned socialist in the 1880s, still produced the highest level of support in the country for the communist presidential candidate in 1995.

Given these divisions, every regime knew that its tenure of power was provisional. Considerable sections of its citizenry – sometimes a majority – considered its claims to legitimacy with scepticism or hostility. Behind every act of political opposition might lurk ideological enmity and revolutionary ambition: there was no 'loyal opposition'. Few were willing to risk their lives or careers to defend a regime that seemed on the way out. Every government had to try to find a balance between conciliating its enemies and alienating its friends: that France since 1789 has had five monarchies, five republics and 15 constitutions shows the difficulty of the task.

Failure of 'moderation': the Restoration and the July Monarchy, 1814–1848

While far from identical in their ideas or practices, the two constitutional monarchies had in common the desire to put up barriers against popular sovereignty without attempting the oppressive authoritarianism of Napoleon I, and to win the support of the property-owning 'notables' who had come out on top after a generation of revolution and war.

The Bourbon Restoration (1814–1830), under Louis XVIII and ministers such as Elie Decazes, tried for opportunistic rather than principled reasons to draw a veil over the Revolutionary period and present the monarchy as a guarantee of peace, order and normality. The Restoration's advantages were that most people were indeed tired of war and upheaval. And yet it was overthrown by the July 1830 Revolution. Why?

The Restoration's acute political problem was that there were active minorities who were unwilling or unable to give up the struggle. On one side were 'ultra-royalists', many of them nobles who had suffered during the Revolution and expected to regain something of their former position. On the other were thinly disguised Bonapartists or republicans who had also lost jobs and status when Napoleon fell. Both sides were nourished by a powerful mixture of ideology, hatred, ambition, pride and fear.

Though the majority of the small electorate and probably of the people at large was willing to accept the Bourbons as the best or only rulers available, few were deeply loyal to the restored monarchy. It had only been able to return to France thanks to the victory of the Allies over Napoleon, which had been accompanied by some executions, a 'white terror' in the south, and mass dismissal of civil servants. Although Louis XVIII had been obliged to 'grant' a constitution, the Charter, in 1814, his return symbolized a largely unlamented old regime of 'feudalism'. The Restoration's enthusiastic partisans condemned the Revolution and Empire, which most Frenchmen had served and many had profited from, as criminal regimes. Rhetoric and ceremonies – such as penitential commemorations of the execution of Louis XVI, hell-fire sermons on the iniquities of revolution, even burning of subversive books – at best brought back unpleasant memories and at worst seemed to threaten wholesale reaction.

Legislation introduced by an ultra-royalist government in the 1820s – including compensation to former émigrés, inheritance laws benefiting eldest sons and capital punishment for sacrilege – seemed to confirm these fears, and created opposition even among moderates who dreaded further upheaval. The succession in 1824 of Charles X, youngest brother of Louis XVI, known to favour the ultras, revived support for the opposition liberals among the electorate – a small group of the 90 000 richest men in France, mainly landowners. In 1827 and 1830 the opposition made large gains in the chamber of deputies. In 1830 they voted no confidence in the king's ministers.

Why this became first a constitutional crisis and then a revolution is explained by the perceptions of the king and his advisers: they interpreted the situation as a repetition of 1789, with the prerogatives of the crown being challenged by a parliament bent on revolution. 'If I gave in this time,' Charles declared, 'they would finish by treating us as they treated my brother.' Hence, the idea of making concessions to try to win over opponents was quickly abandoned as hopeless. Some of the opposition certainly were outright enemies, but most shared the Bourbon's fear of revolution and (as their later conduct showed) would have been perfectly willing to live with a Bourbon monarchy that accepted the hard-won gains of the Revolution: legal equality, security of property (including the *biens nationaux*), equal access to state jobs, and a curbing of the power of the Church.

However, the conflict between the royal prerogative and the majority in parliament led some opponents to evoke the English Revolution of 1688, not 1789, as the real historical parallel. In July 1830 Charles and his ministers tried to override the parliamentary majority by using royal emergency powers which they claimed were legal under the Charter. These ordinances (to dissolve parliament, increase control of the press, and further reduce the size of the electorate) led to riots in Paris in July 1830 – 'the three glorious days' – which turned into revolution with the inability, or unwillingness, of the army to suppress them. In brief, the Bourbon Restoration fell because it could neither reconcile nor repress the deep antagonisms – social, political, emotional – left by the Revolution. On the contrary, it made them the central political issue.

The liberal opposition defused the revolutionary situation by putting forward a substitute monarch, the Bourbon's progressively minded cousin the duc d'Orléans, who became King Louis-Philippe (1830–48). He was presented as a patriotic 'citizen king' who accepted the consequences of 1789:

The Duc d'Orléans is a prince devoted to the cause of the Revolution ... [He] has carried the tricolour under enemy fire ... he accepts the Charter as we have always wanted it. It is from the French people that he will hold his crown.[5]

This was an attempt, directed by men many of whom had served not only the Restoration, but also the Napoleonic Empire and often the First Republic, to steer a pragmatic middle course – a *juste milieu* – between right and left, to synthesize monarchy and republicanism as 'a popular throne surrounded by republican institutions', and so unite the nation.

The practice proved less attractive than the rhetoric. The July Revolution, like all revolutions, had raised expectations. Many patriots, often city workers and the middle class, expected an outcome as dazzling as that of the 1790s, with France again defeating the monarchies of Europe. Workers who had fought in July wanted their claims for economic protection realized at a time when socialist theories had begun to open new egalitarian horizons. The new government disappointed those expectations by keeping on good terms with the European powers, arresting strikers and soon shooting rioters in the streets of Paris and Lyons. Its priorities were to keep the peace and maintain law and order. Few changes were made in the Charter, and the parliamentary electorate was extended only from 90 000 extremely rich elderly men to 170 000 very rich middle-aged men. Neither Louis-Philippe nor François Guizot (chief minister 1840–48) was willing to accept further reform. Like Charles X, they feared that to make concessions to the opposition would lead to instability and disaster. They could never see a right time for reform, and the severe economic crisis of the late 1840s in France seemed a further reason to say no. In fact, their refusal to make concessions probably led more surely to disaster. In February 1848 another Parisian riot, sparked off by a parliamentary reform campaign, developed into another uncontrollable insurrection, and French royalty met its final defeat.

This brief account emphasizes failure and division. To redress the balance, we should note that there were successes too. The Restoration's relative freedom of expression permitted a cultural renaissance in the arts, science, literature and philosophy. The July Monarchy encouraged unprecedented economic development. Although there was much grumbling and some harsh repression of popular disturbances, France could not really be described as groaning under the yoke of despotism. These years, far from being a dead end, were in many ways the beginning of modern politics in France: in 1814 royalty had been forgotten, the Empire had collapsed, Catholicism was withering, the First Republic was barely a memory, representative government an exotic and unpredictable experiment. By 1848 the foundations of modern political culture had been laid. The political lines had been drawn and the ideologies and myths elaborated on which France would function throughout the century. A parliamentary system had become the norm, with permanently important developments in political practices, as will be seen in the second part of this chapter. And yet, as one disillusioned liberal observed, a system of constitutional monarchy that worked perfectly well in Britain had proved impossible in France. We might add that, with a comparable level of social and political discontent, it worked in Belgium and Scandinavia too: it was in fact the norm for the advanced countries of western Europe, which all survived even the economic crisis and political turbulence of the late 1840s.

Why was France different? The failure of constitutional monarchy, Pierre Rosanvallon has argued, was the failure of 'moderation' as a political concept. The French, he believes, were not able to practise or even really imagine a middle way between monarchical absolutism and popular sovereignty. A liberal *juste milieu* based on compromise and gradual change was impossible to find in a country which had not only 'horizontal' social divisions but 'vertical' factional division dividing the political class between Legitimists, Orléanists, Bonapartists and republicans: among the most dangerous enemies of governments were members of the social and political élite. Moreover, the question of *how* state power was to be organized and controlled (the crucial question for liberals) was felt to be far less important than the question of *who* was to possess that power – the perennial issue of French politics, recently reflected in François Mitterrand's notorious comment that the Fifth Republic's somewhat imperial constitution was not dangerous as long as he was in charge of it. When the July Monarchy collapsed in the February 1848 Revolution, the recognition of popular sovereignty became the only alternative.

Harnessing popular sovereignty: the Second Republic and the Second Empire, 1848–1870

The Parisian workers who overthrew Louis-Philippe in the streets in February 1848 insisted on proclaiming a republic with universal male suffrage – two ideas that had come to be synonymous. Many were consciously aiming to prevent a repetition of 1830, when moderate royalists had taken over the revolution. There was a euphoric expectation among republicans and socialists that democracy and liberty would quickly create a harmonious and equal society. Instead, they proved to be the ways in which social and political tensions, greatly aggravated by continuing economic crisis, found open political expression through clubs, newspapers and elections. Confrontation soon emerged between socialists and radicals who wanted a formal guarantee of the 'right to work' and sweeping reforms leading to cooperative 'organization of work', and moderate republicans and conservatives who resisted this as dangerous utopianism. Election of a constituent assembly in April 1848 by the 9 million new electors, who returned a majority of conservatives (mainly crypto-royalists), showed that support for a republic and for expensive social reforms was mainly limited to workers and the lower middle classes in the cities.

This division led to civil war in June 1848, when Parisian workers took up arms to resist closure of the national workshops (a large job-creation scheme with socialist overtones). They were crushed in the bloodiest fighting ever seen in Paris by the army backed up by National Guards from the provinces, who resented paying heavy taxes to create jobs for workers in the towns. This ended the first stage of the revolutionary period, which had been centred on the economic and social concerns of Paris and the cities. Comparable clashes took place in other parts of Europe during the year of revolutions, but nowhere was violence so severe, taking the form of naked class warfare. The difference in France was that social and economic problems fuelled already existing political conflicts, aggravated by fears inherited from the bloody events of the 1790s.

Universal male suffrage was soon to produce unpredicted developments. In December 1848 Louis-Napoleon Bonaparte, nephew of the emperor who had died in 1821, was elected president by a huge majority of 5.5 million out of 7.4 million voting. This was the effect of a Napoleonic myth which presented the emperor as 'the greatest genius of modern times', defender of the fruits of the Revolution, conqueror of Europe, lawgiver and people's friend. This was one of the greatest, and least analysed, legacies of the Revolutionary period. Louis-Napoleon had since the 1830s put himself forward as the man to continue Napoleon's work – 'my name is a programme itself' – but without success. This changed in 1848. A credible candidate for president was needed. True republicans were unpopular or little known. Royalists were no more popular. Louis-Napoleon, however, was able to appeal across party lines: conservatives saw him as a strong man who could keep order; many republicans and socialists saw him as a democrat and a reformer; peasants and workers saw him as a providential figure who would solve their problems. In general, the mass electorate's support for him was a populist rejection of the political class. As the socialist Pierre-Joseph Proudhon put it, 'Napoleon will be their saviour ... So away with the priest, the lawyer, the landlord, the gentleman, the moneylender, the rich!'

Soon afterwards, however, workers and peasants also elected to parliament considerable numbers of a new Democrat-Socialist Party who promised sweeping reform of credit and taxation. They were most successful in 'Jacobin' regions in central and south-eastern France which had supported the Revolution half a century earlier. For the first time since 1789 a substantial and potentially revolutionary movement was growing independently of the cities. Was this a sign of 'modernization' and of urban influence radiating outwards? More probably, its successes were based on the harnessing of grass-roots peasant discontents, not least a suspicion of the cities.

Louis-Napoleon's ministers did their best to repress the 'Démoc-Socs' with the support of a conservative majority in parliament. This culminated in the law of 31 May 1850 disenfranchising 3 million voters, a desperate attempt to keep control by politicians who, 'like river boatmen navigating in mid ocean', had no confidence in their ability to manage a democracy. But the 'prince-president' was playing an assured populist game, touring the provinces to win popular support among voters and in the army. The constitution did not permit him a second term of office, so on 2 December

1851 he carried out a *coup d'état* against both his opponents in parliament (the leaders were arrested and the chamber dissolved) and against the Démoc-Socs, whose armed resistance in rural areas was ruthlessly repressed and followed by 27 000 arrests.

The immediate second phase of the coup, however, was an entirely novel political strategy. The president immediately restored full manhood suffrage and called on the electorate for a mass vote of confidence: 'I appeal to the whole nation ... If you still have confidence in me, give me the means to accomplish the great mission you gave me.' Over 7 million – nearly 80 per cent of the electorate – voted yes. A year later, even more voted to approve the establishment of the Second Empire, with Louis-Napoleon as Napoleon III. The democratic republic, which progressives thought of as the natural culmination of France's destiny, was thus snuffed out with overwhelming popular approval. Yet France set out in a quite different direction from that of Germany and the Habsburg empire, where the 1848 revolutions were followed by a return to traditional conservatism and rejection of democracy.

Bonapartism marked a sea-change in political history, not only in France: it discovered that democracy did not necessarily mean revolution, but that it could be made a tool of the government. Although at least in its first decade Napoleon III's rule was as authoritarian as anywhere in Europe, it also had a genuinely democratic dimension, even though it was, as Frédéric Bluche has defined it, 'active authority and passive democracy'.[6] The authorities did their best to 'manage' democracy by inducements and threats, but support for Napoleon was real and enduring, aided by a surge of economic growth and a foreign policy that seemed to have made France again mistress of Europe. This was the prototype for what Max Weber termed 'charismatic' government; as Louis-Napoleon had put it in 1839, 'it is in the nature of democracy to personify itself in a single man'. His formula has had many imitators in countries having to invent a viable regime, even if few perhaps are aware of the origin of the model. Whereas a parliamentary democracy like the Second Republic requires rules, conventions and a party system difficult to improvise at short notice, 'charismatic' populism simplifies (even if it distorts) political choices and can cut across factional divisions. It needs only a suitable leader – and even some improbable characters have filled that role with the help of the power, prestige and propaganda of the state.

Largely because some of its policies began to go wrong – foreign policy and the economy – the Second Empire faced more effective opposition in the 1860s. It responded by liberalizing its political practices in a way that neither the Bourbons nor Louis-Philippe had dared, even though parliamentary rule by parties was alien to Bonapartist theory. In 1869, Napoleon called on the moderate opposition to form a government, instituting the so-called 'Liberal Empire'. This flexibility was no guarantee of survival. Serious difficulties still remained. But in purely domestic terms, the Empire, still supported by a large majority of the electorate, had a better chance of survival than its predecessors. Its downfall came only through embarking on a reckless and disastrous war with Germany. The war, however, was not simply a bolt from the blue: it was an inherent part of Bonapartism's nationalistic foreign policy, and hence as characteristic of the regime as any of its other features.

The German armies destroyed the Second Empire at Sedan on 2 September 1870, just as the allies had destroyed the First Empire at Waterloo, and as German armies were to destroy the Third Republic, the Empire's successor, in 1940. In a sense, this is a wry testimony to the strength of these much-criticized regimes, which were strong enough to resist any domestic challenge. But they were not strong enough to survive defeat. Bonapartism's strength lay in its ability to synthesize the different strands of French political culture: as Guizot put it, it had managed to be simultaneously a guarantee of the Revolution, a pledge of order, and a symbol of national glory. It combined the features of absolute monarchy and popular sovereignty – the two conceptions of government most strongly rooted in French political culture. Eminent historians have disagreed as to its essential nature: René Rémond classes it as part of the right; Louis Girard considers it as fundamentally on the left. The answer surely is that it was neither, or both. It had managed to be an arbiter between factions, neither 'red' nor 'white' and hence acceptable to an unprecedented and never-equalled majority. It left a deep mark on its successor, the Third Republic, both in what it copied and what it rejected.

1870–1879: coming into port?

The fall of the Empire made the political future once again unpredictable. A provisional republican government of national defence was set up by a bloodless revolution in Paris in September 1870, but it was soon besieged by the Germans, who occupied much of northern France. French surrender in January 1871 left a momentary political vacuum. This was filled by an elected National Assembly in which royalists won 60 per cent of the seats. But Paris and the cities wanted a republic, and were willing and able to fight for it, the Parisian population having being armed and organized to resist the Germans.

This gave rise in March 1871 to the Paris Commune, an insurrection determined above all to defend republican democracy against a possible monarchist coup, although a range of political and social reforms (including disestablishment of the Church, democratization of the state and encouragement to workers' cooperatives) were soon added to its programme. As Marx wrote, its main achievement was 'its own working existence': it was both the first government largely run by 'the people' (white-collar and skilled manual workers and the lower-middle class) and the last major revolutionary upheaval in French history – 'dusk, not dawn', in Jacques Rougerie's phrase. Its unprecedented violent and destructive defeat in 'bloody week' (21–8 May

1871), in which probably about 10000 people were slaughtered and 40000 arrested, marked the end of the 'Revolutionary passion play', that familiar ritual of insurrection that in 1789, 1791, 1830, 1848 and 1870 had been the decisive factor in French politics. François Furet argues that this apocalyptic climax was 'the ultimate exorcism of a violence which had been an inseparable part of French public life since the end of the eighteenth century . . .' in this Paris in flames, the French Revolution bade farewell to history'.

The defeat of Bonapartism and of Paris removed the two queens from the political chessboard. Nothing prevented the large royalist majority in the National Assembly from restoring a monarchy – except their own divisions. They were split between Legitimists and Orléanists, whose conceptions of government were as different as in 1830. Legitimists wanted an absolutist Catholic monarchy in the person of the last Bourbon, the comte de Chambord, 'Henry V'; Orléanists wanted a British-style parliamentary monarchy under one of Louis-Philippe's grandsons. All were aware that their majority might not last, and so the Orléanists agreed to support the restoration of the childless and ageing Chambord, who would adopt as his heir the Orléanist comte de Paris. The French people, exhausted by war and fear of revolution, would probably have acquiesced. But Chambord was determined to be a real king: he insisted on replacing the Revolutionary tricolour with the Bourbon white standard. This was overwhelmingly unacceptable both for sentimental reasons and for what it said about his absolutist intentions.

This gave the republicans their chance. Their weakness was that they were associated with turbulence, war and defeat. Their strength was that royalism was usually no more popular, while Bonapartism, the real crowd-puller, was temporarily out of contention. Adolphe Thiers (1797–1877), a veteran former Orléanist who had come to accept the republic as 'the government that divides us least', was president from 1871 to 1873. He crushed the Commune, proving that a republic could guarantee order, and negotiated a treaty with Bismarck, proving that this republic meant peace. He now proposed a novel and seemingly contradictory political formula: a 'conservative republic'. He urged republicans to reassure the electorate as to their good sense; royalists must abandon their impossible dreams of a restoration and rally to a 'sensible' compromise. This view was tacitly accepted by the republican leadership and by many liberals, who now looked to America as a model. Thiers's strong endorsement of the republic as 'the legal government of the country' whose overthrow would mean 'another revolution, the most dangerous of all', did much to convert a wavering electorate. Republicans began to win more and more parliamentary seats. A last effort by the royalists to organize a restoration failed, and their stand-in monarch, Marshal MacMahon, elected president in 1873 for 7 years, was ousted in 1879 by the republicans when they finally won majorities in both the chamber of deputies and the senate.

During his term, in 1875, a constitution was voted by a temporary alliance of most republicans and most Orléanists, who above all agreed on the need to eschew Bonapartism. It was a compromise: it established the republic legally, but its system of two chambers and a president elected by parliament embodied the conservative 'checks and balances' that Orléanists hoped would restrain dangerous democratic tendencies. Both sides intended to modify it in due course, the republicans to make it more democratic, the royalists to transform it into a monarchy. Ironically, it lasted until 1940, France's most durable constitution so far.

With the republican election victories of 1877 and 1879, says Furet, 'the revolution was coming into port'.[7] The implication is that the Third Republic was the logical, natural, perhaps inevitable culmination of a process begun in 1789. But was it? Could not France have remained a constitutional monarchy, like most of Europe, whether ruled by Bourbon, Orléans or Bonaparte? Republicanism was not an all-conquering movement. It had its fervent supporters, but so did the other factions; and like them, it aroused enmity and suspicion. Its victory in the 1870s was above all due to circumstances: divisions among royalists, the eclipse of Bonapartism, the crushing of the revolutionary Commune. And, far from negligible, the approval of the Germans, who gave no support to royalists and made clear their trust in Thiers. In these circumstances, the 'victory' of the republic is comparable with that of the Bourbon Restoration in 1814: it was the only practical alternative.

Though the Third Republic succeeded over the next 50 years in making its values of secularism and liberal democracy the predominant political values, and made republican symbols (the tricolour, the Marseillaise, the figure of Marianne) into national symbols, it never established a general consensus. Hence its political history is one of periodic crisis. It survived as an 'absolute republic', excluding rivals from power; but those rivals on the right (royalists, nationalists, later fascists) and left (socialists and later communists) maintained a constant opposition to the regime as such.

The 'English history' of French politics: making up the rules

Simultaneously with this 'Jacobin history', concerning ideological struggle and conquest of power, we can identify a different process in which political rules, precedents and conventions were elaborated with the 'recapitulation, assembly and combination' noted by Corbin. In this section, the development of two of the most important areas of politics will be summarized: first, parliament and the executive – the exercise of state power; second, parties, politicians and voters – the organization of popular representation and consent.

Parliament and the executive

In the aftermath of recurrent revolution every regime needed legitimacy, or at least acquiescence. The nineteenth-century recipe for obtaining them was through formal representation in a parliament. But there was no agreement on the proper role or rights of parliament: for legitimists it was an auxiliary of the crown, for Bonapartists a rubber stamp, for radical republicans the mouthpiece of the people. In fact, the French experience shows not theory being put into practice, observes Rosanvallon, but practice being improvised and subsequently justified in theory. Circumstances and partisan conflict were the shapers of practice, and the continuing constitutional theme from 1814 to the present has been a see-saw of dominance between executive and parliament.

The fundamental developments came as early as the first years of the Restoration. Though it broadly wanted to emulate the British system of crown, lords and commons, its 1814 Charter did not formulate even the basic rules of government. Necessity – Napoleon's hundred-days' seizure of power in 1815, and pressure from the allies – laid the foundations. The first cabinet and prime minister (*président du conseil*) were appointed; the convention that ministers, not the king, bore responsibility for policy was established; and the principle that ministers needed the confidence of parliament was asserted. In the lower house, the chamber of deputies, ultra-royalists who at first rejected constitutional government root and branch became defenders of parliamentary prerogatives once in opposition. The royalist François René de Chateaubriand, in his *La Monarchie selon la Charte* (1816), went so far as to define the role of the monarch in a manner anticipating Bagehot's famous formulation in Britain: he could advise, but not insist. The chamber asserted rights not laid down in the Charter to discuss petitions, request legislation, question ministers, vote a reply to the king's speech and – the crucial issues – to examine and vote on the details of the budget.

But Charles X tried to stem the growing power of the chamber and rejected its assertion of the right to overthrow his ministers by a vote of no confidence: he insisted that final authority lay with him – the essence of absolutism. Hence, France's complex political conflicts boiled down to a constitutional crisis in 1830 between executive and chamber, and ended with the fatal attempt at a *coup d'état* to assert the prerogatives of the crown.

The conscious aim of the July Monarchy's supporters among the political élite was to adapt a British model of parliamentary primacy to French post-Revolutionary reality, and so – as in Britain in 1688, an analogy they frequently made – to end the political crisis through modest reforms without a descent into civil war and terror. The July Monarchy, remembered as a parliamentary regime *par excellence*, did not greatly modify the practices established during the Restoration, though in 1830 parliament became the *de facto* principal expression of 'national sovereignty'. Hereditary peers were abolished; the monarchy no longer claimed divine sanction.

The Orléanists subsequently tried to justify in theory what they had improvised in the heat of the moment, but, Rosanvallon has argued, were never able to see parliamentary monarchy as more than a precarious compromise between opposing tendencies. The phrase 'republican monarchy' was used by Louis-Philippe – a sign of the need to synthesize traditions, and a phrase that was to have a distinguished future. But there was never agreement as to what the role of the monarch should be, or how it could be justified in principle. So the monarchy became mainly an *ad hoc* device to block movement towards democracy. Especially after 1840, what was seen as the illegitimate use of the royal prerogative to stifle national sovereignty became again the crucial political issue, and contributed to the fall of the regime in 1848. In short, under the Bourbons it proved impossible to create a system which centred on a traditional, quasi-religious concept of monarchy: Humpty-Dumpty could not be put together again. Under the July Monarchy, the concept of monarchy as a useful legal fiction proved no more viable.

The Second Republic saw an elevation of the role of a single chamber elected by all male citizens as the 'National Assembly', the mouthpiece of popular sovereignty, and (following republican theory) source of executive as well as legislative power. The former was exercised by a committee from among its members – a model later carried to its logical conclusion by the Paris Commune of 1871, the only regime to attempt to return to the pure republican system of the 1790s. However, the 1848 assembly subsequently decided in the aftermath of the June Days insurrection in Paris that a president was necessary to ensure strong authority, and that he should be elected directly, not chosen by the assembly. This led directly to the very unrepublican charismatic regime of Louis-Napoleon Bonaparte, to a struggle for primacy between the president and the assembly, and finally, as we have seen, to a *coup d'état* in December 1851.

The Second Empire was a conscious copy of the First. The emperor, not parliament, now became the representative of the people and the focus of politics. He was responsible for exercising power without prime minister or cabinet and alone was able to introduce legislation. Parliament was downgraded to a technical advisory body; its debates were not even published, and ministers could not sit in it and were not responsible to it. Bonapartism, with its awkward but effective synthesis of popular sovereignty and authoritarianism, gave a very different form to Louis-Philippe's idea of republican monarchy. Opponents stigmatized it as 'caesarism'.

However, in the 1860s, as the regime ran into difficulties at home and abroad, a liberal opposition pressed for increases in parliamentary prerogatives and for what they called the 'necessary liberties' that made proper political representation possible. These were gradually conceded, including publication of debates, parliamentary questioning of ministers, greater press freedom and freedom of meeting. In 1870, the emperor accepted a liberal ministry responsible to parliament, though he insisted on keeping his right to call plebiscites, and hence his own independence of parliament, over whose head he could 'appeal to the people'. This of course left the possibility of conflict between crown and parliament, to liberals' dismay.

Nevertheless, the Empire – pressed by the liberal opposition – had thus established for the first time a working parliamentary democracy based on universal male suffrage. This constituted, in Claude Nicolet's opinion, the 'matrix' of modern French politics. It made universal suffrage a permanent feature of normal political life, practised by a high proportion of the electorate – unlike during the Revolution and First Empire, when most people did not vote even when they had an opportunity. The experiences of the 1860s, in which parliament proved the only viable means of checking the power of the emperor, converted most Orléanists to acceptance of manhood suffrage, and converted most republicans to acceptance of a liberal parliamentary system as the best way of expressing popular sovereignty.

The Third Republic's system grew out of this emerging consensus between moderate royalists and moderate republicans. It owed nothing to the ultra-democratic and potentially authoritarian tradition of urban radical republicanism, briefly resurrected by the Paris Commune. The 1875 constitution was shaped by ideas of 'checks and balances' largely inherited from the July Monarchy: a senate indirectly elected with life members ('republican peers'), and a president elected by both chambers for 7 years – features

Räumung der Rednerbühne in der Nationalversammlungshalle zu Paris nach dem Angriffe der Clubbisten am 15. Mai.

Illustration 2.1 France, 1848: The podium of the National Assembly being cleared after the 'clubbist' attacks on 15 May. The scene captures a sense of the passions and violence provoked by the disputes that year over the form under which France should be governed. (AKG: London.)

republicans accepted unwillingly until they took them over and discovered their advantages. One reason for the system's long stability was the Orléanist device of over-representing conservative rural and small-town France against the radical cities. Stability could mean immobility: for example, republican senators regularly refused the vote to women on the grounds that they were too right-wing and Catholic, and only in 1946 was truly 'universal suffrage' constitutionally established.

The Third Republic was marked by determination to reject the Bonapartist system of a dominant executive. France, said the republican Jules Ferry (1832–93), needed 'weak government'. This tendency was accentuated by the party struggles of the 1870s: the president was largely reduced to a figurehead, and his power to dissolve parliament was abandoned. The effect was to institute parliamentary government in its fullest sense: parliament, strongly reacting against anything smacking of Bonapartism, now dominated the executive. It could overthrow governments without facing elections, so governments had short lives. Its committees dominated ministers. Legislation was long and uncertain.

This was the most durable system France has had since 1789. According to the pioneering political scientist André Siegfried, it corresponded to the tastes, desires and even weaknesses of the French. Yet the system that governs France today is very different, and represents a deliberate reaction against the Third-Republic system, which was criticized as early as the 1880s as partisan, weak and unstable. These criticisms increased amid the stresses and strains of the 1920s and 1930s, but various attempts to strengthen the executive were rejected as quasi-Bonapartist attacks on the Republic. The catastrophic defeat of 1940 led to a widespread rejection of the Third-Republic parliamentary system as a cause of France's weakness and source of division. Parliament itself handed full powers to Marshal Pétain, who cast aside the whole republican and liberal parliamentary tradition. The Fourth Republic, in a reaction against the reaction, returned to that tradition in its 1946 constitution giving even greater preponderance to the lower chamber, now rechristened (as in 1848) National Assembly. But General de Gaulle campaigned vehemently for a system – duly attacked by critics as neo-Bonapartist – that would give the executive greater power and independence from parliament. His opportunity came in 1958, with another wartime crisis over Algeria. He was given full emergency powers to draw up a constitution, that of the Fifth Republic. It places an elected but thereafter practically unaccountable 7-year president at the apex of the state as guardian of the national interest and source of executive authority, and reduces the power of parliament. This is the latest, and so far most successful, version of the idea of 'republican monarchy', the term now widely used to describe the presidential system, and which Michel Debré, main draughtsman of the constitution, declared to be the only hope for French democracy.

Parties, politicians and voters

For most of the nineteenth century the French were by far the most involved in politics of any European people. From 1830 a considerable proportion of male citizens could vote in local elections; from 1848 all male citizens could vote in parliamentary elections. A very high proportion did so, for in the remotest village political defeats and victories could influence the lives and prospects of the humblest: up to 80 per cent of peasant voters went to the polls. Even now, compared with more phlegmatic or apathetic neighbours, a higher proportion of French citizens regularly vote at local, national and (to a lesser extent) European levels. An enduring problem was how this eagerness to take part in political life could and should be limited, channelled and organized.

The starting point was the Revolution. Its political societies, such as the Jacobin Club, provided both a model and an anti-model. A model, in that locally organized clubs holding public meetings to discuss politics and affiliating with others to coordinate propaganda and action was the most familiar pattern. An anti-model, in that many people – especially moderates and conservatives – feared that such organizations could again be a source of subversion and violence. They were therefore tightly restricted by law. The Napoleonic penal code, tightened in 1834, severely limited their size, prevented public activities and forbade wide affiliation. The only permissible activity was small-scale, local, private and under the eye of the authorities. This remained in theory the legal position until the 1901 law on associations. Moreover, both republicans and conservatives had doubts in principle about the organization of 'a state within the state'; the very word 'party' implied faction, subversion and jobbery. To divide and organize citizens into hostile groups was seen as illegitimate, aggravating conflict and causing weakness.

Yet political organization was necessary, above all among those who opposed the government. Individuals and small groups could not stand up to the powerful state machinery of patronage, propaganda, intimidation and gerrymandering. There were three main types of political activity which began during the Restoration, and which shaped organizations throughout this century. First, and most important, to contest elections. Second, to promote and defend a friendly press, commonly the target of prosecution. Third, what Raymond Huard terms 'action societies', often clandestine and with revolutionary aims.

Contesting elections was the first and always most important activity. The local electoral committee was the basic cell of French politics for the whole nineteenth century. Local interests and patronage, local personalities and local independence were crucial. Two- or three-round elections encouraged several candidates and parties in the first round and made large united parties both less necessary and more difficult. With only brief intervals, single-member constituencies were the rule, deliberately encouraging this local focus, in which notables – men who combined social status, economic power and political office – predominated for most of the nineteenth century. From the 1880s onwards, democratization and increasing demands on politicians' time progressively eliminated the traditional land-owning, often titled, notables from national politics, in favour of upwardly mobile middle-class professional politicians. Yet in all regimes a local power base for individual politicians has been an important springboard to a national political career: in this sense, the tradition of the notables survives. At the same time there was a conscious desire to create a trained administrative and political élite, first through the École Libre des Sciences Politiques (founded in 1872) and from 1945 though the ENA (École Nationale d'Administration). This has created a mandarinate unique in the Western world, dominating politics, the civil service and big business. A continuing theme of French politics has thus been the symbiotic relationship between local political élites and the central administrative machine and its agents.

The history of party organization is a jerky one, with bursts of activity at moments of crisis followed by demobilization or repression. Unlike in Britain, political organization grew slowly from the grass roots, not from parliamentary parties down. The restoration saw the beginnings of electoral, press and conspiratorial groups, which were boosted by the crisis from 1827–34. Here the liberal society *Aide-toi le ciel t'aidera* (1827) was the prototype: a network of local groups which registered electors, combatted official gerrymandering and supported candidates. Legal repression in 1834 lasted until another period of mass activity in 1848, almost completely interrupted by Louis-Napoleon's *coup d'état*: Bonapartism had no time for party politics, and even Bonapartists were not permitted to organize. If the liberalization of the 1860s can be seen as the beginning of parliamentary democracy, it was only in the 1890s, when an upsurge in radicalism and socialism was met by defensive alliances among conservatives, that permanent national party organizations were constructed. The final spurt came round the turn of the century, when the Dreyfus affair created further political realignment and further sharp increases in radical and socialist strength. Moreover, in 1901 the law on associations removed legal restrictions. By about 1910 a recognizably 'modern' party system was in place, principally geared towards parliamentary representation, but without anything like the organizational stability of parties in America or Britain.

Seemingly in contradiction, but in fact as the other side of the coin of this fragmented, localized and personalized party system, there has always existed a broader sense of ideological identity, of belonging to what the French call 'political families'. To be for or against the Revolution, or for or against the Church (usually the same thing) were the fundamental poles. The attempt to create class parties in the late nineteenth century only partly modified this picture, which fully survived until the Second World War and still leaves traces. The most familiar expression of this polarity is as 'right' and 'left'. First used during the Revolution itself to denote attitudes towards the monarchy, the terms long applied principally to parliamentary, not grass-roots, groupings: they were only generally used by citizens as descriptions of themselves towards the end of the nineteenth century. The precise point of division between right and left shifted continually according to circumstance. Hence, liberal monarchists were on the left before 1830, but many were on the right afterwards. The easiest definition is probably that the left were those who did not accept that the revolutionary process begun in 1789 had yet been completed; the right were those who either regarded the Revolution as disastrous, or at least believed that it was, or should be, over. The boundary between left and right at any given moment was usually clear (though the prestige of the idea of progress meant that centrist parliamentarians have often tried to squash into the benches at the left-hand end of the chamber): 'How many diverse complexions there are from the extreme right of the centre left to the extreme left of the centre right!' wrote a commentator of the 1840s.[8] Marcel Gauchet has argued that the principal function of the left/ right spectrum was to permit such delicate classification and give seeming coherence to the complexity. At election times it facilitated unity round a single left- or right-wing candidate at the second ballot, essential for victory. Opinion polls in the 1990s show that, although many old political shibbo- leths have disappeared, voters still have a strong sense of themselves as on the right or left. Yet it has never proved possible, especially for the right, to create broad, stable party organizations (such as the British Conservative Party that many envied) which could permanently organize and unite these political 'families' or sensibilities. Inherited ideological differences were too deep: for example, many conservatives were Catholic and anti-republican but other conservatives were not Catholic or not anti-republican (and there were Catholics who were not conservative, and so on).

The First World War had major political consequences. Extreme groups (whether parties such as the post-1920 Communist Party or right-wing *ligues*) condemned parliamentary politics as a corrupt and feeble sham. Moreover, there always remained objections – some going back to the Revolution – that parties were fomenters of division, conservatives usually disdained the term 'party' for their own organizations, preferring words such as alliance, federation, union or *rassemblement*. The wartime Vichy regime condemned parties, but its enemy General de Gaulle, the principal architect of contemporary French politics, was also suspicious, even of his own supporters' organization, and again refused to adopt the term 'party' – a practice that has survived him. His Fifth-Republic constitution, by increasing the importance of the presidency, has made the main function of contempo- rary parties the election and support of a president. Hence their association with a particular individual: the modern Parti Socialiste (1971) was largely associated with François Mitterrand, the neo-Gaullist Rassemblement pour la République (RPR) was founded by Jacques Chirac in 1976, the Union pour la Démocratie Française (UDF) was a vehicle created by Valéry Giscard d'Estaing in 1978, and the Front National has been led since its foundation in 1972 by Jean-Marie Le Pen. There is no reason to suppose that present parties will be more durable than their many predecessors.

Conclusions

I have tried to avoid a 'grand narrative' showing French political history as going in a single direction and reaching an inevitable goal. But I am not suggesting that we should merely substitute two such narratives – 'Jacobin' and 'English' – especially as the latter bears an obvious resemblance to the traditional 'Whig history' of British politics. The French experience should not be seen as linear or logically predetermined. We see abrupt shifts and oscillations between one political pattern and another (from élitist to democratic and back; or from strong to weak executives and vice versa). We also see reversions to earlier patterns (for example the Second Empire's imitation of the First – an influence arguably transmitted to the Fifth Republic). We see a history that is not the rational unfolding of a political blueprint. It has inherited elements from every regime, and borrowed from a variety of ideologies and models, domestic and foreign. It has also been marked by accident, circumstance and the irruption of outside forces through war.

Above all, it is a history that has not ended. This has been amply shown in the 1990s by the rise of Le Pen's populism, the controversies over European integration, and the recent crisis of confidence in the Fifth Republic and its élites. All these phenomena contain new elements, but also have roots in the past – a past of rich ideological contention, party strife and international conflict. As was noted at the beginning of this chapter, French politics today in many ways resemble those of neighbouring countries. Yet France's dramatic past explains why fundamental questions about the role of the state, the sovereignty of the nation, and the rights of citizens are regularly posed with more vehemence than in any other western European country. In France, the unpredictable always seems possible.

Notes

1 Pierre Rosanvallon, *La Monarchie impossible: les chartes de 1814 et de 1830* (Paris: Fayard, 1994), p. 179.
2 Pierre Nora (ed.), *Realms of Memory, Vol. I: Conflicts and Divisions* (New York: Columbia University Press, 1996), pp. 21–3.
3 Rosanvallon, *La Monarchie impossible*, p. 7; Alain Corbin, '(Re)penser le XIXe siècle', *Revue d'Histoire du XIXe Siècle*, 13 (1996), p. 9.
4 Peter M. Jones, *Politics and Rural Society: The Southern Massif Central, c.1750–1880* (Cambridge: Cambridge University Press, 1985), p. 248.
5 Proclamation drafted by Adolphe Thiers and François Mignet, 29 July 1830, in J. P. T. Bury and R. P. Tombs, *Thiers 1797–1877: A Political Life* (London: Unwin Hyman, 1986), pp. 33–4.
6 Frédéric Bluche, *Le Bonapartisme: aux origines de la droite autoritaire, 1800–1850* (Paris: Nouvelles Éditions Latines, 1980), p. 332.
7 François Furet, *Revolutionary France 1770–1880*, trans. A. Nevill (Oxford: Blackwell, 1992), p. 537.

8 Eugène Duclerc and Laurent Paguerre (eds.), *Dictionnaire politique* (Paris, 1842), quoted in Marcel Gauchet, 'Right and Left', in Pierre Nora (ed.), *Realms of Memory: Rethinking the French Past, Vol. 1: Conflicts and Divisions*, English language edn. ed. Lawrence W. Kritzman, trans. Arthur Goldhammer (New York: Columbia University Press, 1996), p. 249.

Further reading

Agulhon, M. *Marianne into Battle: Republican Imagery and Symbolism in France, 1789–1880*, trans. J. Lloyd (Cambridge: Cambridge University Press, 1981).

——, *The Republic in the Village: The People of the Var from the French Revolution to the Second Republic* (Cambridge: Cambridge University Press, 1982).

——, *Marianne au pouvoir: l'imagerie et la symbolique républicaines de 1880 à 1914* (Paris: Flammarion, 1989).

Best, G. (ed.) *The Permanent Revolution: The French Revolution and its Legacy, 1789–1989* (London: Penguin, 1988).

Furet, F. *Revolutionary France, 1770–1880*, trans. A. Nevill (Oxford: Blackwell, 1992).

Gauchet, M. 'Right and left', in Pierre Nora (ed.) *Realms of Memory: Rethinking the French Past*, trans. A. Goldhammer (New York: Columbia University Press, 1996).

Gildea, R. *The Past in French History* (New Haven: Yale University Press, 1994).

Hause, S. and Kenney, A. R. *Women's Suffrage and Social Politics in the French Third Republic* (Princeton: Princeton University Press, 1984).

Hayward, J. *After the French Revolution: Six Critics of Democracy and Nationalism* (London: Harvester Wheatsheaf, 1991).

Hoffmann, S. 'Paradoxes of the French political community', in *In Search of France: The Economy, Society and Political System of the Twentieth Century* (Cambridge, MA: Harvard University Press, 1963).

Huard, R. *La Naissance du parti politique en France* (Paris: Presses de la Fondation Nationale des Sciences Politiques, 1996).

Jones, P. M. *Politics and Rural Society: The Southern Massif Central, c.1750–1880* (Cambridge: Cambridge University Press, 1985).

Nicolet, C. *L'Idée républicaine en France, 1789–1924* (Paris: Gallimard, 1982).

Nora, P. (ed.) *Realms of Memory: Rethinking the French Past* (New York: Columbia University Press, 1996).

Pilbeam, P. M. *Republicanism in Nineteenth-Century France, 1814–1871* (London: Macmillan, 1995).

Rémond, R. *La Droite en France: de la Première Restauration à la Ve Republique*, 2 vols. (Paris: Aubier, 1968).

Rosanvallon, P. *La Monarchie impossible: les chartes de 1814 et de 1830* (Paris: Fayard, 1994).

Tallet, F. and Atkin, N. (eds.) *Religion, Society and Politics in France since 1789* (London: Hambledon, 1991).

Tombs, R. *France 1814–1914* (Harlow: Longman, 1996).

Weber, E. 'Another look at peasant politicization', in *My France: Politics, Culture, Myth* (Cambridge, MA: Belknap Press, 1991).

Zeldin, T. *France 1848–1945*, 2 vols. (Oxford: Oxford University Press, 1973–7).

|3|

Society and people in the nineteenth century

COLIN HEYWOOD

One can trace the 'discovery of society' back to the early nineteenth century. According to Karl Polanyi, this was when people discovered a society that was not subject to the laws of the state, but rather subjected the state to its own laws.[1] In the French case, the Revolution of 1789, and its bid to abolish all intermediary bodies between the state and the individual, was a key influence. The Revolutionary ideal was a nation of free and equal citizens. However, subsequent generations became aware that a sizeable minority of the nation, the poor, was failing to benefit from its new juridical status. Nor was it immediately obvious to contemporaries that the wealth being created by commercial and industrial development would help solve the problem. Indeed, a common assumption was that the *laissez-faire* system favoured a few wealthy capitalists at the expense of a mass of paupers. By the 1830s the way was open for 'the social' to occupy the void left by the formal declaration of individual rights, and the promotion of self-interest by political economists. One of the first indicators was the appearance of various 'social enquiries' concerned with such issues as poverty, the employment of women and children in the workshops, high infant mortality and prostitution. Meanwhile Saint-Simon (1760–1825) and some of the early socialist writers began to think in terms of society as a system. They set out to replace what they considered to be an irredeemably corrupt social system with one based on rational, scientific principles. 'Society', in other words, was becoming an object to be studied and reformed.

If the early nineteenth century was a decisive period in the construction of the idea of society, the late twentieth century has been no less forthright in deconstructing it. Frederic Jameson, for example, dismisses the modernist conception of society as a 'fictive totalizing entity'. To the 'post-modern' mind, the idea that human beings can be confined in a single social system is unconvincing. Rather they are placed in the context of what S. N. Eisenstadt calls 'a multiplicity of only partly coalescing organizations, collectivities and systems'.[2] The emphasis in recent works is on diversity rather than unity, chaos rather than order, the periphery rather than the centre. They depict people sliding in and out of 'imagined communities' such as a class or a nation, rather than being held firmly in a rigid social structure, or being encompassed by overarching entities such as industrial or bourgeois society. This chapter, taking a leaf from the recent shift from 'social history' to a 'history of society', will look at the society and the people of France by exploring some of the divergences between nineteenth- and late-twentieth-century perceptions of social change. Was society disintegrating under the combined forces of the French and industrial Revolutions, as many contemporaries feared? Was it polarizing into two distinct and antagonistic classes, as Karl Marx suggested? Or was it following the liberal ideal and providing increasing opportunities for individuals to improve themselves?

A society in dissolution?

To feel that society is somehow falling apart is common enough at any period of history, though doubtless some have been more pessimistic than others. The first half of the nineteenth century stands out as one such in France. As Pierre Rosanvallon recently noted, most observers under the Restoration and July Monarchy were haunted by the spectre of social dissolution, talking in terms of a society that had turned to dust, or of decomposing social ties. Yielding to no one in their vehemence as prophets of doom were the ultra-royalists of the Restoration. Their starting point was a rather rosy view of social harmony under the strict hierarchies of the old regime. This they contrasted with the social and economic dislocation caused by the spread of modern industry. The vicomte de Bonald (1754–1840), for example, following in the footsteps of the early fathers of the Church, deplored the love of money as the worst of passions. He asserted that money relations were steadily dissolving the social bonds of church, family and village. In his own words, 'we might say that agriculture unites men without placing them in proximity, and commerce, which heaps them together in cities and puts them in continual contact, puts them together without uniting them'.[3]

The late nineteenth century witnessed a further wave of concern over an 'excess of civilization' creating social disorder. Contemporaries became obsessed by fears of 'degeneration', a medical term implying a moral and intellectual decline in the nation, as well as a physical one. A range of experts in new disciplines such as psychiatry and criminology made much of the running in this sphere. They sought to establish a link between the degenerate individual and a range of social problems such as crime, prostitution and insanity. At first sight, nineteenth-century France might seem an odd setting for such fears, given the long drawn-out character of its industrialization and the relatively slow pace to its population increase. We must therefore accept that there was, among observers of European industrialization and urbanization, what Robert Nye calls 'a manifest incongruence between what actually

occurred and how they perceived it'.[4] Their perceptions were important in
their own right for cultural historians, but can one salvage any insights on
social change from them?

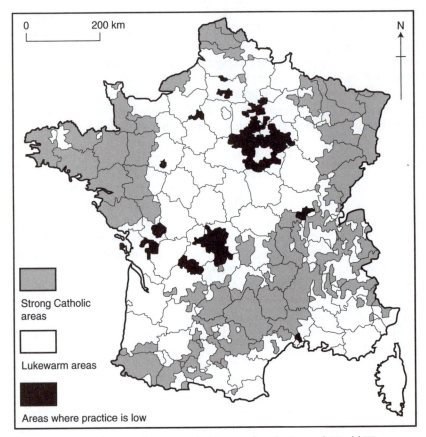

Map 3.1 Religious observance in France after the Second World War

'Dechristianization' of the population?

Consider first the declining hold of the Roman Catholic Church on the
French population. Ruling élites for much of the nineteenth century were
convinced that religion was an essential guarantee of the social order. In 1814
Fontanès, grand master of the university, issued a circular to his rectors which
proclaimed that 'there is only one sure way to control opinion and morality,
and that is to put them under the rule of religion'.[5] Ministers of education
under the July Monarchy and the latter part of the Second Republic, notably
François Guizot (1787–1874) and the comte de Falloux (1811–86), were no

less concerned than he was to ensure that religious teaching suffused the whole of the education system. With hindsight, one can see that they were fighting a losing battle. However, recent historical research indicates that contemporaries often exaggerated the extent of what is loosely termed 'dechristianization' and its impact on moral and civic values.

Religious practice ebbed and flowed over the decades, rather than following a linear decline, with considerable variation according to region, gender and class. As long ago as 1947, Canon Boulard and his map of Catholic religious practice revealed the existence of strongholds of the Church, including Flanders, Brittany and Alsace-Lorraine, besides its well-known disaster areas such as the Ile-de-France and the Champagne. That men left the Church in droves in some regions whilst women were more likely to remain faithful has also been well documented. The disparities were most in evidence in heavily 'dechristianized' areas: on the eve of the First World War, for example, in the diocese of Châlons-sur-Marne, 20.8 per cent of women took Easter communion, but only 3.7 per cent of men. Class differences were more complex. The middle classes began the nineteenth century with a notoriously detached attitude to religion. During the 1830s, as René Rémond observed, a pious woman might be respectable, but it was still ridiculous for a man to be devout. The June Days of 1848 and the depth of class hatreds they revealed are generally thought to have encouraged something of a stampede into the haven of the Church among sections of the bourgeoisie. Henceforth it would be the increasingly bitter divisions within this milieu that stood out. The temptation is to look for a social basis for such divergences, lining up stock characters such as Catholic army officers against 'Voltairian' *petits bourgeois*, but this type of analysis cannot be taken very far. As for the workers, they are generally assumed to have been a group which became resolutely hostile to the Catholic Church, particularly from the 1880s. However, certain qualifications to this picture are revealed by detailed local studies. Small-scale enterprises, located in the countryside, could provide a favourable setting for Catholicism to flourish: the 'Catholic factory' created by Léon Harmel at Val-des-Bois (near Rheims) in the late nineteenth century was the most extreme example. The presence of a Protestant middle class, as in Nîmes or Mulhouse, could sharpen an appetite for Catholicism. Moreover, a combination of factors such as a large female presence and location in a *dévot* region, as occurred in the textile mills of the Nord, might give a Catholic tinge to labour.

By the end of our period, following the separation of Church and state in 1905, those for whom being a Roman Catholic featured prominently in their sense of identity may have formed less than 10 per cent of the population: a distinctly embattled minority, but one whose fervour was impressive enough. Such an allegiance, it might be added, had some tendency to overlap with others, notably conservatism in the political arena. Many others (leaving aside the Protestant and Jewish contingents) retained varying levels of conformity to Catholic teaching, from fairly regular attendance at mass to turning out only for baptisms, weddings and funerals. The position of the Church was therefore by no means hopeless, but French people had certainly strayed further than ever from the model of an orthodox Catholic community. From the point of view of a devout Catholic, there were therefore some grounds for concluding that society was 'going to the dogs' in the nineteenth century. The occasional outburst of violent anti-clerical feeling, as in Paris during the 1830 Revolution or the Commune of 1871, could only have reinforced feelings of an underlying social crisis in this milieu.

It should be added that not everyone in France considered the Catholic Church as a suitable bastion of the social order. Those on the left of the political spectrum generally welcomed the detachment of the population from the Church as a release from ignorance and superstition. Radical republicans, and later socialist militants, arguably followed alternative 'religions', and ones that sought to establish their own bases for holding society together. Leaders of the Third Republic were no less keen than their predecessors to instil the 'good old morality of our fathers' in school texts, stressing the virtues of order and obedience. They also shared the worry that material progress would lead to exaggerated individualism, and so Paul Bert, in his *Manuel général de l'instruction primaire* of 1882, advised teachers to stir patriotic feelings among their pupils.

Breakdown of the family?

The family was considered a bedrock of society by almost everyone in the nineteenth century. Any threats to its stability were therefore seen as boding ill for the future, not least by traditionalists wedded to the principle of social hierarchy. Bonald, for example, liked to compare the authority of the father, the supposedly natural head of the family, with that of the father-king, the 'natural' leader of France. Already in the 1830s the very Catholic (and very conservative) comte Alban de Villeneuve-Bargemont was lamenting the way irresponsible fathers among workers in the towns were neglecting the upbringing of their children. With examples only of 'debauchery, drunkenness and disorder' before them, these young people became in their turn heads of impoverished and demoralized families. The theme of the weakening of bonds between parents and children was taken up again later in the century by Frédéric Le Play (1806–82). As before, one can detect a conservative social and political agenda in the background, in this case hostile to democracy and the emancipation of women. Le Play deplored the rise of what he called the 'unstable family', characteristic of propertyless wage-earners, which started with a marriage, grew as children were born, shrank as they left home and finally disappeared with the death of the parents and the division of the inheritance. He contrasted it with his famous 'stem family' and a vision of paternal authority reinforced by the passing on of property to a single heir. A new twist appeared during the 1890s, when the issue of the declining birth rate or 'depopulation' loomed large in French politics. Social conservatism caused many observers to blame this on the increasing partici-pation of women in the labour force. The economist Paul Leroy-Beaulieu, for example, accused the feminist movement of diminishing women's interest in marriage and maternity by tempting them with 'men's jobs'.

It is indeed all too easy to associate the onset of industrialization with the breakdown of the working-class family. In so doing, there is the risk of being led astray by the alarmist tone that pervaded much contemporary comment. There was admittedly much to shock those of a conservative frame of mind when they surveyed conditions in the slums of the new manufacturing centres. The links between the family and the transmission of property, characteristic of an agrarian society, had certainly weakened in the towns, as wage-earners came to form a growing proportion of the total population. Vulnerable to the periodic crises in the business cycle, industrial workers and their families often struggled to support themselves. In 1828, for example, Villeneuve-Bargemont discovered to his horror that nearly half of the pop-ulation of Lille was estimated to be in poverty. Recent research into inheritances by Adeline Daumard and her team confirm this grim picture. At the beginning of the Restoration, in the major industrial and commercial centres of Paris, Lyon, Bordeaux, Lille and Rouen, 70 to 80 per cent of adults died with no assets whatsoever. In the smaller towns and villages, by contrast, only 30 to 40 per cent of deaths did not require probate declara-tions.

Furthermore, domestic life in the popular *quartiers* did not always con-form to conventional notions of 'respectability'. Unmarried daughters were more likely to become pregnant in towns and 'proto-industrial' areas than in the general run of villages because of the 'hit-and-run' tactics of young men (to adopt the terminology of Edward Shorter), or because marriage plans were thwarted when circumstances forced a lover to depart. Prospective marriage partners had no qualms about living together in 'concubinage' for a few years, producing the odd illegitimate child along the way. Typically, during the 1830s, the Lyonese silk-weavers Louis Bellin and Benoite Mon-teley only married when they could afford to set up their own workshop, by which time they already had a 7-year-old daughter. Most importantly, working-class families frequently expected mothers and children to work for wages, despite all the opprobrium heaped on them for their pains. With fathers disappearing into the workshops and bars for much of their time, and mothers harassed by an unending struggle to make ends meet, relations between parents and children were often strained. Jeanne Bouvier (1865–1964), the daughter of a railway worker, remembered being beaten frequently by her mother, and deprived of physical contact: she was only kissed once a year, on New Year's Day.

Yet there is no need to be so relentlessly negative about working-class families, for in the final analysis one should emphasize their adaptability to changing circumstances. It might even be argued that family ties were strengthened during the industrial age, as the custom of sending children to work as servants or apprentices in other households gradually declined. In the textile town of Roubaix, in the Nord, for example, children generally lived with their parents until they married: the census of 1872 revealed that 86 per cent of girls aged 15–19 were still at home, as were 45 per cent of those aged 20–24. The family remained a unit of production for many, including proto-industrial workers in the countryside and owners of small businesses in the towns. To take one instance from many, the ribbon weavers of Saint Chamond (near Saint Etienne, in the department of the Loire) depended on the efficient cooperation of their wives and children to meet the tight deadlines often imposed by the *fabricants*. The desire to maintain the patrimony intact, and if possible to increase it for future generations, provided an important element of stability for such families. Even where peasants felt obliged to send their daughters to work away from home, most often in the textile industry or domestic service, family links were maintained by regular visits and remittances of money to the home. Under the factory system, parents could sometimes maintain the family unit by employing their own children as assistants, the power-loom weavers of Armentières in the northern linen industry being a case in point. If families expected all but the very youngest to contribute to the family budget, and thereby often skimped on, say, the schooling of their children, this was because of harsh necessity. In 1840 Louis Villermé reported that the 'feeble wages' of many families employed in the textile industry of Mulhouse 'were barely sufficient for the indispensable needs of material life'.[6]

Besides, as Michelle Perrot puts it, the family always involved something more than the soup pot and a budget. It influenced the marriage strategies of the young, helped relatives find jobs and settle into new areas, and provided a basic level of emotional support for its members. The evidence of autobiographies reveals that peasants and workers almost invariably acknowledged the powerful moral influence of their families, and above all their mothers, during the early years. Beneath the façade of strictness there was always a certain warmth, and a determination to help their offspring as best they could. René Michaud (1900–79), recalling a childhood in the Parisian suburbs, noted the infinite kindness that lay behind the brusque exterior adopted by his mother. Throughout the century, therefore, despite all its trials and tribulations, the family remained the principal source of a social identity for French people.

Disintegration of the local 'community'?

A gradual drift of the population from the countryside to the towns provoked further dire warnings of social dislocation. Whereas in 1851 only a quarter of the population lived in a town, by 1911 the proportion had risen to 44 per cent. The theme of a dangerous atomization of society in the towns was as potent in *fin-de-siècle* France as it had been during the 1820s. The almost mythical figures who reflected this unease most dramatically were the Apaches: members of the street gangs whose reputation for violence and disorder sent a frisson through the rest of society. Of course, the inclination to idealize the rural way of life, contrasting the purity of the countryside with the vice and corruption of the towns, can be traced back to antiquity. The record in nineteenth-century France will do as much as any other to expose the fantasies underlying any such vision.

In the first place, although the 'rural community' cannot be dismissed out of hand, it was unlikely to survive as the stable, patriarchal, community envisaged by traditionalists. Witness the fate of the comte Théodor de Quatrebarbes, who used his considerable landed wealth, social status and energy to try to turn the clock back to the *ancien régime* in his village in Anjou. He had some success, winning the municipal elections in Chanzeaux in 1848, but eventually contacts with the towns through emigration upset his plans. Marxist historians provide a useful antidote to any such vision of rustic harmony. They suggest that after 1789 the rural community disintegrated as struggles between capital and wage labour came to the fore under capitalism. These would vary according to local conditions. Closest to the Marxist model would be an area of large-scale cereal farming, such as the Paris basin, where a few wealthy tenant farmers faced numerous, potentially antagonistic agricultural labourers. The countryside can plausibly be depicted as a hotbed of all manner of tensions, feuds and rivalries within and between communities. At the marriage of Pierre-Alain Hélias and Marie-Jeanne Le Goff, in 1913, a fight erupted between the young men from the two Breton villages where the spouses were born over the attention of the local women. There were 'bitter words, challenges, a few isolated fights, and an exchange of the type of insult that can only be washed out with blood'.[7]

Social conflict did not necessarily prevent a spirit of community remaining in the villages. This latter, as Ronald Hubscher reminds us, could be very lively, but also very burdensome: everyone knew each other, and lived in public view. It revolved around work, and the little exchanges of goods and services between villagers that were essential to survival. Women, for example, regularly helped each other out at childbirth and occasional huge washes of linen, or worked together at spinning, mending clothes, lace-making, embroidery, or some other regional speciality. Village sociability was also reinforced by the traditional popular culture, which arguably reached a final flowering during the period 1750–1850. In the department of the Var (in Provence), for example, there was a series of community-based festivals, notably the *fête patronale* specific to each village, and collective activities such as carnival and *charivaris*. The 'rural exodus' of the later nineteenth century drained the villages of some of their vitality. Yet the sedentary nature of the French population remained outstanding, minimizing the disruption of established communities. During the 1890s two-thirds of both men and women aged 45 were still living in the department where they had been born.

One symptom was the tendency for peasants to marry locally, finding their partners within their own or a few neighbouring villages. We also have the testimony of peasant memoirs. Pierre-Jakez Hélias ends his *Horse of Pride* (1975) on a note of nostalgia for his youth in the early twentieth century, a period when the fields of his Breton village teemed with families working together on the harvest, and the farms were full of men and horses: now, he lamented, 'there is no longer any visiting among neighbours, no longer any community'.

In the second place, the stock image of city dwellers as isolated individuals is also worth challenging. There is no denying that the young men and women who moved into the towns faced an uncertain future. The denizens of the *faubourgs* which grew on the edges of the towns were marginal to the rest of society, as John Merriman reveals, being propertyless, transient and short on marketable skills. However, the tendency among historians is to play down the destructive influence of 'uprooting' through urbanization. Much migration was over a short distance, and along well-worn paths: from the impoverished villages of the Dauphiné, the Bugey, the Lyonnais and Savoy to Lyon; or from the southern part of the Haute-Vienne to Limoges, for instance. The efforts made by families, friends and others from the same village or region to help newcomers settle into the towns have been extensively documented. The 'colonies' of Auvergnats and Bretons in the capital were notably effective in this respect. Moreover, the precarious initial stage was only part of the story of migration: marriage was the classic route for the immigrant to integrate in to local society. To take one well-documented case study, by the end of the nineteenth century in Nîmes, temporary migrations were giving way to permanent ones, and migrants were intermarrying freely with natives.

It must also be conceded that the urban 'community' was more informal than its rural counterpart, being based on a few streets and squares that were not always well defined. It was in addition less stable, with populations moving in and out more readily, and often finding employment and entertainment in other parts of town. Ultimately its vitality depended on kaleidoscopic shifts in the fortunes of assorted cafés, theatres, festivals, sports associations, brass bands, political clubs, and so on. Nonetheless, in the older, artisanal type of community, such as those of the cabinet-makers of the Faubourg Saint Antoine in Paris, or silk-weavers of the Croix Rousse in Lyon, groups of men in particular worked, relaxed and lodged in close proximity. The café was an important focus for informal solidarities among skilled workers. W. Scott Haine has investigated the way various 'rituals of camaraderie and resistance' in the Parisian cafés held groups such as metal and construction workers together: new recruits, for example, were welcomed into the fold after they had treated everybody to drinks, and strikes were coordinated from headquarters located in them. Even within the *faubourgs* workers eventually came to develop new forms of solidarity, which crystallized in various leisure and political activities. Many inhabitants of Belleville, a Parisian suburb still dominated by small-scale manufacturing on the eve of the First World War, evidently became attached to the place: they frequently moved house, but mostly within the same neighbourhood, and chose their marriage partners locally. The factory system tended to undermine such tight-knit networks. Yet the miners of the grim Le Soleil *quartier* of Saint-Etienne had plenty of cafés and sporting clubs (for *boules* especially) on their doorsteps in the later nineteenth century. The men and the women of Parisian suburbs such as Saint-Denis and Puteaux could benefit from local commercialized forms of leisure by the early twentieth century, such as dance halls, theatres, and cinemas, plus their own celebrations of Bastille Day.[8] In short, for all the upheavals created by mass movements of population, it seems that most people still identified themselves with a particular village or neighbourhood. As we have hinted, other solidarities, of family, trade or regional background, might serve to reinforce relationships forged in a local community.

To conclude, the inclination here is to stress the elements of stability within nineteenth-century French society, rather than the dislocation and degeneration highlighted above all by conservatives. One can readily understand that members of certain groups, such as landed aristocrats and Catholic priests, might have a jaundiced view of the modern world emerging from the French Revolution and industrialization. This should not be dismissed out of hand: they were right to draw attention to the disruptive effects of early industrialization on workers, and the shift to secular values. All the same, like so many supporters of the Vichy regime during the 1940s, they remained rooted in an idealized version of a rural and agrarian backwater. For all the temptation to lament the coming of a supposedly atomized mass society, it is rather the resilience of institutions and relationships under pressure that stands out, be it the working-class family or even the Catholic Church under a hostile Third Republic. One should also acknowledge their variety: family, neighbourhood, trade, church, music society, sports club, mutual aid society, and the like all provided networks of support for the individual.

A class-based society?

Simonde de Sismondi (1773–1842) was the first person to suggest that industrial society tends to separate into two distinct classes: in his case, defined as those who work and those who possess. By the 1840s this line of thought was common currency in France. The 1848 Revolution added a menacing edge to it, as the 'springtime of the peoples' turned sour. Alexis de Tocqueville (1805–1859) recalled the 'sinister and frightening' atmosphere in Paris after genuine republicans had fared poorly in the April elections: 'Society was cut in two: those who had nothing united in common envy; those who had anything united in common terror.' In similar vein, Karl Marx

(1818–83) concluded that the violence on the streets during the June Days of that year was 'the first great battle ... between the two great classes which divide modern society'.[9] It was of course Marx who provided the fullest exposition of the process of class formation. He was convinced that a distinctive feature of the capitalist era was the simplification of class antagonisms. Landowners, peasants and petty bourgeois were merely 'transitional classes', doomed to be engulfed by the two great classes of bourgeoisie and proletariat. The huge influence of Marxism in academic circles has led to this vision of two antagonistic classes pervading much of the recent literature on nineteenth-century French social history. However, it has not survived unscathed in the 'post-modern' era. William Reddy talks in terms of a crisis of the class concept for the Marxist tradition, which has led to a 'healthy period of reformulation'.

The materialist approach to class and the class struggle

Most historians over the last few years have followed E. P. Thompson in seeing class as a historical relationship, 'embodied in real people and in a real context'. The argument is that classes cannot exist on their own, for they only emerge when people enter into relations with each other to produce and distribute goods. In the Marxist model the outcome was always a dominant and a subordinate class, revolving around ownership of private property in the means of production. However, as Anthony Giddens usefully warns us, this conception of a simple two-class society must be seen as a theoretical construct.[10] Marx in the mid-nineteenth century assumed that until a fully fledged bourgeois society emerged at some point in the future, a more complicated system of relationships would always prevail. He himself devoted a great deal of effort to analysing the complexities of the class struggle in France. He highlighted rivalries between landowners and capitalists, the financial aristocracy and the industrial bourgeoisie, proletarians and lumpenproletarians, and the state bureaucracy and the rest of society. It is not hard to fathom why Marxism in its various forms appealed to intellectuals, for the Marxist model of social change is breathtaking in its scope. Briefly stated, it links all of the ideas, institutions and apparent characteristics of a social system to the material base: the way people earned their living.

The 1960s and 1970s brought a certain reaction against the established Marxist historiography, particularly its emphasis on the impact of mechanization in the early nineteenth century and its heavy bias towards the institutional history of trade unions and socialist parties. The 'new labour history', for example, did much to recover the daily experiences of wage-earners in a series of fine local studies. In retrospect, however, one can see that this generation retained the Marxist focus on the emergence of a class-based society and class consciousness. It also continued to seek the explanation for change largely in the economic sphere, with the familiar tale of proletarianization at the workplace.

Take one of its key innovations: exploring the paradox of working-class consciousness first appearing among the élite of skilled workers rather than among factory proletarians. Outstanding examples from France include the silk-weavers of Lyon, whose insurrection in 1831 reverberated around the continent, and the militant printers, tailors and shoemakers active in Paris during the aftermath of the 1830 Revolution. The 'new' history set out to demonstrate that the problems they faced had little to do with mechanization and the factory system. Yet it was still very much a case of social and economic tensions leading to militancy: that is to say, the threats to skilled workers from flooded labour markets, competition from rural industry, the resort to unskilled labour in 'sweatshops' and restrictions on their organizations. In the words of Bernard Moss, 'neither traditional artisans nor industrial workers, workers in the labor movement were skilled craftsmen undergoing a process of proletarianization'. The Parisian tailors studied by Christopher Johnson provide a classic case study for this 'radical artisan' thesis. During the first half of the nineteenth century, traditional bespoke tailors found themselves under pressure from *confectionneurs*: large-scale manufacturers of ready-made clothing. The *confection* system reduced costs by resorting to a handful of cutters and a small army of low-paid outworkers sewing together the pieces. The upshot was that during the 1830s and 1840s tailors were amongst the most vocal and well-organized militants in the capital.

Social history takes the 'linguistic turn'

A full-blown assault on the Marxist interpretation of class would have to await the 1980s and 1990s. Jacques Rancière gave a hint of what was to come, in disputing the links between skilled workers and a militant working-class culture during the 1830s and 1840s. He accepted that two of the most active trades in the early labour movement were tailors and shoemakers. But he flatly denied that a sense of their own professional worth and the threat of 'deskilling' could have fired them into action. These two trades were, he alleged, among the most contemptible for workers, since they required little strength, skill or technical knowledge. Instead, it seemed likely that the least cohesive trades were the ones the most receptive to republican or socialist values – values that were potentially opposed to those of the trade. In so doing, he countered the orthodox view that militancy sprang above all from tensions on the shop floor. He preferred to locate discourses on workers' unity in the context of a political struggle, to unite intellectuals and militant workers around moderate republicanism. William Sewell also pioneered the line that cultural influences were more important than economic ones in the development of class consciousness among French workers. His influential study argued that the 'pre-existing values' of the old guilds, duly updated during the revolutions of 1789 and 1830, were what shaped the challenge of workers to the new industrial order during the first half of the century.

The way was open for historians to jettison the base–superstructure model of social change, and any vestiges of economic determinism inherited from 'vulgar Marxism'. They would now be prepared to give greater autonomy than before to the political and cultural spheres. In particular, they would pay close attention to language, and the way it shapes people's perception of the world. The result was to deny the socio-economic reality of classes, seeing them rather as discursively constructed during the political struggle. Without a material base, any class allegiances were likely to be temporary and unstable. It became fashionable to deny that class affiliations were at all important for many people during the nineteenth century, particularly for the mass of the peasantry. Rather, the stress was on the multiple identities noted in our previous section.

From class to 'class'

Take the changing contours of the middle class over the nineteenth century. During the Restoration, doctrinaires like Royer-Collard (1763–1845) began celebrating the virtues of a *classe moyenne*, its intelligence and independence contrasting with the greed for power of the upper classes and the ignorance and dependence of the lower classes. The historian Dror Wahrman argues that this appearance of 'middle-class' language in the early nineteenth century had only a tenuous connection with underlying social change. In his view, the latter was proceeding too slowly to account for such a dramatic shift in usage. He insists on 'the considerable space for different representations and interpretations' of social reality. It was a broad range of Frenchmen, more middle than class, who allegedly took the opportunity to assert themselves in the political arena with an appeal to the 'middle class'. What emerges, then, is an 'imagined constituency', to be placed in the context of the 'post-aristocratic political experience' of the period. The *classe moyenne* returned to prominence in public debates at the very end of the nineteenth century, this time very much in a state of crisis. The constituency had now become a *petite bourgeoisie*, consisting of artisans and shop-keepers. Of course there is no disputing the existence of small enterprise at this period, and the efforts made to defend its interests against the encroachments of big business and organized labour. Yet Geoff Crossick adds an element of 'invention' to the proceedings, as Social Catholics in particular idealized the middle as the key to social peace. In 1908, for example, Georges Blondel wrote of 'the ideas of moderation and good sense to which they are naturally inclined'.[11]

We might, then, concede that there was a certain desire among the middling groups in society to distinguish themselves from the masses, particularly in times of crisis. But far more in evidence was the diversity within any 'middle class'. It did after all run from an élite of high finance and top civil servants, which had practically supplanted the old aristocracy, down to a *petite bourgeoisie* still rubbing shoulders with the workers. In the case of Rouen, Jean-Pierre Chaline has isolated a wealthy bourgeoisie, accounting for approximately one-tenth of the population, which hardly conformed to the Marxist model of this class. There were variations in its activities, with landed, commercial, professional and bureaucratic strands. There were variations in its income level, summed up as *petite*, *bonne* and *grande bourgeoisie*. There were also notable political and religious variations, pitting Catholics against Protestants and a conservative majority against a leftist minority. Besides differences in wealth, status, occupation, religion and politics, we should also keep in mind the no less fundamental one of gender. The notion of 'separate spheres' dictated that men would occupy the public one of work and politics, whilst women would be confined to the private one of the family. Such a clear-cut distinction could not be sustained in practice, women in most *petit-bourgeois* families being involved in the running of a business. Even so, Bonnie Smith recorded the gradual exclusion of wives from an active role in the textile mills of the Nord over the course of the century. While many women may have accepted this division of labour between the sexes, others champed at the bit and registered their protest in an early feminist movement.

A much more persistent series of campaigns attempted to persuade wage-earners that they formed part of a 'working class' – with some success. They reached a crescendo during the revolutionary years of 1830–4, 1848 and 1871, and again during the rather different upheavals of the late nineteenth and early twentieth centuries. In the latter case, according to Michelle Perrot, economic influences did come into play, with the depression of the 1880s and the 'second industrial revolution' accelerating the shift to mass-production techniques in industry. At the same time, she observes:

> This working class defined itself by its enemies, its limits, its conscious-ness of a shared 'fate' and a shared exploitation, its vision of the future. All of this, often voiced by militants who were both mediators and spokesmen, was crystallized in words and images, a language that became an instance of reality, a referent that in turn structured the imagination.[12]

Militants were able to concoct a heady brew in their speeches, revolving around suffering workers, rapacious bosses and a glorious struggle for a better world: 'Live by our labour, or die fighting', as one worker proclaimed during a strike.

Yet historians are bound to note that many workers, perhaps the major-ity, rebuffed all such advances from the militants. There was no mass labour party in France until the formation of the SFIO in 1905, whilst even on the eve of the First World War less than 10 per cent of the labour force was unionized (though as Alain Cottereau warns, such figures may fail to reveal the informal means of 'collective defense' widely adopted by French workers). The great diversity of interests among workers should also make us think carefully about who we have in mind when we discuss the 'working class'. The fact is that the leaders of organized labour had a narrow vision of their constituency. Their vision of the future tended to reflect the aspirations of skilled male workers, such as mule-spinners, metal workers, engineers, building workers, railwaymen and coal miners. Historians can in their turn be accused of concentrating on the struggles of this particular group. In so doing, they marginalize huge groups of wage-earners, including domestic servants, casual labour, the unskilled, immigrants and women workers.

Women, for example, accounted for nearly 30 per cent of the industrial labour force in 1866. From the perspective of the (male) leadership, much of their work was casual and unskilled; they were difficult to unionize; and they could be deployed in trades such as printing and leather to undercut the wages of male workers. We know from a study of the garment trades in Paris during the 1830s and 1840s by Joan Scott that seamstresses had their own ideas about how work should be organized, and that these differed from those of the tailors. The women in these trades were determined that they should be able to combine 'the right to work' with child care, and so they opposed the clear separation between work and home proposed by the men. Even so, by the end of the century union leaders were starting to demand a 'family wage', permitting men to support their families without the need for their wives and children to find employment. Most delegates to the workers' congress of Marseille in 1879 supported the position that 'a woman's true place is not in the workshop or the factory, but in the home, within the family'.[13] The 'worker', in other words, was being represented as a man, not a woman, in line with the notion of separate spheres for the two sexes.

French people talked the language of class often enough in the nineteenth century – though it was readily interchangeable with more moral and political divisions, lining up producers and the idle, say, or the people and their oppressors. Historians have become increasingly wary of using this type of language as evidence that there existed two or three socially homogenous groups of actors squaring up to each other: what the Marxist would call classes *in* themselves. They are more prepared to countenance the notion of people perceiving themselves as part of a class, that is to say, a class *for* itself. However, any allegiance to a culturally constructed class of this type, uncoupled from an economic base, must be seen as fluid and ephemeral. The powerful image of a working class marching inexorably to revolutionary consciousness appears dead and buried with the worldwide retreat of communism post-1989. Instead we have a more chaotic picture, as the meaning of class is seen to fluctuate according to the circumstances of period and place.

Illustration 3.1 The General Strike. The years between 1890 and 1914 saw a heightened and more organized labour militancy in France. For anarcho-syndicalists the general strike was much vaunted as a weapon with which to paralyse the capitalist economy and topple the bourgeois, parliamentary Third Republic.

Liberty, equality ... towards a free and equal society?

Besides the pessimists and the class warriors of nineteenth-century France, there were a number of optimists who were no less vocal in public debates. The political liberalism of the French Revolution created the vision of a classless society, that is to say, one of free and equal citizens. The early liberals believed in the inexorable march of progress, though in small stages rather than any revolutionary form. They were, to quote Dieter Langewiesche, the 'innovative section of respectable society'.[14] This meant that they sought to promote stability as well as a measure of change with their reforms. They were quite content to leave the ambitious programme of a 'classless civil society' to the long term. Indeed the sufferings of the poor were something of a blind spot for them, their focus being on political and constitutional issues. During the 1820s Benjamin Constant (1767–1830) was convinced that the progress of civilization and wealth would raise the standard of living among workers and spread enlightenment. One of his biographers notes his 'blind faith in the benefits of liberty', with the easy assumption that social problems would be solved by free competition. His recipe for social harmony lay in the widespread ownership of property, which he felt the Revolution had encouraged. Some inequality was considered inevitable here, but he anticipated that it would be far less than in the earlier 'aristocratic' society. How much evidence, then, will the historical record show of progress in the material and cultural life of nineteenth-century French society?

The changing distribution of wealth

Take first the question of landownership, so important in a traditional agrarian society. Was there a broadening of the ownership of property during the nineteenth century, as Constant so earnestly hoped would occur? It is always tempting to depict nineteenth-century France as a 'republic of peasants'. Taxation records for 1826 do after all suggest that there were approximately 6 million owners of landed property in France, out of a total of 7 or 8 million adult males. The number of taxable property units also rose steadily during the first half of the century, from 9 million in 1815 to 14 million in 1865. One can assume that most families in rural France owned at least a small plot of land. Nonetheless, France was still a long way from the ideal of a democracy of small, independent landowners. In 1884, when the tax records become more informative, only 5 per cent of assessments were for properties which the owner and his family could farm unaided: those from 10 to 50 hectares. What stands out is the concentration of landownership. The majority of assessments (61 per cent) were for properties of less than 1 hectare in size, and a further 33 per cent for those between 1 and 10 hectares: not enough land to support a family in most regions. This leaves large-scale properties of 50 hectares and over accounting for less than 1 per cent of assessments but for over one-third of the land.

Landed wealth naturally declined in relative importance with the onset of industrialization. This provokes the question of how the infusion of new types of wealth influenced the overall distribution among various groups in the population. Did it have a levelling effect? Or did it tend to widen the gap between rich and poor, as critics of industrial society frequently alleged? Again, it is the persistence of earlier inequalities that emerges from the historical record, rather than any dramatic improvement or deterioration. In 1914, no less than during the 1820s, around three-quarters of adults who died in a sample of major cities left nothing to their heirs. Figures for the concentration of wealth in the cities at the two ends of the century are also remarkably similar. To quote Adeline Daumard:

> Around 1820 the poorest 30 per cent of the deceased owned only 0.1 per cent of all assets in Paris, 0.5 per cent in Bordeaux, 1 per cent in Toulouse. The proportions were identical in 1911. At the other end of the scale, 30 per cent of all wealth in the Restoration period was owned by 1 per cent of Parisians, 1 per cent of Bordelais, 2.5 per cent of Toulousains; in 1911, by 0.4 per cent of Parisians, 1 per cent of Toulousains, and 2.5 per cent of Bordelais.[15]

Within this overall stability there were, however, winners and losers among the various socio-economic groups. Not surprisingly, big businessmen stood to gain more than most from the general enrichment. In Paris merchants and bankers profited most, whilst in Lyon and Lille it was manufacturers who emerged in 1911 with the largest fortunes on average. Meanwhile, the *petite bourgeoisie* of small shopkeepers and craftsmen suffered a relative decline in social status. The mean value of their fortunes increased over the century, but insufficiently to keep up with other groups. In Paris, for example, they accounted for 17 per cent of total wealth in 1820, but only 3 per cent in 1911.

A rising standard of living

The nineteenth century brought a modest rise in living standards for the French people as a whole. The best indicator is the growth in product, or income, per head of population. Paul Bairoch estimates that between 1830 and 1910 the gross national product *per capita* grew on average by 1.2 per cent a year. This was slightly ahead of the figure for Europe, which stood at 0.9 per cent. At the beginning of the century the standard of living in France had been perhaps 10 to 12 per cent higher than that of continental Europe (excluding Russia). As Bairoch observes, however, even in the wealthiest traditional societies, only a tiny minority of the population enjoyed any material security: 'For the great majority not only were the average conditions of life close to poverty, but the frequent periods of subsistence crisis were periods of hunger, if not of famine'.[16] The economic growth achieved over the following decades at least made daily existence for most people significantly less precarious.

Above all, the nineteenth century solved the age-old subsistence problem. Toutain estimates that the average calorie intake of the population was below 2000 at the beginning of the century, which still left people vulnerable to undernourishment. A gradual increase in the calorie ration starting in the 1840s meant that a 'desirable' level of 3000 calories had been reached by the end of the century. One should not lose sight of the deficiencies in the popular diet. It remained heavily dependent on bread: 'bread, always bread, and more bread'. A foundry man at Fourchambault during the 1820s would work his way through 2 to 4 lbs of it a day. There was also an endless succession of daily soups to go with the bread. During the 1830s textile workers in Alsace subsisted on a regime of potatoes, thin soup, a little milk and butter, some poor-quality noodles and bread. Later in the century urban workers in particular could afford some milk, sugar, fruit and fresh vegetables, but even so their diet remained excessively reliant on carbohydrates and fats. A lack of calcium and vitamins exposed children to deficiency diseases such as rickets and scrofula. Nonetheless, the terrible food shortages that periodically afflicted people under the *ancien régime* gradually receded at mid-century. There were also certain developments in housing and in public sanitation – but they were painfully slow throughout the nineteenth century.

Social mobility

Whether one should be thinking in terms of 'careers open to talent' in nineteenth-century France, or something of a caste system, remains a conundrum. The stock figure of the 'self-made man', as illustrious in France as in England, suggests an element of social mobility in industrial society. There was, for example, Auguste Badin, who started on the shop floor at the age of 12, and ended as the owner of the huge cotton and linen mill at Barentin in Normandy. There was, too, Marius Berliet, an apprentice silk-weaver in Lyon whose passion for machinery eventually helped him to make a fortune as a motor manufacturer. Louis Bergeron is persuasive in arguing that industrialization encouraged considerable upheaval within the élite, challenging existing forms of authority and allowing in some fresh blood. Yet, as he also notes, the occasional spectacular success story risks diverting attention from the undoubted continuities within the élite, and the existence of formidable 'dynasties' among wealthy bourgeois (and aristocratic) families: the Wendels, Schneiders, Taittingers, and so on. Christophe Charle reveals how the top level of the civil service recruited consistently from the same *bonne bourgeoisie* throughout the century. Even in 1901, under a republican regime, he found that only around one-tenth of directeurs, conseillers d'état and prefects came from the *petite bourgeoisie* or the 'popular classes'.

A very different approach involves dividing society into classes and attempting to estimate mobility between them. In this case, the results tend to show the rigidity of social structures. In Rouen, Chaline asserts that the bourgeoisie gradually became a 'patriciate' or 'bourgeois-nobility' as the cotton industry became concentrated in a few hands during the late nineteenth century. Similarly, a study of Toulouse by Aminzade and Hodson finds a 'very closed' bourgeoisie between the 1830s and the 1870s, and 'very limited' short-range mobility, from working class to petty bourgeoisie, or petty bourgeoisie to bourgeoisie. This is consistent with the findings on the unequal distribution of wealth, but there remains the objection that the proposed schema of classes may tell us more about what is going on in the historians' heads than what mattered for contemporaries.

A recent study by Dupâquier and Kessler, based on 3000 family histories, focuses on the more limited (but safer) ground of occupational mobility. On the one hand, it highlights the existence of a large and stable section of the population employed in agriculture throughout the nineteenth century. Farmers (as opposed to the farm labourers) in the population were something of a caste. No less than 83 per cent of bridegrooms in the sample who described themselves as *cultivateurs* had fathers with the same occupation. On the other hand, the study documents the high level of occupational mobility among artisanal and working-class occupations in the towns. The constant influx of sons and daughters of peasants into urban areas meant that workers whose fathers might also be classified as workers were relatively rare before the 1880s. Of the 168 fathers of miners in the sample, for example, only 35 were miners or workers, the rest being farmers, agricultural labourers, artisans, property-owners and traders. Quite how all such 'movement' translates into upward or downward mobility is unfortunately not confronted in this study.

Towards a more 'civilized' society

Liberals under the Restoration placed great faith in the benefits of education for the masses. Their views were sharpened by debates with extreme royalists, who opposed education for the people beyond a very minimum which could be left to the supervision of the Church hierarchy. François Guizot argued that education was a necessity for all classes, and not least the lower classes. Keeping them in ignorance was dangerous because it left them open to manipulation by factions: far better, then, to give them the means to better their condition. At the same time, Guizot could with a perfectly good conscience recommend that education should reinforce rather than disturb existing social hierarchies. The liberal view was that secondary education should be reserved for a wealthy minority, whilst a very limited primary education would suffice for the masses. The liberals were always outflanked on the left by a humanist element, which from the time of Condorcet and the Revolution believed that the schools could liberate people from the 'obscurantist' influence of monarchs and priests. Yet even with the arrival of a republican regime in 1870, the ideal of unifying all groups in society through the school proved impossible to realize. The upheavals of the early years of the Third Republic produced three antagonistic 'families': a Catholic one, in the private schools run by the Church; a liberal bourgeois one, in the *lycées* (and their elementary classes); and a 'popular' one, catering for the masses, in the state-run primary schools.

Hence the 'progress' of education in the nineteenth century looks decidedly double-edged. A combination of state provision and parental initiative meant the vast majority of children were receiving some schooling by the time primary education was made free and compulsory in the 1880s. Yet the system did little or nothing to encourage the majority to expect that primary schooling would lead into secondary, let alone higher education. The schools had produced a more-or-less literate population by the end of the century. Yet class and gender remained significant influences on what was expected. For the masses, particularly in the countryside, the basics of literacy would suffice, augmented eventually by a little history and geography, plus a heavy-handed dose of religious or republican morality. For girls, too, expectations were limited, the overriding concern being to prepare them for family responsibilities: every law on education in the nineteenth century, for example, expected them to learn needlework.

A similar kind of progress of a sort can be found when looking at the broader transformation of popular culture in the nineteenth century. One can point to the stimulating influence of mass-produced books and newspapers, adult-education classes, cheap travel on the railways, sporting organizations, and leisure facilities such as music halls and *café-concerts*. By the early twentieth century, for example, newspaper reading was firmly established among the 'popular classes' – though men tended to concentrate on the political sections and women on the crime reports and serialized novels. Eugen Weber enthusiastically depicted the peasantry being emancipated from the parochialism, the routine and the 'superstition' that had dominated village life. Once converted to rationalism, the peasant could 'throw away his ragbag of traditional contrivances, dodges in an unequal battle just to stay alive', and become an agent of change.

There is a strong counter-current in the literature which believes that a vibrant popular culture associated with the peasants and artisans of the pre-industrial era was supplanted by the 'mass culture' or even the 'pseudo culture' of modern capitalism. Certainly, political and commercial interests attempted to hijack various cultural activities for their own ends. The public festivals of the Third Republic, such as 14 July and the centennial of 1789, were a case in point: Charles Rearick argues that by 1900 they had lost much of their original sparkle, as the celebration of the exciting ideals of liberty and equality gave way to the glorification of an established regime. More oppressive was the campaign by a number of employers to 'moralize' their workers. At Carmaux, the Marquis de Solages poured thousands of francs into the local church and Catholic schools for his miners during the latter part of the century. In 1897, in similar vein, the steel manufacturers of Lorraine boasted that labour relations had been improved by the 'healthy distractions' on offer, such as music and theatre. This type of evidence readily lends itself to the 'social control' model, so beloved of an earlier generation of historians.

The tendency of late, however, has been to look more from the 'bottom up', using autobiographical material to investigate how ordinary men and women reacted to such efforts to indoctrinate them. Given the fiercely anti-clerical and anti-capitalist elements in the French political culture, it is hardly surprising to find plenty of signs of resistance. To take one example, Antoine Sylvère (1888–1963) asserted that the 'odious' text *The Duties of a Christian*, used in his Christian Brothers school, drove people to anti-clericalism as effectively as any Mason or free-thinker. Evidence abounds that the 'popular classes' adopted a canny, instrumental approach to schools, charities, leisure activities, and so on, trying hard to take what suited them and to leave the rest.

The ideal of a society of free and equal citizens was an exacting one, doubtless honoured more in the breach than the observance. The nineteenth century brought some developments that helped free the poorer members of the population from the extremes of material deprivation and ignorance. The period did after all hum with innovation, pioneering our own age of mass production, mass schooling and mass culture. Yet the inequalities between rich and poor remained stubbornly entrenched. By the end of the century even liberals had come to recognize that freeing up markets would not in itself lead inexorably to universal prosperity. The way was open for state intervention to remedy some of the ravages created by the *laissez-faire* system. François Ewald claims that the 1898 law whereby the state assumed responsibility for industrial accidents was a notable turning point. It revealed how, in facing the destructive side to industrialization, people came up with new ways of thinking about their relationships and their mutual obligations. By the early twentieth century the creeping influence of the state on society was much in evidence, with a growing contingent of schoolteachers, factory inspectors, tax collectors, gendarmes, and so on.

Conclusion

Was the nineteenth century the age of the bourgeoisie, as historians for long concluded? The last few decades have witnessed a gradual retreat from the materialist and class-based interpretations of history that this implies. During the 1980s Roger Magraw made a valiant stand against the tide, reasserting the line that 1789 was a 'Bourgeois Revolution' and emphasizing 'the consolidation of bourgeois hegemony' up until the First World War. Theodore Zeldin denied that France was dominated by 'one man, one class or one set of principles', though he still had the bourgeoisie acting as a class, noting how it fought the Church, controlled the press, entrenched privilege in its families, and so on. Roger Price in his turn talked in terms of a ruling élite rather than a bourgeoisie, but retained economics and demography as 'the most effective means of understanding the structure of society'. Very recently, however, historians have become increasingly impatient with any hint of economic determinism, social structures and classes behaving as actors. 'Society' dissolves into a multitude of groupings and organizations, classes only being one among several possible 'imagined communities'. What holds them all together is the state: in the wake of the French Revolution, to quote Pierre Rosanvallon, it became 'the principal unifying agency for a society of atomized individuals'.[17] The wheel had now come full circle, as the social yielded ground to the political.

Acknowledgements

The author would like to thank Martin Alexander, Olena Heywood, Roger Magraw and Robert Tombs for comments on an early draft of this chapter.

Notes

1 Karl Polanyi, *The Great Transformation* (Boston: Beacon Hill, 1957), p. 111.
2 Frederic Jameson, *Postmodernism, or, the Cultural Logic of Late Capitalism* (London: Verso, 1991), p. 187; S. N. Eisenstadt, *A Sociological Approach to Comparative Civilization* (Jerusalem: Hebrew University, 1986), cited by Zygmunt Bauman, *Intimations of Postmodernity* (London: Routledge, 1992), p. 56.
3 Vicomte de Bonald, 'Pensées', cited in D. K. Cohen, 'The Vicomte de Bonald's critique of industrialism', *Journal of Modern History*, 41 (1969), pp. 479–80.
4 Robert A. Nye, *The Origins of Crowd Psychology* (London: Sage, 1975), p. 1.
5 Cited in Gérard Cholvy and Yves-Marie Hilaire, *Histoire religieuse de la France contemporaine, Vol. 1, 1800–1880* (Toulouse: Privat, 1985), pp. 21–2.
6 Louise A. Tilly, 'Individual lives and family strategies in the French proletariat', *Journal of Family History*, 4 (1979), p. 148; Elinor Accampo, *Industrialization, Family Life, and Class relations: Saint Chamond, 1815–1914* (Berkeley: University of California Press, 1989), ch. 2; W. M. Reddy, 'Family and factory: French linen weavers in the *belle époque*', *Journal of Social History*, 8 (1975), pp. 102–12; Louis Villermé, *Tableau de l'état physique et moral des ouvriers employés dans les manufactures de coton, de laine et de soie*, 2 vols. (Paris: Renouard, 1840), I, p. 49.

7 Pierre-Jakez Hélias, *The Horse of Pride* (New Haven: Yale University Press, 1975), p. 26.
8 Gérard Jacquemet, *Belleville au XIXe siècle* (Paris: École des Hautes Études en Science Sociale 1984), ch. 7; Jean-Paul Burdy, *Le Soleil Noir: un quartier de Saint-Etienne, 1840–1940* (Lyon: Presses Universitaires de Lyon, 1989), pp. 170–4; Lenard R. Berlanstein, *The Working People of Paris, 1871–1914* (Baltimore: Johns Hopkins University Press, 1984), ch. 4.
9 Alexis de Tocqueville, *Recollections* (New York: Anchor, 1971), pp. 123–4; Karl Marx, 'The defeat of June 1848', in David Fernbach (ed.), *Surveys from Exile* (Harmondsworth: Penguin, 1973), p. 58.
10 E. P. Thompson, *The Making of the English Working Class* (Harmondsworth: Penguin, 1968), p. 9; Anthony Giddens, *Capitalism and Modern Social Theory* (Cambridge: Cambridge University Press, 1971), p. 38.
11 Cited in Geoff Crossick, 'Metaphors of the middle: the Discovery of the petite bourgeoisie, 1880–1914', *Transactions of the Royal Historical Society*, 6th series, 4 (1994).
12 Michelle Perrot, 'On the formation of the French working class', in Ira Katznelson and Aristide Zolberg (eds.), *Working-Class Formation* (Princeton: Princeton University Press, 1986), p. 94.
13 Michelle Perrot, 'L'Eloge de la ménagère dans le discours des ouvriers français au XIXe siècle', in *Mythes et représentations de la femme au dix-neuvième siècle* (Paris: Campion, 1976), p. 110.
14 Dieter Langewiesche, 'Liberalism and the middle classes in Europe', in Jürgen Kocka and Allen Mitchell (eds.), *Bourgeois Society in Nineteenth Century Europe* (Oxford: Berg, 1993), p. 54.
15 Adeline Daumard, 'Wealth and affluence in France since the beginning of the nineteenth century', in W. D. Rubinstein (ed.), *Wealth and the Wealthy in the Modern World* (London: Croom Helm, 1980), p. 98.
16 Paul Bairoch, 'L'Economie française dans le contexte européen à la fin du XVIIIe siècle', *Revue économique*, 40 (1989), p. 959.
17 Pierre Rosanvallon, *L'État en France de 1789 à nos jours* (Paris: Seuil, 1990), p. 96.

Further reading

Aminzade, R. and Hodson, R. 'Social mobility in a mid-nineteenth century French city', *American Sociological Review*, 47 (1982).
Bastid, P. *Benjamin Constant et sa doctrine*, 2 vols. (Paris: Armand Colin, 1966).
Bergeron, L. *Les Capitalistes en France, 1780–1914* (Paris: Gallimard, 1978).
Berlanstein, L. (ed.), *Rethinking Labor History: Essays on Discourse and Class Analysis* (Urbana, IL: University of Illinois Press, 1993).
Bouvier, J. *Mes mémoires* (Paris: Maspéro, 1983).
Chaline, J.-P. *Les Bourgeois de Rouen: une élite urbaine au XIXe siècle* (Paris: Presses de la Fondation Nationale des Sciences Politiques, 1982).
Christophe, C. *Les Hauts Fonctionnaires en France au XIXe siècle* (Paris: Gallimard, 1980).
Cottereau, A. 'The distinctiveness of working-class culture in France, 1848–1900', in Ira Katznelson and Aristide R. Zolberg (eds.), *Working-Class Formation: Nineteenth-Century Patterns in Western Europe and the United States* (Princeton: Princeton University Press, 1986), pp. 111–54.

Dupâquier, J. and Kessler, D. (eds.), *La Société française au XIXe siècle* (Paris: Fayard, 1992).

Ewald, F. *L'État-providence* (Paris: Grasset, 1986).

Furet, F. and Ozouf, J. *Reading and Writing: Literacy in France from Calvin to Jules Ferry* (Cambridge: Cambridge University Press, 1982).

Gibson, R. *A Social History of French Catholicism, 1789–1914* (London: Routledge, 1989).

Haine, W. S. *The World of the Paris Café* (Baltimore: Johns Hopkins University Press, 1996).

Heywood, C. *Childhood in Nineteenth Century France: Work, Health and Education among the 'Classes Populaires'* (Cambridge: Cambridge University Press, 1988).

Hubscher, R. 'L'Identité de l'homme et de la terre', in Yves Lequin (ed.), *Histoire des français, XIXe-XXe siècles, Vol. 2, La Société* (Paris: Armand Colin, 1983), pp. 11–57.

Johnson, C. H. 'Economic change and artisan discontent: the tailor's history, 1800–1848', in Roger Price (ed.), *Revolution and Reaction: 1848 and the Second French Republic* (London: Croom Helm, 1975).

Magraw, R. *France 1815–1914: The Bourgeois Century* (London: Fontana, 1983).

Merriman, J. M. *The Margins of City Life: Explorations on the French Urban Frontier, 1815–1851* (New York: Oxford University Press, 1991).

Michaud, R. *J'avais vingt ans: un jeune ouvrier au début du siècle* (Paris: Éditions Syndicalistes, 1967).

Moch, L. P. *Paths to the City* (Beverly Hills: Sage, 1983).

Moss, B. H. *The Origins of the French Labor Movement, 1830–1914: The Socialism of Skilled Workers* (Berkeley: University of California Press, 1976).

Noiriel, G. *Workers in French Society in the 19th and 20th Centuries* (New York: Berg, 1990).

Nye, R. A. *Crime, Madness, and Politics in Modern France* (Princeton: Princeton University Press, 1984).

Offen, K. 'Depopulation, nationalism, and feminism in fin-de-siècle France', *American Historical Review*, 89 (1984).

Perrot, M. (ed.), *A History of Private Life, Vol. 4, From the Fires of the Revolution to the Great War* (Cambridge, MA: Harvard University Press, 1990).

Price, R. *A Social History of Nineteenth-Century France* (London: Hutchinson, 1987).

Procacci, G. *Gouverner la misère: la question sociale en France, 1789–1848* (Paris: Seuil, 1993).

Rancière, J. 'The myth of the artisan: critical reflections on a category of social history', in S. L. Kaplan and C. J. Koepp (eds.), *Work in France* (Ithaca, NY: Cornell University Press, 1986), pp. 317–34.

Rearick, C. *Pleasures of the Belle Epoque: Entertainment and Festivity in Turn-of-the-Century France* (New Haven: Yale University Press, 1985).

Reddy, W. M. *Money and Liberty in Modern Europe* (Cambridge: Cambridge University Press, 1987).

Rémond, R. *The Right Wing in France: From 1815 to de Gaulle* (Philadelphia: University of Philadelphia Press, 1969).

Scott, J. W. *Gender and the Politics of History* (New York: Columbia University Press, 1988).

Sewell, W. H. *Work and Revolution in France: The Language of Labor From the Old Regime to 1848* (Cambridge: Cambridge University Press, 1980).

Smith, B. *Ladies of the Leisure Class: The Bourgeoises of Northern France in the Nineteenth Century* (Princeton: Princeton University Press, 1981).

Sylvère, A. *Toinou: le cri d'un enfant auvergnat* (Paris: Plon, 1980).

Tombs, R. *France, 1814–1914* (Harlow: Longman, 1996).

Wahrman, D. *Imagining the Middle Class: The Political Representation of Class in Britain, c.1780–1840* (Cambridge: Cambridge University Press, 1995).

Weber, E. *Peasants into Frenchmen: The Modernization of Rural France, 1870–1914* (Stanford: Stanford University Press, 1976).

Wylie, L. *Chanzeaux: A Village in Anjou* (Cambridge: Cambridge University Press, 1966).

Zeldin, T. *France 1848–1945*, 2 vols. (Oxford: Oxford University Press, 1973).

|4|

Paris versus the provinces
Regionalism and decentralization since 1789

ALAN FORREST

It has become almost clichéd to portray France as one of the most centralized states in the western world, where the political class made all the decisions that mattered at the centre, and where provincial and regional interests were callously ignored in deference to a centralist – many would say Jacobin – vision of the polity. Writing in 1947, in his somewhat polemical vision of a Paris that creamed off all the nation's talent while many parts of the periphery were doomed to poverty and depopulation, Jean-François Gravier put the case incisively:

> Ignoring both decentralization (that is, local liberties) and deconcentration (or delegating authority to the prefects), the unitary system favoured by the French concentrated all forms of authority in a capital city which emerged as the sole nervous centre of national life.[1]

Gravier's book, *Paris et le désert français*, was bold and apocalyptic in tone, and its central message was an economic one. He called on the infant Fourth Republic to reverse the centuries-old tradition of centralized power which was impoverishing whole areas of the country – like the Massif Central and large parts of the south-west – and would, he warned, lead to the death of many mountain villages and pastoral communities if it were left unchecked. But to check it would not be easy. It could only be achieved if French people learned the lessons of their history and abandoned many of the political, economic and demographic ideas which had underpinned government policy since the Revolution of 1789. For throughout the nineteenth century republicans had consistently equated centralism with progress and modernity, arguing that liberty and equality could only be guaranteed if they were made equally available to all, imposed by national legislation that would apply equally to Picardy and to Perpignan. Peasants, in Eugen Weber's felicitous phrase, had to be turned into Frenchmen, a process which necessarily involved the state. Provincialism was divisive and smacked of special pleading; the republic had to remain the property of all, one and indivisible.

Gravier's argument was fundamentally an economic one, to save rural France from neglect and depopulation, and it was partly answered by the development of regional initiatives for employment and investment during the 1950s. But the regionalist case was also a political one, that Paris and the state had been allowed to grow at the expense of local and regional interests. Many, indeed, would go further and suggest that there has been a fundamental conflict of interest between the capital and provincial France which lies at the very heart of modern French history, and that there is no distortion in presenting the issue as a consistent tussle for power between Paris and the provinces, between the state and regional interests. On the right of the political spectrum centralism has often been presented – by Barrès, Maurras, Renan and a host of others – as a tyranny that had its roots in the French Revolution, with a clear implication that before 1789 things were arranged much better, and provincial liberties were allowed to flourish. But were they? Much of the history of the Bourbon monarchy was consumed by power struggles between Versailles and the local *parlements* and estates; while the work of the *intendants* and the extension of royal justice during the eighteenth century had further antagonised provincial opinion. Indeed, if one of Louis XVI's most promising reforms was the introduction of provincial assemblies in 1787, it was mooted precisely because in many provinces the old estates had fallen into disuse and local interests had been left without any voice in national affairs. And without some representation, the province had little to legitimate its existence. Even in Provence, whose leaders were apt to rejoice in their rights and political inheritance, the 'constitution provençale' was nothing more than a series of texts which had been built up since the end of the Middle Ages and which laid down a number of local privileges and helped define the power structures across the region. This situation had been exacerbated by the reforming decrees of a succession of monarchs. Colbert as much as Robespierre was responsible for France's centralist tradition.

The problem is complicated by the overlapping jurisdictions and shifting frontiers which characterized the internal divisions of *ancien-régime* France. Though provinces were central to the monarchy's conception of France, there was little conformity between them and they were often rather hazily defined. Some, it is true, were proud units that had maintained their identity in the form of provincial estates: such was the case of Brittany and Burgundy, Languedoc and Provence. A few others were recent additions to France, which sought legitimacy in their long and distinct history. Of around 60 provinces at the end of the *ancien régime*, a number had been annexed only during the previous 200 years: among them are Flanders and Artois in the north, Alsace and the Franche-Comté in the east, and Roussillon along the Pyrenean frontier with Spain. Lorraine had become French as recently as 1766, and Corsica 2 years later. But many provinces remained ill-defined, with little administrative or judicial function that could provide them with a clear identity. Aquitaine and Gascony were both vague entities, the first long since abandoned in favour of Guienne, the second split by its geographical ambivalence between the Garonne and the Pyrenees. And in the north, in the region that would become the Nord and Pas-de-Calais in 1790, provincial divisions were characterized by confusion and incoherence. In this part of France Louis Trénard could list around 30 different administrations, and he concludes, not unreasonably, that the province was little more than a 'rassemblement' of 'petits pays', without either common identity or mutual understanding.[2] More generally, the province had long ceased to be an administrative unit of any significance; by the eighteenth century the term was coming to be used to delineate the area of an *intendance*.

Few other than the local élites and aristocratic families had much to gain from provincialism. Neither the state, the Catholic Church nor the military used provincial boundaries for their own local administration, and their jurisdictions often conflicted, sowing seeds of doubt in the minds of ordinary Frenchmen as to where precisely, in provincial terms, they belonged. Justice, in particular, derived more from the jurisdictions of the 13 *parlements* than from any discrete notion of the province. And in a country where few people

Map 4.1 The departments in France in 1790

had much occasion to travel, and where the inhabitants of the countryside were especially immobile, there is little doubt that it was the most local points of geographical reference – the village, the *pays*, the *communauté d'habitants* – that commanded loyalty. Different areas, it is true, enjoyed varying liberties, differing tax levels and tax exemptions. And time could confer a certain legitimacy upon local custom. But it would be wrong to exaggerate the emotional tug of eighteenth-century provinces or to portray the years before 1789 as some sort of golden age for provincial freedoms. As Peter Sahlins has shrewdly observed, national identity had already developed in the farthest-flung corners of the Pyrenees long before it was built there by the centre. 'At once opposing and using the state for its own ends, local society brought the nation into the village.'[3]

Yet the idea of France as a collection of discrete provinces has stubbornly refused to die, in spite of the vagueness of their boundaries and their administrative obsolescence. Indeed, in the last years of the *ancien régime* provincial parlements in those areas which did not have estates began to call for their resurrection as a means of blocking royal despotism and the power of the centre. Their case was at least partly based on the alleged popularity of the provinces as bastions of popular liberty, even if in practice they were more obviously connected with privileges and noble traditions. It was argued that they continued to command strong local loyalties and that – as Vidal de la Blache would claim so persuasively a century later[4] – they also had a personality unique to themselves. The identity of Bretons and Burgundians was presented as being intimately tied up in the history and customs of their provinces, an identity that would be violated by any attempt to impose an artificial national uniformity. Shared culture and history reinforced provincial affinities, while in some regions of France a strong dose of anti-Parisian sentiment helped keep provincial identity alive.

It is the French Revolution which is most commonly identified with the drive to centralize France, to promote the interests of the nation at the expense of any cultural groupings within it. Such a drive was perhaps ineluctable given the Revolution's consistent mission to root out privilege in all its forms. For provincial liberties, whether as traditional rights or collective exemptions, were forms of privilege, often granted in that most explicit format, a charter from the king. What was exemption from the *taille* or the *gabelle* but a special and cherished privilege that gave some Frenchmen benefits that were denied to others? How else could a regime bent on the defence of the rights of man interpret the distinctions between *pays d'états* and *pays d'élections*, or the special trading privileges that had been hard won by port cities like Bayonne and Dunkerque? The fact that often the defence of local liberties fell to élite groups like the nobility or the *parlementaires* served only to harden this identification of provincialism with privilege and to weaken the sympathies of the Revolutionaries for any extension of provincial rights. Often, of course, these liberties were less symptoms of local privilege than desperate measures to salvage the local economy. When the

merchants of Bayonne finally gained freeport status for their town in 1784
after decades of lobbying, they saw it as the least that was necessary to
safeguard their trade against competition from bigger ports like Bordeaux.
And when, in 1787, provincial interests made their case to the king for a local
provincial assembly, it is striking how frequently their argument was about
the economy, which local people saw as the strongest case for a measure of
devolved power. Administrative convenience and their distance from the
courts were, of course, relevant; but, as in Maine, the real argument was the
threat of economic ruin. Their soil is poor compared to that of their
neighbours, and they are incapable of harvesting wheat or vines; to the south,
indeed, the landscape is largely arid, consisting mainly of heathland, pines
and sand. Poor communications made this doubly damaging. 'The province
of Maine does not have a single navigable river', they pleaded; 'the Mayenne,
the Sarthe and the Loir only become so when they flow into Anjou'.[5] Their
only possible salvation lay in greater administrative autonomy and economic
control.

If the Revolutionaries turned a deaf ear to such special pleading, abolishing provincial and municipal liberties as well as the corporate privileges of
the professions, this does not mean that they were committed to a centralist
vision of France. The greatest privilege of all was that of the monarchy, and
much of their early effort was devoted to the destruction of what they
regarded as royal despotism, notably the administrative system that had been
built up around the person of the *intendant* and which was viewed in many
regions as an unwarranted intrusion in their traditional way of life. Moreover, if the early reforms of the Revolution were devoted to the destruction of
privilege, they were also concerned with the guarantee of rights, rights that
should be enjoyed equally by all citizens. The constitution of 1791 was based
on the idea that there was a natural harmony, a unity of purpose shared by all
Frenchmen, and that the new polity was based upon consent. All should
therefore be seen to be equal in rights, equal before the law, with easy access
to local administration and justice. They had rights of political association,
including the right to form clubs and popular societies, and governments
ruled not by placement or privilege but through the expressed preference of
the people. Towns and cities were encouraged to show their political colours
both in addresses to the assembly and in the regionally inspired federations
which blossomed in the summer of 1790. And when local government was
reorganized into departments, districts and communes, a system common to
the entire country and bereft of the associations of privilege which had
encumbered the old provinces, there was no suggestion that local leaders
were to be imposed against the will of local people. On the contrary, at every
level, from the municipal to the national, the Revolutionaries insisted that
those placed in authority should be subject to election and should be
answerable to their electors. Similarly, within the new system of justice, there
should be elections for judges and justices of the peace. The reforms of 1790
were predicated not on centralism but on answerability and devolution.

How, then, did a Revolution whose instincts favoured the devolution of power so quickly become identified with Parisian interests and with an insensitive centralism? The answer cannot lie with the local-government reforms alone, though provincial diversity was weakened and romantic regionalists lamented the passing of their estates and assemblies. After all, the choice of departmental *chefs-lieux*, the claims and counter-claims of local towns and cities, even the decision about the number of districts to be formed, all these were processes that involved local people. They were not choices that could be arbitrarily imposed by the *Comité de Division* of the Constituent Assembly. And Mirabeau's eloquent plea that the lessons of

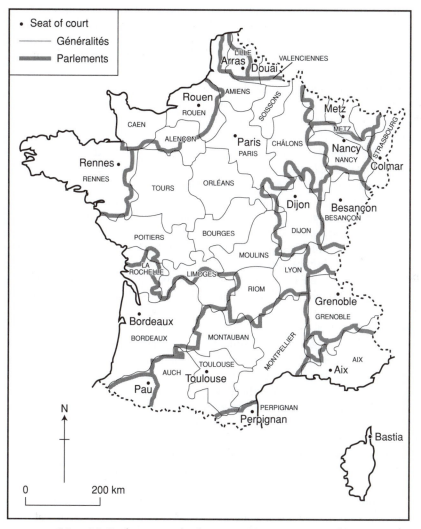

Map 4.2 *Parlements* and other sovereign courts; *généralités*

history should be heeded was answered: habit and convenience took prece-
dence over rationalist demands for the geometrical division of the kingdom.
But in the structures adopted it is undeniable that the seeds of future
centralism were already sown. The communes, districts and departments
might all be run by elected bodies or *conseils-généraux*, but the workings of
local government were highly centralized, with mayors reporting up to
districts, districts to departments, and the entire system answerable to the
person of the minister of the interior. In 1790 much of the initiative still came
from below, and such initiative was officially encouraged in the name of
transparency, of *franchise*. But by 1793 the Republic had little interest in
encouraging such pluralism, while Napoleon would drain any remaining
spontaneity out of the system by reducing the elective element in favour of a
strong executive arm, as represented by the prefect. A process which had
begun as a measure to counter privilege and royal despotism had been turned
into a tool of imperial centralism.

Nonetheless, the abolition of the old provinces and their replacement by
administrative *départements* marks a key moment in the creation of a
modern centralized state. One of the principal justifications for the reform
was precisely to root out cultural and historic differences which stood in the
way of the nation-state to which the Revolution was dedicated. In theory this
was to be done scientifically, as the Committee persuaded itself that it was
possible to divide France into equal administrative units or to guarantee that
all should have equal access to justice. Thus the main towns of both
department and district should be central to the area they controlled; there
was even talk of using the *cadastre* to ensure a perfect equilibrium. But in
practice, of course, choices were often made by local élites: the number of
districts that would best suit local conditions (from three in the smallest
departments like the Ariège to nine in the largest like the Nord); the natural
boundaries between them; and the towns that should be selected for the
major administrative and judicial functions. These choices could be difficult,
involving important economic prizes and the settling of old scores between
rival communities. The many hundreds of petitions that flowed in from every
corner of France pleading for some reward (whether a district or a canton, a
tribunal or a college) demonstrate how much these institutions counted in
both economic and honorific terms and how bitterly imagined slights would
continue to be resented. Yet there were few objections to the overall aim of
the exercise. Local people welcomed the improved access that was promised,
both to government and to the courts; and they rushed to express their
enthusiasm for the principles that underlay the proposed reforms. In the
flood of words that greeted the measure there is little evidence of resistance,
little sense that the abolition of the provinces was occasioning widespread
regret.

Yet with the passage of time the Revolution would come to be seen in
many parts of the French provinces as a regime marked by a strong centralist
imperative and by an equally deep-seated intolerance of provincial differ-

ence. There were good reasons for this. It was, above all, a very urban regime: whether radical or republican, Jacobin or *sans-culotte*, it was dominated by townsmen, and its concern for Paris and Parisian interests seemed likely at any moment to result in a rural backlash, especially in times of dearth and in those areas of the countryside that formed the bread-basket of the capital. This town–country division was ever-present, and with it went an ill-concealed contempt on the part of townsmen – and particularly Parisians – for their less radical, less civic-minded country cousins. It was only too easy for them to think of Paris as the cradle of all that was revolutionary – the Bastille, the Jacobin Club, the radical press; addresses from provincial Jacobin societies had served to reinforce this view, with Paris variously lauded as 'the cradle of liberty' (Château-Vilain) or as 'the home of patriotism and enlightenment' (Le Havre). And it was equally easy to portray the provincial as self-seeking and egotistical, ignorant and superstitious. As circumstances changed, rural France came to be suspected of almost any anti-Revolutionary crime: hoarding grain for profit, starving the cities and the armies, protecting émigrés, holding back their sons from conscription, or listening to the counter-revolutionary siren-calls of their refractory clergy. After the declaration of war and the suspension of the monarchy, the gulf between national and provincial values became increasingly stark.

It was also the period when centralization was greatest and when government sought to legislate in areas that would have been unthinkable under the Bourbons. For if citizens had rights, they also had obligations to the state. This was especially so after the proclamation of the Republic, for if the people were now the sovereign authority, resistance to the will of the people became uniquely hard to justify. Laws were passed to be obeyed equally by all, and under the Jacobin dictatorship of 1793–4 the state gave itself the means necessary to ensure that these laws were enforced. With deputies sent out from the Convention on mission to the provinces, commissioners given the powers to requisition for the armies, and units of the *armée révolutionnaire* entrusted with the delicate job of policing grain convoys, resistance often proved fruitless. Moreover, the state was now intervening in matters of personal faith and family tradition. Not only did it revolutionize provincial space through administrative reforms; it also sought to revolutionize time by imposing a new calendar that would abandon the familiar Christian points of reference. And, driven by a strong dechristianizing mission, the Jacobins closed churches, persecuted priests, renamed villages and threw saints out of their time-honoured shrines. In parts of France which were Protestant or where Catholic observance was already low, these measures might receive a warm welcome; but in deeply Catholic communities they seemed like yet another insult casually thrown at their traditions by an arrogant state authority.

The Jacobins were particularly eager to discredit any sign of independent provincial initiative, which by the summer of 1793 they rather randomly stigmatized as federalist, a somewhat vague term of abuse which demonstrated how far the Revolutionaries had travelled since the libertarian days of the federations of 1790. But if it was vague, it was also deadly: federalism was the most serious political crime of which provincial politicians stood accused in the summer of 1793, when any disagreement with Paris expressed by a departmental or municipal authority could lead to denunciation and arrest. Yet in practice there was no federalist movement, not even in the Rhône valley where local authorities had got into the habit of meeting to discuss future policy. The men guillotined for federalism were committed republicans who, from their vantage-point in Lyon or Marseille or Bordeaux, could argue that theirs was the true republic and that the Convention was being blinded by the violent excesses of popular Paris. In the countryside, meanwhile, opposition merged easily into open counter-revolution, especially in the Vendée, where Catholicism, local community and the crass insensitivity of urban Jacobins created a lethal cocktail that propelled large swathes of the west into open insurrection. Here there was no regional tradition to help explain the rebellion; the Vendée did not exist before the 1790s, when repression and state brutality were responsible for creating a new identity, one that has gained strength through 200 years of memory, of grieving for a generation wiped out by Turreau's *colonnes infernales*. In the Vendée more than elsewhere we see a permanent memorial to the sort of provincial resentment which the Jacobins evoked. There are lesser examples in other areas of terrorization and civil war: in the Cévennes, for instance, or the Comté Venaissin. In every case it was the Jacobins' facile belief that a new French nationalism could be created which would have no place for local sentiment which sparked an indignant reaction locally, the same arrogant dismissal of local difference that led Bertrand Barère to declare that provincialism necessarily spelt opposition. As he famously declared in 1794 when urging that only French was the true language of republicanism, 'federalism and superstition speak Breton, emigration and hatred of the Republic speak German, counter-revolution speaks Italian, and fanaticism speaks Basque'. Barère's answer was predictably blunt: these languages did harm to the revolutionary cause, and they must therefore be destroyed.[6]

If the enduring image of the Revolution in many parts of the provinces was one of intolerant centralism, that image was only strengthened by the years that followed. Under the Directory, it is true, central government was less effective and the Terror was ended. But the regime was in no mood to compromise with provincial demands or to lessen the commitment to the nation-state. Disorder threatened widely with both outbreaks of revenge killing and widespread banditry, while royalists and neo-Jacobins were always ready to exploit government weaknesses. Maintaining the rule of law remained the primary ambition of the state. To achieve it the army was used for local policing on a scale not previously endured; gendarmes were sent into local communities; and troops were garrisoned on recalcitrant villagers. And if there was some relaxation of political controls – some émigrés did return to their homes, and in a number of regions churches were reopened for worship – there was little state encouragement. France remained committed to the ideal of a secular republic where all citizens were equal before the law and where privilege and provincial difference had no part; and the memory of the Revolution that was passed on to the nineteenth century remained one dominated by the power of the state.

That memory could only be reinforced by the experience of the First Empire, of whose centralist ambitions few can have any doubts. Between 1800 and 1804, during the Consulate, Napoleon had negotiated himself into a position of absolute authority, concluding a series of deals with the Brumairians and then with the pope that allowed him to exercise strong personal rule. In the Napoleonic system there was little place for opposition or diversity. Unlike the early Revolution, Napoleon had little interest in opinion expressed from below, and the whole machine of local government became increasingly centralized, increasingly intolerant of dissent. Electoral consultations were now matters of minor interest, as real power was vested at the centre, and the will of the centre was made known to local people through the prefects and sub-prefects charged with the administration of the departments and districts. The system was designed to strengthen ministerial authority: prefects were never local men; their sole loyalty was to Paris; and they could be moved around at the whim of the minister. And if sub-prefects were quite deliberately chosen from amongst the local élite, this was again a device to strengthen the power of the centre, providing the prefect – and indirectly Paris – with precious information about the state of public opinion in the provinces. Long gone were the Revolution's dreams of bringing the people into the process of government, dreams which had emphasized the necessity for democratic control. The war and the Jacobins had long buried such ideals. But now Napoleon built a new structure of local government that was devised to collect information and impose obedience. Provincial France was to be policed more tightly than ever before, the army drafted in when the more conventional forces of the gendarmerie proved insufficient. The French people, who had been subjects of Louis XVI but who had become citizens in 1789, were now, most tellingly, referred to as *administrés*, those 'administered' by the state and hence subjected to its authority. Their rights were very much a secondary matter.

Under Napoleon the relationship between Paris and the provinces was only part of a much wider European picture, in which the ambitions of the state extended far beyond France's traditional frontiers. By the height of the Empire, indeed, in 1811 or 1812, Greater France stretched to 130 departments and reached far beyond even the most extensive ambitions of the old Bourbon monarchy. Prefects now reported back to Paris not just from the farthest corners of the *hexagone* but from departments in Belgium and Holland, Germany and Italy. And they did so on exactly the same basis, respecting the same command structure in the Tibre and the Arno, the Bouches-de-l'Elbe and the Roer, as they did in the departments of metropolitan France. Nor was this centralism restricted to pure administration. Legal and social reforms which had already been introduced in France, often by the Revolution – reforms such as the abolition of feudal tenure and the attack on noble privilege – were now extended to the peoples whom France annexed. They, too, could enjoy careers open to talents, and could rise high in the army or in Napoleonic administration. Other areas of reform, to the law, education and the Church, were also extended to those whom France had annexed, a measure which Napoleon took with the aim of consolidating his control over the population. All these reforms tended to create a new conformity, to reduce local autonomy and the possibility of resistance. And all served to reinforce the power of the state in its day-to-day relations with the increasingly diffuse population of the Empire.

In the history of the often turbulent relationship between the centre and periphery in modern French history, it is easy to present the Revolution and the Empire as a single continuum, a period when Napoleon built on the achievements of the Jacobin Republic and created the most centralized state apparatus that France had ever known. There is little contradiction here. Napoleon was himself a Jacobin during a large part of the 1790s, an officer who owed his rapid promotion to the Republic and who had in 1793 embraced avowedly Jacobin values in his short political tract, *Souper à Beaucaire*. His desire to control was partly the instinct of a soldier, for whom policing and governance could never be matters of compromise; but he was also a modernizer who believed that by root-and-branch reform, imposed on all equally by law, he could enlighten and educate the people into new ways. Resistance to his reforms he dismissed as the result of ignorance or intransigence, and those who put their provincial identity before the interests of the state were easily equated with backwardness and self-interest. Of course it is true that many of the most prominent regional leaders had always been drawn from the local landed aristocracy, from those groups most attached to tradition and most resistant to change. But the net effect of the Revolutionary and Napoleonic years was to identify progress with the centre, and provincialism by the same logic with reaction. It was an identification that would continue to mark French politics for much of the succeeding century, as the left became more strongly *étatiste*, seeing progress as something that must be achieved by national legislation and by the pursuit of power at the centre. It seemed almost tautological that the Republic was the ultimate goal, and that the Republic could only be built on Parisian foundations.

If republicans espoused the cause of the centre, then it followed that the only plausible political outlet for provincial sentiment must lie in opposition to the Republic, or at the very least to a radical, Parisian form of republicanism. Suspicion of the Republic had always centred on fear of Parisian extremism, of the sort of egalitarian radicalism, that emerged from the sections and the Paris Commune during 1793–4, with all the overtones of violence and atheism which so terrified provincial opinion. The image of Paris as the natural home of violence, of lynch mobs and *septembriseurs*, prison massacres and tumbrils, was difficult to eradicate. The resurgence of Parisian revolutionary violence in 1830 and 1848 could only underline the contrast between the capital and other parts of the country, a contrast which provincial politicians were all too likely to ascribe to moral distinctions between Paris and the rest of France. The image of bloodshed and barricades remained, even though the 1830 Revolution was soon taken over by the notables and 1848 subsumed into parliamentary politics. It made it all the more difficult for republicans to stake their claim to the provincial middle ground, despite attempts in 1848 to reassert the specifically provincial heritage of the Girondins (whose reputation Lamartine had done so much to restore during the previous two decades). By the same token it was always easy for politicians to advance provincial interests under the guise of legitimism and other right-wing alternatives to the Republic. In devoutly Catholic areas the religious issue was another which condemned those whose political inheritance had its roots in the French Revolution. Provincial liberties and religious conscience seemed equally safe in the hands of the monarchist right.

There was also, of course, a federalist legacy from the 1790s, both from the federations of the early months of the Revolution and from the federalist revolt of 1793. But opportunities for decentralization would prove rare, since, except briefly in 1849, the state kept financial and decision-making powers under tight control at the centre. And the *coup d'état* of 1851 ended any hopes that devolution might evolve gradually. Napoleon III had no wish to offer concessions to provincial opinion, sticking singlemindedly to the centralist model he had inherited from his more famous ancestor. But this did not prevent regionalist aspirations from progressing during the 1850s and 1860s, both through growing cultural awareness in many provinces and in demands, heard with increasing frequency, that departments be allowed greater responsibility for their own governance. In this campaign the local press played a vocal part, and it reached its highest point in the so-called Nancy Programme of 1865, whereby local councillors in Lorraine and the Franche-Comté issued a plan for decentralization, demanding greater democracy and greater financial control for local government. They presented their case as a measure of public safety, to stem the imperialist ambitions of the red revolutionaries in Paris. In 1870 Emile Ollivier gave some ground to such demands by setting up a government commission on decentralization. Provincial politicians could persuade themselves that their constituency had finally been recognized by those in power.

But it was the outbreak of war in 1870 and the subsequent anarchy of the Paris Commune which most strikingly demonstrated the validity of the regionalist cause. For what was the Commune if not a form of federalism, with one city defying the commands of the national government and establishing *de facto* autonomy in defiance of the democratically expressed views of the united provinces of France? In their rejection of the election results of 1871 the Parisians were seen to be treating provincial France with an ill-disguised contempt, claiming that they alone had a monopoly of patriotism and equating provincial sensitivities with collaboration and defeatism. There could be no clearer signal that Paris considered itself to be above the nation, or that it had little respect for the sovereignty it claimed to defend. It is true that there were short-lived imitations of the Commune in a number of provincial cities, notably Lyon, Marseille and Nîmes, but they lasted only a few days, and often provincial communes wrapped themselves in significantly federalist language, basing their legitimacy on the fact that national sovereignty was seen to have collapsed. The Commune imprinted itself on the mind of the nation as a specifically Parisian movement, and one in which Paris followed all its sanguinary revolutionary instincts. The tactics, the nomenclature, the organization of national defence, all had their roots in a Parisian revolutionary model. So, for many, did the dispossession of the rich and the organization of a siege economy. So did their appetite for destruction and their avowed anti-clericalism. The image of Paris in flames, its proud public buildings torched by the *pétroleuses*, was one which left an indelible impression on provincial minds. Another was the horror of the Commune's last desperate week, when hostages were taken – among them the archbishop of Paris and a number of priests – only to be butchered in the rue Haxo on the eastern edge of the city. In Parisian eyes the capital might be playing out its historic role, defending national pride before a nation of *capitulards*. But provincial France saw things differently. The frenzy of killing and burning with which they associated the Commune convinced them that Paris remained a foyer of anarchy, self-consumed and ungovernable. Many towns responded in 1871 by mobilizing their National Guard units and appealing to the military to prevent the spread of anarchy from the capital.

During the Third Republic fear of Paris remained a constant theme of politics, even if the fact that republican institutions were now assured ended much of the antagonism which many had felt towards the French state. Indeed, one of the achievements of the Republic was to be the devolution of greater powers to local government, notably the right (granted in 1882) to elect their own mayors. Paris was the notable exception to that rule: the people of the capital were still viewed as potential anarchists and disrupters of public order, to the extent that they could not be trusted to elect their own mayor and must remain subject to direct prefectorial authority. In the meantime local politics was opened up to generations of republican notables, many of whom used their local positions to seek national office and to lobby for local and provincial interests with central government. As one of the principal features of the constitutions of both the Third and Fourth Republics would be the relative weakness of the executive arm, the years after 1871 would be a golden age for lobbying, and local businessmen, lawyers and especially schoolteachers, dutifully wrapped in the republican *tricolore*, were quick to take advantage. But in their lobbying they surrendered little to federalist or decentralizing claims. Nor did they challenge the powers of the centralist state. After all, it palpably worked well for them, since after 1880 their right-wing opponents got hardly a sniff of power. As provincial politicians they were proud to associate themselves with their Revolutionary heritage and to stake their claim as the true heirs to the Jacobin legacy.

If the Republic was pleased to grant some powers to local *élus*, it did little to encourage provincial sentiment or cultural identity, both of which had flourished since the middle of the century. But what was this cultural identity? It had little to do with the administrative and legal divisions of the *ancien régime*, except in so far as a shared history had created traditions and mentalities that could be termed provincial. Rather, the sense of provincial identity which grew during the nineteenth century, often in the local societies and clubs frequented by *érudits*, had its roots in shared language and folklore, a common religion or a history of political repression. It was often strongest on the periphery, in areas where local culture ran deep and the ties binding people to the nation were only recently or imperfectly developed. In the Roussillon, for instance, the persistence of the Catalan language and the long history of ties with Aragon conspired to ensure that there would be a deep-seated resistance to attempts at *francisation*, whereas in Gascony language alone proved insufficient to create a unity which had never really existed. It is surely no accident that the regions which responded most positively to the lure of provincialism were those where a sense of Frenchness was least strongly developed – peripheral regions with a strong sense of their own culture, like Brittany, the Basque country, Catalonia, Provence and Languedoc. In Alsace and Lorraine, where again local self-awareness was high, provincial sentiment was tempered by their position on the eastern frontier and their fate in the military struggle between France and Germany in the years after 1870.

There is general agreement among historians that from the mid-nineteenth to the early twentieth century there was a significant change in the character of provincial politics, which might be termed a shift from provincialism to regionalism. The distinction lies largely in the aims of those advocating provincial interests. Instead of seeking to defy the nation-state and stand by certain well-defined provincial values – the approach that had been adopted by provincialism – the new regionalists were more pragmatic. They might emphasize the supposed particularisms of their region and wish that their cultural heritage be preserved; but they also accepted their place within the French nation, and agreed that there were shared characteristics which bound them to other Frenchmen, to those living far beyond the region. But that did not make it any less urgent to defend their own culture against attack. Dialects, *patois*, regional languages, folk tales and literature, all had their place in the lives of the people, all must be defended against the apathy and educational reductionism of the state. Some argued that they should be treated as separate nations, with all the distinction and dignity to be accorded to *nations provinciales*. Almost all put their case in very defensive terms, emphasizing the need to defend their old, traditional ways against attack from the outside, from the state administration on the one hand, and from technology and the forces of modernity on the other. Many were frightened by what they saw as the threat of the modern state, the extension of the tentacles of Paris through the administrative machinery of the Republic. It is all too easy to see them as arch-conservatives, dedicated to a cult of the past in defiance of the new industrial age.

Of course many of the apologists for regionalism argued very differently, presenting their cause as the key to a better and more vital future for France. Even Charles Maurras, who was deeply conservative in his politics and who linked his Provençal sympathies to the cause of monarchy and legitimism, talked in the most positive terms of the need to embrace change to release the energies of the people, to rediscover the 'organic life' of the many local communities that made up the nation. Monarchy for him was part of the tradition of southern France, just as republican nationalism remained a northern, even a Parisian phenomenon. In the provinces the nation could be understood only through the intense bonds that tied a man to his *pays*, to his village, to his parish, to the soil. Maurras grew up to admire the poetry and the patois of the Midi, the cultural ambition of Mistral and the Félibrige, though he would soon became impatient with folklore and press the case for genuine political autonomy. The French provinces, he argued, needed to be set free from the stifling conformity imposed by the state, from the France of prefects and departments. To be effective provincialism had to be focused on political autonomy, not on the adulation of local culture.

In formulating his provincial demands, Maurras leant heavily on Maurice Barrès, another protagonist of the regionalist cause whose love of his native Lorraine helped forge his philosophy just as a love of Provence had etched that of Maurras – the concept of integral nationalism, the notion that every Frenchman had his psychic roots in the earth and the dead of the motherland, that belonging meant bridging the generations, forming a bond between the present and the past, the living and the dead. Barrès, who, unlike Maurras, remained a committed republican, developed this theme in a series of novels that caught the mood of the 1880s and 1890s, novels like *Les Déracinés* and *Sous les yeux des Barbares* which denounced the uprootedness of *fin-de-siècle* society and pleaded for more traditional values. It was a powerful message, and one that spread its appeal across the political spectrum. For, as Robert Soucy reminds us, it was not just intellectuals of the right who found their inspiration in Barrès' writings. So, too, did republicans of the left. Léon Blum, who remained his disciple until the time of the Dreyfus affair, wrote much later of the spell which Barrès had cast over a whole generation. 'He was for me', reflected Blum,

> as for most of my comrades, not only our master but our guide. We formed a school around him, almost a court ... At no period in our history, with the exception of Rousseau, has there arisen a more completely original writer.[7]

In the wake of the Dreyfus affair, however, with Radical republicans united against the values of the army and the Church, there would be little place on the left for either traditionalism or provincialism. Their values were once again those of the rights of man and citizenship, the values of liberty, equality and fraternity which they had inherited from the First Republic, and the appeal of cultural regionalism was treated with scorn, at best as an archaism, at worst as a tool in the hands of the anti-republican right. With the threat of European war approaching, the regionalist lobby was easy to isolate, especially where it embraced the cause of monarchy. Yet it continued to rally its support and publicize its philosophy. Among its most stalwart spokesmen in the immediate pre-war period was Jean Charles-Brun, another southerner and a product of the Félibres who saw the dangers of isolation and refused to divorce himself from the Republic. In 1900 he founded a movement to unite political decentralizers of all political views, the Fédéra-tion Régionaliste Française, which stressed the need for the regions of France to assume more of their own governance but which sought to distance itself from royalism and the more emotive strains of provincialism. His book *Le Régionalisme*, published in 1911, would have some appeal on the left as well as the right and would become one of the bibles of the regionalist movement in the early twentieth century.

Charles-Brun defined regionalism in the sense that the term was now used: it was not quite the same as decentralization, since that implied that powers legitimately belonged at the centre; nor should it be confused with feder-alism, whereby sovereign states chose to delegate to a federal state certain of their proper functions. Rather he saw regionalism in a solidly Maurrassian sense, as a process that allowed the various *pays* which made up France to regain their own organic life. The enemy was centralization from whatever source or political tradition: it had begun under the monarchy, been aggra-vated by the Jacobin Convention, perfected by Napoleon and adopted by every subsequent regime from the Restoration monarchy to the Third Republic. This centralist tradition was, he believed, doubly damaging: it was a formula for despotism on the one hand, while it drained the natural energy of the people on the other. For Charles-Brun what was lost was energy, the natural dynamism and initiative of the French people. Regionalism was not only a policy, it was a way of thinking, an organizing principle for the nation. In his view it was the only way by which disasters like 1870 could be avoided in the future, and he insisted that there was no contradiction between the region and the nation. On the contrary, regionalism was an organizing principle that could give the country a more organic structure and a less mechanistic approach to national unity. This, he claimed, was the true nationalism, since it was the only means of reconciling the imperatives of individualism and unitarism.

With the outbreak of the Great War official tolerance of such views rapidly evaporated, and French politicians once again stressed the integrity of the motherland and the affront to national pride which a strong German Reich necessarily posed. And in 1918, when the war was won, there was little temptation to compromise: Alsace had been triumphantly liberated, and now it must be solidly reintegrated into France, with administrators speaking only French and the education system devoted to the transmission of French culture. There could be no question of a separate statute for Alsace that would take account of its unique heritage or its bilingual culture. Similarly, the state had little interest in compromising with the political demands of Bretons for greater autonomy and a Breton parliament, demands that were first voiced by the new Breton Autonomist Party in 1927. They were even more dismissive of the claims emanating from Provence and Languedoc for a more autonomous Midi, based on what autonomists claimed to be their shared occitan culture. For historically there was no such entity as Occitanie: it had no obvious ethnic or linguistic unity, and it had never had any clear identity or history. Even Mistral had refused to equate the cultural spread of Provençal with a fixed geographical zone, and the more ambitious southern autonomists now spoke of a far-flung occitan mass, to be composed of all the lands of the *langue d'oc*, the territory of the troubadours: for some Occitanie embraced Gascony and Catalonia, the Auvergne and the Limousin. In the interwar years all three movements gained converts among the young and disaffected, just as they did among traditionalists and *érudits*. But they did not yet constitute a popular movement or pose any significant electoral threat. Paris remained largely unmoved. Indeed, the fact that all three movements emphasized a separate linguistic tradition and that they were associated in the public mind with anti-Jacobinism and with a strong popular Catholicism, did little to integrate them into the political mainstream or endear them to the leaders of the Third Republic.

The public identification of regionalist politics with the political right intensified during the interwar years, despite the fact that not all regionalists subscribed to traditionalist values and some, following Ricard, were advocates of a federalist republican polity on the Swiss model. There was a *Midi rouge* as well as a *Midi blanc*, the homeland of the social republic of 1848 and of the winegrowers' revolt of 1907. But this was not the perception of national politicians, nor of the national press. Regionalists were seen as anti-national and anti-urban, as critics of the state and of national government. This perception was increased by the growth of a specifically peasant politics during the interwar years, which blamed the state for peasant misery and attacked the damage done to the countryside by the pursuit of a liberal economy. Peasantism became a part of the political agenda championed by groups like the Parti Agraire, founded by Gabriel Fleurant in Aurillac in 1927, and the more overtly fascist peasant defence committees of Henry Dorgères, whose stronghold was in Brittany. In his highly polemical manifesto of 1935, *Haut les Fourches!*, Dorgères expressed his somewhat maudlin attachment to the soil, urging his supporters to embrace peasant corporatism and to reject what he saw as the harmful influence of parliaments and politicians. In this way taxes could be cut and agricultural imports ended, the role of the state reduced and resources returned to the countryside. He dreamed of a France that would be 'rid of parties and politicians who have weakened and ruined it, a France where the two constants of our lives, our jobs and families, will be safe'.[8] His was a France that valued its rural traditions and which curbed the authority of those servants of republican orthodoxy, the tax man and the *instituteur*, who must stop denouncing or belittling rural beliefs. If Dorgères remained within the republican canon, it was by redefining the role of the republic and reducing the authority of the state to that of an arbiter among organized professions. In his own words, 'Vive la république corporative et familiale!'

Under the Vichy regime between 1940 and 1944 these ideas would find an official favour that they had never enjoyed under the republic. Questions of family, religion and moral authority were at the heart of Marshal Pétain's sense of order, and these were values that were much easier to demonstrate in the security of local life than in the impersonal context of the state. Like the regionalists, Vichy placed a high value on a sense of rootedness and an attachment to the soil; it sought to reverse urban capitalist values which it held to be meretricious, and to appeal instead to the old France of peasant holdings and family cohesiveness. Indeed, the peasant community was held up as a model of moral integrity for the rest of society to emulate. The law

Illustration 4.1 1920 Reconstruction Loan. The immense cost of repairing wartime devastation in northern France led the French government to work with banks, such as the Crédit du Nord, exhorting the public to subscribe to the required debt. Shouldering the financial burden was depicted as a patriotic duty – though the French expected to recoup much of their own outlay from German reparations. (Courtesy of Historial de la Grande Guerre, Péronne, Somme. Photographer: Didier Cry.)

was changed to recreate the authority of the father within the family and to encourage unequal inheritance, while the regime favoured large families and publicly honoured motherhood. It also restored much of the moral standing of the Catholic Church that had been lost under the republic, appealing once more to Breton, Alsatian, Catalan and other provincial groups whose causes had been closely identified with Catholicism and anti-secularism. And if it did not directly challenge Protestant beliefs and practices, it did please regionalists by attacking many of the rationalist assumptions of the republican state and by taking an open stand against Freemasonry. In his economic policies, too, Pétain took up some of the peasantist causes of the 1930s, giving official sanction to the corporatist dreams of the interwar rural militants and extending them to other forms of production. In short, the Vichy regime embraced many of the values of the regionalists: it liked tradition and folklore, it favoured agriculture and religion, and it did nothing to conceal its distaste for the thrusting, impersonal world of urban capital. In the process it played to the rather simple, homely instincts that had characterized so much of provincial and regionalist thinking over the previous 100 years. And it adhered to many of the enthusiasms of the provincial movement. Pétain shared the belief in cultural traditions, in the need to strengthen one's attachment to one's local community in order to love the nation more. On the occasion of the 110th anniversary of Mistral's birth the marshal expressed his admiration for the Provençal writer in unambiguous terms. Mistral, he said, was to be admired as 'the sublime inspiration of both the new France we wish to institute and the traditional France we wish to re-establish'.[9]

The Vichy period ended in violent recrimination and an orgy of blood-letting, and the values to which it had pinned its colours became widely despised. It was no doubt inevitable that this cosy, backward-looking view of the provinces should be among its victims, as the French once again put their faith in the national legislative solutions of the republic. It is surely no accident that when regionalist policies were articulated anew in the years after the Liberation they should have taken a very different form from those espoused by Mistral. Of course the folklorists have not died out, in Brittany, Provence and elsewhere, and cultural regionalism would find a new constituency among the guitar-strumming youth of the 1960s. Meanwhile in Corsica and the Pays Basque demands for regional autonomy would become intermittently violent and bloody, with militants turning to the bomb and the machine-gun in pursuit of their cause. But among the political classes these excesses cut little ice, and the regionalist policies which France adopted, especially during the Fifth Republic, have been largely economic responses to the arguments of Gravier and others, who urged that a pro-active regional investment programme was necessary if the nightmare of the 'désert français' were to be averted. At first such initiatives remained highly centralist, funds being distributed downwards by the government's regional development agency, DATAR, which had a national mission, described as 'l'aménagement du territoire' (the development of the country's infrastructure). To this end the departmental system was revised to provide, for the first time since 1790, a regional structure for France, with regional prefects supplementing the work of their departmental colleagues. But the role of the state remained dominant. Jobs were to be devolved from Paris with the aim of providing alternative regional poles for investment and technology; education and other public-sector services were to be improved; and new infrastructure was to be provided to discourage the population drift away from provincial centres towards the Ile-de-France. But increasingly responsibility, too, has been passed down to these 22 *régions*, which have come to be seen as viable areas of activity in their own right, each investing and competing in a complex supra-national European marketplace. Together, the economists argue, the French regions can compete far more effectively in the new Europe than can a single national unit. Here, perhaps, lies the supreme irony of the regionalist issue. For it is in the face of supra-national regulation and the globalization of the economy that questions of decentralization and region-alism, which for so long were a source of division and conflict within the nation-state, have become assimilated into the polity of the Fifth Republic and merged into the wider quest for efficiency and competitiveness.

Notes

1 Jean-François Gravier, *Paris et le désert français* (Paris, 1947), p. 14.
2 See Christian Gras and Georges Livet (eds.), *Régions et régionalisme en France, du 18e siècle à nos jours* (Paris: Presses Universitaires de France, 1977), pp. 55–85.
3 Peter Sahlins, *Boundaries: The Making of France and Spain in the Pyrenees* (Berkeley: University of California Press, 1989), p. 9.
4 See Gras and Livet (eds.), *Régions et régionalisme*, p. 11.
5 'Mémoire pour les habitants du Mans sur la nécessité d'une administration particulière à la Province du Maine, 1787', repr. in *La Province du Maine à la veille de la Révolution: choix de documents* (Caen, 1971).
6 See Michel de Certeau, Dominique Julia and Jacques Revel, *Une politique de la langue: la Révolution Française et les patois* (Paris: Gallimard, 1975).
7 Robert Soucy, *Fascism in France: The Case of Maurice Barrès* (Berkeley: University of California Press, 1972), p. 2.
8 Henry Dorgères, *Haut les Fourches!* (Paris: Les Oeuvres françaises, 1935), p. 13.
9 Robert Gildea, *The Past in French History* (New Haven: Yale University Press, 1994), pp. 210–11.

Further reading

Ardagh, J. *France in the 1980s* (London: Secker & Warburg, 1982).
Barral, P. *Les Agrariens français de Méline à Pisani* (Paris: Armand Colin, 1968).
Charles-Brun, J. *Le régionalisme* (Paris: Bibliothèque Régionaliste, 1911).
Cobb, R. *Paris and its Provinces, 1792–1802* (London: Oxford University Press, 1975).

de Certeau, M., Julia, D. and Revel, J. *Une politique de la lanque: la Révolution Française et les patois* (Paris: Gallimard, 1975).

Forrest, A. *The Revolution in Provincial France: Aquitaine, 1789–99* (Oxford: Clarendon Press, 1996).

Gildea, R. *The Past in French History* (New Haven: Yale University Press, 1994).

Gras, C. and Livet, G. (eds.), *Régions et régionalisme en France, du 18e siècle à nos jours* (Paris: Presses Universitaires de France, 1977).

Hazareesingh, S. *Political Traditions in Modern France* (Oxford: Oxford University Press, 1994).

Jones, P. *Reform and Revolution in France: The Politics of Transition, 1774–91* (Cambridge: Cambridge University Press, 1995).

Lyons, M. *Napoleon Bonaparte and the Legacy of the French Revolution* (London: Macmillan, 1994).

Ozouf-Marignier, M.-V. *La Formation des départements* (Paris: Éditions de l'École des Hautes Études en Sciences Sociales, 1989).

Paxton, R. O. *Vichy France: Old Guard and New Order, 1940–44* (London: Barrie & Jenkins, 1972).

Perry, S. (ed.), *Aspects of Contemporary France* (London: Routledge, 1997).

Sahlins, P. *Boundaries: The Making of France and Spain in the Pyrenees* (Berkeley: University of California Press, 1989).

Soucy, R. *French Fascism, the First Wave, 1924–33* (New Haven: Yale University Press, 1986).

Sutton, M. *Nationalism, Positivism and Catholicism: The Politics of Charles Maurras and French Catholics, 1890–1914* (Cambridge: Cambridge University Press, 1982).

Weber, E. *The Nationalist Revival in France, 1905–14* (Berkeley: University of California Press, 1968).

——, *Peasants into Frenchmen: The Modernisation of Rural France* (Stanford, CA: Stanford University Press, 1976).

Woloch, I. *The New Regime* (New York: W. W. Norton, 1994).

|5|

Outsiders by birth?

Women, the Republic and political history

SIÂN REYNOLDS

During the French Revolution a dressmaker named Anne Rose Berjot was living in Paris. We know only a little about her. But we do know that she signed a petition in June 1792 calling for the 'punishment of conspirators'; that she was a regular attender at the people's assemblies in her local section, and at meetings of the Society for Social Harmony, which had members of both sexes; that she wrote a letter deploring the way the trials of Danton and Lucile Desmoulins were conducted (1794); and that she was once attacked in the street for being 'a Jacobin and a woman meddling in politics'. Accused later of taking part in the bread riots of *prairial*, Year III (May 1795), she claimed she had only turned up 'out of curiosity'. These haphazard and sometimes contradictory fragments of information nevertheless add up to political activity of a kind. They have been retrieved from the police archives by Dominique Godineau's study (1988) of 'women of the people' during the Revolution, a book with the ironic title *Citoyennes tricoteuses*, referring both to citizenship and to the popular image of women who sat knitting (*tricoter*) as they watched victims go to the guillotine.

Godineau argues that our view of political activity in the Paris of the 1790s is inadequate without reference to women. That argument poses something of a challenge to historians. It is not so much that women have been entirely neglected: it has always been impossible to ignore the role played by individuals such as Charlotte Corday, the assassin of Marat, or Madame Roland, an important member of Girondin circles. Historians have readily acknowledged too that women in Paris and other towns played a part in bread riots, and in the related march to Versailles in 1789. But in the 'grand narratives' of the Revolution written during the twentieth century – that is, the major interpretations which have dominated historical debate, from Soboul through to Lefebvre, Cobban and Furet – women have tended to be not so much absent as irrelevant. Such historians assumed, without saying so explicitly, that gender had no particular significance for political history. It was no part of their interpretation to ask whether a particular form of power, that of men over women, might have been part of the political legacy of the Revolution. So they left relatively unprobed differences between gender relations before and after 1789.

Some of these mainstream accounts were written before the massive expansion of women's history since the 1970s. These days most historians would think it necessary to refer to the many new scholarly works on women and the French Revolution. But today the debate is not simply about including or excluding. The question has been put more than once, and it is a serious question: 'Now that we know there were women taking part in the French Revolution, what difference does it make?' In other words what contribution can such research bring to 'French' history? There are at least two possible answers. Godineau's answer is that we cannot understand the ideas of the French Revolution, or indeed why it took place at all, by studying only the dominant male actors: the Enlightenment élites and the *sans-culottes*. The lower-class women of Paris may provide different evidence about grass-roots opinion and its willingness to react to revolutionary ideas, or to engage in revolutionary politics. While Godineau's work obviously tells us a lot about women, her aim is that it also tell us something new about the Revolution. A second answer has been suggested by historians who have pointed out that some women, especially in the higher orders, had a degree of power under the *ancien régime*; but that such informal, and in a sense illegitimate powers were particularly deplored by the revolutionaries. This helps explain why the Jacobins deliberately excluded from public life all women, even those who had shown support for the Revolution by setting up their own clubs.[1] In both cases, the question of gender can be intimately related to political history.

The purpose of this chapter is to explore that relation further: to link women to French political history since the Revolution, so as to say something new about political history as well as about women. French political history over the last 200 years has given rise to many grand narratives and like those of the Revolution they have not, as a rule, had a great deal to say about women. In mainstream histories of the Napoleonic Wars, the revolutionary episodes of the nineteenth century (1830, 1848, 1871), the Dreyfus affair, the Great War, the Popular Front, the Occupation and Resistance, the colonial wars in Indochina and Algeria, the Fifth Republic's vicissitudes, or May 1968 – to pick out some of the more obvious chapters in this story – one still tends to find only brief references to women. The reason is not hard to seek, and the problem is a real one. The central actors in these events were virtually all men; throughout most of this period, armies, political parties, cabinets, diplomats, the Church hierarchy, the colonial administrators, and so on were practically all male groups. While social history can quite easily accommodate gender becoming a 'useful category of analysis', to quote Joan Scott,[2] political history has found it more difficult. When I give lectures to students on this kind of history, I often find it quite a challenge to say a great deal about women.

Recognizing and perhaps hoping to change this situation, various approaches have been tried from within women's history. There is now a wealth of books and articles specifically relating women to the 1848 Revolution, the Paris Commune, the First World War, and so on. These perform an essential and long-neglected task: they identify women as actors in history, discover source material previously overlooked or ignored, and begin to analyse events from a different perspective. Such projects mostly have what might be called a woman-centred logic. That is, they ask questions about the importance of women's role in the events described, and whether the cause of women's rights was furthered (or not) by such participation. The French Revolution might be described in this perspective as having 'failed to emancipate women', 'excluded them from citizenship', 'driven them into the arms of reaction' and so on. Similarly, books on the First World War, when many women replaced men in civilian jobs, have queried whether this hastened women's emancipation – to which the current answer is maybe, but less than one might think.[3]

These questions are far from exhausted and will continue to be asked. In any case, they can stand alone as subjects of historical enquiry. After all we *ought* to want to know how all these events affected or involved women and what they got out of them, since women made up half the population. But I am here concerned to see if there is more to be done with that awkward question 'What difference does it make?' – not only to women, but to men, and to history as previously written. It often seems as if there is a set of political events out there, the Dreyfus affair for example, within which we can certainly locate women if we look for them. It is not hard to find women *dreyfusardes* and *anti-dreyfusardes*: like the Duchesse de Guermantes and the Princesse de Guermantes in Proust's novel, women in the same family could be on opposite sides. But our discovery may have little impact on the normal narrative(s) describing the affair, since women were only rarely central players.

Since there is a ready-made common-sense answer to this problem, let us start from there. Political history says little about women because they were formally excluded from where politics was going on. In a society like nineteenth-century France, where women were legally constrained by the civil code from all kinds of independent activity, where girls were offered less education than boys, and where women had no political rights, it is hardly surprising if they were rather absent from the stage of political history. So the only time we really meet them is when they are struggling for their own rights, and that struggle is seen as the only history they have. This common-sense approach has governed much recent writing about women and politics.

The story of women's rights has always had a central place in women's history, whether in France, the USA or Britain. It has obvious parallels in the struggles for rights by other groups, such as trade unionists or ethnic minorities, and follows the pattern of the 'liberation narrative'. Its recognizable outline begins with early pioneers, goes on to describe mainstream campaigners and reactionary opponents, strategies and allies, and generally ends in victory and the acquisition of rights – including the right to vote. Nobody could claim that the history of women's suffrage has been neglected, particularly in Britain where spectacular tactics brought suffrage activists much attention. But it is often treated in such a way as to seem the *only* section of political history where the sex of the participants is relevant.

When one turns to France, the topic has a particular twist, appearing to make the French case something of an exception. In France, the first document granting women the right to vote and be candidates in national and local elections was the ordinance of 21 April 1944. This was drafted for the Comité Français de Libération Nationale, the unofficial government in exile in Algiers, headed by Charles de Gaulle. French women voted for the first time in 1945, after the Liberation, and their rights were officially written into the constitution of the Fourth Republic (1946).[4] These dates have prompted the observation that they are comparatively late: France lagged behind other European nations in granting women the vote. The question is generally phrased as: 'Why did it take so long for women to get the vote in France?' If only because it has provoked such a long-lasting debate, this question is our starting point here. I propose first to ask why this question has been so prominent as to eclipse all others relating to French women and politics, how it is usually answered and whether that is the whole story; and secondly to suggest ways of going beyond what has become rather a straitjacket for analysis. How might politics and gender be brought into a more dynamic relationship in future writing on French political history?

The vexed question of women's suffrage in France: keeping the outsiders out

Pierre Rosanvallon's study of universal suffrage, published in 1992, poses the following historical problem. How did it come about in France that

> a whole century separates the recognition of male suffrage (1848) and female suffrage (1944) whereas the gap is much smaller everywhere else? How can we explain why the political rights of women were recognized in France much later than in many other countries which have a less clear democratic heritage or unconvincing feminist credentials ... such as India (1921), the Philippines (1937), or Turkey?[5]

This 'problem' has only been identified as a problem at all in fairly recent years. French women's voting rights were in the past treated as an interesting but not very important footnote to the grander topic of men's voting rights. The term 'universal suffrage' was regularly applied by historians, and sometimes still is, to the decree of 5 March 1848, which granted the vote to all men over 21 under the Second Republic (1848–51). For various reasons outlined below, republican historians in France used to think it was pretty obvious why women had not been given the vote any earlier. If pressed, they might even have argued that it was no bad thing. Although women historians had for some time regarded 1944 as an important date in French history, Rosanvallon was the first French male historian who set out seriously (in 1992) to explain the late granting of the vote to women within the overall question of democracy in France. So there is a double exclusion to explain: a historical one and a historiographical one.

The second point is that the problem has two aspects, short-term and long-term. France was 'late' both when compared in the short term to other countries, and in the long term, when we remember how early France itself granted the vote to all men. This double aspect has all the makings of a good historical debate, and it reinforces the notion that France was somehow different, historically specific. Before going further, we might review the arguments that have been put forward to explain this example of 'French exceptionalism'.

International comparisons confirm that France was out of step with its neighbours. As a recent (if slightly inaccurate) description of the delay puts it, French women voted 'thirty-eight years later than Finnish women, twenty-nine years after the Danes, twenty-six years after the Germans, Austrian and Irish, twenty-five years after the Luxemburgers and Dutch, twenty-three years after the Swedes, sixteen years after the British, thirteen years after the Spanish'.[6] The general point is rarely disputed. But for how long did French women look on, while their counterparts elsewhere voted? It cannot be gainsaid that many European countries and several non-European ones granted women their political rights well before the Second World War. In particular, there was a wave of enfranchisement immediately after the First World War. Whether as a 'reward' for women's war work, or as a result of suffrage campaigns, or both, the years 1918–20 saw women receive the parliamentary vote in no fewer than 21 previously all-male political systems, including the United States. In Britain, where women could already vote in local elections, the parliamentary vote was granted in 1918 to women over 30, and extended to all women over 21 in 1928. Other countries did move faster than France in this period and the chronological gap is not negligible.

Viewed from the vantage-point of the end of the twentieth century, however, the advance made by other European countries loses some of its force. In the 25 years separating the treaty of Versailles in 1919 and the French decree of 1944, Europe had been through some devastating convulsions. Many Europeans, men or women, were for years prevented from voting in a regular democratic process. No elections were held in France between 1936 and 1945, because of the outbreak of war in 1939. The same was true of Britain – where in any case all women over 21 had voted in only three general elections (1929, 1931, 1935). Several countries had totalitarian regimes, ruling out democratic elections altogether. There were no elections in Germany after 1933; Italian women had never voted even before fascism;

Spanish women were briefly enfranchised in the early 1930s but the civil war had put an end to all that. For France's European neighbours, the quarter-century from 1919 to 1944 was a time of patchy enfranchisement and disfranchisement, followed by war, rather than the age of regular democratic elections that a mere comparison of dates without context might suggest. While it makes a good rhetorical point to compare France with its neigh-bours, it creates an artificial distinction, with France on one side and 'everyone else' on the other, as if there were identical forces operating in favour of women's suffrage elsewhere. Other countries had their own chequered history of voting rights: after all Italy, Switzerland, Greece and Portugal enfranchised women even later than France. So France is not the only historically specific country in the world.

What is more, emphasizing the gap avoids the awkward fact that the wave of legislation in favour of women in 1919 did not pass France by. The French chamber of deputies voted by a large majority in May 1919 for full political rights for both sexes. This tells us that plenty of French parliamentarians were persuaded by some of the same arguments used elsewhere in favour of women's rights. What happened in France was that a different set of politicians, in the senate, blocked the chamber's bill in 1922, and went on to do the same to several similar bills in the interwar period, thus providing one short-term explanation for the 'French delay'. The senate's opposition, which is undeniable, may have had more than one cause. But the main one is generally taken to have been fear of 'the clerical vote': fear that women – assumed to be more devout than men – would vote for parties closer to the Catholic Church and therefore opposed to the anti-clerical Republic. Since anti-clerical republicans, in the shape of the Radical Party and its allies, made up most government coalitions of the period, and also controlled the senate, this argument goes, they blocked women's suffrage for 20 years or so, aided by conservative opponents. Some historians have suggested counterfactually that if women had had the vote, the Popular Front would not have come to power and the republic might have collapsed.

With hindsight, we can place this argument too in some kind of historical context. The 50 years after the Dreyfus affair (1894–1944) formed a long-drawn-out, but ultimately finite, period in French history, during which the clerical–anti-clerical hostility was at its height. With unfortunate if inevitable timing, women had begun to press seriously for their rights at the turn of the century, just when the governing parties of the republic, after an unremitting battle against the Church ending in the separation of 1905, felt most vulnerable to attack and feared the impact of a clerical backlash. It is not particularly fruitful to ask whether their fear that women's votes would lead to a clerical revival were justified. No doubt the never-quite-exorcized demons of 1848–51 lay behind the fear among some republicans that women would destabilize the Third Republic – just as those new voters of an earlier time, the male peasants of France, open to Bonapartist persuasion, had destabilized the Second. Perhaps it is no accident that most parliamentary support for women's suffrage came in the 'Indian summer' of the 1920s, when the danger to the Republic appeared to recede after the war. But the storm clouds of the 1930s made even those in favour of women's suffrage reluctant to make it a priority. That is in no sense to 'excuse' the delay, merely to relativize it. Looked at in context then, the short-term aspect of the 'French delay' may be explained by the political issues marking this period of French history, while the 'advance' of other countries turns out on scrutiny to be less striking, and even less conclusive at the time, than strict chronology might suggest.

It is tempting to conclude, looking back from the year 2000, that France's delay was not in the end so very significant, compared to other countries. What is interesting though is that it has certainly operated as a historical irritant, inspiring writers (especially outside France) to try harder to unearth just why the senate was so reluctant, or to put it another way, why the forces of feminism were not strong enough to overcome opposition in the short term. The political context of the interwar period has been closely scrutinized for clues, and the above analysis refined further. Steven Hause, for example, in a long survey of campaigns for women's rights, has analysed the electoral geography of the supporters and defenders of feminism and has argued that the urban–rural divide was of key importance. Paul Smith, in a detailed account of interwar politics, has argued that it was easy for a few well-placed opponents of women's suffrage to keep blocking it, despite several favourable votes in the chamber. Only partly accepting the traditional anti-clerical explanation, he argues instead that not one but several kinds of threat to the Republic surfaced during these years, constitutional reform for example, and that women's suffrage had the bad luck to become entangled in some complex parliamentary battles. Smith departs from previous accounts by pointing out that the issue was practically never off the agenda between the wars. During this age of apparent male monopoly politics, gender was in fact an obsession. When other countries had either resolved the matter, or abolished democracy altogether, only in France did the question rage for so long. One might say that between the wars, France was the country *most* preoccupied with women's suffrage.

Other writers have looked at the French women's suffrage movement, and French feminism generally, from the turn of the century to the Second World War, to see whether part of the explanation lies in its lack of appeal. Historians are no longer quite as ready as they once were simply to write French first-wave feminism off as weak and lacking in militancy. The major study by Christine Bard of the range of feminist groups in the interwar years shows that the women's movement did not lack for numbers, for variety and for energy. Yet as she points out, the links between pre-1939 feminists and the coming of the vote are not obvious. The older generation, from the movement's most active years, had mostly died, retired or changed their priorities by the time war broke out. The younger women in the Resistance, about whose politics admittedly much remains to be discovered, were not primarily concerned with issues like political rights, nor were many such women available to be consulted by the 1944 Algiers assembly.[7] There is no clear progressive narrative linking feminism to the eventual outcome: it does not neatly fit into a 'liberation story'.

The conclusion of all these analyses is that only in the extraordinary circumstances of wartime, when the senate along with all the other institutions of the Third Republic had been destroyed by the Vichy regime, could the short-term blockage be removed. Any Radical Party politicians who found themselves in Algiers were outnumbered (they opposed women's suffrage to the bitter end). New factors too came into play. There is no doubt that admiration for certain particularly heroic women in the Resistance motivated the communist representatives who spoke in their favour in Algiers. The argument that women were to be 'rewarded' for this role, much as in 1919 women were praised for their war work in munitions, tells us something about the mentality of the men who took the decision, explaining their change of heart. There were other short-term pressures too, less openly admitted but not negligible: the desire to convince the allies that France was restoring real democracy after the Liberation, or calculations by the Gaullists that they stood to gain from women's votes. In the end it is not very difficult to answer the historical question 'Why were French women excluded from the vote?' or even the related one, 'Why did it happen in the end?'.

If, taking our cue from these short-term considerations, we rephrase the original question as 'Why was universal suffrage so persistently *resisted* until 1944?', we can open up the longer-term comparison with 1848 and confront our second question: the historiographical exclusion of this topic from political history. If 1944 had been regularly referred to in mainstream French history as 'the coming of universal suffrage', French textbooks would long ago have devised a story of republican progress towards universal enfranchisement, starting with the Revolution, including 1848, combining long-, medium- and short-term explanations, and culminating in 1944.

It is the very absence of such a narrative which has pushed some feminist historians to look more critically at the republic than its own historians do. The history of democracy in France is closely associated with that of the republic. French history since 1789 has been characterized by alternation between, on the one hand, republican regimes which extended the vote to various categories of male citizens, and on the other, authoritarian regimes (the First Empire, the Restoration, the Second Empire, Vichy) which curtailed, manipulated or suppressed these same men's voting rights. As a result, the republic, however fallible in practice, has naturally been seen as a worthy ideal. It had to be defended against its enemies, who included the Catholic Church and authoritarian challengers of every stripe – Bonapartists, monarchists, would-be military dictators. The writers of history have rightly seen the republic as standing for freedom from oppression, championing reason as against 'superstition', elections as against dictatorship. Episodes during which basic freedoms such as the freedom of speech, of belief and of

treatment before the law were threatened have occurred in France sufficiently often over the last 200 years to stimulate plenty of defence
mechanisms. But defence of the republic can lead in some cases to uncritical
admiration.

The contributors to an influential book *Le Modèle républicain* (1992) set
out to explore why 'the Republic is not just a regime, but a true political
model, corresponding to the aspirations of the French'. They agree in
locating the 'golden age' of the model very precisely in French history
between about 1900 and 1930–9 – dates that cause one to reflect. These
dates cover the period between the Dreyfus affair, 'the founding myth' of the
Third Republic, as Michel Winock has called it, and the Vichy regime, 'that
rape of the republic'.[8] Despite that rather sexual imagery, these dates are
remarkable for their gender-blindness. Individual justice had certainly been
the issue during the Dreyfus affair, and political liberty was indeed taken
away under Vichy. But whose liberty? These were exactly the years when
debates raged sporadically about whether women should be admitted to
political rights within the republic, and this question always received the
answer 'no'. And throughout these years married women were also without
many of their civil rights, that is individual justice, with only a timid reform
in 1938. Of course no historian writing today would deny women's civil or
civic rights. But amnesia about the very recent past, going so far as to call it
a golden age, when it had disfranchised every other child born in France, is
bound to have some effect on the way the history of the period is written.

This is why longer-term arguments about gender and the republic are
relevant. In *Le Modèle républicain* gender is simply ignored. But even
Rosanvallon, who takes gender seriously, is inclined to let the republic off the
hook. He argues that simply to look at the senate during the interwar period
is superficial, and concludes that it was the specificity of France's ideas of
citizenship, dating back to the Revolution, which excluded women.

> The obstacle to women's suffrage was much more philosophical than
> political. It was something more than party politics or timing that
> caused reluctance: voting limited to the municipal level does not
> correspond to an alternative approach to citizenship in the framework
> of French principles ... Citizenship cannot be divided up in French
> public law ... So the French delay is not due to greater anti-feminism
> there than elsewhere. It proceeds rather from the restrictive and
> demanding notion of the citizen-as-individual.[9]

One can certainly agree that great value was placed on citizenship in France.
But in the perspective Rosanvallon adopts it is essentially economic (or class)
segregation, rather than discrimination by race, sex or religion, which
'universal' suffrage is seen as remedying. Hence he is concerned not just to
explain, but to explain *away* sex discrimination, seen as a lesser evil compared to excluding certain categories of men – the unpropertied. The logic of
this analysis is that it too rests on a defence of the republic which is both

uncritical and sweeping. It has the effect of suggesting that male republican discourse (which excluded women from voting) was nevertheless universal, idealist, humanist and 'generous', whereas feminist challenges to it (which never after all proposed depriving any category of men of their rights) were partial, particularist and indeed 'bourgeois'. This vision of republican individualism finds it hard to accept that as human beings, men and women might have some interests (and human rights) in common, while as groups in history they might be differently placed and thus have different political interests.

Rosanvallon does make the persuasive point that during the 1789 Revolution, in 1848 and during the Third Republic, the high value placed on male suffrage made it necessary (psychologically?) to have something that was 'not' citizenship: an out-group of – at various times – women, servants, etc. But he does not push this argument as far as feminist historians would towards the idea of a deliberately constructed masculine republic. There is now quite a substantial amount of work both inside and outside France, for example by Joan Landes on the early period, Michèle Riot-Sarcey on 1848 and Karen Offen on the Third Republic, developing an idea which I have also suggested that the French republic was constructed not just without women but in some sense against them. Its universalism was therefore not just flawed: that flaw (keeping women out) was chosen, and went on being chosen repeatedly for many years, at various times, and for various reasons which seemed persuasive enough to people at the time. It requires analysis not in the abstract, but at every chronological turn. As Joan Scott has pointed out, the idea of some kind of timeless republicanism or masculinism, against which feminism was perpetually pitched, is unhistorical. Although gender was always the issue, different contexts produced different conflicts.[10]

On the particular question of women's political rights, therefore, one way to resolve it might be to direct research towards a *multi-factor approach* which would be sensitive to the complex interaction of long-, medium- and short-term factors working both for and against women's suffrage. One would need to analyse which were uppermost at any given time in shaping any given outcome. Among the long-term factors, one could mention the inheritance of the Revolution, the military and secular language of citizenship, the cultural education of the politicians of the Third Republic, the role the Church played in the education of many girls until the end of the nineteenth century, and the newly emerging discourses of feminism. Medium-term factors would include the post-Dreyfus antagonism between republic and Church; the visibility of women's suffrage campaigns; apprehension about women's cultural alienation from republican politics; and priorities at a time of international instability. Short-term factors would relate to the wartime years of Occupation and Resistance, the international context of 1944 and the forces at work on the assembly in Algiers. The eventual decision was taken not by an elected parliament, nor by a referendum, but by a rather haphazard group of people in Algiers. But they had not been living on some other planet before the war, and it is quite legitimate to speculate that the victory of the pro-suffragists was won as a result of the complex chemistry between all these factors. More importantly perhaps, the way that women's right to vote was greeted with virtually no opposition in post-Liberation mainland France – being warmly welcomed in the press and articulated public opinion in 1944–5 – suggests that a process of long-term acclimatization had taken place. Feminist campaigns were part of that acculturation process, though far from the sole explanation.

This would give full weight to the untidiness of real-life historical experience, while recognizing that there may at different times be ways of thinking and writing – discourses and narratives – which shape the perceptions both of historical actors and of historians as we try to reconstruct the past. It would mean nuancing some quasi-mythical dates like 1848, but reviving some forgotten dates like 1914 and 1919, both years in which it looked briefly as though the suffrage campaign in France was heading for victory. Above all, it would mean treating this question as if it were of importance not only to women, but also to men; recognizing that the history of the republic cannot be properly understood without exploring the exclusion zone underlying its universalist pedigree.

In politics there are no outsiders: women and political life

This chapter has spent some time on the issue of voting rights, because in a broad survey of French history this is hard to avoid. But as suggested earlier, this topic can be a straitjacket. It seems to imply that until women had the vote they existed in some kind of shadowy non-political world, and that their omission from the political – as distinct from social – narratives is understandable. Women's history has obligingly provided a great many social narratives to prove that French society just can no longer be described without reference to women. We know a lot more about women as waged workers, partners in family enterprises, mothers, explorers, artists, nuns, and so on, than we once did. But we are still feeling our way with politics.

If we recall though that politics is about the distribution and exercise of power within a society, and start looking, we might find that it is impossible to write a political history of France too, without working out how the sexes stood in relation to it. If women were absent from the corridors of power and could not vote until 1944, that does not mean that gender is irrelevant to the analysis of French politics before that date. We have grown used to the idea that it is virtually impossible to analyse Italian fascism, the Spanish Civil War or the rise of Nazism, for example, without reference to gender. Perhaps it is because events in the Third French Republic never became quite so dramatic that its political history has concentrated on parliamentary and therefore by definition male actors. But politics everywhere is enacted 'on a field of gender'.[11] France is no exception.

Mapping the field of gender means taking a slightly different line from the 'women and 1848' approach. It means asking how firmly a male monopoly was in force, and what it was based on. To illustrate the point, the three examples here will be taken from the interwar years, the ones I know best. It can be argued that the male monopoly was crumbling rather rapidly at this time. But it would be quite possible to take a different period, say the *belle époque* or the early nineteenth century: the examples would be different, the male monopoly would be more solid in some respects, but parallel points could be made. Any kind of explicit male monopoly carries the implicit recognition that there is a female group deprived of rights. The latter may be outside power, but it is conceptually impossible to call it outside politics.

The politics of a given society can be seen as a set of overlapping circles: there is 'the electorate', which may or may not be the same thing as the resident adult population but is sometimes nevertheless called 'the people', or in this case, 'the French' ; there is the highly visible parliamentary arena which figures most in historical accounts of interwar France; and in between, the many political causes and movements that may mobilize people to act 'politically'.

The first question we could ask is what it means to equate 'electorate' with 'the people'. The most striking statistic every student of these years encounters is the loss of close to 1.5 million Frenchmen, in the prime of their lives, in the 1914–18 war. Its consequences for the gender balance of the French population are rarely ignored. Everyone knows that there were many more French women than men of this age-group (young adults in 1918) in the France of the 1920s and 1930s. But the imbalance is normally related to a demographic context: childbearing or the ageing population. The low French birth rate understandably became a national obsession. And the interwar age-pyramid is often scanned for its negative demographic factor in age terms. France, historians tell us, was becoming, most worryingly, a country of the old.[12]

Less remarked on is a different negative political factor: the structure of the electorate. A generation of men was missing here throughout the period. This could be analysed in a different, political perspective, particularly when seen alongside the growing numbers of immigrants in the 1920s. Recent research has drawn much more attention to the immigrant groups than demographers traditionally did. Immigrants to France in the 1920s – chiefly Italians, Belgians, Poles and some North Africans – came in response to the call for reconstruction workers. They were mostly male, young and unmarried. Especially during the 1920s a 'compensatory' male population came to be concentrated in certain areas, made up of men broadly in the age-groups of those who had been killed in the war. But the newcomers had no citizenship or voting rights unless, as some later did, they took out naturalization papers. (In the 1930s, in the wake of the Depression, some immigrants returned to their country of origin, others had become integrated into French society, so that statistically they became less visible.[13])

In the 1920s, then, and rather less so in the 1930s, the French republic's electorate, by being confined to French males over 21, excluded the majority of adults resident on French soil, those who were either not male or not French. The resident population over 21, 'the people', for a while had a profile very different from that of the electorate. The full adult population (containing women and immigrants) was much younger for one thing, while the electorate was indeed ageing. To compound this, serving soldiers, *sous les drapeaux*, were not allowed to vote either. For fear of politics in the barracks, especially after the Dreyfus affair, the army had to be 'politically mute'. This further removed from the electorate in any given year the scores of thousands of young French conscripts who reached their 21st birthday while serving, as well as the 28 000 or so regular officers, plus varying numbers of enlisted men. Within an 'ageing population', France had a significantly older electorate.

Contemporaries were well aware of the surplus of women. But most historical narratives about political events do not mention either immigrants or women, seeing them as irrelevant. The point to be made here is not what might have happened in left–right political terms if the French electorate had been enlarged, rather it is a point about legitimacy. What exactly is meant by 'France' or 'the Republic' in this period? It is perhaps ironic that what is described by political scientists as 'the golden age of the republican model', producing a 'sort of social ecosystem',[14] should have occurred at the time when the electorate represented a smaller proportion of the adult population of France than at any time from 1870 to the present, and one made up exclusively of older men – literally more patriarchal than any electorate of the last 100 years. This shift in emphasis is an example of the fresh understanding we may gain by viewing this period against the field of gender.

Having noted that all electoral politics between the wars was based on a particular minority, the older male group, we may take a different view of the parliamentary politics of the age. While the republic officially excluded more people than it included, the nation's political life was not enclosed within the senate and chamber of deputies. Groups and associations of all kinds operated as political units, whether lobbying for a precise cause or bringing together like-minded people. Then as now, they made up the wider circle of political interest groups and activists, within which party politics operated. Sometimes they met in bleak village halls, sometimes, like the right-wing leagues, they marched through the streets. This was what might be termed 'alternative politics', where French people of both sexes were intermittently active. And that is not even to mention extraordinary surges of political consciousness, such as occurred in 1936. Many of those who took part in the famous strike wave were women, because the strikes occurred above all in industries where women workers were numerous, such as food, light engineering, clothing and department stores. In all these activities, thousands of political apprenticeships were being served by French people of both sexes.

This can perhaps best be illustrated by the second example, the politics of the peace movement. René Rémond has written that:

> of all the feelings that roused, disturbed and mobilized hearts and minds [in interwar France] there is probably none that was so widely shared, or had such a decisive impact on political choices and behaviour, as the attachment to peace and the desire to maintain it.[15]

Yet until recently, little serious historical work had been done on the peace campaigns. It is not hard to see why: they were retrospectively associated with appeasement and weakness in the face of the dictators. What is more, they do not fit neatly into the classic left–right forms of political analysis which structure most narratives. Many peace groups straddled these divisions, and people changed their minds as their pacifism sometimes turned into anti-fascism. The purpose here is neither to blame nor to defend the political judgment of those concerned, but to point out that this was a massive section of the political landscape, and a complex one. The gap in historical research is now being filled as it becomes clear that many French people, of all backgrounds and both sexes, were involved at one time or another in the various peace movements. They ranged from all-male ex-soldiers' associations to the all-female League of Mothers and Educationists for Peace. In between were many associations which had both men and women as members. Their political choices might vary across the spectrum or over time. In the 1920s many supported the diplomatic initiatives of Aristide Briand and placed hope in the League of Nations. In the 1930s left-wing anti-fascist movements took a stance closer to defending the Soviet Union against German aggression than to across-the-board pacifism. Other groups were absolute for peace, echoing Bertrand Russell's view that 'not a single evil that one should like to avoid by war is greater than the evil of war itself'.[16]

Peace campaigning took many forms: official diplomacy, delegations and lobbies of politicians, petitions and rallies, street demonstrations. It was one of the forces behind the rise of the Popular Front, whose original slogan was 'Bread, Peace and Liberty'. Groups were by no means all Parisian, but could be found in all the major cities and in smaller towns. In all these groups an analysis from the point of view of gender helps to explain Rémond's statement. Everyone in France was affected by issues of war and peace. Sometimes quite explicit claims were made about the importance of gender. Many ex-servicemen campaigned for peace, since they knew what fighting had meant; and war widows might campaign in order to spare their sons what had happened to their husbands. In the immediate aftermath of the Great War some writers actually blamed women for having helped the war-effort instead of protesting against the slaughter. By contrast, in 1927 a bill came to the assembly calling for the draft to be applied to both sexes in time of war, and this drew protests from several quarters. As the skies darkened towards the end of the 1930s, some women campaigned (in vain as it turned out) to be allowed to play a role in civil defence in the event of war. Other all-women's groups were particularly active on the international front, lobbying for peace in Geneva. The call for peace was often explicitly linked by such groups to the call for women's suffrage, making the common though not necessarily correct assumption that all women would 'automatically' be against war.[17]

It is now becoming increasingly difficult to narrate the history of these years without including as part of the picture the politics of pacifism: of course plenty of attention has been paid to the topics of international negotiation and disarmament, but essentially under the heading of diplomatic history (all-male) rather than in terms of popular movements (mixed). Once these are fully recognized, after years of sensitive amnesia, then the question of gender simply cannot be ignored: the peace movement not only included many women, they were often leading campaigners. Here is an example of a central issue in political history which has only lately emerged as worth studying at all, and within which gender can be seen as something both explicitly present (soldiers and ex-servicemen, mothers, widows) and implicitly invoked. The fact that women were still non-voters at this time did not mean they were outside politics.

If the peace movement points to the politics of passion and commitment, my third example, the embryonic welfare state, reveals the politics of administration and co-option. To use the expression 'welfare state' is of course anachronistic for interwar France, but the state was intervening more and more in the health and survival of the population during these years, as France moved slowly from being a rural to an urban society. Although one observer wrote of France in 1917 that the social services were 'almost non-existent',[18] there was in fact no shortage of individual welfare associations and projects – most of them run on voluntary lines by women of the bourgeoisie. Their very number made the picture chaotic: in the town of Nancy alone the years 1850 to 1900 saw the creation of 'no fewer than fifty different leagues and charities, from the Pure Milk Society to the Apprentices' Gymnastic Group, by way of the Lorraine Tuberculosis League and the Sheet-Lending charity'.[19] The state had started to move in the direction of legislative provision in the 1880s and 1890s with the Direction Générale de l'Assistance et de l'Hygiène in 1889, but local authorities lacked resources to implement laws, so they regularly appealed to private organizations. Tuberculosis proved to be the spur to greater coordination. Just after the First World War, when the disease was especially prevalent, the Rockefeller mission to France had provided training for the nurses and home-visitors who were employed to combat it. This provided the model of social service between the wars: a mixture of public and private funding for a corps of trained local case-workers, all of them women. The term for a social worker was *assistante sociale* in the feminine. It was initially assumed that like nursing (and many case-workers had nursing qualifications) this work was best done by women.

Women were not only involved at this ground-floor level of the social services, they were also to be found as active members of private charities or sitting on public commissions, committees and statutory bodies of all kinds. Middle-class women with a record of philanthropy would often be invited to sit alongside doctors, civil servants and other professionals, to help organize the growing number of initiatives. One example among thousands was the Office de Protection Maternelle et de l'Enfance de la Seine, a body concerned with eliminating infant mortality in the Paris area in the 1930s. Three women and three men sat on its *comité technique*, meeting weekly to organize the team of case-workers, establish documentation and decide on policy. It could claim some success, since over the decade infant mortality declined by several percentage points.[20]

During the Popular Front this kind of initiative was developed at national level. Léon Blum appointed three women as junior ministers – a surprising step, which was nevertheless welcomed by the public. Their brief tenure of office is generally viewed as more remarkable for having happened at all than for anything they accomplished. But we can see in the role of at least one of them, Suzanne Lacore, who was responsible for 'the protection of childhood' within the team of both sexes created by the health minister, Henri Sellier, a projection at national level of the growing importance of welfare as part of the state's portfolio of domestic responsibility.

It would be argued today that this was type-casting on a massive scale: asking women to deal with babies and children, caring and nursing, health and safety. And so of course it was. But co-opting women into the state apparatus at every level was also an admission of a need. There were areas of need within public administration which the previous all-male model of politics could not handle. Perhaps, too, men were not ambitious to handle welfare: glittering careers were more likely to be made in the Quai d'Orsay or the ministry of finance. But politics itself was changing. One of the major issues relating to power and the distribution of resources in the post-war world was to be what we now call the welfare state. The 'expertise' of women was already being drawn on by men during the pre-war period, when women had no political authority in the abstract. But they were already wielding considerable collective power within the workings of the welfare system, which could not have been operated without them.

Conclusion

It has been the argument of this chapter that gender cannot be ignored in political history. Gender sometimes becomes an explicit issue in politics: examples might be legislation on women's rights or decisions about men's military service. Everyone can agree about these cases. What is less universally accepted is that the sex of the participants in (say) the Munich talks of 1938, the Dreyfus trials of 1894 and 1899 or the Catholic *ralliement* of the 1890s also tells us something about the distribution of political power throughout different layers of society at different times – if only by drawing attention to a greater or lesser degree of male monopoly. This needs to be remembered every time we study such events, unless we are to carry on the gender-blindness of the past – and it is all too easy to fall back into it. But trying to rethink the position can open up challenging new ways to write history.

In recent years the question of the sex of participants in politics has been reformulated in France in the form of the debate about *parité*. In November 1993 a petition to *Le Monde*, signed by almost equal numbers of men and women, a total of 577, the number of seats in the National Assembly, called for equal representation for the sexes in parliament. The cause for such a call, made mostly by intellectuals and artists, was the extremely low percentage of women in parliament since 1945 (never as many as 10 per cent of the total). Since 1993 politicians, constitutional lawyers and feminist groups have joined the debate, which has had considerable exposure in the media, although it is not yet certain whether any permanent change will result.[21] What the *parité* debate in France suggests, whichever side one takes, is that there is no guarantee that formal rights are always translated into equality of participation. While this chapter has cited examples of women participating in political life even when they were formally excluded from it, those who campaign for parity today argue that formal inclusion has not removed long-term structures of *informal* exclusion of women from the real centres of power.

So the questions historians will ask about the Fifth Republic will be different from the ones they ask about the Third. Those who are interested in carrying the insights of women's history into political history, and vice versa, will want to ask questions about all political regimes from the point of view of gender. These investigations should not be conducted as if there is some eternal set of principles at issue. The French republic has never been a set of timeless principles. It has a real history and it has had real exclusion zones. During the first three republics one of those zones was the exclusion of those French people who were born female. The reasons for keeping them out seemed perfectly sufficient to the men who were in power at the time, although we would not agree today. But the result of the exclusion was that the political culture of nineteenth- and twentieth-century France was born and nourished in an all-male environment, and therefore represented the particular interests, habits and priorities that mattered to French men. That is an argument for historical enquiry which does not content itself with the question 'Why did it take French women so long to get the vote?' but tries to understand what was historically specific about power relations at different moments of the past. Sometimes knitting was politics carried on by other means.

Notes

1 See for example Joan Landes, *Women and the Public Sphere in the Age of the French Revolution* (London: Routledge, 1988) and Lynn Hunt, *The Family Romance of the French Revolution* (London: Routledge, 1992). Cf. the inclusion of essays from a feminist perspective in Gary Kates (ed.), *The French Revolution: Recent Debates and New Controversies* (London: Routledge, 1998).

2 Joan Wallach Scott, 'Gender a useful category of historical analysis', *American Historical Review*, 91:5 (1986), pp. 1053–75, and *Gender and the Politics of History* (New York: Columbia University Press, 1988).

3 For the revolution see Olwen Hufton, *The Limits of Citizenship in the French Revolution* (Toronto: Toronto University Press, 1989), and for the First World War see James F. McMillan, *Housewife or Harlot: The Place of Women in French Society 1870–1940* (Brighton: Harvester–Wheatsheaf, 1981).

4 The fullest account of the process of decision-making in Algiers is in Albert and Nicole Du Roy, *Citoyennes! Il y a cinquante ans, le vote des femmes* (Paris: Flammarion, 1994).

5 Pierre Rosanvallon, *Le Sacre du citoyen: histoire du suffrage universel en France* (Paris: Gallimard, 1992), p. 393.

6 Elisabeth Guigou, *Etre Femme en politique* (Paris: Plon, 1997), p. 75. These figures do not quite tally with those of the more exhaustive study by Steven Hause with Anne Kenney, *Women's Suffrage and Social Politics in the French Third Republic* (Princeton: Princeton University Press, 1984), which contains a wealth of comparative material; see for example table p. 253. (NB Guigou's date for Britain refers to the extension of the partial suffrage to all women over 21 in 1928.)

7 The evidence so far is that gender politics was not a priority for women within the Resistance; see Margaret Higonnet et al., *Behind the Lines: Gender and the Two World Wars* (New Haven: Yale University Press, 1986); Karen Adler, 'No words to say it: women and the expectation of liberation', in H. R. Kedward and Nancy Wood (eds.), *The Liberation of France: Image and Event* (Oxford: Berg, 1995); Joan Tumblety, 'Obedient daughters of Marianne: discourses of patriotism and maternity in the French women's Resistance press during the Second World War', in *Women's History Notebooks*, 4:2 (Summer 1997).

8 See Serge Berstein and Odile Rudelle (eds.), *Le Modèle républicain* (Paris: Presses Universitaires de France, 1992), pp. 7 and 32.

9 Rosanvallon, *Le Sacre du citoyen*, pp. 409–10.

10 Joan Wallach Scott, *Only Paradoxes to Offer: French Feminists and the Rights of Man* (Cambridge, MA: Harvard University Press, 1996), see especially the conclusion.

11 The expression 'field of gender' comes from Scott, *Gender and the Politics of History*, p. 49.

12 A particularly clear example of this kind of comment, but far from the only one, is Serge Berstein, *La France des années 30* (Paris: Armand Colin, 1988), pp. 5–7.

13 See Gérard Noiriel, *Le Creuset français: histoire de l'immigration XIXe–XXe siècles* (Paris: Seuil, 1988).

14 See Berstein and Rudelle (eds.), *Le Modèle républicain*.

15 René Rémond, introduction to *Matériaux pour l'histoire de notre temps*, 30 (Nanterre: Bibliothèque de Documentation Internationale Contemporaine, 1993), special number, 'S'engager pour la paix dans la France de l'entre-deux-guerres', p. 1.

16 Quoted from B. Russell, *Which way to peace?* (1936) in Norman Ingram, *The*

Politics of Dissent, Pacifism in France 1919–39 (Oxford: Clarendon Press, 1991), pp. 127–8. Ingram's book, the first thorough study in English of the French peace movement, includes a major section on an all-women's league for peace.

17 The Fonds Gabrielle Duchêne at the Bibliothèque de Documentation Internationale Contemporaine (BDIC) at Nanterre contains essential primary sources for the study of more than one of these groups.

18 Quoted in Lion Murard and Patrick Zylberman, 'L'idée de service social dans la pensée hygiéniste, 1928–36', *Vie sociale*, 8–9 (1987), p. 463.

19 Ibid., p. 467.

20 Discussed in greater length, as are the other examples, in Siân Reynolds, *France Between the Wars: Gender and Politics* (London: Routledge, 1996). The Sellier archives in the *mairie* at Suresnes are the essential primary source both for this and the health ministry under the Popular Front. Cf. Alisa Del Re, *Les Femmes et l'état-providence: les politiques sociales en France dans les années trente* (Paris: L'Harmattan, 1994).

21 On the *parité* campaign, see F. Gaspard (ed.), *Les Femmes dans la prise de décision* (Paris: L'Harmattan, 1997), and the full bibliography in Rose-Marie Lagrave, 'L'exercice de la citoyenneté pour les femmes: parité ou égalité?', in *Liber*, supplement to *Actes de la recherche en sciences sociales*, 120 (1997).

Further reading

Bard, C. *Les Filles de Marianne: histoire des féminismes 1914–1940* (Paris: Fayard, 1995), contains bibliography.

Clio: Histoire, Femmes et Sociétés (journal published twice a year, Toulouse: Presses Universitaires du Mirail, since 1995).

Duby, G. and Perrot, M. (eds.), *A History of Women in the West*, trans. A. Goldhammer (Cambridge, MA: Belknap Press, 5 vols., 1992–5), esp. vols. 4 and 5; contains bibliography.

Duchen, C. *Women's Rights, Women's Lives in France 1944–1968* (London: Routledge, 1994).

Du Roy, A. and N. *Citoyennes! Il y a cinquante ans, le vote des femmes* (Paris: Flammarion, 1994).

Godineau, D. *Citoyennes tricoteuses: les femmes du peuple à Paris pendant la Révolution française* (Aix-en-Provence: Alinéa, 1988).

Hause, S. C. with Kenney, A. R. *Women's Suffrage and Social Politics in the French Third Republic* (Princeton: Princeton University Press, 1984).

Higonnet, M., Jenson, J., Michel, S. and Weitz, M. C. (eds.), *Behind the Lines: Gender and the Two World Wars* (New Haven: Yale University Press, 1986).

Hufton, O. 'Women in revolution', repr. in D. Johnson (ed.), *French Revolution and Society* (Cambridge: Cambridge University Press, 1979); *The Limits of Citizenship in the French Revolution* (Toronto: Toronto University Press, 1989); and 'Voilà la citoyenne', *History Today*, 39 (May 1989), pp. 26–32.

Ingram, N. *The Politics of Dissent: Pacifism in France 1919–1939* (Oxford: Clarendon Press, 1991).

Landes, J. *Women and the Public Sphere in the Age of the French Revolution* (London: Routledge, 1988).

McMillan, J. F. *Housewife or Harlot: The Place of Women in French Society 1870–1940* (Brighton: Harvester–Wheatsheaf, 1981).

Offen, K. 'Women, citizenship and suffrage with a French twist, 1789–1993', in C. Daley and M. Nolan (eds.), *Suffrage and Beyond: International Feminist Perspectives* (London: Pluto Press, 1995).

Reynolds, S. *France Between the Wars: Gender and Politics* (London: Routledge, 1996), contains bibliography.

Riot-Sarcey, M. *La Démocratie à l'épreuve des femmes: trois figures critiques du pouvoir 1830–1848* (Paris: Albin Michel, 1994).

Rosanvallon, P. *Le Sacre du citoyen: histoire du suffrage universel en France* (Paris: Gallimard, 1992).

Scott, J. W. *Only Paradoxes to Offer: French Feminists and the Rights of Man* (Cambridge, MA: Harvard University Press, 1996).

Smith, P. *Feminism and the Third Republic: Women's Political and Civil Rights in France 1918–1945* (Oxford: Clarendon Press, 1996).

Thébaud, F. *Ecrire l'histoire des femmes* (Fontenay/Saint-Cloud: ENS Editions, 1998).

Viennot, E. *La Démocratie 'à la française' ou les femmes indésirables* (Paris: Centre d'Études et de Recherches Féministes, Publications de l'Université Paris-VII Denis Diderot, 1996).

6

The Catholic Church and politics in twentieth-century France

MAURICE LARKIN

The main problem that confronts the newcomer to French politico-religious history since 1900 is how to discern its shape. At the time of writing there would seem to be no detailed survey in English that covers the whole period, while those in French tend to subordinate a clear overall structure to the desire for factual comprehensiveness – a choice French writers can more easily afford to make, given the greater familiarity of their readers with the subject. (See Further reading, p. 170.) The difficulties of the newcomer are further complicated by the fact that the principal points of friction between historians in this field have largely found expression in scattered French periodicals and specialist literature, with only limited reflection in the more general histories of the period. The purpose of this chapter is to outline the chequered relationship between Church and politics in France since the Dreyfus affair, and to indicate the specific areas of scholarly controversy as they occur in the sequence of developments.

The opening years of the twentieth century saw the greatest upheaval in the life of the Church in France since the Revolution of the 1790s. Tens of thousands of monks, friars and nuns were evicted from their communities, and a third of the schools run by the religious orders were closed down. Others survived only by taking on the guise of schools run by laymen, adopting various subterfuges to conceal their ecclesiastical connections. In 1905 Napoleon's concordat with the pope was unilaterally abolished and the Church officially disestablished, thereby dispossessing the parish and diocesan clergy of their state salaries and evicting them from many of the buildings that they had traditionally occupied. To add to their hardship, the death of Pope Leo XIII in 1903 deprived French Catholics of a wise and sympathetic counsellor and saddled them with a new spiritual leader who, understanding little of their particular problems, compounded their difficulties by forcing inappropriate and costly policies upon them.

This traumatic start to the century represented the nadir of two decades of fluctuating antagonism between committed Catholics and the politicians in power, during which ministerial office had been effectively denied to people with strong Catholic sympathies. Moreover, the more politically sensitive branches of the civil service, especially the ministry of the interior and its dependent bodies, were open only to those who were discreet about their religious allegiances. Given these pressures, lukewarm Catholics with ambitions in these sectors found it simpler to abandon Sunday worship and confine their visible contact with the Church to the politically anodyne social round of baptism, weddings and funerals. Indeed, mass-going in some dioceses not only fell to a lower level in those years than it had been since the Revolution, but it was actually lower than it was to be in the interwar period – despite the continuing erosion of religious practice in the western world.

It would doubtless have astonished all but the most optimistic churchgoer in these inauspicious times that the 1940s would see what appeared to be a dramatic turnabout in the Church's political fortunes. Although the favours of the wartime Vichy regime were to prove short-lived, the Liberation of 1944 would bring a practising Catholic to power as head of government; and cabinets thereafter would nearly always contain several committed Catholics, including some who became prime minister. Moreover, in subsequent decades under the Fifth Republic, a majority of presidents and several of their premiers would choose to present themselves to the public as practising Catholics – however varied the reality of their inner convictions. In the same way, committed Catholics would no longer have difficulty in penetrating the traditional bastions of republican secularism in the civil service. From the 1940s the expelled religious orders of the pre-1914 era would be legally entitled to set up schools and other institutions with a potential influence on society – not merely informally tolerated, as in the interwar years. And with the Fifth Republic, the government would actually be paying the salaries and many of the running expenses of Catholic private schools – something that even the ultra-Catholic Charles X had never dared to do in the most *bien-pensant* period of the Bourbon Restoration.

In the middle decades of the century these many signs of government favour and the material advantages that came with them were to be accompanied by a marked rise in religious observance among the general public. In many ways this phenomenon was independent of the changed attitudes of government, and owed much to the anxieties created by the Second World War and its aftermath. Indeed the receding of these anxieties and the coming to adulthood of a generation that had never known them were to see a significant downturn in religious practice in the 1960s. By the 1990s less than 10 per cent of the adult population went regularly to Sunday mass – less than half the population who attended during the anti-clerical high tide at the beginning of the century. Inevitably, the seeming paradox of these divergent trends has puzzled and intrigued historians (see p. 170).

Numbers and factors

Part of the problem lies in the irremediable uncertainty of the actual levels of religious practice during the early 1900s. Although individual bishops, such as Félix Dupanloup of Orléans during the Second Empire, had encouraged their clergy to keep statistical records of church attendance and Easter communion, these initiatives were isolated and short-lived; and it was only after the Second World War that a systematic, nationwide attempt was made to measure the degree and the geographical pattern of religious observance. And even this was transitory. No sooner had the major surveys of the 1950s and 1960s established a firm numerical base than the French national pastime of conducting and answering opinion polls seemed to offer the Church an easy alternative that left the work and expense of collecting and collating evidence to outside, impartial bodies. While these later opinion surveys are a cheap and serviceable measure of overall trends, they suffer from the obvious deficiencies of nationwide polls, using oral questions put to periodic samples of only 1 500 people or so. They depend entirely on the veracity of the replies; and, given the small numbers polled, they can give little or no idea of regional variations. Even so, they are a cornucopia compared to the paucity of information at the start of the century (see p. 170). Although well over 90 per cent of the French population in 1900 had been baptized as Catholics, perhaps only a fifth or a quarter of adults went to mass regularly on Sundays, despite the fact that the Church traditionally taught that deliberate non-attendance was a matter of grave sin. And of these churchgoers, the majority were women. Observance was highest in the remote pastoral areas of France where there was less sustained contact with the secularized nature of life in the main arteries of economic change and development. Yet it was not just the Massif Central, the eastern uplands and the Breton peninsula that could still draw sizeable congregations. Industrial regions that bordered on Belgium and the German Rhineland shared the deep-rooted religious traditions that characterized the populations on the other side of the frontier. Moreover, during its annexation to the German Reich between 1871 and 1918, Alsace-Lorraine was spared the anti-clerical policies of the Third Republic, which weakened the loyalties of less committed Catholics elsewhere in France. Churchgoing was likewise marked in those regions where past centuries had witnessed conflict between Catholics and Protestants – and where on both sides religious observance was an affirmation of tribal identity.

Historians have little trouble accounting for the hostility between the Church and republican governments at the turn of the century. It was largely a battle for the minds of the nation's youth. In the 1870s the Church had openly supported the monarchists, seeing them as a barrier against the secularizing policies of the more militant republicans. Pope Leo XIII instructed French Catholics in 1892 to bow to the inevitable and accept the Republican constitution, if only to keep the left in check, but a large number of them chose to interpret this as merely a tactical shift of ground in the fight against the moderate republicans, as well as against the committed anti-clericals. The government, for its part, viewed with apprehension the growing attractiveness of the more fashionable Catholic schools to otherwise staunchly republican bourgeois families, who saw in them the supposed virtues of the more prestigious English private schools, with their stress on character-building and discipline. Nearly 20 per cent of the entire male secondary-school population in 1898 were taught in schools run directly or indirectly by religious orders, while a further 22 per cent attended other Catholic schools. It is true that in an age when state as well as private secondary schools were fee-paying and followed a rigorously academic curriculum, only 5 per cent of French children went on to full-time secondary education of any sort. Yet this 5 per cent contained the bulk of the future élites who would fill the key positions in public and private employment. Republicans feared that the Catholic private schools were producing a generation of young talents, ready to combat the government through the ballot-box or undermine its cohesion by infiltrating the army and the civil service. Indeed over 15 per cent of the intake into the military academies came from Jesuit schools.

Government apprehension was fanned into vigorous action by the repercussions of the Dreyfus affair. Rumours of a right-wing *coup d'état*, backed by disgruntled army officers and anti-republican Catholics, brought to power a broad-bottomed ministry under René Waldeck-Rousseau (June 1899–June 1902), with a mandate to suppress right-wing subversion and restore public confidence. His successor, 'le petit père' Emile Combes (June 1902–January 1905), took the clean sweep much further; and his obsessive anti-clericalism saw draconian reprisals against those elements in the army and the Church suspected of anti-republican sympathies.

While agreed on what divided Church and Republic, historians have differed on the justifiability of the measures taken against the Church (see p. 170). Despite the suggestions of police-informers – who were always at pains to justify the payments made to them – 1898–9 had found royalists and right-wing nationalists making rival plans to take over the Republic. Nor should the ineptitude of the plotters disguise the reality of their intentions. Yet recent evidence seems to show that no more than half a dozen generals were strongly in favour of a seizure of power; and of these none was prepared to take the initiative in launching a coup. They would merely rally to it, once it was successful (see p. 170). Although previous services to the Church had brought one of them a papal knighthood, while two of the others sent their children to Catholic private schools, there is little to suggest a strong Catholic link between these military dissidents. Indeed a Catholic schooling and outlook were more in evidence among the generals who had rebuffed the various attempts to enlist them in subversion – even if the fact of their being approached at all would seem to indicate their strong distaste for the Republic. And although both the royalist and Bonapartist pretenders made rival claims that a restoration of the monarchy would see new privileges granted to the Church, Leo XIII had long since discounted the possibility of a restoration – seeing compromise with the moderate republicans as the only way forward. The Bonapartist pretender, for his part, had in effect resigned himself to much the same conclusion, whatever the official rhetoric of his followers; and even his impulsive royalist rival, the flamboyant duc d'Or-léans, personally preferred the spas and hunting lodges of central Europe to the endless plans for a seizure of power devised by his entourage. As for the

Illustration 6.1 Caricature from *L'Assiette au Beurre*, 2 January 1904. Jesuit teacher to aristocratic army officer: 'I think this one's now ripe for the barracks'. Dreyfusards and anti-clerical Republicans vehemently denounced links between Church and Army, setting the scene for War Minister General André's hostile treatment of practising Catholic officers in 1900–4.

nationalists and anti-semitic leagues, Leo XIII regarded them as being too disreputable to be worth considering, despite the membership of a number of notable Catholics and despite their pledges to improve the legal position of the Church in France, should they succeed in coming to power. Unfortunately the pope's commitment to working for an accommodation with the moderate republicans was not shared or properly understood by all sections of the Catholic press in France. The Catholic paper with the largest circulation, *La Croix*, had notoriously participated in the anti-semitic campaign against Dreyfus; and although it publicly advised its readers to steer clear of Paul Déroulède's comic opera schemes to overthrow the Republic in 1899, the personal sympathies of the Assumptionist editors of the paper were known to be with Déroulède and his colleagues (see p. 170).

Retribution and its aftermath

Not surprisingly, the Assumptionists were the first religious order to be dissolved by the new-broom policies of the Waldeck-Rousseau ministry. Predictably, but less justifiably, the Jesuits were the next; the fact that so many of their former pupils filled influential positions in the army made them an obvious target for a government determined to ensure that the army remained loyal to the Republic. Thereafter, however, the evictions bore increasingly little relevance to the security of the regime, unless one shared the conviction of the more militant anti-clericals that Catholic education of its nature was an obstacle to the creation of future generations of French citizens committed to democratic and rational ideals. Emile Combes, under whom the evictions reached their height, was himself a former seminarist who was personally convinced that the communal celibate life of the orders was contrary to human nature, making their members unfit for the care and instruction of the young. He was also convinced of the need to apply more strictly the control over bishops and parish clergy that Napoleon's concordat had acquired for the state; and, paradoxically, it was Combes's attempts to bully the Vatican into accepting his stringent interpretation of the concordat that indirectly led to its abolition. Combes's own subsequent claim, and that of many historians, that he was actively seeking its abolition does not square with the evidence (see p. 170). Deadlock with the new pope, Pius X (1903–14), over concordatory procedures for the appointment of new bishops decided him to threaten a unilateral repudiation of the concordat. To Combes's embarrassment the anti-clericals in parliament took his threats more seriously than did the Vatican; indeed his rhetoric against the intransigence of Rome created a groundswell in favour of abolition that he proved unable to control. Both Combes and his more circumspect successor, Maurice Rouvier (January 1905–March 1906), regarded the concordat as an essential means of keeping the French clergy in order; but neither of them dared to confront parliament's demands for abolition – which brought with it the disestablishment of the Church and the cessation of state salaries for the bishops and parish clergy (law of 9 December 1905).

The impact of the separation law on the Church's finances was far more severe than its principal authors had intended – largely because of the intransigence of the new pope and his secretary of state, Merry del Val. The Vatican feared that if the French clergy complied with the law's provisions for the allocation of concordatory Church property to the now disestablished Church, this would imply that the Church had weakly capitulated to an unjust, unilateral measure – with the danger that anti-clerical governments in other countries would be encouraged to follow the French example. The Vatican overrode – indeed concealed – the expressed wishes of the majority of French bishops in the matter, and prohibited French Catholics from forming the *associations cultuelles* which the separation law envisaged as the future legal representatives of the disestablished Church (see p. 170). For two decades the Church in France had no legal embodiment to which the state was prepared to transfer former church property; and although the matter was to be resolved in 1924 by the good sense of later popes, the greater part of the unclaimed property had in the meantime been passed on to various secular bodies of a semi-charitable nature and was irrecoverable. Fortunately for the Church, successive governments decided not to risk public outcry by insisting on the letter of the law in respect of the parish churches and diocesan cathedrals – which the clergy were allowed to occupy as unofficial non-paying tenants until the *dénouement* of 1924.

The Church in France was now faced with the task of providing an income for its bishops and parochial clergy. This was a situation which the British, American and other Catholics in non-state-supported situations had traditionally lived with – and many had regarded as an advantage, since it gave the Church a moral independence of the state, as well as imbuing the laity with a sense of responsibility towards its pastors. It likewise obliged the clergy to take more notice of their parishioners' needs and opinions. But in many Latin countries, where direct or indirect state support had been the norm for centuries, it was found that the churchgoing public would not take their new financial responsibilities seriously if the Church was disestablished. The reality that ensued in France justified both the hopes and fears of the two sides in the debate. The anti-clerical onslaught of the first decade of the century had created a sense of solidarity among many Catholics that disposed them initially to give generously to the *denier du culte* – the diocesan collections for the upkeep of the clergy – in the years immediately following separation. But, of its nature, the Dunkirk spirit is notoriously hard to sustain; and the prudent calculation of self-interest soon replaced generosity, even if the clergy's material situation remained tolerable, albeit with a certain amount of belt-tightening. Even so the uncertain prospects which disestablishment presented resulted in a rapid fall-off in recruitment to the secular clergy – with ordinations dropping to a half of what they had been before Combes came to office. The regularization of the Church's legal position in

1924 helped to relieve this uncertainty, but the subsequent rise in ordinations still left the figure on the outbreak of war in 1939 as only three-quarters of the pre-Combes level.

The predicted psychological benefits were equally mixed. In retrospect, it is hard not to see the separation as a vast, neglected opportunity on the Church's part. The concordatory regime had made the redeployment of parish priests to deal with shifts of population dependent on mutual agreement with an often unsympathetic government; but the Church too had been guilty of failing to appreciate the consequences of the rapid growth of large urban communities, vastly outstripping the capacity of the existing parish structure to cope with such numbers (see p. 171). The result was a new expanding urban working class, with little or no contact with the formal structures of the Church. Conversely many villages were depleted of former parishioners, migrating in search of better-paid work in the towns; yet the Church feared to amalgamate country parishes because a hostile government might not be prepared to balance the consequent saving on village stipends by the creation of new state-paid livings in the towns. Once the initial cold shower of the separation was over, inertia and old habits reasserted themselves. Nearly all the parochial amalgamations that took place in the first half of the twentieth century were forced on the Church by the shortage of priests; few were the outcome of conscious redeployment of manpower in response to the changing demographic map of France. The problems were compounded by the Vatican's suspicion of any attempt to give the French episcopate a national cohesion and identity that would enable it to deal with the church's current problems on an effective countrywide basis. Pius X and Merry del Val were all too conscious of the French bishops' hostility to the self-damaging policies that Rome had forced upon them in the matter of accepting the concessions contained in the separation law; so there was no question of allowing them regular plenary meetings. As a result the French Church continued to be a mosaic of semi-autonomous dioceses, precluding any effective rationalization of resources and policies (see p. 171).

If the Church failed to capitalize on the compensatory aspects of disestablishment, the achievement of separation did at least exhaust the current agenda of anti-clericals, leaving parliament free to deal with other matters, such as state social insurance, and allowing a breathing space for tempers to cool. Yet many committed Catholics still felt at a disadvantage when it came to seeking employment and promotion in several major branches of the civil service. While Catholics had little difficulty in entering and rising in the more technical ministries, where professional skill rather than political commitment was the principal requirement, matters were different in those ministries and *grands corps d'état* where the government felt the need to be assured of the complete loyalty of its servants, especially in the implementation of policies that some *fonctionnaires* might find uncongenial – the most obvious example being the eviction of the religious orders (see p. 171). More seriously, the anti-clerical high tide of the Combes years had also seen a systematic attempt to block the promotion of committed Catholics in the commissioned ranks of the army, irrespective of their political attitude to the government. Although the origins of this scheme dated back to Waldeck-Rousseau's premiership, perhaps even earlier, Waldeck-Rousseau claimed not to have known that the war ministry was employing the network of the Masonic Grand Orient to spy on officers and report on those who were assiduous churchgoers. Such officers were put on the 'Carthage' list and ran the risk of spending the rest of their military careers on their current rungs of the ladder. When the system became publicly known in October 1904, this 'affaire des fiches' caused such a *furore* that it led indirectly to the resignation of the Combes government three months later. It is argued by some historians that the adverse listing of thousands of Catholic officers in this fashion impoverished the professional quality of the army that faced Germany in 1914 (see p. 170). They point out that of the 19 officers whose skill in 1914 earned them unusually rapid promotion to positions of high responsibility, 14 had been the victims of unfavourable Masonic reports – which suggests that their qualities had remained unrewarded in the pre-war promotion lists. Conversely, of the 400 or so senior officers who had enjoyed steady promotion during the anti-clerical purge, nearly half had to be switched to less responsible posts when their limitations were revealed by the realities of war.

War and *détente*

If the First World War revealed the price that a nation pays for marginalizing talent on non-professional grounds, it also helped to soften differences between Catholics and anti-clericals. The German challenge demanded a united French response in which internal differences should be temporarily shelved. On the outbreak of war the militantly anti-clerical minister of the interior, Louis Malvy, suspended the programme of closing Catholic schools that were in breach of Combes's legislation against the religious orders. With the Church disestablished, well over a third of the French clergy were mobilized. Those who had been part of the established Church before the separation of 1905 were allowed to serve as stretcher bearers, ambulance drivers and the like; but those of a post-1905 vintage were treated no differently from other French citizens. Foreseeing such a situation, the Vatican had already temporarily lifted the ban on clergy carrying weapons. Well over 15 per cent of the clergy in uniform were killed – a third of whom belonged to the regular orders of friars, brothers and monks – many having voluntarily returned from exile to serve the country that had evicted them (see p. 171). As so often in times of national emergency or personal crisis, religious practice suddenly increased, especially in the battle areas and in the German prisoner-of-war camps, where Sunday mass celebrated by a fellow-captive French priest provided troops with a focus of solidarity. By 1917, however, churchgoing in the rest of France had reverted to its pre-war levels, as the fear created by the initial German breakthrough of 1914 gave way to the frustrations of stalemate on a static front.

Even so, the camaraderie of the trenches and the euphoria of victory went some way to softening the antagonism between the anti-clericals and committed Catholics – in the short term, if not necessarily in the long – and the elections of 1919 favoured candidates who were popularly seen as having pursued an unquestionably patriotic line of conduct in the war. Those socialists and the handful of Radicals who had favoured coming to terms with Germany emerged discredited, while the traditional anti-German rhetoric of the right in general was remembered more favourably in the polling booths. The new parliament was a body more disposed to be conciliatory towards the Church than its predecessors with their substantial left-of-centre majorities.

But reconciliation between Frenchmen did not necessarily extend to the foreigner, especially if the foreigner had failed to share French perceptions of the nature of the war. And this was certainly how the papacy was regarded in a hard-pressed France, where papal calls for a negotiated peace between the belligerents were seen as ignoring the moral superiority of the allied cause (see p. 171). Yet 1920 brought the re-establishment of formal diplomatic links between France and the Vatican, which Combes had broken off in 1904. This was not so much the result of a post-war generosity of impulse as the indirect outcome of the French recovery of Alsace-Lorraine. These provinces had been in German hands at the time of the French abolition of Napoleon's concordat in 1905, with the result that the sees of Strasbourg and Metz were still subject to the old concordatory methods of episcopal appointment, which required official contact between government and pope. Moreover the government decided to continue paying the concordatory state salaries to the bishops and parish clergy, and likewise forbore from extending to Alsace-Lorraine the pre-war legislation against the religious orders of monks, friars and nuns. Given the relatively high level of religious practice in the regained provinces, this was elementary common sense, if movements of dissident particularism were to be avoided. And when Edouard Herriot's Cartel des Gauches government of 1924–6 made ill-judged moves in the direction of removing these legal differences, it was clear from the lack of public enthusiasm that pre-war anti-clericalism no longer had the rallying power that had made it the cement of the disparate forces of the left during *la république de papa* (see p. 171).

The resumption of diplomatic relations between Paris and the pope in 1920 was rapidly followed by an informal arrangement in 1921 by which the Vatican gave consideration to any objections that the government might have to the pope's choice of candidates for vacant sees in France. While in no way constituting a veto, the Vatican took it sufficiently seriously to substitute a more acceptable candidate on the dozen or more occasions in the three following decades when the government expressed misgivings on Rome's initial choice. The absence of such an arrangement in the 1906–21 period had resulted in the appointment of a series of intransigent individuals as bishops, as Pius X endeavoured to stiffen the episcopacy with men who shared his perception of current issues. Consequently his more flexible successors, Benedict XV (1914–22) and Pius XI (1922–39), found themselves having to deal with an episcopate that was far less open to compromise than their predecessors at the time of the separation. There was therefore a paradoxical reversal of roles in 1924 when the Church belatedly accepted the provisions of the separation law for the transfer of ecclesiastical property to the legal representatives of French Catholicism: the Vatican urged acceptance, while many of the new bishops favoured rejection.

The settlement of the legal status of the Church in France was subsequently matched by a settlement of the Vatican's own anomalous position in Rome. The completion of the unification of Italy in 1870 had seen the pope deprived of all that remained of his territorial sovereignty – leaving him with merely the notional concept of the sovereignty of his person as the sole guarantee that other nations would not accuse him of being under the thumb of the Italian government – and hence no longer worth heeding when it came to dealing with the Church in their own territories. The Vatican had therefore refused to recognize the legitimacy of the Italian presence in Rome and had reduced its dealings with the government to the barest minimum, even to the point of prohibiting Catholics from participating in Italian parliamentary politics. Recent research demonstrates that Leo XIII's advice to French Catholics in 1892 to accept the French Republic had been partly motivated by the hope that France might eventually reward the pope by putting pressure on the Italian government to evacuate Rome and set up shop once more in Florence (see p. 170). The failure of these chimerical hopes had convinced Pius X and Merry del Val that the so-called 'Roman question' had been a millstone around the neck of Vatican diplomacy, inhibiting papal plain-speaking on issues affecting the Church, for fear of alienating governments which Leo XIII had vainly hoped might help him recover Rome. The new masters in the Vatican decided that the future lay conversely in a general *détente* with the Italian government, conducted gradually and carefully, which would free the papacy to speak its mind (see p. 170). Benedict XV and Pius XI broadly shared the same belief that such a *détente* was essential; and in 1929 Pius XI concluded the Lateran treaties with Mussolini, thereby acquiring for Vatican City the formal attributes of a completely sovereign state. Although relations with Mussolini soon became very strained, the sense of moral independence that came with territorial sovereignty greatly increased the Vatican's confidence and its readiness to adopt forthright attitudes in its dealings with secular governments.

The same confidence characterized papal dealings with the rank and file of the Church, where Pius XI displayed a readiness to give a bold lead in the shape and strategies of extending Church influence in the secular world at grass-roots level (see p. 171). The direction of his policies was already apparent in the 1920s, when he showed a predilection for negotiated settlements with established governments rather than working through national political parties representing Catholic interests. To some extent this had always been the preference of the Vatican; and, in so far as popes had veered from it, the shift had usually been one of desperation, resulting from the reluctance of governments to offer terms acceptable to Rome. Moreover, in turning to Catholic political parties, the Vatican had usually been wary about their adopting titles that might make them appear to be the accredited spokesmen of Church views. Leo XIII (1878–1903) had advised French Catholics to cooperate with other 'moderate', socially conservative politicians against the anti-clericals of the left, rather than marginalize themselves as a specifically confessional party. He also had bitter experience of his conciliatory policies towards the Republic being traduced by militant Catholics claiming to speak in his name. And even when the onslaught of the Combes ministry made the creation of a party of Catholic defence seem unavoidable, the resultant Action Libérale (1901) respected his wishes in not having a confessional title, and tried to steer clear – not always successfully – of militant anti-republicans. Pius X and Merry del Val, on the other hand, felt that the Catholic cause in France could not afford to be too choosy in the support it accepted; and, while they continued to recognize the Republic as the established form of government in France, they saw no harm in making use of any ally who was genuinely committed to the defence of the Church. This partly explains their reluctance to denounce the policies of Charles Maurras's Action Française, a neo-pagan, theoretically monarchist movement of the extreme right, which was increasingly recruiting support among the clergy by claiming to be the Church's only reliable protector. It was not until 1926 that the Vatican under Pius XI officially prohibited Catholics from supporting Action Française or reading its newspaper; and even then the condemnation was rapidly revoked by the next pope, Pius XII, in 1939, after an ambiguous display of submission by Maurras.

In the meantime, however, the war years of reconciliation in common cause against the invader, and the rightwards swing of the vote in the 1919 elections, made religious defence a less pressing priority in the concerns of Catholic voters. Conversely the coming to office of Edouard Herriot's Cartel des Gauches government in 1924 – with its clumsy attempts to resort to the pre-war tactic of using anti-clericalism as a banner to unite the divided forces of the left – provoked General Edouard de Castelnau into forming a Fédération Nationale Catholique (FNC) in February 1925, committed to opposing Herriot's proposals. Although it was essentially an extra-parliamentary organization, nearly half of the new parliament of 1928 were to subscribe to its declaration in favour of relaxing the draconian pre-war legislation on private schools and religious communities. By that time, however, the Herriot government's failure to achieve agreement on effective financial and economic policies had removed the enemy that the federation had been founded to fight; and the FNC ceased to count for much after 1930. Its representatives in parliament were a mixed bunch, ranging from 'moderate' republicans committed to Church interests to men whose inner sympathies lay with a monarchy or dictatorship. Otherwise the only parliamentary groups with a professed remit to support Catholic concerns were the dozen to a score members of the Parti Démocrate Populaire – a Christian democrat party with a modest programme of social reform that alienated Catholics of a more conservative stamp – and the even smaller Union Populaire Républicaine which specifically represented the Catholic interests of Alsace-Lorraine. So, as far as voting power was concerned, any measure of specific Catholic concern in parliament had to depend on the sympathies of secular conservative parties such as the Fédération Républicaine and Alliance Démocratique. Significantly three of the four committed Catholics who achieved ministerial office in the 1920s belonged to secular parties with no particular brief for the Church. These were Auguste Isaac, Charles de Lasteyrie du Saillant and Edouard Lefebvre du Prey; Auguste Champetier de Ribes was the only minister to belong to the Parti Démocrate Populaire. Fortunately for the Church, the failure of Herriot's anti-clerical programme in the mid-1920s discouraged the left from raising the old tattered banners of militant *laïcisme* in the subsequent elections of the interwar period. Even the Popular Front victory of 1936 saw very little attempt to regain the ground that die-hard *mangeurs de curés* claimed had been lost to creeping clericalism.

These general circumstances particularly suited Pius XI's predilection for a grass-roots offensive to rechristianize society. His first encyclical, *Ubi Arcano Dei* of 1922, had proposed 'the organized participation of the laity in the hierarchical apostolate of the Church, transcending party politics for the establishment of Christ's reign throughout the world'. And his chosen instruments were the various Catholic action movements that he encouraged to expand in the interwar period. Jeunesse Ouvrière Chrétienne (JOC) spread from Belgium to France in 1927, while its rural equivalent, Jeunesse Agricole Chrétienne, came into being 2 years later. These and other youth movements, such as Jeunesse Étudiante Chrétienne, sought to rechristianize their particular socio-occupational milieux by displaying a persuasive combination of professional progressivism and social conscience; they would challenge the secular world on its own terms and transform it. It was these organizations that were also to provide a generation of articulate spokesmen and women who made their way into the parliamentary politics of post-Liberation France. The JOC was also a recruiting ground for the Catholic trade-union movement, the Confédération Française des Travailleurs Chrétiens, founded in 1919, whose membership was to reach 400 000 by the late 1930s, even if this left it a long way behind the several million of the Confédération Générale du Travail. This wide gap did not deter it from expressing its resentment at being excluded from the Matignon negotiations of June 1936 which led to the implementation of some of the Popular Front's most notable reforms; and although it declared sympathy for a number of the Front's social aims, it later welcomed with considerable warmth what it was

to call Edouard Daladier's more 'national' government of 1938. On the level
of ideology, the 1930s were also notable for the growing influence of
Emmanuel Mounier's 'personalist' philosophy and his review, *L'Esprit*,
which were to provide Catholic socio-political action with an intellectually
appealing theoretical basis, even if its adherents largely belonged to an
educated élite.

Occupation and Liberation: retribution averted

The German invasion of France in 1940 and the 4 years of foreign occupation that followed were a turning point in the fortunes of French Catholicism
– but a turning point with the complexity of a corkscrew. For the Church
historian, the 1940s were a decade of paradox (see p. 171). Half a century
later the French episcopate was to make a public confession that its reticence
during the Occupation towards the persecution of the Jews had been inex-
cusable – despite the outspoken courage of a handful of prelates. Prior to this
tardy admission, bishops had sought to justify their complaisant attitude to
the Vichy government and to the occupying forces by the need to protect
Church-members from German repression. Yet the readiness of the bishops
to profit from the benign attitudes of the Vichy government left them open to
the obvious charge of opportunism, while the hostility of many senior clergy
to the Resistance inevitably made them seem like counter-revolutionaries,
seeking to preserve 'the Pétain miracle' against a return of the secular
republic of the pre-war years. Opportunistic or merely naïve, their behaviour
would have seemed to lead inexorably to a counter-wave of anti-clerical
retribution when Vichy's victims and critics eventually triumphed at the
Liberation. That appeared to be the lesson of the previous century when the
anti-clerical outbursts of 1830, 1871 and the late 1880s had all been the price
paid for the Church's complicity with the Bourbon Restoration, the Second
Empire and the *ordre moral* of the mid-1870s. Yet the great reckoning did
not occur. Counter to the logic of past history, the Church emerged more
powerful, while practising Catholics obtained more ministerial portfolios in
post-war France than they had had since the 1870s – far more than even
Vichy at its most indulgent had ever offered them.

The explanation lies largely in significant changes in popular perceptions
of the Church. The public increasingly drew a sharp distinction between the
senior clergy and the committed laity, whose professional and social lives
were linked with the rest of the community and who were to provide post-
war France with so many of its influential political figures. This distinction
had been much more difficult to make in the past, especially during the anti-
clerical years of the Third Republic, which had brought the bishops and the
Catholic laity into close alliance in defence of Church interests. But the
declining animosity that characterized interwar France had slackened the
defensive discipline within Catholic ranks – so much so that the die-hard

clerics warned that the various enthusiastic initiatives of the laity were escaping Church control. This divergence was to take dramatic shape during the Occupation when a modest but increasingly influential number of Catholic laymen and women took up Resistance activity, which, although directed against the German occupation, was *ipso facto* critical of Vichy policies and the regime's supporters, including most bishops. Though relatively few they played a major organizational role in what was to be the winning side – as most strikingly reflected in the fact that both the internal and external Resistance were led by noted if very different exemplars of Catholic lay commitment, Georges Bidault and Charles de Gaulle. Yet the readiness of the post-war electorate to honour them, and not engage in lengthy recriminations against the opportunism or passivity of the majority of French Catholics and their spiritual leaders, also stemmed from an uneasy recognition that the inglorious role of so many Catholics had also been shared by a large section of the French population as a whole; and, in turning their eyes from the shabby record of the Church, they were also pushing under the carpet the memory of their own inaction or dingy acceptance of short-term advantage.

Turning to Vichy itself, there were few committed Catholics among Pétain's ministers – even if the government in its first year contained a number of tepid churchgoers who saw the Church primarily as a useful bastion of the social status quo. It was mainly at the secondary levels of government that committed Catholics were to be found, notably in the organization of youth and the implementation of the so-called National Revolution. Many were initially seduced by what they hoped would be a vigorous government of national solidarity, in which pre-war class animosities would give way to a common determination to achieve results: at long last problems would be solved that had eluded the Third Republic with its miserable procession of weak cabinets. Catholics were gratified that members of religious orders were now formally allowed to teach once more in France (September 1940), even if this had in practice long since been a *fait accompli*; and the Third Republic's discriminatory legislation against the orders was now officially lifted (April 1942). Access to religious instruction was made easier for the pupils of state schools, albeit on an optional basis and off the premises (March 1941). And the government authorized municipal authorities to give financial help to Catholic private schools, if they were so minded. It nevertheless refused to accede to the bishops' persistent attempts to obtain a regular form of national subsidy for Catholic schools. Even so, these various tokens of government favour encouraged more Catholic parents to resort to the private sector, with the result that its share of the primary-school population rose from 18 to 23 per cent by 1943.

It might have been expected that Vichy would see the last bastions of secular purity in the civil service fall into Catholic hands. But the ministers and the *grands corps* had their jealously guarded ladders of promotion which even a government as undemocratic as Vichy was hesitant to touch.

Although the new regime lost no time in sacking a third of the nation's prefects, over four-fifths of their replacements came from the ranks of sub-prefects who had entered the service in the pre-war period and who consequently reflected the ethos and attitudes of the now despised Third Republic. Admittedly they had to learn very quickly to sing the different tunes required by the change of master, but desperate times brought forth unsuspected skills of adaptation.

Whatever hopes had been raised in the early months of Vichy of a rechristianized France arising from the ashes of the Republic, Admiral François Darlan's government (February 1941–April 1942) brought a ministry unsympathetic to the Church, committed to technocratic planning and dominated by the need to meet Germany's economic demands. He had no time for what he called 'the soft-cheeked altar-boys' who had hung around Vichy, hoping for advancement, during the first six months of the regime – nor did the German embassy staff in Paris. Pierre Laval (April 1942–August 1944) was even less sympathetic to the Church; and during his period of government the episcopate became increasingly concerned about Vichy's growing subservience to Germany. The papal nuncio protested to Pétain in 1942 about France's involvement in Germany's anti-semitic programme, and a few months later a political spokesman for the bishops confidentially suggested to Pétain that he should resign before events made him little more than an instrument of German government. But these fears, increasingly justified, did not shake the loyalty of the bulk of the bishops to Pétain; and only four months before the D-day landings of June 1944, the assembly of cardinals and archbishops condemned Resistance activity as 'terrorism'. This did not prevent individual bishops from publicly denouncing the immorality of Vichy's part in the persecution of the Jews; and several of them were arrested in consequence. Indeed over 1000 priests were deported to Germany, either for criticism of the occupying forces, or by personal choice as a means of giving clandestine moral support to French deportees.

Hopes and disappointments

The Liberation in 1944 seemed to many Catholics to bring promise of a new dawn for the Church in France. De Gaulle's government was not only the first to be headed by a practising Catholic since the 1870s, but nearly a third of its principal ministers were committed Catholics. Of the 25 subsequent governments of the post-war Republic, 11 were likewise Catholic-headed; and the Catholic-inspired Mouvement Républicain Populaire (MRP) was to hold an average of four to five portfolios over the next decade. If, as already indicated, this seemed to run counter to legitimate expectation after the unhappy compromises of the Vichy period, it in effect represented victory for precisely those elements in French Catholicism who had not followed the uneasy leadership of their official spiritual leaders. And it was this that seemed to offer hope of regeneration. The fact that the MRP was now the second largest party in the post-war assemblies admittedly owed much to the enfranchisement of women in 1944–5 – and likewise owed much to the discrediting of the traditional conservative parties by the unedifying record of many of their members during the Occupation. But the influx into the MRP of many conservative Catholics who did not share the ideals of the party's founders was insufficiently recognized by enthusiasts as a potential perversion of the party's initial aims. The more naïve saw it as a change of heart on the part of many traditionalists, a belated recognition of the moral bankruptcy of the old alliance between inherited property and the Church, finally discredited by the self-interest and hypocrisy of the Vichy experience, presided over by an octogenarian who outwardly displayed deference to a religion which meant little to him personally.

Conservatives had no particular objection to the MRP's professed aim to reconcile the working classes with the Church – and to reconcile the Church with the republic – but they differed from the party luminaries in the amount of ground that the Church and the propertied classes were expected to relinquish in this desirable reconciliation. Nor did they see much harm in singing the virtues of a pluralist society in a country where pluralism had clearly come to stay. But once again their concept of pluralism was limited to a wary co-existence rather than an enthusiastic sharing of the values of post-war secular society. All these reservations were to become increasingly apparent in the post-Liberation years; but in the meantime the conscience bearers of the MRP looked to what seemed bright prospects (see p. 171).

Regeneration also seemed to be promised by the growing independence of the progressive elements in French Catholicism from the domination of Rome and the control of the French episcopate. While loyalty to the pope as head of the Church was not in question – except for the usual departure of individuals who chose to leave the formal structures of the Church – there was a much greater readiness to take initiatives without reference to the Vatican or the bishops. Like the conservative parties in France, the bishops had lost respect through their complaisant attitude to Vichy, while Pius XII was deeply disliked in Liberation France for his diplomatic record in the 1930s before becoming pope and for his overly reticent attitudes towards Nazi atrocities. Given this situation, neither the bishops nor the Vatican were tempted to reassert their authority at a time when their credit was so low; a low profile seemed the wisest strategy, until the clouds of opprobrium dispersed. Symptomatically the MRP had come into being (November 1944) without prior consultation with either the bishops or the Vatican – unlike the Catholic parties of the pre-1914 period. Moreover the loudest demands for the removal of bishops with tarnished Occupation records came from the MRP – Bidault himself, now foreign minister, demanding the resignation of a dozen, even if he finally had to settle for four. With the ecclesiastical authorities keeping a discreet silence, the intellectual life of French Catholicism blossomed.

While the tactical reticence of Pius XII had little in common with the tolerant intellectual curiosity of Leo XIII, the mid-1940s saw a vibrant expectancy in French Catholic writing and its readership, reminiscent of the 1890s, before the 'modernist' witch-hunt unleashed by Pius X and Merry del Val muzzled speculative religious literature. If much of it stemmed from the innovatory work of *les non-conformistes des années trente*, it flourished in the invigorating climate of Liberation France; and progressive Catholic writers found a following that extended well beyond the confines of Church membership. At the same time, the growing acceptance of Catholicism as a political factor in post-war French politics encouraged many middle-class Catholics to be less reticent about the expression of their religious commitment, particularly in those sectors of public employment where it had periodically been regarded as something of an encumbrance under the Third Republic. In fact church attendance among *fonctionnaires* and the professional classes was probably more widespread in the post-war decade than it had been since the nineteenth century. Nor should the impact of the experience of war be forgotten. As in the First World War, fear and uncertainty engendered a rise in religious practice that was distinct from the growth in churchgoing that stemmed from Vichy's formal benevolence towards the Church. And the feeling of euphoric gratitude that swept much of France at the Liberation likewise filled churches, until the morose drudgery of dealing with day-to-day shortages and problems in the following years reduced congregations to a more familiar size – if still remaining higher than in the pre-war period.

While these external factors also had an impact on the fluctuations of working-class religious practice, it was less marked and shorter-lived than the rise in middle-class churchgoing. During the war, in January 1944, the archbishop of Paris had inaugurated the worker-priest movement as a response to alarming evidence of the extent to which working-class contact with the Church had evaporated during the gradual industrialization of France. There had been individual initiatives in this direction in pre-war years; but, inspired by the example of French priests in German prison-camps and factories, upwards of 100 priests were permitted to seek full-time employment in industry and other secular workplaces in the post-war decade, with the intention of establishing links with a generation of workers that had little or no contact with religion (see p. 171). The rise and fall of this bold experiment was to be in many ways a parallel image of the trajectory of progressive French Catholicism under the Fourth Republic.

It was the coming of the Cold War that chilled the burgeoning hopes of the Liberation years. In the realm of French politics it resulted in the exclusion of the communists from the left-wing coalition of socialists, MRP and PCF (Parti Communiste Français) that had governed France since 1944. As no government could survive without the support of at least three parties, this obliged the coalition to open the alliance to the Radicals – which effectively ended hope of any further extension of the Liberation programme of social

reform. Sharing government with the Radicals enabled the socially conservative elements in the MRP to become increasingly influential – a process
that gathered momentum in the early 1950s, when the socialists dropped out
of government, obliging the MRP and Radicals to turn to the conservatives
to make up the ruling coalition. The emergence of a formal Gaullist party in
1947 likewise pushed the MRP in a conservative direction, since it now had
to compete with the Gaullists for the traditional Catholic vote.

On the international front, the Cold War encouraged the western nations
to close ranks on a mutual programme of anti-communism – a situation that
gave the Vatican its chance to come out of the cold, since its anti-communism
had never been in doubt. This in turn encouraged it to reassert its authority
over the various segments of the Church – an inclination that was further
strengthened by the growing power of the Christian Democrat party in Italy,
assuring the pope of a secure position at home, thereby enabling him to be
tough in his dealings with the Church in other countries. French progressivism was among the early victims, notably the worker-priest movement. The
trade-union activities of a number of worker-priests, some of whom did
committee work for the communist CGT, gave the more conservative
elements in the Vatican the opportunity to press for the imposition of very
tight restrictions on the movement. This in effect made its continuation in
any meaningful form impossible (January 1954). At the same time, tight
discipline was reasserted by Rome over other aspects of Church life in
France, including the revocation of three provincial heads of the Dominican
Order and the purging of the leadership of various lay organizations.

Renewed hopes – and further disappointments

1958 brought the death of the Fourth Republic and the death of Pius XII.
Both events were to have important if indirect repercussions for the Church
in France. Shortly after General de Gaulle became president of the new
republic, the Debré law of December 1959 effectively established substantial
state subsidies for Catholic private schools – a prize that the Church had
vainly sought since it lost its landed property at the Revolution. French
absorption in the Algerian crisis and parliament's fears of a possible civil
war, should de Gaulle's authority be undermined, enabled him to realize this
concession, which in previous years would have been quite impossible.
Despite the initial *furore* that it created in secular circles, the very size of the
concession paradoxically gave it an air of semi-finality which more or less
discouraged a recrudescence of the traditional feuding over the issue that had
divided French politics for so long. Even when the left returned to power
with a large majority in the early 1980s, its assault on the concession
envisaged modification rather than abolition.

The 1960s were a watershed for the Catholic Church in the western
world. While the accession of Pope John XXIII (1958–63) was an important

element in these changes, the principal factor was the coming-of-age of a post-war generation that had little or no memory of the fears and privations of the 1940s and was reaching adulthood in a period of unprecedented affluence – and sexual liberty – when the here-and-now seemed to offer as much promise of future happiness as did the traditional prospect of the ineffable but uncertain serenities of the after-life. Weekly attendance at mass fell from well over 20 per cent of the adult population in the early 1960s – men and women combined – to less than 15 per cent by the end of the decade – while the late 1980s were to find it down to 10 per cent. The tumble in the 1960s was unquestionably part of the much wider rejection of old-established forms of authority and constraint that hit the western world. Apart from the unparalleled material prosperity of those years, the development of the contraceptive pill was putting women on a closer par with men; and it seemed to many that the only impediment to a paradise on earth was the joyless timidity of those who wielded power, weary oldsters without the vision to maximize the unprecedented possibilities of the new age – and who, moreover, were responsible for a series of bloody wars, including the current devastation of Vietnam. If the churches were just part of the spectrum of deep-rooted authority that was in question, this scrutiny was especially searching in the Catholic Church where obedient membership entailed a much greater personal price – celibacy for the clergy, weekly mass for the laity, no contraception and distressing agreements imposed on non-Catholic marriage partners.

The situation was paradoxically further complicated by the Second Vatican Council (1962–5) which gave rise to widespread hopes of substantial liberal reform which for the most part remained unfulfilled. The new pope, John XXIII, had been nuncio in Paris during the heady years of the Liberation, and was well aware of the disappointed hopes that progressive Catholics had experienced during the Fourth Republic. While sharing only some of the enthusiasms of the *avant-garde*, he recognized the need for substantial changes in the Church, an *aggiornamento* which among other things would lay greater emphasis on 'collegiality' – collective authority within the Church, as distinct from the strict top-down leadership that had characterized most of his predecessors and their immediate advisers in the twentieth century. While the council immediately gave rise to various liturgical changes that made the Church's services and sacraments more comprehensible to the less-educated sections of society, its declaration of principle on greater devolution of authority depended on various post-conciliar commissions to work out the practical means of making them a reality; and this in turn depended on the readiness of the Pope to encourage their labours and implement the results.

Unfortunately for the progressives, the death of John XXIII saw the tiara pass to Paul VI (1963–78), Pius XII's former secretary of state whom critics unkindly called 'Pius XII writ small'. For all his virtues of patience and conscientiousness, he was intellectually timid and unwilling to open the windows to the winds of change any wider than was ordained by a minimum interpretation of the council's prescriptions. A heavy programme of foreign travel was his main contribution to the reformed style of papal government; and, although it was expected that these new-found opportunities for listening to the concerns of clergy and laity in different countries would see these concerns respected and reflected in subsequent Vatican policy, the visits increasingly became occasions for mass displays of loyalty to the pope – especially under his successor, John-Paul II (1978–) – strengthening rather than qualifying the monarchical character of Church authority. Lukewarm or restless Catholics who had postponed quitting the family home in the early 1960s to see whether council improvements would render it more habitable and to their taste, were disappointed and packed their bags, while progressive Catholics were especially disillusioned, with considerable numbers joining the emigrants. The biggest disappointment was Paul VI's encyclical, *Humanae Vitae* of 25 July 1968, reaffirming the church's prohibition of contraception – other than the optimistically named 'safe period'. A majority of the pope's advisory committee on the matter had recommended change, and hopes were high in the laity that change would come. In reality many committed Catholics had long since adopted contraceptive stratagems condemned by the Church, while others expecting a relaxation of the prohibition had begun to use them. Paul VI's reassertion of the traditional Vatican position was not only a disappointment for western family life but it prolonged the gigantic dilemma of the Third-World countries where the progress of development and relief-aid was continually offset by population growth. Although it was only a minority of practising Catholics who left the Church at that point, a sizeable proportion of those who remained turned a blind eye to the encyclical, justifying their attitude as in line with what had been the majority opinion of the pope's advisers on birth control. Sample polls in the early 1990s revealed that some 80 per cent or so of regular mass-going Frenchwomen were ignoring the Vatican's views on contraception.

The drift to pick-and-mix

The Church thereby suffered a double loss – a loss of membership and a loss of authority over those who stayed. A pick-and-mix attitude towards papal teaching increasingly characterized the laity – in sacramental and liturgical issues, as well as in sexual matters (see p. 171). Regular attendance at weekly mass was often replaced by a once-or-twice-a-month routine, while confession (soon to be benignly termed 'reconciliation') was abandoned altogether by many Catholics – on the grounds that the realities of married life and the moral dilemmas of the secular world were beyond the experience of seminary-trained priests with little acquaintance with modern psychology. Indeed by the early 1980s only 1 per cent of adult practising French Catholics went to monthly confession – as against some 20 per cent in the 1950s.

Priests themselves were starting to query their own role as moral advisers in an increasingly professional world where personal problems seemed better treated by qualified counsellors, social workers and psychiatrists. These and other doubts – notably on the issue of celibacy – resulted in a dramatic diminution in secular priests in France from about 40 000 in the mid-1960s to 27 000 two decades later. In their instructions to priests, the French episcopate counselled caution in the confessional in matters of birth control, lest close questioning or a hard line should discourage parishioners from going to confession or indeed to church at all.

But the arrival in the Vatican of Pope John-Paul II confronted them with a charismatic travelling pope who rapidly unleashed a vigorous campaign to reaffirm traditional Vatican views on sexual matters. Progressive Catholics made a brave attempt to devise a survival strategy for what promised to be a tough pontificate. In effect they adopted a dialectical view of the Church: they regarded the Vatican with its traditional views as the thesis; and they presented themselves, the theological *avant-garde*, as the antithesis. They boldly suggested that the conflict between the thesis and the antithesis would give birth to a series of mutually acceptable syntheses when the time was ripe for each to emerge. Nor did it worry them unduly that the pope for one did not always seem to appreciate the nature of the role they had conferred on him.

With practising Catholics becoming a decreasing proportion of the population, religion declined as a divisive force in French politics. Catholic political allegiance was increasingly split between parties whose leading concerns were not religious. With the Gaullists and their allies solidly in power from 1958 to 1981, and still enjoying the credit of having obtained the greatest financial concessions to Catholic education since the *ancien régime*, the MRP no longer seemed necessary for the defence of Catholic interests. Its transformation into the Centre Démocrate in the mid-1960s, and its subsequent cannibalization by other parties, obliged Catholics to look elsewhere – and the Gaullists and Giscardians were the principal beneficiaries.

The first three presidents of the Fifth Republic – two Gaullists and a Giscardian – openly claimed to be practising Catholics; and if their prime ministers were harder to pin down, there were several committed Catholics among them and among their cabinet colleagues. More importantly, the question of whether they were Catholic or not no longer seemed to be of significant concern; their policies, styles and tactics were not noticeably any different from those of their free-thinking or Protestant colleagues. Symptomatically, if paradoxically, it was during the presidencies of two churchgoing Catholics, General de Gaulle and Valéry Giscard d'Estaing (1974–81), that contraception and abortion were securely and unambiguously established in French law. Given this situation, governments of the left as well as of the right saw no reason to be concerned over the influx of committed Catholics into what had been the jealously guarded secular strongholds of state service; their religious convictions were no longer seen as relevant to whether they were suitable to be a prefect, a councillor of state or whatever their professional abilities matched.

There are, however, many historians who believe that religious issues are far from dead in French politics. Indeed several claim that deep-rooted religio-cultural differences are still the prime determinant of current French voting patterns. They point to the legislative elections of 1997, when government changed from right to left; and they quote the opinion polls of the time, which indicated that roughly 70 per cent of practising Catholics supported the parties of the right as against 30 per cent who supported those on the left. Sceptics reply that these opinion polls leave unresolved a fundamental question. Was it the Catholicism of the right's supporters that determined their overall attitude to the political programme of the right? Or was their Catholicism a product – or part-product – of the socio-cultural milieu to which they belonged? If the latter, it was arguably their milieu, rather than their Catholicism, that drew them to the right, with its offers of financial and economic policies that were more congenial to people of their material standing. At the same time, churchgoers of the left vigorously rejected the implication that left-wing Catholics were in some way 'less intrinsically Catholic' than the Catholic supporters of the right.

Historians who claim that religious issues still weigh heavily in French politics make much of the schools question, asserting that this lays bare one of the great geological fault-lines that continue to cut across the opposing rock faces of socio-economic interests that dominate French parliamentary debate. They argue that this invalidates the idea that French politics have 'come of age' and are now on a par with the politics of Britain and Scandinavia, where stability is guaranteed by the solid dominance of confronting forces whose differences are mainly over socio-economic policy. These commentators point to the gigantic demonstration that took place in Paris on 24 June 1984, protesting against greater state control over those private schools that were in receipt of public funds. Over a million people took part, an unprecedented total in French history. Other historians have replied that the demonstrators' prime concerns were not religious – even though religious issues were unquestionably a contributory factor. Barely one in five who bought a Catholic private education for their children was a practising Catholic. Most of the rest opted for the private sector for reasons that were broadly similar to those current in Britain. The local state school might have social problems or immigrant language difficulties; or parents might be disappointed with the state school's decision on how their child should be streamed – and consequently turned to a Catholic private school in the hope of securing the level of education they wanted. Right-wing politicians, however, led by the mayor of Paris, Jacques Chirac, sought to use the demonstration as a stick to beat the government by presenting it as a crusade to protect religious freedom. This was a major embarrassment for the many bishops who privately felt that the proposals of the government were broadly acceptable, with certain minor adjustments. The fact, however, that the rally intimidated President Mitterrand into imposing an anodyne compromise on his ministers – and led indirectly to a change of premier – encouraged observers, both then and thereafter, to claim it as evidence of the surviving power of clericalism to threaten the integrity of republican policies. The debate continues.

Further reading

The best comprehensive survey is Gérard Cholvy and Yves-Marie Hilaire, *Histoire religieuse de la France contemporaine*, 3 vols. (Toulouse: Privat, 1985–8). The same journey in English involves changing trains several times: Ralph Gibson, *A Social History of French Catholicism, 1789–1914* (London: Routledge, 1989); John McManners, *Church and State in France, 1870–1914* (London: SPCK, 1972); Adrien Dansette, *Religious History of Modern France, Vol. II: Under the Third Republic* (Edinburgh: Nelson, 1961); James F. McMillan, 'France', in Tom Buchanan and Martin Conway (eds.), *Political Catholicism in Europe, 1919–1965* (Oxford: Clarendon Press, 1996); and, for the post-1965 period, the relevant chapters in the more specialized works mentioned below. A general overview of the period 1890–1994 is given in the course of Maurice Larkin, *Religion, Politics and Preferment in France since 1890* (Cambridge: Cambridge University Press, 1995) – but the book mainly concerns the problems of practising Catholics in public employment.

The controversies surrounding the numerical strength of Catholicism in France are summarized in Fernand Boulard and Jean Rémy, *Pratique religieuse urbaine et régions culturelles* (Paris: Éditions Ouvrières, 1968), and in Gérard Cholvy, *La Religion en France de la fin du XVIIIe siècle à nos jours* (Paris: Hatchet, 1991), while the statistical methods are critically scrutinized in L'Association Française d'Histoire Religieuse Contemporaine, *L'Observation quantitative du fait religieux* (Lille: L'Université Charles de Gaulle, 1992).

The best contemporary statement of the case against the Church was put by Antonin Debidour, *L'Eglise catholique et l'état en France sous la Troisième République*, II (Paris: Alcan, 1909) – a view challenged by a succession of Catholic writers and later debated in Dansette's well-balanced *Religious History*, II. The involvement of Church members in anti-republican activity in the late 1890s is examined in Larkin, *Religion, Politics and Preferment* and in Larkin, *Church and State after the Dreyfus Affair: The Separation Issue in France* (London: Macmillan, 1974) which also analyses Combes's religious policies and how the separation came about. Both books look at how papal policy towards France in the period 1890-1914 was influenced by 'the Roman question' and the Vatican's relations with other countries. For a chronological view of the period from the perspective of a leading Catholic spokesman, see Benjamin F. Martin, *Count Albert de Mun: Paladin of the Third Republic* (Chapel Hill, NC: University of North Carolina Press, 1978).

The attempt to purge the army of Catholic influence in the Combes era is closely analysed in François Vindé, *L'Affaire des fiches, 1900–1904* (Paris: Éditions Universitaires, 1989) – and more briefly in Larkin, *Religion, Politics and Preferment*, which mainly deals with parallel issues in the civil service.

On the French Church and the First World War, see James F. McMillan, 'French Catholics: *rumeurs infames* and the Union Sacrée, 1914–1918', in Frans Coetzee and

Marilyn Shevin-Coetzee (eds.), *Authority, Identity and the Social History of the Great War* (Oxford: Berghahn, 1995), pp. 113–32. The only major study is Jacques Fontana, *Les Catholiques français pendant la Grande Guerre* (Paris: Cerf, 1990), to which should be added Francis Latour, 'De la spécificité de la diplomatie vaticane durant la grande guerre', *Revue d'histoire moderne et contemporaine* (April–June 1996).

The reasons for the Church's failure to modernize its administrative structure in France, both before and after separation, are examined in Dansette, *Religious history*, II, Larkin, *Church and State* and, in more specific detail, Adrien Dansette, *Destin du catholicisme français, 1926–1956* (Paris: Flammarion, 1957).

The improvement in church–state relations in the 1920s is described in Harry W. Paul, *The Second Ralliement: The Rapprochement between Church and State in France in the Twentieth Century* (Washington: Catholic University of America Press, 1967), while Martin Conway, *Catholic Politics in Europe, 1918–1945* (London: Routledge, 1997) has illuminating comments on the period in general. Like James McMillan's 'France', it is more critical of Pius XI than was the scholarship of earlier decades. Specific aspects of Catholic attitudes towards the politics of these years can be followed more closely in James F. McMillan, 'Catholicism and Nationalism in France: the case of the Fédération Nationale Catholique', in Frank Tallett and Nicholas Atkin, *Catholicism in Britain and France since 1789* (London: Hambledon Press, 1996), pp. 151–64; R. W. Rauch, Jr., *Politics and Belief in Contemporary France: Emmanuel Mounier and Christian Democracy, 1932–1950* (The Hague: Martinas Nijhof, 1972); John Hellmann, *Emmanuel Mounier and the New Catholic Left, 1930–1950* (Toronto: University of Toronto Press, 1981); and O. L. Arnal, *Ambivalent Alliance: The Catholic Church and the Action Française 1899–1939* (Pittsburgh: University of Pittsburgh Press, 1985).

The role of the Church in the Vichy years has been excellently described in Wilfred D. Halls, *Politics, Society and Christianity in Vichy France* (Oxford: Berg, 1995) and in his *The Youth of Vichy France* (Oxford: Oxford University Press, 1981).

Catholicism during the Fourth and early Fifth Republics is comprehensively surveyed in William Bosworth, *Catholicism and Crisis in Modern France: French Catholic Groups at the Threshold of the Fifth Republic* (Princeton: Princeton University Press, 1962). See also Ronald E. M. Irving, *Christian Democracy in France* (London: Allen & Unwin, 1973); O. L. Arnal, *Priests in Working-Class Blue: The History of the Worker Priests (1943–1954)* (New York: Paulist Press, 1986); and Jean-Marie Mayeur, 'De Gaulle as politician and Christian', in Hugh Gough and John Horne (eds.), *De Gaulle and Twentieth-Century France* (London: Arnold, 1994).

Developments within the Church after the 1960s are closely analysed in Danièle Hervieu-Léger, *Vers un nouveau christianisme?* (Paris: Cerf, 1986) and in Jean-Marie Donegani, *La liberté de choisir: pluralisme religieux et pluralisme politique dans le catholicisme français contemporain* (Paris: Presses de la Fondation Nationale des Sciences Politiques, 1993). The major issues are very briefly surveyed in Larkin, *Religion, Politics and Preferment*.

|7|

The 'Jewish question' from Dreyfus to Vichy

VICKI CARON

Come on now, let's be serious; we're in France and not in a country of racism, and no Frenchman could ever conceive of the idea of proposing a law to strip French Jewish citizens of their status and their civil rights.

> Oscar de Férenzy, 1935

One can't distinguish between Jews who have recently immigrated and those who've lived in France for many generations. As for the latter – who claim to be completely assimilated – one can only respond: 'If it's been 150 years that you've been in France, that has been 150 years during which you've ruined the country.'

> M. Taillefeur, speaker at a meeting of the Anti-Jewish Committee of France, May 1937

For a long time, the republic did not understand that anti-semitism was only the mask donned by a weakened and discredited clericalism, and that what was hiding behind the war against the Jews was the war against the Republic ... From the moment this long misconceived danger was understood, the republic returned to its principles and traditions against which anti-semitism stood as the direct negation .... Now, the battle was no longer between anti-semitism and the Jews, but between anti-semitism and the ideas of the [French] Revolution. From that point on it became inevitable, it became a matter of the force of circumstance, that anti-semitism would be vanquished.

> Isaïe Levaillant, 1907[1]

In recent years the history of anti-semitism in modern France has become a veritable cottage industry. This spate of interest has been generated in part by the centennial of the Dreyfus affair (1894 through 1898–9), which has provided the occasion for reflection upon the affair's long-term significance. It has also been fuelled by the prolific scholarship of a younger generation of

French researchers, many of whom are Jewish. These scholars, motivated by the belief that their parents' generation swept under the carpet one of the most shameful episodes of modern French history, namely the anti-semitic policies of the Vichy regime and that regime's collaboration with the Nazi 'final solution', have committed themselves to uncovering this past and to raising critical questions regarding the place of anti-semitism within the broader arena of French history.

While this flurry of scholarly activity has greatly enhanced our under-standing of anti-semitism, it has also served to highlight several on-going debates in the historiography of modern French anti-semitism. First, scholars remain sharply divided over just how central anti-semitism has been to the larger themes of French history. On one end of the spectrum stand those who diminish the importance of anti-semitism. This camp's most outspoken proponent is Eugen Weber, who has argued that 'to most French during the 19th century and to many French in the 20th century, it [the Jewish question] was a minor question, or no question at all'. According to Weber, although the Dreyfus affair witnessed an outburst of anti-semitism, the affair itself had little to do with actual Jews, who numbered only about 75 000 at the time, less than 1 per cent of the total population. Weber is even more dismissive of twentieth-century anti-semitic movements. To be sure, in his most recent book, *The Hollow Years*, he concedes that 'by late 1938 and early 1939 anti-Semitism had become endemic' (p. 109), but the fact that he folds his discussion of anti-semitism into a chapter entitled 'Foreigners' suggests that he sees anti-semitism merely as a variant of xenophobia. The prominent French diplomatic historian, Jean-Baptiste Duroselle, similarly discounts the anti-semitism of the right-wing leagues during the interwar years. While recognizing the royalist Action Française as the principal conduit of anti-semitism from the Dreyfus affair era into the twentieth century, Duroselle nevertheless insists that the Action Française 'never made anti-semitism the very essence of its doctrine'. Moreover, since the Action Française, despite its considerable influence on Vichy officials, 'never acceded to the antechambers of power, even in 1940', Duroselle concludes that 'French anti-semitism never found its Hitler'. Most strikingly, Henry Rousso and Eric Conan have recently argued that historians of the Vichy era are now devoting too much attention to the Jewish question. In truth, according to Rousso and Conan, Vichy officials never considered Jews more than a matter of secondary importance.[2]

At the other end of the spectrum are scholars, including Pierre Birnbaum, Michel Winock, Stephen Wilson, Jean-Denis Bredin, Zeev Sternhell, Ralph Schor, Michael Marrus and Robert Paxton, who see anti-semitism as central to the broader themes of modern French history. According to this camp, while the Dreyfus affair or the Vichy regime did not revolve exclusively around the Jewish question, that question was by no means peripheral. Rather, these scholars argue that anti-semitism became a major weapon in the nineteenth-century attack against capitalism, a struggle proclaimed as early as 1845 in the popular treatise of the utopian socialist publicist, Alphonse Toussenel, *Les Juifs, rois de l'époque, histoire de la féodalité financière*, but carried to new heights by the chief theoretician and spokesman for late nineteenth-century anti-semitism, Edouard Drumont.

But in addition to this economic critique, which was common to all western and central European anti-semitic movements, French anti-semitism assumed a political dimension as well. As Birnbaum, Sternhell and Winock have illustrated, anti-semitism emerged as the principal weapon in the assault against liberalism and the republican state. Thus, according to Birnbaum, the Jewish aspect of the Dreyfus affair was not a secondary issue; nor was it separable from the larger issue at stake: the question of whether the government would uphold the principle of individual justice, even if that meant besmirching the honour of the army, long a bastion of conservative, aristocratic and Catholic values. Rather, according to Birnbaum, it was precisely because a Jew, Alfred Dreyfus, had penetrated the highest echelons of the army command that the attacks against him swiftly escalated into a full-fledged assault against the Republic itself. Thus, as Birnbaum suggests, the Jewish question came to epitomize the values the Republic stood for: the secular state; the equality of all citizens before the law, irrespective of religious or ethnic background; and the promise of careers open to talent rather than birth. In the twentieth century this coalescence of anti-semitism and anti-republicanism resurfaced in the vitriolic campaigns waged against the nation's two Jewish prime ministers – Léon Blum, who served as premier under the Third Republic (4 June 1936 to 21 June 1937, and 13 March 1938 to 9 April 1938) and Pierre Mendès France, who served under the Fourth Republic (18 June 1954 to 2 February 1955). While not all the above-mentioned scholars would go as far as Birnbaum in melding anti-semitism to anti-republicanism, they nevertheless would agree that Jews, especially during the Third Republic, became potent symbols of those movements that threatened social and political change: economic and political liberalism, and, in the twentieth century, socialism and communism as well. Thus, according to these historians, it was no accident that the Vichy regime, in its campaign to destroy the republican legacy of the Revolution of 1789, moved swiftly to dismantle Jewish emancipation.

In addition to the question of the centrality of anti-semitism, the second major debate that has informed recent historiography of French anti-semitism is the issue of continuity. For some scholars, most notably Winock and Sternhell, the essential features of anti-semitism and the social and political conditions that gave rise to this prejudice were fixed during the Dreyfus affair, and all subsequent expressions of anti-semitism were merely repetitions of this basic paradigm – 'the Dreyfus affairs', as Winock calls them. Thus, with reference to the 1930s, Winock declares, 'everything happened as if all the conditions of another Dreyfus affair were reunited'. Similarly, according to Sternhell, 'the anti-Semitic movement between the wars added nothing original to the themes of its late nineteenth-century forerunner. In the course of that half-century, neither the fundamental problems nor the function of anti-Semitism changed significantly'. And, finally, Michael Marrus has even argued that there was scant difference between the anti-semitism of the late Third Republic and that implemented by Vichy, since the latter 'drew directly upon the experience of the 1930s, notably the last two years of Republican government under [Edouard] Daladier'. Vichy's innovations in anti-Jewish policy began, Marrus argues, only 'in the summer of 1942, when the Nazis' deportation programme thrust new dilemmas upon the French government and the police'.[3]

By contrast, Birnbaum and Stephen Schuker argue that anti-semitism in the 1930s and under Vichy reflected significantly different concerns than its nineteenth-century antecedent. In his book, *Anti-Semitism in France*, Birnbaum argues that nineteenth-century anti-semitism was primarily economic, focusing its attacks primarily on the Rothschilds, while anti-semitism in the twentieth century was primarily political, targeting Jews as the pre-eminent symbols of the secular republic, a theme that culminated in the hate campaigns against Léon Blum and Pierre Mendès France. Schuker similarly argues against overemphasizing continuities in anti-semitism. As he states, 'The more closely one examines French anti-semitism in the 1930s, the more different it appears in inspiration and character from the type of Jew-hatred that had marked public life in France during the late 19th century.' Like Birnbaum, Schuker stresses that nineteenth-century anti-semitism was based primarily on the theme of the Jew as capitalist exploiter, a theme he claims had no basis in social reality since the majority of Jews were not well-to-do. With regard to the 1930s, however, Schuker sees the major theme of anti-semitism – the identification of Jews with the left – as reflecting social reality, since he believes most Jews were in fact adherents of left-wing parties.[4]

The aim of this essay is therefore to re-examine these two questions – the centrality of anti-semitism and the issue of continuity – in light of new evidence regarding the interwar period, and especially the 1930s. As we will show, anti-semitism during this period was by no means peripheral to the larger themes of French history. Rather, it was deeply embedded in the social, political and economic crises of this era – the impact of the Depression; the fervent desire for appeasement; and the growing political polarization between the left and right, which exploded at the time of the Popular Front's electoral victory in 1936. If anti-semitism is perceived not as an isolated intellectual current, but rather as an integral element of a broad matrix of political, social and economic forces, it becomes clear that its reach extended well beyond the ranks of the radical right, hitherto the principal focus of scholarly attention. Moreover, while admitting the remarkable continuity of anti-semitic themes and even personnel between the Dreyfus affair era and the 1930s (indeed, many leading anti-semitic spokesmen of the interwar years, such as Charles Maurras and Léon Daudet, launched their careers during the Dreyfus affair), there is nevertheless a danger in reducing all manifestations of twentieth-century anti-semitism to a series of 'Dreyfus affairs'. To do so is to deny the specific function of anti-semitism at a particular point in time. While certain anti-semitic themes in the 1930s undoubtedly had their roots in the nineteenth century – especially the complaints of Jewish economic domination and the link between Jews and the allegedly corrupt republic – others, such as the charge of Jewish war-mongering, or the identification of Jews with bolshevism, were quite specific to the 1930s. Moreover, an overemphasis on continuity fosters the view that the history of anti-semitism should be studied primarily as the history of ideas. While this approach can be quite fruitful, it nevertheless neglects the socio-economic and political functions of anti-semitism. Finally, an over-emphasis on continuity, especially between the Third Republic and the Vichy era, masks the degree to which Vichy anti-semitism constituted a rupture with the past. Never before in modern French history had any regime, whether royalist, Bonapartist or republican, repudiated Jewish emancipa-tion, which had been passed into law by the National Assembly in 1791. Hence, an examination of the continuities and discontinuities between anti-semitism during the Third Republic and the Vichy period reveals what happens when a popular prejudice is institutionalized as the ideology of the state, a transformation for which no French Hitler was required.

Since the Dreyfus affair has served as the paradigm against which all subsequent anti-semitic movements in France have been compared, it is useful to review briefly the way in which the Affair catalysed anti-semitism into a modern mass movement. In ideological terms the affair, which exploded on the French scene in late 1897 and 1898, as the army's case against Captain Alfred Dreyfus, who had been convicted of treason in 1894, began to unravel, added little new to the existing arsenal of anti-semitic rhetoric. Nearly every theme of modern anti-semitism – the Jew as capitalist exploiter; the Jew as enemy of the Catholic Church; the Jew as corrupter of parliament; the Jew as symbol of the craven materialism of modern urban life; and the Jew as responsible for France's decline since its humiliating defeat at Sedan in 1870 – had already been articulated in the 1880s and early 1890s. Nevertheless, the affair did much to reinforce the themes already introduced by anti-semitic theoreticians, and especially Edouard Drumont, whose 1886 treatise, *La France juive*, achieved overnight success. In partic-ular, anti-semites pointed to Dreyfus's alleged treason as proof that Jews, no matter how assimilated, could never be truly French. In the words of Jules Soury, mentor to the nationalist leader, Maurice Barrès, 'But they [the Dreyfusards] are right, because a Jew is never a traitor, he is not of our nation, how can he betray it?'[5] Moreover, the fact that the republican government ultimately rallied to Dreyfus's defence merely confirmed for anti-semites that the real power behind the state was not the democratically elected parliament, but a secret cabal, the Jewish–Protestant–Masonic syndi-cate, whose aim was to use the Rothschild fortune to conquer the world.

But while the Dreyfus affair introduced few new themes, it nevertheless was of immense significance with respect to the political mobilization of anti-semitism. In sociological terms the affair crystallized an alliance between two erstwhile political enemies – traditional conservative élites – the old aristocracy and supporters of the Church – and the lower middle classes – small shopkeepers, artisans, white-collar workers and some professionals.

Illustration 7.1 Anti-Dreyfus propaganda. From a hand-coloured lithograph of 1900 by V. Lenepveu in *Freak Show (Musée des horreurs)* this is No. 6, *The Traitor*. Alfred Dreyfus is represented as the mythological monster, the Hydra, symbolizing a many-headed evil that regenerates itself and is difficult to eliminate. (Courtesy of Bibliothèque nationale de France.)

Although these groups had stood on opposite sides of the barricades for most of the nineteenth century, during the 1880s and 1890s they increasingly found themselves united in opposition to the existing republican regime. The lower middle classes had become disenchanted with liberalism, and especially liberalism's promotion of economic modernization. For these social classes, the spread of industrialization and capitalism – symbolized above all by the department store – threatened their traditional livelihoods and signaled the onset of what Drumont referred to in 1899 as *La Fin d'un monde*. Since Jews as a group had clearly benefited from those economic processes so many others perceived as threatening, it was only a short leap for many to conclude that they had instigated those trends as well. Thus, for those social classes who perceived modernity as a threat, anti-semitism, with its populist anti-capitalist message, offered an attractive alternative to liberalism. It also offered an alternative to the nascent socialist threat, since what these social classes wanted was not the destruction of private property, but rather its protection against the ravages of Jewish 'financial feudalism', that is, unrestricted capitalism.

For conservatives, who primarily represented the remnants of the old aristocracy and supporters of the Catholic Church, anti-semitism became attractive for different reasons. In ideological terms conservatives had traditionally despised Jews, since Jews were identified with the French Revolution and the demise of the *ancien régime*, upon which their traditional privileges had been based. Moreover, these groups shared the lower middle classes' disdain of capitalism, industrialization and modernity in general, which they believed had ushered in the age of Mammon and the degeneracy of modern urban life. Above all, they resented the fact that capitalism had given rise to a new social class – the bourgeoisie, symbolized especially by the Jews – whose power and prestige now rivalled their own. And finally, in political terms, anti-semitism provided traditional élites with a means of appealing to the masses, enabling them to remain politically viable in an age of universal male suffrage. Hence, anti-semitism served as the perfect 'liaison agent' between conservatives and the anti-capitalist lower middle classes, despite the long-standing rift that had divided these groups prior to 1870.[6]

This alliance became the cornerstone of what historians have called the new right, which erupted on the French political scene with full force at the time of the Dreyfus affair. In contrast to traditional conservatism, the new right embraced mass politics and advocated a chauvinistic brand of nationalism – integral nationalism – which extolled violence, called for the overthrow of the existing parliamentary regime, and proposed the creation of a new social order based on Christian values, a hierarchical social order, and the restoration of authoritarian, and perhaps even monarchical, government. Jews and other *métèques*, or foreigners, would either be expelled or relegated to inferior social status, and the twin villains of modern society – capitalism and socialism – would be sharply restricted in favour of a third economic alternative, corporatism, which would preserve small-scale private property and would encourage workers and owners to negotiate amicably rather than engage in class conflict.

Despite the backward-looking nature of this vision, the political tactics embraced by the new right – the use of the mass-circulation press, street rallies and parades, and violent street action – were entirely modern, and in many respects prefigured trends that would become commonplace with the advent of fascism and Nazism in the twentieth century. Not only did the affair inject new energy into existing nationalist leagues, such as Paul Déroulède's Ligue de Patriotes, which numbered some 600 000 in 1899, but it spawned new and far more radical leagues, such as Jules Guérin's Ligue Antisémite Française, which counted some 11 000 members in mid-1898 and engaged in direct street action. Partly as a result of the proliferation of these leagues, anti-semitic violence, which had remained relatively subdued since the revolution of 1848, erupted anew. According to Stephen Wilson, anti-semitic riots or disruptions broke out in nearly 70 different localities in metropolitan France in January and February of 1898, and Algeria became the scene of even more virulent anti-semitic attacks. Finally, this new aggressive anti-semitism surfaced even in parliament. In January 1898 158 deputies voted for a bill calling for the exclusion of all Jews from public employment who could not prove three generations of forebears born in France, and in February of that year 198 deputies – nearly one-third of the chamber – supported a move to interpellate the government regarding 'What measures it intended to take to end the predominance of Jews in the various branches of the administration?' In 1899 another bill was introduced calling for the repeal of the Crémieux decree, which had granted emancipation to the Jews of Algeria in 1870.[7] Although none of these measures was implemented at the time, they would all reappear in the anti-semitic programme of the Vichy regime.

After the government of René Waldeck-Rousseau granted Dreyfus a pardon in 1899, anti-semitism seemed to be on the decline. To be sure, it continued to play an important role in extreme right-wing circles, and especially among adherents of the royalist league, the Action Française, which emerged from the Dreyfus affair as the foremost proponent of integral nationalism. At the same time, anti-semitism continued to be embraced by some dissident factions of the socialist movement, although the majority of socialists followed Jean Jaurès in breaking with anti-semitism at the time of the affair, having come to the realization that attacks on Jewish capitalism did nothing to weaken the capitalist system as a whole. Nevertheless, most Jewish leaders by 1914 shared the view of *Les Archives israélites* that 'The heroic period of anti-semitism is definitely over.'[8] Most significantly, France's experience in the First World War, during which thousands of Jews, immigrant and native, fought and died for their country, seemed to signal a major shift in the overcoming of anti-semitic prejudice. In 1917 Barrès published *Les Diverses familles spirituelles de la France*, in which he argued that Jewish valour during the war qualified Jews to be considered one of the nation's 'diverse spiritual families', on a par with Bretons, Provençals, or Alsatians. That Barrès, one of the foremost exponents of anti-semitism during the Dreyfus affair, had repudiated his former views was heralded by Jewish leaders as a sign that *union sacrée*, the setting aside of internal divisions for the sake of national unity, would endure into the post-war era.

During the 1920s these expectations seemed to be borne out. Despite the fact that the Jewish community grew dramatically in size, increasing from 150000 in 1919 to 200000 in 1930, primarily as a result of immigration, anti-semitism nevertheless remained subdued. France desperately needed foreign workers in the 1920s to compensate for the devastating loss of 1.4 million men in the First World War, and the government, with the encouragement of big business, actively recruited foreign workers. As a result of these liberal immigration policies, France's immigrant population grew to 2.7 million by 1931, or about 7 per cent of the total. To be sure, as Ralph Schor has illustrated, there was a dramatic upsurge in xenophobia during these years, which was accompanied by repeated attempts by the radical right to impose limits on immigration and naturalization. Nevertheless, these efforts were counteracted by the pressing need for foreign labour, and in 1927 the parliament even passed an extremely liberal naturalization bill, which reduced residency requirements from 10 to 3 years. Moreover, to the extent that xenophobia surfaced, Jews were not singled out. According to Richard Millman, most right-wing leagues in the 1920s, with the notable exception of the Action Française, endeavoured to reach out to native Jews, particularly those who had served in the war, despite their visceral xenophobia. Thus, the journal *Gringoire*, which only a few years later would become one of the most virulently anti-semitic publications, could comment in 1931 that 'There are no more anti-Dreyfusards . . . . They're either dead, or they've converted.'[9]

In the 1930s, however, this climate of tolerance swiftly gave way to a wave of anti-semitism, which may even have surpassed that which had surfaced during the Dreyfus affair. At first glance this anti-semitism appeared merely to be a replay of those earlier events. On the occasion of Dreyfus's death in 1935, the well-known critic Julien Benda, who also happened to be a Jew, compared the political tensions of his day to the virtual civil war that had raged at the time of the affair. As Benda declared in the Jewish paper, *L'Univers israélite*, 'The attitude of the reactionary forces has resurrected in a striking fashion that of our adversaries of 40 years ago . . . . Alfred Dreyfus belongs to the martyrology of Israel.'[10]

Despite these apparent similarities, a closer look at the anti-semitism that erupted during the 1930s reveals that this movement was motivated by somewhat different concerns. The wave of anti-semitism that took place during this period must be seen against the backdrop of the specific events of the 1930s – the impact of the Great Depression and the central-European refugee crisis; the escalating political polarization between left and right at home, which mirrored broader international tensions between fascism and Nazism on the one hand and bolshevism on the other; and the mounting threat of war. Thus, notwithstanding many similarities between the anti-semitic movements of these two eras, the anti-semitism of the 1930s was in many respects unique, and deserves to be analysed within its own political context. Indeed, such an understanding is essential if we are to appreciate the extent to which it paved the way for Vichy's anti-semitic programme.

While historians have focused on the political dimensions of anti-semitism in the 1930s, there can be no doubt that the Great Depression played a critical role in shaping debates over the Jewish question. Although the Depression hit France late, with the first signs of economic downturn appearing only in 1930, it nevertheless hit hard, and by 1935 nearly 1 million people were out of work. To be sure, the Depression gave rise not only to anti-semitism but to a general wave of xenophobia: as early as 1932, in response to pressure from labour unions, parliament enacted legislation restricting the number of foreigners who could work as wage labourers in a wide range of occupations. Moreover, although the radical right was most vociferous in demanding the elimination of foreign workers, many liberals and socialists shared the view that the best remedy for the Depression was to reduce the number of foreigners, although the socialists opposed admin-istrative efforts in 1934–5 to repatriate foreign workers by force.

Yet it was primarily in the urban middle-class professions – commerce, artisanry, and the liberal professions, especially law and medicine – that the anti-semitic dimension of this campaign surfaced most sharply. Unlike the vast majority of immigrants in France, who were manual labourers, Jews tended to concentrate in these middle-class professions, and the fact that the Depression coincided with an influx of approximately 25 000 Jewish refu-gees from Nazi Germany in 1933 ignited a sharp anti-semitic backlash. Within weeks after the arrival of the first wave of refugees, French business associations and local chambers of commerce, especially in Paris and in Alsace and Lorraine, began to complain bitterly of refugee competition. As the Metz chamber of commerce declared, these 'foreign competitors, highly undesirable, have become a veritable plague for honest French merchants'. Similarly, in 1934 the president of the Alsatian chamber of artisan trades condemned as 'revolting', the 'insouciance with which a large number of foreigners have engaged in a competitive struggle, without mercy and often without loyalty, against their French competitors'. It was up to the govern-ment, he proclaimed, to prevent the devastation of French production 'by an army of foreigners who have come to France with business concepts and commercial values that are incompatible with the traditions of French artisanry'. Fearful of alienating its middle-class constituencies, the central government in Paris caved in to these protectionist demands: in 1935 Pierre Laval's government imposed quotas – generally 10 per cent – on the number of foreigners allowed to practise artisanry, and in mid-1938 Edouard Dala-dier's government similarly restricted the number of foreigners allowed to practise commerce. As the then minister of the interior, Albert Sarraut, explained, such harsh sanctions were necessary 'to protect French commerce, which is ever more invaded by foreign elements'.

No less insistent in their demands to limit the threat of foreign competition were those in the liberal professions – especially doctors and lawyers. In early 1935 medical students throughout the country staged a strike to protest against 'unfair competition' from foreign students, many of whom were central- and east-European Jews. So blatantly anti-semitic were these demonstrations that the Radical paper, *L'Oeuvre*, noted that 'a pogrom-like atmosphere' prevailed, while *L'Ere nouvelle*, another Radical paper, reported that '[d]octors and [medical] students of Jewish origin have been cruelly beaten and molested'. At the same time, national syndicates of doctors and lawyers lobbied relentlessly to reinforce already stringent legislation restricting the numbers of foreigners allowed to practise those professions. In response, laws were passed in 1934 and 1935 barring even naturalized immigrants from taking up either of these professions for 5 to 10 years following their naturalization. Keenly aware of the prevailing atmosphere, the director of the French Committee for the Protection of Persecuted Jewish Intellectuals deemed it 'dangerous to welcome too many German Jews in France'. To do so, he declared, 'would provoke a backlash of jealousy among unemployed French intellectuals'.[11]

These middle-class protectionist campaigns did much to inculcate popular anti-semitism and to orient public policy in an increasingly anti-semitic direction. Although extreme right-wing groups since the early 1930s had been demanding the imposition of a *statut des juifs*, or Jewish statute, to curb naturalizations and Jewish occupational behaviour, such demands had initially garnered little popular support. By the end of the decade, however, this situation changed dramatically, in part because of widespread sympathy for these middle-class professional associations. In 1938 several prominent conservatives, including Louis Marin, Fernand Laurent and Robert Schuman, sponsored legislation demanding the revision of all naturalizations granted either since 1933, the year the refugees began to arrive, 1927, the year the liberal naturalization law was passed, or even 1919. Such measures were necessary, they explained, since 'recently naturalized citizens ... in commerce in addition to certain liberal professions, and especially in medicine, engage in inadmissible competition with French citizens'.[12]

Conservatives and even some Radicals also began to demand the imposition of a *numerus clausus*, or quota, to limit the number of Jews practising a wide range of middle-class professions. In 1938 Joseph Rossé, an influential Catholic autonomist deputy from the Upper Rhine, claimed that Jews had taken over the region's cultural and economic life, and as proof he alleged that the proportion of Jewish lawyers in the Alsatian bar had risen from 10 to 30 per cent since 1918. As a result of 'this colossal increase', Rossé argued, 'many Christian lawyers have been pushed to the brink of starvation, so they revolt and anti-semitism begins to take hold'. Rossé therefore proposed the imposition of a quota on the number of Jews, immigrant and native alike, allowed to work in middle-class professions. More striking is the fact that an organ of Radical opinion, *L'Ere nouvelle*, also recommended the imposition of a *numerus clausus* on foreign Jews allowed to work in the liberal professions. In a November 1938 editorial the paper's editors explained that such a measure was necessary since they had been deluged with letters 'from doctors from large cities or the Paris suburbs who have provided us with stupefying statistics regarding the proportion of Jewish doctors and foreign Jewish doctors in the medical corps of the large urban centres'.

While this socio-economic critique of Jewish economic activities thus constituted one major strand of anti-semitism in the 1930s, no less important were two political themes: the identification of Jews with the far left, a theme that emerged with particular virulence in the spring of 1936 with the election of the Popular Front, led by the socialist prime minister Léon Blum; and the theme of Jewish war-mongering, which reached fever pitch in the autumn of 1938 at the time of the Munich crisis. To be sure, the identification of Jews with the far left did not begin in 1936. As early as 1933 right-wing groups began to excoriate the refugees from Germany as bolshevik agents sent by Hitler to foment revolutionary discord in France. Thus, according to Gaëtan Sanvoisin, a journalist for the extreme right-wing paper *Le Figaro* (owned by the perfume magnate François Coty), the participation of many refugees in the left-wing demonstrations of 12 February 1934, which had been staged as a counter-protest against the massive right-wing demonstrations of 6 February linked to the Stavisky affair,* demonstrated that 'Hitler has sent us some 50,000 German Jews who are, for the most part, extremely dangerous revolutionaries.' The sole means of dealing with these 'compatriots of Léon Blum', Sanvoisin insisted, was to throw them into concentration camps. Moreover, when a coalition of right- and left-wing parliamentarians had sought to secure an academic chair for Albert Einstein in late 1933, Coty himself objected, claiming that these efforts would 'install communism at the Collège de France'. And in 1935, at the time of the medical students' protests, the Reverend Joseph Bonsirven, despite his self-proclaimed philosemitism,†

---

* In late 1933 the press revealed that a well-known swindler, Serge Stavisky, an east-European Jew, had been floating fraudulent Bayonne municipal bonds with the knowledge and backing of prominent members of parliament and the administration. When Stavisky committed suicide in January, the Chautemps government resigned and a new cabinet led by the Radical politician Edouard Daladier came to power. On 6 February, following Daladier's dismissal of the Paris prefect of police, Jean Chiappe, a hero of the political right, the right-wing leagues decided the moment was ripe to stage a massive demonstration against the detested Republic. When the demonstrators marched on the chamber of deputies, the police returned gunfire, killing 15 and seriously wounding 200. In an effort to quell these tensions the Daladier cabinet resigned, and a new national unity government was created on 9 February under the premiership of the centrist politician Gaston Doumergue.

† Philosemitism was a position adopted by some Catholic leaders to argue against anti-semitism. Generally, however, this attitude was riddled with ambivalence, since these Catholic spokesmen were, for the most part, extremely hostile to the political left, and they tended to identify immigrant Jews, and after Blum's election native Jews as well, with left-wing movements.

nevertheless argued that it was time to curb the number of Jewish medical students. According to Bonsirven, 'honest and conscientious' Jews, by whom he meant native Jews, would not be harmed by this campaign; rather these protests were aimed exclusively at 'the parvenus[,] ... the Polish, Romanian, Russian, [or] German Jews, who shamelessly indulge in communist propaganda and display a clear intention to take over every available job in France'.[13]

This brand of anti-semitism, however, became significantly more widespread in the spring of 1936 with the election of the Popular Front government, which sharply polarized French political life. One need not agree with Stephen Schuker or Eugen Weber, who suggest that anti-semitism was a legitimate response to specific policies or ideas advocated by Léon Blum, to concur with their view that Blum's coming to power generated a huge anti-semitic backlash. Never before in French history had any prime minister been subjected to such a vitriolic hate campaign, and extreme forms of anti-semitism, previously limited to the far right, now began to penetrate into conservative and even Radical and socialist circles. To many in France, the so-called 'Jewish invasion' now seemed to have taken over the government itself, and these claims acquired a particular saliency in light of charges that Blum had stacked his cabinet and administration with Jewish appointments. Although there were only four Jews besides himself in his first cabinet (Cécile Léon Brunschvicg, Marx Dormoy, Jules Moch and Jean Zay, who was half-Jewish) and four in his second (Dormoy, Moch, Zay and Pierre Mendès France), even Blum's supporters admitted that Jews had been named to a large number of lower-level administrative posts. As a result, the philosemitic journal, *La Juste parole*, reported that French youth felt they had been 'eliminated from positions for the benefit of Jews who have only just become French and scarcely even know how to speak our language'.[14] Moreover, the fact that Blum's election coincided with the onset of a massive wave of labour unrest as well as the beginning of the Spanish civil war instilled among conservatives a sense of being under siege. Ultimately, the question of whether Blum was targeted primarily as a Jew or a socialist is irrelevant, since for many on the right these identities had become one and the same. As Louis-Ferdinand Céline declared in his scatological anti-semitic treatise, *Bagatelles pour un massacre*, 'for me Jews and communists are synonymous'.[15]

Not surprisingly, the most violent attacks on Blum came from the extreme right. Shortly after the election of 1936 *L'Action française*, the newspaper of the league, advocated 'that Blum be guillotined', a statement that echoed Maurras's attacks against Blum the previous year, in which he had declared, 'That's a man to be shot, but in the back.' Another leading exponent of extreme right-wing anti-semitism, Louis Darquier de Pellepoix, who had just been elected to the Paris municipal council and who would serve as Vichy's second commissioner general for Jewish affairs from 1942 to 1944, similarly threatened to kill Blum, while declaring that 'Hitler was right to kick the

Jews the hell out.'[16] Even the chief rabbi received threats regarding Blum, as if the Jewish community were somehow responsible for the turn of events. In one of these letters, written during the labour strife that erupted after the Popular Front election, an anonymous group of business leaders, who claimed to represent all religious groups, called on the chief rabbi to issue a public denunciation of Blum, whom they referred to as 'a sick sadist'. While claiming that they 'do not pretend to hold Jews in general responsible for this atrocious situation', they nevertheless issued an ominous warning: 'Beware that the crimes of Léon Blum and his band not redound upon your entire race.' Although such a public denunciation was never forthcoming, the Jewish community did apparently intervene with Blum privately to dissuade him from assuming office. According to André Blumel, one of Blum's closest advisers, the chief rabbi even offered the newly elected prime minister a lifetime pension equivalent to his salary as head of government if he would agree to step down.[17]

But for the French Jewish community, the most disquieting aspect of this hate campaign against Blum was the way in which it normalized anti-semitism as an element of political discourse. Anti-semitism now surfaced not only in the Paris municipal council, which after Darquier's election in 1935 became a forum for the most extreme anti-semitic views, but in parliament itself, which since the Dreyfus affair had been relatively immune to rhetorical outbursts of anti-semitism. As early as 1934 Xavier Vallat, the conservative deputy of the Ardèche and a prominent member of the right-wing league the Croix de Feu, who would later serve as Vichy's first commissioner general for Jewish affairs, excoriated Blum on the floor of the chamber of deputies as representing 'the voice of Israel'. When a Jewish war veteran complained privately to Vallat that Léon Blum did not speak for all French Jews, Vallat responded that while it was perhaps true that all Jews were not bolsheviks, it was nevertheless the case that

> the immense majority of your coreligionists are found enlisted in the ranks of the international and revolutionary army for which they increasingly furnish the most frightening leaders. Léon Blum personifies them to such a degree that he's currently turning members of his own group into anti-semites. That man isn't French; his thought isn't French.

After the Popular Front victory, Vallat carried this theme even further. In June 1936, just as Blum was assuming office, Vallat explained to his colleagues in the chamber of deputies why he had voted against Blum's cabinet. Turning directly to Blum, Vallat declared: 'There's another reason that prevents me from voting in favour of the ministry of M. Blum: that's M. Blum himself. Your ascendance to power is incontestably a historic date. For the first time this old Gallo-Roman country will be governed by a Jew.' When the president of the chamber, Radical Party leader Edouard Herriot, demanded a retraction, denouncing Vallat's language as 'inadmissible in a

French tribune', Vallat not only refused, but he went on to declare that Jews could never be truly French:

> I have no intention of forgetting the friendship that binds me to my Jewish comrades in arms. Nor have I any intention of denying to members of the Jewish race the right to acclimatize here, just like everyone else who has come here to be naturalized. Nevertheless, I must say ... out loud what everyone else is thinking to themselves – that in order to govern this peasant nation that is France, it is preferable to have someone whose origins, no matter how modest, disappear into the bowels of our soil, rather than a subtle talmudist.

While the left of the chamber vehemently protested at Vallat's remarks, silence prevailed elsewhere, suggesting that Vallat's assertion of speaking for the majority was indeed correct.[18]

Vallat's views did in fact mirror those of a large sector of conservative opinion, and even conservative groups that had previously shied away from anti-semitism, such as the Croix de Feu, the largest right-wing league in the 1930s, increasingly embraced it after the Popular Front victory. Prior to 1936 Colonel François de La Rocque, the league's leader, tolerated anti-semitism only in so far as it focused exclusively on foreign Jews, but he repeatedly reassured native Jews, especially those who had served in the army, that they had a secure place in his movement, and indeed, the Croix de Feu counted a sizeable Jewish membership and several of La Roque's major benefactors were Jewish. Beginning in 1936, however, La Rocque's position became more ambivalent, despite his repeated denials of anti-semitism and his frequent condemnations of the extreme anti-semitism advocated by the Algerian and Alsatian branches of the movement, which failed to distinguish between native and foreign Jews. Thus, at a Croix de Feu meeting in April 1936, La Rocque firmly denounced anti-semitism and declared that 'if a wave of anti-semitism were to break out, our Jewish comrades would unjustly become the victims of it. That would be fratricide, and you'd find me there trying to stop to it.' But he then proceeded to blame Blum himself for igniting the current wave of anti-semitism in France. Moreover, as head of the Parti Social Français (PSF), the political party that supplanted the Croix de Feu after the Popular Front dissolved the right-wing leagues in 1936, La Rocque frequently defined French patriotism as Christian in character, a trend that could not have pleased the party's Jewish membership. At the same time, La Rocque's distinctions between native and foreign Jews also began to break down. In a 1939 interview La Rocque excused the anti-semitism of the Alsatian and Algerian branches of the PSF by claiming that these regions had been inundated by an 'uncontrolled, larva-like invasion' 'of recently immigrated, non-assimilated, Jewish elements, who have voluntarily made themselves foreign to the national community'. But when asked to define precisely what he meant by 'foreign', La Rocque declared, 'We consider as foreigners everyone who, by their attitude, their sentiments and their conduct, hold themselves aloof from the nation, even if they've acquired French citizenship.' By labeling as foreign recently naturalized citizens, as well as anyone whose political views differed from his own, La Rocque's position had become indistinguishable from that of Maurras, who had railed against Blum as 'that naturalized German Jew or son of someone naturalized' despite the fact that Blum was a native-born Jew, whose parents and grandparents had been born in France.[19]

Catholic opinion, too, became increasingly anti-semitic in the aftermath of the Popular Front victory. Although many scholars have argued that Catholic attitudes towards Jews in the 1930s were overwhelmingly sympathetic, in sharp contrast to the extreme Catholic anti-semitism of the Dreyfus affair era, this view requires significant modification. While there were indeed Catholic leaders who spoke out strongly against anti-semitism throughout the 1930s, such as Cardinal Jean Verdier, archbishop of Paris, the vast majority of Catholic spokesmen expressed deeply ambivalent views, which became even more so once Blum came to power. Although this anti-semitism was sometimes expressed overtly, as when Cardinal Alfred Baudrillart, Rector of the Catholic Institute of Paris, accused 'Jewish moscovites' of having ignited the bloody civil war in Spain, it ironically surfaced more frequently in statements intended to rebut anti-semitism. The most notable example of such ambivalence is the explanation offered in 1937 by the prominent Catholic writer and publicist François Mauriac as to why he had joined the patronage committee of the philosemitic journal, *La Juste parole*. Although Mauriac criticized anti-semitism as a 'sin against charity', he nevertheless insisted that Jews themselves were largely responsible for anti-semitism. As he declared:

> The Jews cannot perpetuate themselves, marry amongst themselves, jealously isolate themselves from Christians, without creating a state of defence and hostility.
>
> They cannot monopolize international finance without making others feel they are being dominated by them. They cannot sprout up wherever one of their own has been successful (Minister Blum), without evoking hatred because they themselves have indulged in [anti-Christian] reprisals . . . .
>
> In conclusion, I associate with the fight against anti-semitism, but I believe it ultimately depends on the Jews themselves to render themselves less violent.[20]

Most surprisingly, this anti-semitism directed against Blum surfaced even among left-wing circles. Although several historians, most notably Ralph Schor and Eugen Weber, have argued that the anti-semitism of the left in the 1930s was as virulent as that of the right, this claim is vastly overstated. Despite some sporadic outbursts of anti-semitism by communist leaders, especially after the signing of the Nazi–Soviet non-aggression pact in August 1939, which drove yet another wedge between French socialists and communists, the Communist Party for most of the decade was relatively immune to anti-semitism. Rather, left-wing hostility towards Blum, which found an expression in anti-semitism, was principally the domain of the neo-socialists, a faction that had broken with the Socialist Party in 1933 over demands to reorient the party more towards nationalism, authoritarianism and a more middle-class social base. As early as 1933 Marcel Déat, the principal leader of this group, who after the French defeat of 1940 became a Nazi collaborator, had decried Blum's 'subtle byzantinism' and his 'thoroughly oriental passivity', and in a 1934 interview Déat went even further in expressing his anti-semitic views. In response to a query regarding the role of anti-semitism in the neo-socialist movement, Déat declared:

> We aren't anti-semites, but we've noticed the detrimental effects of Jewish solidarity on the nation and even on the party of unified socialism. Blum's entire escort is composed of Jews. This poses a danger even in a party of the avant-garde.[21]

The third theme of the anti-semitic revival of the 1930s was the charge of Jewish war-mongering, a theme that gained widespread currency in 1938 and 1939 as Nazi aggression brought Europe to the brink of war. The popular tendency to blame the deteriorating international situation not on Hitler but on his victims, the Jews and the communists and socialists, was due to the confluence of two events. First, the influx of Jewish refugees, which had tapered off significantly in 1936–7, reached new heights in the late 1930s. By 1939 the number of Jewish refugees in France neared 60000 as a result of the Nazi incursions into Austria and Czechoslovakia, as well as Hitler's fierce anti-Jewish crackdown at home, which climaxed with the anti-Jewish pogroms of November 1938, commonly known as Kristallnacht. Although this war-mongering theme had surfaced in several right-wing works of the early 1930s, such as Jean and Jérôme Tharaud's popular essay, *Quand Israël n'est plus roi*, which charged that Jewish refugees felt no qualms about 'setting Europe on fire in order to appease Israel',[22] it was only after 1936, when the Germans remilitarized the Rhineland, and especially in 1938 and 1939, that this view acquired widespread currency. As Arthur Koestler noted in his memoirs, the anti-Nazi opinions of the refugees 'condemned us to the always unpopular, shrill-voiced part of Cassandras. Nobody likes people who run about the streets yelling "Get ready, get ready, the day of wrath is at hand." Least of all when they yell in a foreign accent'.[23]

Yet the worsening international situation was not the only factor that encouraged charges of Jewish war-mongering. These accusations were also fuelled by the Popular Front victory and the growing tendency to identify Jews with the forces of the far left. As a result of the Popular Front victory, even many moderates became convinced that the extreme left constituted a far greater threat than the extreme right, a fear summed up by the popular slogan, 'Better Hitler than Blum'. Moreover, many moderates also came to share the extreme right-wing view that a major by-product of war would be social revolution at home, which in turn would lead to communist, and *ipso facto*, Jewish hegemony. As the fiercely anti-Nazi deputy and publicist Henri de Kérillis noted, this brand of pacifism, which perceived the enemy within – the Jews and the communists – as a far greater threat than the enemy without did much to encourage a defeatist mentality on the eve of the war, and indeed, the Nazi propaganda machine poured significant sums of money into finding French agents to propagate such views. After 1940 this tendency to blame the outbreak of war on Jews and communists was swiftly transmuted into the accusation that they were responsible for the defeat as well, a view that suggested these groups deserved the harsh punishments meted out to them by the Vichy regime.

It was in the immediate aftermath of the Nazi remilitarization of the Rhineland in 1936 that the theme of Jewish war-mongering began to receive considerable attention. Already at that time, a British embassy official in Paris reported that

> In political circles of [the] centre and right and even in the press, allusion is being made to a Jewish conspiracy to drag the country into a war at the behest of Moscow, and I should not be surprised if there were to be an increase of anti-Jewish agitation within the next few days.

This same official also noted that La Rocque had recently delivered a speech in which he had declared that 'France must not allow herself to be rushed into war with Germany by an oligarchy of Jewish financiers or by the partisans of the Soviet alliance.' This charge also constituted the central theme of Céline's murderous anti-semitic treatise, *Bagatelles pour un massacre*. According to Céline, France, following the Popular Front victory, had become 'a colony for Jewish international power', and he alleged that the Jews, in order to promote their revolutionary goals, were prepared to plunge the world into another world war, even more devastating than that of 1914–18. While such an upheaval might satisfy the thirst for revenge of 'those little Jews [who had been] kicked out of every good German job', it was not in France's interests. Indeed, Céline exclaimed, there was no 'humiliation worse than having to die for the yids'. Given a choice between Jewish and German domination, Céline affirmed that he would 'prefer the German peace any day'.[24]

As long as the threat of war remained distant, however, such views had limited support. In 1938, however, as Nazi incursions into central Europe made war seem all but inevitable, these charges reached fever pitch. At the time of the Munich crisis in September, as French troops anxiously mobilized, the extreme right and growing numbers of centrists lashed out not against the Germans but against the Jews and the political left, whom they blamed for dragging France into a war that was contrary to France's interests. According to *L'Action française*, 'The French do not want to fight

– neither for the Jews, the Russians, nor the Freemasons of Prague'; and it suggested that the sole reason Jews desired war was to re-establish their former positions of dominance over Germany and Austria. Similarly, *Je suis partout*, the mouthpiece of the young guard of the radical right, went so far as to argue that the Jews be made to pay for the mobilization.[25]

But more serious than these verbal spars was the fact that the mobilization was accompanied by widespread anti-Jewish violence on a scale not witnessed in France since the Dreyfus affair. According to reports of Jewish defence organizations, anti-Jewish attacks, targeted primarily at immigrant Jews, broke out in Paris, as well as in Rouen, Dijon, Lille, Nancy, and towns and cities throughout Alsace and Lorraine. As one Jewish defence organization noted: 'Foreigners, Jews have been molested, despoiled, and battered on the streets of Paris, accused of sometimes having shouted "Vive la guerre!" and sometimes even "Vive Hitler!"' The International League against Antisemitism (LICA) reported that Jewish shops in the Montmartre district of Paris, as well as in Strasbourg and Metz, were pillaged 'on the pretext that the Jews fled to the rear'. At the same time the fact that 15 000 foreign Jews enlisted for military service served as yet another pretext for attack. As the LICA noted, Jews were damned either way. If they enlisted, people said: 'Naturally, the Jews desire war!' And of those who might be waiting to see how events turned out before enlisting: 'Naturally, the Jews are shirking their military service!' In Dijon a particularly violent incident broke out: a crowd of 500 persons sacked and pillaged the shop of a Polish Jew named Lerner, since he had allegedly shouted 'Vive la guerre'. The crowd became so unruly that Lerner and his family had to be escorted out of town secretly by the police. Georges de la Fouchardière, a popular columnist for *L'Oeuvre*, went so far as to suggest the Lerners deserved worse than pillaging; they deserved to be hanged!

Although the war scare temporarily subsided with the signing of the Munich accords at the end of September, events of the next few weeks further enflamed the situation. In October the French foreign minister, Georges Bonnet, began secret negotiations with the Germans to conclude a bilateral security pact, but just as Bonnet was preparing to announce the successful conclusion of these negotiations, a 17-year-old illegal Jewish refugee youth, Herschel Grynszpan, shot and killed the third secretary of the German embassy in Paris, Ernst vom Rath. For the Germans, who were endeavouring to force the remainder of the German Jewish community to leave, Grynszpan's crime provided the pretext for launching the Kristallnacht pogrom of 9–10 November, which was intended to bring this campaign to a conclusion. In this assault, which constituted the most violent Nazi anti-Jewish action to date, 91 German Jews were killed, 267 synagogues burned, over 7 000 Jewish stores plundered and 35 000 Jews arrested and sent off to concentration camps. The Nazis unleashed a similar wave of terror in Austria, where an additional 20 000 Jews were arrested and some 2 000 were sent to Dachau.

Illustration 7.2 Anti-semitic policy during the German occupation and the Vichy era was far-reaching in its persecutory zeal. Here Victor Fajnzylberg, age thirty-four, is pictured with his children. Like her father, the daughter, who is over the age of six, is required to wear the Star of David. The son, under six, is exempt. Victor Fajnzylberg lost a leg fighting for France in 1940, and was decorated for his valour. He was nevertheless deported to Auschwitz on 10 February 1944. (Courtesy of Centre de documentation juive contemporaine, Paris.)

In the wake of Grynszpan's crime, which threatened to shatter forever Bonnet's dream of Franco-German *rapprochement*, charges of Jewish war-mongering reached hysterical levels. According to *L'Action française*, the administration of Edouard Daladier was to blame for having allowed France to become 'the battlefield for all the *métèques* of Europe and the entire world', and it warned that Kristallnacht serve neither 'as a pretext for us to be inundated with Jews ... nor as a pretext for war'. 'The prestige of France', Maurras declared, 'isn't threatened when one burns down a synagogue somewhere. One can burn them all. It's not our business and it has no impact whatsoever on us. No diplomatic intervention, no war for the Jews.' According to Lucien Rebatet of *Je suis partout*, all the refugees, whom he excoriated as 'a band of filthy lice vomited up by Poland', were to blame for Grynszpan's crime. 'That the Jews feel the need to settle their quarrels with the Germans, that's entirely comprehensible,' he declared. 'But that they've chosen Paris for this end, that's intolerable.'

Notwithstanding the increasingly violent tone of these attacks, these themes were not new for the radical right. What most distinguished the debate over the Jewish question in 1938 and 1939 from the debate over this issue earlier in the decade was the degree to which many moderates, including not only conservatives but even many Radicals and a few dissident socialists, began to move towards the extreme right. Calls for a radical 'cleansing' of 'the international underworld' appeared frequently in the mainstream conservative press, and many of these papers shared the view of the conservative daily, *Le Matin*, that Grynszpan was working on behalf of the 'war party', a secret cabal directed by Moscow, whose aim was to drag France into an 'apocalyptic battle'. Similarly, the centre-right paper *Le Temps*, generally considered the mouthpiece of the Quai d'Orsay, was drawn into the anti-refugee frenzy during the 1938 war scare, despite the paper's earlier sympathy for the refugee cause. After vom Rath's assassination, *Le Temps* railed against the refugees, who had 'used our territory to indulge in either the most shady sorts of political manoeuvres, or in the most criminal acts, without giving the least thought ... to ... French interests'. Unless the government immediately barred the entry of additional refugees, *Le Temps* predicted that 'xenophobic and anti-semitic movements would become widespread'.

Clerical spokesmen also expressed increasingly anti-semitic views, and many of them joined Rossé in demanding the imposition of a *numerus clausus* on all Jews, French and foreign alike. In September 1938, just prior to the Munich crisis, Léon Merklen, editor-in-chief of the principal Catholic daily, *La Croix*, reiterated the claim that Jews themselves were responsible for anti-semitism. In times of revolution and social crisis, Merklen argued, 'many Jews, out of a spirit of vengeance or revenge, side with the instigators of disorder'. Moreover, he claimed, the manifold faults of the Jews, among which he listed 'their tendency to monopolize, their habit of pushing themselves into influential posts ... , their solidarity that transcends [national] borders, ... [and] their materialist conception of life', provided 'sufficient motives for defiance and hostility against them'. Although the Church opposed Nazi-style anti-Jewish violence, Merklen nevertheless insisted that 'The Church accepts the fact that Christians need to adopt measures of defence against their [the Jews'] invasion into civil or political life' – measures such as the *numerus clausus*.

Yet it was the manifestation of these attitudes among Radical circles, and even among some socialists, that most sharply delineated the anti-semitic tendencies of the late 1930s from earlier trends. In the aftermath of the Munich crisis, Emile Roche, executive editor of the Radical daily *La République*, sternly warned the refugees not to become involved in French politics: 'France's affairs have nothing to do with you. Don't share your quarrels and hatreds with those who have welcomed you.' Moreover, it was immediately after vom Rath's assassination that *L'Ere nouvelle* issued its controversial call for a *numerus clausus*. Although the economic critique we have already examined was one of *L'Ere nouvelle*'s concerns, the paper also expressed consternation about the refugees' political proclivities, and especially their alleged Marxist sympathies. At the time of the Munich crisis, Léo-Abel Gaboriaud, one of the paper's leading editorialists, had railed against the refugees, who, he claimed, have 'Everywhere ... push[ed] the French out of all prestigious posts ... all the disciplines that have constituted their grandeur, in order to better destroy them'. To curb these dangerous excesses, Gaboriaud called on native Jews to join their Christian compatriots to stop 'the dangerous invasion of wanderers who have besieged us' and to 'advise those who sin through their excessive behaviour ... that they had better not push the citizens of this country into having to impose a numerus clausus'.

Even some voices further to the left joined the anti-refugee and anti-Jewish chorus. Among the fiercely pacifist neo-socialists, the view that Jews were dragging France into an unwanted war was especially pronounced. Adrien Marquet, who subsequently became Vichy's first minister of the interior, insisted that French soldiers not be allowed to die in a 'war for the USSR and Jewry'. Even more surprising was the fact that several mainstream socialists, motivated either by intense pacifism, hostility to Blum or even an attraction to certain aspects of Nazism and fascism, began to articulate their pacifist views in similarly anti-semitic terms. At the time of the Munich crisis the socialist deputy, Armand Chouffet, railed against his Jewish colleagues, Salomon Grumbach and Jules Moch, claiming that he had 'had enough of the Jewish dictatorship over the party .... I won't march off for the Jewish war'. Another socialist activist, Ludovic Zoretti, blamed Blum personally for the mounting war fever in the autumn. The French, he proclaimed, 'have no desire to kill millions of men, to destroy an entire civilization, solely to make life easier for 100 000 Sudeten Jews'. Even Paul Faure, editor-in-chief of the Socialist Party's paper, *Le Populaire*, and secretary-general of the Socialist Party, attributed Blum's increasingly militant stance towards Germany to his Jewish background: 'Blum would have us all killed for his Jews,' he declared.

To be sure, not everyone was swept up by this wave of anti-semitism. On the left, the majority of socialists and communists, the League for the Rights of Man and Citizen, France's principal civil-rights organization; the Catholic left; and the left wing of the Radical Party continued to denounce anti-semitism and warned that it posed a threat to the survival of liberal democracy in France. According to Albert Bayet and Léon Archimbaud, two leading spokesmen for the left wing of the Radical Party, the growing tendency to label anyone opposed to appeasement as a Jew or a communist constituted 'a harbinger of dictatorship in France'. Similarly, the newspaper *L'Oeuvre*, despite its support for Franco-German rapprochement, condemned the signing of the Franco-German non-aggression pact on 6 December, only weeks after Kristallnacht. In an article entitled 'Peace Cannot be Founded on the Pogrom', *L'Oeuvre* asked whether the German foreign office 'could really believe that Franco-German rapprochement, no matter how desirable, could be based on a French anti-semitic campaign "in alignment" with the German anti-semitic campaign'. Nor were such protests restricted to the left. Henri de Kérillis, despite his staunch anti-communism, also warned that anti-semitism was exacerbating internal divisions in France, thus playing into Nazi hands. At the same time he claimed that France's craven pursuit of appeasement regardless of the Nazi anti-semitic campaign was driving a wedge between France and her democratic allies, Great Britain and the United States. If France were to fall into the Nazi camp, Kérillis warned, anti-semitism throughout Europe would swell to unprecedented proportions. '[T]omorrow', he prophesied,

> Nazi Germany will demand that every European nation implement exceptional measures against the Jews or even their mass expulsion, their internment on some faraway continent, something akin to a colossal recommencement of the Babylonian captivity after the destruction of the Jerusalem Temple.

These voices, however, were few and far between, and there can be little doubt that anti-semitism had become widespread by the end of the decade. In 1936 the Jewish Consistory established its first self-defence organization, the Centre de Documentation et de Vigilance, to combat anti-semitism in France itself, a move it had previously resisted, even at the height of the Dreyfus affair. Foreign observers, too, voiced growing concern. As early as April 1938 Sir Eric Phipps, Britain's ambassador in Paris, noted that one of the principal 'by-products of the long drawn out political crisis in France is a certain revival of anti-Semitism. This is the more regrettable', Phipps added, 'in that since the Dreyfus affair, anti-Jewish feeling has, on the whole, remained dormant in French life, and has been mostly confined to the Salons and to the higher ranks of the Army.' Moreover, when the American undersecretary of State, Sumner Welles, met Blum in March 1940, 'he received more than three thousand letters from Frenchmen complaining of the honor he had bestowed on a Jew by his visit'.[26] Finally, this anti-semitic animosity surfaced with particular vehemence with the outbreak of war. In September 1939, when the French government interned all German and Austrian refugees as 'enemy aliens', the refugees were not only branded as communists but as German spies, a charge that was fuelled by the signing of the Nazi–Soviet non-aggression pact in August 1939. In May 1940, when German troops invaded the Low Countries and began to move southward towards France, these fears reached fever pitch. As trains carried thousands of central-European refugees from the Nazi-occupied Low Countries to internment camps in southern France, crowds of onlookers threw stones and called the refugees 'dirty *boches*'. One refugee actually expressed relief at being sent to a camp, claiming 'It's our only defence against the popular indignation.' Another reported, 'I have never seen such a fear of spies, no, not even in 1914.'[27] In his famous memoir of this period, *Scum of the Earth*, Arthur Koestler recounted that the French officer who escorted him to an internment camp told him, 'We're going to line you up and shoot you ourselves before the Germans come.'[28]

There can be no doubt that such attitudes did much to pave the way for Vichy anti-semitism, particularly since the new administration of Marshal Pétain had close ties to groups like the Action Française and the Croix de Feu, which had been propagating these views in the 1930s. Although we cannot examine Vichy's anti-semitic legislation in depth, it is clear that the legal measures against the Jews, as well as the decision to intern foreign Jews, were motivated by indigenous French concerns and reflected the anti-semitic themes of the 1930s. In July 1940 the Vichy government passed a law permitting anyone naturalized since 1927 to be stripped of their citizenship, and in August and September it forbade the exercise of medicine, dentistry, pharmacy and law to all persons not born in France of French fathers. Many of the individuals targeted were liberal professionals, and a large proportion – over 40 per cent – were Jews, notwithstanding the fact that the French Jewish population, which in 1940 numbered between 300 000 and 350 000, constituted less than 1 per cent of France's total population. Moreover, Vichy's two *statuts des Juifs* of 3 October 1940 and 2 June 1941 barred Jews from an even wider range of professions including all civil and military service posts, many commercial professions and all professions having an impact on public opinion. And in the summer of 1941 the government imposed quotas of 3 per cent on the number of Jewish students allowed to attend French universities and 2 per cent on the number of Jews allowed to practise law and medicine. According to Vallat, then commissioner general for Jewish affairs, such measures were necessary since Jews constituted 'a parasitical element, dissolving and revolutionary'. These measures were also justified as punishments for the alleged role played by Jews in France's defeat. As the preamble to the first *statut des Juifs* explained:

In its work of national reconstruction the government from the very beginning was bound to study the problem of Jews as well as that of certain aliens, who, after abusing our hospitality, contributed to our defeat in no small measure. In all fields and especially in the public service ... the influence of Jews has made itself felt, insinuating and finally decomposing.

In October 1940 Jewish emancipation suffered yet another blow when the Vichy government rescinded the 1870 Crémieux decree, which had granted civil rights to Algerian Jews.[29]

Despite these obvious threads of continuity, analogies between the Third Republic and Vichy should not be pushed too far, particularly in so far as government policy is concerned. To be sure, the legislation of the Third Republic did provide some legal precedents for Vichy's anti-semitic initiatives. Most significantly, the concept of two-tiered citizenship, which granted recently naturalized citizens fewer rights than long-standing citizens, constituted a major break with the republican tradition of treating all citizens as equal before the law. This legal precedent, which began with the 1934–5 laws restricting the right of recently naturalized citizens to practise law and medicine, was extended in 1938, when another decree law* stipulated that newly naturalized citizens wait 5 years before being allowed to vote. These initiatives clearly paved the way for Vichy's denaturalization policies, and they had a devastating impact on Jews, since no fewer than half of France's Jewish population was foreign-born. Moreover, the Daladier administration's anti-immigrant decree laws of 2 May 1938 and 12 November 1938, which mandated strict prison sentences for illegal aliens and provided for the creation of internment camps for them, also paved the way for Vichy's harsh crackdown against foreign Jews. Finally, at least one member of the Daladier administration, the foreign minister, Bonnet, frequently expressed anti-semitic views, albeit in a private capacity. Just after the assassination of vom Rath, Sir Eric Phipps described a phone conversation he had with Bonnet, and he noted that 'M. Bonnet is rather perturbed at the growing anti-semitic feeling. He says it's due to the fact that the public is realizing more and more that prominent Jews here desired war at the time of the last crisis.'[30]

Still, the fact remains that anti-semitism was never embodied into law under the Third Republic, and this distinction is no mere technicality. None of the above-mentioned laws from the 1930s referred specifically to Jews, and the goal of the Third Republic with respect to unwanted refugees, including the creation of internment camps, was to provide for their ultimate emigration, although in truth this was Vichy's goal as well. Moreover, in the months immediately preceding the outbreak of war the Daladier administration began to perceive anti-semitism as a national-security threat because it served as a wedge for the introduction of Nazi propaganda into France. On

---

* A decree law was a law enacted by the administration without the consent of parliament. During the interwar years the parliament voted this power to the administration so that the latter could enact legislation deemed necessary, particularly with respect to economic measures, but which lacked popular support.

21 April 1939 the government enacted the Marchandeau Law, which outlawed racial or religious discrimination in the press, paving the way for the
arrest of several prominent anti-semites, including Darquier de Pellepoix.
Furthermore, once war broke out the administration regarded anti-semitic
comments as defeatist propaganda, and as such they became grounds for
arrest. In February 1940 the Sûreté Nationale even investigated a Lyon
couple for purportedly having remarked, 'In the end, we're fighting for the
English and the Jews.'[31]

Having completed this survey of anti-semitism from the Dreyfus affair to
Vichy, it is necessary to return to the two questions raised at the beginning:
how central was anti-semitism to the broader historical themes of the
interwar period; and to what degree can the Dreyfus affair serve as a
paradigm for all subsequent manifestations of anti-semitism in France? With
respect to the first question, the evidence in this chapter strongly suggests that
anti-semitism was not a peripheral issue, as Eugen Weber and Jean-Baptiste
Duroselle have argued. Rather, this theme lay at the heart of the major
debates of the interwar period, and especially the 1930s: the impact of the
depression; the wave of anti-communist hysteria, which reached fever pitch
at the time of the Popular Front victory; and the growing anti-war sentiment,
which climaxed at the time of the Munich crisis and Kristallnacht. To ignore
the centrality of anti-semitism to these debates would constitute a distortion
of the historical record, and it would furthermore obscure the extent to
which anti-semitism in the 1930s paved the way for Vichy anti-semitism.
Moreover, as we have seen, anti-semitism had a currency far beyond the
ranks of radical right-wing parties, previously the focus of scholarly attention. It is therefore clear that if we are ever to understand the pervasiveness of
anti-semitism in the 1930s we need to look beyond those groups that defined
themselves as such. Finally, in response to claims by commentators such as
Rousso and Conan that recent histories of Vichy have become too 'judeo-
centric', since anti-semitism could not have played more than a minor role in
the day-to-day affairs of that regime, the evidence simply does not support
this point of view. In light of the fact that Jews constituted so tiny a
proportion of the French population, what needs to be explained is why the
Vichy regime devoted as much attention as it did to the Jewish question.

Why this preoccupation existed does require explanation, and if we turn
to the question of continuity there are indeed striking parallels between the
anti-semitic movement of the Dreyfus affair era and that of the interwar
years. In both cases Jews were vilified as the pre-eminent symbols of the
liberal economic system – capitalism – with its commitment to careers open
to talent. At the same time they were vilified as the pre-eminent symbols of
the bourgeois republican state. As Birnbaum has noted, the fact that both
Dreyfus and Léon Blum (and later Pierre Mendès France) rose to the heights
of military and political power reveals the extent to which the revolutionary
forces unleashed in 1789 had destroyed the caste system of the *ancien régime*,
which had excluded Jews entirely from the political system and had relegated

them to the lowest rungs of economic activity. Moreover, the degree to which the state in the nineteenth and twentieth centuries was willing and able to resist anti-semitic impulses can also be seen as a barometer of its commitment to republican principles, especially the principles of careers open to talent and the equality of all individuals before the law, regardless of their ethnic, racial or religious backgrounds. Thus, in a general sense, the anti-semitic movements of the Dreyfus affair era and of the interwar years constituted battles between competing visions of what kind of society constituted 'true France'. Would France remain a liberal, republican, capitalist and secular society, based on democratic values and individual rights, or would it return to the hierarchical, corporatist and Christian values of the *ancien régime*, a system in which economic and political rights were determined by birth rather than talent, and in which ethnic and religious background played a decisive role? Summing up this position in his post-war memoirs, *Le Nez de Cléopâtre*, Vallat once again explained that Vichy's *statut des Juifs* had been necessary:

> It would be unreasonable to allow them [Jews], in a Christian State, to run the government and oppress Catholics by means of their authority. It is therefore legitimate to forbid them access to public offices; legitimate as well not to admit them to the University and to liberal professions except in fixed proportions.[32]

Clearly, the contentious debates over Jewish emancipation that had erupted during the French Revolution had not been resolved, even in 1940, as Vichy's revocation of Jewish emancipation poignantly demonstrates.

Despite these similarities, there remain major differences between these anti-semitic movements. While the animosity aimed at Jews in middle-class professions had begun well before the Dreyfus affair, the tendency to link Jews to the political left, which climaxed in the vitriolic attacks on Blum, together with the theme of Jewish war-mongering, were more specific to the interwar years. Thus, we cannot understand anti-semitism in the 1930s without situating it against the backdrop of the Great Depression and the sharp political polarization between extreme right and left, which numbed the sensibilities of many conservatives and liberals to the dangers of fascism and Nazism, which they perceived as the sole bulwark against the communist threat. Hence, to see all manifestations of anti-semitism as the unfolding of a series of 'Dreyfus affairs' is to ignore the concrete social, political and economic circumstances that shaped anti-semitism at a particular historical juncture. Above all, it is imperative to keep in mind the tremendous gulf that separated the state-sponsored anti-semitism implemented at Vichy from earlier manifestations of anti-Jewish hostility. Even during the most difficult moments of the 1930s, few French Jews could have imagined the cruel irony that would befall them in 1942. Only 1 year after the 150th anniversary of their emancipation, French Jews experienced their greatest tragedy when the French government acceded to Nazi demands to assist in the deportation of first foreign Jews and ultimately French Jews to the death camps in Poland. As one German refugee presciently remarked at the end of 1940, 'France of 1940 has nothing in common with pre-war France. A country which was proud to be a refuge for freedom, a place of shelter for all persecuted people in Europe, has now become selfish and intolerant due to the changed situation.'[33] Although this refugee's view of the 1930s is far too rosy, his comment nevertheless suggests that even the refugees, whose situation had deteriorated sharply by the end of that decade, were keenly aware of the momentous change that had occurred with Vichy's coming to power.

Notes

1 Oscar de Férenzy, *Les Juifs, et nous chrétiens* (Paris: Flammarion, 1935), p. 176; M. Taillefeur, cited in André Marion, 'Racisme français pas mort!', *Droit de vivre*, 22 May 1937, pp. 1, 4; Levaillant, cited in Pierre Birnbaum, 'La Citoyenneté en péril: Les Juifs entre intégration et résistance', in P. Birnbaum (ed.), *La France de l'Affaire Dreyfus* (Paris: Gallimard, 1994), pp. 505–42, p. 528.

2 Eugen Weber, 'Reflections on the Jews in France', in F. Malino and B. Wasserstein (eds.), *The Jews in Modern France* (Hanover, NH: University of New England Press), p. 8; Jean-Baptiste Duroselle, 'L'Antisémitisme en France de 1886 à 1914', *Cahiers Paul Claudel*, vol. 7 (Paris: Gallimard, 1968), pp. 49–70, esp. pp. 69–70; Eric Conan and Henry Rousso, *Vichy un passé qui ne passe pas* (Paris: Fayard, 1994), pp. 269–70. [This book has recently appeared in English as, *Vichy An Ever-present Past*, trans. Nathan Bracher (Hanover, NH: University of New England Press, 1998).]

3 Michel Winock, *Nationalisme, antisémitisme et fascisme en France* (Paris: Seuil, 1982), Part 2, ch. 6, pp. 157–85, esp. p. 169; Zeev Sternhell, 'The roots of popular anti-semitism in the Third Republic', in Malino and Wasserstein (eds.), *The Jews in Modern France*, p. 129; Michael R. Marrus, 'Vichy before Vichy: antisemitic currents in France during the 1930s', *Wiener Library Bulletin*, NS, 33:51/2 (1980), pp. 13–19.

4 Stephen A. Schuker, 'Origins of the "Jewish problem" in the later Third Republic', in Malino and Wasserstein (eds.), *The Jews in Modern France*, pp. 146, 148.

5 Cited in Maurice Barrès, *Mes Cahiers* (Jan. 1896–May 1902), *L'Oeuvre de Maurice Barrès*, vol. 13 (Paris: Plon, 1931; Club de l'Honnête Homme, 1968), p. 246.

6 Jean Levaillant, cited in Stephen Wilson, *Ideology and Experience: Antisemitism in France at the Time of the Dreyfus Affair* (Rutherford, NJ: Fairleigh Dickinson University Press, 1982), p. 333.

7 Zeev Sternhell, *La Droite révolutionnaire, 1885–1914: Les Origines françaises du fascime* (Paris: Seuil, 1978), pp. 236–7; Wilson, *Ideology and Experience*, ch. 8, pp. 213–29.

8 Cited in R. Millman, *La Question juive entre les deux guerres: Ligues de droite et antisémitisme en France* (Paris: Armand Colin, 1992), p. 33.

9 Cited in *ibid.*, p. 275.

10 Cited in Birnbaum, 'La Citoyenneté en péril', p. 509.

11 Minutes, meeting to discuss the creation of the Comité National, late June 1933, Leo Baeck Institute Archives, New York City, AR-C 1698/ 4099, p. 20. On these middle-class protectionist movements, see Vicki Caron, 'The antisemitic revival

in France in the 1930s: the socio-economic dimension reconsidered', *Journal of Modern History*, 70:1 (March 1998), pp. 24–73.

12 V. Caron, *Uneasy Asylum: France and the Jewish Refugee Crisis, 1933–42* (Stanford, CA: Stanford University Press, 1999), pp. 237–8; Marrus, 'Vichy before Vichy', p. 18; M. Marrus and R. O. Paxton *Vichy France and the Jews*, p. 50.

13 For above citations, see Caron, *Uneasy Asylum*, chs. 2, 4, 12; Caron, 'The antisemitic revival'.

14 'On sollicite des éclaircissements', *La Juste parole*, no. 7, 20 Feb. 1937, p. 6.

15 Louis-Ferdinand Céline, *Bagatelles pour un massacre* (Paris: Denoël, 1937), p. 96.

16 On Maurras, see 'La France sous le juif', *L'Action française* (*AF*), 5 June 1936, cited in Georges Batault, *Israël contre les nations: Essai d'histoire contemporaine* (Paris: Gabriel Beauchesne, 1939), p. 59; *AF*, 9 Apr. 1935, cited in 'Dossier de la provocation', *Les Cahiers des Droits de l'Homme* (*CDH*), 20 Feb. 1936, pp. 100–5. On Darquier de Pellepoix, see 'Les Provocations antisémites des amis d'Hitler continuent', *Le Populaire*, 28 May 1936, p. 3.

17 Jacques Bonhomme, 'La France Libre; Lettre ouverte à M. le Grand Rabbin de France', in Alliance Israélite Universelle, Archives, Paris (AIU), Ms 650, Boîte 15 (51). On the chief rabbi's intervention, see Phipps, to the British foreign office, 13 Apr. 1938, Public Records Office, London (PRO), FO 371/21634 .C3205, pp. 207–10; J. Lacouture, *Léon Blum*, trans. G. Holoch (New York: Holmes and Meier, 1982), p. 267.

18 On these incidents, see Caron, *Uneasy Asylum*, p. 270; P. Birnbaum, *Anti-Semitism in France: A Political History from Léon Blum to the Present*, trans. M. Kochan (Oxford: Blackwell, 1992), pp. 66, 130, 243–4; R. Schor, *L'Antisémitisme en France pendant les années trente: Prélude à Vichy* (Paris: Editions Complexe, 1992), pp. 172–3; Lacouture, *Léon Blum*, pp. 271, 390.

19 On La Rocque's anti-semitism, see 'Les "Croix de Feu" et l'antisémitisme', *L'Univers israélite* (UI), 17 Apr. 1936, p. 472; 'Le Parti Social Français et la question juive', *La Juste parole*, 5 Apr. 1937, No. 10, pp. 15–16; 'Le Parti Social Français et la question juive', Centre de Documentation et de Vigilance (CDV), Bull. No. 29, 15 Apr. 1937, pp. 3–4, AIU, Ms. 650, Boîte 1 (2); 'Congrès fédéral du PSF en Afrique du Nord', 23 Oct. 1938, CDV, Bull. No. 74 [Nov. 1938], p. 7, in Documents of French Jewish History, Box 11, Archives, Jewish Theological Seminary, New York City (JTS); Robert Soucy, *French Fascism: The Second Wave, 1933–1939* (New Haven: Yale University Press, 1995), pp. 152–8, 202; William D. Irvine, 'Fascism in France and the strange case of the Croix de Feu', *Journal of Modern History*, 63:2 (June 1991), pp. 290–3. For Maurras's statement, see *AF*, 9 Apr. 1935, cited in 'Dossier de la provocation', *CDH*, 20 Feb. 1936, pp. 100–5.

20 On Catholic opinion, see Caron, *Uneasy Asylum*, pp. 281–5; Birnbaum, *Anti-Semitism in France*, pp. 178–87.

21 Schor, *L'Antisémitisme en France*, pp. 47–8; Lacouture, *Léon Blum*, p. 201; 'Néo-Socialisme et antisémitisme', *Droit de vivre*, no. 20, June/July, 1934, p. 2; 'Socialisme et antisémitisme', *UI*, 8 June 1934, p. 311; 'Nos Echos', *UI*, 15 June 1934, p. 345.

22 Jean and Jérôme Tharaud, *Quand Israël n'est plus roi* (Paris: Plon, 1933), p. 142.

23 Arthur Koestler, *The Invisible Writing* (New York: Macmillan, 1954), p. 189.

24 'Bagatelles pour un massacre', *Je suis partout*, 4 March 1938; Céline, *Bagatelles pour un massacre*, pp. 81–2.

25 *AF*, cited in Wladimir Rabi, 'De 1906 à 1939', in Bernhard Blumenkranz (ed.), *Histoire des Juifs en France* (Toulouse: Privat, 1972), p. 382, and Jean-Pierre

Azéma, *From Munich to the Liberation, 1938–1944*, trans. Janet Lloyd (New York: Cambridge University Press, 1984), pp. 9–10; *Je suis partout*, 14 Oct. 1938. All citations here and below on popular reactions to the Munich crisis and Kristallnacht are from Caron, *Uneasy Asylum*, chs. 9 and 12, and Caron, 'Prelude to Vichy': France and the Jewish refugees in the era of appeasement', *Journal of Contemporary History*, 20:1 (Jan. 1985), pp. 157–76.
26 Phipps, to the foreign office, Apr. 13, 1938, PRO FO 371/21634 .C3205, pp. 207–10; John M. Sherwood, *Georges Mandel and the Third Republic* (Stanford, CA: Stanford University Press, 1970), p. 244.
27 Caron, *Uneasy Asylum*, pp. 259–60.
28 Arthur Koestler, *Scum of the Earth* (New York: Macmillan, 1941), p. 176.
29 Caron, *Uneasy Asylum*, ch. 14, pp. 321–53.
30 Phipps, to the foreign office, 11 Nov. 1938, PRO FO 371/21637 .C13793.
31 Sûreté Nationale report, 12 Feb. 1940, Archives Nationales, Paris, F^7 14822 (propos défaitistes).
32 Xavier Vallat, *Le Nez de Cléopâtre: Souvenirs d'un homme de droite (1919–1944)* (Paris: Les Quatre Fils Aymon, 1957), pp. 226–75, esp. p. 247.
33 Walter Baum, Rept., 'Jewish Refugees in France', 10 Dec. 1940, Joint Distribution Committee Archives, New York City, No. 618.

Further reading

Birnbaum, P. *Anti-Semitism in France: A Political History from Léon Blum to the Present*, trans. M. Kochan (Oxford: Blackwell, 1992).
——, (ed.) *La France de L'Affaire Dreyfus* (Paris: Gallimard, 1994).
——, *The Jews of the Republic: A Political History of State Jews in France from Gambetta to Vichy* (Stanford, CA: Stanford University Press, 1996).
Bredin, J.-D. *The Affair: The Case of Alfred Dreyfus*, trans. J. Mehlman (New York: George Braziller, 1986).
Burns, M. *Dreyfus: A Family Affair, 1789–1945* (New York: Harper Collins, 1991).
Byrnes, R. F. *Antisemitism in Modern France* (New Brunswick, NJ: Rutgers University Press, 1950).
Caron, V. 'Prelude to Vichy: France and the Jewish refugees in the era of appeasement', *Journal of Contemporary History*, 20:1 (January, 1985), pp. 157–76.
——, 'The antisemitic revival in France in the 1930s: the socioeconomic dimension reconsidered', *Journal of Modern History*, 70:1 (March, 1998), pp. 24–73.
——, *Uneasy Asylum: France and the Jewish Refugee Crisis, 1933–42* (Stanford, CA: Stanford University Press, 1999).
Hyman, P. E. *From Dreyfus to Vichy: The Remaking of French Jewry, 1906–1939* (New York: Columbia University Press, 1979).
——, *The Jews of Modern France* (Berkeley: University of California Press, 1998).
Kleeblatt, N. L. (ed.), *The Dreyfus affair: Art, Truth, and Justice* (Berkeley: University of California Press, 1987).
Lacouture, J. *Léon Blum*, trans. G. Holoch (New York: Holmes & Meier, 1982).
Malino, F. and Wasserstein, B. (eds.), *The Jews in Modern France* (Hanover, NH: University of New England Press, 1985).
Marrus, M. R. 'Vichy before Vichy: antisemitic currents in France during the 1930's', *Wiener Library Bulletin*, NS, 33:51/2 (1980), pp. 13–19.

——, Paxton, R. O. *Vichy France and the Jews* (New York: Basic Books, 1981; Stanford, CA: Stanford University Press, 1995).

Millman, R. *La Question juive entre les deux guerres: ligues de droite et anti-sémitisme en France* (Paris: Armand Colin, 1992).

Nord, P. *Paris Shopkeepers and the Politics of Resentment* (Princeton: Princeton University Press, 1986).

Schor, R. *L'Antisémitisme en France pendant les années trente: prélude à Vichy* (Paris: Éditions Complexe, 1992).

Soucy, R. *French Fascism: The Second Wave, 1933–1939* (New Haven: Yale University Press, 1995).

Sternhell, Z. *La Droite révolutionnaire, 1885–1914: les origines françaises du fascisme* (Paris: Seuil, 1978).

——, *Neither Right nor Left: Fascist Ideology in France*, trans. D. Maisel (Princeton: Princeton University Press, 1986).

Weinberg, D. H. *A Community on Trial: The Jews of Paris in the 1930's* (Chicago: University of Chicago Press, 1977).

Weber, E. *The Hollow Years: France in the 1930s* (New York: Norton, 1994).

Wilson, S. *Ideology and Experience: Antisemitism in France at the Time of the Dreyfus Affair* (Rutherford, NJ: Fairleigh Dickinson University Press, 1982). [For the English translation, see Winock, M. *Nationalism, anti-semitism, and fascism in France*, trans. J. M. Todd (Stanford, CA: Stanford University Press, 1998)].

Winock, M. *Nationalisme, antisémitisme et fascisme en France* (Paris: Seuil, 1982).

Zuccotti, S. *The Holocaust, the French and the Jews* (New York: Basic Books, 1993).

8

The clash of ideas
Political thought, intellectuals and the meanings of 'France', 1890–1945

JEREMY JENNINGS

The year 1896 marked not the opening of the Dreyfus affair – the innocent Captain Alfred Dreyfus, imprisoned on Devil's Island, had to wait a further 2 years before Emile Zola penned his open letter *J'accuse* – but rather another event of immense symbolic importance: the 1400th anniversary of the baptism of Clovis, first king of the Franks and founder of the Merovingian dynasty, at Rheims in 496. It was this act that subsequently secured France's place as the 'eldest daughter' of the Church and which, when celebrated at the end of the nineteenth century, provided Catholics with the opportunity to re-assert that Christianity represented the inescapable destiny of France. As Eugène Léotard commented in one of the many texts published to celebrate the centenary: 'France will be Christian or it will no longer be France.' On this view, the baptismal act had tied not merely Clovis but the entire French nation to the Church, bequeathing a spiritual principle that would permanently define the collective identity of France and her history. 'Whatever have been our weaknesses and our faults', wrote the Jesuit Jules Pacheu in *Eglise et Patrie*, 'the governance, word, heart and sword of France appear in history as a power, a word, a heart and a sword faithful to the cause of the Church and of God.' If France should turn away from this primordial reality, the result would be chaos.

The primacy accorded to Catholicism in this description of the meaning of France ran up against one major, if not insurmountable, problem: in 1789 and since France had contradicted her vocation and mission, the Revolution and the Republic denying France's ancient faith and history. Moreover, this violation of France's Catholic destiny came armed with its own conception of France's identity, forged by the experiences of the Revolution and the Napoleonic Empire and resting upon less essentialist and more voluntaristic assumptions. The French nation, *la grande nation*, was transmuted into an ideal and an idea, into the *patrie* of republican liberties and the vehicle of humanity in the era of nation-states, its destiny now wedded to the new doctrines of liberty, equality, justice and the rights of man.

Few writers gave better voice to this creed than the historian Jules Michelet (1798–1874), for whom France's interests and destiny were at one with those of humanity and the 'salvation of mankind'. Like his close friend Edgar Quinet (1803–75), he saw in this gospel of equality and brotherhood a new religion that would supersede Christianity. France, Michelet declared, is 'a religion'. Michelet also believed that nations possessed 'moral characteristics' and, by the same token, that France had a 'personality'. It was part of the very process of escaping from a world dominated by fatality, he argued, that races intermingled, that civilizations mixed and that peoples fashioned themselves into nations. This process, he believed, had achieved its apogee in France. 'This intimate fusion of races', Michelet wrote in his *Introduction à l'histoire universelle*, 'constitutes the identity of our nation'. The genius of France lay in its unity and diversity and in its capacity for assimilation.

Defeat in the Franco-Prussian war of 1870 and the subsequent secession of the territories of Alsace and Lorraine proved as much a psychological trauma for the adherents of such a *nationalisme ouvert* as it did, as we shall later see, for the advocates of a Catholic France. For Michelet, the tearing away of France's eastern provinces was an affront to her 'organic unity'. Of all peoples, he believed, the French were *le moins démembrable*. Yet dismembered France was, and with this came not only a searching reappraisal of the nature of the nation but also an analysis of the causes of France's humiliation that would shape political thought through much of the remainder of the Third Republic.

Michelet's own account, written at the end of his life, emphasized the defeated Napoleon III's lack of Frenchness. By contrast, Hippolyte Taine (1828–93), in his multi-volumed *Les Origines de la France contemporaine*, focused upon the corrupting consequences and 'spontaneous anarchy' engendered by the Revolution itself and witnessed again in the Paris Commune. It was, however, the historian and philologist Ernest Renan (1823–92), one of the most important writers of his generation, who provided the most articulate witness to what, in *La Réforme intellectuelle et morale de la France*, he described as France's 'fatal crisis'. 'Weakened by democracy, demoralized by her prosperity', France had fallen prey to 'bourgeois materialism' and a consequent loss of 'military spirit'. France, Renan wrote, 'has become the most pacific country in the world'. If the remedies to these ills lay in part in aping Prussia's model of the *ancien régime*, Renan was equally adamant that, in defining the meaning of the French nation, he could dismiss Prussian claims to France's lost provinces. This he did in 'Qu'est-ce qu'une nation?', a lecture given at the Sorbonne in March 1882.

Prussian claims to Alsace and Lorraine rested upon the grounds that in terms of race, culture and language they were German. Renan, like fellow historian Fustel de Coulanges before him, disputed each of these defences, preferring rather to emphasize that a nation was 'a soul, a spiritual principle'. The components of that soul, he argued, were twofold: a past and a present. The past was a shared past, 'the possession in common of a rich legacy of memories'. The present was one of 'actual consent', made manifest 'in the desire to live together, the will to continue to value the heritage that has been received'. On this view, as Renan eloquently expressed it, 'man is the slave neither of his race, his language, his religion nor of the course of rivers or the direction of mountain ranges'. As such, the nation was nothing else but 'a plebiscite of every day' (*un plébiscite de tous les jours*).

Not everyone was prepared to go along with this definition of the nation. Indeed, there were those ready to deny the reality of the nation, and therefore of France, altogether. The self-proclaimed anarchist Pierre-Joseph Proudhon (1809–65), rejecting both the 'republic, one and indivisible, of the Jacobins' and what he contemptuously described as *la topographie politique*, went so far as to comment: 'The Frenchman is a figment of the imagination: he does not exist.' This was a pattern of thinking that persisted well into the Third Republic. A Ligue des Antipatriotes appeared in the 1880s and later had its anti-patriotic message continued by firebrand Gustave Hervé, editor of *La Guerre sociale*. 'Our country', Hervé proclaimed, 'is our class.' Revolutionary syndicalism, at its height in the first decade of the twentieth century, likewise combined its anti-capitalist and anti-militarist teachings with anti-patriotism. For theoretician Hubert Lagardelle, editor of the influential *Le Mouvement socialiste*, the idea of *la patrie* was the supreme symbolic expression of collaboration between classes, whilst for the movement's militants there appeared little to recommend either the supposed virtues of the French nation (to which as workers they did not fully belong) or the patriotic duty of all Frenchmen to defend the cultural patrimony of France. As leader of the Confédération Générale du Travail (CGT) Georges Yvetot remarked, for the workers of France the lost provinces were not called Alsace and Lorraine but Life and Liberty. This was a theme that also found expression in more literary quarters. In his *Vie de Jeanne d'Arc*, the writer Anatole France not only did much to debunk many of the myths surrounding one of the consummate images of 'national unity', *la Pucelle*, but also contended that the propertyless workers could not and did not possess a sense of national belonging. This 'new class', he argued, 'unlike the peasant and the bourgeois produced by the revolution, does not fear that the foreign enemy will plunder it and, not having any wealth to defend, regards foreign peoples without fear or hatred'. Disputed by socialist leader Jean Jaurès – whose internationalism was combined with a deep sense of France's mission as the land of democracy and progress – such reluctance to attach any meaning to France remained a powerful voice up to and beyond the *union sacrée* of 1914–18.

Nevertheless, Renan's diagnosis of France's ills and his description of the nation continued to find an audience in the decades that followed. In particular, his reference to the nation as a 'spiritual principle' was sufficiently vague to appeal to all sides in any future debate about the meaning of France. Moreover, Renan pointed the way to a new form of political engagement, that of the intellectual, and one in which the meanings of France would again be at the fore.

It has been Christophe Charle who, in a series of path-breaking studies, has done most to extend our knowledge of the changes in the conditions of intellectual life that gave rise in France to the emergence of the intellectual at the very end of the nineteenth century. What he has established is that, as the century progressed, the figures of the poet, the artist and the spiritual messiah were replaced by that of the *savant*, the scientist or scholar, as the guide of humanity. This was a vision fully articulated by Renan. In his *L'Avenir de la science*, not only did he proclaim that 'my religion is now as ever the progress of reason, in other words, the progress of science' but he also stipulated that 'enlightenment, morality, art, will always be represented among mankind by a magistracy, by a minority, preserving the traditions of the true, the good and the beautiful'. On this view, it was an understanding of science that conferred the 'title of nobility'. The universities, therefore, would function as 'the nurseries of aristocrats'. Subsequently, scientists such as Marcellin Berthelot, Louis Pasteur and Claude Bernard, each lionized by the nascent Republic, would give flesh to this model, providing examples of hard work, dedication and intelligence as well as proof of the positive value and social utility of science itself.

Yet, as Charle has shown, for this model of the intellectual to be used with telling political effect – as it was in the Dreyfus affair – required an evolution in the structures of what he, following Pierre Bourdieu, defines as the 'intellectual field'. A 'passive given', of great importance in facilitating collective action, was the geographical concentration of France's intellectual élite in Paris or, more specifically, in certain parts of the capital. To this was then added a significant increase in numbers in both the university and literary sectors combined with an extension of professional, social and cultural autonomy that allowed independent political action. By the end of the century, therefore, there was widespread agreement amongst this group itself that it had a duty to speak out on general issues and to intervene in political debate: as events were to show, the dispute lay in the definition of the function of the 'intellectual' and over the values that were to be defended.

The curtain was raised on 13 January 1898, when novelist Emile Zola (1840–1902) published his open letter to the president of the republic denouncing the acquittal of Esterhazy and all those in the army who had been responsible for the wrongful imprisonment of Alfred Dreyfus. It was, he announced, 'a revolutionary means of hastening the explosion of truth and justice'. The following day, under the title *Une protestation*, there appeared in the newspaper *L'Aurore* a document which subsequently became known as the 'manifesto of the intellectuals' and which announced: 'We, the undersigned, protest against the violation of judicial procedure at [Dreyfus's] trial of 1894 and against the mystery surrounding the Esterhazy affair and persist in demanding revision.' The undersigned comprised a significant proportion of France's academic and artistic élite, many of whom proudly appended their institutional affiliation and qualifications to their names.

Through this act the 'intellectual' was born. How, for political purposes, they cashed in the prestige accorded to them as *savants* is well illustrated by Emile Duclaux, director of the prestigious Institut Pasteur and one of the signatories of the 1898 manifesto. In his *Propos d'un Solitaire* he responded to the request of the vice-president of the senate, Auguste Scheurer-Kestner, for an assessment of the evidence used to convict Dreyfus and did so 'as a scientist'. In concluding his case, Duclaux argued,

> I believe that I have remained moderate and impartial ... I accept that Dreyfus was judged and condemned without reference to his Jewishness ... However, I believe that I have shown that ... the trial was carried out in conditions hostile to the discovery of the truth.

He insisted that this was not to attack the army but to establish that the investigation had confused art for science. In exposing judicial error, his concern was less with the individual fate of Dreyfus than with dissenting in the name of proper scientific procedures.

More, however, was at stake in the Dreyfus affair than the professional autonomy and status of the intellectual. France too was at the heart of the issue. This is, for example, clearly visible in Zola's own *Lettre à la France*. Rehearsing already familiar themes, Zola's argument was that France herself was being insulted by the daily lies associated with the Dreyfus case. 'How', he asked, 'can you want truth and justice when all your legendary virtues, the clarity of your intelligence and the solidity of your reason are being destroyed?' Worse still, France was 'returning to the Church', returning 'to the past, to the past of intolerance and of theocracy that the most illustrious of your children had combatted, had believed killed, through the gift of their intelligence and their blood'. France, he implored, wake up, re-discover yourself, become again *la grande France*, 'the nation of honour, the nation of humanity, of truth and of justice'.

For those more obviously situated on the left rallying to the Dreyfusard cause faced its own obstacles. Why should socialists be concerned by acts of illegality committed by the bourgeoisie against one of its own when the proletariat daily suffered from anti-working-class legislation and repression? Why should the republic be defended when it was demonstrably a corrupt regime? To this the socialist leader Jean Jaurès (1859–1914), if not others, had answers and again they were framed in the context of the meaning of France. Through the sheer weight of the injustice heaped upon his person, Jaurès argued, Dreyfus has ceased to be an army officer and a bourgeois and had become 'nothing less than humanity itself'. Faced with this outrage only one 'institution' had remained upright and that was 'France herself'. 'For a moment', Jaurès contended, 'she was surprised, but she recovered her balance and, even if all official lights have been extinguished, her clear good sense can again dissipate the night.' Never, he argued, had France been obliged to sacrifice 'the legal guarantees that it instituted for all its children and its duties as a civilized nation' in the interests of 'the humiliating calculations of a false international prudence'. Justice, therefore, was required in the name of 'the salvation of the innocent, the punishment of the guilty, the education of the people, the honour of the *patrie*'.

Yet no sooner had the intellectuals intervened to call for Dreyfus's release than their act was denounced by their fellow writers (for the most part those drawn from the Ligue de la Patrie Française). Leading the way was Ferdinand Brunetière (1849–1906), editor of *La Revue des deux mondes* and member of the Académie Française. Already a controversial figure because of an article 'Après une visite au Vatican' in which he had proclaimed the bankruptcy of science, Brunetière added fuel to the fire in 1898 with his anti-Dreyfusard pamphlet *Après le procès*. Here he addressed three questions: the causes of anti-semitism, the place of the army in France's democracy and, finally, the claims of the 'intellectuals'. His answer to the first was that, in part, Jews themselves were to blame. On the second, his contention was not only that the army was compatible with the existence of democracy but that 'the army of France, today as before, is France herself'. Against the intellectuals, he denied their special authority to speak out on the 'most delicate questions concerning human morality, the life of nations and the interests of society'. Why, he mocked, should a professor of Tibetan be able to teach his fellow citizens about politics? But there was, he believed, an even greater danger lurking behind the protestations of the Dreyfusard intellectuals. 'Scientific method, the aristocracy of intelligence, respect for truth, all these grand phrases', he argued, 'only served to conceal the pretensions of *Individualism*.' And it was this, according to Brunetière, that was 'the great sickness of the present time'. 'Intellectualism', in short, led to anarchy.

Brunetière subsequently continued this argument in a series of pamphlets and speeches, of which 'Les Ennemis de l'âme française', delivered in 1899, is the most important. His basic premise was that such a thing as the 'French soul' existed and that it could be defined as a 'hereditary communion of sentiments and ideas'. Here he referred specifically to the opinions of Renan. The nation was not something transitory and unstable. Nevertheless, France was divided and internally weakened. By whom? '*Politicians, Intellectuals, Free Thinkers*, who, in their desperate assault on all our traditions, confound liberty of spirit with independence of the heart; *Individualists*, finally, who glory in being born for themselves.' All had worked to 'denature the French soul'.

There were, however, three traditions that informed this soul, that ensured the continuity of the *patrie*, of France. The first was France's military tradition. 'No nation', he declared, 'without an army.' The second was a 'literary and intellectual' tradition. Great literature had given the French soul 'a truthful expression, a durable expression, an immortal expression'. The watchword was to remain true to 'our own history'. The third tradition, and on this account by far the most important, was religion. Specifying that here he spoke as 'neither believer nor moralist but simply as an historian and observer', his conclusion was, nonetheless, unequivocal:

What I determine in both fact and history is that ... in the same way that Protestantism is England and 'orthodoxy' is Russia, so France is Catholicism. What I determine, in both fact and history, is that for twelve centuries the role of acting as a protector and propagandist of Catholicism has belonged to France.

And this, therefore, was Brunetière's conclusion:

everything that we do, everything that we allow to be done against Catholicism, we allow to be done and we do it to the detriment of our influence in the world, against the grain of our history and at the expense of the qualities which are those of the 'French soul'.

You could not, Brunetière affirmed, be 'French and "anti-Catholic"'.

It was these traditions, he resumed, that had made France what she was and to that extent they were 'neither monarchical nor republican, but French, uniquely French'. However, he was in no doubt that 'the best of governments will always be one which respected them most, the best institutions will be those which help them most to develop and to renew themselves'. The tragedy was that the 'essentially sociable' French soul had been perverted by individualism: the French had become individualists.

In a footnote to his text Brunetière was careful to point out that being a Protestant, a Jew or a Muslim was not what he meant by being 'anti-Catholic'. He had in mind, he assured his readers, the 'militant and active' anti-Catholicism of groups such as the Freemasons. Likewise, in his text *L'Idée de patrie* he made it plain that he did not believe that 'races' formed nations. 'The French race', he argued, 'is not the producer but the creation or, rather, the creature of the history of France.' Nevertheless, it is clear, despite the ambiguities of his position and his attempt to perceive French history as one long continuum, that for Brunetière the Catholic religion was considered a fundamental dimension of the identity and meaning of France. The French Revolution, by contrast, figures alongside such phenomena as romanticism, the morality of competition and the theory of art for art's sake, as causes of France's dread malady, individualism.

Where these, and similar, meanings of France could lead are best illustrated by Brunetière's fellow member of the Ligue de la Patrie Française, novelist Maurice Barrès (1862–1923), author of *Scènes et doctrines du nationalisme*. Here too there is an attempt to encompass all aspects and features of French history, be they Catholic, Revolutionary, Bonapartist, and so on. 'Let us leave these tales', Barrès writes; 'we find greater profit in merging ourselves together with all the moments of the history of France, in living with all her dead, in not placing ourselves beyond any of her experiences.' All these conflicting experiences, he continued, 'proceed from the same source and lead to the same goal; they are the development of the same seed and the fruits of different seasons on the same tree'. No 'conception' of France could prevail over 'the France of flesh and blood'. Yet this generosity of spirit and vision quickly vanishes when Barrès comes to speak of Protestants, and especially Jews. 'The Catholic world', Barrès writes,

> is where my forebears grew to maturity and prepared the way for me. As a consequence I find it the least jarring to my nature: it can best accommodate my various roles and best promote the life suited to my nature.

Moreover, this was why he could celebrate 'the destruction of the Protestant forces': 'I intend to preserve the benefits of this victory with all the power at my command, for it enables the tree of which I am one leaf to continue to be.'

The Jew, as a member of 'a race antagonistic to my own', fared even worse in the Barrèsian scheme of things. The Jews, Barrès argued, had no 'native land' in the way the French understood it. For them, 'it is only the place where they find the greatest profit'. Thus, Barrès had no difficulty comprehending the nature of Dreyfus's crime. 'In psychological terms', he writes, 'it is sufficient for me to know that he is capable of treason' and this Barrès 'deduced from his race'.

On this view, the actual guilt or otherwise of Dreyfus appeared almost irrelevant. What mattered, as Barrès never tired of repeating, was that the question should be resolved 'in the light of the interests of France'. And by these standards Dreyfus *was* guilty. For 5 years he and his supporters, with their 'anti-French campaign', had weakened 'the army and the entire nation'.

Moreover, this was a position that the 'intellectuals', with their passion for metaphysics and abstract truth, could not understand. An intellectual, Barrès announced, is 'an individual who convinces himself that society should be founded on the basis of logic; and who fails to see that it rests on past exigencies that precede and are perhaps foreign to individual reason'. This, for example, was the case with the central figure in Barrès's famous novel *Les Déracinés*, the professor of philosophy Bouteiller. The charge was that he, and those like him who taught what Barrès regarded as the 'official doctrine' of the French state, approached man as 'an abstract universal entity' and encouraged their students to become 'citizens of humanity, free spirits, initiates of pure reason'. All as a result were 'uprooted' from their race and their land. All were incapable of bearing witness to 'French truth and French justice'. The intellectual thus functioned as 'the enemy of society', producing a 'decadence' that derived from a 'lack of moral unity' and the absence of 'a common understanding of our goal, our resources, our centre'. 'As for ourselves,' Barrès commented, 'we are happier to be intelligent rather than intellectual.'

Nationalism, therefore, was defined by Barrès as the acceptance of a 'particular kind of determinism'. It was a 'sense of descent', a way of seeing things deeply rooted in the soil of France, her history and her 'national conscience'. Correctly observed, it provided a series of 'fixed points' and 'landmarks' that 'over the preceding centuries had educated our reflexes'. So, for example, Zola's position on Dreyfus could be explained by the fact that he was not French but an 'uprooted Venetian'. The outrage in occupied Alsace and Lorraine was that the Germans were preventing 'little French children from thinking like Frenchmen'. Those 'too recently' accepted into the French nation had troubled the 'national conscience' precisely because they bore with them the blood of their non-French ancestors.

This carried with it a clear political programme. Nationalism, Barrès argued, was a form of 'protectionism'. The nationality laws were to be tightened to reduce 'the interference of the foreigner into our politics'. Laws on ownership were to be designed to prevent foreigners possessing 'the soil of France' and to limit their commercial and industrial activities. The 'financial feudality', the Protestants and 'the kingdom of Israel' that comprised 'the dangerous *plutocracy* of exotics from which France could die', were to be challenged and defeated. The union of the 'race' and the earth was to be sealed by granting to every family 'a corner of the land'. 'Our salvation', Barrès concluded, 'lies in ceasing to be uprooted and dispersed individuals.'

To these opinions the Dreyfusards had an immediate response in the shape of Lucien Herr, librarian at the École Normale Supérieure. 'Your idea', he told Barrès, 'is that the French soul, French integrity, is today being insulted and compromised, to the advantage of foreigners, by the infernal machinations of other foreigners, aided by the complicity of second-rate intellectuals de-nationalized by a second-rate culture.' This, Herr believed, was nonsense. But, more tellingly, he turned his fire against Barrès's conception of France. 'At the core of your national patriotism', he went on, 'you would find not the old France . . . but a conquering, proud and brutal France, Napoleonic France, the jingoistic chauvinism of our large cities, the passionate instinct for warlike glory, barbarous exaltation, hatred and the arrogance of force.' This, he made plain, was not his France. 'The French soul', he continued, 'has only been truly great and strong at those moments when it has been welcoming and generous.' Nor was it the France of the 'young people' who had rallied to the Dreyfusard cause. They, just like Barrès, did not claim to possess the whole truth 'but they have within themselves something which is absolute: the faith in a human ideal'.

The common meeting place of these young people was the bookshop of Charles Péguy (1873–1914) in the heart of Paris's Latin Quarter. It was here not only that Péguy's remarkable journal, the *Cahiers de la quinzaine*, was produced but where, with passionate intensity, they followed unfolding events and that, on the rock of the Dreyfus affair, their friendships were broken. Victory and the release of Dreyfus turned quickly to disillusionment as, in their eyes, triumph was sullied by politicians intent on reaping their personal reward. The mood was captured by Georges Sorel's *La Révolution*

dreyfusienne, published in 1908. The outcome of the Dreyfus affair, he
argued, was to put an end 'to the passable functioning of the parliamentary
regime' and to secure the ascendency of 'the philosophy of the cowardly
hypocrite'. The full sense of betrayal, however, was first articulated in Daniel
Halévy's *Apologie pour notre passé*. The 'our past' of the title is the past of
a small group of young men (which included future socialist prime minister
Léon Blum, novelist Marcel Proust and critic Julien Benda) for whom the
affair acted to define them as human beings. 'A single, redoubtable crisis',
Halévy writes, 'took hold of us and marked us.' Yet the account is tinged
with melancholy. He and his friends, he recalls, became involved in the
Dreyfusard cause not just to save an innocent man but to save France, an
'innocent France' whose honour was being destroyed by 'a small number of
men poisoned by fear, by hate'. At issue, then, was 'the salvation of France'.
Yet, from within their own number and as a result of their own efforts, a
'demagogic bloc' had emerged and had taken control of the state: hence the
need to make apology.

If Halévy's text remains known today it is largely because in response it
elicited one of Charles Péguy's greatest works, the lyrical evocation of *Notre
jeunesse*, published in 1910. 'My past', Péguy proclaimed, 'has no need of
apology.' Here it is difficult to do justice to the richness of Péguy's prose but,
beyond this, what attracts our attention is that Péguy too situates his actions
in the context of the 'eternal salvation of France' and that he does so by
invoking both the Christian and republican meanings of France.

To do this Péguy framed his famous distinction between *mystique* and
politique. Very simply, one died for a *mystique* but one lived off a *politique*:
the first was principled, the second self-interested. *Politique* is the devouring of
the *mystique* that gave the movement its original force. All movements, Péguy
contended, began as *mystiques* and ended as *politiques*; the point of comparison was like with like, *mystique* with *mystique*, *politique* with *politique*.

He and his friends, therefore, participated in the *mystique* of the Dreyfusard movement. 'Deep down within us', Péguy writes, 'we were concerned
that France should not fall into a state of mortal sin.' Their virtues were those
of justice, courage, charity, perseverance and self-sacrifice. And these virtues,
Péguy wanted to argue, were not simply 'French' virtues; they were also
'Christian virtues': the Dreyfusard movement, in other words, encompassed
both the republican and the Christian *mystiques*. Both were part of what he
constantly referred to as *l'ancienne France* and he, therefore, refused to see
'the 1st January 1789 (Paris time)' as the great divide of French history.

In this Péguy was fortified by a provincial and rural education in which, on
his account, school masters and priests, for all their 'metaphysical' differences, taught the same morality and the same discipline, taught the virtues of
'the French race'. Yet his point was that this France was coming to an end, as
the termination of the Dreyfus affair showed. The Dreyfus affair, he believed,
represented the 'last operation of the republican *mystique*'. This was so
because France was entering a period of 'demystification'. To that extent,

'de-republicanization' went hand in hand with 'dechristianization'. The same 'sterility' afflicted 'the city of men and the city of God'. For the first time we were living in a world that 'opposed all culture'.

So, for Péguy, the dividing point came 'around 1881'. There was no dramatic event, but it was at this time that the republic ceased to be the republic, that it had lapsed into 'caesarism' and demagogy. More specifically, it had fallen prey to its 'worst enemy', 'the domination of the intellectual party'.

Péguy's denunciation of this 'tyranny' knew almost no bounds. It was a system of oppression, of corruption, of depravity, of lying, of *raison d'état*. For 30 years it had tried to overthrow 'God, the Church, France, the army, morals, law'. The unfortunate Jaurès was singled out for particular condemnation and reproach as 'the bourgeois intellectual' who had subverted and corrupted the workers' movement.

Yet Péguy's text contains another theme of great resonance. Péguy repeatedly states that he and his friends were inspired by 'warlike virtues'. And this he identifies as a need, 'a very profound need ... a need for heroism which seizes an entire generation, our generation, a need for war, for sacrifice to the point of martyrdom'. In this evocation of the 'saintliness' of the Dreyfusard is already written Péguy's own later religious pilgrimage to Chartres and his own death, leading his troops forward, in the first battle of the Marne in September 1914. 'Happy', he wrote in *Eve*, 'are those who die for an earthly land, when a just war calls.'

Georges Sorel (1847–1922), the principal theorist of revolutionary syndicalism, also believed that 'a great foreign war' might renew France's 'lost energies'. His preferred solution, articulated in *Réflexions sur la violence*, was a renewed bout of proletarian class struggle directed against a timorous and humanitarian bourgeoisie. So too he shared Péguy's preoccupation with the decline of France's culture and morality, speaking repeatedly of her 'decadence' and blaming it upon the nefarious influence of intellectuals and of parliamentary democracy. Disillusioned with the proletariat, between 1909 and 1914 he, and his close friend Edouard Berth, participated in a series of publishing initiatives that brought together thinkers from both the left and the right and which hammered home the message that France's classical and Christian traditions were being overturned by Protestants, Catholic modernists, parliamentary socialists, feminists, Jews and Freemasons. French greatness was being devoured by an international plutocracy. In these years, as Christophe Prochasson and Anne Rasmussen explain in *Au nom de la patrie*, there appeared

> a new type of intellectual, no longer the washed-out figure of the Dreyfusard intellectual, converted into the guardian of democracy and taken naturally to be cowardly and feminine, but rather that of the fervent defender of the values of a civilization constantly threatened by the corrosion of decadence or barbarism.

The outbreak of the First World War, with its display of German 'barbarism', hardened this vision, narrowing it down to a single cause: the defence of the nation. For those intellectuals prepared to take this course, France, whether as the 'elder daughter of the Church' or the land of the 1789 Revolution, again figured as a nation not like any other, as an entity whose fate was of universal significance. France's defeat would be humanity's loss.

On one side, for example, lay Maurice Barrès. Rallying to the nation, he abandoned his fierce and bitter invective against his fellow citizens and in texts such as *Les Traits éternels de la France* and *Les Diverses familles spirituelles de la France* portrayed the French nation, in all its diversity, as united against the common enemy and in a common sacrifice. All – Catholics, Protestants, socialists, traditionalists and even Jews – subsumed 'their religion and their philosophy with France'. 'Eternal France' thus again became visible and for Barrès there was little doubt what this 'eternal' France was. 'The French,' he wrote,

> in defending France ... fight for their land filled with graves and for a sky where Christ reigns ... They die for France, to the extent that French ends can be identified with the ends of God or even the ends of humanity. And it is thus that they make war with the sentiments of martyrs.

On the other side, and giving a different meaning to France, were the philosophers, for whom the war was a 'war of ideas'. Leading the way was Henri Bergson (1859–1941), a Jew and as such much reviled by the nationalist right. *Bergson politique*, as the late Philippe Soulez has shown in a book of that name, was a man deeply wedded not just to the republic but also to France. A fluent English speaker, he led, for example, several diplomatic missions to America designed to secure US entry into the war. Beyond this he used his immense prestige as the world's most famous living philosopher to trumpet France's cause and to portray her 'idealism' as 'the essence of the French spirit'. His general theme was that Prussian militarism and industrial power were to be defeated by and through the spiritual renovation and energy of France. There is a rhetorical inclusiveness that placed France's soldiers in the traditions of both Jeanne d'Arc and the Revolution, but when Bergson speaks of the 'soul of France' he speaks of 'the need to philosophize' and of its conflation with 'the philosophical spirit'. And here, as he demonstrated in a piece that appeared in a collective volume devoted to praising *La Science française*, he believed France had made a major contribution as *la grande initiatrice*. France's *élan*, he contended, had always rested in 'the double ideal of liberty and of justice with which she had always identified herself'.

Many other philosophers joined the fray, the pages of France's philosophical journals being littered with articles comparing the national psychologies and philosophies of France and Germany. The land of Descartes and of reason was unfailingly thought superior to a country where, from Kant to Nietzsche, philosophy had corrupted the national conscience. A typical example is Emile Boutroux's *L'Idée de liberté en France et en Allemagne*. A member of the Académie française, Boutroux had no hesitation in putting forward the argument that each country operated with opposed conceptions of liberty. The Germans, he argued, had removed any sense of individual judgement from their definition, equating liberty with 'the power, expansion and domination of Germany'. By contrast, the French idea of liberty, drawing upon the twin traditions of 'Greco-Latin civilization' and Christianity, emphasized free will and the capacity of each individual to be 'master of himself'. To the charge that this made France a nation of 'ungovernable individualism' his response, like that of so many of his colleagues, was that, through the use of reason, the French acknowledged their duties towards their fellows and towards humanity as a whole. 'Our flag', Boutroux proclaimed, 'signifies, in equal measure, *patrie* and liberty ... The virtue of this symbol of our faith has not been exhausted.'

To this extent, as Nobel-prize-winning author Romain Rolland (1866–1944) commented, 'since the beginning of the war, [the intellectuals] brought so much violence and passion to bear upon it, that it might almost be called their war'. They demonized the enemy, recounted endless tales of selfless heroism in the idealized trenches and exalted, sometimes simultaneously, both the Christian and humanitarian missions of France. Not everyone, however, went along with this. Exiled in Switzerland, Rolland himself remained, as the title of his famous book indicated, *Au-dessus de la mêlée*, producing a stream of articles which, while condemning German militarism, not only criticized the intellectuals themselves but refused to endorse their message. 'The idol of race, or of civilization, or of Latinity,' he wrote, 'which [the intellectuals] so greatly abuse, does not satisfy me.' Nevertheless, not even Rolland could resist indulging in some familiar rhetoric, talking of the 'true France' and commenting that 'I wish France to be loved, I wish her to be victorious not only by force, not only by right ... but by that large and generous heart which is pre-eminently hers'. Others, most notably combatant Henri Barbusse in his Goncourt-prize-winning novel *Le Feu* of 1916, chose to describe the full horrors and reality of the war. Conversely, many intellectuals – for example, Proust, André Gide and poet Paul Valéry – simply remained silent. Some fought and died. There were very few defeatists.

All hope that the spirit of unity forged during the war would endure after the end of hostilities was quickly dashed. The signs were already there in the favourable, if understandably naïve, reception given to the Russian revolution of 1917 by large sections of the French left and the subsequent creation of the French Communist Party in 1920. The Soviet Union was quickly cast as the promised land, a vision enhanced by the numerous official visits to Moscow undertaken by intellectuals eager to be impressed by what they saw. The 1930s saw similar trips to Nazi Germany.

The terms of post-war political debate were set by the mid-1920s; bolshevism, colonialism, the threat of war and, later, the rise of fascism, galvanizing intellectuals into action. In January 1919 Barbusse published his *Manifeste des intellectuels combattants* and later that year, in May, launched his movement Clarté, described as 'A league of intellectual solidarity for the victory of the international cause'. In the following years he and his group canvassed for active support of the Russian revolution whilst Barbusse himself sought to redefine the role of the intellectual, emphasizing the need not just for 'lucidity' but for intellectuals to be prepared to subordinate themselves to the needs and political will of the masses. Barbusse's launch of Clarté in its turn provoked the publication by Romain Rolland of another manifesto, subsequently known as the *Déclaration d'indépendance de l'esprit*. This time the target was those intellectuals who, during the war, 'had put their science, their art, their reason in the service of governments'. Intellectuals, it argued, should be servants only of the 'mind' and should have no other master. 'Our role, our duty', the manifesto proclaimed, 'is to preserve a fixed point, in the midst of the turmoil of passions to reveal the pole star.' Although Barbusse signed this document it was soon clear that he was out of sympathy with its ethos. While Barbusse sought political commitment from intellectuals, exemplified by his own membership of the Communist Party in 1923, Rolland looked for an engagement that was less militant and which defined intellectuals as an independent moral conscience. If the controversy came to a head in 1921–2, when Rolland refused to support the new journal of the Clarté group and Barbusse declined to participate in Rolland's planned international congress of intellectuals, it foreshadowed a debate about the commitment of the intellectual that would flourish for decades to come.

This, however, was not the end of the matter. On 19 July 1919, the nationalist (and, for the most part, Catholic) right published their own manifesto, *Pour un parti de l'intelligence*, condemning 'the Romain Rollands, the Barbusses, who accuse French writers of having corrupted, debased and degraded thought by putting it at the service of the homeland and its just cause'. Affirming France as 'the guardian of civilization', they saw their task as defending the humanist and Christian 'west' in order to protect 'the spiritual future of civilization in its entirety'. Their motto, against 'the Bolsheviks of literature', was straightforwardly simple: 'national intelligence in the service of the national interest'.

Left and right clashed again in 1925 over the Rif war in North Africa. Once more Barbusse led the way, publishing an anti-colonialist manifesto entitled *Aux travailleurs intellectuels. Oui or non, condemnez-vous la guerre?* and proclaiming 'the right of peoples, of all peoples, of whatever race they belong, to govern themselves'. The right responded with *Les intellectuels aux côtés de la patrie*, a petition addressed 'to the French troops who fight in Morocco for Law, Civilization and Peace' and which specifically condemned those 'who have the audacity to disfigure the lofty and generous duty to progress and humanity displayed by France on the soil of Africa'.

Ten years later it was the Italian invasion of Ethiopia and the threat of sanctions imposed by the League of Nations against the aggressors that provided the opportunity for a virtual re-run of the same arguments. The right (including such luminaries as Robert Brasillach, Pierre Drieu la Rochelle, Pierre Gaxotte, Thierry Maulnier and Charles Maurras) produced a *Manifeste des intellectuels pour la défense de l'Occident*. Condemning what was described as 'a false legal universalism which placed the superior and the inferior, the civilized person and the barbarian, on the same footing of equality', it justified the right of all European nations, in the name of civilization, to possess colonies. The response of the left came first in an appeal headed by writer Jules Romains and then a *Manifeste pour la justice et la paix*, penned by philosopher Jacques Maritain. Supporting the League of Nations, both denied that a 'civilizing mission' could be accomplished by force of arms. The following 3 years – 1936–8 – saw the Spanish Civil War given the same treatment, those for and against Franco claiming to defend civilization.

The issues raised by the Barbusse/Rolland controversy received their most articulate airing in Julien Benda's 1927 text *La Trahison des clercs* and Paul Nizan's later essay *Les Chiens de garde*.

The intellectual outlook that informed Benda's classic text received its clearest articulation in his volume of memoirs, *La Jeunesse d'un clerc*. The first two sections of the book concentrate upon Benda's family and school years. What emerges is a picture of someone whose Jewishness was felt through an attachment to certain values rather than as a religion and where these values are also felt to be those of the French republic. As he expresses it: 'In truth, what my father liked about France was French civilization, the French moralists ... the great liberal tradition, the Revolution.' His republican education reinforced his sense of attachment to these values, producing a 'mandarin' with no sense of 'the particularity of his nation, his ancestors or his race'. The result was a conception of the intellectual whose role was 'not to do but to think'.

The Dreyfus affair – the decisive event in Benda's life – confirmed his belief that 'truth' and 'justice' were 'abstract values' separate from the interests of either 'time or place'. Hence his disagreement with the position of Barrès, whose views were not only 'profoundly anti-French' but constituted the systematic destruction of everything that had sought to raise men above their 'individual or group egoisms'. The function of the intellectuals, therefore, was to protest in the name of truth as an act of 'pure intellectuality' and then 'return to their cells, cleaning their spectacles and leaving society to struggle as best it could with the truth'.

In *La Trahison des clercs* Benda's complaint was that from 'about 1890 onwards' the intellectuals had ceased to operate in this way and had subordinated their mission 'to the service of their political passions', abasing the values of knowledge before the values of action. Doing nothing to resist the passions of race, class and nationality, Benda argued, 'the modern intellectuals have proclaimed that the intellectual function is respectable only to the extent that it is connected to the pursuit of concrete advantage and that the intelligence which is disinterested in these ends is to be scorned'.

The response – in the shape of the first full formulation of the doctrine of 'commitment' – came from Marxist Paul Nizan (1905–40). 'Every philosopher,' Nizan argued, 'though he may consider that he does not, participates in the impure reality of the age.' Thus Benda's talk of the abstract and eternal verities of truth and justice denoted a refusal to talk about the things that really mattered, was 'less a choice made by eternal man than the decision of a partisan'. For Nizan, the choice facing the intellectual was a simple one: to be either for the oppressed or for the oppressors, for humanity or against humanity. The task therefore was to develop 'the closest possible ties with the class that is the bearer of revolution' and to become a 'technician of revolutionary philosophy'. Turning the argument against Benda, he concluded: 'If we betray the bourgeoisie for the sake of mankind, let us not be ashamed to admit that we are traitors.'

As political extremes came more to the fore Benda subtly changed his position. By 1937, for example, he was prepared to argue that 'the *clerc* must take sides'. What this meant was sympathy for the communists, even if, as an intellectual, he reserved the right 'to keep his critical spirit'. The bourgeois Nizan, by contrast, became ever more critical of the Communist Party, breaking with it in 1939 over the signing of the Nazi–Soviet pact. Killed at the front in 1940, he was the subject of a vicious slander campaign orchestrated by his former comrades.

Yet the debate that came to dominate the 1930s was not that between supporters of liberal democracy and communists but rather that between left and right. Jean-Louis Loubet del Bayle has spoken of *les non-conformistes des années trente*, meaning by this the young intellectuals who, from a variety of different perspectives, sought to escape from what they regarded as a crisis of civilization. Critical of Marxism and of the Soviet Union, they were nevertheless anti-capitalist, anti-liberal and also anti-parliamentary in inspiration. This fed into a powerful sense of dissatisfaction with the democratic institutions of the so-called *République des professeurs*, a malaise that received graphic political manifestation in the right-wing riots of 6 February 1934 in Paris. The left intellectuals responded with the creation of the Comité de Vigilance des Intellectuels Antifascistes whilst the electorate answered by producing the left-wing Popular Front government in 1936. The extreme right, now with Jewish prime minister Léon Blum as one of their principal scapegoats, only intensified their campaign against what they saw as a corrupt and degenerate regime.

Their mood was brilliantly captured in Robert Brasillach's autobiographical account, *Notre avant-guerre*. For Brasillach the Popular Front was nothing less than a 'revolution of intellectuals' leading to 'the ruin of the state'. Hope for France, he believed, lay in following the example of Nazi

Germany and in the 'birth of fascist man', young, virile, proud of 'his race and his nation'. Here was the basis of an intellectual collaboration that followed the fall of France in 1940 and which, in Brasillach's own case, led to his execution for treason in 1945.

There is a question mark over how extensive such collaboration was. Jeannine Verdès-Leroux in her *Refus et violences: politique et littérature à l'extrême droite des années trente aux retombées de la Libération* has, for example, recently argued that there were 'few true writers ready to declare themselves collaborators'. Those who did, she believes, were mostly the second-rate. Others would disagree, pointing to such intellectuals as Drieu la Rochelle and Lucien Rebatet as evidence of widespread collaboration.

What is undoubtedly true is that it was the monarchist doctrines of Action Française and of its principal theoretician Charles Maurras (1868–1952), rather than the temptations of fascism, that received the greatest interest from those eager to defend *la seule France*. Maurras converted to monarchism before the end of the century, seeing it as a political order 'conforming to the nature of the French nation and to the rules of universal reason'. A leading anti-Dreyfusard, from his *Enquête sur la monarchie* in 1900 onwards he hammered away at the same themes, mixing the positivism of Auguste Comte with a strident xenophobia and anti-semitism, to produce a monarchist doctrine that held immense appeal in the interwar years. Only a 'hereditary monarchy' that was 'Catholic, anti-parliamentary and decentralized', it was argued, could protect France from what Maurras described as the 'four confederal states', Jews, Protestants, Freemasons and foreigners. Despite an acceptance of the *Union sacrée*, Maurras quickly returned to the fray, pushing his 'integral nationalism' to new excesses of anti-republicanism. 'The republic in France', he wrote, 'is the reign of the foreigner.' In 1940, despite his anti-Germanism, he had no hesitation in calling for unconditional support for Marshal Pétain and Vichy's national revolution (including its later anti-semitic legislation). 'It is the revenge of Dreyfus,' Maurras cried, when found guilty of treason in 1945.

More than this, Maurras's career demonstrates the durability as well as the ultimate bankruptcy of one of our 'meanings of France'. Like many before him, Maurras was convinced that France was being weakened by an individualism that had its sources in Protestantism, German philosophy, the romanticism of Rousseau, the Revolutionary tradition of 1789 and, of course, their common origin, Judaism. The nation, conceived not in Renan's terms of contract but as a 'natural society', was therefore to act as the supreme sovereign power over the individual. Yet, as the abject failure of Vichy's political programme reveals, Maurras's own conception of France, of an 'old France' whose classical traditions were mediated by the Catholic Church, no longer had a significant purchase upon the real world. The clock could not be turned back to pre-1789. And Maurras himself illustrated the nature of the problem, for his was a Catholicism without Christianity. He was an unbeliever.

What of the France of individual rights, liberty and justice? The Second World War dramatically changed the terms of political and philosophical debate, producing not just Sartrean existentialism but an admiration of the Soviet Union that turned Marxism into a near political orthodoxy. However, none of this, as Tony Judt has shown in his *Past Imperfect: French Intellectuals 1944–1956*, diminished the predilection amongst intellectuals to describe France in terms of a special, universal destiny. France remained the predestined guide of humanity. For some it is probably still so.

Further reading

Primary Sources

Barrès, M. *Les Traits éternels de la France* (Paris: Emile-Paul Frères, 1916).

——, *Les Diverses familles spirituelles de la France* (Paris: Emile-Paul Frères, 1917).

——, *Scènes et doctrines du nationalisme* (Paris: Plon, 1925).

Benda, J. *La Trahison des clercs* (Paris: Grasset, 1927).

Bergson, H. *Mélanges* (Paris: Presses Universitaires de France, 1972).

Boutroux, E. *L'Idée de liberté en France et en Allemagne* (Paris: Éditions de Foi et de Vie, 1916).

Brasillach, R. *Notre avant-guerre* (Paris: Plon, 1941).

Brunetière, F. *Après le procès* (Paris: Perrin, 1898).

——, *Discours de combat* (Paris: Perrin, 1920).

Duclaux, E. *Avant le procès* (Paris: Stock, 1898).

——, *Propos d'un solitaire* (Paris: Stock, 1898).

Halévy, D. 'Apologie pour notre passé', *Cahiers de la quinzaine*, 10th cahier of the 11th series (1910).

France, A. *Vie de Jeanne d'Arc* (Paris: Calmann-Lévy, 1908).

Herr, L. 'A Maurice Barrès', *La Revue blanche*, 15 (1898).

Jaurès, J. *Les Preuves. Affaire Dreyfus* (Paris: La Petite République, 1898).

——, *L'Armée nouvelle* (Paris: Imprimerie Nationale, 1992).

Maurras, C. *La Seule France: chronique des jours d'épreuve* (Paris: H. Lardanchet, 1941).

——, *Oeuvres capitales: essais politiques* (Paris: Flammarion, 1954).

Nizan, P. *Les Chiens de garde* (Paris: Maspéro, 1976).

Pacheu, J. *Eglise et patrie* (Paris: Plon, Nourriet et Cie, 1897).

Péguy, C. *Oeuvres en prose, 1909–1914* (Paris: Pléiade, 1961).

Renan, E. *La Réforme intellectuelle et morale de la France* (Paris: Michel-Lévy Frères, 1871).

——, 'Qu'est-ce qu'une nation?', *Oeuvres complètes*, I (Paris: Calman-Lévy, 1947).

Rolland, R. *Au-dessus de la mêlée* (Paris-Neuchâtel: Ollendorff-Attinger, 1915).

Sorel, G. *Réflexions sur la violence* (Paris: Rivière, 1908).

——, *La Révolution dreyfusienne* (Paris: Rivière, 1909).

Thibaudet, A. *La République des professeurs* (Paris: Grasset, 1927).

Zola, E. *Lettre à la France* (Paris: Fasquelle, 1898).

Secondary sources

Charle, C. *Les Élites de la République 1880–1900* (Paris: Fayard, 1987).

——, *Naissance des 'intellectuels' 1880–1900* (Paris: Les Éditions de Minuit, 1990).

——, *Les Intellectuels en Europe au XIXe siècle* (Paris: Seuil, 1996).

Compagnon, A. *Connaisez-vous Brunetière? Enquête sur un antidreyfusard et ses amis* (Paris: Seuil, 1997).

Jennings, J. (ed.), *Intellectuals in Twentieth-Century France* (Basingstoke: Macmillan, 1993).

Judt, T. *Past Imperfect: French Intellectuals 1944–1956* (Berkeley: University of California Press, 1992).

Julliard, J. and Winock, M. (eds.), *Dictionnaire des intellectuels français* (Paris: Seuil, 1996).

Leroy, G. (ed.), *Les Ecrivains et l'affaire Dreyfus* (Paris: Presses Universitaires de France, 1983).

Loubet del Bayle, J.-L. *Les Non-conformistes des années 30* (Paris: Seuil, 1969).

Ory, P. and Sirinelli, J.-F. *Les Intellectuels en France, de l'Affaire Dreyfus à nos jours* (Paris: Armand Colin, 1986).

Prochasson, C. *Les Intellectuels, le socialisme et la guerre* (Paris: Seuil, 1993).

—— and Rasmussen, A. *Au nom de la patrie: les intellectuels et la première guerre mondiale (1910–1919)* (Paris: Éditions La Découverte, 1996).

Schalk, D. *The Spectrum of Political Engagement* (Princeton: Princeton University Press, 1979).

Sirinelli, J.-F. *Génération intellectuelle: Khâgneux et Normaliens dans l'entre-deux-guerres* (Paris: Fayard, 1988).

——, *Intellectuels et passions françaises: manifestes et pétitions au XXe siècle* (Paris: Fayard, 1990).

Soulez, P. (ed.), *Les Philosophes et la guerre de 14* (Paris: Presses Universitaires de Vincennes, 1988).

Verdès-Leroux, J. *Refus et violences: politique et littérature à l'extrême droite des années trente aux retombées de la Libération* (Paris: Gallimard, 1996).

Winock, M. *Nationalisme, antisémitisme et fascisme en France* (Paris: Seuil, 1990).

9

1940 and the crisis of interwar democracy in France

JULIAN JACKSON

History is not Tragedy. To understand historical reality, it is sometimes necessary *not to know the outcome*.

Pierre Vidal Naquet[1]

It has become a habit to look for signs of decomposition in the France of 1920–1935 ... Our epoch is in the process of constructing a representation of itself to cut the ground from under the feet of historians.

Jean-Paul Sartre, 1940[2]

On 12 June 1940 the French cabinet convened at the chateau of Cangé, in the Loire valley, to hear the commander-in-chief, General Maxime Weygand, announce that the war was lost and an armistice inevitable. No one had doubted the seriousness of the situation, but Weygand's announcement caused consternation heightened by the background of chaos. The government had evacuated Paris two days earlier, and was now scattered around the Loire. Some ministers had arrived late at the meeting, having no idea where Cangé was; others had muddled it up with the chateau of Candé, recently celebrated because the Duke of Windsor had married there.

No decision about an armistice was taken at Cangé. The debate continued over the next four days. The premier, Paul Reynaud, opposed an armistice, arguing that the fight must continue from the French empire in North Africa. But the pro-armistice faction gained ground, and was much helped when Marshal Pétain joined it and threatened to resign if an armistice was not signed. How could mere politicians oppose France's most famous soldier? On 16 June, in Bordeaux, Reynaud lost heart. He tendered his resignation to the President of the Republic. Pétain was appointed to replace him. An armistice was signed on 22 June at Rethondes. After the most humiliating defeat in her history, France was out of the war.

Ostensibly, the argument between the pro- and anti-armistice factions concerned the possibility of continued military resistance. Historians are still divided today about whether France could have continued effective military resistance from North Africa. Hitler certainly thought so, and it was for this reason that, to Mussolini's annoyance, he offered relatively lenient armistice terms. But whether or not continued resistance was possible, the government had taken almost no measures to prepare it, and the debate about the armistice was not really military but political. An armistice was a political act engaging the responsibility of the government to end hostilities in all French territories. The alternative was capitulation where the government would leave metropolitan France, taking whatever forces could be salvaged, and allowing the army to capitulate in the field and sign a cease-fire. This solution, which had occurred in Holland, was proposed by Reynaud. Weygand objected on the grounds that it shifted responsibility for the defeat to the army. He refused any analogy between the departure of the Dutch monarch and the head of an ephemeral Third-Republic government. The political assumptions behind this attitude were barely disguised. What started at Cangé on 12 June, then, was not a debate as to whether the army could fight on, but one over the responsibility for defeat. That debate has gone on ever since.

The debate on 1940

On one point there is agreement: in its rapidity and totality this was a very 'strange defeat', to quote the title of the book by the historian Marc Bloch. Everyone had their diagnoses. 'Too few children, too few allies, too few arms,' was Pétain's. De Gaulle blamed defeat on the superior armed might of the Germans. The right claimed that the rot went back to the socialist-led Popular Front government of 1936, and the Vichy regime staged a trial of the Popular Front leaders. The left claimed that France had been betrayed by a bourgeoisie which had become so frightened of the left that it preferred a Nazi victory: 'Rather Hitler than Blum'.

Among historians there have been two schools. First, there are those for whom 1940 was the result of deep-seated problems in the Third Republic. France, it is argued, was a divided and demoralized country whose population was unwilling to fight another war, whose economy was unable to sustain rearmament, whose political institutions were unable to provide stability, whose politicians were too discredited to provide leadership. How different this was from 1914 when the nation rallied to the 'sacred union' against Germany. The classic attempt to link 1940 to longer-term social and political problems is Bloch's *Strange Defeat*, written soon after the armistice and published in 1946. The distinguished French diplomatic historian J.-B. Duroselle called his history of French foreign policy in the 1930s *La Décadence*. The title says it all.

More recently, historians have started to re-evaluate the 1930s positively. Robert Young has argued that in the 1930s French policy was a rational attempt to match objectives with resources: the French prepared intelligently for a long war which would exploit allied economic superiority. Martin Alexander has demonstrated French military planners' awareness of the problems of modern warfare and the impressive efforts they made to prepare France for them. He has even taken on the thankless task of rehabilitating General Maurice Gamelin, the chief of general staff since 1931, a task, one might think, as difficult as that facing Gamelin in 1940. But the fact remains that France did lose the battle of 1940. If the revisionists' favourable reassessment of French military planning and policy is correct, how do we explain the defeat? Displacing the problem from poor leadership, outmoded military thinking or inflexible institutions seems to suggest some fundamental imbalance between France and Germany which no planning could overcome.

Another approach is suggested by Jeffery Gunsburg, who argues that the defeat of 1940 was as much an allied (Franco-Belgian-British) defeat as a French one. France was defeated because the western alliance was not yet sufficiently coordinated. The logic of Gunsburg's argument has been pushed further by Robert Frank's suggestion that in the long term the assumption behind French planning in 1939/40 was sound: the allies did win the war through their superior economic resources. De Gaulle, in leaving for London, remained faithful to that assumption; Pétain, remaining in France, abandoned it.

However one judges these arguments, the importance of the revisionists lies in their attempt to rescue the history of the late Third Republic from the teleology of reading it only in the light of 1940. It would be absurd to deny that all was well with France in the 1930s, and it is legitimate to take 1940 as a vantage-point for examining the 1930s crisis, but we must keep an open mind on the question of the causes and consequences of defeat, at least until the nature of the 1930s crisis has been established.

The crisis of the 1930s

The origins of the crisis go back to 1919. French confidence had been profoundly shaken by the war and French society destabilized by it. No country had suffered a higher proportion of casualties, and this came after a century in which the French birth rate had been declining. The young novelist Pierre Drieu La Rochelle was one of many who emerged from the war obsessed with French decadence. As he put it: 'The war killed France. She will not recover.' Paul Valéry's famous remark that the war had revealed the mortality of civilizations was the expression of a widespread cultural *malaise*. Writers also became obsessed with the threat posed by American mass culture to French civilization.

Although France had not experienced the revolutionary turmoil of postwar Germany, there had been major strikes in 1919 and 1920. The war had caused a considerable expansion in the French working class. The newly formed Communist Party was not a major political force in the 1920s but its very existence was enough to terrify French conservatives, especially after it made gains in the threatening new industrial suburbs which had sprung up around Paris in the war. The prospect of a political red belt around Paris existed in bourgeois imaginations well before it became a reality. When a left-wing government decided in 1924 to translate the remains of the pre-war socialist leader Jaurès to the Panthéon, and the cortège was accompanied by a procession of communist workers from the suburbs, there was a panic which spoke volumes about the fragility of post-war bourgeois self-confidence. This confidence was also hit by inflation caused by the huge government expenditure necessary to finance the war and the post-war cost of reconstruction. Alarmists wrote that the *rentier* was dead. The cultural changes which the war seemed to have brought were no less alarming. These crystallized around the image of the 'new woman' with her short skirts, short hair and supposed defiance of traditional morality. Victor Margueritte's *La Garçonne* (1922), a novel depicting this new woman, became one of the scandalous best-sellers of the decade.

Conservatives did not have any single party to defend their values and interests. As before 1914, conservative politics was fragmented. Conservatives were not reassured by the vacillations of the centrist Radical Party which preferred to ally at elections with the socialists on its left even though its *petit-bourgeois* electorate shared many of the social interests of the right. This was a factor for instability. After the left-wing victory of 1924 and a worsening financial crisis, conservative electors looked to more radical politics. Anti-parliamentary leagues developed, some inspired by Italian fascism. In 1926 when the financial crisis spiralled out of hand, the Radicals in parliament panicked, ended their alliance with the socialists and allowed the conservative Raymond Poincaré to come back to power and restore confidence. The political crisis dissipated and the leagues lost influence. This occurred because, despite the financial instability, the economy was growing rapidly. Economic growth for the moment absorbed the political and social tensions.

In 1931 the Depression arrived. France was now confronted with an economic and social crisis which rapidly developed into a political/ institutional crisis. The Depression hit France later than the rest of the world, but having arrived later, it lasted longer. Indeed, the economy never fully recovered. In 1939 industrial production was still below its 1929 levels. The main reason for the prolonged nature of the Depression in France was that despite the devaluations of sterling (1931) and the dollar (1933), the French refused to devalue and the economy was throttled by an overvalued currency. By mid-1933 the value of French exports had fallen by two-thirds since 1928. Businesses could only export by selling at unremunerative prices. But devaluation was associated in people's minds with the inflation of the 1920s which had left deep scars. Apocalyptic visions were conjured up of the final ruin of the *rentier* and the collapse of social order. Politicians compared the defence of the franc to the defence of Verdun.

Another peculiarity of the economic crisis in France lay in the nature of its social impact. Even if official figures underestimated unemployment levels, which peaked at about 1 million in 1935, this was still far below the comparable figures elsewhere – 2.6 per cent of the working population as opposed to 12.75 per cent in America, 9.4 per cent in Germany, 7.6 per cent in Britain – and those who remained in work experienced an increase in real wages. Thus the working class suffered least although its sense of grievance was exacerbated by largely unsuccessful attempts to cut wages, and by employers' attempts to rationalize work practices in order to reduce costs. Those who suffered most from the crisis were peasants, shopkeepers, small businessmen and artisans. The agricultural depression was particularly intense: wheat prices fell by 40 per cent and wine prices by 60 per cent. Among industrialists, exporting luxury industries suffered worst: in 1935 French silk exports were only worth 20 per cent of their 1928 value. Thus while the crisis hit sections of the conservative (and Radical) electorate, it did not, as in other countries, significantly weaken the strength of organized labour. This created the conditions for maximum social polarization.

For governments the most immediate impact of the crisis was to cause massive public-finance difficulties as revenues fell and social expenditure rose. But the two parties of the left which had won the elections of 1932 had entirely different responses to this problem. The Radicals believed it was necessary to cut government expenditure and eliminate the budget deficit; the socialists believed this would only make the crisis worse. Logic dictated that the Radicals govern with the right whose economic views they shared, but this was impossible so soon after having won elections on a left-wing slate. So the Radicals were obliged to try and obtain socialist support for conservative policies. The result was deadlock: six ministries in 18 months.

With no effective government possible, there was an explosion of competing interest groups intervening directly to protect themselves. There were demonstrations, often violent, of *fonctionnaires* (public employees), peasants, shopkeepers and small businessmen. The agricultural protests were organized by the extreme right-wing agitator Henry Dorgères who founded the Peasant Front (greenshirts); shopkeepers were organized by the right-wing Fédération Nationale des Contribuables. These organizations crossed the frontier between interest-group representation and political extremism, tapping into the tradition of anti-parliamentarianism. The Federation declared in February 1933: 'we will converge on this lair which is called parliament, and if necessary we will use whips and sticks'.[3] The anti-parliamentary leagues, dormant since 1926, returned to the scene. Perhaps more significant was the growing consensus, even within the moderate and parliamentary right, that France's political and social crisis had become an institutional one – that the regime was no longer working. The conservative politician André Tardieu launched a crusade in 1933 for a fundamental reform of France's constitution. An entire generation of young intellectuals turned away from the Republic and from politics itself. 'There is nothing to be done', said the Catholic philosopher Emmanuel Mounier, 'with present political structures'.[4] The first novel of Jean-Paul Sartre, born in the same year as Mounier (1905), was called *Nausea*. Its title embodies the mood of his generation.

This dual social/economic and political/institutional crisis exploded on the night of 6 February 1934 when a right-wing demonstration turned nasty, the police panicked and 15 deaths followed. There is no doubting the epochal nature of this moment – the worst political violence in France since the 1871 Commune – and it could be described as the beginning of the French civil war. When, in 1940, the French fascist novelist Robert Brasillach wrote his autobiographical memoir *Notre avant guerre*, he dated the preface '6 February Year VII'. As in all civil wars, each side invented a myth about what had occurred, thus permitting it to demonize its opponent. For the left, 6 February was a fascist plot to storm parliament; for the right it was a massacre of innocent patriots by the police of the Republic. The immediate result of the riots was to cause the resignation of the government, and the Radicals once again switched their allegiance and supported a conservative government of national union under the veteran politician Gaston Doumergue. The right now had the chance to impose its solution to the crisis.

The right-wing solution: 1934–1936

That solution had two components: deflation and constitutional reform. Deflation meant cuts in government spending in order to restore business confidence and lower interest rates. It was also hoped that this would have the beneficial side-effect of lowering wages and prices in order to make France competitive again without having to devalue. The idea of constitutional reform was indirectly linked to the deflation policy since it was clear that a policy which hit many sectional interests would be easier to carry out if the power of the government were strengthened. For a while it looked as if the government would be able to create a consensus around constitutional reform but this foundered on the opposition of the Radicals, who suspected anything redolent of Bonapartism. As a result Doumergue resigned in the autumn. But the right-wing coalition remained in power, and when in 1935 the new premier, Pierre Laval, carried out another wave of deflation – cutting all government expenditure by 10 per cent including war pensions and the income on bonds – he had to rely on special decree powers. For lack of fundamental constitutional reforms, the government resorted to these emergency measures, rather as Brüning had done in the last days of Weimar Germany to carry out similar policies.

The return of conservatives to power did not, as in 1926, bring the antiparliamentary agitation to an end. On the contrary it intensified it, and this demonstrated how much more serious the crisis was. The main agent of this agitation was the Croix de Feu (CF), a league founded as a war veterans' organization in 1928. Its leader, Colonel de La Rocque, took the movement away from its lobbying beginnings in an increasingly political direction, even creating paramilitary sections. The left in the 1930s was in no doubt that the CF posed a fascist threat. Historians have been less sure. Taking their lead from René Rémond, most historians argue that the CF was too conservative to be fascist, and they see it as a manifestation of the Bonapartist tendency in French politics. As for its paramilitary aspects, Rémond dismissed these as 'boyscouting for adults'. Recently Rémond's view has been contested. Robert Soucy has suggested that fascism's claim to radicalism was itself largely phoney and that the overlap between fascism and conservatism is considerable: in this light he reinterprets the CF as a fascist movement. More recently still Kevin Passmore has argued that both views are wrong, the former in underestimating the radical populism of the CF and the latter in underestimating the radicalism of fascism. This debate needs to be considered briefly because upon it turns our interpretation of the depth of the crisis of liberal democracy in France.

It was between 1934 and 1936 that the CF became easily the largest of all the leagues, with probably over 300000 members at the end of 1935. What therefore made it different from the development of previous leagues in the 1920s was that its maximum growth occurred while the right was in power. In other words, it was directed against the traditional right as well as the left. For La Rocque the Doumergue government was only a 'poultice on a gangrenous leg'.[5] The main feature of La Rocque's programme was its studious vagueness, and in this, at least, it was similar to the Nazi and Italian fascist programmes which never allowed themselves to be trapped into specific commitments which could narrow the basis of support or limit the scope of future action. The same tactical fluidity characterized La Rocque's attitude to democracy in general. As well as ritual denunciations of Masons and communists, the CF rejected any 'fetishism' of electoralism (it refused to stand in elections), and denounced all political parties as 'lying, parasitical, bribed, outdated'. It presented itself as a moral and political élite, guided by a charismatic leader and ready to regenerate the nation. How La Rocque intended to take power was unclear. He warned his followers against premature action and stressed his commitment to order. But he also kept them ready for action with frequent references to H-hour and the organization of paramilitary mobilizations and parades. As far as membership was concerned, the CF seems to have drawn on the urban lower middle class, but also some managers and salaried engineers. It represented a revolt of rank-and-file conservative voters against their leaders.

At the very least the CF was an authoritarian-populist movement which represented a significant revolt against liberal politics. Whether it is seen as fascist depends of course on how one defines fascism, but one should avoid being trapped into some essentialist notion of fascism. As Passmore suggests, all fascist movements were a conflictual combination of radical and reactionary elements. Certainly the CF was less stridently anti-democratic than the Nazis and less violent in the streets than the Italian fascists. But we should remember that Mussolini himself was very ambiguous until 1925 in his attitude to the liberal state, and the dream of liberals that he might be 'tamed' was not absurd even if in the conflict between radical and moderate elements, it was ultimately the radicals who prevailed. In the CF the balance of forces may have been different, but so was the context. As Passmore reminds us, in Italy and Germany fascism developed *after* the mobilization of the left; in France the rise of the CF pre-dated the mobilization of the left in the Popular Front, and the success of that mobilization seemed to indicate the failure of the radical–fascist option. The Popular Front was the left's answer to the CF and to the crisis of the 1930s.

1936–1938: The left-wing solution: the Popular Front

What became the Popular Front was born out of the left's response to 6 February. On 12 February there had been a general strike in defence of the Republic. What channelled this into something more durable was a change in the politics of the Communist Party. Since 1928 the communists had pursued a sectarian political line, refusing to associate with the socialists – whom they called 'social democratic vomit' – and denouncing the Republic as bourgeois. In 1934 all this changed. The arrival of Hitler to power had shown the dangers of disunity on the left, and the lesson was not lost in Moscow. 1934 also saw a reorientation of Soviet foreign policy as Stalin began to court France as an ally against Hitler. In these circumstances it made no sense for Moscow to encourage the communist parties to weaken French democracy. Thus the communists adopted the 'Popular Front' policy, aiming to build the widest possible coalition of parties dedicated to defending the Republic and reuniting the left around patriotism and national defence. Where communists had previously sung the Internationale and waved the red flag, they now draped themselves in the tricolour and sang the Marseillaise. The Popular Front policy was enormously successful: in July 1934 the communists signed a unity pact with the socialists; by the beginning of 1936 they had won over the Radicals, and the three parties signed a joint programme. An alliance between the communists and the Radicals was an extraordinary event, and it demonstrated the extent to which the antics of the Croix de Feu had frightened law-abiding republicans. Support for the Popular Front was also generated by the Depression and the social impact of the government's deflation policy. The Popular Front was both a social response to the Depression and a political response to 'fascism'.

The communists may have talked the language of moderation, but the rise of the Popular Front represented a major radicalization of French politics. Huge street demonstrations occurred. They showed that the left could mobilize larger numbers than the right: the Croix de Feu had lost the battle of the streets. The Popular Front won the elections of 1936 and for the first time ever France had a socialist premier, Léon Blum; communist seats in parliament rose from 12 to 75. The elections were followed by the outbreak in June 1936 of a wave of strikes and factory occupations on a scale never seen before in France, (1.8 million strikes, and over 12 000 strikes in June 1936 alone) and to conservatives it seemed France was on the verge of revolution. In fact these strikes were a mixture of elation at the left's victory and an attempt to profit from a favourable political moment to obtain concessions. The frightened employers met the unions in the presence of Blum, and the signing of the Matignon agreement granted the workers a whole series of concessions: two weeks' paid holidays, the 40-hour week, wage increases, recognition of collective bargaining and union rights. This was a remarkable shift in power to organized labour, accompanied by a massive increase in trade-union membership.

The Popular Front was no more successful than the right, however, at solving the economic/social and institutional/political crisis of the 1930s. Its economic policy was to reverse deflation and increase demand. At first the stimulus to the economy represented by the Matignon agreement did have positive effects in increasing industrial production and lowering unemployment once the government had devalued the franc. But this did not last, for reasons that are controversial. The root cause of the failure of the Popular Front's economic policy was the 40-hour week. It made no sense to increase demand and at the same time restrict the capacity of factories to meet that demand. The theory was that the 40-hour week would provide jobs for the unemployed, but once an initial pool of about 70 000 unemployed had been absorbed, the rest of the unemployed lacked the necessary skills. Instead of pulling the economy out of depression the Popular Front sparked off inflation. The result was financial crisis, forcing Blum to resign in June 1937. Although the Popular Front coalition still remained in power, under a more conservative premier, the writing was on the wall.

The Popular Front's answer to the political/institutional crisis was to rehabilitate the idea of republican democracy in France. Its use of the traditional iconography of republicanism – for example its big demonstration on 14 July – proved that the republican idea was much less discredited than had seemed the case 4 years earlier: France was not Weimar. The Popular Front government was not an experiment in socialism but an attempt to demonstrate that the republican state could be as effective and innovative as the regimes of Germany and Italy. One of the most striking features of the government was its ambitious cultural agenda to democratize culture, sport and leisure – whether in promoting the youth-hostel movement or sponsoring workers' educational projects. Many intellectuals were enormously excited by this enterprise and they entered politics on a scale not seen since the Dreyfus affair. Some of those who had been disillusioned by politics were, briefly at least, inspired by the idealism of the Popular Front.

Despite these successes, in the end the Popular Front did more to weaken than strengthen the Republic because it accentuated the polarization of politics beyond even the situation which had existed before 1936. The strikes had terrified conservatives, who felt that they were living through something close to a revolution fomented by the Communist Party. The outbreak of the Spanish Civil War in July nourished these fantasies of revolution: Spain, where the 'reds' were burning churches, seemed to French conservatives an ominous sign of what the future might hold for them. Within France, the Popular Front was experienced by conservatives as an assault on bourgeois order in all its forms. The massive demonstrations were an invasion of urban space by the proletarian suburbs on a scale beyond the worst nightmares of 1924; the arrival on the beaches of workers enjoying their first-ever paid holidays presaged an era when no social space would be sacrosanct.

In response to this there was a radicalization of the right which manifested itself in many ways. The most extreme was the terrorist organization, the Cagoule; another was the formation of the Parti Populaire Français by the former communist Jacques Doriot. Even those historians sceptical about the existence of fascism in France are willing to accept that this organization, which peaked at about 70000 members in the middle of 1937, was fascist. Ostensibly La Rocque's evolution in a less extreme direction modifies this picture of radicalization. Since the Popular Front had outlawed the leagues, he turned the CF into a political party, the Parti Social Français (PSF). The PSF grew rapidly and by 1937 was estimated to have about 700000 members, making it by far the largest party in France. The significance of this has been much debated. Rémond argued that the PSF's success demonstrates the 'immunity' of French society to extremism, since La Rocque's greatest success occurred after he turned to conventional politics; Soucy argues the contrary, claiming that the PSF remained fascist. The most convincing case is that of Passmore, who argues that having renounced the violence, para-militarism and apocalyptic rhetoric of the CF, the PSF was no longer fascist, but that it nonetheless remained an authoritarian-populist movement, ambivalent about democracy and with sympathy for fascist Italy and Nazi Germany. Although the main enemy remained 'Masonic communism', the CF also attacked other right-wing groups and even disrupted their meetings. Thus, even if it had abandoned violence, the PSF's extraordinary success is still testimony to the radicalization of politics in this period. In terms of membership, it was briefly the most successful political movement in French history.

That the Popular Front radicalized the right and gave shape to its fear of communism is perhaps not so surprising. More striking is the way in which it created a new anti-communism of the left. Many Radicals had gone into the Popular Front alliance with misgivings; others had rallied to it because they feared the threat to order caused by the right. The *grande peur* of June 1936 now made the left seem more frightening than the right. The Radical Party became increasingly worried about communism. Even more startling was the evolution towards anti-communism of a number of socialists and trade unionists. One must remember there was no love lost between the socialists and communists. The Popular Front had been a marriage of convenience which had benefited the communists, who for the first time overtook the socialists in party membership. But the most fundamental reason for the turn to anti-communism by some of the left – both Radical and socialist – was disagreement over foreign policy, a disagreement so profound that socialists who had in 1936 seen fascism as enemy number one came to feel that communism was as bad, if not worse.

What crystallized this feeling was the association of communism with war. To understand this, it is necessary to see how foreign policy came to interconnect with the general 1930s crisis. Traditionally the right had been anti-German and believed in security through alliances. The left had been internationalist and committed to the League of Nations. In the late 1920s these issues became blurred as Briand's pursuit of reconciliation won considerable consensus. Briandism was underpinned by a defensive military strategy (the Maginot Line, on which construction began in 1929) and the ambient pacifism of a society traumatized by the memories of the war. Among some intellectuals of the left pacifism was an ideology – 'rather servitude than war' – but for the mass of the population it was an instinct. Hitler's arrival in power, however, undermined the Briandist consensus. The left governments between 1932 and 1934 cut defence spending and laid its hopes in disarmament; after 1934 Doumergue's government renounced disarmament and set about consolidating France's eastern alliance system, resulting in the Franco-Soviet pact of May 1935.

This is how the left and right would have been expected to behave. But when the Franco-Soviet pact came up for parliamentary ratification in February 1936, 174 conservatives voted against it, inaugurating a dramatic evolution of conservative foreign policy where fear of communism began to displace fear of Germany. This evolution was exacerbated by the events of 1936 and the communist campaign for intervention in Spain. Were the communists not trying to drag France into war for the sake of Stalin? If anti-communism pushed conservatives into neo-pacifism, pacifism was pushing many socialists into anti-communism. When the Popular Front had been formed, it had been axiomatic among its supporters that there was no contradiction between a commitment to peace and opposition to fascism. But Hitler's increasing belligerence raised the possibility of fighting a war against fascism, requiring a choice to be made between political values. Since the communists were clearly committed to the possibility of war against Hitler – this for them was one of the points of the Popular Front – those for whom pacifism remained an absolute value moved towards anti-communism.

These conflicts crystallized in September 1938 during the Munich crisis. The most ardent supporters of Munich were an unholy alliance of neo-pacifist conservative anti-communists and left-wing pacifists. Munich was supported in parliament by a massive majority, with only 75 communists (and two mavericks) voting against, but this apparent unanimity disguised the existence of considerable doubts among many anti-fascist socialists and many anti-German conservatives. For its committed supporters, Munich was only the beginning of a total French disengagement from eastern Europe, to be compensated for by a fallback on the resources of the empire (*le repli impérial*). For those who were more doubtful, Munich was the end of the road: there must be no more concessions.

A resolution: 1938–1940

The political alignment around Munich allowed the Radicals to break the Popular Front alliance with a clear conscience, which many of them had been wanting to do for a long time. The communists were now in opposition. Daladier, the Radical who had taken his party into the Popular Front, now became premier of a government opposed by the communists whose idea the Popular Front had been. The new finance minister, Paul Reynaud, was a leading figure of the right. The social corollary of the new political alignments was the destruction of the powerful labour movement which had emerged in 1936. The chosen issue was the 40-hour week, seen by most workers as the symbol of the 1936 victory. The government passed a series of decrees revoking the 40-hour week. This provoked a general strike which was repressed with ferocity. Thousands of workers were sacked. Union membership, which had stood at 4 million in 1937, was down to 1.5 million at the start of 1939 and falling fast.

In the post-Munich mood of crisis, Daladier was able to govern France more like a dictator than anyone since Clemenceau during wartime. Daladier was helped after Munich by a widespread feeling that the Republic was sick and in need of a greater dose of authority. Capitalizing upon such sentiments, he largely ignored parliament by having himself voted successive sets of decree powers: from October 1938 to September 1939 he ruled by decree for over seven months. These previously emergency powers became a permanent system of government and Daladier used them with little respect for legal niceties. On 27 July 1939 he issued a decree proroguing parliament and suspending by-elections until June 1942, a measure unprecedented in peacetime. In 1914 no such decision had been taken until four months into the war, and it had been taken by parliament itself.

There was also a new mood of resolution in attitudes towards Germany. An opinion poll in July 1939 asked if any German attempt to take over Danzig should be met with force: only 17 per cent replied negatively. The changed mood was partly a response to Hitler's occupation of Prague, but it was also caused by Italy. On 30 November deputies in the Italian parliament rose to their feet shouting 'Tunisia, Corsica, Nice'. This was the start of an orchestrated anti-French campaign whose objective was to secure some

Italian gains in France's North African empire. Daladier visited Tunisia and Corsica to reaffirm France's fidelity to its empire, and this was given extensive press and newsreel coverage. Suddenly the empire became the theme of the moment. There was a flurry of popular films about empire and foreign legion; Edith Piaf had a hit with her song 'Mon légionnaire'. By a process of transference, the imperial theme, which was directed against Italy, contributed to a rehabilitation of patriotic values which made people less willing to contemplate further concessions towards Germany. This was ironic given that many *Munichois* had conceived of the *repli impérial* going hand-in-hand with a rapprochement with the Axis. The new French confidence was also demonstrated by Daladier's firm rejection in the summer of British pressure to pursue a conciliatory line towards Mussolini. For the first time in years, the French had defied the British. Halifax, the British foreign secretary, worried that Daladier was behaving like a new Poincaré. Daladier would certainly have been flattered by the comparison. He had become the most popular leader since Clemenceau, using the radio to great effect, and his straightforward style was perfectly suited to the medium.

It was also under Daladier's government that French rearmament began to take effect. The issue of rearmament needs to be looked at carefully because, quite apart from its centrality to any discussion of 1940, it was at the nexus of the social and political problems of the 1930s. Although a timid rearmament programme had been voted by Doumergue's government in 1934, the first serious one was voted by the Popular Front: 14 billion francs over 4 years, aiming to produce 3200 tanks. Blum, who had hoped to spend on butter, was forced to spend on arms, and the scale of this spending contributed to the financial crises which brought him down. So it was not true, as the right alleged, that the Popular Front refused to finance rearmament. It was true, however, that these spending programmes had very little immediate effect. Industry could not cope with the sudden influx of orders. Total tank production actually fell from 467 in 1936 to 403 in 1938. Conservatives alleged that this was the fault of Popular Front policies: the nationalization of the arms factories, the constant industrial unrest, the 40-hour week. In fact nationalization had only covered a small proportion of industries working for national defence and the factories in question were discovered to suffer from outdated plant and artisanal production methods. Industrialists had had little incentive to invest, given the lack of steady government orders and hesitations by the military about what models to order. In the long run the nationalizations led to modernization, but not immediately. As for the 40 hours, it was true that by early 1938 many arms factories were suffering from labour shortages, but it was not entirely the case that the unions refused to work longer than 40 hours. The issue was as much one of profits as hours – whether or not the extra hours would be remunerated at overtime rates – in other words, whether or not the principle of the 40 hours would be respected.

These problems were gravest in the aviation industry. Rearmament plans had been voted in 1934 (Plan I: 1100 planes) and in September 1936 (Plan II: 1500 planes). But the factories could not cope. In the last quarter of 1937 average monthly production was 40 planes; in January 1938 it was 35. Plan-I aircraft were still being produced in 1937, by which time they were obsolete anyway. France, which at the start of 1936 still enjoyed supremacy over the Luftwaffe, no longer had it a year later. This created a sense of urgency, and, after two other abortive rearmament programmes, a new plan was approved in March 1938 (Plan V: 4700 planes). In this year, for the first time, the air ministry took the largest proportion of defence spending (42 per cent). But Plan V called for high-speed planes which were still only at testing stage. So in the aviation industry, until the end of 1938, it is not true that the 40-hour week was blocking production, since the industry was not yet equipped to produce planes in mass quantity. One of the reasons why Daladier signed the Munich agreement was the gloomy warnings of General Vuillemin, air chief of staff, that the airforce would be obliterated in days.

Although many important spending decisions had been taken between 1936 and 1938, it was under Daladier that the first results started to appear. The pretext for the government's assault on the 40 hours had been rearmament, and in the conflict between profits and hours Daladier decided against the unions. This helped create an entirely new financial climate. Capital exports which had blighted the Popular Front were reversed, and the government was able to fund rearmament in a non-inflationary manner. But not all the Popular Front's reforms were abandoned. The air minister, Guy La Chambre, appointed the engineer Albert Caquot, an effective industrial administrator, to run the nationalized aircraft companies. In the process the companies lost much of the autonomy that the Popular Front had left them, and they were required to specialize their production in order to maximize efficiency. In September 1939 Raoul Dautry, formerly head of the state railways, was appointed minister of rearmament to coordinate the whole process.

In 1938 French military spending as a proportion of national income (8.6 per cent) had been half Germany's (17 per cent); in 1939 the proportions were equal (23 per cent). The production results were also impressive: 403 tanks in 1938; 1059 in 1939; 854 in the first six months of 1940. As for aviation, a modern industry had been created from scratch in almost 2 years. In 1937 the state had spent 116 million francs on plant modernization; between January 1938 and June 1940 the figure was 4 billion francs. The workforce in the aviation industry rose dramatically: 58 300 in January 1938, 85 300 in January 1939, 171 000 in January 1940, 250 000 in June 1940. Monthly production of planes had risen from 41 in November 1938 and 137 in March 1939 to an average of 330 per month in the first quarter of 1940. These successes, it should be noted, were achieved not only as a result of the abandonment of Popular Front policies in favour of *laissez-faire*. Proto-technocrats like Caquot and Dautry built on the Popular Front nationalizations. Their work was a continuation of the Popular Front policy of rationalization of the state.

In short, the Daladier government had produced a resolution to the 1930s crisis centred around anti-communism, authoritarian government, imperial rhetoric and an economic recovery stimulated by rearmament. The novelty was that for the first time it was the Radical Party which presided over this turn to the right rather than, as previously (1926, 1934), being prisoner of it. In the process the party moved sharply to the right – some historians talk of 'neo-Radicalism' – seeming ready to abandon some of its most cherished values such as anti-clericalism, and presiding over tough measures to restrict the rights of foreigners and refugees whose presence in France had led to a considerable wave of xenophobia. In these ways the Radicals were also able to defuse the threat from the PSF, whose support was diminishing. In all this there is no sign that the Third Republic was on its last legs; on the contrary it seemed healthier than at any time for almost a decade, even if the values it traditionally represented had not emerged unscathed from the crisis. Nothing, then, seemed to predestine France to defeat.

The war

The prefects described the mood of the population on the outbreak of war as one of 'resolution', 'gravity' and 'calm', terms very similar to 1914. The number of soldiers refusing the call-up was infinitesimal. The peace movement, so strong a year earlier, collapsed. This apparent unanimity should not be exaggerated. The pacifist socialists and neo-pacifist conservatives had not changed their views, but were forced to keep quiet. Twenty-two deputies had unsuccessfully tried to provoke a debate on the war before voting war credits. In the corridors of parliament there was an active peace faction which plotted against Daladier. Daladier himself was racked with doubts. One adviser noted on 24 September: 'On Wednesday he was for peace; on Thursday for war; Friday, on his return from London, he thought it might be possible to stop the war, counting on Mussolini to overcome British objections.'[6]

Daladier's method of defusing any parliamentary *fronde* was to deflect it towards the PCF. On 23 August Hitler had signed a non-aggression pact with Moscow. The communist press was immediately banned in France and the party outlawed on 26 September; communist municipalities were suspended and over 3400 activists were arrested. What was striking about this major intensification of post-Munich anti-communism was that it was launched before the PCF had reversed its policy from supporting to opposing the war in line with the new Soviet position: the communists did vote war credits. If Daladier's priority had been to keep the communists within the national community it would have made sense not to move against the party until it unequivocally repudiated its previous *bellicisme*, thus playing on the doubts many communists felt about the new policy rather than encouraging them into reflexes of solidarity with their persecuted comrades. The government's real purpose, however, was not to rally the communists who could be 'saved' but to win over the right. It was difficult for conservatives to advocate a positive response to possible German peace proposals when the communists were to be outlawed for doing the same. In return for accepting a war it did not much like, the right was rewarded with a campaign against communist traitors, and in the coming months the press gave itself over to an orgy of anti-communism.

This reached a crescendo after the Soviet Union attacked Finland in November. The government saw this as a chance of combining economic warfare and anti-communism by means of an operation into Scandinavia which would both help the Finns and cut off Swedish iron-ore exports to Germany. Such plans were received cautiously by the British, who saw no reason to risk antagonizing the Soviet Union, with whom the allies were not at war. Such issues were discussed by the allies in the joint Supreme War Council. Although this body turned out to be a forum to air differences rather than agree, the fact that it existed was itself an improvement on the First World War when no such organization had been set up before 1917. It was also the case that the two governments had been very quick to organize economic coordination. Jean Monnet was sent to London to look after this.

When possible operations were discussed, the French were keener on action – in the Balkans, in Salonica, in Scandinavia – than the British. This was partly due to the fact that the French had mobilized their full armies much faster, and it was necessary to keep up morale. During the winter morale both among the soldiers and civilians had declined alarmingly. Jean-Paul Sartre picked up the mood in his diaries of the period: 'the men who left with me were raring to go at the outset . . . now they are dying of boredom'.[7] There were many practical reasons for this decline in morale apart from boredom – the exceptionally cold winter, organizational problems which meant that the army was unable to provide enough socks and warm clothes, price rises, and so on – but it was fundamentally a failure of communication. Later there was much recrimination against government propaganda, which was the responsibility of the writer Jean Giraudoux. His operation was underfunded and his own radio broadcasts too literary to touch people, but the real problem was that Giraudoux was given no clear guidance as to why the war was being fought: the anti-communist obsession hardly provided reasons to be fighting Germany. The most potent illustration of the propaganda failure was the extraordinary impact of the German propaganda broadcasts from Stuttgart by the French journalist Ferdonnet. His theme was that Britain would fight to the last Frenchman. Not many people heard the broadcasts, but by reputation they inspired much fear.

The defeat of the Finns finally allowed Daladier's enemies in parliament to prevail. He was brought down on 20 March by a coalition between those who wanted to prosecute the war more vigorously and those who wanted peace. Daladier's successor, Paul Reynaud, had long believed himself to be the man destined to save France. In the 1930s he had been one of the few conservatives not to allow anti-communism to blind him to the threat from Germany. The problem was that this had cut him off from his own party, and his parliamentary base was weak. He felt the need to prove himself, to Gamelin's irritation: 'After Daladier who couldn't make a decision at all, here we are with Reynaud who makes one every five minutes.'[8] Reynaud did get the British to agree to a Scandinavian operation, but the allies were pre-empted by the Germans, who invaded Norway first on 9 April. Reynaud tried to use this débâcle to sack Gamelin, in whom he had no faith, but before he could do this the Germans at last launched their offensive in the west, on 10 May.

What happened next can be described very briefly. The French sent their crack troops into Belgium where they expected the main German assault. But in fact the brunt of the German attack came further south through the Ardennes, which the French high command had believed to be protected by the natural barriers of the Meuse river and the Ardennes forest. The troops guarding this sector were among the weakest in the army (many of them old B-division reserve troops), entirely unprepared and ill-equipped to respond to the massive assault of German panzers supported by demoralizing air attacks. Within three days the French line had been breached; on 15 May Rommel was advancing so fast that he was overtaking the retreating French; on 16 May nothing lay between the Germans and Paris, and the government considered evacuating the city.

In fact the Germans decided instead to head for the Channel and cut off the French and British forces in the north-east, but probably the battle of France was already lost on 16 May. The playing out of the final stages took another three weeks. Reynaud sacked Gamelin and replaced him with General Weygand. Weygand's plan, which had already been Gamelin's, was that the British in the north-east should link up with the French from the south and cut the German corridor. When this counter-attack failed in an atmosphere of Franco-British recrimination, the north-eastern armies headed for the Channel, where 320000 men were evacuated at Dunkirk. Meanwhile Weygand formed a new defensive line on the rivers Aisne and Somme, but he knew this could be no more than a last-ditch defence. The Germans breached the line on 6 June and the French retreated south. The government evacuated Paris on 10 June, and two days later it met at Cangé to hear Weygand admit that the battle was over.

The defeat: 'causes', 'consequences' and counterfactuals

The allied strategy had been to play a waiting game in order to build up their economic and military strength to win a long war, but the French had lost the short war before they could win the long one. What were the reasons for this débâcle? It was not true that France was beaten owing to inferiority in armaments. The success of the French rearmament effort meant that by the spring of 1940 French arms factories were outproducing German ones. In terms of quantity and quality of tanks there was little to choose between the two sides. In the air the French were still dramatically inferior to the Germans. But although this was important in the Ardennes breakthrough, it was probably not a decisive factor in the victory.

What about the way the arms were used? Here the accusation is that the French dispersed their tanks instead of forming them into the rapid and powerful heavy armoured divisions (DCR) which de Gaulle had been advocating since 1934. Martin Alexander has shown that the idea of a farseeing de Gaulle pitted against a hidebound French general staff is too simplistic. There were other modernizers in the French army, Gamelin possibly included, and de Gaulle may have hindered the modernization cause by linking it unnecessarily to the idea of a professional army, which alarmed politicians. But revisionism can be pushed too far. Whatever Gamelin's views about DCRs, and as so often with the mysterious Gamelin it is difficult to be sure, the fact is that the first DCR did not come into operation until January 1940. Two more were formed before May 1940 (and another improvised in the battle) but these were not fully trained. In total the DCRs included only one-sixth of all French tanks. The other tanks were incapable of offensive action. In general the French military had failed to see the degree to which new technology had transformed the possible speed of war. Too few tanks had radios; Gamelin's own command post only had telephone communications; the army lacked motorized gun transports. In short, having been strategically outmanoeuvred, the army lacked the *tactical* flexibility to respond quickly and effectively.

But it was the *strategic* error which was most serious. Dispatching the cream of the army into Belgium and neglecting the Ardennes sector was a fatal error. Gamelin compounded this by sending General Henri Giraud's crack Seventh Army, which had previously formed the bulk of the strategic reserve, through Belgium to join up with the Dutch at Breda, despite the opposition of other senior commanders. Giraud was therefore stranded in the north-east when the Germans broke through in the south. As a result of this infamous 'Breda variant', when Churchill asked Gamelin on 16 May 'Where is your strategic reserve?' he received the answer 'There is none'. (In fact there were also reserve troops behind the Maginot Line but Gamelin did not move these, fearing a possible German attack through Switzerland.) The greatest irony of Gamelin's career is that having built up a reputation as a man of caution, the only time in his life he took a gamble, it failed.

The defeat of 1940 can, therefore, be satisfactorily explained in military terms alone. Of course, it is true that the military are part of a society and that rigidities in military thinking cannot be unrelated to the social and intellectual context, but beyond this rather general statement it becomes difficult to link the defeat of 1940 to the crisis of the 1930s. It would be quite wrong to talk of a chronic decadence, a steady decline into defeat, a straight line from Paris in February 1934 via Munich in 1938 to Rethondes in 1940. The mood and prospects of the country had been transformed almost beyond recognition in the year since Munich. The Daladier government had provided a resolution to the crisis, and this 'Daladier moment' must not be allowed to disappear between the drama of the crisis which preceded it and the catastrophe which followed it.

Certainly there were many problems in the conduct of the phoney war, but these link to the defeat only tenuously. One approach to this problem might be to offer two counterfactual speculations. The first relates to Britain in 1940. Many of the alleged deficiencies of the French war-effort also existed in Britain. Giraudoux's propaganda was accused of being out of touch, but it was no more so than those British propagandists who produced the infamous poster 'Your courage and your ardour will bring us victory'. British propaganda had time to improve; France's did not. The French may have listened to Ferdonnet, but a poll showed that 62 per cent of British radio-listeners were tuning into the broadcasts of the traitor Lord Haw-Haw. It is what happened in 1940 which turned the folk memory of Lord Haw-Haw into a joke and Ferdonnet into a sinister and malign force. There were many pacifists in France, but we hear little about the luminaries such as Bernard Shaw, G. D. H. Cole and John Gielgud who signed an appeal for peace in February 1940, or the many pro-Nazi sympathizers described in Richard Griffiths's book *Fellow Travellers of the Right*, or the group of about 30 MPs in the pacifist Peace Aims Group, or the defeatist comments chronicled in the diaries of Harold Nicholson or Chips Channon. Britain, it is said, had Churchill presiding over a strong war cabinet and Reynaud over a weak and divided one. In fact Churchill was hated by most of his own party when he came to power, and there was a strong peace lobby in his own government led by Lord Halifax. The myth of Churchill was as much the consequence of success as it was its cause. Andrew Roberts has recently shown that one of the most obsequious celebrators of that myth, Sir Arthur Bryant, had in the 1930s been a pro-Nazi appeaser. If Britain had lost – if, dare one say, the Channel had not been there – it is all too easy to imagine Bryant playing the same sycophantic role to whoever might have emerged as the British Pétain (Lloyd George?) as in France the writer René Benjamin was to play towards Marshal Pétain.

The second counterfactual relates to France in 1914. Had France been defeated in 1914 our perspective on the French Republic of 1914 would be very different. The infamous Plan XVII of 1914 was quite as disastrous as Plan D in 1940. Joffre had to sack so many generals in August 1914 that a new word was coined for the purpose (*Limoger* – send to Limoges). In 1914 the French inferiority in armaments, especially artillery, was dramatic: French arms expenditure was 5 per cent of French national income in 1939, 0.67 per cent in 1913. The atmosphere of Bordeaux, where the government had taken refuge, was hardly better in September 1914 than in 1940. The relations between generals French and Lanrezac in 1914 were certainly as bad as between Gort and Weygand in 1940 – with the difference that the allies had set up some organisms of coordination in 1940. The premier in 1914, René Viviani, was an ineffectual neurasthenic whereas Daladier and Reynaud were men of stature. In short, when one knows the outcome, the narrative writes itself too temptingly. In narratives of 1940 the fact that General André Corap, unfortunate commander of the Ninth Army, was so fat he could barely get into his car functions as a symbol of his sluggishness in responding to the German breakthrough; in narratives of 1914 Joffre's no less considerable bulk functions as proof of unflappable moral solidity.

The Third Republic in 1914 was much less ready for war than it was in 1940, but luckily it had the time to adapt. In 1940 it did not. At the Marne the French were saved possibly by the Russian alliance – Moltke diverted six army corps to the eastern front on 25 August 1914 – and by a German mistake when Kluck wheeled his armies to the east of Paris, exposing his flank to counter-attack. Of course, the Marne was also won by the tenacity of the *poilu*. But again one must be careful of retrospective vision. J.-J. Becker's study of public opinion has shown us that the crowds shouting *À Berlin* in 1914 were a minority. The French soldier in 1914 went to war in a spirit of resignation not enthusiasm – not so different in this from his successor in 1940. The dip in morale in the winter of 1940 had been overcome by the spring; the soldiers of 1940 were to fight no less bravely than those of 1914 when they were properly led. Certainly the style of patriotism had changed. One observer noted that the preferred songs of the soldiers during the phoney war were current hits; attempts to revive the First-War hit 'Madelon' were a failure and people who tried to sing the Marseillaise were shouted down.[9] But these were merely reactions against showy manifestations of chauvinistic patriotism on the model of 1914. One should remember in this context that the Germans had also experienced Verdun and the Somme. There was no greater enthusiasm for war in the streets of Berlin in 1939 than there was in Paris. If the German mood changed, it was a result of victory, not a cause of it.

As for the contrast between the heroic *poilu* and his 1940 successors, one should not forget that in 1914 there were many worries about the combativity of the Midi troops of the 15th corps, and indeed allegations that they had not fought properly. If this has been largely forgotten – though not in the Midi – it was because of the Marne. Similarly one must not judge the French army of 1940 by the undertrained, underequipped and old troops (the 55th and 72nd infantry divisions) who faced the Germans in the Ardennes. The troops who fought three weeks later on the defensive line of the Aisne–Somme did so just as tenaciously as their 1914 predecessors, and their commanders had already started to adapt to the new methods of warfare. But it was too little and too late to provide victory. Nonetheless, 100 000 soldiers were killed in the six weeks of the battle of France, only slightly less than in the first six weeks of war in 1914. This is hardly the sign of an army unwilling to fight. It is true that some 1.6 million French prisoners were taken in 1940, but most of them after Pétain's broadcast saying that France would be seeking an armistice.

The Battle of France, then, was lost because of the errors of the high command, errors hardly greater than those of 1914, but errors that in this case could not be remedied. Many of the alleged 'causes' of the defeat could equally be seen as its consequences. As for the crisis of the 1930s, it should be seen not so much as a cause of defeat as the cause of that defeat's consequences: the Vichy regime. There was a serious crisis of liberal democracy in the France of the 1930s, and the kind of resolution that Daladier offered to that crisis – authoritarian and technocratic government, celebration of empire, racism – prefigured many aspects of Vichy. It is also true that the Daladier government had not been in existence long enough to erase the memories of the 1930s civil war. The defeat of 1940 turned that government from a resolution of that civil war to a respite in it. The economist Charles Rist noted the following episode in his diary on 28 May 1941: 'Madam Auboin tells me that after the armistice she received from a reactionary friend a letter containing these words: "At last we are victorious". She says it took her a moment to understand.'[10] Soon the meaning of the letter would be only too clear. Few French people had wished for defeat in 1940, but there were many who were only too ready to profit from it.

Notes

1 P. Vidal Naquet, *Les Juifs, la mémoire et le présent* (Paris: Seuil, 1991), p. 87.
2 J.-P. Sartre, *War Diaries: Notebooks from a Phoney War November 1939–May 1940* (London: Verso, 1984), p. 175.
3 P. Milza, 'L'Ultra-droite des années trente', in M. Winock, *Histoire de l'extrême droite en France* (Paris: Seuil, 1993), p. 160.
4 M. Winock, *Histoire politique de la revue 'Esprit', 1932–1950* (Paris: Seuil, 1975), p. 36.
5 R. Soucy, *French Fascism: The Second Wave* (New Haven: Yale University Press, 1995), p. 112.
6 P. de Villelume, *Journal d'une défaite* (Paris: Fayard, 1976), p. 42.
7 Sartre, *War Diaries*, pp. 46–7.
8 Quoted by M. S. Alexander, 'The fall of France 1940', in J. Gooch (ed.), *Decisive Campaigns of the Second World War* (London: Cass, 1990), p. 26.
9 G. Sadoul, *Journal de guerre. 2 septembre 1939–20 juillet 1940* (Paris: Les Editeurs Français Réunis, 1977), pp. 101, 123, 139.
10 C. Rist, *Une saison gâtée. Journal de guerre et de l'occupation 1939–1945* (Paris: Fayard, 1983), p. 165.

Further reading

Adamthwaite, A. P. *Grandeur and Misery: France's Bid for Power in Europe 1914–1940* (London: Arnold, 1995).
Alexander, M. S. *The Republic in Danger: General Maurice Gamelin and the Politics*

of French Defence, 1933–1940 (Cambridge: Cambridge University Press, 1993).

Blatt, J. *The French Defeat of 1940: Reassessments* (New York and Oxford: Berghahn, 1998).

Bloch, M. *Strange Defeat* (New York: Octagon, 1968).

Chapman, H. *State Capitalism and Working Class Radicalism in the French Aircraft Industry* (Berkeley: University of California Press, 1991).

Crémieux-Brilhac, J.-L. *Les Français de l'An 40*, 2 vols. (Paris: Gallimard, 1990).

Duroselle, J.-B. *La Décadence, 1932–1939* (Paris: Imprimerie Nationale, 1979).

Frank, R. *Le Prix du réarmement français, 1935–1939* (Paris: Publications de la Sorbonne, 1982).

Gunsburg, J. *Divided and Conquered: The French High Command and the Defeat of the West* (Westport, CT: Greenwood Press, 1979).

Jackson, J. *The Popular France in France: Defending Democracy, 1934–1938* (Cambridge: Cambridge University Press, 1988).

Passmore, K. *From Liberalism to Fascism: The Right in a French Province, 1928–1939* (Cambridge: Cambridge University Press, 1997).

Rémond, R. *The Right Wing in France from 1815 to de Gaulle* (Philadelphia: University of Pennsylvania Press, 1969).

Soucy, R. *French Fascism: The First Wave 1924–1933* (New Haven: Yale University Press, 1986).

Young, R. *France and the Origins of the Second World War* (Basingstoke: Macmillan, 1996).

|10|

Renewal, repression and Resistance
France under the Nazi occupation, 1940–1944

NICHOLAS ATKIN

The Nazi occupation of 1940–4 remains the most traumatic episode in contemporary French history. The defeat of June 1940, the signing of the armistice, the division of France into two principal zones, the destruction of the Third Republic and the creation of an authoritarian regime at Vichy forced the population to make some agonizing choices: whether to support the new administration of Marshal Pétain; whether to collaborate with the occupier; whether to join the Resistance; or whether to wait on events, a phenomenon known as *attentisme*. These choices proved so distressing that for several years after the Liberation most French writers depicted Vichy as a parenthesis in their country's history, a foreign regime visited on an exhausted France by a triumphant Hitler. By the late 1960s, however, it was difficult to sustain this view. Work on Nazi archives, conducted by American and German scholars, together with the findings of the under-acknowledged researchers of the Centre de Documentation Juive Contemporaine in Paris, revealed that Berlin was uninterested in the Vichy unoccupied zone so long as the Wehrmacht's security remained steadfast.[1] Although both the French public and the political establishment found such reappraisals difficult to stomach, before long a fresh generation of scholars had unveiled the autonomy enjoyed by the Pétain government. No longer an aberration in its country's history, Vichy was shown to have drawn from existing French traditions, most embarrassingly an indigenous anti-semitism. It is this fact – Vichy's complicity in the Holocaust – that now dominates the remembrance of the war years. Today, the Occupation is rarely recalled through the events of Franco-German relations: the armistice at Rethondes; the Hitler–Pétain meeting at Montoire; and the Syrian protocols agreed at Paris. It is instead remembered through the actions and choices of individuals, not so much the Darlans, Weygands and Lavals, but the Touviers, Leguays and Bousquets, lesser officials who have all been recently charged with 'crimes against humanity' for their part in persecuting Jews.

There remains one man whose legacy is inextricably bound up with that of the Occupation. Introducing him to children in 1941, one school primer announced: 'He is a handsome old man, solid and upright like the tree of the Druids ... this is Marshal Pétain, our marshal, the father of all French children who has given the gift of his person to France.'² Throughout the Occupation such idolization was the norm, not the exception. As the novelist Alphonse Boudard has his schoolboy hero caustically reflect in his 1977 novel *Les Combattants du petit bonheur*, 'our marshal' was everywhere in wartime Paris, 'at the town hall, at the church, in the bistrots, in the brothels, the portrait of the marshal ... the immortal phrases of the marshal! The white moustache of the marshal.'³ In October 1941 the minister of education announced that sales of the old man's picture, calendars and posters had totalled 18 846 000 francs. Moreover, this was a hero whom the public could see and hear. His frail voice was frequently on the radio, and the marshal

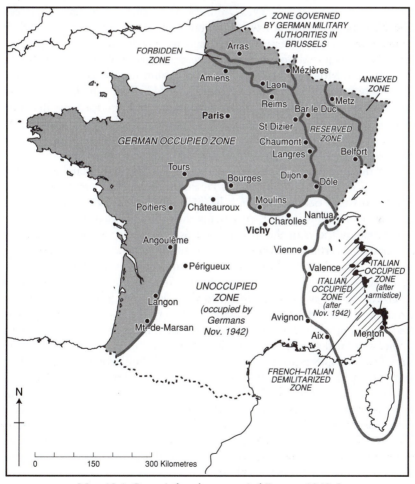

Map 10.1 Occupied and unoccupied France, 1940–2

himself regularly toured the towns and villages of the southern zone. Additionally, he received visitors at his residence, the Hôtel du Parc, in the centre of Vichy. When, on 10 July 1942, 70 Catholic children belonging to the youth group Fanfare Jeanne d'Arc de Langogne journeyed to the temporary French capital, they sang the Pétainist anthem, 'Maréchal, nous voilà', to which the old soldier modestly replied, 'Eh bien, le maréchal le voilà'.[4]

The writer Henri Amouroux has since suggested there were '40 million Pétainists' in 1940, yet this claim remains questionable. Tiny in number, there were those brave few prepared to question the marshal's wisdom, even at the time of the armistice, thus constituting the beginnings of a fledgling Resistance movement. Detailed local studies have also shown that the ruralist propaganda of Pétainism had a greater resonance in the largely agrarian southern zone than it did in the industrialized north where, in any case, the German presence made it difficult to present the old soldier as a saviour. Historians such as Yves Durand have further distinguished between 'active' Pétainists, the minority, who subscribed to the political tenets of their leader, and 'passive' Pétainists, the majority, who valued their hero as a symbol of security. Although later events in the war – notably the handshake with Hitler at Montoire, the recruitment of labour for German factories and the total occupation of France in November 1942 – forced many to question the marshal's decisions, his underlying popularity propped up his ramshackle government. Through innovative use of oral testimony, Rod Kedward has shown how this loyalty to Pétain was one of the trickiest obstacles resisters had to overcome when recruiting to their ranks.

Why this popularity? Part of the answer lies in the cult of marshalship that originated in the First World War. During that conflict Pétain rescued his country on two occasions: when he held Verdun in 1916 and when he quelled the mutinies in the French army the following year. In 1918 he was one of the architects of the final victory over Germany, and received enormous public gratitude. There was thus a cult of Pétain before 1940, and it is no surprise that some of his most fervent supporters during the Occupation were old soldiers, men who, as the English journalist Neville Lytton observed, openly wept when they heard their former leader announce the armistice on the radio,[5] and who later flocked to the veterans' organization, the Legion Française des Anciens Combattants. In 1940 Pétain's popularity further stemmed from the *exode*. Frantically trying to escape the German onslaught, up to 8 million men, women and children took to the roads, a harrowing experience vividly recounted in Jean-Paul Sartre's novel *Iron in the Soul* and René Clément's 1954 film *Jeux interdits*. Seemingly deserted by their government and stranded in unfamiliar locations, these refugees looked to their saviour, the patriot who would restore order amid the chaos. Pétain was, then, as Paxton argues, the right man for the moment. In this respect, it helped that during the interwar years he had said little to puncture people's illusions and was untainted by close connections with the Third Republic, a regime damned by defeat. In 1940 virtually everyone, save the Gaullists in

London and the pro-Nazi sympathizers in Paris, saw something in Pétain to admire.

Few realized it at the time, but the 'real' marshal was far removed from the images of Vichy propaganda. As the present author has argued elsewhere, to Catholics he was the product of *enseignement libre*, a man who would restore religious liberties and halt the tide of dechristianization; few recognized that he went rarely to mass, was a dedicated roué, and was married to a divorcée. To peasants he was one of them, a man of lowly origins, not someone who spurned his roots in northern France for a comfortable house in the sunnier south and the fashionable salons of Paris. To soldiers he was the great patriot, an able strategist and humane leader, not a man whose outmoded military thinking had left France badly prepared for war in 1940, and whose pessimism and anglophobia nearly cost France victory in 1918. To those on the left he was, in the words of Léon Blum, 'the most compassionate and republican of the high command', not an intensely ambitious politicker eager for power. That he was a republican cannot be questioned, yet his preference was for an authoritarian republic, free from the shackles of parliamentary democracy. Convinced that socialism, liberalism and individualism had ruined his country, Pétain looked to the army, the school, the workplace and the family to instil the traditional French values of discipline, order and obedience.

The marshal also looked to his ministers to bring about 'national renovation', the term he favoured for the much-vaunted national revolution, Vichy's ambitious programme for domestic reform. Historians have since tried to make sense of this most contradictory of governments. Those keen to rehabilitate the marshal have claimed Vichy was merely a 'government of wartime expediency', holding the fort and protecting France from the worst excesses of Nazism. Unquestionably, the regime's freedom of manoeuvre was severely limited: two-thirds of the most prosperous parts of French territory were under occupation; the demarcation line between the two principal zones served, in the words of General Stülpnagel, as a 'bit between France's mouth' which could be relaxed and tightened whenever Berlin chose; foodstuffs, economic resources and manpower were ruthlessly plundered; and 1.6 million prisoners of war languished in German camps. After the total occupation of France in November 1942 Nazi controls became even stiffer; according to Jean Tracou, one of the marshal's personal entourage, by 1943 Vichy resembled a prison with its own *Gauleiter* and division of SS guards.

Nevertheless, Vichy was clearly more than a 'holding operation', otherwise there would have been no need to launch a series of domestic reforms. Conscious of this fact, historians have pointed to similarities between Vichy's projects and the values of a traditional right, leading to suggestions that the regime constituted a counter-revolution, a rejection of France's republican heritage. Superficially, there is evidence to support this view: the administration's renunciation of parliamentarianism and universal male suffrage; its attempted reconciliation with the Catholic Church; its organicist rhetoric; its denial of women's rights; its *retour à la terre* philosophy; its celebration of regionalism; and its promotion of the family. Nonetheless, as Paxton states, while the values of a traditional right were often at the forefront of national-revolution propaganda, epitomized in the slogan 'work, family, country', the regime was never a 'bloc'; rather it encompassed a wide body of political traditions, among them social Catholicism, positivism, Orléanism, modernism and republicanism. Indeed, republican politicians – Flandin, Laval and Peyrouton – were well represented at Vichy, ensuring that government implemented many of those schemes that had fallen foul of parliamentary *immobilisme* in the 1920s and 1930s. In economic affairs, Vichy experimented with economic planning through the Délégation Générale à l'Equipement National, even though there was little the regime could do in the economic sphere without Nazi permission. In educational matters, Vichy risked the wrath of academy inspectors, committed to a rigorous and demanding curriculum, by displaying a greater concern for vocational training, sports and outdoor activities. In the social domain, Vichy improved facilities for post-natal care and established a state pension, something that the Popular Front had promised but failed to deliver.

To the ingredients that comprised the national revolution it is possible to add fascism. During the Occupation itself communist resisters, recalling Pétain's handling of the mutineers in 1917, denounced the regime as 'fascist', the stooge of big business and the *haute bourgeoisie*, a view repeated by left-wing historians since the war. That the marshal's government included fascists is not in doubt. Notwithstanding the debates over whether a French fascism ever existed, Vichy also embraced several of the 'anti' characteristics that define generic fascism: it was anti-parliamentarian, anti-liberal, anti-capitalist, anti-communist and anti-Jewish. It is only when one scrapes beneath the surface that ambiguities arise. To begin with, there is the problem of the national revolution itself which, as Paxton states, comprised 'competing visions'. Another difficulty is Pétain. While a cult of leadership might be an essential ingredient of fascism, the marshal was no Mussolini or Hitler, but an ageing soldier whose political philosophy was little more than a half-baked appreciation of Maurrassian ideals. Nor was Vichy prepared to challenge social élites in the manner of the Nazis, preferring to rely on existing hierarchies. Fascist regimes were 'youthful', yet Vichy was a gerontocracy: in 1940 Pétain was 84 years old, Weygand 73. As Richard Vinen has shown, when in 1941 Vichy brought young men into power, these technocrats, or so-called *jeunes cyclistes*, were appreciated more for their economic expertise than their youth.[6] Vinen has further demonstrated that Vichy's attitude to violence separated it from fascist states. Although the marshal's government used force to crush its enemies, it did not celebrate struggle in the same way as German Nazism and Italian fascism. Vichy propaganda was terribly muddled; unlike fascist states, it had little notion about how it wished to be portrayed. Nor did the regime promote a single party, another vital characteristic of fascism. When, in July 1940, Marcel Déat suggested the possibility of a *parti unique* to Pétain, the old man dismissed the idea, fearful such an organization might form a rival power base. Instead, the regime established a number of veteran and youth groups such as the Légion and the Chantiers de la Jeunesse to counteract the threat of a one-party state. In 1941 Déat founded the Rassemblement National Populaire (RNP), the first political body of note to have been set up since the defeat, yet its activities were restricted to the unoccupied zone and it never commanded universal support among collaborators.

While there is considerable scepticism as to whether Vichy was fascist, debates over the nature of the regime have been helpful in that they have pointed to its inchoate nature. Today there is a growing certainty that Vichy was, as Stanley Hoffmann first suggested, a *dictature pluraliste*, a faction-ridden government, unclear of what direction to pursue in either domestic or foreign policy other than to clamp down on its enemies and ensure its own survival. That said, historians have been able to plot the regime's evolution. In summer 1940 the government was essentially the rump of Reynaud's cabinet, comprising former parliamentarians, military men and odd members of the left. Through a series of reshuffles, notably those of 6 September and 13 December 1940, the occasion on which Pétain dismissed Laval, government came to include traditionalists such as Jacques Chevalier and Xavier Vallat, and yet more military figures. It is no surprise that in early 1941 the national revolution was at its height. Then, in February 1941, anxious for foreign-policy success, the marshal handed over considerable power to Admiral Darlan, who introduced his own people, young *dirigistes* in the shape of Pierre Pucheu and François Lehideux. In April 1942, as part of another desperate attempt to reinvigorate Franco-German relations, the marshal reluctantly recalled Laval, who appointed trusted friends, notably former parliamentarians and syndicalists, for instance Max Bonnafous and Hubert Lagardelle, men who would not dare repeat the coup of 13 December. Thereafter, only lip-service was paid to the ideals of the national revolution and in the course of 1943–4 the regime completed its transformation into a police state, calling on the services of Joseph Darnand, Philippe Henriot and Déat.

If there is a theme which unites these phases of Vichy's existence, it is the regime's desire to purge France of 'unreliable elements', leading to a growing belief among historians that the regime was one of 'exclusion'. Although there is some truth in apologist claims that the government's police powers were designed to highlight the regime's autonomy and resist German meddling, the marshal and his associates always believed that tough measures were necessary for national renovation. In their view, Vichy had inherited an enfeebled society, corrupted by the individualism, secularism and moral permissiveness of the Third Republic. It was thus necessary to purge the country of the 'anti-France': Jews, Freemasons, communists, free-thinkers and parliamentarians. Yet, as Paxton first observed, not all of the right's bugbears were victimized, notable exceptions being Protestants. Pétain respected the Protestant Church and enjoyed good personal relations with Marc Boegner, head of the Fédération Protestante. Several prominent Protestants, among them Paul Baudouin, René Gillouin and Maurice Couve de Murville, worked for Vichy, and Protestant institutes of higher education received government subsidies, even though Laval suspected them of being hotbeds of Resistance. Freemasons were not so lucky. Masonry remained inextricably linked with past episodes in French history going back to the Revolution of 1789. Vichy was quick to exact revenge, abolishing lodges and forcing Freemasons to declare membership of secret societies. Nonetheless, as Vinen states, 'the conflict between the Masons and the government was blunted by the fact that most Masons were property owners who feared Marxism as much as they feared "reaction".'[7] Vichy also enjoyed an ambivalent relationship with ex-parliamentarians. While many former rightist deputies, notably Marquet, Flandin and most famously Laval, found their way into cabinet, others, especially those connected with the Popular Front, were openly persecuted. Vichy took a sadistic pleasure in placing Daladier and Blum on trial at Riom, accusing them of having lost the Battle of France.

Less ambiguity surrounds Vichy's relationship with communism. As Kedward has remarked, Vichy was indelibly marked by its 'rejection of the left and trade unionism'.[8] Even though much of the Popular Front's progressive legislation had been unpicked before 1940, the victory of the Blum government had deeply unsettled the French right. Small wonder that Pétain was eager to put Blum into the dock at Riom; small wonder, big business and high finance were especially prominent at Vichy; small wonder, the regime was anxious to amplify the anti-communist legislation of the Daladier government. Historians have demonstrated how Vichy's attack on the left entered an exceptionally savage phase after June 1941 when Hitler's invasion of the Soviet Union prompted French communists to engage in widespread Resistance. Thereafter, much Resistance activity was conveniently blamed on the left and Pucheu, as minister of the interior, gladly handed over communist hostages to the Nazis in response to the killing of German soldiers.

Among the groups targeted by Vichy, it was the Jews who received the most savage treatment. While Germany was busy spreading its poisonous brand of racist laws in the occupied zone, Vichy was doing likewise in the south. During summer 1940 the Crémieux decree of 1875 bequeathing French citizenship to Algerian Jews was repealed. The 1938 Marchandeau law banning racism in the press was also abrogated, thus opening the way for a particularly nasty type of journalism favoured by such collaborationist newspapers as *La France Socialiste* and *Le Gringoire*. Additionally, those not of French parenthood were debarred from holding public office; and all naturalizations conducted since 1927 were reviewed. In October 1940 Vichy introduced the first *Statut des juifs*, limiting the types of jobs Jews could perform. The next year the Commissariat Général aux Questions Juives (CGQJ) was established under the directorship of Vallat, a veterans' leader and ardent xenophobe. June 1941 witnessed the second *Statut*; July saw the seizure of Jewish property and businesses.

This legislation used to be put down to Nazi pressure, yet research by Michael Marrus and Robert Paxton has established beyond doubt that Vichy's anti-semitism stemmed from an indigenous racism that dated back to the Dreyfus affair and beyond. The same authors have also shown how Vichy's dislike of Jews arose from a traditional fear of foreigners, a fear that was heightened during the interwar years when governments actively encouraged immigration to compensate for a low birth rate and welcomed refugees fleeing fascist oppression in Germany and Spain. More importantly, the regime's anti-semitism derived from the Maurrasian conception 'that Jews lacked the communal and local associations that formed the *real nation*'.[9] Vichy's apologists have, in turn, claimed that the government's racism was more cultural than biological. Whereas the Nazis viewed all foreigners as a threat to racial purity, Vichy believed that certain groups – Jewish ex-soldiers and French-born Jewish families – could assimilate French traditions and should therefore be tolerated. Nonetheless, as several historians have been quick to point out, Vichy's definition of a Jew was a racial one and, as the occupation progressed, the distinctions between Vichy and German anti-semitism evaporated. Confronted with the Reich's plans for the 'final solution', Laval hit upon the morally indefensible policy of exchanging the lives of foreign Jews for French ones, a move epitomized by the infamous Vél d'Hiv round-up when in July 1942 some 16 000 Jews, among them 4000 children, were interned in appalling conditions in a Parisian sports hall before being shipped to their deaths in the east. When Germany occupied all of France, it became harder to resist German demands for all categories of Jews. Recent work on the French police under the leadership of René Bousquet, and the CGQJ under the fanatic Louis Darquier de Pellepoix, has proved that Vichy played a key role in the round-up of Jews. It was in this context that lesser officials such as Maurice Papon in the Gironde and Paul Touvier in the Savoy worked alongside the German authorities. Without this sort of assistance, it is unlikely that some 75 000 Jews would have been deported from France; few, maybe 2–3 per cent, returned alive.

Thus, by 1943 Vichy had largely completed its metamorphosis into a police state. The intensification of measures against the Jews, the total occupation of France and the recruitment of labour for Germany, first through the voluntary *relève* in 1942 and then through the compulsory Service du Travail Obligatoire (STO) the following year, brought the 'language of deportation' and 'persecution into the village squares and rural towns' that had hitherto experienced little state interference.[10] In 1943 Vichy was compelled to establish a special paramilitary force, the Milice, under the control of the distinguished war veteran Joseph Darnand, to root out resisters and deserters from STO. The brutality of Darnand's cut-throats, chillingly depicted in Louis Malle's 1974 film *Lacombe Lucien*, undoubtedly troubled the marshal and his ministers, yet they tolerated such behaviour as they feared social disorder the more. Vichy never understood that, in doing the Germans' sordid business for them, France was in danger of becoming another Poland, a brutalized and submissive state, subject to the Nazis' every whim.

This was never the intention. Through its foreign policy, Vichy attempted to reach an accommodation with Germany. Much controversy, however, exists over what the Pétain government wanted out of negotiations with Berlin, and it is in this arena that the marshal's apologists such as Louis-Dominique Girard and Louis Rougier have been at their busiest, leaving behind them a trail of obfuscation and, on occasion, forged documents. Echoing the arguments first deployed by Jacques Isorni, the most eloquent lawyer on Pétain's defence team in 1945, it is argued that the old man was secretly playing a double game with the Germans. While de Gaulle acted as 'the sword' of France, conducting resistance overseas, the marshal constituted 'the shield' at home, protecting his people from the worst excesses of Nazism by hoodwinking the Germans and secretly working with the allies. If anyone was keen on collaboration, then it was Laval and Darlan, the other two Vichy ministers chiefly responsible for foreign policy. Naturally enough, the supporters of these two men have vigorously denied these charges: Laval and Darlan were likewise beguiling the enemy.

The release of German, French, British and American archives has conclusively demolished the double-game theory, and has displayed that the initiatives for collaboration came from Vichy not Berlin. Moreover, the released documents have shown that Pétain, Darlan and Laval had remarkably similar objectives. To begin with, the three men believed collaboration would ease the demands of the armistice and pave the way for a conclusive peace treaty by which France would recover something of its former standing. They also saw collaboration as a means of ridding France of its ties with 'perfidious Albion'. Each man was possessed with a burning anglophobia: Pétain through his dealings with Haig in the First World War; Laval through his negotiations with Sir Samuel Hoare in the 1930s; and Darlan through his career in the French navy, a traditional well of anti-English sentiment. If they sought connections with the Anglo-Saxon world, then it was with the United States of America, a country all three admired. The other country they hated was, of course, the Soviet Union. Even greater than their hatred of Britain was their dislike of communism. Pétain still smarted from communist criticism of his handling of the mutinies in 1917 and of his suppression of Morocco's Rif tribes in 1925. As a former socialist, Laval despised the sectarianism of the left and, through his foreign-policy dealings in the 1930s, concluded that it was the fascist regimes, not the liberal democracies, which constituted the greatest protection against bolshevism. Darlan, a member of the respectable bourgeoisie and himself an experienced diplomat, concurred, and in 1941 readily persecuted communists. Thus, when on 22 June 1942 Laval delivered his infamous speech 'I desire the victory of Germany for without it bolshevism will install itself elsewhere', the speech for which, as Kedward has observed, he would be pilloried and tied to an execution post in 1945, he was saying nothing new, and nothing which contradicted the sentiments of either Darlan or the marshal.

Although the three men had much in common, there were differences. Through his dislike of bloodshed and reading of history Laval had concluded that unless France and Germany reached some kind of lasting *modus vivendi* they would clash 'every 20 years on the battlefield'; and because of its demographic and economic advantages Germany would always emerge the winner. Thus, for Laval, collaboration was a means to achieve his long-term aim of Franco-German reconciliation, and he busily worked to make France an equal partner in Hitler's New Order. Darlan also possessed a longer-term vision. He foresaw that at the end of the war global politics would be dominated by two camps: on the one hand, Germany, all-powerful on both the European and African continents; on the other, the USA supported by a gravely weakened Britain. Darlan's apologists claim that their man attempted to steer a middle path between these two camps. In truth, his preference was for the Germans, and he hoped that France would be able to play a naval role in this new world order. Only in November 1942, cornered by the allies in North Africa and under intense American pressure, did he go over to the Anglo-Saxons. By contrast, Pétain saw collaboration in domestic terms, a means of consolidating his much-cherished national revolution, a project for which Laval and Darlan felt nothing but contempt. The marshal also appreciated how collaboration would secure him another chapter in posterity. By obtaining a favourable peace with Germany and through the overhaul of his country's institutions, he would be recalled as the man who had pulled France back from the abyss. As he himself acknowledged, this would be no military success such as that he achieved at Verdun in 1916; instead, to use Girard's memorable phrase, it would be a moral triumph, a *Verdun diplomatique*.

Of the triumvirate, it was Laval, an accomplished wheeler-dealer, who achieved most success in exploiting channels of communication with the Germans. He enjoyed especially cordial relations with Otto Abetz, the German ambassador to Paris, himself a former socialist and advocate of Franco-German *rapprochement*. In 1942 it was largely thanks to German pressure that Laval was recalled to office, although the newly reinstated minister would have no success in fending off Nazi demands for workers and Jews. During 1941 Darlan had been equally unsuccessful in resisting German demands. He had conceived of a policy of 'give-and-take', *donnant-donnant*, yet at his meeting with Hitler at Berchtesgaden in May and in his encounters with Ribbentrop, he found that he was merely giving, and forgot Laval's maxim that it was always important to keep something in reserve in order to strike a bargain. Thanks to Darlan, France nearly re-entered the war on the side of the Axis. It is, however, Pétain who most illustrates the folly of collaboration. As several biographers relate, he was incapable of understanding the dynamics of Nazism, believing the Germans to be 'honourable men'. So long as he could meet personally with Hitler, he could hammer out a deal. His opportunity came on 24 October 1940 when the Führer, returning from Spain, agreed to see the marshal. The interview, conducted at the little railway station of Montoire, was unscripted, resulting in nothing more than an exchange of platitudes and a much-publicized handshake.

Historians have recently speculated whether Vichy, through its residual ties with Britain and its initial maintenance of a large empire and fleet, could have obtained more concessions out of the Germans, at least in 1940. The real problem was that the marshal and his ministers never appreciated that France always had more need of Germany than Germany had need of France. It was only on the odd occasion – October 1940, when Hitler was intensifying his campaign against Britain in the Mediterranean and planning his invasion of the USSR, and May 1941, when Rommel required French air bases in Syria – that Berlin entertained French overtures of collaboration, and even then it had no intention of honouring any agreements. Hitler despised France. Although at the armistice he was prepared to grant Vichy some freedoms, fearing that a harsher settlement might foment that country's revolutionary tradition, he was determined to exploit French economic resources for all they were worth, and ultimately, in his plans for a *Mitteleuropa*, he envisaged the disappearance of France from the map altogether, a policy apparent in the German seizure of Alsace-Lorraine in 1940 and the creation of forbidden and annexed zones in the north-east of the main occupied zone, territories designated for the resettlement of Prussian farmers. Small wonder that the Germans encouraged separatist movements in Brittany and Languedoc. Elsewhere, too, the many German authorities dealing with France – the armistice commission at Wiesbaden, the military command in Brussels, the embassy at Paris – faithfully heeded Hitler's plans, playing the French off against one another. The overlapping responsibilities and rivalries between the occupying agencies considerably eased Berlin's task as Vichy representatives were often confused as to whom they should be negotiating with.

At least the French pro-Nazi sympathizers of the 1930s had no doubt where they were most welcome, quickly making their way to the German embassy on the rue de Lille in Paris where they were lavishly entertained and flattered by Abetz, a man who had assiduously cultivated French contacts before the war. For their part, scholars have followed the signposts of Stanley Hoffmann, supporting his distinction between the *collaboration d'état* of Vichy and the ideological *collaborationisme* of the Paris fascists. Yet, as historians have pointed out, important links remained between the two French capitals. When in Paris, which was often in late 1940, Laval happily mixed in collaborationist circles and employed de Brinon and Luchaire as 'messenger boys' between the two zones. In 1941 Darlan welcomed PPF

Illustration 10.1 Family photograph taken during the Occupation of 1940–4. Many French homes had German soldiers billeted on them. Relationships between occupied and occupier ranged from intimacy to uncompromising hostility, with the latter more marked the longer the war went on and the harsher the conditions of occupation. (Photograph reproduced with the permission of the copyright holder, EDMEDIA.)

members such as Paul Marion and Pucheu into his cabinet; by early 1944 several fascists held office at Vichy. Moreover, there were ideological links between the regime and the *collabos*. All desired a German victory; all feared social disorder; all hated Britain; all (or most) abhorred Jews; all despised bolshevism. In 1941 the marshal himself reputedly sent a letter of support to the newly formed Légion des Volontaires Français contre le Bolchevisme (LVF), Doriot's organization which recruited Frenchmen to fight on the eastern front.

When not in the uniforms of the Waffen SS, the Paris fascists presented a bewildering picture. Journalists, writers, artists, *liguers*, eleventh-hour opportunists and various n'er-do-wells all competed for influence and German patronage. One of the most penetrating analyses of this *demi-monde* is that recently provided by Philippe Burrin.[11] He has identified several tendencies, one of which congregated around Marcel Déat, an ex-schoolteacher and aspirant *homme des lettres*, who deserted the left in the 1930s for the cause of 'neo-socialism', and who, as leader of the RNP, edited the newspaper *L'Oeuvre* which criticized Vichy for its timidity and traditionalism. Supported by other ex-socialists such as Georges Albertini, Déat's RNP favoured a totalitarian republic which would redress social inequalities and bridge the gap between left and right. To this end, it cultivated links with the extreme rightist Eugène Deloncle, a former naval engineer who in the 1930s had swum in the murky waters of terrorist politics, establishing the violent Cagoule organization which had attempted to torpedo liberal democracy by planting bombs in Paris. In 1940 Deloncle was back to his old tricks, setting up the Mouvement Social Révolutionnaire (MSR), attacking synagogues and murdering his opponents.

Alongside Déat and his cronies, Burrin has identified an intellectual collaborationist tendency, fronted by writers such as Jean Luchaire, Alfred Fabre-Luce, Robert Brasillach and Alphonse de Châteaubriant. A devout Catholic, de Châteaubriant founded the circle Groupe Collaboration, and possessed the bizarre dream that Hitler would create a Catholic Europe akin to that of Charlemagne! Although the Catholic Church was compromised by its open admiration for the Pétain government, it was fortunate that it included few out-and-out collaborators: the octogenarian rector of the Institut Catholique, Cardinal Baudrillart; the bishop of Arras, Mgr Dutoit; the LVF chaplain, Mgr Mayol de Lupé; the broadcaster, Henriot; and small fry such as Touvier.[12] Nor were such Catholic pro-Nazi sympathizers necessarily respected by the remaining collaborationist tendency outlined by Burrin: a hardcore headed by Jacques Doriot. Like Déat, Doriot had begun political life on the left, albeit as a communist and not a socialist. Paradoxically, he was expelled from the Communist Party for urging a Popular Front alliance against Nazism before Moscow had given the nod. Soon after, he established the Parti Populaire Français (PPF), taking a sizeable chunk of working-class support with him. Historians are undecided whether the PPF was truly fascist before 1940; there is no doubt that it was under Vichy. Alongside other hard-line organizations such as Marcel Bucard's Francisme, it represented what Burrin calls *une droite musclée*, uncompromising in its support for a Nazi victory.

In the event, these collaborationist organizations failed to become truly popular. Predominantly male in complexion and over-represented in the Parisian region and occupied zone, Burrin estimates that, for the period 1940–4, the total of those belonging to such groupings, including the Milice, numbered no more than 250 000, the same as the Socialist Party at the time of the Popular Front. Nonetheless, like all fascist phenomena, Doriot and others were not averse to exaggerating their support. Parisians joked that people bought copies of collaborationist newspapers because German subsidies ensured they were printed on better-quality paper than other titles, and thus burned better in the fireplace. Certainly relations between the collaborationists were of an incendiary nature. So-called 'collaborators', the one thing these men could not do was work with one another. Many pre-war quarrels and ideological disputes lingered into the occupation. Personal rivalries also created sparks. Déat and Doriot detested each other, and the former discovered that he lacked the charisma and personal authority to transform the RNP into a single party. He soon fell out with Deloncle, who himself fell out with MSR supporters. Vichy, fearing that these men might form a rival government in Paris, also did its bit to foment division yet, as in the case of *collaboration d'état*, the success of *collaborationisme* ultimately depended on the German position, and this remained as inflexible as ever. Hitler, misjudging the mood of French public opinion, considered that these movements might become a rallying point for *revanchiste* nationalism. It was thus the job of Abetz to play a game of 'divide and rule' among collaborators, a task he executed with considerable aplomb but with few thanks from Berlin, which was suspicious of his francophilia.

Now that historians have become confident about the nature of collaboration and collaborationism, they have turned their attention to other things, notably the state of public opinion. Before the release of local archives it was often assumed that the French public grew tired of Vichy sometime in 1942. Without doubt, 1942 was a pivotal year. W. D. Halls has recently shown how the return to power of Laval and the overt persecution of Jews forced many Catholics, including members of the Church hierarchy, to reconsider their loyalty towards Pétain's government.[13] The allied invasion of North Africa and the subsequent occupation of all of France was also significant as, in future, there was a rival administration developing in the shape of the provisional government in Algeria. Nonetheless, there is now a growing conviction that the French began to lose faith in Vichy, if not in the marshal, as early as January 1941. Although it is hazardous to generalize about a country as geographically diverse as France, a number of observations can be made. In the annexed and forbidden zones, it appears that the public's rejection of collaboration was 'immediate'; here even Pétainism struggled to put down roots. A report produced in September 1940 by the Wehrmacht on the situation in the occupied zone reveals that the population there was on the whole 'calm', on occasion 'welcoming', but for the most part 'reserved', often 'unfriendly' and to a degree 'hostile'.[14] This hostility was increasingly focused on the marshal's government as it became obvious that Vichy was incapable of acting as a protector. South of the demarcation line dissatisfaction was also setting in. Once public opinion in the Vichy zone recovered from the shock of the defeat, it was soon fretting about other matters. Abroad, the conflicts in the colonies between Free French and Vichy forces raised the prospect of civil war, while the invasion of the Soviet Union was a stark reminder that the war, and its attendant upheavals, was far from over. Meanwhile, at home the handshake at Montoire, spiralling inflation, food shortages, deteriorating town–country relations and the rightward drift of the marshal's government boded ill for the future.

Through the *contrôle technique*, a system whereby Vichy opened people's mail and listened in to their telephone conversations, the marshal's regime was fully aware of its unpopularity. With Resistance activity on the increase, in August 1941 Pétain complained that 'an evil wind' was sweeping through France and urged the population to show restraint. His words went unheeded. Perhaps the one area where the marshal's harmful current did not blow was in the sweltering heat of Algeria, the most prestigious of French colonies. Here, as Vinen records, Vichy's popularity remained high thanks to the fact that Algeria never experienced direct German occupation; the area also escaped many of the material hardships that crippled the mainland. It further helped that Vichy's delegate in North Africa, General Weygand, appeared to be reconstructing the French army, thus restoring a sense of national pride, even though he had no plans to use force against the Axis. Aware of Algeria's sentiments, in November 1942 the Americans involved a number of former Vichyites, most notably Darlan, in their liberation plans. As Vinen concludes, the territory thus escaped the bitter infighting between Vichy and the Resistance which overtook the mainland. Small wonder that at the time of the Algerian war of independence French settlers looked back on the Vichy years with a certain nostalgia, often drawing on Pétainism for their political philosophy.

Public disenchantment with Vichy did not automatically translate itself into resistance. Despite Gaullist claims of 40 million resisters, Paxton suggests that maybe only 400000 individuals, or 2 per cent of the population, actively belonged to underground organizations. Whatever the truth of these figures, the obstacles to joining the Resistance were formidable. As noted, there was first the loyalty to Pétain. In 1940 it was understood that he had made logical decisions; it would take the wider developments of the war for people to deconstruct the mythology surrounding his position. The demarcation line also had a bearing, an impact, on resistance behaviour. It might have been thought that dissidence would have been most marked in the occupied zone where the German presence was concentrated; yet, as Kedward has demonstrated, Resistance movements were stronger in the unoccupied zone precisely because they did not fall under the vigilant eye of the occupying authorities.[15] It is Kedward, too, who has demonstrated the other geographical factors governing the emergence of resistance. In its early stages, he writes, protest tended to be urban-based: it was the towns that suffered most from material hardships; it was the towns that offered the best hiding places; and it was the towns that contained the printing presses, a critical form of resistance activity. Rural resistance would not emerge until late 1942/early 1943 when many young men, escaping work service in Germany, fled to the countryside where they established *maquis* units in the scrubland. According to Kedward, resistance further originated in those areas of France, such as the Cévennes, which had a long tradition of defying central authority, a history dating back to the 1789 Revolution and beyond. Eager to articulate a justification for their opposition to both Vichy and Nazism, resisters frequently trawled their nation's past for moral sustenance, and it is significant that the titles of many of their journals – *Valmy, Père Dûchesne* – recalled past struggles against oppression.

Of all the resisters, it is de Gaulle who remains the best-known. Commemorating the centenary of his birth in 1990, the Institut Charles de Gaulle conducted an opinion poll among the British public.[16] Among those who knew the general at all, the majority remembered that he led the Free French/ Fighting French in London. Far fewer recalled his presidency of the Fifth

Republic or events in 1963 when he said *non* to Britain's application to join the EEC, testimony that some 50 years after the event the British were still struck by his courage in defying both Vichy and the Germans. This admiration had clearly existed in 1940, yet Churchill had initially struggled to sell this little-known and junior general to the public, and always hoped that a more senior and less arrogant figure – a Blum, Daladier or Reynaud – would cross the Channel. Within France, de Gaulle was also an unknown. Despite what was claimed afterwards, hardly anyone listened to his now famous broadcast of 18 June 1940 in which he urged Frenchmen to join him in continuing the fight. His connections with the British, who were perceived to have deserted French soldiers at Dunkirk and who had then shelled the French fleet at Mers-el-Kébir in July 1940 to prevent it from falling into German hands, undoubtedly counted against him. As several historians have pointed out, so too did his reputation compared to Pétain's. The marshal was the most successful of France's First-World-War generals; the marshal was his country's military guru; the marshal was politically experienced; the marshal was the legitimate ruler of France, having been granted power by the national assembly's vote of 10 July 1940; the marshal headed an internationally recognized government. De Gaulle was a temporary general, the author of some little-known books on tank warfare, a minor office-holder in Reynaud's brief-lived cabinet of June 1940, and a disloyal citizen whose claims to incarnate French sovereignty rested on highly dubious grounds. Only a minority – discontented junior officers, ex-colonial officials and adventurers – initially rallied to his 'call of honour'. Even the French community in Britain was divided in its attitude to the general, and the bulk of those French servicemen, rescued at Narvik and Dunkirk and stationed at various camps in England, chose repatriation or action in the British armed forces rather than enrolment in the Free French. Nonetheless, over the course of 1941, support for the Free French improved, thanks to Churchill's backing, thanks to the declining popularity of Vichy, thanks to the globalization of the war, and thanks, most of all, to the political acumen of de Gaulle himself, who was determined to become leader of the Resistance both inside and outside of France.

As Kedward has demonstrated, within France resistance was initiated by individuals, usually acting independently and unknown to one another. It was inevitable, however, that such men drew on existing political and professional networks for support, a point recently illuminated by the examples given by Jean-François Muracciole: in the occupied zone Ripoche, a little-known engineer, recruited among officer pilots to found Ceux de la Libération in September 1940; later that year Colonel Heurteaux assembled civil servants and industrialists in the Organisation Civile et Militaire; and in Paris academics such as Lewitzky and Odolon gathered around the young ethnologist Vildé to create the network Musée de l'Homme. Other initiatives in the occupied zone, too many to list here, likewise recruited in familiar *milieux*, although, as already remarked, the watchful eye of the Germans ensured that these groupings were small and hazardous enterprises. Over in the unoccupied zone, Resistance movements were larger but again recruited among existing professional and personal circles; Catholics gravitated to Combat, the work of two prominent pre-war Christian Democrats, Henri Frenay and François de Menthon; socialists and trade unionists were prominent in Libération, initially established by Emmanuel d'Astier de la Vigerie, an ex-naval officer. Franc-Tireur, another prominent organization in the south, recruited in a more diverse constituency, counting ex-communists and members of Action Française in its ranks; yet it was not uncommon to find left and right alongside one another in the Resistance. Whereas many right-wingers were sympathetic to Pétainism, their patriotism made them determinedly anti-German.

The one movement associated closely with a political party and to function across both zones was the communist-dominated Front National, established in May 1941 on the eve of Hitler's invasion of the USSR. Much debate centres on the communist involvement in the Resistance, and it is frequently pointed out that the Nazi–Soviet pact of August 1939 prevented the Moscow-influenced Communist Party (PCF) from entering resistance until the German attack on the USSR. It should be remembered, however, that the pact was an embarrassment to a party which, as Kedward writes, had an 'excellent record of anti-fascism'. It should also be noted that several individual communists, Charles Debarge and Charles Tillon among others, engaged in underground activity long before Operation Barbarossa. In Autumn 1940 communist leaders were influential in forming the Organisation Secrète (OS), and the following year helped organize strikes among miners in the Nord-Pas-de-Calais. It was, however, the invasion of the USSR which gave the PCF its cue to enter into full-scale resistance and, thanks to its habits of secrecy and history of persecution at the hands of the Daladier and Vichy governments, the party was able to place its nationwide networks at the disposal of the Front National.

Communists were also to be found in the *maquis* bands that proliferated in the countryside. It used to be thought that this type of resistance did not begin until February 1943 when Vichy introduced the STO. Yet, as noted, the total occupation of France in November 1942 and the growing authoritarianism of Pétain's government had already forced numbers of young people to take refuge in the hillsides. It is also apparent that the *maquis* offered an 'alternative lifestyle' that might well have appealed to the young, a lifestyle that transcended class boundaries, offering a community of spirit not to be found in Vichy's youth groups where the mawkish morality of the national revolution still dominated. Admittedly, however, it was STO that swelled the ranks of the *maquis*. Some 650000 workers eventually boarded the train for Germany, ensuring that France was only behind Poland in the supply of labour to Hitler's war machine. It is generally agreed that this legislation was the most unpopular ever initiated by Vichy. While the prospect of work in Germany appealed to the very poor, few wished to contribute to the Nazi war-effort, and now understood how far Vichy had gone in aligning itself to the Nazi cause. How many escaped to join the *maquis* is unknown; one estimate suggests 40000. Until recently their lifestyle was also improperly understood, and it is largely thanks to the efforts of Kedward that their 'outlaw culture' has been rescued from obscurity. Young, sometimes urban in origin, rebellious and occasionally ill-disciplined, not all *maquisards* were welcome among rural communities. Yet by late 1943 public disillusionment with Vichy was so deep-rooted and the regime's authority so dilapidated that most local people were willing to support and supply *maquis* groups. Kedward suggests that these bands had become so well established that in 1944 we should speak of 'Resistance France' rather than 'Vichy France' as being the principal determining factor in the life of the countryside.

Resistance activity was extremely varied. At the start of the Occupation the publication of clandestine newspapers was especially important. The empty white columns that often appeared in national papers such as *Le Temps* and *La Croix* were a constant reminder of censors at work and of the need to get across a different point of view to that of the authorities. The establishment of escape networks for allied airmen shot down over France was another vital form of Resistance action, as was the collection of intelligence. Yet not all Resistance behaviour was so dramatic. Listening to the BBC, scrawling 'V' signs on the walls, giving wrong directions to German soldiers, as when one of the characters in Jean Dutourd's Paris-based novel *Au bon beurre* misdirects an officer to the Bastille – these were all acts of 'passive resistance', acts that were taken seriously by the Germans. Nonetheless, as the allied invasion drew nearer, military operations became increasingly important, and the Resistance responded by setting up the Forces Françaises de l'Intérieur (FFI), which boasted its own high command to direct operations come the Liberation. Anticipating the allied invasion, in February/March 1944 *maquisards* of the Haute-Savoie amassed on the Glières plateau where they fought an unwinnable battle against the Milice and German troops. Fully aware of the limited supplies available to resisters and reluctant to entrust partisans with precious information, the masterminds behind the D-day landings of 6 June 1944 assigned a restricted role to the Resistance. It has since been argued that more effort should have been made to have integrated underground groups in allied plans; yet at least in August 1944 American forces, landing in southern France as part of Operation Dragoon, took care to work closely with the FFI.

Certainly, the Resistance was marked by diversity. Personal jealousies were rife, with some Resistance leaders creating their own spheres of influence. Other resisters were troubled by the arrival of 'Johnny come-latelys', and there was always a suspicion of potential police informers. Gender differences also intruded. Given that many males were held as POWs in Germany or had been deported via STO, women were less conspicuous than men in Vichy France and were thus able to play a critical part in underground activity, collating intelligence material and helping allied airmen, a role that is only now beginning to be recognized by historians. At the time, women were not necessarily rewarded for their efforts. Marie-Madeleine Fourcade, head of the network Alliance, was one of the few women to become a Resistance leader, and at the liberation only six women were granted the honour of the Compagnon de la Libération: 1 057 awards were made in total.[17] Events of 1944 also created tensions among the predominantly male *maquisards*. Whereas some were happy to abandon their irregular status and occupy posts vacated by Vichy officials, others cherished their 'outlaw status' and were reluctant to re-enter respectable society.[18] It was, however, political quarrels that did most to divide the Resistance, especially those between communists and non-communists. It was not just de Gaulle, but a wide range of resisters, who feared that the PCF would monopolize protest against Vichy and the Germans, exploiting resistance as a means to kill its enemies and pursue its own agenda. Such behaviour notwithstanding, the public appreciated the importance of the far left in defying the occupier, and during the early years of the Fourth Republic the Communist Party enjoyed an electoral popularity unparalleled in its history.

Remarkably, the Resistance did succeed in achieving an impressive measure of unity. In 1943 Jean Moulin, a former prefect of Chartres, later murdered by the SS man Klaus Barbie, 'the butcher of Lyon', worked with de Gaulle to create the Mouvements Unis de la Résistance (MUR), an informal partnership of non-communist organizations in the southern zone. Later that year, he helped found the Conseil National de la Résistance (CNR) which brought together resistance groupings throughout France, including the communists, who following the recent demise of the comintern were less influenced by Moscow directives. Outside of France, moves were also being made to coordinate resistance activities, involving de Gaulle in a protracted struggle with the Anglo-Saxons. Following their invasion of North Africa in November 1942, the Americans governed Algeria first with the cooperation of Darlan and then with Henri Giraud, a general of Vichyite sympathies and little natural political instinct. It was not long before de Gaulle outwitted Giraud. May 1943 saw the creation of the Comité Français de Libération Nationale (CFLN) in which the two generals were supposed to share power, yet by October de Gaulle had become president. Thereafter, Algiers formed the nucleus of an alternative French government. The politicians there quickly announced their intention of punishing all those who had worked for the Pétain government and, looking ahead to the liberation of their country, began to 'rethink France', debating plans for the nationalization of key industries, the democratization of education and the restructuring of the state, ambitious projects of reform which had first been discussed in the 1930s.

De Gaulle himself did not necessarily have much sympathy for these schemes. His concern was to ensure a smooth transfer of power between himself and Vichy, and to guarantee that he emerged as France's next political leader. He was only partially successful in his aims. Following the allied landings in France, the Vichy government disintegrated, left for Germany and then returned to France for trial. Some ministers, notably Pétain and Laval, were sentenced to death, although the marshal escaped execution on the grounds of old age and spent the remainder of his senile years in captivity on the île d'Yeu. Overall, the purge (*épuration*) was a limited affair; perhaps some 10000 people were arbitrarily killed, not the 100000 that Vichyites sometimes claim, and many former Pétainist officials returned to public life. Consequently, France was spared the indignity of a civil war. It was not, however, spared further political upheaval. For just over a year after the Liberation, de Gaulle governed with extensive personal powers, confident that he could construct a new republican system which allowed for a strong presidency and a weak legislature. In the event, his designs were stymied by the consultative assembly, empowered with the drafting of a fresh constitution. While the representatives there might have been at sixes and sevens over a constitutional structure, they shared an intense suspicion of de Gaulle, whom they suspected of being a Boulanger-in-waiting. Such misgivings ensured that, in 1946, the deputies ended up bestowing France with a political system eerily akin to that of the Third Republic.

Although de Gaulle might have misjudged the political mistrust he generated in 1944, he clearly understood the ways in which Vichy had divided the French, and when he returned to power in 1958, as president of the Fifth Republic, he took care not to reopen the wounds of the Occupation. Since his death in 1970 historians have not been so squeamish, and have gone a long way in diagnosing what has been dubbed the 'Vichy syndrome'. In so doing, they have conclusively proved that the Pétain regime was far from being a quirk in France's history. Indeed, there exists today so much agreement among historians about the nature of the marshal's government that researchers are fast running out of new areas to investigate. The historian of the Occupation has thus become a skilled physician, well aware of the physiology of Vichy. Yet, like a cancer specialist, the historian has struggled to devise a cure which will heal the divisions within France. Similar to a dreadful illness, the 'Vichy syndrome' still strikes fear among the French public and political establishment. The trials of such Pétainist functionaries as Touvier and Papon, and the stunning revelations about President Mitterrand's Vichy past, have shown that many people, even in the 1990s, have yet to come to terms with this most controversial episode in French history, especially the treatment of the Jews. There are those who argue that it is wrong to haul such elderly and silver-haired Vichy officials before the courts. Bygones should be bygones. Yet, as others contend, so long as France vaunts the largest neo-fascist party in the whole of western Europe in the form of Jean-Marie Le Pen's unashamedly xenophobic Front National, it is vital that the Occupation years should remain at the forefront of public debate and scrutiny.

Notes

1 Most importantly, see R. O. Paxton, *Vichy France, Old Guard and New Order, 1940–44* (New York: Alfred A. Knopf, 1972).
2 R. Descouens, *La Vie du maréchal Pétain racontée aux enfants de France* (Nice: Éditions de la Vraie France, 1941) cited in J.-P. Azéma, *De Munich à la Libération, 1938–1944* (Paris: Seuil, 1979), p. 104.
3 A. Boudard, *Les Combattants du petit bonheur* (Paris: La Table Ronde, 1977), p. 72.
4 *La Quinzaine Catholique du Gévaudan*, 17 (31 July 1942), p. 256.
5 N. Lytton, *Life in Occupied France* (London: Macmillan, 1942), p. 17.
6 R. Vinen, *France, 1934–1970* (London: Macmillan, 1996), pp. 41–2.
7 *Ibid.*, p. 64, and for much that follows on Vichy's repressive side.
8 H. R. Kedward, 'Introduction: ideologies and ambiguities', in H. R. Kedward and R. Austin (eds.), *Vichy France and the Resistance: Culture and Ideology* (London: Croom Helm, 1985), p. 1.
9 Vinen, *France*, p. 66.
10 H. R. Kedward, *In Search of the Maquis: Rural Resistance in Vichy France, 1942–1944* (Oxford: Oxford University Press, 1993), p. 7.
11 P. Burrin, *La France à l'heure allemande, 1940–1944* (Paris: Seuil, 1995), pp. 365–464.
12 K. Chadwick, 'A broad church: French Catholics and National Socialist Germany', in N. Atkin and F. Tallett (eds.), *The Right in France, 1789–1997* (London: I. B. Tauris, 1998), pp. 215–29.
13 W. D. Halls, *Politics, Society and Christianity in Vichy France, 1940–1944* (Oxford: Berg, 1995).
14 Burrin, *La France*, p. 187 and p. 188.
15 H. R. Kedward, *Resistance in Vichy France. A Study of Ideas and Motivation in the Southern Zone, 1940–1942* (Oxford: Oxford University Press, 1978), and his brilliant essay, 'The French Resistance', supplement to *History Today*, 34 (June 1984), pp. not numbered, for much that follows on resistance and to which the present chapter is deeply indebted.
16 J. and M. Charlot, 'Le général de Gaulle dans la mémoire des Britanniques', in Institut Charles de Gaulle, *De Gaulle en son siècle, Sondages et enquêtes* (Paris: 1992, Institut Charles de Gaulle), pp. 297–319.
17 J.-F. Muracciole, *Histoire de la résistance en France*, 2nd edn. (Paris: Presses Universitaires de France, 1996), p. 97.
18 Kedward, *In Search of the Maquis*, p. 203.

Further reading

Azéma, J.-P. *From Munich to the Liberation, 1938–1944* (Cambridge: Cambridge University Press, 1979).
Azéma, J.-P. and Bédarida, F. *Vichy et les français* (Paris: Fayard, 1992).
——, *La France des années noires*, 2 vols. (Paris: Seuil, 1993).
Burrin, P. *Living with Defeat* (London: Edward Arnold, 1996).
Griffiths, R. *Pétain*, 2nd edn. (London: Constable, 1994).
Kedward, H. R. *Resistance in Vichy France: A Study of Ideas and Motivation in the Southern Zone, 1940–1942* (Oxford: Oxford University Press, 1978).
——, *Occupied France: Collaboration and Resistance, 1940–1944* (Oxford: Basil Blackwell, 1985).

——, *In Search of the Maquis: Rural Resistance in Vichy France, 1942–1944* (Oxford: Oxford University Press, 1993).

Marrus, M. and Paxton, R. O. *Vichy and the Jews* (New York: Basic Books, 1981).

Ousby, I. *Occupation: The Ordeal of France, 1940–1944* (London: John Murray, 1998).

Paxton, R. O. *Vichy France: Old Guard and New Order, 1940–44* (New York: Alfred A. Knopf, 1972).

Rousso, H. *The Vichy Syndrome: History and Memory in France since 1944* (Cambridge, MA: Harvard University Press, 1994).

Vinen, R. *France, 1934–1970* (London: Macmillan, 1995) for a brilliant chapter on Vichy.

Webster, P. *Pétain's Crime* (London: Papermac, 1990).

11

Defending France

Foreign policy and the quest for security, 1850s–1990s

MARTIN S. ALEXANDER AND J. F. V. KEIGER

Overview

Despite defeat and occupation at the end of the Napoleonic Wars, France's post-1815 security dilemma was a matter of facing age-old conundrums rather than new problems. France required security on the European continent. Yet she also needed the maritime trade and global 'reach' commensurate with a country possessing an Atlantic and a Mediterranean seaboard. Since emerging as a modern, unified state in the seventeenth century, France had pursued ambitions that were both continental and worldwide. The quest for colonies and naval power developed simultaneously with France's consolidation as the greatest unitary state possessing an organized army. Thus from the wars of Louis XIV onwards, French ambitions in and beyond Europe brought frequent conflict with British naval and colonial interests on the one hand and, nearer home, with the still-fragmented Germanic states. The seeds of an enduring dichotomy for French statesmen since Napoleon were thus sown under the *ancien régime*.

France, not unlike Britain, faced the quandary of securing scattered global interests whilst facing existential threats closer to home. In the Bourbon, Revolutionary and Napoleonic years the dangers to the east were successfully mastered by diplomatic combinations, the acquisition and fortification of a defensible frontier on the Rhine and a powerful military machine. Crucial was the absence of a unified Germany. Even as late as 1806 Napoleonic France quite easily inflicted crushing defeat on a respected but still overly small Prussia. Revolutionary and Napoleonic France was a superpower before the term had been invented. Successive allied coalitions required over 20 years to wrestle her into submission. In some respects the wars of 1793–1815 prefigured, in their length and worldwide scale, the struggle that France herself would have to wage a century later, first politically and then militarily, to contain and defeat the new European hegemon, Germany, between 1891 and 1918. Moreover, just as it took coalitions to subdue France in the early nineteenth century, so the taming of Germany in the early twentieth was a task beyond France alone, requiring an alliance of France and her erstwhile rival, Great Britain, as well as Russia and even the United States.

The key change in France's position occurred with the successful wars fought by Bismarck's Prussia against Denmark (1864) and Austria (1866), establishing the North German Confederation (1867). France's defeat by Prussia in 1870 enabled the proclamation of the second German Reich in January 1871, in the hall of mirrors at the palace of Versailles (the venue calculatedly symbolizing the German usurpation of French power). German unification overturned the European equilibrium. France was no longer pre-eminent, for Germany's territory, population and economic potential surpassed her own. As one contemporary noted, 'Europe has lost a mistress and gained a master'.

Geo-strategic realities behind French diplomacy

Paul Kennedy has rightly emphasized that statesmen do not enjoy the luxury of starting with a clean slate when making external policy or planning for war and peace. A nation's friends and enemies set an international context to its foreign policy. National resources – financial, industrial, geographic and demographic – dictate the limits and the potential for a state's aggrandize-ment. France, as many of her nineteenth- and twentieth-century leaders remarked ruefully, had been dealt a poor hand by the vagaries of geography. From the time of Louis XIV and his 20 million French people, until at least 1813–14, France had been larger, more populous and better organized administratively than her neighbours. As late as the 1790s she stood head and shoulders above the myriad small states on her borders (as prone, in any case, to warring among themselves as to fighting France). As Paul Reynaud nostalgically recalled in 1939, Revolutionary France had been 'a giant among pygmies'.[1] Between 1815 and 1870 France's political unity and geographic homogeneity, bolstered by overseas territories, assured her standing as a great power. But, as will be discussed in more detail below, the war with Prussia in 1870–1 and the resultant German unification decisively upset the balance of power. Even before this catastrophe, however, French population growth had tailed off (and would become an annual deficit of births over deaths in one-third of France's departments during the nineteenth century's last quarter). Germany meanwhile – unified, confident and vigor-ous – enjoyed rapid population growth and equally rapid industrialization in the 1880s and 1890s. France steadily slipped down the international league table of industrial powers as the century waned. Indeed France fell not just behind Britain, the 'first industrial nation', but also behind the USA and Germany and could feel further challengers such as Italy and Japan breathing down her neck. Demographic weakness translated into alarm over the strength of the army that France could maintain in peacetime and mobilize for war. By 1905 Germany was able to field about half as many troops again as France, if general mobilization were ordered.

Moreover, international stature was no longer measured solely by a nation's total number of men in uniform. With the growing pace of technological change, defence was becoming an arena of scientific and industrial competition too. Possessing accurate, reliable and penetrative artillery, for example, was a function of industrial productive capacity and was closely tied to the modernity of the nation's steel-making plant, the quality of its machine-tools and the availability of skilled engineering workers. France was deficient in each of these areas. French firms in the nineteenth century and the first half of the twentieth remained largely under family control. Factories were generally smaller, plant and machine-tools older and less up-to-date, than in rival American, German or British companies.

Geography and geology had saddled France with further disadvantages. The vital raw materials for a powerful industrial economy – notably coal and iron-ore deposits – occurred chiefly in northern and eastern France. Some lay in Alsace and Lorraine. These were lost to France's industrial base (and, by the same token, added to Germany's) through Bismarck's annexation of the provinces in 1871. France's remaining industrial assets were dangerously near her north-eastern frontiers: the Longwy-Briey ore basin, the steel and engineering heartland at Pont-à-Mousson, Nancy, Charleville-Mézières, the coal mines around Douai, Lens, Valenciennes and Armentières. The Low Countries almost invited an invasion from the east aimed into the Nord and Picardy. Not only was this natural terrain flat and difficult to defend, Belgium's small army was a flimsy human barrier to a German attack. An aggressor could march on Lille, Douai and Arras inside a week and seize control of much of France's coal and steel production. Small wonder that Charles de Gaulle, writing in 1934 about the region's invasion in 1708–9 and 1814–15, described Flanders as a fatal high road to France, slicing straight to the heart of the nation.

Nor was this the end to French geographic vulnerability. As Reynaud warned parliament in 1937, the advent of aircraft made northern and north-eastern industries doubly vulnerable – to destruction by bombing as well as to physical capture. Since the 1890s, French industrialization had grown disproportionately around Paris, driven by the capital's sizeable labour pool, its transport and distribution networks and proximity to the ministries that generated lucrative government orders. By the interwar years suburbs such as Aubervilliers, Billancourt, Courbevoie and Levallois hummed to the sound of electrical-component factories, aircraft assembly, motor manufacturing and armaments. 'The capital of France', bemoaned Reynaud, 'is not, alas, Bourges or Clermont-Ferrand.'[2] Steps could be taken to disperse the government in an emergency and prevent air strikes destroying the nation's administrative nerve-centre. But preventing an enemy delivering a knock-out blow upon French industrial concentrations, the country's productive capacity for war, posed a far greater challenge.

Policy-machinery and decision-making in French external affairs

Foreign and strategic decision-making was straightforward in the age of Napoleon – the emperor personally took command of France. In the later nineteenth century, and more so during the twentieth, it became impracticable for leadership to be directly exercised by one person. As other nations learned too, the conduct of foreign and defence policy and the waging of war necessitated collaboration between many individuals. Making grand strategy required politicians, economists, statisticians and scientists to work together, alongside diplomats, generals and admirals. But it also increasingly required the creation of a permanent bureaucracy or administrative machine to coordinate the actions of civil servants, ministers, uniformed military chiefs, industrialists whose firms manufactured the nation's armaments, and so forth. The phenomenon known as 'defence by committee' arguably emerged first in Britain, with her uniquely complex defence imperatives arising from possession of the world's largest and most dispersed empire. But it appeared in France, too, after 1871. Indeed, humiliation at the hands of Prussia spurred the French to create many institutions that became the normal management apparatus of external relations and defence for all states in the twentieth century. According to the historian Allan Mitchell, many of the French reforms deliberately copied German practice. The establishment of the higher war council in 1872, later followed by the superior council of national defence, helped systematize French defence planning. The re-introduction of compulsory conscription in 1874 had both practical and symbolic significance. On the first count it enlarged the pool of military manpower by requiring 2 years' service and subsequent annual reserve training for all able-bodied Frenchmen. On the second, it strengthened the bonds between army and society – bonds which had loosened whilst the army was an all-professional force under Napoleon III from 1852 to 1870. According to Richard D. Challener, this revitalized the 'French theory of the Nation-in-Arms'.[3]

Meanwhile in foreign policy the president of the republic had considerable powers, even if many required a ministerial countersignature. The president commanded the armed forces, appointed to military and civil posts (including ambassadors), negotiated and ratified treaties and only informed parliament when the interests and security of the state permitted. As the career foreign service acquired prestige and was professionalized from the 1880s, so selection for the diplomatic corps became fiercely competitive. A rigorous annual *concours* or entrance examination was instituted in 1877. Originally intended to republicanize the aristocratic diplomatic corps and open it to merit rather than birth, it attracted the Parisian élite, mainly graduates from the prestigious but nationalistic École Libre des Sciences Politiques, who were intent on pursuing their own policies often independently of their political masters. Between 1881 and 1914 some 297 attachés were recruited via the annual entrance examination. This replaced the amateurish aristocratic diplomat by a new Parisian technocrat, thereby transforming the methods and politics of the diplomatic profession. The 10 embassies abroad ceased to be social sinecures. Certain republican ambassadors became better known and more powerful than their ministers. Ambassadors received extensive support staff after the 1890s in the persons of military, naval and commercial attachés. A far-reaching reform in 1907 of the central administration of the foreign ministry, located at the Quai d'Orsay in Paris, was intended to put the diplomatic machine on a more efficient footing. The new-style recruits and the reform did not always have the desired effect, leading the experienced ambassador to Berlin, Jules Cambon, to remark in 1911: 'All these wretched people are sabotaging foreign policy as they have sabotaged the organization of the "firm".'[4] The drive for professionalism continued after the war so that by the 1920s and 1930s major posts such as London, Berlin, Rome and Washington were further reinforced by financial, press and cultural attachés as the skills of a range of specialists were deployed abroad to promote French national interests. In keeping with French aspirations as a world power, the Quai d'Orsay became one of the two or three most prestigious and desirable of government posts.

The importance of a well-oiled coordination of the administrative machine was revealed during the 1914–18 war. Not all the lessons were absorbed, however. A certain amateurishness or lack of system persisted. For instance, the Third Republic continued, after 1918 as before, to keep no official minutes of cabinet meetings. This freed politicians from the discipline of seeing their views in cabinet placed on the record and it made voting on key issues unaccountable. This meant that decisions were made under the protective shroud of individual anonymity. Nor was responsibility bred in a system marked by short-lived governments and frequent swapping of portfolios among ministers. Admittedly some historians insist that, in practice, the civil service gave more continuity to French policy than the 'revolving doors' of ministerial to-ings and fro-ings would imply. Yet it is hard to deny that, even between the wars, France had nothing to compare with Britain's legendary 'Whitehall machine' established in 1916 when the cabinet office was added to the committee of imperial defence, both run till 1938 by their ubiquitous secretary, Maurice Hankey.

Nevertheless, in the aftermath of the First World War France did develop a stronger apparatus for integrating strategic and foreign policy. The navy possessed an equivalent of the army's higher war council and a consultative committee for the defence of the colonies was established. In 1928 an air ministry was formed, heralding the advent of a third military service which acquired full independence in 1933 with an air staff and higher air council. Gradually the coordination of the three armed services was improved, as was liaison with French military intelligence. In 1932 André Tardieu, then prime minister, assembled the ministers for war, air and the navy, along with the three service chiefs of staff, in the higher military committee (renamed the permanent committee of national defence in 1936, the year in which a college for higher national defence studies was founded to train administrators, generals and admirals in the management of national security). Regrettably, however, subsequent prime ministers did not convene these coordinating bodies with any regularity. They preferred *ad hoc* gatherings of personal advisers to decide policy when a crisis arose. This was plain in France's wavering response to fascist Italy's aggression against Abyssinia in 1935 and in her vacillation when Germany remilitarized the Rhineland in March 1936. Many writers indeed ascribe a major part in France's defeat in 1940 to the shortcomings of her government machinery. But others note that the Franco-British leaders in 1939–40 began the war with a top-level inter-allied Supreme War Council and an agreement on sharing the financial costs of war, and were thus better prepared for the lengthy conflict than had been their predecessors of 1914.

The shocking defeat of 1940, in an echo of what had occurred after 1870, prompted further institutional reform after 1945 in the area of foreign and defence policy-making. The establishment of the Ecole Nationale d'Administration in 1945 reinforced the tradition of a highly educated technocratic élite and provided a unified governing culture. With the constitution of the Fourth Republic in 1946, a *comité de défense nationale* was set up. This at last provided an inner advisory and decision-making executive to improve the efficiency and coordination of national security planning. In 1958 de Gaulle's Fifth Republic took centralization a step further in making foreign and defence policy a 'reserved domain' of the president of the republic. Thenceforth presidents of France have been – almost on the American model – the nation's 'commander-in-chief'. With France's defence resting overwhelmingly on nuclear weapons from the mid-1960s, this further concentrated authority over national-security decisions with the president, creating what Edmond Maire termed in 1980 'a sort of nuclear monarchy'.[5] Ironically in the light of de Gaulle's anti-American posturing, the Fifth Republic has closely imitated American executive power in foreign and defence matters with just one finger on the nuclear button.

France and the German problem

Unification for Germany was forged in war and victory – the Second Reich being proclaimed on 28 January 1871 at the palace of Versailles, symbol of the glories of French power since Louis XIV. This underlined France's prostration and decisively punctured the myth of French military supremacy which had been cultivated, and widely believed abroad, from Napoleon I to Napoleon III. The treaty of Frankfurt which ended the Franco-Prussian war exacerbated the new power imbalance by annexing Alsace and Lorraine to Germany, thereby creating the running sore that periodically broke out to remind European politicians of the deep wound inflicted on French pride. During the late 1880s under General Georges Boulanger and again from 1912, Alsace-Lorraine would contaminate Franco-German relations and lead some to call for a war of revenge.

The war-mongers were restrained, however, by cooler French statesmen and strategists who understood that the calculus of power was not to France's advantage. Léon Gambetta, who directed France's war-effort in 1871 and was the leader of the republicans in the 1870s, counselled his compatriots to 'never speak of the foreigner [the German], but let it be understood that we are always thinking of him'.[6] French efforts at rehabilitation initially focused on repaying the 5 billion gold francs war indemnity by 1873 and reforming the army. In the 1880s French policy fluctuated repeatedly as competing views of how to deal with the German threat sought ascendancy. From the 'war scare' of 1875 onwards, bellicose elements periodically urged a pre-emptive strike for revenge. More cautious spirits advocated reconciliation with Germany through customs union and closer economic cooperation or by diverting France's energies into colonial acquisition, particularly in North and West Africa, Madagascar and Indochina. The more accommodating diplomatic approaches were matched by a more defensive strategic posture. This was based on replacing the lost natural frontier of the Rhine with a belt of fortifications from Verdun to Belfort within sight of the 'blue line of the Vosges' on the eastern horizon. Other statesmen again sought to restore France's position and escape the isolation imposed by Bismarck's alliances (particularly the triple alliance of Germany, Austria–Hungary and Italy) by seeking diplomatic partners, the first of which would be Russia in 1891.

Indeed Bismarck's dismissal in 1890 opened the way for the French to loosen the straitjacket in which Germany had encased them. German diplomacy itself became less adroit. Along with France's new friendships, this meant that Germany felt more threatened. France consolidated the alliance with Russia through financial investments and naval-port visits. Tensions between Paris and Berlin rose once more. Seeking to nip France's revival in the bud, Kaiser Wilhelm II provocatively landed in 1905 at Tangier in Morocco, where France was seeking to extend her informal empire. This show-down was resolved in 1906 through an international conference at Algeçiras at which France was crucially backed by Britain, her new-found partner since the colonial settlement in the *entente cordiale* of 1904. This startled the Germans and prompted a new round of cooperation ending in a diplomatic agreement under French Foreign Minister Stephen Pichon in 1909. But German fears mounted again as the 1907 Anglo-Russian agreement's implications sank in, enhancing France's security as part of a triple *entente*.

Further provocations by France and Germany saw relations deteriorate into the second Moroccan crisis at Agadir in 1911. Again France crucially received British support and was granted a protectorate over Morocco in 1912. The German government, now feeling encircled, responded by a rapid army expansion and extension of conscription to 3 years. France took her own counter-measures which included passing a 3-year-service law in 1913. This raised tensions further. German war-preparations in the form of the Schlieffen plan, stressing a swift knock-out blow against France, contributed to the slide into hostilities during the July 1914 war crisis.

France's allies, Russia and Britain, played crucial parts in saving her from defeat at the Battle of the Marne in September 1914. This close brush with disaster at the war's outset, risked by the inappropriate strategy of the offensive, shocked the French into a more defensive posture that was only reinforced as her armies suffered huge casualties. The new strategy was epitomized by the successful defence at Verdun in 1916, organized by the cautious and reputedly compassionate General Henri-Philippe Pétain. Two more years of trench warfare defeated Germany, but bled France white in the process. Victory in 1918 owed more to allied men and money (the USA joining in 1917) than to France's own exertions. French leaders came to the Versailles peace conference keenly aware that Germany's prostration would be temporary and French security dependent on continuing alliances.

Allies in 1918 (as indeed in 1945), however, did not view Germany through French eyes. British and American economic interests demanded a rapid resurrection of Germany as a commercial partner and counterbalance to France's revived status. For France the problem was one of treaty enforcement – to avoid winning the war but losing the peace. As predicted in 1919 by Marshal Ferdinand Foch, the allied supreme commander, Versailles was not a peace 'but merely a 20-year truce'. Singlehandedly enforcing the terms proved illusory, as the Ruhr crisis of 1923 demonstrated. Advocates of conciliation then held sway for the rest of the 1920s, notably the foreign minister, Aristide Briand. Economic *rapprochement* and early withdrawal of French occupation garrisons from the Rhineland were tokens of this *détente*. Briand's plans even envisioned a federal European union (abhorrent to British officials) to bind up Germany, limit her sovereignty and internationalize her coal and steel industries.

From 1930 the wind of economic depression swept away such idealistic solutions, though not some more narrowly conceived schemes of Franco-German appeasement. Indeed the decade continued to see real tensions – for the historian Robert Young an 'ambivalence' – between appeasers and champions of a tough attitude in dealing with Germany. Although this was now a Germany of Adolf Hitler, treaty revision, rearmament and annexationist expansion (Austria 1938; Bohemia-Moravia 1939), appeasers thought themselves heirs to an honourable tradition of Franco-German conciliation, as Joseph Caillaux had earlier. Likewise, the champions of a harder line saw themselves as descendants of nineteenth-century nationalists and patriots such as Raymond Poincaré. French public opinion became as divided as the political élites over how to meet Hitler's challenge. Among numerous ministers who called for firmness towards Germany from the moment Hitler gained power in 1933 were Louis Barthou, architect of France's 3-year military-service law in 1913; Georges Mandel, political aide to Clemenceau in 1917–20; Tardieu, Poincaré's successor as prime minister in 1929; and Edouard Herriot, prime minister in 1924–5 and 1932. After 1934 policies of rearmament and *rapprochement* were both attempted. But neither was ever pursued wholeheartedly. The rub, according to Maurice Vaïsse, was that advocates of firmness, whilst analysing the German problem lucidly, were 'unclear about the methods to use' to fix it.[7] France lacked the political unity to make a now-emboldened Hitler feel she would go beyond diplomatic protests to halt Germany's resurgence. Nor, in practice, did France have the army to stage a 'police action' (her troops being defensively trained and aligned behind the fortifications of the Maginot Line). As a result France reached the eve of another war with Germany in 1939 with her public opinion profoundly divided and her armed forces incompletely prepared. Worse, her politicians were ideologically divided. Left-wingers wanted to oppose war and oppose fascism. Conservatives wavered between accommodating a Germany that stood for anti-communism and their ingrained fears of the colossus across the Rhine.

A defeat for France was not inevitable in 1939–40. But 20 years of vacillation and domestic divisions had left France again vulnerable to a German knock-out blow – this time not deflected or diminished by any eastern counterweight (Hitler having secured his flank by the August 1939 non-aggression pact with Stalin). Few ordinary French people welcomed another war with Germany in 1939, given the 1.4 million French dead of 1914–18, though most felt Hitler's conduct had become intolerable. But indecisive national leadership and public rows between ministers and the high command deepened the uncertain mood of the French during the 'phoney war' (September 1939 to May 1940). Unclear whether to shed further blood by fighting again, or to make terms with Hitler's Germany, France was once again somewhat adrift and felt friendless. Though the British were engaged at France's side, their military effort was modest (less than one-tenth the size of France's army). The USA remained resolutely neutral (its ambassador, Robert Murphy, staying accredited to the collaborationist Vichy regime until 1942). The Soviet Union was neutralized by the Nazi–Soviet pact; most small French allies, such as Poland, were rapidly engulfed by Germany. This sense of betrayal to the German terror was skilfully exploited after the collapse in June 1940 by a poster depicting a Wehrmacht infantryman cradling an infant child, over the slogan: 'Abandoned peoples, trust the German soldier!'

The 1940 débâcle ushered in a political upheaval not seen since the Paris Commune of 1871, which followed a previous defeat by Germany. France, as earlier, was traumatized. A wave of revulsion swept away the Third

Republic, a regime widely perceived as 'decadent' and to have led the nation to catastrophe. On 10 July 1940 its senators and deputies voted it out of existence at one of Napoleon III's favourite spa towns, Vichy, vesting constitutional powers in Marshal Pétain, the 84-year-old saviour of Verdun. The marshal demanded scapegoats, blaming defeat on 'Too few arms, too few allies, too few children'. Making the best terms possible with Germany's armistice delegation, Pétain retained two-fifths of metropolitan territory, the powerful French navy and the colonies. Infamously shaking hands with Hitler in October 1940 at Montoire, he 'entered into the path of collaboration' with the Nazi Reich. It was the apotheosis of the 'conciliator/appeaser' tradition of tackling the German problem.

Yet the wartime years if anything saw the French attitude to Germany lose rather than gain in clarity. The two competing policies of accommodation (Vichy) and firmness (Resistance), characteristic from the 1870s to 1939, now became three. For many French leaders under the occupation did not embrace collaboration as such, but rather a policy of 'wait-and-see' (*attentisme*). This was the case with General Maxime Weygand, Vichy pro-consul in North Africa, and with the admirals who scuttled their warships in Toulon in November 1942 rather than see them fall into German hands. The problem for Vichy's external and defence policy-makers, as for its ministers engaged in domestic policy, was that Germany did not share their goal of a

Illustration 11.1 Christmas Eve at the French Army postal sorting-office, December 1939. A satirical view of the military's tendency to become bogged down in paperwork, combined with a hint at the tensions between France and its ally, Great Britain, during the so-called Phoney War – the caption reading: 'It's the King of England on the phone .... . He's sending four million Christmas cards to our troops ... '. (© Service historique de l'armée de terre, 27 N, Fonds 'Clemenceau'.)

privileged place for France in Hitler's new European order. Moreover, defeat in 1940 and partial occupation (extended to complete occupation in November 1942) ensured that a wholly unequal power relationship underlay the putative partnership.

By late 1942 it was apparent to all except the ultra-collaborationists that a restoration of France's rank in the world could occur only with the external assistance of France's Anglo-Saxon allies. This assistance, combined with the Red Army's pressure on Germany once Hitler attacked the Soviet Union in June 1941, was accompanied by the activity of the powerful French Communist Party in opposing Vichy. Communist and non-communist Resistance and Free French leaders warmed to the prospect of France regaining her 'traditional' counterweight to Germany in the east. This policy reversion was underlined by the treaty with the USSR in December 1944 that de Gaulle concluded whilst head of the provisional government of the republic. He explained that Franco-Russian solidarity 'conformed to the natural order of things, as much in relation to the German danger as to Anglo-Saxon attempts at hegemony'.[8]

The war's end in 1944–5 saw the pendulum of French foreign policy swing decisively to the tradition of firmness towards Germany, as Hitler's defeat became only a matter of time. With British help de Gaulle lobbied successfully for a French zone in occupied Germany (including Berlin, located in the Soviet zone of Germany as a whole). These were key political symbols of French recovery. All de Gaulle's efforts in foreign and defence policy would concentrate on rebuilding France's standing and grandeur – 'without which France is not France', as he wrote in his *War Memoirs*.[9] But de Gaulle resigned in January 1946, having fallen out with the main political parties over the constitution for France's new Fourth Republic.

Down to 1954 his successors sought mainly to contain Germany through the treaties, whilst re-integrating France into alliances with former wartime partners in a more enduring manner than their predecessors, Clemenceau and Poincaré, had managed in 1918–22. Thus France concluded the treaty of Dunkirk with Britain in 1947, joined the Brussels treaty (the embryonic Western European Union) in 1948, and NATO in 1949. Many French would not have disagreed with the quip attributed to Lord Ismay, NATO's first secretary-general, that the alliance was 'a device for keeping the Americans in, the Soviets out and the Germans down'. As understandably nervous, still, about Germany in 1945–6 as she was alarmed by the signs of the emerging Soviet threat, France determined at all costs not to repeat the policy errors of the early 1920s and successfully avoided diplomatic isolation as the Cold War began.

The Cold War was, of course, not confined to Europe though it impacted seriously on France's relations with West Germany. The onset of the Korean war, in 1950, pitted communist North Korea against pro-western South Korea. A divided Korea in which one half, communist-led, invaded the other half was interpreted as a dummy run for a similar scenario in which Soviet-backed East Germany decided to test the defences of West Germany. Supporting South Korea had diverted many of Britain's and America's best military forces and commanders to the Far East by 1952–3. The West German Federal Republic, formed in 1949, had no armed forces of its own. The arguments for West German rearmament by 1951–3 appeared overwhelming to France's Anglo-American allies. This worried the French, for whom the spectre of a rearmed Germany was anathema. It came hard on the heels of French military and financial commitments to war in Indochina from 1946, ruinous to French economic recovery plans at home. But American concern to 'contain' communism gave France leverage to maintain her empire in Indochina and have four-fifths of the cost paid by Washington. Nevertheless, troops in south-east Asia could not defend West Germany or France's eastern borders. French strategists and politicians had, therefore, to acknowledge that theirs was a short-weight contribution to western Europe's security so long as France remained snared in colonial entanglements. The favoured solution in 1951–3 was the establishment of a European Defence Community (EDC), to permit limited West German rearmament within an internationalized command structure, avoiding a sovereign rearmed Germany. Others, however, found the memories of 1940–4 too fresh to contemplate any German armaments, notwithstanding the new Soviet threat. Others still feared that Germany would come to dominate the proposed EDC by its economic and military potential. For them, the spectre of Prusso-German militarism was a genie that dared not be released from the bottle a third time (after 1906–14 and 1933–9). For different reasons, EDC thus encountered insuperable Gaullist and Communist Party opposition in the French National Assembly in 1954 and the project failed.[10]

The question remained what to do with Germany. On a military level, the Americans, irritated by the EDC fiasco, moved swiftly to support the reestablishment of West German armed forces in 1955. The French, steered by Pierre Mendès France, then prime minister, secretly decided in December 1954 to proceed with the development of France's atomic-weapons programme. Meanwhile, on a politico-economic level, other French politicians such as Robert Schuman and Jean Monnet, associated with Franco-German industrial cooperation (the 1950 European Coal and Steel Community), asserted the need to bind West Germany into an economic community. This would, in Schuman's phrase, make all prospect of war with France 'not only impossible but unthinkable'. The result was the European Economic Community (EEC) established by the treaty of Rome in 1957. De Gaulle, returning to power in 1958, did not overturn this policy for he saw in it a means to claw back France's ability to speak for Europe and thereby enhance her world standing. At the same time he accelerated France's atomic-weapons programme. 'Hurrah for France, this morning she is stronger and prouder,' intoned de Gaulle triumphantly on 13 February 1960, as he announced the news of France's first atomic test in the Sahara.

At the same time he did not want French leadership in the EEC diluted or challenged by British membership – for, after his rocky wartime experience with the Anglo-Americans in 1940–5, de Gaulle suspected Britain of being a 'Trojan horse' for the 'Americanization' of not only NATO but also the European Community. In both 1963 and 1967, therefore, de Gaulle used France's veto to exclude Britain. 1963 also saw the culmination of de Gaulle's *rapprochement* with West Germany, pursued as part of his project to lead the EEC in foreign policy while Germany looked to the industrial and economic agendas. The Franco-German treaty signed at the Elysée with Chancellor Konrad Adenauer in January 1963 perhaps represented the triumph of the middle-way policy of Franco-German partnership through mutual respect and reconciliation.

It became apparent, however, that Germany would not acquiesce in French leadership. In 1965 de Gaulle in a fit of pique instructed his delegation to boycott EEC committees (the 'policy of the empty chair'), thereby paralysing all EEC decision-making. He was disinclined to compromise with the 'Anglo-Saxons' any more, and set France on the quest for grandeur by her own efforts. De Gaulle in fact ended his presidency in 1969 disillusioned with any possibility of a French-led Europe.

Whilst Helmut Schmidt was West German chancellor and Valéry Giscard d'Estaing was president of France (1974–81), personal cordiality between the leaders in Paris and Bonn led to a picking up of the pieces of the Franco-German partnership.[11] Yet even in the 1970s and 1980s critics commented that bigger differences between France and Germany existed than were implied by images of solidarity such as Chancellor Helmut Kohl and President François Mitterrand in 1985, arms linked, paying respects to the war dead of 1939–45, or the Franco-German brigade joining in the 1995 Bastille Day (the first German troops to parade in Paris since Hitler's conquering armies in 1940). Giscard, Mitterrand (1981–95) and Jacques Chirac (president after 1995) had not learned the lessons which de Gaulle himself, as early as 1965, had experienced, viz. Germany's unwillingness to cut defence links with the USA. Even though the policies themselves had something slightly unreal about them, in the main the French foreign and defence consensus showed a popular and élite support for de Gaulle's 'security revolution' from the 1960s until the time of the Gulf War of 1990–1. Around that point, however, new doubts surfaced in France about containment of Germany after her reunification – as did alarm at the cost and ethics of France's heavy reliance on a nuclear defence.

The Anglo-Saxons

Before 1900 Britain and France mostly regarded each other more as likely enemies than as potential friends. Despite allying to curb Russian ambitions during the Crimean war of 1854–6, memories of the Revolutionary and

Napoleonic wars were strong. In the 1860s Britain had undertaken a serious fortification of the Royal Navy's base at Portsmouth against the supposed danger of a French attack. The United States, on the other hand, was literally and metaphorically far too distant and beyond the revival of sentimental ties by gestures such as France's gift of the Statue of Liberty to New York in 1876. America aroused little interest among French élites or the general public. The making of the *entente cordiale* in 1904 saw changes afoot, the accord settling Franco-British imperial differences and raising possibilities of cooperation against the German threat. In the 1914–18 war, France paid for much of her military expenditure by borrowing in London and New York. This left her heavily dependent, financially as well as militarily, on Britain to begin with – and then on the USA after 1917. France feared that wartime Anglo-American predominance would eventually dilute French control of a peace settlement. This fear led French leaders to agree an armistice rather than fight on to defeat the German armies completely, as some hard-liners such as Poincaré and Foch urged.

After 1919 French foreign policy was characterized by a persistent but futile quest for an alliance with the USA and Britain which would strengthen her position against Germany. Disintegration of the wartime economic *entente* between the United States and its European partners after the November 1918 armistice was, as William Keylor has emphasized, 'a major disappointment to France'.[12] Clemenceau relinquished security on the Rhine in exchange for an Anglo-American guarantee treaty, only to see this slip like sand through his fingers as the US senate refused to ratify the Versailles treaty in 1920 and America returned to its traditional isolationism. Since the British guarantee was contingent on US participation, the French found themselves empty-handed.

Worse than this, because Anglo-American financial interests dictated a recovery of German prosperity, their approach to enforcement of the reparations clauses of Versailles differed sharply from the more punitive-minded French. As France was, however, encumbered with considerable wartime debts owed principally to the US and Great Britain, her freedom to enforce German repayments to her fell victim to Washington's and London's more magnanimous policy. Consequently the only remaining instrument for controlling Germany slipped from France's grasp, as the unavailing Ruhr intervention in 1923 starkly revealed.

Without the support of the Anglo-Saxons and with her traditional eastern ally Russia having become communist in 1917 and an international pariah, France spent the 1920s building a network of lesser European allies. Located chiefly in eastern Europe and the Balkans, these were envisaged as a counterweight to possible German recovery, which many French leaders saw as only a matter of time. Although this grouping of eastern allies looked superficially impressive, states such as Poland, Czechoslovakia, Romania and Yugoslavia were divided among themselves. Furthermore, French treaties with these states frightened British governments anxious not to be drawn into the quarrels of 'small far-away countries' of which Britons knew little and cared less.

French leaders nonetheless remained ever anxious to rebuild the elusive alliance with Britain. Yet they faced a dilemma: abandoning their eastern friends would signify France's acceptance of second-class international status, whereas a British alliance would only have been possible if France relinquished her commitment to the east. Lacking firm support at the time of Germany's remilitarization of the Rhineland in March 1936, France stepped onto the path of appeasement already being trodden by Britain. Historians such as François Bédarida used to argue that the years from 1936 onwards saw France concede all diplomatic independence to the tutelage of 'an English governess', seeing French appeasement policy as 'made in London'.[13] Writing more recently, however, Robert Young has argued that France retained some capacity for initiatives. In 1938 France admittedly offered only a diplomatic protest to German annexation of Austria and, at Munich in September, colluded with Britain to induce Czechoslovakia (France's ally by treaty), to accept dismemberment by Germany – a precursor to Hitler's destruction of the Czechoslovak state in March 1939. But whilst suffering diplomatic defeats France did at least rebuild her armed strength. In 1939, with another ally, Poland, under attack, French military chiefs advised a return to firmness and were confident enough to stand up to Germany. To Hitler's astonishment, Edouard Daladier's government took France into war that September. It was only in these extreme circumstances of renewed hostilities against Germany that Britain agreed to resume the alliance with France. Even then, as in 1914, Britain's pre-war aloofness from the continent and her imperial priorities ensured that her military aid to France in 1939–40 was modest and did not compensate for Germany's greater number of mobilized troops.

Aware of their need of an arsenal abroad, and notwithstanding American isolationism in the 1930s, some French leaders such as Foreign Minister Georges Bonnet and Jean Monnet (the latter a member of the Tardieu–Joffre mission to Washington in 1917–18) appealed to the US president, Franklin D. Roosevelt. The 'spirit of Lafayette and Rochambeau', a 200-year tradition of Franco-American friendship, was invoked to recall how France had assisted America in its war for independence. Roosevelt, however, though sympathetic to France, was prevented by congressional hostility to US entanglement in Europe from providing practical assistance. Even in the crisis of June 1940, desperate telegrams containing personal pleas from Reynaud, the French premier, failed to draw the USA into war alongside France.

1940 saw a rupture in Franco-British relations once again. Dunkirk symbolized, for many French, the perfidiousness of an Albion ready to cut and run from the continent, leaving France to fend for herself in a German-controlled Europe. The Americans, too, were objects of suspicion. Not only did they retain ambassadorial relations with Pétain's Vichy France, but de

Gaulle's Free France got short shrift in Washington. 'How can one deal with a man who thinks himself Napoleon and Joan of Arc?' asked a bemused and irritated Roosevelt. The British, largely because Churchill admired de Gaulle's stubborn courage, gave more support to Free France. They put BBC broadcast facilities at de Gaulle's disposal to help him rally resistance inside occupied and Vichy France, and supplied weapons and training facilities for de Gaulle's Fighting French forces. The Americans remained sceptical, even hostile. They put up an alternative to de Gaulle in 1942, the more senior General Henri Giraud, and did not recognize de Gaulle's leadership of the French committee of national liberation until 1943. This legacy soured de Gaulle's long-term view of the United States. He decided that the Americans were driven by non-European interests and were potentially untrustworthy. He was incensed in early 1944 to discover well-advanced plans to impose an Allied Military Government of Occupied Territory (AMGOT) regime on liberated France, currency even having been printed and prepared for distribution. Through unyielding negotiation, de Gaulle narrowly averted this humiliation. Instead he secured the administration of liberated France by commissioners of the republic acting in the name of the provisional government which he headed; he also won the right for Free French tanks to lead the return to Paris in August 1944 to symbolize France's 'liberation by itself'.

These achievements were consolidated by de Gaulle's desire to carry on the fight against Germany and gain recognition of France's status as one of the 'big four' powers whose decisions would shape the post-war European settlement. Although excluded from the conferences at Yalta and Potsdam in 1945 between the USA, the Soviet Union and Britain, de Gaulle nonetheless achieved a remarkable amount of this ambitious agenda. He also laid blame for the post-war division of Europe squarely on the Yalta decisions and specifically at the feet of Americans with their 'non-European' perspective. This jaundiced view by de Gaulle of US behaviour in the war's latter stages conditioned the general's thinking on foreign and defence policy. Indeed it marked his outlook both in his 'wilderness years' of 1946–58, when he was out of office, and in his presidency (1958–69). Most saliently, it prompted French desires for an independent foreign and defence policy. These were most potently epitomized by France's atomic- and nuclear-weapons programmes which de Gaulle prioritized after his return to power in 1958. 'It is indispensable that it be a French defence and that France defends herself by herself, for herself, and in her own manner,' he declared in November 1959.

De Gaulle found a broad welcome among the French political community and public for his more independent external and defence policy. This was in part because the years of the Fourth Republic (1946–58) had witnessed further setbacks for French national pride at the hands of the Anglo-Saxons, and particularly the Americans. During the final crisis of the Indochina war, with a French garrison at Dien Bien Phu on the verge of surrender to the Vietminh communists in April 1954, the ostensibly anti-communist

Eisenhower administration refused pleas from a desperate French foreign minister, Georges Bidault, to provide US atomic weapons to break the encirclement. Two years later, in 1956, US hostility to the Franco-British-Israeli military intervention against Egypt's President Nasser at Suez forced French and British withdrawal from the canal zone.

The French and British governments drew radically divergent lessons from this débâcle. Whereas London toed the US line thereafter, drawing especially close in nuclear cooperation and procuring US Polaris missiles via the Anglo-American Nassau agreement of 1962, France resolutely pursued her own independent nuclear deterrent. First the French developed Mirage bombers, operational from 1964. These were, in practice, more symbolic than truly threatening. Critics scathingly referred to the French atomic weapon as *une bombinette*.[14] Nevertheless, de Gaulle persevered, aided by his defence minister, Pierre Messmer, a distinguished Free French combat veteran. From 1960 a ground-to-ground strategic ballistic missile was developed.

Basking in French economic success ('the 30 glorious years' after 1945), military revival and world recognition, de Gaulle felt sufficiently confident to withdraw France from NATO's integrated military command. In 1966 he instructed NATO personnel and bases to leave French territory. A maverick in the eyes of his western allies, he delivered a series of calculated snubs to the USA. In 1966 he visited Moscow and championed third-world interests against 'American imperialism'. He openly criticized American involvement in Vietnam, sided with the Arabs against Israel in the six-day war of 1967 and, in the same year, outraged Britain by using a visit to Canada to encourage Quebecan separatism. As part of his now-independent foreign and defence policy, de Gaulle launched the first nuclear-powered submarine, the *Redoutable*, in 1967 (even if it could not deliver a nuclear warhead till 1971). Not until the year after de Gaulle's death in 1970, ironically, did France complete the elements of a superpower-in-miniature's strategic triad: land-based medium-range missiles on the Plateau d'Albion, and a ballistic-missile-armed nuclear-submarine flotilla, complementing the Mirage force. In the last two decades of the Cold War, therefore, albeit at dauntingly great expense, France possessed a significant independent nuclear deterrent. This, even more than her permanent membership of the UN security council, restored France to the 'club' of great powers, a status she had arguably not enjoyed since 1914. France felt she had pulled herself up and could once more look the Anglo-Saxons squarely in the eyes. The nuclear weapon had come to replace the empire as the most important trapping of French great-power status.

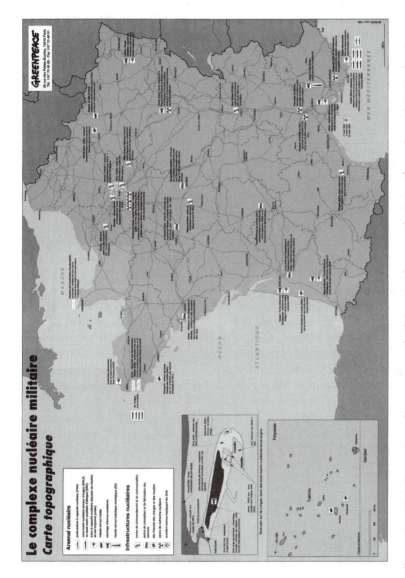

Illustration 11.2 France's nuclear weapons facilities. A schematic depiction from the mid 1980s by Greenpeace, highlighting the quantity and geographical spread of French nuclear assets and test sites in an era when President Mitterrand's government was spending lavishly on weapons-system upgrades and expansion of stocks of fissile materials. (Courtesy of Greenpeace, 21, rue Godot de Mauroy, 75009 Paris, France.)

Empire

De Gaulle thus exploited the coincidence of French nuclear industrial take-off with the decline of the imperial idea. In many respects it was this French nuclear-weapons capability which for de Gaulle offered a replacement for the colonial empire – France's strategic-power make-weight in the era from 1881 to 1961. The colonies had always represented another French vision of their role – one in which global presence combined with cultural and linguistic influence to rival Britain as the leading world player.

Colonies had been a part of France's power base since the *ancien régime*. Under the Bourbons, from the 1690s to 1789, the territories of France's first colonial empire in the West Indies, Canada and India were continually fought over in a global struggle with Britain. This contest for naval, commercial and colonial supremacy was renewed in the Revolutionary and Napoleonic wars. By 1815 France had been vanquished overseas, as she was in Europe. But her empire, albeit reduced, was not lost completely. A second imperial expansion occurred in the late nineteenth century, prefigured by French seizure of control over Algeria in 1830. However, after France's crushing defeat by Germany in 1871, interest in empire really revived. Some colonial lobbyists practised a forward policy, not always officially sanctioned by governments in Paris. This brought about the acquisition of Tunisia (1882), Indochina (1879–85) and Madagascar (1899). Writing in 1880, Paul Leroy-Beaulieu urged more overseas expansion, warning that without a big empire France's awful fate would be to fall below the rank of Spain or Portugal. In the 20 years from 1880 to 1900 the French empire expanded tenfold in terms of surface area and population, and became second only to Britain's. An inter-party parliamentary group of some 90 to 100 members, known as the 'Parti Colonial', was established in 1892 and fostered pro-imperialism even though this was not always official policy. The empire was further enlarged by the peace treaties of 1919. The acquisition of Syria, the Lebanon and parts of Germany's former West African colonies marked the climax of French imperial expansion and was welcomed as an apparent enhancement of France's great-power status. Among scholars there is a consensus that, at least until the First World War, France's empire made a net economic and financial loss, whatever the prestige and strategic value.

Between the wars, however, French trade and investments with the overseas territories markedly increased. By 1939–40, estimates Jacques Marseille, the empire was taking 50 per cent of French foreign investment and in general a serious economic exploitation of the colonies was under way. The share of French total foreign trade increased substantially to 26.9 per cent of French imports and 27.2 per cent of French exports in 1938. Economic activity was matched by propaganda and promotion of the empire by French governments. The colonial exhibitions of 1922 in Marseille and 1931 in Paris drew scores of thousands of metropolitan visitors for whom overseas France had hitherto been an unknown quantity. Surprisingly, however, this greater profitability of empire did not translate into any major investment in imperial defence, the Dakar and Mers-el-Kébir naval bases excepted.

National leaders trumpeted the overseas territories as a 'greater France' of 110 million inhabitants, the potential salvation of a demographically enfeebled post-1918 mainland. Articles appeared in influential journals extolling the empire's strategic value. 'Imperial policy will save France,' boasted the newspaper *Le Grand Echo* on 20 January 1939.[15] However, the colonies were always a defence liability as much as a strategic asset. Whilst they offered resources for war (especially manpower to reinforce France's metropolitan army), they also required protection. This gave a voice to the advocates of French naval expansion. These lobbyists provided a momentum for French naval build-up through the rise of the *jeune école* who urged in the 1880s that British naval mastery be challenged. From then on France maintained a significant fleet, partly based at Brest to cover the Atlantic and partly at Toulon in the Mediterranean. Following the *entente* with Britain in 1904, however, the focus of French maritime strategy shifted away from potential conflict against the Royal Navy. Thereafter, as the fourth-ranking naval power (by fleet tonnage), France reached agreement with Britain in 1912 to assume responsibility for Mediterranean defence against the triple alliance, in exchange for the Royal Navy's concentration in the North Sea.

Arguably the French navy's chief contribution in the First World War was that it assured safe passage for colonial troops to fight on the western front and in major peripheral theatres such as Gallipoli and Salonika. In August 1914 only 65 000 soldiers stood ready for service in French North and West Africa. But the war saw mass mobilization in the empire. Contingents were recruited in Morocco, Algeria, Tunisia, Madagascar and Indochina. Some helped seize Germany's African dependencies in Togoland and Cameroon. But most were shipped to France to fight in the mud of Flanders, the Aisne and Verdun. A vast reservoir of indigenous manpower, *la force noire* as it was termed by General Charles Mangin, one of the leading colonial commanders, eventually provided 569 000 North African and colonial soldiers – crucial infusions of strength to fill the gaps caused by the casualties France suffered in 1914–15.

The French fleet's role in securing lines of communication between empire and metropole in 1914–18 kept it at the forefront of national-security planning between the wars. However, the 1921–2 Washington naval conference set new international fleet parities: Great Britain 5; USA 5; Japan 3: France 1.75; Italy 1.75. France felt humiliated at an essentially Anglo-American-imposed equality with Italy. At a more practical level, she worried about defence and communications with the empire. The French navy lobbied for fleet expansion in the early 1930s. From 1930 the minister of marine, Georges Leygues, and naval chiefs such as Admiral François Darlan, secured funding second only to the army's (with the airforce, despite being crucial to the security of the metropole, coming a poor third till 1938). New

battleships to dominate the western Mediterranean in face of a threat from
Italy (also modernizing her navy by 1935) were built as evidence grew of
Mussolini's ambitions in North and East Africa – areas France regarded as in
her sphere of influence.

Defending the empire as a whole proved beyond France in 1939–45. The
combination of Nazi Germany, fascist Italy and imperial Japan was too
strong, and its menace too widespread. France found that, even allied to
Britain, it could not protect its colonies and ward off German invasion. Even
before 1939 the naval theorist Admiral Raoul Castex warned that Indochina
and French Polynesia were indefensible if Japan turned hostile. North Africa
provided military reinforcements again in 1939–40 as in 1914–18. But
France had failed to develop military–industrial facilities there against the
eventuality of defeat in Europe. Consequently Vichy could do no more than
guard the unoccupied status of North Africa after the 1940 armistice.
Meanwhile Indochina, cut off from metropolitan assistance, had to bow to
Japan's will and eventually suffered complete Japanese occupation in March
1945.

The French empire did not declare unanimously for Vichy, however. In
sub-Saharan Africa support emerged in the summer of 1940 for de Gaulle
and Free France. Troops based in Chad, the French Congo and Djibouti
formed the nucleus of units that eventually grew into the Free French corps in
Italy in 1943–44 and the Free French first army in France in 1944–5.
Colonial support for Free France, albeit limited in comparison with the many
overseas territories loyal to Pétain, was crucial to Gaullist myth-making.
Also, and more dispassionately, it allowed French people a measure of pride
in their empire's contribution to the allied triumph over the Axis powers.
'The Empire', in the words of Marc Michel, 'was a vital element in the
restoration of national prestige, just as it had been after 1870.'[16] In 1945
Gaston Monnerville, deputy for French Guyana and pre-war under-secretary
of state for the colonies, was appointed to draft a new constitutional status
for the overseas territories. Echoing Ferry, he told the National Assembly in
Paris that the empire had ensured France's status as a victor; without it
France would be just another liberated country.

More problematically, however, in the immediate post-war years, the
French had only the empire as a material sign of greatness. Consequently
they clung to the colonies for more than they were worth. The trauma of
defeat in 1940 meant that, for the army especially, nationalist independence
movements which surfaced from 1945 were brutally repressed. French
commanders set their faces against further 'retreats and defeats'.[17] Indigenous peoples therefore lost hope that their part in liberating France would be
matched by their own early liberation. Indeed Martin Evans argues that the
example of Second-World-War resistance by the French against German
occupation inspired resistance by the colonized to a continuation of French
rule after 1945.

Unlike the pragmatic British, France stubbornly opposed decolonization and what she saw as another loss of face. This had high opportunity costs, for expending so much energy on retention of empire meant France was unable to provide foreign-policy leadership in western Europe, play her full part in meeting the growing Soviet threat after 1949 or upgrade her armaments and military doctrine. Not till 1954 did France escape the war in Indochina and then only as a result of a humiliating military débâcle at Dien Bien Phu. Imperial crisis resurfaced much closer to home when, in November 1954, nationalist violence erupted in Algeria. Unable to countenance another defeat the French army responded with ruthless counter-measures. The crisis was not strictly imperial. Algeria was not a colony but three departments of France, its million European settlers (and a few Muslims) represented in the French parliament. Paradoxically, French foreign policy would be enlisted to convince other powers and the United Nations that Algeria was purely a French domestic problem. The Algerian war proved unwinnable, however. The strain it placed on French society brought down the Fourth Republic in 1958 and by the war's end in 1962 had divided and demoralized the French army. De Gaulle, back in power in 1958, understood that world rank was now measured less in terms of square kilometres of empire than in mega-tonnage of nuclear warheads. He swiftly cut the formal imperial ties. French sub-Saharan Africa was granted independence in 1960 – the very year that France exploded its first atomic bomb.

The French empire, however, mutated rather than disappeared. After decolonization France retained extensive informal influence – a continuation of empire by other means. A vague notion of French worldwide outreach, a loose 'French commonwealth', was established. This rested partly on the franc as a common currency, partly on the persistence of French as the lingua franca. French influence was buttressed by educational and cultural links as well as a network of military training and basing agreements which gave France a role as 'gendarme' in Africa until the 1990s. Known officially as *la Francophonie* ('those nations having in common the use of French'), this French commonwealth has been cynically decried as mere neo-colonialism.

As in other areas of specifically French post-1945 foreign and security policy, this final manifestation of empire embodied a burning ambition to preserve and promote French language and universalist ideals. Most distasteful to the French were the encroachments of Anglo-Saxon, and specifically American, economics and culture. Though many French people criticized the bombast and costly nuclear projects of de Gaulle's presidency (1958–69), many more shared a revulsion at what they saw as the debasement and 'Coca Cola-ization' of the arts, culture and language. Indeed it was the politician and journalist Jean-Jacques Servan-Schreiber, an outspoken opponent of the attempt to hold onto Algeria by force 10 years before, who struck a populist chord with this theme in his best-selling polemic of 1967, *The American Challenge* (actually addressed mainly to industrial-technological issues).[18]

In the aftermath of de Gaulle's liquidation of the empire, it seemed that successive presidents (Pompidou, Giscard d'Estaing and Mitterrand) could resolve France's continental/imperial dilemma by concentrating France's energies on Europe. However, the vestiges of the 'civilizing mission' and the universalist pretensions of French republicanism lured French foreign and defence policy into entanglements in Chad and other former colonies in the 1970s and 1980s, often by invitation of a beleaguered local despot such as Jean-Bedel Bokassa in the Central African Republic. France even acted outside her former empire. No episode better illustrated the Fifth Republic's muscular interventionism than the paratroop drops into Zaïre in 1977 and 1978 to evacuate Europeans caught up in civil war. The former colonial power, Belgium, was notified only when the action was under way. In other actions French mercenaries, with or without French-government assent, have helped mount *coups d'état* in Africa, replicating the unofficial work of the colonial lobby in the French scramble for Africa in the nineteenth century.

Since the early 1960s France has intervened some 20 times in Africa, usually after a technical invitation from the country concerned and using the justification of protecting European expatriates and property (or under the guise of UN peacekeeping or 'humanitarian interventions', as in the controversial deployments in Zaïre in 1991 and Rwanda in 1994). Down to the early 1990s, France maintained some 8000 troops and 1200 military advisers around Africa. This reaffirmed France's claim that francophone Africa remained within its sphere of external influence. In 1997 a 40 per cent reduction in French troop levels in Africa was announced, linked to President Chirac's decision to end conscription in favour of a smaller professional army by 2002. Ghosts of past military failures in the colonies continued to haunt the offices of the Quai d'Orsay, however. Hubert Védrine, France's foreign minister, touchily denied that these cutbacks marked a 'retreat', insisting that France merely sought to move 'to a smaller, more flexible and more effective force'.[19]

The former colonies still swallowed most of France's overseas-aid budget in the mid-1980s, sub-Saharan Africa taking 54.4 per cent and North Africa 12.4 per cent. France's trade patterns, too, continue to reflect flows established in the empire's heyday. By 1997 the French were spending nearly US $1 billion a year promoting the French language and culture, despite the fact that (or because) Chinese, Arabic, Spanish and Portuguese – and of course English – are spoken more than French. Empire as an instrument of foreign and defence policy continues subtly to underpin French claims to grandeur and world status. But the imperial idea has been repackaged by emphasis on the defence of cultural particularisms, not the retention of territory. Asserting French cultural specificity in the face of Americanization was one of the roles assigned to the secretary-general of *la Francophonie*, the former UN secretary-general, Boutros Boutros-Ghali, on this post's creation in 1997. When the seventh francophone summit conference met in Hanoi that year it was attended by 46 countries (many of whom had only tenuous links with French, as in the case of Portuguese-speaking Sao Tomé). As in the nineteenth century the organizers claimed that English was the language of commerce; but French, they asserted, was the language of 'culture and fraternity'.

Conclusions

Since Napoleon's time, world influence and French security on the continent of Europe have competed for priority in French foreign and defence policy. For most of the nineteenth and twentieth centuries, notably from 1871–1945, France swung between the two poles – the overseas mission and the European. An equilibrium appeared to emerge from about 1960 to 1990. Formal withdrawal from empire was offset by acquisition of nuclear weapons and a partnership with West Germany. From about 1989, however, the certainties of this Gaullist consensus crumbled. In 1990 German reunification reminded the French of old demons. Awareness of French demographic and economic inferiority re-emerged. Nerves showed again about 'the German problem'. The senior editor of the influential French weekly, *L'Express*, wrote a book evoking a 'return to a Bismarckian system'.[20] De Gaulle and his successors may have thought they had resolved the strategic dilemma of an overseas and a European role. Yet in a book published in 1996, Jean-Pierre Chevènement, Socialist Party parliamentary deputy for Belfort – an ancient fortified city bordering Germany – and defence minister from 1988 to 1991, warned that Europe's geo-politics risked being upset. The scenarios facing France were, he estimated: 'A Europeanized Germany, a German Europe or an American new world order.'[21] One approach was for France to draw closer to Germany through the European Union's formal institutional structures; but popular disquiet about German domination of the EU may explain the narrow margin by which the French government carried the day in the referendum on the Maastricht treaty (51/49 per cent). Evidently fear as to whether partnership with Germany meant French subservience resonated in the 1990s as it had a century before.

Simultaneously, the defence consensus started to unravel. On the one hand the *furore* over Chirac's round of nuclear tests in 1995 revealed the fragility of agreement on nuclear weapons. On the other hand the republican tradition of the 'nation in arms' seemed incapable of fitting the French armed forces for post-Cold-War challenges, as her feeble contribution to the coalition to defeat Iraq in 1990–1 underlined. The twentieth century closed rather like the nineteenth, with French people nervous about the country's role, its dependency on allies and its problems in providing for its own security. Evidently the Cold-War consensus was but a parenthesis in France's historic dichotomy between defending the 'blue line of the Vosges' and pursuing wider world ambitions.

Notes

1 In headquarters journal of General Maurice Gamelin, 9 October 1939, Service Historique de l'Armée de Terre, Vincennes, Fonds Gamelin 1K 224/9.

2 *République française: Journal Officiel – Chambre des Députés: débats* (Paris: Imprimerie Nationale), 27 Jan. 1937, pp. 169–72.

3 R. D. Challener, *The French Theory of the Nation-in-Arms, 1866–1939* (New York: Columbia University Press, 1955).

4 J. F. V. Keiger, 'Patriotism, politics and policy in the Foreign Ministry 1880–1914', in Robert Tombs (ed.), *Nationhood and Nationalism in France: From Boulangism to the Great War 1889–1918* (London: Harper Collins, 1991), p. 263.

5 Quoted in Samy Cohen, *La Monarchie nucléaire: Les coulisses de la politique étrangère sous la Ve République* (Paris: Hachette, 1986), p. 16.

6 Quoted in Frederic H. Seager, 'The Alsace-Lorraine question in France, 1871–1914', in Charles K. Warner (ed.), *From the Ancien Regime to the Popular Front: Essays in the History of Modern France in Honor of Shephard B. Clough* (New York: Columbia University Press, 1969), p. 112.

7 M. Vaïsse, 'Against appeasement: French advocates of firmness, 1933–8', in W. J. Mommsen and L. Kettenacker (eds.), *The Fascist Challenge and the Policy of Appeasement* (London: Allen & Unwin, 1983), pp. 227–35.

8 C. de Gaulle, *Mémoires de guerre. III: Le Salut, 1944–46* (Paris: Plon, 1959), p. 54.

9 C. de Gaulle *Mémoires de guerre. I: L'appel, 1940–1942* (Paris: Plon, 1954), p. 1.

10 See Denise Artaud, 'France between the Indochina War and the European Defense Community', in Lawrence S. Kaplan, Denise Artaud and Mark R. Rubin (eds.), *Dien Bien Phu and the Crisis of Franco-American Relations, 1954–1955* (Wilmington, DE: Scholarly Resources, 1990), pp. 251–68.

11 Haig Simonian, *The Privileged Partnership: Franco-German Relations in the European Community, 1969–1984* (Oxford: Clarendon Press, 1985), pp. 247–306.

12 W. R. Keylor, 'France's futile quest for American military protection, 1919–22', in M. Petricioli and M. Guderzo (eds.), *A Missed Opportunity? 1922: The Reconstruction of Europe* (Berne: Peter Lang, 1995), pp. 61–80.

13 F. Bédarida, 'La "gouvernante anglaise"', in René Rémond and Janine Bourdin (eds.), *Edouard Daladier, chef de gouvernement (avril 1938–septembre 1939)* (Paris: Fondation Nationale des Sciences Politiques, 1977), pp. 228–40.

14 Quoted in D. Johnson, 'De Gaulle and France's role in the world', in H. Gough and J. Horne (eds.), *De Gaulle and Twentieth-Century France* (London: Arnold, 1994), p. 91.

15 Eugen Weber, *The Hollow Years: France in the 1930s* (London: Sinclair-Stevenson, 1995), p. 180.

16 M. Michel, 'Decolonisation: French attitudes and policies, 1944–46', in P. Morris and S. Williams (eds.), *France in the World* (London: Association for the Study of Modern and Contemporary France, 1985), p. 83.

17 M. Vaïsse, *1961: Alger, le putsch* (Brussels: Editions Complexe, 1983), pp. 51–3.

18 J.-J. Servan-Schreiber, *Le Défi Américain* (Paris: Editions Denoël, 1967); English edn. (trans. Ronald Steel), *The American Challenge* (London: Hamish Hamilton, 1968).

19 Quoted in David Owen, 'France set to lower its guard in Africa', *Financial Times* (31 July 1997), p. 2.

20 Georges Valance, *France-Allemagne: Le retour de Bismarck* (Paris: Flammarion, 1990).
21 J.-P. Chevènement, *France-Allemagne, parlons franc* (Paris: Plon, 1996), pp. 36–9, 143–61. For continuing evidence of these neuroses, see Joseph Rovan, *Bismarck, l'Allemagne et l'Europe Unie, 1898–1998–2098* (Paris: Éditions Odile Jacob, 1998), esp. pp. 129–231; Pierre M. Gallois, *La France, sort-elle de l'Histoire? Superpuissances et déclin national* (Lausanne: L'Age d'Homme, 1998), esp. pp. 105–35, 137–58.

Further reading

Adamthwaite, A. P. *Grandeur and Misery: France's Bid for Power in Europe, 1914–1940* (London: Arnold, 1995).

Alexander, M. S. *The Republic in Danger: General Maurice Gamelin and the Politics of French defence, 1933–1939* (Cambridge: Cambridge University Press, 1993).

Andrew, C. M. and Kanya-Forstner, A. S. *France Overseas: The Great War and the Climax of French Imperial Expansion, 1914–1924* (London: Thames & Hudson, 1981).

L'Aventure de la bombe: de Gaulle et la dissuasion nucléaire, 1958–1969 (Paris: Plon, 1985).

Bell, P. M. H. *France and Britain, 1900–1940: Entente and Estrangement; France and Britain, 1940–1994: The Long Separation* (Harlow: Longman, 1996–7).

Bozo, F. *La France et l'OTAN: de la guerre froide au nouvel ordre européen* (Paris: Masson, 1991).

Chipman, J. *French Power in Africa* (Oxford: Blackwell, 1989).

Chuter, D. *Humanity's Soldier: France and International Security, 1919–2001* (Providence, RI and Oxford: Berghahn, 1996).

Cogan, C. G. *Oldest Allies, Guarded Friends: The United States and France since 1940* (New York: Praeger, 1994).

——, *Forced to Choose: France, the Atlantic Alliance and NATO – Then and Now* (New York: Praeger, 1997).

Cooke, J. J. *New French Imperialism, 1880–1910: The Third Republic and Colonial Expansion* (Newton Abbot: David & Charles, 1973).

De Gaulle, C. *Vers l'armée de métier* (Paris: Plon, 1934).

Doise, J. and Vaïsse, M. *Diplomatie et outil militaire: politique étrangère de la France, 1871–1969* (Paris: Imprimerie Nationale, 1987).

Gordon, P. H. *A Certain Idea of France: French Security Policy and the Gaullist Legacy* (Princeton: Princeton University Press, 1993).

——, *France, Germany and the Western Alliance* (Boulder, CO: Westview, 1995).

Hitchcock, W. I. *France Restored: Cold War Diplomacy and the Quest for Leadership in Europe, 1944–1954* (Chapel Hill, NC: University of North Carolina Press, 1998).

Hoffmann, S. 'The foreign policy of Charles de Gaulle', in G. A. Craig and F. L. Loewenheim (eds.), *The Diplomats, 1939–1979* (Princeton: Princeton University Press, 1994).

Hogenhuis-Seliverstoff, A. *Une alliance franco-russe: la France, la Russie et l'Europe au tournant du siècle dernier* (Brussels: Bruylant, 1997).

Howard, M. E. *The Franco-Prussian War* (London: Hart-Davis, 1961).

Hughes, J. M. *To the Maginot Line: The Politics of French Military Preparation in the 1920s* (Cambridge, MA: Harvard University Press, 1971).

Keiger, J. F. V. *France and the Origins of the First World War* (London: Macmillan, 1983).

——, 'France and international relations in the post-Cold War era: some lessons of the past', *Modern & Contemporary France* NS, 3:3 (1995), pp. 263–74.

Kennan, G. F. *The Fateful Alliance: France, Russia and the Coming of the First World War* (New York: Pantheon, 1984).

Kennedy, P. M. *The Realities behind Diplomacy* (London: Fontana, 1983).

Kolodziej, E. A. *French International Policy under de Gaulle and Pompidou: The Politics of Grandeur* (Ithaca, NY: Cornell University Press, 1974).

Kuisel, R. F. *Seducing the French: The Dilemma of Americanization* (Berkeley: University of California Press, 1993).

Maguire, G. E. *Anglo-American Relations with the Free French* (London: Macmillan, 1995).

Marseille, J. *Empire colonial et capitalisme français: histoire d'un divorce* (Paris: Albin Michel, 1984).

Michel, M. *L'Appel à l'Afrique: contributions et réactions à l'effort de guerre en AOF, 1914–1919* (Paris: Publications de la Sorbonne, 1982).

Mitchell, A. *Victors and Vanquished: The German Influence on Army and Church in France after 1870* (Chapel Hill, NC: University of North Carolina Press, 1982).

Mongin, D. *La bombe atomique française, 1945–1958* (Brussels: Bruylant, 1997).

Paxton, R. O. and Wahl, N. (eds.), *De Gaulle and the United States: A Centennial Reappraisal* (Providence, RI: Berg, 1993).

Schuker, S. A. *The End of French Predominance in Europe: The Financial Crisis of 1924 and the Adoption of the Dawes Plan* (Chapel Hill, NC: University of North Carolina Press, 1976).

Soutou, G.-H. *L'alliance incertaine: les rapports politico-stratégiques franco-allemands, 1954–1996* (Paris: Fayard, 1996).

Stevenson, D. *French War Aims against Germany, 1914–1919* (Oxford: Oxford University Press, 1982).

Thomas, M. *The French Empire at War, 1940–45* (Manchester: Manchester University Press, 1998).

Vaïsse, M. *La Grandeur: la politique extérieure du général de Gaulle, 1958–1969* (Paris: Fayard, 1998).

Vaïsse, M., Mélandri, P. and Bozo, F. (eds.), *La France et L'OTAN, 1949–1996* (Brussels: Complexe, 1996).

Wall, I. M. *The United States and the Making of Postwar France, 1945–1954* (Cambridge: Cambridge University Press, 1991).

Woodhouse, R. 'France's relations with NATO, 1966–1996', *Modern & Contemporary France* NS, 4:4 (1996), pp. 483–95.

Young, J. W. *France, the Cold War and the Western Alliance, 1944–1949* (Leicester: Leicester University Press, 1990).

Young, R. J. *In Command of France: French Policy and Military Planning, 1933–1939* (Cambridge, MA: Harvard University Press, 1978).

——, *France and the Origins of the Second World War* (London: Macmillan, 1996).

|12|

France's cultural clashes
Arts and taste since the impressionists
CHARLES REARICK

Fruitful oppositions

Through the history of modern French culture, amid the many brilliant innovations, some fundamental traditions from the old regime have endured. One of those traditions is strong state support for the arts and literature. Since the seventeenth century French governments have pursued a policy of enhancing a prestigious élite culture at home and abroad. During recent centuries the state in all its diverse forms has supported, for example, a national theatre (the Comédie-Française) to keep classic plays alive, and it has sponsored the Académie Française, whose 40 honored luminaries ('the immortals') work to uphold the country's literary standards and language (in part by producing a dictionary). Another old-regime legacy is the sense of France as a leader of civilization. That claim to leadership originated with French writers in the eighteenth century who used their newly-coined word *civilisation* to point up their country's accomplishments in the arts, manners and sociability. They also hailed the language and literature of France as superior.

In the following century, when the painters now known as impressionists were beginning their individual careers, the self-made Emperor Louis Napoleon patronized traditional high culture just as the old-regime kings had – for the glory of France and of his own reign. Like the kings, he used a system of official schools, exhibitions and prizes to foster that culture and also to control it. To enhance France's international image, his administrators displayed France's fine arts, along with its modern machinery, in the 1867 Paris World's Fair. Although his government prized new technology and engineering, it still adhered to the old view of the arts as a hallmark of civilization, and it held to old standards for judging quality. Paintings selected for the official exhibition were traditional in subject and style; some were even reproductions of old art. The jury that chose the paintings did not appreciate such innovators as the controversial Édouard Manet, who set up his own independent exhibition, or the younger painters Claude Monet, Auguste Renoir and Paul Cézanne – all of whom were rejected. Several years later, under the young Third Republic, state officials and salon juries were still unreceptive to the paintings and painters that a hostile critic dubbed 'impressionist' in 1874.

At the time the movement was so christened, the impressionists were holding their first exhibition, mounting it in a former photographic studio in the heart of Paris. It was the first of eight such showings. Subsequent innovators of note held similar independent exhibitions, outside the old state system of prizes and salons. Cut off from the patronage of king and Church, they tried to sell their paintings through dealers, and most of them ended up selling very few. But now they did not have to tie their works to the ideologies of the old patrons: they were free to pursue their individual visions.

The impressionists turned from traditional subjects – history, mythology, religion – and instead set their gaze on the contemporary world, fast changing around them. They captured scenes of modern life, especially the modern city that Paris became under Napoleon III. They painted a renovated city of new parks and avenues, railway stations, commercial entertainments and other places of leisure – from simple cabarets and cafés featuring popular singers (*café-concerts*) to racetracks and the opera. Painted with new brush and colour techniques, their pictures were lighter and apparently more spontaneous than earlier works. The impressionists captured fleeting moments of ordinary life without depicting anecdotes or moralizing. They also found subject matter outside Paris – in scenes of the countryside, riverbank resorts and the seashore, places especially important to Monet, Cézanne and Camille Pissarro. There too the impressionists gave their attention to contemporary life, not idealized pastoral scenes but rather places being transformed by city dwellers and commercial developers.

Most people preferred the conventional old styles, just as the salon juries and state officials did (the latter went so far as to refuse a large donation of impressionist works in 1894). Like the critics writing in newspapers, many middle- and upper-class French people considered themselves connoisseurs, priding themselves on their refined taste, their capacity for distinguishing quality. Paris had long been known as the centre of fine taste, fashion and intellectual life. In the second half of the nineteenth century it enjoyed the reputation of being a world 'capital of art'. With its great museums and many studios, schools, galleries and exhibits, Paris was the home of thousands of artists struggling to create and to win favour with critics and buyers. Paris had more art galleries than any other capital, most of them catering to conservative tastes. Only after several decades at least did the French public come to accept what at first seemed so shocking. Not until the turn of the century did the impressionists receive wide recognition and favour at home. For years the impressionists sold most of their works abroad – to Americans, Russians, Germans and Britons. Subsequent avant-garde painters also found foreigners more receptive than the French.

Illustration 12.1 L'étoile, by Degas (1878). French Impressionist painting flourished during the early decades of the Third Republic (1870s–1900s), helping to restore France's international image as a cultural and artistic leader as the nation rebuilt itself after the Franco-Prussian War. (Photo: AKG London, Erich Lessing.)

In the nineteenth and twentieth centuries, then, the famed capital of France was a place both of entrenched tradition and of fertile experimentation. No other city in France came close to rivalling the capital's cultural ferment and concentration of talent. Since the Middle Ages Paris had been a distinguished centre of learning, with its great university, its many scholars, brilliant writers and book publishers. It was also historically home to a vibrant social life in which wit, quick keen intelligence and eloquent conversation brought prestige. That kind of sociability, which had developed in old-regime court and salons, lived on through the nineteenth century in salons of middle-class patrons and in cafés on the bustling boulevards. Out in the provinces, ambitious and gifted young people dreamed of becoming part of that cultural ferment, and many moved to Paris to realize their dreams, finding there the stimulation of others sharing their interests. They took cheap lodging in neighbourhoods of the poor, found meeting places in cafés and cabarets, and produced their creations, hoping to gain recognition in competition with many others. Many of the artistic innovators of Paris, it must be added, drew on ideas and inspiration from foreign cultures. The impressionists, for example, learned from seeing English paintings by Turner and Constable as well as from viewing Japanese prints.

Paris the cultural capital was also the historic centre of the French Revolution, where a legacy of freedom and a tradition of bold *contestation* lived on. That possibility of freedom extended to artistic creation and artists' ways of living individualistically in community – in that loose community and unconventional lifestyle known as Bohemia (*la Bohème*). The artists of Bohemia revelled in jokes and provocation, shocking the guardians of tradition and the bourgeois who did not like novelty in art. In the 1880s and 1890s the heartland of Paris's Bohemia was Montmartre, a low-rent district full of artists and models, dance halls and music halls, cafés and brothels. A renegade nobleman from Albi, Henri de Toulouse-Lautrec, became the most assiduous and penetrating painter of the pleasure haunts of Montmartre, beautifully capturing both their gaudy exteriors and the underlying ennui. In that district of social diversity and freedom, Bohemian artists, writers and musicians thrived on sociability and shared delight in bold experimentation, working on the margins of art and society – often with path-breaking results.

Early mass culture

The cabarets and music halls of Montmartre were part of a growing urban entertainment industry catering to modest people in addition to the moneyed. All over Paris and throughout France ordinary people frequented cafés that featured the continuous performance of songs. Some of those *café-concerts* evolved into music halls on the English model, offering variety shows of singing, comedy, trained animals, juggling and acrobatics, and magic acts. The Folies-Bergère was one of the earliest and most successful; in the 1890s the Moulin Rouge and the Olympia also flourished. The Folies-Bergère and the Moulin Rouge, where admission was uncommonly expensive, became glittery shrines for provincials and foreign tourists wanting to sample a distinctly Parisian popular culture.

Another new form of entertainment, the 'movies', made its début in Paris in 1895. Invented by the Lumière brothers of Lyons, cinema spread quickly throughout the country as a fairground amusement and an added attraction in music halls before it became a principal entertainment with its own halls. By 1908 France had more than 10 000 movie theatres along with many itinerant projectionists serving the countryside. In cinema as in other arts, this period before the First World War was one of astonishing French creativity and vitality. Early film-maker Georges Méliès, formerly a magician, created the first science-fiction movies and invented many techniques and special effects still in use today. Graphic artist Emile Cohl created the first animated cartoons. French film-makers also pioneered the westerns, selling them even in the big American market. French comedies and the comic Max Linder were worldwide favourites – before Charlie Chaplin. The French cinema industry was the world leader in production and distribution until a couple of years before the First World War.

New sporting events, too, became part of the leisure of the masses around the turn of the century. Masses of spectators followed football and rugby games (imported from England) and bicycle races. The longest and most followed race was the Tour de France, organized by a newspaper publisher for publicity purposes and held annually from 1903 on. A fast-growing sports press stimulated the interest of masses of fans – mostly men – who could not actually attend the events. For most horse-racing fans, for example, the place to be was not the racetrack but a local café where they placed bets and talked over the competition with friends. These new kinds of entertainment – which were added onto such older kinds as theatres, circuses and fairs – became an integral part of the cultural life of the masses around the turn of the century.

To some observers these innovations amounted to a happy democratization of pleasure and culture. To others they represented decadence. New music halls offered bigger and bolder spectacles that offended conservative tastes. Turn-of-the-century revues and early strip-tease sketches featured a semblance of female nudity. Song lyrics in ordinary *cafés-concerts* trafficked in the bawdy and obscene – with frequent jokes about cuckolds, drunks, constipation and diarrhoea. Early movies on fairgrounds often provided sexual titillation along with slapstick comedies and melodramas. This expanding mass culture seemed to moralists and conservatives to threaten standards of decency and civilization. The republic's leaders, while habitually using the rhetoric of democracy, offered no encouragement to the new cultural forms and continued to subsidize the old-élite establishments, the opera and the Comédie-Française.

More importantly, the early Third Republic created new bases of a democratic mass culture by establishing state-run elementary schools for the entire nation. One of their fundamental contributions was to make almost all the population literate for the first time by the turn of the century. In the process, lay schoolteachers also imparted their reverence for literature and their admiration for great writers and artists. The state paid its highest tribute to writers upon their death by giving them huge national funerals and burial in the national temple of geniuses, the Panthéon. Victor Hugo received those honours when he died in 1885 (as Voltaire had in the preceding century), and in the twentieth century Anatole France, Paul Valéry, Colette, and others have followed. In the same period of emergent mass literacy, advances in technology brought production costs of publications down. A growing industry of cheap mass-circulation newspapers, illustrated magazines and books catered to the interests of the new readers. Ordinary people bought books in railway stations, newspaper stands and local grocery stores, as well as in a growing number of bookstores. By the end of the nineteenth century, masses of new readers read works by Victor Hugo, Jules Verne and Emile Zola along with vast quantities of now-forgotten novels – romances, adventure tales and detective stories. Readers also bought increasing quantities of tourist guides, practical household manuals, cookbooks and regional studies. So a new national culture based on print came into existence, serving widely divergent tastes and interests.

Despite commonplace optimistic rhetoric about 'progress' in the *fin-de-siècle* years, high anxiety about social antagonisms and fear of decadence was widespread among the better-off people in France. Progressive republicans and conservative social leaders found a fresh role for the arts in their effort to respond to the nation's problems in the 1890s. They sponsored a new kind of art – an *art nouveau* – as a way of bringing the French people together in the production and aesthetic enjoyment of high-quality craft products. The new-style creations – furniture, jewellery, vases, ornate subway entrances – represented a reconciliation of old French tradition and new materials (such as industrial iron and glass). Old organic and curvilinear feminine forms found a place in the burgeoning machine-age – until the exuberant style fell out of fashion several years after its triumph at the 1900 Paris World's Fair.

Avant-gardes and modernists

Other forms of new art came from foreigners who immigrated to Paris, leaving behind distant parts of Europe and Russia to be a part of the renowned cultural vitality in the 'city of light'. The immigrant artists quickly joined in the Bohemian camaraderie and the excitement of untrammelled creativity centred in Montmartre and Montparnasse. Vincent Van Gogh arrived in Paris from his native Holland in 1886. Pablo Picasso came to Paris from Spain in the early years of the twentieth century. The Romanian Constantin Brancusi settled in Paris in 1904; Amedeo Modigliani and Gino Severini came from Italy in 1906, and Juan Gris from Spain the same year. Marc Chagall arrived from Russia in 1910. The list of other notable immigrants could go on and on.

In the decades around the turn of the century, some of those newcomers along with some young French artists made more radical innovations than the impressionists had. Impatient with traditional art and the past, they wanted to break through to new aesthetic experiences and even to a new society. They yearned for a close natural relationship between art and life – or no boundary at all between the two. In diverse forms of art, they wanted to liberate themselves from academic traditions. Though they did not form a single group or coordinated movement, they have become known as 'modernists'. Poet Stéphane Mallarmé and others tried out free verse and a stream-of-consciousness style. Claude Debussy broke with clear melody in his opera *Pelléas et Mélisande* (1902) (also in his orchestral tone poem *La Mer* of 1905) and substituted a free fluidity for the traditional forms of the classical-romantic symphony. Henri Matisse and other painters whom a critic called 'the fauves' (wild beasts) in 1905 produced canvases filled with passionate patches of bright colour without realist detail. In 1907 Pablo Picasso and Georges Braque produced startlingly unconventional paintings of human figures with faces and bodies flattened into juxtaposed facets, disregarding traditional devices for showing perspective, the natural way of seeing and painting since the Renaissance. In abandoning representational art, those first 'cubist' painters turned away from the historical past and drew inspiration from 'primitive' art and their own imagination. In 1913 the Russian composer Igor Stravinsky and the Ballets Russes filled the Théâtre des Champs-Elysées with dissonant brasses and wild crescendos and pulsing drumbeats with bizarrely dressed ballet dancers acting out a primitive dance for the earth's renewal and the sacrifice of a virgin – in a first performance of the *Rite of Spring*. Outraged critics attacked modernist works as anarchic and revolutionary. Newspapers played up the conflicts between old and new.

Some movements and artists, however, were not so locked in polarizing battle. Some, like the sponsors of art nouveau, sought to reconcile old and new. Many artists worked veins of both high and popular culture. Cubists drew inspiration from music-hall dance routines and variety acts, caricature and broadsheets. Bridging the gulf between high art and the vernacular, they included pieces of newspaper, wallpaper and advertising signs in their paintings and collages. The whimsical composer Erik Satie combined ancient and new, classical and popular forms of music in his pieces. Despite their love of provocation and jokes, most modernists did not want to isolate themselves and their work from the public.

Nonetheless, conservative critics sustained a fierce antipathy to the new, a reaction which in part sprang from political concerns. In the 1880s the nationalist programme of General Georges Boulanger's backers included attacks on Wagner's music and its supporters. But by the turn of the century Wagner's operas with their grand heroic and mythic themes aroused enthusiasm on the political right, over-riding anti-German sentiment. In reaction, Debussy's opera of 1902 found favour on the left and among nationalists who delighted in finding a *French* answer to the German master. In the minds of the avant-gardes as well as in the minds of conservatives, cultural innovation was often linked to revolutionary causes. Such neo-impressionists as Maximilien Luce, Camille Pissarro and Paul Signac (and evidently Georges Seurat, too) embraced anarchism, which gave critics of their art all the more reason for hostility. During the Dreyfus affair, many writers and artists sympathetic to new art (for example, Emile Zola, Anatole France, Marcel Proust) sided with Captain Alfred Dreyfus, while such culturally and politically conservative writers as Maurice Barrès, Charles Maurras and Paul Valéry supported the army and church against the accused. Ever since the Dreyfus affair, historically conscious intellectuals and artists on the left have commonly shared a sense of special responsibility to take courageous moral stands in political life – to be *engagé* in the fight for truth and justice against prejudice and abuse of power.

Embattled culture

The outbreak of the First World War ushered in an austere climate of clamorous nationalism and national emergency that undermined the bold high spirits of the avant-garde. Artists scattered – some to the front, some abroad. Those remaining in civilian life, mostly foreigners like Picasso and Juan Gris, became more cautious and embraced a new classicism, a style and subjects that were figural rather than abstract. The individualistic and cosmopolitan outlook associated with the avant-garde came under fire. Conservatives attacked cubism and other modernist art as the work of foreigners, indeed as German. Strident wartime nationalists pointed up the superiority of French civilization and the barbarism of the Germans. For most of the war, the reigning ethos called for every activity to serve the fatherland and the war-effort. In music-hall revues and movies, patriotic moral tableaux and tales became standard fare – with 'La Marseillaise' as the favourite finale.

Painter Fernand Léger moved away from abstraction and reached out to ordinary people, painting them sympathetically in a more accessible modern, figural style. Hoping to bring the avant-garde and the public closer together, Jean Cocteau created his novel ballet spectacle *Parade* in May 1917. Picasso painted the stage curtain and designed the costumes and cubist sets; Erik Satie composed the music, incorporating dance-hall melodies; and Diagalev's Ballets Russes performed. The audience failed to appreciate the more classically French qualities of the production and instead responded negatively to the many foreigners associated with it, noting particularly Russians now identified with revolutionaries and self-indulgent élitist artists. The performance provoked an uproar (*un scandale*), which was by then a Parisian tradition for important premières.

In November 1918 the French celebrated the end of the war as 'victory', but the long ordeal had left France grievously wounded. In addition to the terrible loss of 1 400 000 men and the staggering economic costs incurred, the nation's contemporary culture suffered. One of the casualties was the nation's film industry, which had already begun losing its world-market supremacy to Hollywood several years before the war. From 1914 to 1918 American movies flooded onto the French market, now undersupplied by domestic producers. In other domains of art as well, foreign artists and their stimulating influences were cut off. Under such circumstances, France was no longer the place of astonishing creativity that it had been in the decades before the war.

Disquiet and shock

In 1920 some radical artists called Dadaists came to Paris from central and eastern Europe as well as from New York and found receptive comrades in the French capital. Rejecting all conventions, they had produced shocking works to signal that the drawn-out war with all its senseless carnage was destroying all meaning and tradition. Marcel Duchamp had offered the world such 'ready-made' art as a urinal signed 'R. Mutt' (1917). In France as earlier abroad, such Dadaists as Duchamp, Francis Picabia and Man Ray (an American expatriate) rejected conventional morality, traditional art and the common nineteenth-century interpretation of history as progress.

After several years, some of those writers and painters of the Dadaist revolt found new hopes for renewal. Going beyond provocative protests and jokes, they set great store on tapping the power of the unconscious and the imagination. They worked to create a new art and new way of living in accord with a vision they called surrealist. Above all they wanted freedom, life and art untrammelled by society, its conventions, aesthetic standards and morality. In 1924 a group of those writers and artists around the writer André Breton proclaimed their hopes and new ideas in the first surrealist manifesto. Following Freud, they took dreams and the unconscious seriously as sources of truth and beauty. They set out to open their creativity up to the play of chance, spontaneity and fantasy. In one of the most famous surrealist movies, *L'Age d'or*, directors Salvador Dali and Luis Buñuel featured shockingly violent and sexual scenes mocking the Church and society. A public screening in Paris on 3 December 1930 drew angry right-wingers of the Ligue des Patriotes, who violently disrupted the show. Unlike the Dadaists, many surrealists had political hopes and commitments, framed by Marxism with new hope raised by the Russian Revolution and the communist effort to create a just society in the young Soviet Union. As politically engaged artists, they protested against war and militarism, nationalism, and after 1933 the Nazi dictatorship and terror. Breton and others had joined the Communist Party in 1927, but they found it difficult to live with the party's rigid ideological line and discipline, especially the rule of Stalin and the aesthetic orthodoxy of social realism. A complete rupture between surrealists and the party took place in 1935.

Paris was still the capital of the art world – with Montparnasse the new centre within the capital – but artistic creation suffered from the impact of the nation's post-war economic difficulties. Art buyers were more wary than ever of avant-garde works. Many of the artists themselves were more subdued. A group of composers called *les Six* – including Francis Poulenc, Darius Milhaud, Arthur Honegger and Georges Auric – grafted popular music and jazz onto classical tradition, producing modernist works that were less provocatively experimental than before the war.

In post-war literature, moral concerns inspired some distinguished creativity – novels by Romain Rolland, who had been a pacifist even during the war, and probing narratives by André Gide, for example. Gide created controversy with his writing about homosexuality (*Si le grain ne meurt*, 1926) and anti-colonialism. At the same time some remarkable innovations emerged without making shocking ruptures in literary tradition. Novelist Marcel Proust won the Prix Goncourt (1919) and fame with the second volume of his seven-part work *À la Recherche du temps perdu*, published over the years 1913–27. His novels told stories of upper-class society in Paris and in a small town nearby, bringing to light a rich inner life of reverie and memory conveyed in an elaborate, flowing style. Roger Martin du Gard carried on the classic narrative tradition with his eight-part novel *Les Thibauts* (published from 1922 to 1940), telling the lives of two families from the beginning of the century to the end of the First World War. Other new riches for French literature came from the pens of the foreign-born who wrote brilliantly in French, among them Samuel Beckett, Julien Green, Eugène Ionesco and Fernando Arrabel.

Although Weimar Germany with its influential Bauhaus took the lead in propagating a modern style in the 1920s, France was not far behind. In 1925 Paris hosted an *Exposition des arts décoratifs et industriels modernes* where visitors saw displays of the modern home, studded with sleek ornaments and furniture in cubist shapes, chromium tubing and bright flat colours. Through the 1920s the Swiss-born architect Le Corbusier published his ideas for a rational modern architecture, and he designed modern furniture for a new world of machines instead of craftsmen.

Other currents of the 1920s were far from rational and cool. In the last year of the war the French picked up jazz (ragtime) from the Americans, and a few years later they imported such sexy new dances as the shimmy and the Charleston. The looser, syncopated rhythms resounded at a time when many women were pushing for greater freedom, symbolically showing their modernity in their short haircuts and shorter skirts as well as the latest dance steps. Victor Margueritte's novel *La Garçonne* (1922) provoked controversy by portraying one such 'boyish' bachelor woman, who led a life of independence and marriage-free love that deeply disturbed upholders of tradition. Several years later, the young African-American Josephine Baker emerged as another exemplar of new boldness and freedom: she created a sensation with her frenetic, erotic dancing in a show at the Théâtre des Champs-Elysées in 1925 and went on to become a star singer and movie actress in France.

Mass culture, comfort and danger

While the better-off people in France dallied with modern fashion and bought sleek furnishings for the rational home, ordinary people embraced a culture of nostalgia for pre-war life. They listened to phonograph records and singers of songs about old-fashioned little Parisians – shopkeepers, flower girls and young apprentices in close-knit neighbourhoods, their loves and heartbreaks.

In the 1930s French masses also listened to such songs on radios in homes and cafés. A small young singer nicknamed Piaf ('sparrow'), who lent her beautiful voice and emotional flair to songs about streetwalkers and sorrowful lovers, won fame in 1937 with a music-hall triumph and subsequent hit recordings. Audiences followed populist stories in new sound movies, too – in René Clair's *Sous les toits de Paris* (1930) and *Quatorze juillet* (1932), for example. In 1929 Eugène Dabit's populist novel about the inhabitants of his parents' cheap hotel – *L'Hôtel du Nord* – had become a best-seller; 9 years later an adaptation of the story became a major movie, directed by Marcel Carné. Some of this turn to an idealized French past of the 'little people' was a reaction against a tide of American films featuring big-city life, luxurious nightspots, and gangsters of Chicago and New York.

In the struggle against competition from Hollywood, French film directors made many movies adapted from classic French novels of the nineteenth century and successful plays as well as popular romances and detective stories. Literature enjoyed a respectability that film-makers wanted to borrow for their art, and French stories offered audiences familiar places, characters, language and accents. Writer Marcel Pagnol, a native of Marseille, brought a number of his plays to the screen; some of them were among the most popular movies of the 1930s – notably the trilogy, *Marius*, *Fanny* and *César*, presenting the story of romantic love, family conflicts and long-delayed resolutions among ordinary people of the port of Marseille.

As the economy went into depression and politics grew more embittered, songs and films offered relief in the form of fresh themes and settings – excursions in the French countryside and life deep in the provinces. Youthful and energetic Charles Trenet soared to stardom in the late 1930s singing his own upbeat poetical lyrics about love and adventure, set to fresh jazzy rhythms. Comedy was also a staple of entertainment in great demand – notably, songs and movies by the clownish but clever Georges Milton and Fernandel and the zany wordsmith and singer called Georgius.

In the 1930s listening to radio at home became a central leisure activity and cultural source for the masses, providing music, news, plays and serials. The number of radios in France grew from 500 000 in 1929 to 1.9 million in 1935 and then to 5.5 million in 1939, each radio serving three or four listeners. The airwaves conveyed some serious plays and classical music but also many popular songs and serial 'soap operas'. Here was one more growing cultural force at work that state authorities tried to control but did not yet fully accept or utilize.

As political passions heated up during the early 1930s, many writers and artists on the left grew more militantly activist in organizations against fascism and war. New revolutionary songs took hold; militant choruses and theatre groups flourished. Those cultural activities proliferated as anti-fascists united in a Popular Front in 1935 and won power in the legislative elections of May 1936. The victorious Popular Front unleashed exuberant energies and hopes through the spring and summer of 1936. Masses of supporters filled the streets regularly, demonstrating, singing, celebrating. Inspired by those extraordinary events, a film-making collective that included director Jean Renoir made a big-cast feature movie, *La Marseillaise* (released in 1937), in an effort to recapture the courageous, patriotic spirit of the ordinary people as revolutionaries in 1789.

The Popular Front government undertook much more in the cultural domain than its predecessors had. It showed more favour towards contemporary art, and it did more to enlarge the cultural life of the masses. It made museums more accessible, opening them in the evenings and allowing group visits. The government of Léon Blum also created a new national folklore museum in Paris, the Musée des Arts et Traditions Populaires, and it allocated unprecedented sums for sports programmes and youth hostels. After the summer of 1936, bitter political strife, persistent economic troubles, and a mounting Nazi threat brought an end to the brief euphoria that had accompanied the triumph of the Popular Front, and the new cultural programmes suffered budget cuts and neglect.

The most innovative commercial feature films reflected that darkening time. From the mid- to late 1930s, leading man Jean Gabin starred in successful movie after movie playing a likeable but hapless working-class man who meets defeat and is killed or commits suicide – from director Julien Duvivier's *La Bandera* (1935) and *La Belle Equipe* (1936) to Marcel Carné's *Quai des Brumes* (1938) and *Le Jour se lève* (1939). That difficult period for France turned out to be an age of classic French cinema – of brilliantly made films suffused with a keen social consciousness about working people, French-style works of quality made to compete with the onrush of captivating Hollywood productions.

The counter-revolution of Vichy

After the German Blitzkrieg of May and June 1940 defeated the French armies, and the Third Republic gave way to a new state headed by Marshal Philippe Pétain, partisans of the new order denounced commercial popular culture and foreign influences for having weakened and corrupted France. Above all they attacked Anglo-Saxon and Jewish influences. They also condemned the works of the modernist artists, whom conservatives had been assailing since the nineteenth century. German and Vichy authorities banned American and English films, and they excluded all cultural figures having Jewish ancestry from public life – from film-making, from the theatre, art exhibits, radio and publishing. Under the banner of a 'national revolution', Pétain's government at Vichy undertook a counter-revolution which included efforts to revive folklore (old local dances, music, costumes) and other non-Parisian traditions. It also encouraged new creativity in the provinces by supporting local theatre companies, writers, musicians and artists – a cultural decentralization continuing similar efforts by the Popular Front. Breaking with the Third Republic's traditional anti-clericalism and state–Church separation, the Vichy government worked closely with the Catholic Church in an effort to give cultural activities for youth a moral and religious tone.

Many of France's literati and artistic élite supported the national revolution. Novelist Louis-Ferdinand Céline contributed ferociously anti-semitic writing. Some writers (for example, Pierre Drieu la Rochelle and Robert Brasillach) advocated for Nazi Germany's project of a new Europe. In Paris, German artists, singers and actors received star treatment. In the Vichy zone, Pétain – as an old patriot and austere patriarch – and Joan of Arc – as a religious patriot courageously devoted to her king – were the objects of orchestrated hero-worship.

The Vichy programme amounted to waging 'cultural war' from the right, but overall it was far from thorough-going for a number of reasons. Vichy controlled only the south during the first 2 years – with the north under direct German occupation. Further, the shapers of Vichy policy were divided. Some of them favoured close collaboration with the Germans in a new Europe, while others sought a national renewal above all. The public, though generally approving of Pétain, the 'hero of Verdun', soon became sceptical of ideological preaching. After the first year, increasing numbers of ordinary French people favoured some form of resistance. French culture of the 'black years' reflected the nation's divisions as well as its confusions and indecision. Some of Vichy's 'revolution' in fact continued work begun in the decades before, even carrying on projects of the now-vilified Popular Front. For example, Vichy organizations and programmes for youth, sports and folklore had their roots in the Popular Front years, though that link went unacknowledged.

German-occupied Paris was still a flourishing cultural centre. Under the depressing and difficult wartime conditions, the demand for entertainment was huge. Theatres, music halls and cabarets flourished. Cinema attendance reached all-time highs. Throughout the country, radio was more important than ever to ordinary people.

Film-makers had to contend with the enormous difficulties of working under conditions of wartime disruptions, restrictions of electricity and shortages of materials. But at least French films now did not have to compete with American productions. Many of France's best-known directors (Jean Renoir and René Clair, for example) and actors fled the country to escape German rule, to seek opportunities in Hollywood, or to avoid persecution for being Jewish, but a talented younger generation of directors quickly emerged – directors such as Robert Bresson, Jacques Becker and Henri-Georges Clouzot. They made some fresh high-quality movies, mostly in a dark vein. Clouzot's *Le Corbeau*, to take one of the most notable, presented a suspenseful story of an anonymous letter writer cruelly frightening and hurting people in an ordinary French town, depicted as rife with scandals and malevolent suspects; this disturbing psychological drama, now considered a masterpiece, provoked protests from partisans of Vichy and the Resistance alike. Even more common and popular were literature-based costume dramas and fairy-tale romances (for example, Marcel Carné's *Les Visiteurs du soir*). Film-makers had to submit to German and French censorship, but most (by far) of the movies they made were not vehicles of ideology.

While Radio-Paris offered much German propaganda, the BBC carried broadcasts of Charles de Gaulle's Free French movement of Resistance, based in London. Listening to those broadcasts, people in France first heard the song 'Le Chant des partisans', which became the most important song of the Resistance. The lyrics urge saboteurs to use their dynamite and other 'comrades' to take up rifles, machine-guns, grenades and knives – and to 'kill quickly'. Underground newspapers, tracts and stories ambiguous enough to get past the censors filled a growing part of the cultural life of the French, as support for Vichy waned and the German conqueror began to suffer setbacks, especially from 1943 on. While Vichy propagandists made a hero out of the peasant and the dutiful traditional mother, Resistance writers did the same for the urban worker and the anti-German fighting woman.

Waves of the new

After the unprecedented destruction of the Second World War and the horrors of the Nazi death camps, French confidence in European civilization and its good conscience was shaken. When the war and the German occupation ended in 1944, France had a greatly weakened economy and a diminished political status in a world now dominated by the non-European superpowers, the United States and the Soviet Union. Post-war New York City emerged as a strong challenger to Paris's tradition of being capital of the art world. Dynamic artists in the new world were producing paintings in a vigorous non-representational style known as abstract expressionism. New French works rooted in Parisian avant-garde traditions did not match the excitement generated by the bold canvases of Jackson Pollock, Mark Rothko and Willem de Kooning in New York. Money for new art, further, was much more abundant in the United States.

Many French post-war plays and novels focused on human alienation and told stories of the solitary individual colliding with the absurd. Irish-born expatriate Samuel Beckett wrote in French an array of works treating those themes – from novels and stage plays (notably, *Waiting for Godot*, 1952) to plays for radio and television. Novelist and philosopher Albert Camus also depicted a world with no inherent meaning or pattern of 'progress', a world in which the best that individuals can do is to revolt against the absurd and celebrate life with all its possibilities of pleasure and creativity. In philosophical writing, plays and novels, Jean-Paul Sartre and Simone de Beauvoir expounded their existentialist ideas, stressing the necessity for individuals to make their own choices and shape their own lives in an unnerving freedom without hope of knowing any essential givens or divine purposes. These literary and philosophical giants did much to renew the sense of Paris as an intellectual centre, but with the bleak mood and economic weakness of post-war France there was no general cultural flowering like that of the turn of the century.

With the left back in power, post-war governments resumed the project of making culture more accessible to all, giving the lead responsibilities to the ministry of education. Numerous organizations on the left – associations for popular education, youth centres and cinema clubs – pursued that democratic ideal, offering cultural programmes aimed at workers, peasants and students alike. The state-supported Théâtre National Populaire (created back in 1920) and seven new national dramatic centres in the provinces brought classic plays at low admission prices to spectators who had not been theatre-goers. In the private sector, inexpensive paperback books – Hachette's *livres de poche* – came onto the market (1953), making more accessible than ever the classics as well as contemporary best-sellers. Still, the traditional genres of popular literature along with entertainment and news provided by radio and the movies remained the cultural mainstays for the vast majority. Overall it was not so much the masses that were changing, but rather the élites and their culture that were opening up more to arts hitherto disdained. Detective fiction, for example, began to receive serious attention from critics and prestigious publishers such as Gallimard after the Second World War. Song lyricists such as singers Charles Trenet, Jacques Brel (Belgian, but popular in France) and Georges Brassens gained critical recognition as gifted poets. Old cultural boundary lines were blurring.

The first new movie released after the liberation buoyed hopes for a strong new national cinema: Marcel Carné's *Les Enfants du paradis* was an instant classic, an extraordinarily well-received big historical drama about Parisian actors, crowds and love in the romantic era. French cinema generally, however, faced grave economic problems and braced anew for stiff competition from Hollywood. The state provided help. It reduced cinema taxes and created a Centre National de la Cinématographie (1946) to ensure that a percentage of film profits went back into French film-making. The state also began giving subsidies to encourage new film projects of quality. French film-makers succeeded in staking out an important part of the market with their art films, but American films continued to win a larger share of the mass audience.

In the late 1950s about 50 new young film-makers produced a 'new wave' (*nouvelle vague*) of small-budget movies with big box-office appeal. The directors worked like individual authors, each with his own style, doing personal artistic work unlike that of Hollywood's studios and commercial producers. Their movies ranged from François Truffaut's almost classic narrative form to Jean-Luc Godard's shock-producing works of social criticism and satire. Among the most notable in the *nouvelle vague* were Claude Chabrol's *Le Beau Serge*, Truffaut's *Les 400 coups*, Alain Resnais's *Hiroshima mon amour* and Godard's *À bout de souffle*. The new cinema appealed to young people particularly and sustained their interest in movies through the 1960s – even as television became a part of ordinary French life.

In that period of the 'new wave', the Gaullist Fifth Republic replaced the critically weakened Fourth Republic and raised new hopes for France's future. Resuming ambitious cultural policies, President de Gaulle created the first ministry of cultural affairs in 1959 and gave the portfolio to novelist and Resistance hero André Malraux. The new ministry pursued the old policy of supporting the classical arts to enhance the prestige of France. Malraux also worked to bring high culture to the masses, continuing the previous republic's ideal of cultural democratization. To that end, his administration built eight *maisons de culture* and envisioned dozens more. Malraux viewed the new cultural centres as 'cathedrals' for a religion of culture with artistic masterpieces offering meaning to life. Over the 10 years that he held office, however, his ambitious plans suffered from small budgets and political conflicts with municipalities, and in the end his ministry produced quite limited results.

Around 1960 a fast-growing post-war generation of youth and young French singers discovered American rock 'n' roll, introducing a huge disjuncture between the culture of young and that of older people in France. Through the 1960s unprecedented numbers of students gained access to quickly overcrowded universities and looked ahead to only dim prospects for career opportunities. With the society on a conspicuous binge of consumption, and the government led by an ageing patriarchal figure from the past, the discontents of youth and cultural critics mounted. The songs of such singers as Jacques Brel and Colette Magny along with films by Godard and others fed the critical spirit. Some influential writers and artists who took part in a broad movement called the Situationists International (founded in 1957) shared the surrealists' hope for a cultural revolution and a transformed everyday life. Guy Debord and other situationists looked hopefully to potentially fruitful *situations* or creative moments when people could glimpse an integrated, playful kind of urban living, free of the oppression of existing political and economic systems. Some of the situationists took an active role in the rebellion of spring 1968.

The events of May 1968 awakened new interest in democratizing culture (again). With the feminist movement beginning to make itself felt, women film directors (Agnès Varda, for example) and women's roles took on new importance. Immigrants and other workers received more attention in movies. Interest in regionalist and ecological causes also grew. The songs of Marti (Occitan) and the music of Alan Stivell (Breton), for example, became popular even outside their own regions. And in the 1970s the ministry of culture began granting funds for the study of 'minority cultures and languages'. In the 1980s state funds also went to the promotion of traditional music, regional linguistic research and new regional art.

The old disdain for popular culture diminished further in the aftermath of 1968, and a more inclusive appreciation gained ground. Comics, for example, acquired a respectable status in France that is rare elsewhere. More adults read them – and more people who are highly educated – than in other countries. The state lent its support: the ministry of culture began giving subsidies to comic-strip artists and began to support the Centre National de la Bande Dessinée et de l'Image, which opened in 1990 in Angoulême, the city where an international comics salon had taken place annually since 1973. In the 1980s under President Mitterrand, the dynamic minister of culture Jack Lang went on to confer new legitimacy and respectability on other arts that were low in the traditional hierarchy – pop and rock music, photography and circus acts – giving them subsidies for new national centres, shows and schools.

Yet overall the changes were not large or dramatic. The left lost much of its hope and fire after the exhilarating near-revolution of 1968, and the avant-gardes had difficulty recapturing the historic hope of radically changing society through the combined action of the arts and political revolution. By the late 1970s the new-wave directors were much less influential and less successful in meeting the American challenge than they had been earlier. Hollywood and commercial concerns were clearly winning, and a sense of crisis once again returned to the French cinema.

Some of the critical spirit of the 1960s went into opening up memories of the Vichy regime and of collaboration with the Nazis – memories that had been repressed or covered over with the legend of Pétain as 'father-protector' and the legend of virtually all the French people as resisters. Marcel Ophuls's path-breaking documentary *Le Chagrin et la pitié* of 1971 presented ordinary people recalling everyday life under Vichy – with little or nothing heroic about it. Even though the documentary began as a government-sponsored television project, it turned out to be too disturbing for those in power, and it was not allowed to be shown on television for many years. Yet it did find a large audience in movie theatres in the early 1970s. Over the next two decades, amid a stream of historical works, a series of commercial feature films also revisited the troubling 'black years' – for example, Louis Malle's *Lacombe Lucien* (1974), about amoral young Frenchmen joining the Milice, and Malle's *Au revoir les enfants* (1987), focusing on one case of the persecution of Jews in France.

In recent decades the state has continued to play a strong role in supporting culture – now with an especially keen interest in the economic, tourist and leisure benefits that the arts bring to France. In 1977 the state-supported Centre National d'Art et de Culture Georges Pompidou opened in Paris, occupying a modernist building of bright-coloured metal and glass, housing a collection of now-classic modernist art along with temporary exhibitions of contemporary works and a large open-stack public library (hitherto non-

Illustration 12.2 La Grande Arche (La Défense), Paris. Grandeur remains an abiding theme in French public architecture, the Grande Arche at La Défense being built in the 1980s – one of several *grands projets* conceived by President Mitterrand as a cultural legacy to stand with such earlier edifices as the Arc de Triomphe, the Sacré Coeur Basilica at Montmartre, the Eiffel Tower, and the Pompidou Centre. (Photo: AKG London, Stefan Drechsel.)

existent in the city). It quickly became one of the most visited sites in the capital. In the 1980s François Mitterrand's socialist government sponsored a series of grand projects for Paris, including a new 'popular' opera at the Place de la Bastille, a new museum of nineteenth-century art in the former train station Orsay, and a huge new national library, the Très Grande Bibliothèque (now called the Bibliothèque Nationale de France). Government subsidies continue to go to the cinema industry as well as to other non-traditional arts noted earlier. In the last decade of the century, however, the state's role has diminished as a result of weaknesses of the French economy, national budget problems and political gains by the right. Private support has become more important.

Vitality of French civilization and its defence: a continuing debate

French alarm about foreign cultural 'invasion', which dates from the inter-war period, reached new highs in the last third of the twentieth century. Fears about the decline of French culture – and the French language as the vital core – are best understood as part of a complex of old fears about a general decline of France and its loss of importance in the world. In recent decades the English language and American popular music and movies have loomed as the biggest threats. France's cinema industry produces more than 100 films a year – more than any other country in Europe – but they do not draw even half the French audiences, while American films have been attracting more than half. Since the early 1980s, American and British rock and popular songs have gained a large presence on the radio and in recordings sales. In November 1981 private radio stations gained the right to operate alongside the state-controlled radio, and they proliferated rapidly (by 1986 there were about 1500 of them). Many of them played American music much of the time. In the 1990s still another new cause of alarm for defenders of the French language and culture emerged: the dominance of English on the internet.

The government has taken some defensive measures, none of them very effective. Under President de Gaulle in 1966 it created the Haut Comité de la Langue Française to find new French words to take the place of invading English terms. Over subsequent decades, several efforts to legislate against English in public life followed. In January 1996 a law went into effect requiring that radio stations play French songs at least 40 per cent of the time. Broadcasters lambasted the new law and argued that there were not enough French songs to fill out the daily programme. The cultural battle continues.

The opening of a Disney theme park near Paris in 1992 touched off new outcries against 'American cultural imperialism'. The number of customers for Europe's first Disney park fell far short of expectations in the early years (one reason: its high admission price), yet generally the French public consumes American cultural products with relish. Even the French government shows its appreciation of the 'invaders' periodically: the ministry of culture has honoured such Hollywood stars as Sharon Stone, Clint Eastwood and Sylvester Stallone, making them knights of the Order of Arts and Letters. American popular culture – music, dance, movies – remains an important part of contemporary French entertainment and exerts strong influence on French cultural producers. African and Arab influences are also important in present-day France, particularly in music. French culture has long borrowed from other cultures, but now the foreign imports are more conspicuous than ever and more than ever a challenge to state policy-makers, as they try to adapt to the more media-connected global conditions of the present era.

At the end of the twentieth century the French state still assumes major responsibility for promoting French culture and provides support in ever-expanding forms. For example, the culture ministry in 1997 began awarding grants to *haute-cuisine* restaurant chefs, recognizing them as artists. The arts in France continue to command a depth of respect rare elsewhere. Film directors, writers and literature in particular enjoy extraordinary prestige. In many countries near and far, French creativity in many forms is highly prized – from contemporary music and modern dance to cartoons. French fashion and taste are still followed with special respect around the world. And like a strong magnet, Paris still attracts talented exiles and expatriates who contribute richly to their new homeland's culture. Yet overall, in the more decentralized contemporary world, the French arts no longer occupy the prestigious primary place that was theirs historically. At home, national popular pride fastens not so much on the arts as on French technological achievements (Concorde; 'very high-speed' trains), French scientists' Nobel prizes and international sporting victories, such as the World Cup soccer triumph in 1998. In the more globalized economy and multi-centred world of our time, those who cherish France's past glories in the arts alternate between an uneasy acceptance of new realities and defiant efforts of resistance.

Further reading

Abel, R. *French Cinema: The First Wave, 1915–1929* (Princeton: Princeton University Press, 1984).
——, *The Ciné Goes to Town: French Cinema, 1896–1914* (Berkeley: University of California Press, 1994).
Barrot, O. and Ory, P. (eds.), *Entre deux guerres: la création française entre 1919 et 1939* (Paris: Éditions François Bourin, 1990).
Brody, E. *Paris: The Musical Kaleidoscope, 1870–1925* (New York: George Braziller, 1987).
Dillaz, S. *La Chanson sous la Troisième République (1870–1940)* (Paris: Tallandier, 1991).
Donnat, O. *Les Français face à la culture: de l'exclusion à l'éclectisme* (Paris: La Découverte, 1994).
——, *Les Pratiques culturelles des Français* (Paris: La Découverte, 1990).
Duval, R. *Histoire de la radio en France* (Paris: Éditions Alain Moreau, 1979).

Ehrlich, E. *Cinema of Paradox: French Film-making Under the German Occupation* (New York: Columbia University Press, 1985).

Forbes, J. and Kelly, M. (eds.), *French Cultural Studies* (New York: Oxford University Press, 1995).

Hayward, S. *French National Cinema* (London: Routledge, 1993).

Herbert, R. L. *Impressionism: Art, Leisure, and Parisian Society* (New Haven: Yale University Press, 1988).

Hewitt, N. and Rigby, B. (eds.), *France and the Mass Media* (London: Macmillan, 1991).

Holt, R. *Sport and Society in Modern France* (Hamden, CT: Archon Books, 1981).

Jeancolas, J.-P. *Quinze ans d'années trente: le cinéma des français, 1929–1944* (Paris: Stock, 1983).

Kedward, R. and Austin, R. (eds.), *Vichy France and the Resistance: Culture and Ideology* (Totowa, NJ: Barnes & Noble, 1985).

Martin, J. W. *The Golden Age of French Cinema, 1929–1939* (Boston: Twayne Publishers, 1983).

Ory, P. *L'Aventure culturelle, 1945–1989* (Paris: Flammarion, 1989).

——, *La Belle Illusion: culture et politique sous le signe du Front populaire, 1935–1938* (Paris: Plon, 1994).

Rearick, C. *Pleasures of the Belle Epoque: Entertainment and Festivity in Turn-of-the-Century France* (New Haven: Yale University Press, 1986).

——, *The French in Love and War: Popular Culture in the Era of the World Wars* (New Haven: Yale University Press, 1997).

Rioux, J.-P. (ed.), *La Vie culturelle sous Vichy* (Brussels: Éditions Complexe, 1990).

Rousso, H. *The Vichy Syndrome: History and Memory in France since 1944* (Cambridge, MA: Harvard University Press, 1991).

Seigel, J. *Bohemian Paris: Culture, Politics, and the Boundaries of Bourgeois Life, 1830–1930* (New York: Viking, 1986).

Shattuck, R. *The Banquet Years: The Origins of the Avant-Garde in France 1885 to World War I*, rev. edn. (New York: Random House, 1968).

Silver, K. *Esprit de Corps: The Art of the Parisian Avant-garde and the First World War, 1914–1925* (Princeton: Princeton University Press, 1989).

Weiss, J. *The Popular Culture of Modern Art: Picasso, Duchamp, and Avant-Gardism* (New Haven: Yale University Press, 1994).

Williams, A. *Republic of Images: A History of French Filmmaking* (Cambridge, MA: Harvard University Press, 1992).

Yonnet, P. *Jeux, modes et masses 1945–1985* (Paris: Gallimard, 1985).

|13|

What about the workers?
The trade unions' 'short century'
SUSAN MILNER

Decidedly, perceptions of the notion of time are strange and fluctuating things. The CGT is only one century old. It is a very short time in the history of societies. [But] this first century, which began and ends with the turn of the century, will have seen everything: industrialization, the development of the service sector, the rise of the big company, a mass labour force including women, and today deindustrialization, downsizing, the erosion of public services and unemployment and social exclusion.[1]

Much of the debate about trade unionism in France concerns its 'exceptional' history, which is linked with the specific economic conditions in which it grew. Unlike many other western European countries, France has always had a numerically weak (and pathologically divided) trade-union movement, and yet its workforce has traditionally been seen as militant or at least potentially militant. The reason is generally held to be the relatively slow development of industrial capitalism in France. A further factor is the heavy hand of the French state, which stifled workers' organization, first by repressive means and later through legislative regulation of workplace relations.

Beginnings

The right to join with other workers in trade unions was not granted until 1884, thanks to a long history of distrust of what were called 'corporations' (craft-based associations dating from medieval times). The pre-capitalist 'corporations' gave time-served skilled workers control over the mode of production, as well as production itself, and entry into the craft. In 1776 a first attempt was made by the state to prepare the way for capitalism by abolishing the *corps de métier*, but Turgot's law was withdrawn in the face of resistance from these bodies, and it was left to the French Revolution to outlaw corporations, with the 1791 Allarde law. Those attempting to organize their fellow-workers to obtain better pay or working conditions could expect a harsh response, as in the case of Denis Monnet, guillotined in 1793 for leading a movement by silk-workers in Lyon. State repression aimed both to promote capitalism, by removing restrictive practices hampering the creation of capitalist relations of production, and to prevent the new dispossessed workers ('proletarians') from joining together to obstruct its smooth functioning.

Napoleon followed this up with the 1803 Le Chapelier law, which outlawed strikes (*coalitions*) and tightened sanctions against workers who stepped out of line: mayors gained new powers and responsibility to put down local unrest, and the *livret ouvrier* or workers' logbook was introduced to enable employers to bar 'trouble-making' workers from their trade. Employers' organizations were now allowed, however. Placement bureaux appeared in Paris in 1804, with the aim of reducing workers' control over hiring, and industrial tribunals (*conseils de prud'hommes*) were introduced in 1806 in order to settle disputes 'in the family' (since they were composed mainly of local employers). Repression tightened under the restored monarchy, and an 1834 law sharpened anti-assembly and anti-association provisions: meetings of five people of more were banned.

Despite illegality, workers' societies survived throughout the nineteenth century. Two forms in particular may be seen as the forerunners of modern French trade unionism: *compagnonnages* (networks of skilled workers, especially in the building trades) and *mutuelles* (mutual-aid societies in case of sickness, accident or unemployment). These were exclusive associations which aimed to protect the status and conditions of their members and mark them off not only from capitalist merchants but also from other workers without their skills. Moreover, deep and antagonistic divisions existed within each trade, between Catholic, Protestant and 'free-thinking' *compagnons*. But the nature of workers' associations changed as production became more industrialized. So too did their activities: whereas craft corporations had boycotted certain 'masters' deemed to have dealt harshly with apprentices and workers, workers now became more likely to strike against employers. Mutual aid lent itself to strike funds. Such associations and activities built solidarity and helped to break down the old divisions between different trades and between different religions within each trade.

The nineteenth century saw the emergence of a fledgling (male) workers' movement which still retained many features and customs of older ways of working. Movements which could draw on the structures of *compagnonnages* and *confréries* (ancient forms of mutual-aid societies), i.e. those involving skilled workers or previously skilled workers, tended to be better organized and had more chance of winning concessions from employers than had those based on newly proletarianized peasants. Such structures depended, of course, on the local economy. In 1851 official figures showed over half of the active population (53 per cent) living from agriculture, with only around 5 per cent in large industry, and 21 per cent in small-scale industry.

By 1881, the proportion of farmers and agricultural workers had dropped below half (48 per cent), and industry's share had risen slightly to 27 per cent. Broadly, three main types of labour market existed: rural populations offering labour according to family needs and labour demand ('proto-workers', working often in terrible conditions and for low pay because employers thought they did not need as much money as urban workers); small-scale urban craft production (*artisanat*) which formed the backbone of the *compagnonnages*; factory workers, essentially deskilled artisans or newly recruited peasant labour. These three co-existed uneasily until the last quarter of the nineteenth century, when the industrialized workforce took over. Thus began the decades – slightly less than a century – of the 'heroic' working class, which were to end in the 1970s.

The Third Republic and the workers' movement

It is difficult to pinpoint the precise moment when workers looked beyond their narrow craft and status divisions and expressed their solidarities in terms of class. For some historians, as well as the development of capitalistic work relations, the experience of revolution – the 1848 Revolution and later the Paris Commune – was crucial in creating working-class consciousness. Some would even locate the origins of class consciousness further back, in disillusionment with the failed Revolution in 1830. In 1848 demands were explicitly made not in the name of the nation or the people but the working class. Of the 80 members of the Commune, 35 were workers (mainly artisans), and craft workers were reported to represent nearly 45 per cent of those arrested in the aftermath. Class consciousness was also inspired by the ideas of early 'utopian' socialists such as Fourier and Saint-Simon's procla-mation of the importance of the industrial working class, and by Proudhon's vision of autonomous workshops.

Class consciousness is above all evident in strike figures. Industrial conflict flared as workers acquired both a growing antagonism towards employers and elementary solidarity between themselves. Around 1880, the number of strikes increased: between 1830 and 1870 between 20 and 30 strikes a year were recorded; by 1881 this had risen to 121. With the legalization of trade unions, the right to form and join labour organizations itself became an issue of conflict between workers and employers. At the same time, the increasing strike rate reflected the accelerating pace of changes in work organization and related issues of job control. The number of strikes rose steadily in the 1890s (annual average of 200), and then again in the early 1900s (annual average of 250–300). After 1904 there were always more than 1000 strikes per year. A significant number of strikes were sudden (not preceded by warnings or bargaining), indicating surges in the rate of industrial change and the turbulence of social relations, as well as the fragility of trade unions' presence in the workplace.

Strikes had been legalized in 1864, but not union organization (so union-sponsored strikes were illegal). The bronze-worker Tolain and his fellow-workers who represented France in the First International were still campaigning for freedom of association at home, as in the 1864 'manifesto of the 60' which demanded the right for labour to organize, and Napoleon III's Empire used the courts to dissolve French sections of the International. But the legalization of labour organization was a logical consequence of the 1864 law, which had let the genie out of the bottle. Successful strikes in the 1860s left numerous trades (an estimated 65 in Paris) with money which they used to build a lasting organization. A further impetus to organization was the influence of the International Working-Men's Association (First International), whose French sections were set up in 1865. The IWMA created a union structure which already by the 1870s was beginning to develop craft federations, and a central coordinating body. The Empire and later post-Commune crackdown had the effect of diverting these organizations from political action but did not break the structures. By 1876 the movement had almost returned to its pre-1870 strength, with 86 local unions (*syndicats*) and 14 other trade societies representing over 20000 workers in Paris and perhaps 80 000 others in the provinces.

The legalization of trade unions (along with the later amnesty of Communards) in 1884 formed part of the new Republic's break with the past. It also marked the tentative beginning of a new approach to labour relations on the state's part. Suppression of unrest did not disappear, however; on the contrary, it was legitimized by the state's attempt to regulate union activity and bring it into the public sphere. But the 1884 act did create a space for autonomous working-class action. In 1892 came France's first legal procedures for collective bargaining, mediated by the local justice-of-the-peace. However, employers proved reluctant to bargain, and very rarely instigated the justice of the peace procedures. Employer refusal to recognize unions and enter into negotiations had two consequences: first, trade unions looked increasingly to the state to force concessions, and tended to organize street demonstrations rather than workplace actions; second, contrary to the spirit of the 1884 and 1892 laws, frustration with employer intransigence led to a hardening of positions and often to violent conflict. This attitude on the part of employers has been a specific feature of French labour relations and shaped their development throughout most of the twentieth century.

The labour movement thus emerged in France as a meeting-point between skilled male workers with a history of independent organization and a growing but still highly internally differentiated mass of industrial workers. If opposition to specific forms of the capital-labour relationship united these workers, their relationship with politics and the republican state was more ambiguous. The legacy of revolution and the experience of monarchist repression, together with the resonance of French variants of socialism, created a link between labour activism and the Republic. The discourse of republicanism and democracy was used to promote the idea of social and economic democratization, to match the progress made in the political sphere (universal male suffrage since 1848). Yet the state's failure to respond led many to reject the 'Bourgeois Republic' in favour of more radical solutions.

Under monarchy and Empire, the embryonic labour movement had been obliged to limit its activities to self-help. An increasingly radicalized generation of labour leaders emerged, many of them autodidacts who frequented 'free-thinking' reading circles and were influenced by the ideas of Proudhon and the activism of the Communard Édouard Vaillant and other disciples of the insurrectionist Auguste Blanqui, or Jean Allemane's Revolutionary Socialist Workers' Party. A common strand of all these was a distrust of bourgeois parliamentary politics and respect for autonomous workers' action. Allemane's followers put their energy into local activism, and together with early municipal socialism in some cities this led to the creation of local labour centres (*bourses du travail*) which provided unions with offices and meeting-rooms, as well as other facilities for workers such as libraries and labour exchanges. First appearing in Paris (1887), then Nîmes, Marseille and Saint-Étienne, and rapidly spreading to cover most major towns (51 by 1898, and 157 in 1908), the *bourses du travail* came to form a decentralized union structure and an important power base within the labour movement after the creation of a federation of *bourses du travail* in 1892.

Meanwhile, three of the main socialist parties had the epithet 'workers' in their title and sought to recruit among trade unions, although one strand of socialism in particular actively sought to organize unions within the party: the French Workers' Party, led by Jules Guesde (the closest thing France had to a Marxist leader at that time, although his links with Marx were tenuous). The first national federation of trade unions, convened in 1886, fell into Guesdist hands but factionalism ensured an early death. When the first confederation of unions was set up in 1895 (the Confédération Générale du Travail, or CGT, which still exists today), it represented the coming-together of union leaders with diverse political affiliations, working-class men who were primarily committed to trade-union rather than political activity. Their aim was both to build solidarity through practical actions and to increase the impact of the working class on French society, rather than to lobby for reform (as in Britain) or to create a mass political movement (as in Germany).

The rivalry between Guesdists and other currents of French socialism culminated in the organization of two separate international congresses in 1889. The Second International, created as a result of these contacts, actively sought to unite French socialism and bring trade unions under its wing (this being, of course, the German pattern of organization embodied in the mighty Social-Democratic Party) and encouraged negotiations within a coordination committee. But this only strengthened the determination of the core of labour leaders to keep the unions free of party-political influence. In the

1900s, the CGT had a relatively cohesive leadership with important power bases in building and metal working, a guiding principle – workers' autonomy – and a doctrine: revolutionary syndicalism, a heady mixture of inflammatory rhetoric and practical organization-building. Its merger with the federation of *bourses du travail* in 1902 strengthened its structure and its autonomy. Nevertheless, its membership base was weak (barely half a million members) and the revolutionary syndicalist leadership, kept in place only by favourable voting rules, was challenged from within by reformist and socialist unions. In 1906 the leadership staved off an attempt to bring the CGT into closer relations with reformist socialists by securing congress support for a declaration of independence from employers and the state: the Amiens Charter, a major reference point for the French unions which is still invoked today. The Amiens Charter defined the double task of trade unionism as being, on the one hand, to coordinate workers' efforts to improve their daily lot through increased wages and better working conditions, and on the other, to prepare the way for 'total emancipation, which can only come about through capitalist expropriation', by means of the general strike. According to the CGT, 'the trade union, now an organization of resistance, will in future be an organization of production and redistribution' and the basis for rebuilding society.[2] There was little room for political parties or political action in this vision of the future.

Victor Griffuelhes, CGT general secretary at the time and one of the authors of the Amiens Charter, embodied the contradictions of revolutionary syndicalism: a former shoemaker, he represented craft traditions but also embraced modernity and, together with the metal workers' leader Auguste Merrheim, criticized French industrialists as 'backward'. Above all a strike leader, he saw strikes as the means to raise workers' consciousness and empower them in the face of aggressive bosses and a hostile state, as well as to strengthen organization, as he explained in 1908:

It won't be long before all trade unionists recognize that the real revolutionary action is that which, practised every day, increases the revolutionary value of the proletariat. Exercised by a working class which has grown stronger because of its struggles, thanks to powerful and active trade unions, the strike can achieve more than the content of any library; it educates, it hardens, it trains and it creates.[3]

The state's response to the syndicalists' maximalist logic (especially under the 1906–9 Clemenceau government) was to send the army in, often with tragic consequences, as in 1906 when troops killed two strikers in their strike headquarters in Draveil, and four demonstrators at the subsequent protest march in Villeneuve-Saint-Georges. In these conditions, it is not surprising that the unions sought to make virtue out of necessity by proclaiming autonomy, but in reality their position was more sophisticated and unity of action with the major socialist parties, with whom they shared many members, was commonplace. However, the CGT's elevation of the strike weapon into a mobilizing myth was to prove its undoing, as it found itself increasingly caught between an insurrectionist wing out of touch with workers' day-to-day fears and a reformist socialist wing only too ready to leap on the former's excesses. Revolutionary syndicalism may also be seen as the victim of its own rhetoric in the sense that it hides the real, painstaking work of union-building and consolidation which had taken place within the space of a generation. The new structures worked out in 1906–9 reflected the transition from craft to industrial unions, and the tensions inherent in this shift. But the belated legal recognition of unions gave them little chance to adapt to rapid economic and technological change; in Great Britain, in contrast, deeper-rooted craft unions had been able to organize within industry. After 1909 the movement was in the doldrums. When war in 1914 called the CGT's bluff and forced it to choose between insurrection and cohabitation, its then general secretary, Léon Jouhaux, joined the 'sacred union' and even, for a while, the government, leading to recriminations which prepared the way for the later split.

Impact of the First World War

In the early decades of the twentieth century, changes in France's economic structure and the evolving role of the state posed new dilemmas for the fledgling labour movement, which the war accentuated. The imperative of organizing munitions production obliged the state to intervene directly in industrial relations for the first time. Already, the 1890s had seen the first hesitant steps towards regulation of workplace relations, notably the 1893 law on health and safety, giving new powers to labour inspectors. The first socialist minister Alexandre Millerand (with the help of his colleague Jean Jaurès) had attempted to encourage collective bargaining, but his planned law (1900) introducing workplace delegates in large companies failed, and neither the centrepiece of his bargaining structure – a tripartite national labour council – nor plans for compulsory arbitration schemes ever got off the ground, thanks to employer resistance. Progress thereafter was slow, although 1910 saw the adoption of the first pensions law and the labour code (eroding employers' absolute power to hire and fire). Some of the pre-war ideological uncertainty of the CGT must be attributed to this very limited social reform, which encouraged workers' tendency to look to the state in the face of employer resistance but left them unsatisfied. Despite its initial antipathy to Millerandism, the CGT was in favour of collective bargaining and labour legislation, for example on working hours.

The new contractual style of industrial relations ushered in during wartime amounted to little more than the creation of consultative committees in armaments production (in 1916) and a 'policy of confidence' associated with Interior Minister Louis Malvy (until 1917) which was criticized by the right as too conciliatory to labour's wage demands. Nevertheless, it was enough to set CGT leaders like Léon Jouhaux and Auguste Merrheim dreaming of social partnership, and they saw a chance to integrate labour in post-war economic planning.

Meanwhile, the war accentuated trends towards economic concentration. An industrial latecomer, France became the most dynamic of all industrial economies in the first three decades of the twentieth century, especially 1913–29. In the metal-working industry, France gained second or third place in world production, thanks largely to its steel and automobile pioneers. The new industries were based in large factory units and used new American methods of production, with their resultant deskilling and proletarianization. Whereas textiles had accounted for over half of all industrial work in the nineteenth century, by 1930 textiles and metal-working each accounted for around a quarter of the industrial workforce. The proportion of service workers, especially in the burgeoning civil service, rose too. New urban centres developed around key industries. Simultaneously, the social and spatial distance between rich and poor increased in large cities as the 'dangerous' and infirm populations were removed to the periphery. Class relations hardened.

Two new types of worker were emerging. The 'heroic' figure of the working class was no longer the craftsman but the semi-skilled metalworker employed in large plants such as the emblematic Boulogne-Billancourt factory built by Renault in 1899. Correspondingly, the interwar period saw the beginnings of a new form of union activity (developed particularly in the period after the Second World War) based on large firms: what one scholar has called twentieth-century trade unionism *à la française*. Such local unions developed a powerful corporate culture and militant solidarities, akin to other traditionally solidaristic professions such as miners or railway drivers. The big industrial-union federations strengthened. Mechanization and Taylorization undermined traditional worker autonomy and led to a new division of labour: Renault brought in time management in 1913. Low-skilled machine operators (later to be known as OS or *ouvriers spécialisés*) represented a third of Renault's workforce in 1913, and well over half in 1925. Many of them were immigrants. If mechanization provided the first answer to France's labour shortage (chronically exacerbated by wartime losses), organized immigration was the second. In the 1920s over a million foreign workers (plus another million family members) arrived in France. By 1930 immigrants represented around 15 per cent of the workforce, but in mining and heavy industry their numbers reached 40 per cent. In many large factories (especially automobile plants) they outnumbered French nationals by the 1930s.

The second type of worker to become increasingly important was the white-collar worker, especially in the civil service. The burgeoning tertiary sector employed a relatively high proportion of women, but since the new jobs barely compensated for job losses in textiles, the female participation rate actually fell during this period. Tertiarization of employment also had a major and lasting effect on trade unions. Postal workers', civil servants' and teachers' unions all joined the CGT in the period 1918–20. By 1936 the public sector was predominant in French trade unionism. If the industrial workforce became increasingly radical, the service-sector unions' proximity to the state made them more favourable to reformist solutions such as state planning of the economy.

The new recruits joined the ranks of an already swelling labour movement: by 1920 the CGT had well over a million members and became a real force to be reckoned with. Not only had work intensification and wage pressure radicalized the workforce during the war, leading to mass unrest in 1916–17, but the end of the war provided an opportunity to put pressure on the state to fulfil workers' demands, channelled through the unions. However, the central dilemma about unions' relationship with the state was only sharpened by the new post-war conditions. At the first post-war national congress in 1918, the CGT adopted the reformist – and productivist – 'minimum programme' calling for state management of industry and transport, and Jouhaux announced that the labour movement must substitute a 'policy of presence' for its habitual 'policy of the clenched fist'. In 1919 workers obtained the eight-hour day for which the CGT had campaigned so vigorously, and the right to elect works' delegates. A powerful minority in the industrial federations, buoyed by the recent Bolshevik Revolution in Russia, strengthened its attacks on the reformist leadership. In 1921 the CGT expelled the dissidents, who set up a rival confederation, the Confédération Générale du Travail Unitaire (CGTU). The workerist CGTU reached out to the new proletarians, especially in metal working. Under the influence of the Bolshevik Third International, the CGTU grew close to the Parti Communiste Français (PCF), formed after a split with the socialists in 1920. Although membership fell immediately after the split, communism provided an ideological cement (and, perhaps more importantly, a convivial solidarity) and efficient organizational structures based on factory 'cells', which allowed the CGTU to build important power bases among disaffected workers. Labour militancy broke out in important strike movements, as in metal working in 1919 and the railways in 1920.

Meanwhile, the CGT's policy of presence brought its leaders closer to the organs of the state. But further legislation giving workers rights did not appear. In the workplace, collective bargaining, which the 1919 law had attempted to stimulate, failed to develop because of entrenched employer resistance. Membership slumped: the CGT lost half its members following the split, and struggled to recover them during the economic depression of the 1920s. It took left-leaning government to deliver the social and economic benefits which the unions could not themselves achieve by either revolution or reform. In 1925 the centre-left Cartel des Gauches government instituted the National Economic Council for which the CGT had so long pressed. The creation of a tripartite forum represented a symbolic victory for the CGT rather than a practical achievement, although it foreshadowed the much more developed state corporatism of the post-1945 period. But it was the Popular Front government which brought about a sea-change in labour relations.

Left unity was prepared by Stalin's abandonment of the Leninist 'class traitors' policy of confrontation with non-communist groupings in favour of class alliance against fascism. In France following the Cartel des Gauches victory in 1932, the anti-fascist campaign not only brought socialists and communists together (left unity was proclaimed in 1934) but allied them in defence of the Republic. On 24 February 1934 the CGT and CGTU launched a general strike against far-right putschists: 'the day when workers' action saved the Republic', according to the CGT's own recollection of events and the beginnings of a new phase in the union movement's history. From now on, the CGT (and later the other union confederations) would define themselves as defenders of democracy, allowing them to claim a wider social role beyond strict representation of their members. In March 1936 the CGT was reunified. The threat of fascism, together with new-found unity and a sense that political victory was in the air, brought workers flooding into the unions. Already by 1935 the CGT had seen its membership rise to 2.5 million, signalling the end of the organizational difficulties which had until then marked the Depression years. Following reunification, membership soared to 5.5 million.

With the Popular Front victory at the polls in May 1936, mass euphoria erupted in factories and workshops across the country, as strikes and occupations spread in the expectation of radical social reform. Although most of the workers involved were not union members, the strikes marked the birth of mass unionism in France. One month later the unions took their place at the negotiating table for the first time. The leading employers' organization, the Confédération Générale de la Production Française, participated in the talks and signed the resultant agreement out of fear. As well as an average 12 per cent rise in wages, the 'Matignon' agreement (backed up by a series of laws) granted workers a 40-hour limit to the working week and annual paid holidays, and reformed the 1919 law on bargaining by introducing elected works delegates to represent workers. For CGT leader Léon Jouhaux the agreement marked 'the beginning of a new era, an era of direct relations between the two great economic forces of the country'.[4] The agreement did not immediately stop the strike movement, but it ensured CGT support for a return to work, and gradually the movement was brought under control. Faced with worker unrest, the government also embarked on a radical new approach to industrial conflict, with the introduction of compulsory arbitration which recalled Millerand's abortive attempts at the turn of the century. This time the CGT was in favour of such a move, because with a favourable government in power the union leaders felt it would give them greater power over employers. Compulsory arbitration was counter balanced with recognition of the right to strike, brought in under the government of Camille Chautemps in 1937.

The Popular Front government was short-lived; its economic impact had been minimal, and the limits of social reform soon became apparent. By 1938 the most important gain (40-hour law) had been effectively dismantled, and the mass strike organized in protest at this measure ended in failure. Trade-union membership began to fall once again. Employers recovered from their panic and exacted their revenge; most resisted the implementation of the bargaining laws in the workplace. Organizationally, they regrouped their forces and sought to lobby the state more effectively. Yet enough remained of the Matignon agreement (paid holidays, the principle of working-time reduction, the beginnings of an institutional structure and practice of bargaining) for it to remain a reference for future action. And the climate had changed in the 1930s, to allow ideas of economic planning into the mainstream. The nationalization of the railways (by the Chautemps government in 1937) was not overturned: along with the 1936 nationalization of armaments production, it paved the way for other economic policies advocated by the unions, and which gave them a powerful membership base.

The union movement did not face the oncoming war years completely united. Antagonism between communists and non-communists resurfaced during the Nazi–Soviet pact, and although ideological differences were put aside during the war and Resistance this key division was to remain a fundamental fault-line in French unionism. The interwar years also saw the development of a further fault-line: the division between Christian and non-Christian unionism. Catholic trade unionism emerged in the late nineteenth century (and particularly after the papal encyclical *Rerum Novarum* in 1891), sometimes directly sponsored by Catholic employers. It was especially strong in the industrial regions of the north and the Lyonnais. In 1919 a Catholic confederation, the Confédération Française des Travailleurs Chrétiens, was set up. Catholic trade unionism preached harmony between workers and employers, although it also looked to the state for social reform, especially where this could be seen as encouraging family life (such as working-hours limitation). Originally recruiting among white-collar workers and traditionally reformist communities like miners, by the 1930s the CFTC was making inroads into construction and heavy industry and thus beginning to compete more directly with the CGT/CGTU. Its numbers remained small, but like its non-confessional counterparts the CFTC benefited from the membership boom of the mid-1930s, so that by 1937 it had perhaps half a million workers enrolled. The roots of fragmentation in the French labour movement run deep.

From war and Vichy to Liberation and the post-war settlement

Once again, the war-effort required trade unions to set aside their demands, and once again the CGT complied, having expelled the communists in

September 1939. As in 1914–18, wartime brought about an intensification of work, a drastic drop in the standard of living and a marked deterioration of working conditions. But there were two major differences: after the armistice with Germany, the war-effort was effectively enlisted on the side of Nazism (including forced labour and even deportation of workers to Germany after September 1942), and the labour policy of the Vichy government could not tolerate autonomous unions. In November 1940 a Vichy decree dissolved the CGT and CFTC, as well as the employers' organization, the CGPF; strikes were outlawed. Only local labour unions which fitted into the Vichy corporatist model (essentially, channels of a state policy based on collaboration between workers and employers) could survive. Ideologically, Vichy was revenge for the Popular Front: nation against class.

As a result of state repression, an important part of the trade-union movement was driven underground and in some cases into active Resistance. Immediately following the dissolution of the union confederations, three CFTC and nine CGT leaders courageously put their names to the 'manifesto of the 12', in which they reaffirmed the need for collective class action and the principle of labour autonomy. Local studies suggest that workers, especially trade unionists, formed a disproportionately large part of the

Illustration 13.1 French strikers in 1936. The wave of factory occupations by workers followed the May election to government of the left-centre Popular Front. Often spontaneous, the strikes were quickly taken over by the Communist Party whose clenched fist salute, newspaper and flag – alongside the French tricolour – are much in evidence here. (Photo: AKG London.)

Resistance movement. The main rallying point for these workers was the Communist Party, and in some cases communist and Catholic unionists resisted side by side, whilst in others Catholic unionists organized separately.

On the other hand, Vichy continued the rationalization of the French economy which had already begun earlier in the century, and injected it with a social paternalism which proved tempting to some labour leaders, most notoriously René Belin, who became minister of labour. Belin's labour charter of October 1941 introduced compulsory 'social committees' in large firms, intended to encourage harmony between management and employees. At first distrusted by employers, social committees were accepted in a majority of firms by the end of the war. Similarly, the Popular Front's elected works' delegates disappeared, but were replaced by representatives designated by approved trade unions. The role and function of the committees and representatives varied enormously, depending on employers' and unions' attitudes. State paternalism also included the introduction of a minimum wage and health benefits for workers. Other Vichy measures established immigration quotas (formalizing the policy pursued since the early 1930s, which had mitigated the effects of the Depression on the French workforce) and financial incentives for women to stay at home. The moral, political and social ambiguities of such institutions were characteristic of French society during this period.

For the trade-union movement, the dilemmas posed by its relationship with the state were resolved in ideological terms by the Liberation, and especially for communist unionists in the CGT. The CGT's early dissolution and its association with the 'manifesto of the 12' and minor and major acts of Resistance gave it huge popular and political legitimacy, which its Catholic counterpart also shared to a lesser extent: the Liberation saw the peak of union membership in France, with at least 5 million flocking to the CGT and perhaps a million joining the CFTC. The wartime experience, coupled with a workerist organization based on industrial plants, brought the CGT closer to a PCF also legitimated by Resistance as the former *unitaires* of the CGTU gradually marginalized the reformist Léon Jouhaux and his allies. Jouhaux himself, imprisoned in an internment camp for half of the war years, grew isolated from the union movement. The end of war saw a new generation of activists, many close to the PCF, take over the leadership of the united CGT: distinguished Resistance figures like Louis Saillant and Alain Le Léap, and foremost among the communists Benoît Frachon (formerly general secretary of the CGTU from 1933 to 1936, but who was 14 years younger than Jouhaux and who also enjoyed the post-war prestige of his Resistance role) and his allies, such as Julien Racamond and Henri Raynaud.

Post-war politics and the peacetime settlement brought the PCF–CGT alliance closer to political power, rather than confining it to the revolutionary margins. Employers and politicians who had embraced the subordination of labour now fell into complete discredit, none more so than the collaborator Louis Renault, whose company was nationalized. From now until the 1980s, Renault would be a pioneer company in another sense: a laboratory for state-sponsored modern industrial relations, although the results did not always live up to expectations. Trade unions' commitment to the republican state found its reward in the preamble to the 1946 constitution, which recognized five fundamental rights of workers: equal treatment for women; the right to employment, regardless of background or beliefs; freedom to belong to the trade union of one's choice; the right to strike; and the right to take part in determining working conditions and even the management of business, through works delegates. These constitutional rights are still valid today, although the 1958 constitution relegated them to an annexe. They gave trade unions an inalienable place in the republic, regardless of their economic position: thus, even during the period of membership crisis in the 1980s and 1990s, opinion polls showed that a majority of French people believed trade unions to be indispensable to the functioning of a democratic system.

In other respects, the post-war settlement resembled elements of Vichy's corporatism. In 1945 elected works committees (*comités d'entreprise*) became obligatory in all companies with over 50 employees, in order to encourage collaboration between workers and management (it was not until 1982 that this reference to collaboration was removed) and to promote social activities. The significant difference with Vichy was that now independent trade unions were allowed to present candidates, and indeed had exclusive ownership of the electoral lists in the first round (with non-union candidates being allowed to stand in a second round). As with the election of workers' delegates, works committees legitimated trade unions' presence in the workplace at a time when employers were still not obliged to recognize unions for bargaining purposes (this came in 1969). Moreover, workplace representation granted vital benefits to trade unions otherwise dependent on membership dues. In the absence of check-off arrangements (by which employers collect union dues directly, thus making payment easier and more regular), workplace representation has constituted an important employer subsidy to unions in the post-war period.

Even more important for the future of the union movement was the institution of the social-security system. Unlike in several north European countries, benefits were not tied to union membership, but to occupation and status. But they reinforced the unions' role in two ways. First, the administration of social security was set up on a tripartite basis, with employers' organizations and trade unions directly managing the funds established by employer and employee contributions, together with the state which oversaw and underwrote the whole system. In addition, a series of joint employer–union committees was later created to manage other funds financed by employment-based contributions (such as unemployment benefits and vocational training funds). Participation in the management of state-funded and insurance-funded schemes altered the basis of union activity, at national level at least, and gave unions an important alternative source of funding. According to some scholars, this new activity caused the union leaderships to become bureaucratic and turn away from less easily controlled grass-roots activity. Second, the mushrooming civil service provided a major source of employment for French workers (male and, increasingly, female) and a recruiting ground for trade unions. Civil servants' special status, acquired in 1946 thanks to the communist leader Maurice Thorez (minister of state in charge of administrative reform, then deputy prime minister), gave them job security and promotion through seniority. As we saw earlier, the effect of trade unionism in the public sector was to focus attention on state policies and tie unions to a discourse of public service and state provision which also had the effect of widening their potential public appeal.

Similarly, nationalization of mines, the Banque de France and four deposit banks, the national airline and the major utilities went a long way towards satisfying union demands, as well as giving them new power bases. In terms of economic policy, nationalization also signalled a move towards a more interventionist state which chimed not only with the unions' desire for a greater economic role but also their critique of a backward-looking *patronat* more interested in social control than innovation. Alongside employers and other social groups, trade unions acquired a seat on the planning commissions set up after 1946. The attraction of these new roles quickly palled as unions found their influence limited, and certainly subordinated to that of employers. In the longer term, unions' economic role was much less important than their part in the administration of social affairs, although here too they could not alter the direction of policy. But, together with the presence of communists and socialists in the first post-war governments, the new structures helped to enrol unions in the productivist effort.

In the immediate post-war period, unions' confidence was at its highest. Workers had become indispensable for the reconstruction of the economy, and the working class grew steadily in absolute terms and as a proportion of French society: from just over 6 million in 1945 to nearly 7 million in 1960. The economy started to grow at an astonishing rate, with industrial output increasing fivefold between 1945 and 1960, and France's 'economic miracle' (the '30 glorious years' from 1945) owed much to human capital: the skills and productivity of its workforce. But this effort did not come without sacrifice. Wages rose, ushering in the 'consumer society' of the 1960s, but higher productivity meant increased intensity of work, sometimes to the detriment of working conditions.

Industrial concentration continued: in 1931 a quarter of the workforce was employed in units of over 500 employees, and by 1962 the proportion had risen to 37 per cent. The CGT's workerist discourse was appropriate for a movement based in areas of high industrial density and ports. Mass production provided communist activism, which had taken root in the union movement in the 1930s, with a major stronghold. The workforce was still relatively homogeneous, and the wartime experience, far from disrupting the pre-war communist stranglehold over CGT organization, strengthened and legitimized it.

The price for the communists' ideological and organizational capture of the CGT was a hardening of internal opposition, particularly once the climate of Cold War set in at the end of the 1940s. On the heels of a mass strike which started at Renault in April 1947 and led to the dismissal of communist ministers from government (even though the CGT had originally tried to stop the strike), an anti-communist minority left the Confederation to set up the 'CGT-Force Ouvrière' (CGT-FO, or simply FO). FO took with it a membership of less than half a million, around the same number as the CFTC. The creation of separate, professionally based confederations for supervisory staff (Confédération Générale des Cadres or CGC) in 1946 and for teachers (Fédération de l'Éducation Nationale or FEN) in 1948 also changed the shape of the union movement, although it had less impact on the CGT than the setting-up of FO because numbers were small (200000 for FEN, 100000 for the CGC), many teachers' unions retained dual membership of FEN and the CGT, and the CGT retained its own federation of supervisory staff. Taken together, the splits weakened the CGT, whose membership was by 1950 down to 1.5 million, a far cry from its peak in 1946. Thereafter, however, membership continued to grow slowly until the 1970s.

1960s and 1970s: the trade unions' heyday, or the swan-song of collective action?

Industrial conflict had changed during the post-war period. The violence of earlier phases, on the part of the state as well as strikers, reappeared in the early strikes immediately after the war. But after 1950 strikes became more orderly and controlled, and although they usually broke out spontaneously they were often taken over by the CGT and channelled into a particular policy direction. Strike figures show an overall decrease from 1949 to 1962, but the pattern is uneven because of the importance of large strikes, mainly in the public sector or in large factory units. Such strikes could last a long time because they often involved a show-down with government, which now controlled a significant part of heavy industry and became the dominant employer in several regions. Thus, the summer of 1953 saw a wave of civil- and public-service militancy (especially railways and electricity) which drove the annual number of days lost through strikes up from 1.75 million in 1952 to 9.75 million in the following year.

Public-sector strikes, a long-established feature of French industrial relations despite being illegal until 1946, changed too: these were increasingly associated with trade unions, and as public-sector strikes involved less risk than in the private sector because of job security, they became central to the confederations' political demands, especially on social policy. In the civil service and public transport and energy, 24-hour strikes became a central feature of unrest. In the civil service and the public sector (except energy and railways), organizational pluralism presented a challenge to CGT dominance. However, common opposition to government proposals led to a convergence – if not real unity – of action, particularly during the 1960s.

The structure of the trade-union movement was changing. Important sections of the CFTC leadership had been moving towards a progressive view of social action based on grass-roots democracy, more in tune with the 'alternative' movements emerging in the 1960s than the teachings of the Catholic Church. In 1964 the confederation decided to rename itself Confédération Française Démocratique du Travail, dropping the reference to Christianity in its title as well as its statutes. A minority of more traditional activists left and reclaimed the name of CFTC for themselves. The new CFDT soon aligned itself with the alternative (non-communist) left and reached out to the marginal workers often neglected by CGT discourse: unskilled, women and immigrant workers, as well as the technical staff said by some scholars to constitute the 'new working class'. Both the CGT and the CFDT opposed Gaullist plans for a reduction in coal production and social-welfare cuts and called for wage indexation, opening the way for joint action. An agreement on basic demands was concluded in 1966 and joint protest actions took place in 1967. But unity of action remained too fragile and uncertain to constitute a real threat to government.

In the private sector, the workplace seemed relatively peaceful in the 1950s and even into the 1960s. On the one hand, the union confederations found it easier to organize in a handful of huge companies than in France's myriad small- and medium-sized firms, and to focus strategy on the state rather than the workplace. On the other, it proved relatively easy to trade wage rises for social peace during a period of prosperity. Whether trade unions took part in this process through bargaining or were excluded, the result was the same. For some observers, workers had been lulled into quiescence by the promises, if not the reality, of consumer society.

Signs of growing discontent increased after 1962, however. Miners at Decazeville stayed on strike for three months in the winter of 1961–2 in protest at the planned closure of the pit. In 1963 a miners' strike, initially planned for 48 hours, prompted the Gaullist government to call up the striking miners. The conscription order, signed by President de Gaulle, backfired badly: the miners stayed out for over a month, whilst the strike spread to other public services (railways and gas). Many would later recall this event as a harbinger of the confrontations to come. In 1966 a bitter strike broke out at the Peugeot works at Sochaux, and in 1967 shipbuilding at Saint-Nazaire was brought to a standstill. In hindsight, what appeared to be social peace was latent hostility waiting to surface.

From the middle of May until the end of June 1968, France saw the biggest strike movement of its history. The numbers of strikers and days lost through strikes were so great as to escape official count (the country was in any case in political and administrative turmoil), but estimates range between 6 and 10 million strikers: at least half the workforce was on strike at some time, and the strike wave cost around 2.4 per cent of national output. In many cases, strikers occupied company premises and some even 'sequestered' (locked in) the owner or manager. The big confederations, especially the CGT, swung in behind the movement and sought to channel it, but they could not control it. Government's reflex action was to convene a 'summit' (the Grenelle talks) bringing together unions and employers. However, the concessions won were of more importance to the unions and the industrial-relations system than the workers themselves: wage gains were substantial in some cases, but the strikers had challenged the very foundation of management's power, and the legal recognition of unions in the workplace (1969) provided only a partial solution to such pent-up grievances and distrust. Famously, CGT leader Georges Séguy's address to Renault's workers at Billancourt – the Confederation's heartland – immediately after the Grenelle talks failed to persuade them back to work. Eventually the strikers grew weary and by the start of the summer vacation France returned to normal. For many, May–June 1968 represented a missed opportunity, and the union confederations (especially the CGT) with their old habits and fear of uncontrolled mass movements seemed to bear a lot of the responsibility for this.

The 1970s saw continuing unrest, often focusing on 'qualitative' issues concerning control of production and work organization rather than quantitative (more pay). Even wage demands were often presented in terms of equality (differentials) rather than simple increases. Many commentators stress the 'bottom-up' nature of these strikes, involving lower-status workers in many cases. Many of the strikes also involved key issues of control, with unions fighting to gain the *de facto* recognition already acquired in law. The Joint Français (1972) and Lip (1973) strikes stand out as emblematic of this new wave of unrest, influenced by the ideas of May 1968. At Le Joint Français (a Breton subsidiary of the electrical construction giant CGE), a largely low-skilled and mainly female workforce went on strike for two months, at one point confining the local managers for three nights. Wage demands mixed with wider concerns about work organization and conditions, under CFDT leadership. Crucially, the management's hard-line tactics strengthened the strikers' resolve and swung public opinion in the workers' favour. A contemporary song expressed the strikers' distrust of both management and government:

> Listen everyone, people of Basse-Bretagne.
> The lads and lasses of Saint-Brieuc
> have stopped work
> because they weren't paid enough.
> The riot police attacked them,
> sent by the government.
> Great anger there was against the manager

and he was shut in his office.
[...]
Against the merciless boss,
we march to the four corners of the country.
Forward, Bretons! forward, Bretons!

CHORUS
At the Joint Français, at the Joint Français
The Breton workers say b— to the boss.[5]

Thanks to massive local support, the strike ended successfully. At Lip, a bankrupt Besançon watchmaking factory threatened with closure, workers went even further: they took over production. Widespread popular support made the government hesitate before sending in troops to evict the workers, but by then a business plan drawn up by the CFDT laid the basis for an agreement allowing the factory to continue production and saving most of the jobs.

The union confederations enjoyed renewed support in the climate of worker unrest, but the rise in membership was less marked than, say, in 1936. Total membership rose to nearly 5 million, with the CGT (2 million), the CFDT (close to 1 million) and FO (around 0.75 million) claiming the lion's share. The fragmentation of the union movement stood in stark contrast with the 1930s, the heyday of communist activism. Direct action was taking place without necessarily feeding into union organization, although local unions (especially the CFDT and to a lesser extent the CGT) played an active part in leadership. One of the reasons put forward to explain this gap between local militancy and national union membership is that national labour leaderships were too caught up elsewhere: either in bureaucratic office-holding or in political activity.

Following de Gaulle's departure, a new team under President Pompidou and Prime Minister Chaban-Delmas (aided for a time by Jacques Delors) attempted an ambitious and innovative overhaul of the industrial relations system: industry-wide bargaining was encouraged by a top-down process of national framework agreements, and productivity deals were reached in the public sector. The policy undoubtedly helped to stimulate bargaining at all levels. The number of sectoral agreements (providing a basic floor for pay and conditions in a given sector or industry) rose to over 1000 a year in the 1970s, whereas previously they had been few and far between, and plant-level bargaining more than doubled.

However, just as unions were beginning to make inroads into the workplace, economic crisis struck. After 1973, plant-level bargaining virtually stopped and industry-level agreements were increasingly ignored. Mass redundancies became commonplace. Probably the key to the unions' failure to translate militancy into membership is not so much bureaucratic inertia (although it undoubtedly reduced their attractiveness to potential recruits) as the radically changed climate of the crisis years. The 'qualitative' demands of the 1970s, which at the time were taken to constitute a radical challenge to capitalism, may have been a shock response to job threats: traditional wage demands had not been superseded, they simply belonged to the 'glory' years.

For a while unions went along with the general view in believing that the crisis would soon blow over. Faced with employer retrenchment in the workplace, the CGT and CFDT followed the Communist and Socialist parties into joint action, counting on a left victory at the 1978 legislative elections to reverse austerity policies and give the unions new legal rights. This strategy compounded their problems, however: it made them appear even more remote from their grass-roots membership. In opposition to the 'big two', FO dedicated itself to workplace bargaining, which became the central plank of its leader André Bergeron's policy, and it started to gain members as quickly as the CGT and the CFDT lost them. In any case, the left lost the elections in 1978. The CFDT reacted by 'recentring' its action and promoting a more moderate, more workplace-oriented image. François Mitterrand's victory in 1981 came as the union movement, more divided than ever, faced its future with no clear sense of direction.

The end of trade unions in France?

Ironically, the decline of the French labour movement has taken place since the election of a socialist president and left-wing government in 1981. Between the early 1970s and early 1990s, union membership halved. In the late 1990s France had barely 2 million union members (8 per cent of the workforce) and fragmentation continued, with the creation of new autonomous unions, particularly in the public sector. Workplace elections (of workers' delegates, representatives on works committees and industrial tribunals) showed decreasing turnout and a dwindling base for unions within the firm, as more and more elected representatives were non-union members. With privatization and the dismantling, decentralization and downsizing of large firms, the model of trade unionism *à la française* was disappearing. Strike figures dwindled to below 1 million days per year on average in the 1980s, and an annual average of around 0.5 million in the early 1990s.

Initially, the prospects for union renewal after 1981 looked promising. With its interventionist economic policy and extensive nationalizations, its close ties with sections of the union movement (especially the CFDT, and the CGT through the four communist ministers in Pierre Mauroy's government) and its promise to modernize industrial relations by giving workers new rights, the government seemed set to reverse the setbacks of the late 1970s. But the turnaround in economic policy lasted only a few months, and nationalization did not fundamentally alter power relations within the big companies; after 1986, the process of privatization began anyway. The 1982

Auroux laws offered more: as well as granting workers a say in work organization (through mandatory 'expression groups'), they sought to revitalize bargaining and fill the glaring gaps in coverage, especially by encouraging plant-level bargaining in small and medium-sized companies. They also attempted to modernize the system of workplace representation, making the works committee a more active participant in the life of the company by obliging employers to inform it of major economic, financial and technological decisions, rather than simply a social-events organizer. In many ways the Auroux laws caused a sea-change in industrial relations, dissipating a climate of distrust and bringing the employers round to a more participatory way of dealing with their employees. In terms of bargaining, the obligatory nature of the laws had an immediate effect on the number of agreements reached and levels of coverage, particularly as the laws were later accompanied by other laws encouraging flexible bargaining on new subjects, notably working time. Some even identify in the Auroux laws the seeds of a new 'micro-corporatism': negotiation in the workplace, with pay rises being traded for job enrichment, or leisure time, or (temporary) job security. So why did they not help the unions to surmount the crisis? At a simple level, the unions started from such a weak power base that they did not have the capacity to shape the new social-relations structure, as conversely the employers did: many expression groups resemble management-led quality circles. Some argue that the rights granted by the Auroux laws, based on individuals rather than collective modes of representation and expression, actually disadvantaged unions. Others argue that the Auroux laws were simply the latest in a series of interventions by the state, demonstrating once again by their very existence the failure of 'social' actors to seize the initiative. Others still note that the Auroux laws were accompanied by a general climate of deregulation, with the emphasis on flexibility for employers: under such conditions, and with the general threat of mass unemployment hanging over them, unions could do no better than hold a defensive position.

It is possible to see the new climate of deregulation as the beginnings of a new economic order. If the old order was characterized by organization (institutions designed to minimize uncertainty), the new order means insecurity and disorganization. It is true that the history of French trade unionism shows a tandem (if not always perfectly synchronized, and always uneven on both sides) development of institutions such as social insurance, rationalized work practices and instititionalized industrial relations, and state-sponsored collective bargaining. In this sense, the period after 1973 marks the end of an epoch, although it is also important to remember the discontinuities and the incompleteness of the process before then.

The 1980s certainly saw the end of a particular type of French trade unionism – mass and class unionism – associated with a strong, workerist, communist subculture. The mass and class model was strongly linked with the growth of the French state and the economy. And yet, although it corresponded to a particular phase in French history, in terms of political culture it drew on much earlier traditions of revolutionary action and practical solidarity. The value of solidarity remains strongly rooted in French culture today, despite the individualistic impact of social and economic trends. For this reason, unions will continue to have a role to play, although they have been remarkably slow (in comparison with their counterparts in other countries) to develop locally based or direct services which would help them to draw on the solidaristic tradition.

The mass and class model was also to a large extent based on a myth, albeit an extremely powerful one: French trade unionism has never really been a mass movement, although the aspiration to mass membership is an understandable aspiration. When it did acquire mass membership, it quickly lost it again.

Notes

1 T. Hirszberg, 'Si c'était à refaire', in CGT, *Le Premier Siècle 1895–1995* (Paris: VO Éditions, 1995), pp. 7–15, p. 7.
2 'La Charte d'Amiens', reproduced in J.-D. Reynaud, *Les Syndicats en France*, vol. 2 (Paris: Seuil, 1975), pp. 26–7.
3 Cited in J. Julliard, *Clemenceau Briseur de Grèves* (Mestril-sur-l'Estrée: René Julliard, 1965), p. 31.
4 Cited in R. Mouriaux, *La CGT* (Paris: Seuil, 1982), p. 75.
5 J. Capdevielle, E. Dupoirier and G. Lorant, *La Grève du Joint Français* (Paris: Presses de la Fondation Nationale des Sciences Politiques, 1975), pp. 78–9.
Note: all translations by the author.

Further reading

Confédération Générale du Travail *Le Premier Siècle 1895–1995* (Paris: Voix Ouvrière Éditions, 1995).
Horne, J. *Labour at War: France and Britain 1914–1918* (Oxford: Clarendon Press, 1991).
Lequin, Y. *Histoire des Français XIXe–XXe siècles: la société* (Paris: Armand Colin, 1983).
Magraw, R. 'Socialism, syndicalism and French labour before 1914', in D. Geary (ed.), *Labour and Socialist Movements in Europe before 1914* (Oxford: Berg, 1989), pp. 48–100.
——, *A History of the French Working Class*, 2 vols. (Oxford: Blackwell, 1992).
Milner, S. 'France', in S. Berger and D. Broughton (eds.), *The Force of Labour* (Oxford: Berg, 1995), pp. 211–44.
Mouriaux, R. *Les Syndicats dans la société française* (Paris: Presses de la Fondation Nationale des Sciences Politiques, 1983).
Noiriel, G. *Les Ouvriers dans la société française XIXe–XXe siècle* (Paris: Seuil, 1986).
Reynaud, J.-D. *Les Syndicats en France*, vol. 1 (Paris: Seuil, 1975).
Shorter, E. and Tilly, C. *Strikes in France 1830–1968* (Cambridge: Cambridge University Press, 1974).
Willard, C. (ed.), *La France ouvrière, Vol. 1: Des origines à 1920* (Paris: Éditions Sociales, 1993).

|14|

'Not backward but different'?
The debate on French 'economic retardation'

ROGER MAGRAW

Introduction

Until the 1970s historiographical debate about the performance of the French economy was dominated by unfavourable comparisons with a British paradigm which was assumed to comprise several essential elements:

1 A precocious 'agricultural revolution' engendering large-scale capitalist farming capable of producing surpluses to feed growing towns, of generating capital for industrial investment and of 'freeing' surplus labour for industry.
2 Rapid, widely diffused technological innovation and the concentration of production into factories.
3 An industrial 'take-off' in the period 1780–1820 – with cotton as the 'leading sector'.
4 Rapid urbanization – with 50 per cent of the population inhabiting towns by 1850.
5 Mass production of low-cost consumer and capital goods both for export and for an expanding domestic market created by a good internal transport system, rapid population growth and the rising purchasing power of sizeable 'middling classes'.
6 Colonial and naval hegemony established during the 'second hundred years' war' with France (1714–1815) which provided raw materials, markets and mercantile profits for domestic investment.
7 A dominant laissez-faire ideology which eroded nostalgia for paternalism, the 'moral economy', guild controls and mercantilism, and which fostered free-markets, competition and entrepreneurial individualism.

Gerschenkron suggested strategies by which 'latecomers' could subsequently attempt to narrow Britain's lead by using the State and industrial banks to provide the capital requirements of railways and heavy industry. Yet, despite some interest in the Saint-Simonian spurt of the French economy during the

Second Empire (1851–70), his focus was on Germany, Russia and Italy. France was treated with a degree of condescension – as an 'old' economy that had lost its long struggle for supremacy with Britain and subsequently failed to summon sufficient vitality to confront the challenge of 'younger', more vigorous newcomers.

The much-criticized 'French model' was thus presented as battered and tired – a rather pitiful 'other' with which the narratives of 'success' first of Britain and later of Germany or the USA could be contrasted. Its characteristics, portrayed as a virtual mirror-image of those of Britain, included:

Survival of an 'archaic' peasant sector

Although the anti-seigneurial Revolution of 1789 was a key 'moment' at which peasants won the right to stay on the land throughout the nineteenth century, peasant survival had, O'Brien argued, deeper roots in the peculiarities of French agrarian development. As eastern Europe evolved towards intensified serfdom and Britain towards agrarian capitalism – and a landless proletariat – French élites kept peasants on the land, in part because wine, the main cash crop, was more labour-intensive than sheep-farming which produced England's main cash crop, wool. Aristocrats then extracted surplus value via seigneurial dues and monopolies. However, when *seigneurs* sought to appropriate common lands and erode communal rights the *ancien-régime* state, reluctant to see its peasant tax-base undermined, defended peasant usage rights – as the British state ceased to do after 1660.

British agricultural productivity pulled ahead of that of France during the *ancien régime* because Britain's soil and climate were better suited to fodder crops. Hence more livestock could be sustained and more manure (fertilizer) produced. However, 'pessimists' argue that the post-1789 survival of a peasantry now freed from seigneurial burdens, its landholding augmented by acquisition of church property and its debts reduced by the hyper-inflation of the early 1790s, constituted the major obstacle to subsequent agricultural – and to wider economic – development. Lacking capital and technical expertise, peasants were unable or unwilling to innovate, making agricultural modernization impossible outside a few atypical regions of agrarian capitalism – Flanders, Picardy, Ile-de-France. Yields remained 'medieval' in parts of the west and the south. Peasant reluctance to leave the land led to exploitation of low-yield, marginal land, to labour-supply bottlenecks in industry and to slow urbanization. Peasants obstructed agrarian individualism by clinging tenaciously to communal and forest rights. Economic crises remained of the 'traditional' type – triggered by grain deficits, rising food prices and consequent falling demand for textiles. Moreover, reluctant to see farms sub-divided amongst numerous heirs under the inheritance provisions of the Napoleonic code, peasants practised 'Malthusian' fertility controls. The resultant sharp decline in demographic growth contributed to inelasticity of consumer demand – as did the quasi-subsistence nature of much peasant farming.

Precocious peasant enfranchisement (1848) made subsequent governments reliant on peasant votes. Hence, faced with falling agricultural prices
and rising import penetration in the 1880s and 1890s, politicians cushioned
'inefficient' peasant farmers by protective tariffs – thereby increasing domestic food prices, stimulating wage-demands and raising the costs of industrial
exports. In 1914 41 per cent of French labour was still in agriculture, as
against 8 per cent in Britain – where output per agricultural worker was
twice as high.

Prevalence of small-scale industry
Critics emphasized that the French non-agricultural economy remained
similarly dominated by 'archaic' small-scale industries. In 1900 30 per cent
of the French industrial labour force was employed in units of 10 or under,
54 per cent in units of under 50. Whilst 9 per cent of British labour was
classified as 'self-employed' the French figure was 40 per cent. Production in
cities such as Paris, Lyon and Toulouse remained dispersed amongst a
multiplicity of 'artisanal' workshops. 'Sweated' domestic industries and
rural 'proto-industry' remained widespread.

Failure to achieve a 'take-off' based on 'advanced' large-scale industry
Despite claims that France achieved its Rostowian 'take-off' in the 1850s to
1860s or after 1896, many historians argued that this was not achieved until
the 1950s. Nineteenth-century France did have a handful of major industrial
companies, but these were isolated exceptions. Its industrial regions – the
Nord, Alsace, the Stephenois-Lyonnais region – were pale imitations of
Lancashire, Yorkshire or the Ruhr. French steam-power stood at a mere 13
per cent of British levels in 1815 and had increased only to 24 per cent by
1850. Levels of metallurgical production achieved in Britain in the 1820s
were not matched in France until 1870. By 1850 Britain was 50 per cent
'urban' – and six of its 10 largest cities were industrial. At that date France
was barely 25 per cent urban – and all but three of its 25 largest cities
remained essentially administrative, ecclesiastical or agricultural market
centres.

To explain such 'backwardness' historians invoked a range of geographic,
technological, cultural and socio-political factors.

1 France's coal resources were modest, ill-suited to conversion to coke for
new iron and steel processes and remote from her iron-ore deposits. Coal
production reached 5 million tons per year by 1850 – one-tenth of British
levels – and grew to some 40 million tons – one-seventh of British levels – by
the 1900s, after the opening of the Pas-de-Calais coalfield. France had to
import one-third of her coal in the 1870s and fuel comprised 60 per cent of
the costs of French iron production in 1850 – as against 18 per cent in South
Wales.

2 As a large land mass with numerous mountain regions France had
greater transport problems than did Britain with its long coastline and

navigable rivers. Unification of the internal market was achieved only belatedly with the main-line rail network in the 1850s. Until then coal from the Loire cost nearly four times its pithead price in Alsace. Thus, as Price argues, the impact of railways on the French internal market was greater than was the case in Britain.

3 'Pessimists' such as Crouzet support the classic thesis that it is Britain's technological superiority – in steam-power, textile machinery, iron processes – which explains France's growing 'inferiority' in the crucial 1780–1840 decades. A hitherto narrow 'gap' widened to a chasm as war cut France off from British innovations. Le Creusot did import British coal-fuel technology but such technology transfers often foundered on the inability to assimilate expertise and know-how. Some modern forges collapsed in the late-1820s slump and in 1850 half of French iron was still being produced by charcoal forges. French textile mills were consistently two decades or more behind Britain in adoption of state-of-the-art machinery. Power-looms, for example, were commonplace in Britain by the 1820s but in France not until the Second Empire.

4 Whereas 'coal men' analysed French retardation in terms of inadequate mineral resources, 'culture men' emphasized deficiencies in entrepreneurial culture. Rejecting 'Marxist' stereotypes of a 'bourgeois' French Revolution paving the way for the hegemony of nineteenth-century industrialists, historians portrayed a French bourgeoisie singularly deficient in red-blooded capitalist dynamism. Post-Revolutionary élites were, instead, categorized as *grands notables* – a composite stratum amongst whom industrialists and financiers were both less prominent and less influential than surviving aristocrats, *rentiers*, bureaucrats and lawyers whose cultural values remained those of 'traditional' France. The education system directed sons into the bureaucracy or the professions. Landownership continued to confer status and security – so that mercantile élites in Bordeaux redirected investment into vineyards in the hinterland and the Rouen textile manufacturers evoked by Chaline retired to leisurely lives as country gentlemen in Normandy châteaux.

Even those who remained in industry – such as the Motte textile dynasty in the Nord – were cautious, undynamic, committed to bequeathing the family firm intact to the next generation. Hence, Landes argued, they were reluctant to become 'corporate' businessmen, to disclose family secrets to outside shareholders by re-launching their firms as joint-stock companies. Though sectors more capital-intensive than textiles – steel, railways – did require outside capital, French banking allegedly remained keener on investment in state bonds or abroad than in domestic industry. Moreover, banking was associated with 'marginal' groups – Jews, Protestants – and both the Catholic right and the left viewed 'finance capital' with suspicion, as 'parasitic', 'usurious', 'un-French'.

5 Despite the apparent triumph of free-market ideas in the aftermath of 1789 – when guilds, corporate monopolies and internal tolls were swept

away and property rights affirmed – liberal critics argued that the nineteenth-century state retained too many of the 'Colbertist' *dirigiste* assumptions of the *ancien régime*. Thus protectionist and interventionist policies inflicted avoidable self-mutilation on the economy – distorting the free market by protecting the nascent machine-building industry in the 1830s, by subsidizing shipbuilding, by 'cushioning' archaic small producers during the Great Depression or by sponsoring counter-cyclical public-works projects.

6 Finally it is claimed that British hegemony was built on relative internal political and social stability and on successful colonial and military policies. Crouzet argues that whilst France competed well in the 'race' until the 1770s – with comparable growth rates in iron, woollens and foreign trade – she subsequently fell badly behind. The financial pressures of funding both a continental military strategy and colonial/naval rivalry with Britain imposed fatal strains on the tax structures of the *ancien régime*. Two decades of internal revolution and incessant warfare then left France, by 1815, on balance further 'behind' than in the 1780s. Coal and iron production had declined. The British blockade and the loss of Latin American and colonial markets – most damagingly St Domingo – destroyed trade links which had sustained eighteenth-century expansion and led to de-industrialization around the west-coast ports. The Napoleonic Empire offered the ephemeral compensation to eastern France of militarily imposed economic penetration of Europe. Lille businessmen invested in Mons coalmines, Strasbourg flourished as an entrepôt between Germany and Italy, Alsace industrialists imported raw materials via the Rhine. But Waterloo deprived France of this economic empire – hence the understandable mood amongst business groups after 1815 was a preoccupation with defending, via tariffs if necessary, the much-reduced national economic 'space' of the hexagon.

Subsequent attempts to 'catch up' were disrupted by internal instability or by war. The politico-social crisis of 1846-51 undermined business confidence and halted railway construction. Whereas 'mid-Victorian prosperity' eased the social conflicts of the Chartist years and enabled British employers to offer concessions to 'responsible' trade unionism, the Bonapartist state and the French *patronat* – with less room for flexibility given France's relative backwardness – could afford fewer industrial or political concessions to labour. Thus the on-going cycle of alternating periods of repression (1830s; 1850s) and of worker militancy (1848–51; 1869–71) was perpetuated and the emergence of a 'normal' industrial-relations system delayed.

The de-industrialization of the once-flourishing textile towns of lower Languedoc provides graphic evidence of the potential impact of class conflict on regional economic development. Whereas the decline of Midi textiles has often been attributed to local élites' 'atavistic' preference for landed investment, C. Johnson identifies the 1848 Revolution as the crucial watershed. The militancy of textile workers in Lodève threatened, in conjunction with that of local small *vignerons*, to make the region a socialist bastion. The Bonapartist regime subsequently took its revenge on these 'red' workers by shifting orders for army uniforms to regions with more docile labour forces – a strategy of 'hopscotch capitalism' which has been refined and globalized in the past century and a half. The prolonged agonies of the region's textile sector – and the partial stifling of its emerging mining industry – were also, it is true, due to deficiencies in transport infrastructure. It was deprived of projected rail links to Paris via the Massif Central by the machinations of Paris-based financiers seeking to maximize their revenues from the Paris–Lyon–Marseille railway.

The Franco-Prussian war caused further economic disruption. France lost industrial Alsace, whilst the 5.5 billion franc war indemnity reduced industrial investment, necessitated tax increases and deepened the early stages of the Great Depression. Subsequent military expenditure to prepare for *revanche* took a disproportionate share of state budgets.

The revisionist critique

Towards a reassessment

The net conclusion of the historiography of the 1950 to 1960s was, thus, that French economic performance in the period 1789–1914 was, at best, modest – hence France's inexorable decline from being the dominant power in 1700 to second-rank status. Not only did the rise of Germany and the USA consign her to fourth place in the world economic league, but 'newcomers' (Japan, Russia) appeared more dynamic in heavy industry and smaller neighbours (Belgium, Switzerland) more efficient. Occasional periods of respectable growth were interspersed with periods of disruption or stagnation (1789–1815; 1846–51; 1865–96).

However, major historiographical reassessment during the 1970s saw the 'French model' – *la voie française* – treated with growing respect. No longer characterized as the perennial also-ran, France was now perceived as running (almost) neck-and-neck or, indeed, as running an entirely separate race – one of greater relevance than the British to the wider world. Some now argued that the French experience should seen as one of the earliest and most successful cases of sustained economic growth rather than as an anaemic and imitative effort to 'follow' Britain. The French pattern of growth combining industrialization with continuation of handicrafts and of peasant agriculture came to be portrayed not as a failed effort to imitate British achievements but as an entirely appropriate response to the domestic situation.

Before analysing the resultant debate it is important to emphasize that, despite their 'scientific' verbiage and positivistic quantification, economic historians are just as subjective, just as influenced by the assumptions of their age, as any other historian. They, too, present grand narratives, tell stories, use metaphors of 'organic growth' borrowed from biology – or of 'take-off' borrowed from aviation. Their preferences for *dirigisme* or *laissez-faire*, for

greater or lesser degrees of social inequality, for asceticism or social hedo-
nism reflect their underlying ideologies and value systems. Crouzet, the
doyen of comparative Anglo-French historiography, has his own idiosyncratic 'agenda'. He is an Anglophile, an admirer of British 'civility',
'moderation', constitutionalism – and of Thatcherite free-market ideology.
He continues to contrast Britain's 'success story', her 'majestic and splendid
course', with the 'sinister buffoonery', the 'tragi-comic rhapsody of lost
opportunities and wasted chances' of his homeland – a France corrupted by
Jacobinism, Marxism and endemic social conflict which somehow managed
to survive for two centuries after 1789 but whose 'chances of survival (were)
greatly diminished' by the election of a socialist government in May 1981
which finally condemned it to underdevelopment and to banana-republic
status! It seems bizarre, therefore, for Crouzet to accuse Tom Kemp – who,
from a very different perspective, shares similar 'pessimistic' views about the
French economy – of allowing his 'Marxist bias' to distort his 'scientific'
economic analysis.

The agenda of 1950s 'pessimism' was set by Cold-War liberals alarmed
that France's NATO duties might be incompatible with aspects of her
national culture – enthusiasm for state planning, the existence of a powerful
Communist Party, the reluctance of peasants and small businessmen to
appreciate the virtues of unregulated free markets, widespread suspicion of
American cultural hegemony. The thesis about French 'backwardness' made
perfect sense, Fohlen cryptically observed, to the 'average impatiently-
chauvinistic American tourist'! Pessimistic readings of French economic
performance were sustained by anti-Marxist re-interpretations of the French
Revolution. Insistence that this was made neither *by* nor *for* an emerging
industrial bourgeoisie fitted neatly with claims that the *ancien-régime* economy had been flourishing until the 1770s, that the Revolution damaged
France's economic competitiveness and that the post-Revolutionary élites
remained essentially *rentiers* with traditionalist values.

The context for a more 'optimistic' re-interpretation of French economic
performance was provided by four significant factors:

1 By the mid-1970s France had experienced nearly three decades – subsequently dubbed the *trente glorieuses* – of sustained economic growth
created, in part, by *dirigiste* planning and a mixed economy. This encouraged some to challenge the supercilious condescension of Anglo-American
'pessimists'.

2 Meanwhile the 'British model', against which French 'retardation' had
been measured, was itself being reappraised. Crafts estimated that growth
rates in the crucial 1780–1820 decades may have been lower than once
assumed, new technologies restricted to a narrow range of industries,
'hand-technologies' more widely used. Victorian education may have been
increasingly pervaded by anti-industrial cultural values, and aristocratic
hegemony may have persisted. Moreover, 'gentlemanly capitalism' –

whose bastion was the City of London, not the industrial north – may have systematically exported capital to the detriment of domestic industrial investment.

3 Simultaneously questioned were automatic assumptions of one optimum *route royale* to the modern world. Perhaps the 'British model' was not *the* one rational model to which to aspire? Had not its social costs been unacceptably high? Were not foreign observers correct to be appalled by the social conditions and harsh Poor Law of industrial Britain, to view Manchester as more dystopia than ideal? Did not Thomas Hardy memorably contrast the sturdily independent peasant of France with the broken, demoralized figure of 'Hodge' – the dispossessed landless labourer of southern England? To dub the former a product of French 'labour-market failure' appeared particularly absurd.

4 Meanwhile the decline of 'Fordism' and the flourishing during the 1970s to 1980s of small-scale industries in, for example, northern Italy, caused historians to reassess the viability of nineteenth-century rural proto-industry, 'artisanal' production and peasant agriculture. As teleological assumptions, of liberals and Marxists alike, about the inevitable 'progressive' triumph of large-scale industry came under scrutiny, so France's socio-economic *Sonderweg* came to be less harshly judged.

Comparisons with other 'latecomer' economies suggested that there was no single 'correct' path. Each nation had to utilize its own blend of resource endowment, culture and skills. Belgium had metal-working traditions, abundant coal and a dominant business élite. Holland, with little coal or iron, relied on financial and commercial expertise, efficient agriculture and a good transport system, whilst the Swiss, similarly deficient in minerals and with a difficult terrain, relied on their financial sector, on an educated, skilled and relatively cheap labour force and on using imported British yarn to embroider and print up-market textiles.

French macro-economic performance re-evaluated

Revisionists accused 'pessimists' of diagnosing a 'retardation' which they had failed to measure or prove. Statistical comparison of national growth rates remains, inevitably, a highly approximate science. French regional monographs invariably raise doubts about the status of local statistics – assembled by bureaucrats' subordinates – from which 'national data' are compiled and on the basis of which complex, esoteric calculations are made by cliometricians. Nevertheless the evidence of researchers at the Applied Economics Institute (ISEA) from 1960 onwards did suggest that French 'backwardness' had been exaggerated.

France, the researchers suggested, had enjoyed periods of quite impressive growth – 1820–45; 1852–65; 1896–1914. Overall growth rates in the 1820–65 period were around 2 per cent per annum, possibly 2.5 per cent in industry. Since the post-1896 expansion had continued into the late-1920s, Aldrich even suggested that 'historians seeking the start of the long acceleration of growth could situate it as validly in 1900 as in 1950'.

However, the most striking results derived from per-capita statistics. Judged on overall production figures France's performance often looked very modest – with, for example, 1.41 per cent per annum growth in GNP 1860–1910, as against 1.87 per cent in Britain and 2.57 per cent in Germany. However, the sharp decline in French birth rates in those decades meant that French population growth (0.16 per cent p.a) had almost ceased, whereas the European average stood at 0.92 per cent p.a. At 1.25 per cent p.a. French per-capita growth remained slightly below Germany (1.37 per cent p.a) but ahead of both the British and European average (0.96 per cent p.a.). The crucial difference between Britain and France thus became the fact that Britain's population had quadrupled between 1800 and 1914, whilst that of France had grown by barely one-third. Not only was growth in French per-capita productivity – 1.2 per cent p.a. across the century – only marginally lower than British, but it was higher both in some 'old' sectors (construction; clothing; leather) *and* in some 'new' sectors (automobiles; electricals). Lévy-Leboyer's subsequent calculations have lowered French growth estimates during the Great Depression. But revisionists have continued to cling to this general argument.

The fall in the French birth-rate from above 30 per thousand in the late eighteenth century to well under 20 per thousand by 1914 – at a time when it remained 29 per thousand in Germany – caused alarm amongst French nationalists, army commanders, 'natalists' and Catholics. Many perceived such 'Malthusianism' as symptomatic of a loss of vitality and self-confidence, as both the product of a lack of economic opportunities and the cause of sluggish growth in internal markets and of failure to embrace mass production. The 'virility' of newcomer nations aroused a mix of envy and fear. Whilst such views are still echoed by right-wing historians – Chaunu; Crouzet – who appear to view family limitation as one key to France's decline to 'third-class' economic status – these phenomena are open to other interpretations. In the first half of the century – during which the population rose from 27 million to 35 million – élites were still denouncing the 'rabbit-like' breeding of the lower classes as proof of their brutality and fecklessness and as cause of land-hunger and poverty. Yet with birth-rates already in decline France was in the vanguard of a shift to 'modern' fertility patterns, already escaping the high fertility/high mortality model typical of Europe's demographic *ancien régime*. Birth control – via delayed marriage, coitus interruptus, abortion – became commonplace not only amongst the bourgeoisie but in large strata of artisan and peasant classes outside the Catholic west. Whilst clergy lamented this as a symptom of post-Revolutionary cultural and moral decline, others might view it as a healthy sign of secularization and 'modernity'. A low birth rate enabled France to have the highest percentage of married women in Europe in paid employment. Maximum rates of economic growth were achieved precisely in those years (1886–1914) when the birth rate was falling the fastest. Only in the twentieth century has the rest of Europe begun to 'catch up' with the French demographic model.

The 'French path' to the twentieth century

Whilst part of the revisionist argument was to claim that France performed well in some sectors of large-scale industry, an alternative strategy was to admit that France faced specific 'problems', but that these should be viewed not as 'obstacles' to a 'British' model of development but rather as stimuli for imaginative, creative responses. French entrepreneurs thus acted in ways appropriate to the particular constellation of factors which they confronted.

A FLOURISHING RURAL PROTO-INDUSTRY?

Rural industry, once cited as symptomatic of French 'archaism', has been re-evaluated. Given difficulties of access to cheap, high-quality coal did it not make sense for industry to locate close to wood and water-power? With water-power safe, cheap and clean France became, as Woronoff emphasizes, a leader in and exporter of water-turbine technology. In the late nineteenth century Alpine valleys witnessed innovative hydro-electricity projects. Rural charcoal-forges were capable of producing quality steel needed for precision medical equipment.

During the *ancien régime* textile 'proto-industry' had flourished in Lower Languedoc, Normandy, the west and the north. Evading urban guild restrictions and stimulating the skills and entrepreneurial potential of peasant spinners and weavers, it had been central to the quintupling of French exports to Latin American and Levant markets. Obsessed with the Lancashire factory model, orthodox economic historians lamented the 'failure' of many of these proto-industrial regions to develop concentrated/mechanized production in the nineteenth century. Revisionists such as Chassagne or Lewis, by contrast, have praised rural industry's adaptability – whilst emphasizing, too, that in Normandy and the Nord many entrepreneurs who did go on to establish textile mills had honed their organizational skills and raised their initial capital whilst coordinating rural textile outwork.

Rural manufacture continued to flourish because it suited both peasant workers and merchant capitalists. The system should not be idealized. Cambrésis rural weavers were often those pauperized by loss of their small farms. At the bottom of the village hierarchy, they were highly dependent on the merchants. However, for many, proto-industrial work provided that essential supplement to earnings from farms and from seasonal agricultural labour which allowed them to remain in the village. In the Pays-de-Caux, near Rouen, – an area of fertile soil but of many tiny farms – men worked in agriculture but women's employment in spinning allowed families to stay on the land. As Gullickson emphasizes, although marriage age was high, marriage rates, too, were high because there were jobs for children in spinning and carding. In the Mauges Liu has shown how peasant weavers' resistance forced cotton entrepreneurs to withdraw mule-jennies in the 1840s. Thus hand-weaving revived in the subsequent years – just as it was declining in northern France. Despite the arrival of power-looms in the 1860s, male weavers clung tenaciously to their 'independence' – albeit only with aid from their sons, employed in the nearby shoe industry, and at the expense of wives and daughters whose toil kept the households functioning.

Entrepreneurs could benefit from such survivals because they minimized their fixed capital outlay and because peasant workers, with access to agricultural resources, were usually both cheaper and less militant than urban workers. In Haut-Rhin, as Hau has emphasized, mill-owners tapped a pool of rural weavers as a reserve army of labour which was laid off first during slumps. From the 1820s the cheaper, simpler cloths of the Lyon silk industry, still the world market leader, were moved from the city itself – notorious for the militancy of its skilled weavers – into the surrounding countryside. Thus cost-cutting strategies, designed to preserve France's export markets, involved not concentration into urban factory production – although silk-preparation and dyeing processes were concentrated – but, Cayez shows, an accelerated rural diaspora.

Nor was rural industry technologically stagnant. Villages around St Etienne utilized both Jacquard looms and *métiers à la barre* which allowed ribbon-weavers to operate several looms. The Troyes bonnet industry utilized sophisticated hand-frames. Textiles were not the only rural industry to flourish. Shoemaking dominated the villages around Fougères in western France and glove-making those near Grenoble. In Oyonnax (Ain) a flourishing village comb-making industry survived into the interwar period. Monographs on such industries emphasize their durability, flexibility and skill in adjusting to ever-changing market trends. The Bourgeois family of peasant watchmakers in the Doubs developed their 'farm-workshop' to specialize in watch-cases – constructing a forge and a polishing shed, using their land as collateral for loans from Swiss financiers and from local *notaires*. They synthesized local metal-working traditions with Swiss expertise, adopted steam and electric power (1890s), pioneered techniques for veneering metal and collaborated with Besançon University science faculty. They diversified into barometer cases, car clocks, cigarette lighters – and use of advertising and commercial travellers won them national and, briefly, international sales. They appear to be the natural heirs of the resourceful peasant weavers of Cambrésis villages who had taken to capitalism like ducks to water a century earlier.

AN ADAPTABLE, MARKET-ORIENTATED PEASANT AGRICULTURE?

As Heywood observes, analysis of French agriculture often simply reiterated Arthur Young's mantra – peasant farming was a 'great evil' engendering 'very bad agriculture'. Hence its survival was, in itself, bound to have harmful effects on the wider economy.

Revisionists accepted that France's agrarian structure differed markedly from that of Britain. However, they emphasized that France also had erratic rainfall, much hilly terrain, a higher proportion of inferior soil. Yet, despite such problems, peasant agriculture kept millions on the land, occupied and fed them – albeit with difficulty in the grain crises of 1816–17 and 1846–7 – during decades when French industry could offer little alternative employment, when population growth was still quite strong – from 27 million in 1800 to 35 million in 1850 – and when 'Malthusian' dangers persisted. The relative stability of grain prices suggests that food production kept pace with demographic growth. There is evidence, Newell claims, of a decline in fallow land, increased use of fertilizers and real, if modest, gains in agricultural productivity of perhaps 1.2 per cent p.a. 1820–70 – below Britain's 1.4 per cent p.a. but substantially above the European average of 0.6 per cent p.a.

From different ideological perspectives two recent studies of peasant agriculture have questioned the stereotype of routine-bound archaism. Hilton Root portrays Burgundian peasants as eagerly seeking to maximize market opportunities, whilst the Marxist Ado claimed to detect a 'peasant path' towards rural capitalism, and not just in those areas of Picardy dominated by larger tenant-farmers. Peasant cash-crop agriculture was already established in some regions before the railway revolution of the 1850s, analysed by Price, which encouraged further market specialization – so that the Midi concentrated on cheap table-wines, the Charentes on dairy farming, and so forth. Rising agricultural prices allowed peasants to pay off debts. Moreover, as agricultural wages crept upwards in the 1860s, with falling birth rates and gradual rural exodus reducing labour supply, peasants' ability to tap family labour proved an advantage, particularly in labour-intensive vineyards.

Undoubtedly prolonged agricultural depression (1870–90s), compounded by the phylloxera disaster, slowed overall economic growth. Reduced rural purchasing power depressed consumer demand. However, it is important not to condemn the return to protectionism as an economically illiterate attempt to cushion 'inefficient' small rural producers – for 'dynamic' Wilhelmine Germany similarly resorted to tariffs to protect its sizeable rural *Mittelstand*.

Indeed, recent studies of peasant farming no longer offer a monolithically gloomy picture. Agricultural growth rates of 0.9 per cent p.a. in 1880–1914 were still marginally above the European average. Mesliand suggests that the sturdy, politically radical peasantry of the Vaucluse, actively involved in cash-crop farming, was more productive than the department's larger estates. Hubscher's analysis of monograph studies undertaken by students at *instituts agronomes* showed peasants increasing yields, improving livestock, switching between crops as market demand fluctuated, marketing a rising percentage of their crops. Attitudes towards machinery and innovations exhibited a 'wait-and-see' pragmatism rather than deep-seated suspicion. Midi *vignerons* survived the phylloxera crisis by developing a network of wine cooperatives. Moreover, continuing peasant 'pluri-activity' – temporary and seasonal job-migration, part-time work in mining – provided additional resources. Acute indebtedness to 'usurers', which had exacerbated social relations in the mid-century, had eased. *Notaires* acted as credit-brokers and neighbours and relatives formed 'personalized' credit networks.

Thus while French agriculture – with 5 million male 'actives' – still employed 'too many' in 1914, its productivity per hectare had risen by 70 per cent since 1800. There was, of course, no rustic idyll. Deep-seated tensions persisted in the countryside – as the *crise du Midi* (1905–7) in the Languedoc vineyards illustrated. But potential access to the land still offered the lure of independence and status, of an adequate livelihood built on hard work, fertility restriction and austerity. Peasants actually *gained* land in the Depression as falling profits prompted larger owners to sell land. As growers of fruit, dairy produce or industrial crops they were often effective market producers. Burgundy – whose peasants produced fine wines – since 1850 has experienced not stagnation but 'development without industrialization'. Undoubtedly the quality and variety of French agricultural produce, the outcome of heavy use of labour at a micro-level, has benefited French cuisine – and gastronomic tourism!

THE VITALITY OF 'QUALITY' ARTISANAL PRODUCTION?

Nye's research has indicated minimal correlation between firm-size and productivity in nineteenth-century France. As Sabel and Zeitlin emphasize in the Lyonnais-St Etienne region – just as around Birmingham or Sheffield – a vigorous, innovative industrial culture flourished around a critical mass of variegated, small-scale industries which interacted, borrowed and adapted technologies from each other and were alive to organizational and technical innovations. Lyon's silk industry easily eliminated its British counterpart after the 1860 Free-Trade treaty and, at its apogee, produced 30 per cent of the value of all French exports. Yet the bulk of quality weaving was done in tiny *canut* workshops. And, as T. Smith shows, supply of skilled labour was maintained by the imaginative strategies of local élites who supported appropriate technical training courses and a welfare system designed to maintain a pool of experienced labour within the region during slump years – a system dismantled only as the silk industry began to mechanize in the years before 1914.

Historians once spoke of a 'hiatus' in the Parisian economy between the decline of textiles around 1820 and the rise of heavy engineering in the outlying faubourgs after 1860. Its small-scale industry was dismissed as incapable of functioning as the motor of growth. Only recently, as Radcliffe argues, has Paris been re-evaluated as one of the world's great 'artisanal' centres – specializing in 'high value-added' clothing, furniture, leather goods, jewellery, bronze, precision surgical instruments and toys, and in 'finishing' clocks, pottery and wooden fans prepared in the provinces. With 3 per cent of France's population in the 1850s, Paris produced 25 per cent of the value of French manufactured exports. Its success relied on a complex division of labour, sub-contracting, constant product innovation and a variegated labour force of artisans, migrants – often ambitious and industrious – and women. Some 10 per cent of London women were involved in industry, 25 per cent of *Parisiennes*. Some 57 per cent of the city's population was 'active' – compared with 47 per cent in London. A low birth rate, the 'export' of infants to rural wet-nurses and the influx of young provincial migrants meant a city with relatively few children or aged.

Paris's culture encouraged exchange of ideas. Industrial *expositions* were hosted. Jacquard looms, sewing machines and electric motors revitalized workshop and domestic production through small but incremental changes. Attentive to changing customer tastes, small firms proved adept at maintaining a wide range of short runs of products which could be changed rapidly. Although aided by its position at the hub of the new rail network, Paris's 'success' suggests that 'comparative advantage' need not be determined by geography or mineral resources but may be socially and historically induced.

In short, small-scale production was, as Faure emphasizes, not 'a system waiting to die' but one with its own logic which achieved a second wind in the nineteenth century to remain an 'actor' in the changing present. Attempts to establish a factory system in Thiers in the 1860s failed – yet in the town and the surrounding hill-villages a complex division of labour between small masters and home workers involved in forging, mounting and polishing processes maintained a flourishing knife-making industry employing 18 000 in 1900.

FRANCE – A PIONEER IN 'CONSUMERISM'?

Consumption was once the great forgotten factor of economic history. However, our own consumerist culture has prompted historians to shift their focus from the technologies of the industrial revolution towards the role of consumer taste and consumer demand. The consensus has been that Britain led the way because of the size of its relatively affluent 'middling sort' and because mass-produced textiles became affordable by the popular classes. There is, however, no real historiographic consensus, as yet, on the chronology of French 'mass consumption'. Many still emphasize that, at the earliest, this came only with the belated rise of real wages in the 1880–1914 period and that until then families in the popular classes were spending up to 70 per cent of income on food. Others, however, have identified the emergence in the last decades of the *ancien régime*, at least in Paris, of a widespread popular taste for clothing, furniture and household utensils. Whilst the balance of evidence still suggests inelastic consumer demand for most of the nineteenth century, what is clear is that France was a leader in a retailing revolution. Department stores – some employing thousands – became the symbol of the Paris of Haussmann and of the *belle époque*. Most of their initial customers came from the city's middle and lower-middle class, from the provincial bourgeoisie – ordering from mail-order catalogues – or from tourists. There was an important correlation, as Walton has shown, between the tastes of such consumers for well-designed goods and the survival of a vigorous 'craft' sector in French industry. Avoiding cheap, mass-produced wallpapers, furniture and clothing, these consumers filled their apartments with a range of ornaments, furniture from the Faubourg St Antoine, silver-plated cutlery and pots. At the Crystal Palace exhibition (1851) France won more prizes than any nation but Britain, along with countless plaudits for the design and workmanship of her goods – prompting some economists to argue that France should concentrate her efforts on maintaining supremacy in such niche markets.

ENTREPRENEURSHIP AND BIG BUSINESS IN NINETEENTH-CENTURY FRANCE

Recent historiography has also questioned the 'deficiencies' of French big business. Freedeman has challenged assertions that company law inhibited the growth of large corporations, that family firms remained dominant and that industry was starved of investment by banks which exported capital. Certainly the law of 1807 requiring *Conseil d'État* approval for a joint-stock company did limit formation of these to only 11 per annum – mainly in transport and insurance – until 1867. However, the Société de Commandite par Actions (SCPA) – which gave control of a company to a *gérant* with unlimited liability whilst leaving shareholders *with* limited liability without an active say – functioned as a viable form of corporate enterprise for firms such as Le Creusot and was widely copied on the Continent. A more liberal law of 1867 permitted joint-stock companies to flourish. By 1900 400 per year were being established. By 1910 France had over 6000 corporate enterprises – more than Germany, though the average size of a German corporate firm was larger.

Also 'relegated to the dustbin' is the 'myth' of banks' supposed indifference to industry's needs. France was, by 1914, the world's second-largest capital exporter, with some £1500 million invested abroad. However, there appears little truth in accusations, peddled by populist-nationalists and socialists, that industry was 'starved' of capital. Peaks of capital export

(1850s and 1860s; 1896–1914) coincided with periods of rapid domestic growth. French interest rates remained below those in Britain, suggesting that modest domestic demand for capital was being met. Not only were returns on overseas investment generally 1 per cent to 2 per cent above those on domestic investment but overseas lending probably stimulated foreign orders for French exports. Some firms – including the Lens coalmines – continued to rely on self-financing – ploughing back profits, paying modest dividends, borrowing when necessary from family and suppliers. But this was a *chosen* option – not one imposed by any capital market inadequacy. High profits in metallurgy in the 1860s or after 1896 made 'auto-financing' possible. However, Freedeman insists, 'informed contemporary opinion (which) historians are well-advised to heed' believed that the capital market functioned 'rather efficiently' – as the rapid re-equipment of the steel industry with Bessemers or the financing of Alpine hydro-electricity projects suggests. Even the traditional *haute banque* had not disdained industrial investment. Rothschild backed the Grand Combes mines, whilst Seillières invested in Le Creusot. It had been argued that the 'Saint Simonian' vogue for industrial banking during the Second Empire proved ephemeral and that after the collapse of the Crédit-Mobilier (1867) surviving joint-stock banks heeded the warning of Henri Germain of Crédit Lyonnais against the risks of long-term industrial investments. However, younger bankers such as Dorizon of Société Générale rejected such caution, even if his bank's industrial involvements remained more *ad hoc* than systematic.

A further 'myth' is that the rise of joint-stock banks signified the decline of regional banks. Whilst the number of these did decline from their apogee in the 1860s, the survivors proved both robust and responsive to the needs of local industry. The Société Nancéenne de Crédit Industrielle et Commerciale was one of five banks supporting eastern metallurgical and chemical industries. Similar regional roles were played by the Banque Charpenay in Grenoble, and by the Société Marseilleise du Crédit – which invested in the port's sugar-refining and electrical sectors. By contrast the much-vaunted German industrial *Grossbanken* lent only to established firms and were less supportive of local business.

The final 'myth' questioned is that of France as a country of family firms. Certainly she experienced little 'American' merger-mania nor any unilinear trend towards industrial concentration – levels of which were quite high in glass, chemicals and electrical equipment but modest in construction, metal working and automobiles. The share of production of the 10 largest iron and steel firms rose from 55 per cent to 70 per cent between 1870 and 1912 – but that of the largest coal companies fell. However, it was to the cartel that French business turned when faced with pressure from falling profits and competition. Although the 1810 Code outlawed cartels, both courts and governments came to accept them as a sensible compromise between the instabilities of unregulated markets and the 'monster' American corporation. They avoided sales' duplication and excess production, permitted joint purchase of raw materials and – by maintaining domestic price levels – allowed the 'dumping' of surpluses abroad. By 1900 France had over 100 cartels – notably in sugar, aluminium, glass, chemicals, cotton-spinning and in the northern coal fields. After 1876 the Comptoir de Longwy monopolized Lorraine pig-iron. Cartels for a range of steel products – beams, rails, tubes – gave French firms clout in export markets.

It would be naïve to seek to boost the reputation of French industrial capitalism simply by citing evidence of cartelization or by claiming that banks can be taken as proxies for economic development. Nevertheless, broader, albeit impressionistic, evidence confirms the need to question older stereotypes. Whilst accurate 'measurement' of French 'managership' may be difficult, it is – as Fohlen emphasized – almost certainly 'not at level of enterprise and entrepreneurs that the problem of the assumed "lags" of French industry is to be explained'.

Textile manufacturers were frequently the butt of the historiography of the 1950s to 1960s – accused of excessive caution, obsession with family-firm autonomy, over-reliance on protective tariffs and 'atavistic' yearnings for *rentier* lifestyle. Revisionists, however, emphasized the specific difficulties which they faced – most acutely that of low aggregate demand. It was simply inappropriate for them to ape their British rivals. It is too easy to become mesmerized by the Lancashire model, to endlessly emphasize the 'lag' of several decades in the introduction of new textile technologies. Yet British textile machinery was quite well-known and accessible. Spies were sent to Britain – and British engineers were imported. The capital required for textile mechanization was modest and, as Chassagne insists, most entrepreneurs were deficient neither in know-how nor in access to capital. Alsatian mill-owners, as Hau illustrates, could borrow from local merchants and, if necessary, from Swiss banks. But technology transfers only make sense if they fit into a matrix of related capacities. Lancashire, faced with rising overseas demand, had solved a crisis of labour supply through introduction of machines and factories and by tapping abundant coal supplies. France's 'factor mix' was very different – sluggish demand, scarce coal but relatively cheap, flexible labour supply, often rural. Thus, Heywood argues, French manufacturers produced strategies appropriate to the specific situations which they faced. High transport costs and British dominance in cheaper cottons made concentration on up-market goods – *indiennes*, printed cotton, calicos – perfectly 'rational'. These could utilize French strength in design quality and in cotton-printing. Similarly, rural weavers and water supply were harnessed. Overall France's cotton sector was a 'modest success story'. Between 1780 and 1850 growth averaged 5 per cent per annum, and the industry was twice as large as any Continental rival. Whilst some Rouen mill-owners did retire to Normandy châteaux, similar aspirations were scarcely unknown in Lancashire. Moreover, both the Catholic textile dynasties of the Nord and their Jewish and Protestant counterparts in Alsace remained proud of their industrial calling. By 1845 the average Alsatian mill employed 230 workers whilst Dollfuss-Mieg – which integrated bleaching, dyeing, spinning and weaving – employed 2500.

Studies of individual firms and sectors appear to confirm this reassessment of French industrialists. St Gobain adjusted to the loss of its *ancien-régime* glass monopoly, diversified into chemicals, and introduced new product ranges – mirrors, plate-glass windows. As Gordon argues, St Etienne's industrial élites adapted imaginatively after 1880 to the challenges of prolonged economic depression and severe international competition and of rising labour militancy. They 'modernized' their politics by adopting a moderate republicanism capable of attracting working-class voters and their industrial strategy by switching towards specialized steels because Lorraine's abundant iron-ore deposits were giving eastern France clear advantages in basic iron production. Single-industry mining and heavy-metallurgy company towns coped with labour-supply problems both by systematic importation of immigrant workers – of whom France had 1 million by 1914 – and by paternalist schemes designed to retain 'loyal' and 'docile' company workers.

Moreover, French employers' notorious 'individualism' was gradually modified in the face of the 'threat' of organized labour. Employers' associations became larger and more cohesive and even the Comité des Forges, long fragmented by conflicts between large and small firms and between protectionists and engineering firms seeking lower tariffs on imported raw materials, began to achieve a degree of unity.

It is now accepted that by 1890–1914 France was performing creditably in such key 'modern' sectors as aluminium, electrical goods, hydro-electricity and rubber. It was also the world's second car producer – and largest car exporter – and an aviation-industry pioneer. Such real – if patchy – successes would be incomprehensible were one to accept the standard critique of an education system dominated by pre-industrial cultural values. Indeed the 'renewal' of the entrepreneurial élites during the 'second industrial revolution' can only be understood in the context of a higher education system at the apogee of which stood the *grandes écoles*. Their initial goal had been to produce artillery officers and bureaucrats for Napoleon's Empire and many of their graduates felt too superior to waste their talents in modest provincial industry. Yet it was École Polytechnique graduates who planned the railway network – and the rail companies became models of a new style of corporate, technocratic management involving a quasi-military command structure and systematic recruitment of engineers and bureaucrats from the Polytechnique and the École Centrale des Arts et Métiers. The 'technology gap' with Britain was substantially narrowed after the 1830s as the *grandes écoles* trained *patrons-techniciens* to head firms such as Fourchambault or the Cail locomotive company. Nearly half of 800 graduates of ECAM between 1825 and 1871 went into industrial management. And, as industries such as steel and chemicals became more science-based, the practice of *pantouflage* – the interchange of technocrats between bureaucracy and industry – increased.

Taylorism and 'scientific management' – although adopted only in an *ad hoc* fashion before 1914 – won converts amongst managers such as Renault. Comparative analysis has suggested that the divorce between the 'older' cultural and professional strata of the bourgeoisie and its 'economic' strata – between *Bildung und Besitz* – was actually wider in Germany than in France, where there was *more* intermarriage between these groups and *more* likelihood that sons of the professional class would enter business.

THE STATE AND THE ECONOMY

Laissez-faire economists such as P. Leroy-Beaulieu preached a gospel of free markets, of cheap government playing a minimal role in the economy or in social welfare. This was imbibed by students at the École Libre des Sciences Politiques, who carried it with them into careers as officials in the ministry of finance. However the 'official' consensus never fully accepted such dogmatism. Bonapartists, Radicals and social-Catholics, despite their many disagreements, all accepted that the state had a role in cushioning vulnerable groups against rapid change, in funding transport infrastructure, in regulating the pace of industrial development. 'The State', liberal Jules Simon reluctantly conceded, 'must do all the good that individuals cannot do.'

The 'weight' of the state was light by subsequent standards – taking around 10 per cent of national physical product until 1870, 15 per cent by 1913. As the state assumed responsibility for primary education – to mould a literate and productive labour force – education's budget share doubled to 7 per cent after 1880. Furthermore, as Gueslin emphasizes, concern for socio-political stability led to gradual acceptance of some role for a 'welfare state', albeit smaller than that of Bismarckean Germany. The state – which also ran arsenals, naval dockyards and the tobacco industry – had a larger economic role than in Britain.

Liberals continue to argue that the state intervened excessively and usually harmfully – citing subsidies to sailing-ship builders, ill-judged investment in the Freycinet Plan for rail construction in 1878–82 and featherbedding of inefficient industries by tariffs. However, *balanced* analysis of the net impact of such policies is needed, analysis which avoids *laissez-faire* dogmatism. In coal-mining, for example, the 1810 act appears to have provided an effective structure. The state – unlike in Britain – retained rights to subsoil minerals but leased mining concessions to firms which had sufficient capital and expertise. State engineers retained inspection rights. In the Gard, as Lewis has shown, this law provided the necessary framework for the expansion of deep mining after 1820 after a long, chaotic period during which such projects had been thwarted first by the seigneurial system and the need for court favours and then by emphasis, after 1789, on rights of individual landowners – which had allowed proliferation of undercapitalized petty mining schemes.

Even Adam Smith – unlike his recent 'disciples' – accepted the necessity of public involvement in transport infrastructure. The 'liberal' Orléanist regime sponsored road and canal projects, including the Rhône–Rhine canal which reduced coal costs in Alsace. However, the peaks of public expenditure coincided with rail construction (1850s; 1880s). Although a backlash against the 1848 Revolution led to the discrediting of plans for nationalized railways, the involvement of state *ponts et chaussées* engineers in rail planning showed a clear *dirigiste* orientation. The state purchased the land and funded the rail infrastructure. Private companies furnished rolling-stock and were guaranteed 99-year concessions and minimum returns on capital. But the railways remained under the supervision of state engineers and rail companies were expected to take responsibility for less profitable branch-lines. The state encouraged rail-company mergers, pressured for reduced freight rates to benefit peripheral regions and was prepared – as in the west after 1875 – to take over ailing networks. Again the net impact was broadly positive. The rail network united the national market and stimulated French heavy and capital goods industries in the 1860s – when rail orders accounted for 20 per cent of iron sales – and provided stable domestic orders to allow the emerging locomotive industry to move into exports markets. Two decades later the Freycinet Plan provided a – brief – countercyclical boost for depression-hit heavy industry.

One persistent criticism of French governments is that – except for the free-trade interlude of 1860-80 – they consistently overprotected inefficient industries with tariffs. However, any balanced assessment of tariff policies needs to consider four points.

First, as Nye has shown, the stereotype of a clear contrast between successful, free-trading Britain and stagnant ultra-protectionist France is misleading. The Anti-Corn Law League was a high-profile crusade utilizing stirring free-trade rhetoric. Yet, with what the French saw as typical hypocrisy, Britain continued to impose high tariffs on beet-sugar, luxury imports and French wines and spirits which challenged British brewing and distillery interests. Moreover, French tariffs were, on average, *below* those of Britain both in the early 1840s *and* in the 1850s.

Second, most continental liberals agreed that nascent industries were delicate hot-house plants which had to be protected if they were to survive. F. List's critique of free trade as a British ideology was translated from the German. Whilst some French sectors – the ports, silk, industries reliant on imported raw materials – did favour free trade, most, understandably, did not. It is also worth remembering that for much of the period 1780–1840 Britain restricted export of her textile machines and skilled workers – whilst French governments financed attempts to smuggle these into France! Mulhouse calico-printing and Roubaix worsteds were successful sectors saved in their infancy by tariffs. Tariffs may have slowed the construction of the railways – but they ensured that it was *French* engineering which benefited once these were being built.

Nor should the return to protectionism after 1880 be dismissed as economic illiteracy. France's continental competitors *and* the USA pursued similar strategies. It was Britain's unique circumstances – lack of a peasantry and the hegemonic position of the City of London with its global financial interests – which made her resist this tide. Moreover, the period 1896–1914 witnessed higher rates of growth than the preceding free-trade years. Tariffs helped cut France's trade deficit and were, as M. Smith argues, generally nuanced and flexible. Bilateral deals were made and low rates charged on imported coke, wool and flax needed by French industry.

Above all tariff policies must be judged not in narrowly economistic terms but, Lebovics argues, as part of wider strategies of socio-economic and political stabilization. The Méline tariff (1891) was a conscious attempt by the republican élites to be seen to protect 'national labour' in a context of unemployment and labour unrest. The wider strategy encompassed 'social-imperialist' policies designed to persuade workers that employment – and welfare provision – were dependent on colonial markets. Meanwhile attempts were being made – with limited success – to construct a new republican consensus by reconciling various class factions – Republicans and Catholic-royalists, industrialists and landowners, large capitalist interests and those of small business – on the lines of similar efforts being made in Wilhelmine Germany to build a broad anti-socialist alliance of 'Iron', 'Rye' and the *Mittelstand*.

But 'Mélinism' was also a variant of an on-going tradition which accepted the state's role in maintaining a balance between liberalism and *dirigisme*, in reconciling economic modernization with the preservation of a 'balanced' society – because small businessmen and peasants were viewed as the backbone of the 'real' France. 'France', Méline insisted, is '*at once* an agricultural, a manufacturing and a commercial country – and it is important for ... its national genius (and) strength to sacrifice *none* of the major elements of its life.' The English model – proletarianization and rural exodus – was simply unacceptable. France simply would not be France without peasants – any more than Britain is now truly Britain without its coal miners!

Tariffs did stabilize agricultural prices. But they were only one element in a wider republican agricultural strategy. The state subsidized irrigation and re-afforestation projects and established departmental 'professors of agri-culture'. *Syndicats agricoles* were sponsored and the Bank of France and the newly created Crédit Agricole were encouraged to support rural credit schemes. Tax exemptions were granted to farmers for mutual insurance schemes. With the agriculture ministry (founded in 1881) subordinate to the financial orthodoxies of the finance ministry, the 2 per cent of government expenditure allowed for agriculture was never sufficient. But such efforts were not insignificant and played some role in the renewed viability of peasant agriculture in the pre-1914 years.

Towards a post-revisionist balance sheet

In retrospect one can discern that the high-water mark of revisionist 'optimism' came in the mid-1980s. As with all such historiographical debates, there came a point when the pendulum appeared to have swung back too far. An implausibly rosy picture was in danger of emerging of a harmonious French society which blended modernity and stability, whose creative craftsmen secured niches in world markets, where peasant workers engaged in flexible 'pluriactivity' and yet where technocratic managers and engineers secured France a vanguard role in new industries!

Inevitably something of a backlash followed. Crouzet – after a brief flirtation with revisionist ideas during which he talked of 'not brilliant but quite creditable growth' – reverted to more 'pessimistic' views. Just as revisionism had been nurtured by France's post-1945 economic miracle, so now the perceived crisis of the French model – and, indeed, of French identity – in the face of threats of globalization, Americanization, mass unemployment and de-industrialization, has influenced the historiographical debate. Woronoff's recent history of French industrialization, which offers a reasonably positive judgement on the 'French path', concludes, sadly, that 'we are probably living through the last days of (French) exceptionalism'. In a global economy dominated by free-market ideology and practices, France's nostalgia for *dirigiste*, corporatist and social-democratic policies appears increasingly quaint and unsustainable. Historians now emphasize that gloomy interpretations of French economic performance had not originated with post-1945 American liberals. In the late nineteenth century technocratic managers were already lamenting France's anti-industrial culture, 'natalists' were alarmed at her 'Malthusian' demography and fearful of German efficiency. Some syndicalists came to argue that France's conflictual industrial relations were engendered by low wages which were themselves the result of French entrepreneurs' failure to match the productivist dynamism of their American counterparts. As Kuisel emphasizes, from the First World War onwards a range of would-be modernizers, including wartime ministers (Clémentel), reformist socialist advocates of 'planning', conservatives (Tardieu) and industrial technocrats (E. Mercier) drew up blueprints for productivist strategies designed to re-invigorate the 'stalemate society'.

Thus a new provisional consensus is emerging among historians who accept *some* of the revisionist evidence about, for example, the flexibility of small-scale production but who conclude not only that interwar depression exposed the bankruptcy of the 'French model' but that the strains were already clearly apparent before 1914. Hence the 1896–1914 economic upturn should be interpreted less as proof of renewed vitality than as the last gasp of an outmoded system. Similarly O'Brien has now re-emphasized that although many peasants *were* resourceful cash-crop farmers and France did export 'high value-added' goods – wines, spirits, dairy produce – nevertheless her agriculture was not internationally competitive in grain or livestock and the slow pace at which labour was leaving that sector meant that there remained sizeable unrealized potential for economic growth – not tapped until after 1945. And although the crisis in proto-industry was sometimes delayed until the 1930s – when, for example, Swiss competition hit peasant watchmakers in the Doubs – elsewhere the writing was on the wall before 1914.

For decades 'artisanal' industry was at the hub of a system in which France produced a smaller quantity of goods but of a higher overall quality, variety and unit-value than technologically advanced Britain. Yet there were ominous signs that this sector could no longer bear the burden of 'carrying' the French economy. Lyonnais silk, now losing its world-market dominance to technologically more advanced competitors, had become, Cayez argues, 'an industry ... partially paralysed by the weight of its past' – though on the outskirts of Lyon heavy engineering and chemical sectors were developing strongly. Although the fashion industry remained proud of the 'artistry' of French design, it was uncomfortably aware, as Green observes, that if foreign and domestic 'taste' deteriorated to levels commonplace in America then the future might belong to competitors better attuned to mass consumer markets. Some revisionist historiography had appeared to stand Gerschenkron's thesis on its head, arguing that since France was not a 'latecomer' but an 'early developer' it had not required support from state or banks to nurture heavy industry but could continue to develop on the basis of its small-scale consumer industries. However, some critics argued, the resultant 'growth' – however respectable – did not constitute the type of *qualitative* industrial transformation needed to maintain France's relative world position. Perhaps it was true that France exhibited precocious 'modernity' in the spread of birth control or pioneered bourgeois consumerism and department stores or maintained niche markets for quality craft exports. But, Locke observes, the harsh facts of the social-Darwinist world of global Realpolitik were that the relative strength of 'great powers' was calculated on the basis of population size and of levels of production in strategic heavy industry – not on contraceptive practices or exports of ladies' fashions.

And, for all its apparent success in sectors of the 'second industrial revolution', France had crucial weak spots. Though she *was* Europe's premier car producer – and despite flirtations by car manufacturers with 'scientific management' – she remained a producer of luxury cars built by teams of skilled workers for élite markets and, even beyond 1918, adapted slowly to the Fordist world of assembly lines, interchangeable parts, concentration and mass markets. Though Lorraine was the continent's second-largest iron and steel region, her firms failed to integrate production processes as efficiently as their German rivals. In basic chemicals, machine-tools and heavy engineering France was marginally inefficient in international terms. In 1913 13.4 per cent of German exports were of machine-tools, only 3.6 per cent of French. Manufactured goods made up 73.9 per cent of French exports in the 1850s, only 58 per cent by 1913 –

during which period her share of world trade fell from 12.8 per cent to 7.2 per cent. There was a danger of being 'squeezed' between technologically superior western competitors and the lower-wage economies of eastern and southern Europe. The decline of the apprentice system left a gap in training of skilled workers which was only partly filled by state-sponsored technical training schemes.

In part – as in Britain – such weaknesses were obscured by the growing role of the colonial empire in the French economy. Although barely 10 per cent of French trade before 1914 was with her 'formal' empire, the percentage was growing – and would expand faster in the interwar period. Colonies did supply important raw materials – rubber, nickel for the steel industry – as well as duplicating some metropolitan products (e.g. wine). But with France controlling two-thirds of all the trade of her colonies these were, as Marseille observes, already providing a 'cushion' which allowed less efficient sectors to find markets whilst delaying rationalization.

Whilst the French economy was clearly capable of bursts of quite impressive expansion, it also appeared peculiarly prone to long, painful downturns such as the three decades after 1865. The collapse of exports to the USA during the Civil War and the ending of the rail-construction boom were followed by a series of blows including the loss of dynamic Alsace. Construction, the accepted 'barometer' of the economy, went into prolonged recession with the curtailment of Haussmann's urban-renewal projects. Phylloxera devastated the vineyards for more than two decades and pebrine destroyed the raw silk crop. The Freycinet Plan revived orders to heavy industry – but these fell back again after the mid-1880s, leaving a prolonged 'hangover' in terms of a budgetary deficit which pushed up taxes and reduced investment. Low passenger and freight usage of the new branch-lines suggested, too, an 'overbuilding' of railways.

Admirers of the 'French model' have too often ignored its socio-political costs. Available statistics do suggest that France was slipping behind major competitors both in productivity and in per-capita income (see tables 14.1 and 14.2).

Table 14.1 Labour productivity

	1855–64	1905–13
Britain	56	90.4
Germany	39	106.8
France	51	83.1

Thus social realities for many obliged to 'live' the 'French model' were less than idyllic. Although French historians have been better at accumulating than at analysing statistics on incomes and wealth, it is clear that economic inequalities remained enormous in industrial cities like Lille. Infant mortality

Table 14.2 Per-capita income

	1870	1910
Britain	904	1302
Germany	579	958
France	567	883

fell only slowly and life expectation rose only very gradually. Conditions in heavy industry for immigrant workers were frequently harsh. Nearly 40 per cent of the labour force was female, and a much higher proportion of married women than in Britain or Germany had paid jobs. But women were paid barely half male wages in textile mills and were often 'sweated' in the garment industry. Many 'artisans' survived – but most had lost any real independence and were being forced to accept falling rates of pay and a measure of sub-division of tasks and of deskilling.

One possible consequence was endemic social conflict. Despite low levels of unionization strikes averaged over 1000 per annum in the 1900s. Nor was social conflict limited to major cities. 'Proto-industrial' female silk-weavers in the Isère countryside were increasingly militant. It was alarm at such social unrest that prompted Méline to seek to slow the pace of industrialization – whilst conversely some syndicalists came to argue that endemic conflict was a product of economic backwardness which was the fault of France's undynamic business class.

In view of the standard liberal critique of 'excessive' French *dirigisme*, it is ironic that Kuisel's persuasive analysis should conclude that the *real* problem in the period after 1880 was not too much governmental interference but too little. Republican élites showed rather less enthusiasm for forcing the pace of economic modernization than their Bonapartist predecessors. Many who studied France's problems concluded that the state's role had become too modest. Whereas Germany had 'modern', 'rational' economic plans, claimed Jean Cruppi (1908), '(here) things run by chance. We depend on our traditions, resources, our refined taste, our soul . . . , our inventive genius.' Ministers were advised by senior civil servants whose doctrinaire *laissez-faire* prejudices warned them that even the post office was an example of creeping state socialism! The republic appeared to lack the will, the ideology, the data or the bureaucratic resources to respond positively to those diverse but vocal critics who argued that there were major flaws in the 'French model' and that the state *had* to play a more direct role in remedying these.

Further reading

Aldrich, R. 'Late-comer or early starter? New views on French economic history', *Journal of European Economic History*, 16 (1987), pp. 89–100.

Cameron, R. 'Was England really superior to France?', *Journal of Economic History*, 46 (1986), pp. 1031–9.

Cameron, R. and Freedeman, C. 'French economic growth: a radical revision', *Social Science History*, 7 (1983).

Cayez, P. *Métiers Jacquards et hauts-fourneaux* (Lyon: Presses Universitaires de Lyon, 1978).

——, 'Une protoindustrialisation décalée: la ruralisation de la soierie lyonnaise dans la première moitié du dix-neuvième siècle', *Revue du Nord*, 63 (Jan.–Mar. 1981), pp. 95–104.

Chaline, J.-P. *Les Bourgeois de Rouen* (Paris: Presses de la FNSP, 1982).

Chassagne, S. *Le Coton et ses patrons: France 1760–1840* (Paris: Editions de L'École des Hautes Études en Sciences Sociales, 1991).

Crafts, N. 'Economic growth in France and Britain, 1830–1914', *Journal of Economic History*, 44 (1984), pp. 48–67.

Crouzet, F. *Britain Ascendant: Comparative Studies in Franco-British Economic History* (Cambridge: Cambridge University Press, 1990).

——, 'France', in M. Teich and R. Porter (eds.), *The Industrial Revolution in National Context* (Cambridge: Cambridge University Press, 1996).

Daviet, J.-P. *Un destin international: la compagnie de St Gobain, 1830–1939* (Paris: Éditions des Archives Contemporaines, 1988).

Deyon, P. 'Protoindustrialisation in France', in S. Ogilvie and M. Cerman (eds.), *European Protoindustrialisation* (Cambridge: Cambridge University Press, 1996), pp. 38–48.

Faure, A. 'Petit atelier et modernité économique', *Histoire, Économie et Société*, 5 (1986), pp. 531–7.

Fohlen, C. 'Entrepreneurs and management in France in the nineteenth century', in P. Mathias and M. Postan (eds.), *Cambridge Economic History of Europe, Vol. VII* (Cambridge: Cambridge University Press, 1977).

Fox, R. *Education, Research and Industrial Performance in France, 1850–1940* (Lancaster: University of Lancaster Press, 1983).

Freedeman, C. *The Triumph of Corporate Capitalism in France 1867–1914* (Rochester, NY: University of Rochester Press, 1993).

Gerschenkron, A. *Economic Backwardness in Historical Perspective* (Cambridge, MA: Harvard University Press, 1962).

Gordon, D. *Liberalism and Social Reform: Industrial Growth and 'Progressiste' Politics in France 1880–1914* (Westport, CT: Greenwood Press, 1996).

Green, N. 'Art and industry: the language of modernisation in the production of fashion', *French Historical Studies*, 18:3 (1994), pp. 722–48.

Gueslin, A. *L'Etat, l'économie et la société française* (Paris: Hachette, 1992).

Gullickson, G. *Spinners and Weavers of Auffay, 1750–1850* (Cambridge: Cambridge University Press, 1986).

Hau, M. *L'Industrialisation de l'Alsace, 1803–1939* (Strasbourg: Publications de l'Université, 1987).

Heywood, C. *The Cotton Industry in France: An Interpretative Essay* (Loughborough: Loughborough University Press, 1972).

——, *The Development of the French Economy 1750–1914* (London: Macmillan, 1992).

Hohenberg, P. 'Change in rural France in the period of industrialisation', *Journal of Economic History*, 32 (1972), pp. 219–40.

Hubscher, R. 'La petite exploitation en France: réproduction et compétivité', *Annales Économie, Société, Civilisation*, 40 (1985).

Johnson, C. *The Life and Death of Industrial Languedoc: 1700–1920* (Oxford: Oxford University Press, 1995).

Jonas, R. *Industry and Politics in Rural France: Peasants of the Isère* (Ithaca, NY: Cornell University Press, 1994).

Kaelble, H. 'French bourgeoisie and German Bürgertum 1870–1914', in J. Kocka and A. Mitchell (eds.), *Bourgeois Society in Nineteenth-Century Europe* (Oxford: Berg, 1993).

Kemp, T. 'French economic performance: some new views critically examined', *European History Quarterly*, 15:4 (1985), pp. 473–8.

Kuisel, *Capitalism and the State in Modern France* (Cambridge: Cambridge University Press, 1981).

Landes, D. 'French business and the businessman: a social and cultural analysis', in H. Aitkin (ed.), *Explorations in Entrepreneurial History* (Cambridge, MA: Harvard University Press, 1965).

——, 'Religion and enterprise: the case of the French textile industry', in E. Carter, R. Forster and J. Moody (eds.), *Enterprise and Entrepreneurs in France* (Baltimore: Johns Hopkins University Press, 1976).

Laux, J. *In First Gear: The French Automobile Industry to 1914* (Liverpool: Liverpool University Press, 1976).

Lebovics, H. *The Alliance of Iron and Wheat: 1860–1914* (Baton Rouge, LA: Louisiana State University Press, 1988).

Lévy-Leboyer, M. and Bourguignon, F. *The French Economy in the Nineteenth Century* (Cambridge: Cambridge University Press, 1990).

Lewis, G. 'Protoindustrialisation in France', *Economic History Review*, 47 (1994), pp. 150–64.

——, *The Advent of Modern Capitalism in France, 1770–1840* (Oxford: Oxford University Press, 1994).

Liu, T. *The Weavers' Knot: Contradictions of Class Struggle and Family Solidarity in Western France, 1750–1914* (Ithaca, NY: Cornell University Press, 1994).

Locke, R. 'French industrialisation: the Roehl thesis reconsidered', *Explorations in Economic History*, 18 (1981), pp. 415–33.

Magraw, R. 'Producing, retailing, consuming: France 1830–70', in B. Rigby (ed.), *French Literature, Thought and Culture in the Nineteenth Century: A Material World* (London: Macmillan, 1993).

Marseille, J. *Empire colonial et capitalisme français: histoire d'un divorce* (Paris: Albin Michel, 1984).

Mesliand, C. *Les Paysans du Vaucluse* (Aix-en-Provence, 1989).

Newell, W. 'The agricultural revolution in nineteenth-century France', *Journal of Economic History*, 33 (1973), pp. 687–731.

Nye, R. 'Firm size and economic backwardness: a new look at French development', *Journal of Economic History*, 47 (1987), pp. 648–68.

——, 'The myth of free-trade Britain and fortress France', *Journal of Economic History*, 51 (1991), pp. 23–46.

O'Brien, P. 'Path dependency, or why Britain became an industrialised economy long before France', *Economic History Review*, 49 (1996), pp. 213–49.

O'Brien, P. and Keydor, C. *Economic Growth in Britain and France: Two Paths to the Twentieth Century* (London: Allen & Unwin, 1978).

Petiteau, N. *L'Horlogerie des bourgeois conquérants, 1789–1939* (Paris: Les Belles Lettres, 1994).

Price, R. *The Modernisation of Rural France* (London: Hutchinson, 1983).

Ratcliffe, R. 'Manufacture in the metropolis: the dynamism and dynamics of Parisian industry in the mid-nineteenth century', *Journal of European Economic History*, 23 (1995), pp. 263–328.

Reid, D. 'Industrial paternalism: discourse and practice in French mining', *Comparative Studies in Society and History*, 27 (1985), pp. 578–607.

Roehl, R. 'French industrialisation: a reconsideration', *Explorations in Economic History*, 13 (1976), pp. 233–81.

Root, H. *Peasant and King in Burgundy* (Berkeley: University of California Press, 1987).

Sabel, C. and Zeitlin, J. 'Historical alternatives to mass production: politics, markets and technology in nineteenth-century industrialisation', *Past and Present*, 108 (1985), pp. 133–76.

Smith, M. *Tariff Reform in France: 1860–1914* (Ithaca, NY: Cornell University Press, 1980).

Smith, T. 'Public assistance and labor supply in nineteenth-century Lyon', *Journal of Modern History*, 68 (1996), pp. 1–30.

Walton, W. *France at the Crystal Palace: Bourgeois Taste and Artisan Manufacture in the Nineteenth Century* (Berkeley: University of California Press, 1992).

Williams, R. *Dream Worlds: Mass Consumption in Nineteenth-Century France* (Berkeley: University of California Press, 1982).

Woronoff, D. *Histoire de l'industrie en France* (Paris: Éditions du Seuil, 1994).

|15|

The French economy since 1930

KENNETH MOURÉ

L'horreur économique. One year after publication in 1996, Viviane Forrester's essay with this title had sold 330 000 copies and was being translated
into 15 languages. It is an impassioned critique of the triumph of market
capitalism and *la pensée unique* – the seemingly absolute dominance of free-
market principles in policy discussion. Forrester argues that globalization
has increased opportunities for speculation and dissimulation and moved us
from industrial capitalism to a *capitalisme électronique* with little need for
employees, less social responsibility, and no means for public control. In an
economy in which capitalist profit no longer requires employees, and a
society in which employment determines social status and utility, only a few
short steps are needed to pass from exploitation to exclusion, and from
exclusion to elimination. Sceptics claim that the title alone made Forrester's
essay a surprise best-seller, and that few readers ventured beyond the
opening pages. Yet more than the title struck a chord. An affluent audience
feared that France was particularly vulnerable to the adverse consequences
of global economic change. Growth of the French economy (in terms of gross
domestic product, GDP) had slowed to an annual average of 1.1 per cent in
the period 1991–6, unemployment exceeded 12 per cent, and economic
pessimism ran high. The slump was the worst in France since the 1930s.

Just as Forrester warns of the dangers of post-industrial capitalism, some
observers in the 1930s feared that industrialization tended inevitably to
produce massive unemployment and underconsumption, and that compensatory action by the state was necessary to preserve a traditional
economy and guarantee citizens 'the right to work'. They were less dramatic
in their critiques of economic development: Forrester warns against the
revival of a 'latent barbarism' revealed in the eliminationist policies of
governments during and after the Second World War. Superficial comparisons between the French economy in the 1930s and the 1990s would note
similarities in the rising unemployment, slower growth, lower investment,
economic pessimism, and fears that France was losing rank in the world

economic order. Viewed historically, however, the transformation of the French economy since 1930 has been massive, and in conjunction with the changes to the global economy, the differences between the French economy in the 1930s and the 1990s are far more striking than the similarities. The French economy has undergone a process of transformation notable for its rapidity and for its success. The similarities are not without significance, but they must be seen in the context of dramatic changes in the global economy and in the structure and resources of the national economy in France.

This chapter surveys the development of the French economy since 1930, treating French experience in three periods. The first covers the years of Depression and war, singular for the duration of the slump in the 1930s and for the impact of occupation and war, resulting in significant decline for an economy only partially modernized. The second section covers from 1945 to 1973, the economist Jean Fourastié's *trente glorieuses* (thirty glorious years),[1] a period of rapid and in most respects successful modernization of the French economy and society. The third section considers French experience since 1973 to assess how continuing changes in the French economy have produced the current malaise – the point of departure for Forrester's essay.

The overview highlights two key factors in French modernization: the contribution of government policy and the opening of the French economy to world trade. French economic development since 1945 has been directed by an interventionist state. The state contributed substantially to the speed and success of French economic modernization in the years after the war; it now plays a large part in current difficulties, as its size and its influence in the economy are a part of the problem and thus must inevitably play a role in any solution. The French response to the world Depression in the 1930s was to intensify protectionist policies and to retreat from world markets. The reopening of the French economy and its progressive liberalization since 1945 have been essential to the modernization process, and France's economic future has been linked securely to the development of the European Union. These changes have encouraged competition and growth, but have rendered the economy more vulnerable to economic shocks from abroad.

Les années noires, 1930–1945

In January 1930, as other industrialized countries succumbed to the worst depression in history, the French economy enjoyed its third year of strong growth. Since 1918 France had repaired most of the material damage suffered during the First World War and had achieved a surge of new growth after the stabilization of the franc in 1926. French observers took pride in their country's immunity to depression. Their economy, they claimed, exhibited a perfect balance between agriculture and industry (agriculture still employing nearly one-third of French workers). They praised French producers for having refrained from the abuse of credit, overproduction and overconsumption that had generated the artificial level of prosperity now crumbling elsewhere, particularly in the United States and Britain. The Depression abroad was seen as the inevitable consequence of overexpansion; France would be spared the pains of economic contraction because it had eschewed the quick profits of a *prospérité factice* (artificial prosperity). (Many French producers were less sanguine about French immunity to the crisis and prospects for recovery than commentators in the press and parliament.)

But France was not immune to the Depression. Industrial production peaked in May 1930; French GDP then fell by more than 10 per cent, and industrial production fell 30 per cent to touch cyclical lows in 1932 and again in 1935. Most developed countries began to recover in 1932, and surpassed 1929 levels of production in the later 1930s. The French economy slumped from 1933 to 1935, stalled in 1937–8, and did not regain its 1929 level of industrial production until 1950. Defeat and occupation plunged France still deeper in decline. France never fully escaped its depression in the 1930s, going from a limited recovery to full mobilization, and then to 4 years of severe economic exploitation under German occupation. The duration of the slump and the pillaging of the French economy during the war mark the period from 1930 to 1945 as one of exceptional decline: industrial production in 1944 stood at 30 per cent of its 1929 peak, and GDP per capita had fallen by nearly half since 1938. Figure 15.1 shows this decline in comparison with indexed real GDP (1913 = 100) for Germany, Britain and the United States from 1920 to 1944. Midway through this period, from 1932, the French path clearly departs from the upward trend for other industrialized nations, remaining flat through the rest of the 1930s and dropping steeply during the war.

Several factors cushioned the impact of the Depression in France. The size of the agricultural sector rendered the national impact of industrial contraction less severe, but it hurt recovery prospects as falling agricultural prices reduced demand from one-third of the population. (Estimates of the decline in agricultural purchasing power from 1929 to 1935 vary from 10 per cent to 33 per cent. Prices had already fallen significantly since 1926, and purchasing power would have fallen further but for increased output and protectionism.) Many foreign workers recruited in the 1920s were put out of work in the 1930s; working time was reduced in some industries; only limited relief programmes were available for the unemployed. All these factors reduced the officially recorded levels of unemployment. The undervaluation of the franc in 1926 encouraged economic growth in the late 1920s, as did government spending, increased in the belief that tax receipts would continue to rise, producing 'involuntary' deficit spending from 1929 to 1931.

The lessons learned from currency instability and inflation in the 1920s were then applied to the problems of economic contraction and overvalued currency in a world of falling prices. State policy in the 1930s was contradictory and erratic. It applied a mixture of orthodox financial measures and protectionism, and resorted to decree powers to circumvent parliamentary divisions when chronic financial difficulties provoked monetary crises. Economic policy in the Third Republic had been dominated by liberal ideals of minimal state intervention, seeking to preserve the balance of the nineteenth-century economy and to protect French agriculture and business. The ministry of finance sought to balance the state budget, not to promote economic growth. From 1931 to 1936 French governments focused, with a singlemindedness worthy of a better cause, on preventing a second devaluation of the franc. Restrictive monetary and fiscal policies curtailed investment, production and commerce, increased unemployment, and raised real interest rates, in a vain effort to match devaluations abroad through domestic deflation. At the same time, protectionist tariffs and import quotas were employed to protect politically sensitive sectors of the French economy against falling world prices, agriculture in particular, countering state efforts to lower domestic prices.

There is substantial agreement among historians on the origins and nature of the slump in France. The strength of the French economy in 1928–30 was thanks in part to a deliberate undervaluation of the franc in order to reduce

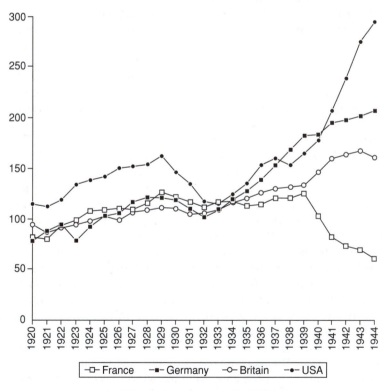

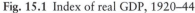

Fig. 15.1 Index of real GDP, 1920–44

the domestic economic adjustment to stabilization. It was also a product of Premier Raymond Poincaré's fiscal policies, which promoted a surge in public and private investment in 1929–30. Export industries stimulated by the fall of the franc suffered contracting markets as soon as the franc was stabilized, but it was global depression in 1929 that brought sharp decline. The contraction of world trade was aggravated by the depreciation of sterling and other currencies after September 1931, which further curtailed French exports, and clearly overvalued the franc. Why the French were determined to remain on gold and defend the *franc Poincaré* is also clear: policy-makers were convinced that inflation and devaluation were inextricably linked, and that it was essential to avoid both in order to maintain a secure basis for economic recovery.

More controversial is the degree to which not just the policy-makers but the French business world can be characterized as 'Malthusian' at this time. Alfred Sauvy used the term to link France's slow population growth to an economic mentality fearing change and promoting stagnation rather than growth, a state of mind that 'produced actions aimed at the destruction of riches or the limitation of production'.[2] Revisionist research has undermined the Malthusian case; as Jean Bouvier has noted, 'the constant litany of retardation ... in the end renders inexplicable the visible, sustained growth, and the changes to and the deepening of French capitalism'.[3] But revisionist attention to the dynamic elements in French capitalism cannot efface the contrary examples of protectionism, low investment, and a willingness to sacrifice economic growth to concerns for social and political stability in what Stanley Hoffmann characterized as a 'stalemate society'. The charge of Malthusianism carries particular weight for the 1930s, when legislators passed measures to restrict competition and protect inefficient producers. As Sauvy admits, 'Malthusianism' can be difficult to distinguish from simple bad policy.

In May 1936 France elected a Popular Front coalition headed by Socialist Party leader Léon Blum that promised to abandon deflation without recourse to devaluation and seek recovery through reflation. The left's electoral victory prompted massive wildcat strikes, involving some 2 million workers, in anticipation of working-class gains. The unexpected and uncoordinated strikes radicalized the Popular Front's social programme, and in so doing aggravated tensions between capital and labour and provoked powerful *patronat* (employers') resistance to the social-reform measures passed in June 1936 to end the strikes. It also increased the inflationary pressures inherent in the Popular Front programme, driving the already overvalued franc off gold in September 1936. The most contentious reform was a reduction of the working week to 40 hours without loss of pay. According to Sauvy and other critics, the 40-hours law choked off the recovery that should have taken place after devaluation. The law, intended to increase employment, curtailed production instead, its intent frustrated by inflexibility in its application on the part of both unions and employers. In his analysis of the law's impact,

Jean-Charles Asselain concludes that the law was economically mistaken, but politically unavoidable.

The socialists progressively abandoned reflation, reform and finally power. The subsequent dismantling of Popular Front reforms, the reassertion of *patronat* authority in 1938–9, and subsequent Vichy measures against organized labour and Popular Front leaders were seen by many as a 'revenge of the bosses' for the Popular Front's challenge to their authority. After a deliberate undervaluation of the franc in May 1938 and the failure of a general strike in November (to protest about the suspension of Popular Front reforms, particularly the 40-hour week), business confidence revived, easing the financial constraints on the treasury and facilitating increased state investment in defence and rearmament that helped fuel a new recovery. But 1929 levels of production had not been regained when mobilization for war reallocated productive resources to national defence, and converted the French economy to a war footing.

War severely dislocated the French economy; the Nazi occupation brought brutal exploitation. Germany extracted resources from France in two forms: cash payments, via inflated occupation costs, and goods seized outright or purchased at exploitative prices. As one treasury official put it, 'the Germans seized our finances in order to buy our economy'.[4] French cash payments to Germany totalled over 860 000 billion francs. The occupation costs and an exploitative exchange rate made these payments impossible without recourse to inflation. French production was geared for the Nazi war economy, with labour and raw materials allocated according to the importance of particular goods for German needs. The armaments, transport and construction sectors were particularly useful for German military purposes. French output fell dramatically owing to a smaller labour force (1.8 million prisoners of war; 700 000 workers on labour service in Germany) and sharply reduced supplies of raw materials, energy and foodstuffs. The most heavily industrialized regions in the north and north-east were either annexed outright (Alsace and Lorraine) or placed under direct German military control (the Nord and Pas de Calais). German policy sought to maximize output with minimal concern for maintenance and reinvestment. Germany drew more from France than from any other occupied country, and at relatively low cost; in 1943, in addition to occupation costs and compulsory labour, Germany took 40 per cent of French industrial output.

By 1944 French industrial production had fallen to a miserable 30 per cent of its 1929 peak; agricultural production had fallen by nearly half. Official rations allowed French citizens only 1200 calories per day in 1944; per-capita consumption of meat, vegetables and sugar had fallen by half since 1938; real wages had fallen more than 40 per cent, partly to encourage French labour to work in Germany. When liberated in 1944, the French economy had suffered serious deterioration of infrastructure and capital equipment. Reconstruction would have to repair not only the damage done by the war, but the decline produced by low investment during nearly a decade of Depression. Frances Lynch comments of this period 1930 to 1945 that 'No other major economy had fallen so far behind in such a relatively short period of time.'[5]

The defeat in 1940 demonstrated not just that social and political stability were at stake in economic performance, but that the economic strength of the nation played a critical role in its very survival. The meagre results achieved by orthodoxy in the 1930s prompted a rethinking of policy and the role of the state, which began during the 1930s and accelerated significantly when the fall of France dramatized the consequences of economic decline. This rethinking marked an important shift away from the essentially financial concerns that had dominated interwar thought, towards state economic planning to encourage growth.

Within France, the Vichy administration sought to work with German authorities to build a place for France in the Nazi New Order. Vichy increased state intervention in order to allocate scarce productive resources and forestall direct German control over the French economy. New administrative structures were created, most notably a planning commission (the Délégation Général à l'Équipement National) and a ministry of industry, staffed by a younger, technocratic élite that believed state management essential to recreate France as a modern economic power. But Vichy planning had little impact. The planners had no real power, and their room for manoeuvre was narrowly constrained by the need to meet German exactions that had nothing to do with modernizing the French economy. Furthermore, Vichy plans were contradictory. Marshal Philippe Pétain claimed Vichy would preserve French social and economic life by a 'return to the soil'. His constitutional reform promised that 'France will become once more a predominantly agricultural and peasant nation, and will reap the benefits from this return'.[6] Yet any plans to restore France as an economic power would inevitably require industrialization, with greater efficiency and fewer workers in agriculture. Vichy collaboration facilitated German exploitation without gaining more than palliatives for the French economy. As Henry Rousso notes of the apologetic wartime aphorism that one could not reconstruct one's house while it was in flames, 'To reconstruct a burning house is difficult enough; to do so with he who has just set fire to it smacks of recklessness, complicity, or perversion.'[7] Vichy did, however, develop a state apparatus for collecting economic data and directing the economy, and it drew energetic new personnel into state planning. It also made a significant negative contribution in the discredit earned by collaborationist administrators and encouragement of businesses to work for the Germans. The political and social consensus in favour of extensive nationalizations, shared by liberals and socialists, was a by-product of Vichy and business collaboration.

Economic planners in Charles de Gaulle's Free French forces, too, realized that national strength and independence required modernization. They also recognized that social and political problems could be more easily managed by sharing the product of a growing economy than by reapportioning wealth in an economy stagnating to preserve stability. Resistance planners were interested not only in European integration (of independent states, not under German hegemony), but in developing Atlantic economic relations with France's wartime allies. This would create an economy more open to trade than the Vichy planners intended; it would also open the tap for allied resources to finance reconstruction and renewal after the war. Resisters called explicitly for a fundamental change in monetary and financial policies, using these as tools to foster growth rather than to preserve stability, and they advocated the creation of a permanent state council to direct investment. Their plans for modernization were not contradicted by a rhetoric of 'return to the soil'. Wartime studies showed how poorly maintained French industrial plant had been even before the war. In 1939 the average age of French machinery was 25 years; in SNCF (nationalized railway) workshops it was 30 years; in 'new' industries it was 20 years for the automobile industry, 16 years for the machine-tool industry, 14 years in the aircraft industry. In contrast, British plant was estimated to have an average age of under 7 years, American plant less than 5.

At the end of the war, in grim material circumstances, French planners faced reconstruction committed to economic modernization, a more open and liberal economy, and a stronger state role, particularly in directing investment to maximize growth, raise productivity and increase the standard of living. Nationalizations were accepted as a necessary means to restore order to the French economy, facilitate control of key sectors, and punish collaborationist owners. The scale of the reconstruction and modernization necessary, the paucity of physical and financial resources, and the immediate needs of a population suffering from the war and 4 years of occupation made state economic planning and direction essential, in order to make optimal use of limited financial resources and to recover the ground lost in the previous 15 years. Unlike 1918, no one wished a return to pre-war experience, distinguished as it was by stagnation. One French planner, Robert Marjolin, stated that for him and others such as Raymond Aron, Jean Fourastié and Alfred Sauvy, the interwar years had been a history of 'complete moral and intellectual bankruptcy'.[8] The task ahead was formidable: 25 per cent of French capital had been destroyed, compared to an estimated 10 per cent in the First World War. If France was to aspire to greatness, planner Jean Monnet told Charles de Gaulle, economic modernization was essential. They faced an urgent choice between economic modernization and national decline.[9]

Modernization, 1945–1973

For some post-war observers, the dismal performance of the French economy since 1930 seemed to be the latest chapter in a tale of chronic French failure to meet the challenges of industrialization and modernization. David

Landes, Herbert Leuthy, Warren C. Baum and Jessie R. Pitts, among others, saw France as a country whose economic development was stalled (or worse) by anti-economic attitudes that retarded the modernization and growth of the French economy. Since then, economic historians have recognized that to seek an imitation of British or American practice is to miss distinctive characteristics of French economic development, and that processes of industrialization and modernization need not follow a single path. The gloomy prognoses for French economic retardation were contradicted by the dramatic successes of post-war modernization. In the 30 years following the war, France accomplished a rapid and successful modernization, with sustained growth that increased in tempo in the 1960s, surpassing West German growth rates in the period 1960–73.

Jean Fourastié termed the changes a *révolution invisible*; French sociologist Henri Mendras, fixing on the social changes resulting from economic modernization, described the period 1965–84 as a 'second revolution', the greatest change in French society since the Revolutionary era of 1789–1815. Employment in agriculture declined sharply, and urbanization and rising real wages established the basis for a society and economy based on mass consumption. The economy was opened significantly to international competition, and exports were reoriented towards technologically advanced goods for a European market. The colonial empire France was losing played a diminishing role in its external trade. Higher education expanded dramatically, providing a more highly skilled labour force. State intervention through nationalizations and indicative planning established a more powerful role for the state in the economy, and the extension of state responsibility for social welfare provided greater social security.

Several statistical indicators for the period covered in this chapter illustrate the magnitude of change:

1 The decline of employment in the agricultural sector is perhaps the most significant indicator of modernization. Table 15.1 shows the changes from 1870 to 1993 in the structure of the French labour force as divided between agricultural, industrial and service-sector employment. From 1950 to 1990 agricultural output more than doubled, while the agricultural workforce fell from 6 millions to 1 million and France became the world's second-largest exporter of agricultural goods. From 1949 to 1969 productivity per man hour in agriculture increased at an annual average of 6.4 per cent, compared to 5.3 per cent in industry. From 1946 to 1975 agriculture's share of the national labour force fell by 72 per cent; industry's increased by 20 per cent and the service sector's by 66 per cent.

2 The transfer of labour from agriculture to industry and services took place with remarkably little change in the size of the labour force. In 1913 the labour force exceeded 21 million, a level it would not regain until the 1970s. From 1918 to the mid-1960s it remained at roughly 20 million workers. A post-war population boom ended decades of population stagnation (over 38 million in 1870, the French population reached 40 million in 1924 and did

Table 15.1 Structure of the labour force (%)

Year	Agriculture	Industry	Services
1870	49.0	28.0	23.0
1913	37.4	33.8	28.8
1929	32.5	36.6	30.9
1938	31.4	32.3	36.3
1946	36.0	32.0	32.0
1968	14.6	38.9	46.5
1979	8.6	35.3	56.1
1993	5.1	27.7	67.2
Germany, 1993	3.3	37.6	59.1
USA, 1993	2.9	24.0	73.1

Sources: Carré, Dubois and Malinvaud, *French Economic Growth*; Organization for Economic Cooperation and Development (OECD), *Economic Surveys: France*

not show sustained increase until the mid-1940s), increasing to 50 million in 1969 and to 58 million in 1995. But French baby-boomers did not enter the labour market until the mid-1960s, making the 20 years after 1945 a period of population growth that increased demand while the labour force remained stable. This encouraged investment and improvements in productivity, and facilitated the maintenance of full employment. After 1965 the labour force increased steadily as baby-boomers sought employment and women's participation rate increased. From 1965 to 1995 the labour force increased from 20 to 25 millions. Demand for employment thus increased as economic growth slowed, making it more difficult to accommodate new workers.

3 The exceptional character of French growth in GDP in the 30 years after 1945 is readily evident in comparing medium-term periods before and afterwards (see Table 15.2). GDP growth averaged 1.9 per cent per annum in the 'strong' growth from 1896 to 1913; from 1913 to 1938 it averaged barely 1 per cent, declining in the 1930s, and it fell steeply during the occupation. From 1945 to 1975 GDP growth in France averaged 6.8 per cent per annum, with rapid recovery during the period of reconstruction to 1950, slower but steady growth at over 4 per cent in the 1950s, then rapid growth of 5.7 per cent in the 1960s and of 5.6 per cent to 1973, exceeding that of West Germany after 1960. In France, and elsewhere in Europe, these rates reflected a 'catching up' to American growth, which had consistently exceeded European growth rates from 1870 to 1945.

These rates substantially surpassed the historic norms for annual GDP growth in Europe, and French growth rates in the period 1945–73 were better than the European average, surpassed only by Japanese and German

Table 15.2 Key economic indicators, trends over time (average annual % increase)

Date	GDP growth	Unemployment	Productivity	Inflation (CPI)
1896–1913	1.9		2.0	
1913–1929	1.5	1.8	2.4	
1929–1938	−0.3	3.3	2.1	
1945–1951	8.7	< 1.0		28.2
1952–1959	4.2	2.0	4.3	3.3
1959–1969	5.7	1.8	4.8	3.9
1969–1973	5.6	2.6	6.3	6.2
1973–1979	3.0	4.5	4.8	10.7
1980–1991	2.1	8.4	2.0	6.6
1991–1996	1.1	11.3	1.3	1.9

Sources: IMF, World Economic Outlook; Asselain, *Histoire économique de la France*; Carré, Dubois and Malinvaud, *French Economic Growth*; OFCE, *L'économie française 1997*

growth rates. Even more impressive was the increase in productivity. The historical norm for European members of the OECD in 1870–1950 had been an average of 1.2 per cent per year. From 1950 to 1973 the OECD Europe average was 4.1 per cent; French productivity increased at an average rate of 5.5 per cent.

4 The French economy was opened to world trade and the share of traded goods in French GDP increased. French foreign trade grew slightly faster than GDP from 1896 to 1913; from 1930 to 1945 it fell sharply. Exports peaked at 18.9 per cent of GDP in 1926, encouraged by the fall of the franc; by 1936 they had retreated to less than 5 per cent. In the 1930s French trade turned to the protected markets of its empire, unable to compete elsewhere. Table 15.3 shows the post-war shift in French trade from its colonies to the OECD and Europe; from 1952 to 1984 the share of French exports going to colonies and former colonies declined from 42.2 per cent to 9.3 per cent, while the share of trade (chiefly in manufactured goods) with its Common-Market partners increased rapidly. Until the creation of the European Common Market in 1959, the French economy was protected by an elaborate network of tariffs and quantitative controls. An attempt to lower French trade barriers prematurely in 1950–1 produced a large trade deficit and prompted a hasty retreat. Fears that French industry could not compete with production abroad stalled French acceptance of proposals for a European customs union until the mid-1950s. Two further devaluations in 1957 and 1958 and a narrowing of the productivity gap during the 1950s made French industry more competitive, and joining the Common Market was one way of pushing producers to meet foreign competition within controlled conditions.

From 1959 to 1974 French trade increased by 10.8 per cent per year (in volume), and the export share of French GDP climbed from 10 per cent in 1958 to 17 per cent in 1970. Thus the strongest phase of sustained growth coincided with the opening of the French economy and strong export growth.

Table 15.3 Share of French exports by destination (%)

Year	French Overseas Union	OECD	Original EEC
1952	42.2	43.2	15.9
1958	37.5	46.6	22.2
1963	19.6	66.3	38.3
1968	13.5	70.0	43.0
1973	9.2	76.1	48.6
1979	9.5	69.6	42.6
1984	9.3	68.0	37.3
1991	7.0	81.7	43.7
1995		79.6	40.6

Sources: Adams, *Restructuring the French Economy*; OECD, *France 1997*

5   Modernization involved a major increase in government participation in economic activity and economic planning. Total government disbursements (state spending, local authorities and social security) as a percentage of French GDP had climbed from 8.9 per cent in 1913 to 21.9 per cent in 1930 and to 26.5 per cent in 1938. After 1945 government spending increased through greater economic intervention and social-welfare spending. It climbed from 40.8 per cent in 1947 to over 50 per cent of GDP during the Algerian war, and has fluctuated close to 50 per cent thereafter. The share of national state spending in total expenditure declined from 35.8 per cent in 1956 to 26 per cent in the early 1970s, while local-government and social-security expenditure both increased significantly. Social-security spending, less than 1 per cent of GDP in the interwar period, jumped to 8.1 per cent in 1947, doubled by 1980 to 16.1 per cent, and has climbed since then to more than 20 per cent. Since the mid-1970s, an ageing population and slower GDP growth has meant social spending takes an ever larger share of GDP.

How were these sweeping economic changes accomplished? Consciousness of the extent and the cost of French economic retardation and a strong consensus on the need for increased government direction provided the point of departure for a strong state role in French economic recovery and renovation after the war. The Vichy state had established statistical services, planning bodies and organizational committees to enable state direction of the economy; Free French planners emphasized modernization, an economy open to trade, and state planning to direct investment and promote modernization. In the months immediately following the war, the state increased its role in the economy through a wave of nationalizations (December 1944 to May 1946) and the adoption of a plan for economic modernization.

The nationalizations brought key sectors of the economy under state control – credit, in order to prevent the use of financial resources for political ends and to mobilize them for purposes of modernization; energy, particularly coal, electricity and gas, as public utilities; transport, mainly aircraft (the railways had been taken over in 1937); and a handful of firms either guilty of collaboration or of significance for national defence purposes. The charter of the National Resistance Council (CNR) had called for nationalizations in order to create 'a true economic and social democracy' in France; to bring public services, monopolies and the nation's financial resources under public control. Direction by the state was intended to remedy the dismal entrepreneurial performance of the 1930s, to punish *patronat* collaboration and profiteering during the war, and to facilitate state direction of economic renewal. French business leadership could not mount effective opposition, as it had been discredited by its collaboration with Germany and cooperation with the Vichy state. The nationalizations were less extensive than the CNR had desired, but by 1948 the state employed one-quarter of the workforce outside of agriculture, and the output of state enterprises accounted for 14 per cent of French industrial production.

State direction of economic renewal was considered essential in order to overcome *patronat* resistance and 'Malthusianism', and to put scarce financial and productive resources to the best possible use. Resistance planners estimated that up to 30 per cent of GDP would need to be channelled into investment in the years following the war, which would entail a reduced level of consumption for a public that had already suffered 4 years of wartime deprivation, and state-directed allocation of limited financial and material resources. The system of French 'indicative planning' – state-defined objectives for investment and goals for production at a sectoral level, with relevant industries cooperating to achieve sectoral targets – was the product of a substantial consensus on the need for a break with the dismal performance of the previous 15 years.

Charles de Gaulle, awed by American prosperity when he visited the United States in August 1945, was persuaded that France had to modernize to survive. In January 1946 he created the Commissariat Général du Plan (CGP), responsible directly to the head of government rather than the ministry of finance, to draft a plan for economic modernization. The CGP was instructed to develop a plan that would increase production and trade, improve productivity to a level competitive with major industrial countries, ensure full employment and raise the standard of living. Its director, Jean Monnet, held a key position to link modernization planning and the possibilities for external finance, and he was uniquely qualified to take advantage of this opportunity. He brought to his post expertise in international banking, business, state finance and international cooperation, and strong connections with the administrative and financial élites in London and Washington. Rather than use the CGP as a central planning agency for a command economy, Monnet's approach was to consult widely and seek consensus among the industries to be affected, and to coordinate investment plans with opportunities for external financial assistance. The CGP's temporary appointment – initially for six months – and its responsibility to the head of state rather than to the ministry of finance freed the CGP from established institutional controls and supervision in developing its plan, although ultimately it needed to persuade the government and parliament to adopt the plan devised.

The first plan, developed under Monnet's direction, called for investment in six sectors on which future economic growth would depend, seeking to modernize plant and break production bottlenecks in coal, steel, electricity, transport, cement and agricultural machinery. Light industry and consumer goods would have to wait until the heavy industrial base and transportation had been renewed. The plan was extended to 1953 in order to coincide with the term of the European Recovery Programme (ERP; the American programme for Marshall-Plan aid to Europe), and overfulfilled most of its targets. The post-war nationalizations made the direction of investment by the Monnet Plan somewhat less critical; state investment would in any case have concentrated in the state-owned sector. But Monnet and the CGP provided coordination in two significant directions. Within France, they worked with modernization commissions drawing on hundreds of businessmen, farmers, administrators and consumers to make the planning a collective process. Outside France, they coordinated French planning to capitalize on the opportunities for financial assistance, particularly through American lending and the ERP. American aid to France from 1945 to January 1953 totalled nearly $11 000 million. Even when these funds were not directly invested in modernization or in machinery and energy imports, they eased the tight financial constraints on the French state, freeing resources for investment.

Subsequent plans broadened their scope to French manufacturing in general and sought to develop French industry to face foreign competition, to open the economy to European and world trade, and to encourage investment from the private sector. The state role in financing investment was reduced, and the planning process became ever more technical, shifting from macro-economic to micro-economic management and becoming increasingly politicized as policy formulation by professional planners gave way to ministerial influence. The results were mixed, with real success in the critical first decade in laying the foundations for growth, encouraging competitiveness and opening the French economy. In the 1960s indicative planning yielded ground to an industrial policy designed to create 'national champions' through increased industrial rationalization and concentration, and improved international competitiveness, in fields such as the aerospace, telecommunications, computer and petroleum industries. In addition, *grands projets* such as the Concorde aircraft, the new airport at Roissy, the Airbus, and nuclear technology, were undertaken in part for reasons of prestige.

Active state intervention and management was not the only fundamental difference from interwar experience. A second was the change in attitude towards the place of France in the international economy. In the 1930s France had retreated from world commerce behind protectionist tariffs and import quotas; the French share of world exports fell by nearly half between 1929 and 1937, with a large share of remaining exports going to the French empire. After 1945 French planners realized that economic progress required re-integration into the world economy, and aimed at modernizing and expanding French manufacturing to be competitive internationally. French trade policy remained protectionist until the end of the 1950s; liberalization then opened the economy and trade became a motor for economic growth.

A third difference was a new willingness to yield ground on monetary and price stability, giving priority to investment and economic growth. This willingness was never unequivocal or uncontroversial; inflation was the most persistent problem successive governments had to face, and the choice between inflation and austerity had to be made repeatedly. The inflation rate in France ran slightly higher than the OECD average throughout this period (see Table 15.4), and significantly higher than the West German rate. The higher levels of inflation in France were compensated in international exchange by a series of devaluations of the franc. By the late 1960s inflation in France was again rising, pushed by labour costs (real wages increased at an annual rate of 6.2 per cent from 1970 to 1973; wages had been increased by 10 per cent in the rue de Grenelle accords that helped end the general strike in May 1968).

Table 15.4 Inflation-rate trends, average annual percentage change

	1948–52	1952–61	1961–9	1969–73	1973–9
France	14.1	3.3	4.0	6.2	10.7
Germany	0.4	1.3	2.5	5.3	4.6
UK	5.2	2.4	3.8	8.0	15.6
OECD Europe	5.1	2.3	3.7	6.4	10.9
US	2.5	1.3	2.6	4.9	8.5

Source: Christopher Allsopp, 'Inflation', in Boltho (ed.), *The European Economy*

The 30 years after 1945 were 'glorious' for most western economies. No single factor can explain this growth, which was the product of a combination of elements and circumstances that varied in different countries. Labour supplies were relatively elastic and wage demands moderate; in the French case the new labour for industry and services came mainly from the under-employed in the agricultural sector. Population growth increased demand for housing, household goods and services. The capital for reconstruction and modernization, often drawn from the United States, facilitated higher levels of investment in infrastructure and capital goods than would otherwise have been possible, and the import of capital goods helped narrow the European 'technology gap' with American producers. Increased government spending on capital projects, social welfare and defence boosted demand and invest-ment. Countercyclical policies and a commitment to maintaining full employment stabilized demand and sustained growth. International efforts to reduce trade barriers and stabilize currencies, implemented in stages, encouraged trade and economic interdependency without causing excessive domestic strains through systemic rigidities.

The French experience was distinctive for the sustained growth that took place, particularly in contrast to previous French experience. Early accounts such as those by Aron and Kindleberger stressed the importance of new men and new attitudes in reshaping public policy, private enterprise and public acceptance of rapid modernization in the context of a mixed economy with significant state intervention. Subsequent studies (Fourquet, Kuisel, Mar-gairaz, Sautter and others) have generally sustained this view, and even economists using quantitative approaches (Caron and Malinvaud) have given substantial credit to public policy and planning. William James Adams tested three hypotheses to assess the extent and reasons for the structural transformation of the French economy since 1945. He found first, that structural reform did take place (rather than economic growth without reform), and second, that government policy played a significant part in resource allocation and structural reform in targeted industries, although its impact was limited to a narrow band of industries within a wider band of growth. Third, he found that market competition played a significant role in driving structural reform, with competition against European competitors in particular forcing the pace of French modernization. Adams argues that government policy and market competition complemented each other, and that this complementarity was 'essential to French success'.[10] Successful government policy and private-sector development in this period were built on a social consensus accepting modernization on the assumption that 'everyone would benefit from growth, that growth was self-sustaining and continuous and that adaptation and inflation were acceptable costs'.[11] After 1973, however, inflation became much less acceptable, growth did not prove to be self-sustaining or continuous, and the costs and benefits of adaptation no longer seemed to be distributed equitably.

Adjusting to slower growth

For western economies accustomed to steady growth at near full employment the shock of inflation, slow growth and higher unemployment after 1973 provoked sharp swings in economic policy, with a turn towards restrictive monetary policies, fiscal restraint and the privatization of public enterprises. 'Keynesian' management to maintain full employment was abandoned in favour of monetarist policies to control inflation, a move seen most clearly in Prime Minister Margaret Thatcher's Britain. In France the state had been more consistent and more successful in guiding economic growth and providing public goods. The change in state policy took place in a different fashion; surprisingly, it did so with a government of the left, not the right, in power.

The first 'oil shock' in 1973 – the quadrupling of the price of crude oil by petroleum-exporting countries – gave a powerful push to inflationary pressures already at work. Since 1950 France had turned to petroleum as its main energy resource, a logical choice given easy availability and falling price. In 1973 imported fuels provided 76 per cent of France's energy needs. In 1974 the cost of imported petroleum jumped from 1.5 to 4.5 per cent of French GDP. Conservation measures and shifting to alternative energy sources cut French petroleum consumption by nearly half between 1973 and 1986, and reduced petroleum's share of French energy consumption from 70 per cent to 43 per cent. But the oil shock was an aggravating factor, not the origin of the slow-down in western economies.

The inflationary current under way since the late 1960s was accelerated in France not just by rising energy prices, but by high wage-demands – nominal wages increased 20 per cent in 1974 and 16 per cent in 1975, and rising labour costs cut into competitiveness and profits. The trade balance deteriorated and investment declined. By 1979 unemployment had reached 6 per cent and GDP growth had slowed to an annual rate of 3 per cent. State policy attempted countercyclical demand stimulus in 1974–5, treating the slow-down and rising unemployment as a temporary, cyclical crisis. This fuelled inflation, and in 1976 President Giscard d'Estaing (1974–81) called on the economist Raymond Barre to take over as prime minister and minister of the economy. Barre implemented an austerity programme that curbed inflation and checked the deterioration of the balance of payments, and adopted liberal measures to encourage private-sector initiatives.

But by the end of the Giscard presidency slower growth, rising unemployment, reduced profits and declining investment led to widespread discontent with state policy. Seeking to maintain employment, state support had shifted from promoting 'national champions' to providing emergency assistance to 'lame ducks' (firms unable to survive without assistance) in the declining sectors of the French economy, particularly textiles, shipbuilding and the steel industry. State-led investment since the war had produced overcommitment in sectors involving medium technology, and France was losing out to

Germany, Japan and the United States in high-technology industries, particularly information and business technology. Restructuring was needed to cut costs and production in declining sectors. The open French economy was more vulnerable to global recession, to French costs rising more rapidly than those abroad (particularly labour costs), and to sustained overvaluation of the franc. In 1979 Barre also brought the franc into the European Monetary System (EMS), the European Community's replacement for the Bretton Woods system for fixed exchange rates that had collapsed in 1971. This limited France's ability to use devaluations to offset domestic inflation, tightening the external constraint on domestic policy.

The slow-down after 1973 prompted economic historians to compare French experience in the 1970s with that in the 1930s. The differences were more striking than the similarities. Despite rising unemployment and slower growth of output, the context in the 1970s was one of rising rather than falling prices; expanding employment (although not quickly enough to satisfy the accelerated growth of the labour force); rising productivity and trade growing more rapidly than domestic output. The 'welfare state' (*état providence*) eased the impact of unemployment, its benefits to the unemployed sustaining domestic demand. Increasing budget deficits mainly resulted from built-in stabilizers rather than discretionary spending, and public expenditure as a percentage of GDP did not rise significantly, although spending shifted from investment to debt servicing and subsidies. Stephen S. Cohen termed French policy in response to the crisis one of 'informed bewilderment'.[12]

François Mitterrand's election as president in May 1981 and his dissolution of the National Assembly to obtain a socialist majority offered the political basis for a significant change in policy. Mitterrand inherited an unenviable economic situation: a franc overvalued by 15 per cent, high unit labour costs, an external deficit and a steady decline in the competitiveness of French industry. The socialist government attempted to revive French economic growth with demand stimulus, counting on a revival of the global economy to reinforce the domestic stimulus. It increased minimum wages, child benefits and old-age pensions, reduced the working week to 39 hours, lowered the retirement age to 60, and planned to increase public-sector and youth employment. But the world economy slumped, interest rates climbed, and the augmented purchasing power leaked out via increased imports. Higher inflation in France increased the overvaluation of the franc.

The socialist leaders decided not to devalue the franc before they took power. The trade and payments deficits rose, speculation increased pressure on the franc, and central-bank reserves declined sharply. Three devaluations, from October 1981 to March 1983, were ultimately necessary within the confines of the EMS, with each successive negotiated adjustment requiring tighter constraints on domestic spending. Wages and prices were frozen in June 1982, imposing a policy of *rigueur*; in March 1983, 'rigour' became 'austerity' as the government cut back sharply on spending and raised taxes to maintain a *franc fort* within the EMS (the franc still slightly overvalued). This meant following the German mark and imitating the monetary policies of the (then West German) Bundesbank. After 2 years in power the Mitterrand administration had reversed its policies, adopting a regime of monetary and fiscal orthodoxy, justifying the reversal as necessary to maintain the franc.

The transformation of socialist industrial policy was less striking, but equally significant. In 1981–2 the state nationalized 36 banks, 2 investment banks (Suez and Paribas), and 12 industrial firms, 7 of which were among France's 20 largest, increasing the proportion of industrial production under public-sector control from 18 to 32 per cent. (Nationalized firms included the Compagnie Générale d'Electricité, Thomson Brandt in electronics, Rhône-Poulenc in textiles and chemicals, and Péchiney-Ugine-Kuhlman in aluminium and chemicals; the state acquired a 51 per cent interest in firms including Dassault-Breguet and Matra in armaments manufacture and CII-Honeywell Bull in computers.) Since 1945 the socialists had advocated nationalization to replace market-based regulation of the economy with state control; nationalization survived in the socialist programme as a means to extend control over public services, firms dependent on the state, and firms controlling sectors important for national economic development and defence. Initially the nationalization programme exacerbated state–private sector tensions. One director of a stock brokerage firm compared the situation to Vichy versus London, equating those working for the state with those who had worked with Vichy.[13] (Recall that the nationalizations in 1945 had been provoked in part by the Vichy sympathies and the willing collaboration of French businesses with Nazi Germany!)

In fact, the nationalizations proved to be a significant 'capitalist success' in most cases, taking corporations that were supposed to be leaders in technology, socializing their losses, and providing greater investment funds for restructuring than would have been available in the private sector.[14] The new state firms were given greater autonomy, and after the socialist u-turn in 1983 they were permitted to shed excess labour to a degree impossible in the 1970s. Management personnel differed little from the private sector; the directors of private and public firms shared similar training and career paths, and moved easily between the two sectors. Profitability replaced maximizing employment as an overall objective, and by 1988 most of the nationalized firms had been turned around to operate with healthy profits. Structural reform was advanced, enhancing the competitiveness of many French firms that had been suffering decline in the 1970s. One socialist adviser commented, 'We went from the idea of a break with capitalism to the very different idea of a break with the failures of capitalism.'[15] Others saw it as more than that: a break with socialism.

When Jacques Chirac led a centre-right government 'cohabiting' with President Mitterrand after the socialists lost their parliamentary majority in 1986, a wave of privatizations signalled a return to liberal policies. But privatizations had begun unofficially under the previous socialist government and were continued when the socialists returned to power in 1988; they were a logical extension of the retreat of the state from direct economic management since 1983. Changes during the Chirac–Mitterrand cohabitation were often a matter of degree rather than direction. Progress on cutting back the size of the large public sector was slow and encountered strong resistance. French exports remained heavily committed to medium-technology industries such as armaments, transportation equipment and nuclear-power technology, as well as to foodstuffs, none of which has been a strong growth sector. In the high-tech industries with rapid growth, such as aeronautical equipment and computer and information technologies, French producers have gained only a small market share compared to producers from the United States and Japan.

The consistency of the *franc fort* policy through changes of parliamentary and presidential power has been even more notable. Until 1983 devaluations had been used repeatedly to restore the external balance when French inflation raised unit costs above competitors' price levels; on several occasions – 1926, 1938, 1949, 1959 – the franc had been deliberately undervalued to strengthen domestic economic recovery and growth. Inflation had provided a means of reducing the burden of state debt and stimulating growth. From 1979, exchange-rate policy was bound by the rules of the EMS (though France could have left the EMS temporarily, as Britain and Italy would do in 1992). Since 1983, France has refused currency realignment and has tailored fiscal policy to win credibility in international markets. The resulting fiscal restraint and high real interest rates have been justified on the grounds that low inflation and a strong franc would achieve two goals: provide the basis for durable long-term growth and a recovery of employment, and maintain a strong French role alongside Germany in leading the continuing integration of the European Union.

The *franc fort* was slow to produce stronger growth or reduce unemployment. Despite success in controlling inflation, which for 4 years was lower in France than in Germany (Figures 15.2 and 15.3), unemployment climbed from 8 per cent in 1983 to over 12 per cent in 1996 (Figure 15.4). When reunification costs pushed up German prices and the Bundesbank raised interest rates to curb inflation, France chose to maintain the franc's exchange rate with higher interest rates. Devaluations by Britain and Italy (which left the EMS), Ireland, Spain and Portugal in 1992 demonstrated that the 'competitive disinflation' pursued in France could be all too easily countered abroad. Given the low level of inflation, real interest rates in France rose above 7 per cent in the early 1990s, and total employment declined for 3 successive years, 1992–4. Persistent, rising and increasingly long-term unemployment, with notably higher rates for youth and women (in 1995 the overall unemployment rate was 11.6 per cent; the rate for women was 13.9 per cent; for men aged 15–24, 19 per cent; for women aged 15–24, 29 per cent), has become the most distinctive feature marking off French experience from that of its European partners in the 1990s.

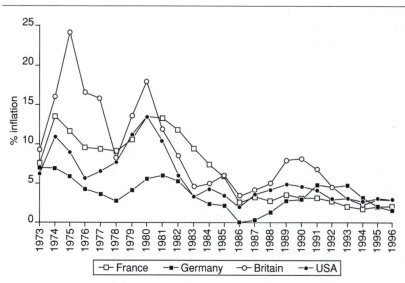

Fig. 15.2 Consumer prices, 1973–96

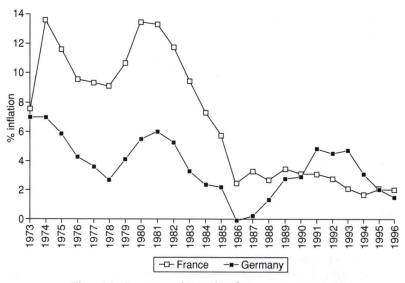

Fig. 15.3 German and French inflation rates, 1973–96

The socialist u-turn in policy combined with a renewed commitment to Europe to justify tighter fiscal and monetary policy, needed in any case to control inflation. François Mitterrand and the French president of the European Commission, Jacques Delors, thereafter played leading roles in further integration to create the single market in 1992 and establish the conditions for economic and monetary union (EMU) in 1999. But the *franc fort* as the symbol of French commitment to and influence in the European

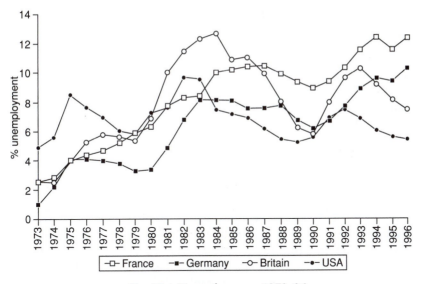

Fig. 15.4 Unemployment, 1973–96

Union has been costly. High interest rates in the 1980s encouraged a shift from industrial to financial investments to take advantage of increased yields. In the early 1990s real interest rates in France climbed higher still to compete with German rates. The franc held its ground against the Deutschmark, at a significant cost of higher unemployment, increased social

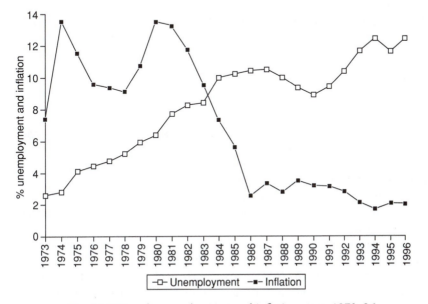

Fig. 15.5 French unemployment and inflation rates, 1973–96

expenditure, reduced government revenue, and aggravation of the problems of social fracture and exclusion. The increased budget deficit imperilled French participation in the first round of monetary union, and public opposition to austerity forced a government retreat from measures to curb social expenditures. A transport and civil-service strike paralysed French cities for three weeks in late 1995 with very strong public support. The credibility of French policy and commitment to Europe were endangered by the persistent failure of the state to solve the problem of rising unemployment.

In one sense French policy had, in the mid-1990s, come full circle from the 1930s when the commitment to maintain the *franc Poincaré* had necessitated high interest rates, produced a prolonged recession and increased unemployment, and narrowed the realm of debate on economic policy to ways to defend the franc. But the unemployment problem in the 1990s is more intractable. The increased role of the state in the economy has been counterbalanced by liberalization and globalization, which have narrowed the state's freedom to direct policy. Jean-Paul Fitoussi argues that the dominant discourse on the necessity of 'disinflation' and the *franc fort* has rendered policy debate more difficult. 'No one can seriously argue that it is necessary to accept a weak franc, a rupture of Franco-German cooperation and the decline of European integration. Conceived in this way, any 'other policy' would be evidently absurd.'[16] When Jacques Chirac dared criticize Bank of France interest-rate policy as harmful to employment during the presidential election in 1995, an immediate weakening of the franc forced him to beat a hasty retreat. Chirac the candidate promised to reduce unemployment as his 'priority of priorities'. Chirac the president discovered that austerity had to take priority if France was to join EMU in its first phase. Thus *L'horreur économique*: a powerful, interventionist state promises repeatedly to reduce unemployment, which, impervious to rhetoric, continues to rise.

Conclusion

The commercial success of Viviane Forrester's essay is a sign of French economic anxieties rather than sharp analysis of what has gone wrong. Its economic foundations and logic are naïve; it eschews statistical evidence and analysis in favour of polemic and alarmist warnings of the coming apocalypse. Forrester offers no solutions to the problems she describes; she seeks to provoke discussion and depends, implicitly, on renewed state direction to save France from post-industrial capitalism.

Social scientists employing a historical approach give better insight into the reasons for French fears of economic change. Robert Castel has provided a long perspective on the evolution of employment relations and their role in social identity and cohesion since the Middle Ages. He highlights the exceptional character of the 30 years after 1945 in providing full employment and durable employment contracts, and explains how employment relations have changed since the 1970s, changes he characterizes as a 'degradation' of conditions of employment. The decline of indefinite employment contracts, the increase in short-term and part-time employment, and increasingly frequent changes of employment have, in his view, transformed employment relations and undermined social cohesion, increasing the precariousness and the insecurity of life for the salaried middle classes. Pierre Rosanvallon has examined the 'new social question' to explain the decline of the 'guardian state' through a series of crises – financial, ideological and finally philosophical – which have progressively weakened social solidarity. Both authors see the role of the state as fundamental, and seek a reformulation of social responsibilities and solidarity that can only be directed by the state. Interest in Forrester's *L'Horreur économique* reflects declining certainty and security with regard to employment and social protection in France, both of which are threatened by slower growth and the need to compete in global markets.

French economic development since 1945 has been founded upon state-directed planning and investment in modernization, and on a progressive liberalization of the French economy. Beyond narrow limits, progressive liberalization could only be accomplished in conjunction with a retreat of the state. The success of French modernization since 1945 has been in sharp contrast to the decline marked in the 1930s. The role of the state has been in constant evolution, beginning from a consensus that only state direction could overcome the constraints and handicaps impeding modernization in the immediate post-war period. The importance of state planning diminished after the 1950s, and state industrial policy has shifted between statist and liberal currents. The socialist experiment of 1981–2 marked a brief revival of heroic state planning. Since 1983, and largely under socialist direction, the French economy has been further liberalized to an extent without precedent and opened to European and world trade. The future of the French economy has been linked to development of the European Union, portending a further retreat of state power and narrowing of freedom of manoeuvre. Yet the state remains a predominant force in the French economy with powerful means to influence development. Liberal and statist currents have co-existed in French policy throughout the changes in government since the Second World War. There are strong public expectations that the state, rather than the market-place, must solve the critical problems of unemployment and social exclusion in contemporary France. The mixed economy will require the cooperative engagement of both.

Acknowledgements

I should like to thank my colleagues, John Majewski and Jack Talbott, for their comments on an earlier draft of this chapter.

Notes

1 The phrase exaggerates the changes in this period, which Fourastié claimed transformed France, 'from millenarian poverty and a vegetative traditional life to the standards of living and style of life of the contemporary world'. Jean Fourastié, *Les Trente Glorieuses ou la révolution invisible de 1946 à 1975* (Paris: Fayard, 1979), p. 28.

2 Alfred Sauvy with Anita Hirsch, *Histoire économique de la France entre les deux guerres*, rev. ed. (Paris: Economica, 1984), vol. 2, p. 398.

3 Jean Bouvier, 'Une démarche révisionniste', in Patrick Fridenson and André Straus (eds.), *Le Capitalisme français, 19ᵉ–20ᵉ siècle: blocages et dynamismes d'une croissance* (Paris: Fayard, 1987), pp. 11–27.

4 Cited in François Caron, *An Economic History of Modern France*, trans. by Barbara Bray (London: Methuen & Co., 1979), p. 268.

5 Frances M. B. Lynch, *France and the International Economy: From Vichy to the Treaty of Rome* (London: Routledge, 1997), p. 10.

6 Cited in Annie Moulin, *Peasantry and Society in France Since 1789*, trans. M. C. and M. F. Cleary (Cambridge: Cambridge University Press, 1991), p. 152.

7 Henry Rousso, 'Les paradoxes de Vichy et de l'Occupation: contraintes, archaïsmes et modernités', in Fridenson and Straus (eds.), *Le Capitalisme français*, p. 79.

8 Robert Marjolin, *Le Travail d'une vie: mémoires 1911–1986* (Paris: Robert Laffont, 1986), p. 161. Fourquet notes the role of 'anti-model' that treasury policy and personnel from the 1930s played for post-war French planners; François Fourquet, *Les Comptes de la puissance: histoire de la comptabilité nationale et du plan* (Paris: Encres, 1980), p. 25.

9 Defending his investment plan in 1947, Monnet warned that without modernization France 'would become another Spain'. Cited in Robert Frank, 'The French dilemma: modernization with dependence or independence and decline', in Josef Becker and Franz Knipping (eds.), *Power in Europe? Great Britain, France, Italy and Germany in a Postwar World, 1945–1950* (Berlin and New York: Walter de Gruyter, 1986), p. 266.

10 William James Adams, *Restructuring the French Economy: Government and the Rise of Market Competition since World War II* (Washington, DC: The Brookings Institution, 1989).

11 Richard Kuisel, 'French post-war economic growth: a historical perspective on the *trente glorieuses*', in George Ross, Stanley Hoffmann and Sylvia Malzacher (eds.), *The Mitterrand Experiment: Continuity and Change in Modern France* (Cambridge: Polity Press, 1987), p. 23.

12 Stephen S. Cohen, 'Informed bewilderment: French economic strategy and the crisis', in Stephen S. Cohen and Peter A. Gourevitch (eds.), *France in the Troubled World Economy* (London: Butterworth & Co., 1982).

13 Cited in Marie-Paul Virard, *Comment Mitterrand a découvert l'économie* (Paris: Albin Michel, 1993), p. 23.

14 Élie Cohen, *Le Monde*, 23 Feb. 1993; Cohen terms the nationalizations 'an ideological failure and a capitalist success'.

15 Lionel Zinsou, cited in W. Rand Smith, 'Nationalizations for what? Capitalist power and public enterprise in Mitterrand's France', *Politics & Society*, 18:1 (1990), p. 80.

16 Jean-Paul Fitoussi, *Le Débat interdit: monnaie, Europe, pauvreté* (Paris: Arléa, 1995), p. 149.

Further reading

Aron, R. 'Myths and realities of the French economy', in idem., *France, Steadfast and Unchanging: The Fourth to the Fifth Republic*, trans. J. Irwin and L. Einaudi (Cambridge, MA: Harvard University Press, 1960).

Asselain, J.-C. *Histoire économique de la France du XVIIIe siècle à nos jours*, vol. 2, *De 1919 à la fin des années 1970* (Paris: Éditions du Seuil, 1984).

Bloch-Lainé, F. and Bouvier, J. *La France restaurée 1944–1954: dialogue sur les choix d'une modernisation* (Paris: Fayard, 1986).

Boltho, A. (ed.), *The European Economy: Growth and Crisis* (Oxford: Oxford University Press, 1982).

Boyer, R. (ed.), *Mouvement social*, 154 (1991), special issue on 'Paradoxes français de la crise des années 1930'.

Carré, J.-J., Dubois, P. and Malinvaud, E. *French Economic Growth*, trans. J. P. Hatfield (Stanford, CA: Stanford University Press, 1975).

Castel, R. *Les Métamorphoses de la question sociale: une chronique du salariat* (Paris: Fayard, 1995).

Eichengreen, B. (ed.) *Europe's Postwar Recovery* (Cambridge: Cambridge University Press, 1995).

International Monetary Fund, *World Economic Outlook* (Washington: IMF, various years).

Kindleberger, C. P. 'The Postwar Resurgence of the French Economy,' in Stanley Hoffmann, et al., *In Search of France* (New York: Harper Torchbooks, 1965 [Harvard University Press, 1963]).

Kuisel, R. F. *Capitalism and the State in Modern France: Renovation & Economic Management in the Twentieth Century* (Cambridge: Cambridge University Press, 1981).

Landes, D. S. 'French business and the businessman: a social and cultural analysis', in E. M. Earle (ed.), *Modern France: Problems of the Third and Fourth Republics* (Princeton: Princeton University Press, 1951).

Lévy-Leboyer, M. and Casanova, J.-C. (eds.), *Entre l'État et le marché: l'économie française des années 1880 à nos jours* (Paris: Éditions Gallimard, 1991).

L'Histoire *Puissances et faiblesses de la France industrielle, XIXe–XXe siècle* (Paris: Éditions du Seuil, 1997).

Loriaux, M. *France after Hegemony: International Change and Financial Reform* (Ithaca, NY: Cornell University Press, 1991).

Machin, H. and Wright, V. (eds.), *Economic Policy and Policy-Making Under the Mitterrand Presidency 1981–1984* (London: Frances Pinter, 1985).

Margairaz, M. *L'État, les finances et l'économie: Histoire d'une conversion, 1932–1952* (Paris: Comité pour l'histoire économique et financière de la France, 1991).

Mouré, K. *Managing the Franc Poincaré: Economic Understanding and Political Constraint in French Monetary Policy, 1928–1936* (Cambridge: Cambridge University Press, 1991).

Organisation for Economic Co-operation and Development, *OECD Economic Surveys: France* (Paris: OECD, various years).

Rosanvallon, P. *La Nouvelle Question sociale: repenser l'État-providence* (Paris: Éditions du Seuil, 1995).

Ross, G., Hoffmann, S. and Malzacher, S. (eds.), *The Mitterrand Experiment: Continuity and Change in Modern France* (Cambridge: Polity Press, 1987).

Sautter, C. 'France', in Andrea Boltho, ed., *The European Economy: Growth and Crisis* (Oxford: Oxford University Press, 1982), pp. 449–71.

Schmidt, V. A. *From State to Market? The Transformation of French Business and Government* (Cambridge: Cambridge University Press, 1996).

Shennan, A. *Rethinking France: Plans for Renewal 1940–1946* (Oxford: Clarendon Press, 1989).

Sicsic, P. and Wyplosz, C. 'France, 1945–92', in N. Crafts and G. Toniolo (eds.), *Economic Growth in Europe Since 1945* (Cambridge: Cambridge University Press, 1996).

Suleiman, E. N. *Les Ressorts cachés de la réussite française*, trans. S. Bleize (Paris: Éditions du Seuil, 1995).

|16|

From colonialism to
post-colonialism
The French empire since Napoleon
MARTIN EVANS

It is a fact that Guesde and Clemenceau, the representatives of the working class and the *petite bourgeoisie* respectively, particularly in rural areas, could fight against the expeditions to Tunisia and Tonkin in the last century. It is a fact that, at that time, they struck a chord with the masses. And it is equally true that since then both those parties – the Radical Party and the Socialist Party – have become tainted by imperialist ideology, the ideology of the dominant nation, of the colonial power.

Generation upon generation of French children were taught at school – and the lesson sank in – that the republic had founded a great colonial empire bringing civilization and prosperity to the poor savages, to the Vietnamese, or the Tonkinese as they were then called – as well as to the Algerians. This being the case people were genuinely at a loss to comprehend why the ungrateful recipients of the advantages and benefits lavished upon them by France should rise up in revolt.

Addressing the central committee of the French Communist Party in October 1958, the then general secretary, Maurice Thorez, was frank about the obstacles confronting opposition to the Algerian war. The Radical deputy Georges Clemenceau and the socialist leader Jules Guesde might have been able to stir up genuine anti-colonial sentiment during the 1880s, but, Thorez admitted, since the beginning of the nationalist rebellion in November 1954 the working class had not identified with the Algerian struggle. In part this indifference was testament to the way in which, in the intervening years, a colonialist mentality had successfully saturated the popular imagination, producing a network of prejudices about Algeria and Algerians. In part, too, it was due to the fact that right up until the end of the war in 1962 the vast majority of French soldiers were conscripts, mostly from a proletarian

background, and the combination of these two factors could not fail to lead
to an 'us' and 'them' mentality where Algerian nationalism was widely
perceived as the enemy. The reticence of its popular base meant, Thorez
explained, that the Communist Party had to adopt a prudent approach. Rash
action, such as direct aid to the Algerians, would, he warned, be misunder-
stood, cutting the party off from the masses, and for this reason the official
line carefully avoided a militant anti-colonial language, preferring instead to
talk in vague terms about the need for 'peace in Algeria'.

Thorez's remarks provide an intriguing snapshot of popular attitudes and
as such they exemplify the principal theme of this chapter, namely the impact
of colonialism within France. Moving outwards from the Algerian war
period it will focus upon the following interconnected questions. First, what
motivated the dramatic expansion of empire at the end of the nineteenth
century? Second, what impact did empire have upon popular consciousness
within the metropole? And third, how has decolonization and the legacy of
empire affected French society? In considering these issues it will be argued
that the phenomenon of empire has been underestimated within mainstream
histories of modern France. The most recent studies of the inter-war period,
Anthony Adamthwaite's *Grandeur and Misery: France's Bid for Power in
Europe 1914–40* and Eugen Weber's *The Hollow Years: France in the 1930s*,
both published in 1995, make little mention of the colonies. When discussed
the colonies are treated as a marginal phenomenon, peripheral to the
development of metropolitan France. In contrast this chapter will argue that
politically, economically and culturally colonization has had a significant
impact. However, in doing so the intention is not to offer up an alternative
orthodoxy where suddenly colonialism is everywhere in French society.
Rather it is to take the line that France since Napoleon cannot be properly
understood without a balanced consideration of the colonial encounter and
its legacy.

Acquisition of empire 1815–1871: accident or design?

1930–1 marked the hundredth anniversary of the French invasion of Algeria
and, when this is added to the fact that it was also the fiftieth anniversary of
the annexation of Tunisia and the Congo, it is not surprising that the Third
Republic used the convergence of these dates to make an emphatic statement
about colonialism. In Algeria, the jewel in the crown of the empire, the
centrepiece of the celebrations was a lavish recreation of the original landings
at Sidi-Ferruch in July 1830. Not surprisingly the tone of the occasion was
self-congratulatory and confident. Before 1830 Algeria had been an empty
desert. Thereafter, in the form of education, roads, transport and cities,

France had transformed the country beyond recognition, bringing civilization to territories which, from 1848 onwards, were legally an extension of the metropole. For this reason, the centenary commemorations solemnly emphasized, all Algerians should be eternally grateful to the mother country.

The themes enunciated at length during the Algeria commemorations were reiterated on an even grander scale with the colonial exhibition in Paris. Set in 110 hectares around the Lac Daumesnil in the Vincennes park in the east of the city, the exhibition was inaugurated by the minister for the colonies, Paul Reynaud, in May in 1931. Lasting until November of the same year, it was visited by 8 million people who found within the exhibition a seductive vision of empire as the 'greater France'. The exhibition projected France as a great imperial power, second only to Britain, whose colonies (totalling 100 million inhabitants and stretching to 11 million square kilometres of land) were inseparable from the metropole. This indeed was the apogee of empire, but what in concrete terms did these vast overseas possessions consist of?

First and foremost there was Algeria, whose status as an integral part of France meant that it came under the auspices of the ministry of the interior. The rest, administered by the colonial ministry, was made up of the other North African territories of Morocco and Tunisia; Madagascar; Indo-China; the French West Indies and the Pacific dependencies. The federation of French West Africa, founded in 1904 with its capital at Dakar, Senegal, brought together Dahomey, Guinea, the Ivory Coast, Mauritania, French Sudan, Niger, Senegal and Upper Volta, whilst French Equatorial Africa, founded in 1910, was centred in Brazzaville and grouped together the territories of Chad, the French Congo, Gabon and Oubangui-Chari. Territorially speaking the empire reached its height after the First World War when the ex-German colonies of Togo and the Cameroons, along with the former Ottoman possessions of Syria and the Lebanon, were placed under French control by the League of Nations.

The 1930–1 celebrations gave the acquisition of empire a sense of cohesion and purpose. Yet it is important to understand that the imposition of any such grand design was purely retrospective. The colonial exhibition might have rewritten history to present the image of a nation united behind the colonial mission, but in reality the empire was acquired by accident with little or no direction from Paris. From the restored Bourbons and the Orléanist monarchy through to the Second Republic and the Second Empire, the steady expansion into Africa, Asia and the Pacific was *not* the result of a systematic policy. There was no global vision which French people could respond to or identify with. Instead pressure to colonize came largely from a motley set of explorers, missionaries and army men, each acting on their own initiative to the indifference of governments and public opinion.

The invasion of Algeria in July 1830, for example, was not part of a grandiose strategy to conquer all of North Africa. Initially it was a limited operation to restore the faltering prestige of the Restoration king, Charles X. But once the invasion had begun it unleashed a process of escalation which successive governments found impossible to stop. This meant that although the new Orléanist monarch, Louis-Philippe, could see little utility in continued colonization, withdrawal was not feasible because it would have involved an unacceptable loss of face, and here the impetus for such an uncompromising policy came from the army on the ground. Embroiled in a war which honour dictated the expeditionary force could not lose, French troops became a law unto themselves. One incident consisted of asphyxiating 500 men, women and children in a cave, and when the reins of command were passed on to General Thomas Bugeaud this scorched-earth strategy was immediately intensified, eventually snuffing out Algerian resistance in 1847. However, Bugeaud's vision was always much wider than a merely military one. In the truest sense of the term he styled himself as a builder of empire, creating the basis for lasting colonization. Ruthless, relentless, singleminded, he was candid about the need to push aside the indigenous population, addressing the National Assembly thus in 1840: 'Wherever there is fresh water and fertile land, there one must locate settlers, without concerning oneself to whom these lands belong.'[1] In this way the army, which ran Algerian affairs for the first 40 years after the invasion, was instrumental in defining the early colonization in Algeria, with the effect that between 1841 and 1870 the settler population rose dramatically from 37000 to 279000.

Bugeaud was the archetypal colonial officer and thereafter strong-willed men of his kind played a pivotal role in the drive for empire. Bugeaud's equivalent in West Africa was Faidherbe, who, between 1854 and 1865, had a sense of mission which was similarly all-encompassing. Again and again he presented the Parisian authorities with *faits accomplis* which they could only sanction. Not only did he extend French authority eastwards and southwards, he also founded the port of Dakar in 1857, developed indigenous agriculture and created a corps of Senegalese troops. The extent to which Faidherbe was given a free hand is indicative of Napoleon III's lack of interest in empire. Preoccupied with attaining great-power status on the continent, Napoleon III appeared to have no consistent colonial policy. Thus whilst on the one hand Cochin-China was annexed in 1862 and a protectorate established over Cambodia, in Algeria Napoleon III condemned the confiscation of native land for the settlers. Declaring Algeria to be an Arab kingdom in 1863, he made sure that colonization was reduced to a trickle.

Impact of the Franco-Prussian war 1870–1871

The muddle and contradiction of the Second Empire gradually gave way to a new imperial policy under the Third Republic and the major reason for this

Illustration 16.1 Poster advertising the Colonial Exhibition in the Parc de Vincennes, Paris, 1931. Visitors were promised that they could 'Do a World Tour in One Day' – the implicit exoticism being designed to arouse curiosity, and even voyeurism, towards an empire that had hitherto left most French people unmoved. (Photo: AKG London.)

change in attitude was defeat in the Franco-Prussian war. It is no exaggeration to say that the loss of Alsace-Lorraine traumatized France, producing a mood of self-doubt and self-flagellation. The quest to restore the territorial unity of France became a national obsession and in this very precise sense the 1870–1 catastrophe is intimately connected to the evolution of a full-bodied colonial doctrine. It was the starting point for a new imperialism where the acquisition of colonies would signal an end to political and social decadence, proving beyond doubt that France was still a great power.

The most significant propagandist of the new imperialism was Paul Leroy-Beaulieu. As a professor at the prestigious Collège de France in Paris his writings and lectures held considerable intellectual sway amongst certain sections of the educated élite. Intermingling a belief in Enlightenment values with the language of social Darwinism, his interpretation of history fused notions of biological and cultural destiny. The unquestionable superiority of French civilization meant, he argued, that the Gallic race had a manifest duty to colonize the weaker, bringing science and technology to the non-European world. For Leroy-Beaulieu imperialism was the next stage in the racial struggle for survival and his views were steeped in a crude sexual imagery where overseas expansion symbolized the restored virility of the French nation. Reflecting the growing fears about demographic decay, Leroy-Beaulieu's *De la colonisation chez les peuples modernes*, written in 1874, was forthright:

> Colonization is the expansive force of a people; it is its power of reproduction; it is its enlargement and its multiplication through space; it is the subjection of the universe or a vast part of it to that people's language, customs, ideas and laws.[2]

Colonial ideas of this nature were taken up and further developed by a small number of journalists and academics during the 1870s and 1880s. On the right of the Radical Party, Gabrial Charmes disseminated colonial arguments through articles in *La Revue des deux mondes* and *Journal des débats*. Writing in 1882 he called on his compatriots not to baulk at the imperial challenge. The expansion of races was the defining characteristic of the late nineteenth century and fixation with Alsace-Lorraine, Charmes warned, must not lead the French to lose out in the dash for colonies. At the University of Dijon Paul Gaffarel mirrored Charmes's views. Rehabilitating the *ancien-régime* empire through a succession of books published between 1875 and 1880, his message was simple. Either French people rediscover the imperial instinct of their forebears or France will fall behind Britain, Holland, Spain or – even more humiliatingly – Portugal. On a much wider scale metropolitan interest in empire was also stimulated by the vogue for exotic literature which, in mixing images of jungles and cannibals with those of the brothel, the harem and oriental 'vices', popularized notions of a racial hierachy, with its crude equations between achieved levels of civilization and innate characteristics The novels of Pierre Loti and Alphonse Daudet made the empire into a familiar setting, whilst Jules Verne's best-selling hero, Captain Nemo, was the very model of colonial exploration. Tough, resourceful, adventurous, he drew upon science and technology to conquer alien environments.

Writings of this nature point to the gathering importance of new colonialism as a current of thought, but the most powerful expression of this expansionist impulse was the explosion of geographical societies during the early period of the Third Republic. Between 1871 and 1881 11 geographical societies were founded in France and two in Algeria with a membership of 9500. Working in unison they formed a geographical movement which aimed to give the imperial idea stimulus and momentum. Through conferences, meetings and publications the movement set out to convince the governing class of the need for colonization and rarely has the relationship between geography and imperialism been so manifest. In speech after speech the leader, Guillaume Depping, espoused a heady imagery of exploration, adventure and exoticism. Blending the quest for scientific discovery with the rudimentary desire for commercial exploitation, his grandiose schemes, most notably the one to bind West Africa with North Africa by rail, aimed to fire the French imagination, making colonialism into a brave new world.

Although it is difficult to measure the impact of these pressure groups, what is not in doubt is that significant parts of the local and Parisian élites, dominated as they were by the trauma of the 1870–1 defeat, were psychologically receptive to ideas linking colonial expansion to national salvation. Amongst the political leaders of the early Third Republic the most powerful advocate of empire was Jules Ferry. As a member of the republican governments of the period 1879–85, including two periods as prime minister in 1880–1 and 1883–5, Ferry was the moving force behind the annexation of Tunisia in 1881 and the completion of the conquest of Indo-China. He also sanctioned the acquisition of the Congo and Madagascar. Speaking in 1885 Ferry advanced a triple justification for colonialism, all of which bore the hallmarks of Leroy-Beaulieu and Charmes. First, there was the economic argument. For Ferry colonial policy and industrial policy were inseparable because colonies represented captive markets and a source of raw materials. Reflecting the way in which the economic downturn of the mid-1870s had produced a protectionist mentality, Ferry took the view that acquiring colonies and then organizing them into an imperial bloc was the only way to insulate France against the growing Depression. Second, there was the humanitarian dimension. In expanding overseas France was engaged in a crusade, raising inferior races to the level of French civilization. And lastly, and most importantly, there was the question of national prestige. Ferry believed that a great power was by necessity a colonial power and for him no other image of France was acceptable.

Although Ferry's colonial vision won over many converts, in equal measure it provoked widespread hostility. On the left Jules Guesde, founder of the Parti Ouvrier Français in 1879, called on workers to oppose colonialism because it only provided fantastic financial opportunities for the bourgeoisie. On the monarchist right, anti-colonialism was heavily coloured by anti-semitism. If colonialism was the expression of Jewish financial interests, the monarchist deputy Langle maintained, why should French soldiers spill their blood in the pursuit of such expansion?

Within the National Assembly Ferry's opponents attacked his policy as dangerously misguided. Wasting precious resources in colonialism played straight into Bismarck's hands because power outside Europe could not compensate for a lack of power within Europe. This hostility climaxed in 1885 when, fearful that expansion into Tonkin would lead to a colonial equivalent of the Franco-Prussian war, Ferry's enemies engineered his downfall. Shortly after, in July, colonial policy was discussed in a wide-ranging debate in the National Assembly and here Ferry was rounded upon in a bitter and acrimonious fashion. The conservative deputy Paul Déroulède had already famously retorted that by exchanging Alsace-Lorraine for empire Ferry was offering him 20 black servants for two lost sisters and gut reactions of this type dominated the parliamentary exchanges. The tone of Georges Clemenceau, the left-wing Radical Party leader, was especially unforgiving:

> My patriotism lies in France. . . . While you are lost in your colonial dreams, there are at your feet men, Frenchmen, who call for useful and beneficial efforts to develop French genius. . . . Do you not think that (the social question) provides a sufficient domain for human ambition, and that the idea of increasing knowledge and enlightenment in our own country, of developing our well-being, increasing the exercise of liberty, the right to organise a struggle against ignorance, vice, misery, to organise a better use for our social forces – do you not think that it is enough to occupy the activities of a politician or party?[3]

Even more provocatively, Clemenceau reiterated the accusation that Ferry was the dupe of Bismarck. Expansion into Tunisia, he explained, had provoked the hostility of Italy, whilst on a more general level colonialism had renewed rivalry with Britain, two developments which diverted France away from the Alsace-Lorraine question.

Yet, if in the short term anti-colonial hostility led to the fall of the Ferry government, in the long run it was the pro-colonial argument that prevailed. The 1884 Congress of Berlin, where the major European powers effectively agreed to partition Africa amicably, inaugurated the new era of colonialism and thereafter the scramble for territory became the dominant aspect of the age. By 1895 only one-tenth of Africa was not appropriated and undoubtedly this international momentum had a considerable impact upon the political élite, turning erstwhile opponents into imperial converts. Soon there was a consensus that France must not lose out in the race for empire and the result was that between 1880 and 1895 the size of the empire grew from 1 million to 9.5 million square kilometres.

In large part this new mood reflected the growing role of the colonial lobby (*parti colonial*). This last phrase was first used by journalists in 1894 to describe a broad coalition of pro-colonial interest groups both within and without the National Assembly, and taken at face value such a term might give the impression of a tightly disciplined unit. In reality it would be more accurate to talk about the colonial lobby as a diffuse phenomenon where the diverse circles of propagandist associations and pressure groups overlapped at common points of interest. Within the political sphere a colonial caucus was founded within the National Assembly in the summer of 1892, uniting deputies from across the political spectrum under the leadership of Eugène Etienne. The fact that two-thirds of the lobby was from the left, and that professionally speaking it was composed of lawyers (28 per cent), business-men (18 per cent), journalists (13 per cent) and public servants (10 per cent), shows how no one party or particular interest group had a monopoly on colonialist language. All, whether left or right, were infused by the same imperial spirit.

In terms of exerting influence and control many of the group's members were prominent within all the various committees pressing for expansion. The committee for French Africa set up in 1890, the committee for Mada-gascar established in 1895, the committee for French Asia organized in 1901, the committee for French Morocco founded in 1905: each had strong links not only with the National Assembly but also with commercial and eco-nomic interests, and in this respect the key individual was Eugène Étienne. Parliamentary member for Oran in Algeria, a seat he held on to from 1881 to 1919, Étienne's career is emblematic of the way in which the colonial lobby straddled many spheres. Government minister, businessman, journalist: in each context Étienne was the leading champion of colonialism and the fact that he was variously minister of the interior, minister of war and vice-president of the chamber of deputies indicates the extent to which the colonial lobby had successfully penetrated the political élite by the eve of the First World War.

Beyond the realm of party politics, the military made up the next element of the colonial lobby. For the army and navy the empire came to represent a private fiefdom, intimately connected to patterns of career structure and promotion. There royalist supporters, of which there were many in the officer ranks, could keep a distance from the hated Third Republic, derided as strife-ridden and petty minded, and recreate a hierarchical society that would ultimately defeat Germany. Likewise within both Protestant and Roman Catholic circles colonialism was seen as an opportunity to escape the forces of secularism at home. Moreover, in opening up the rest of the world to the Christian message colonialism turned the late nineteenth century into the classic age of missionary endeavour. Converting the heathen to the true faith now became a sacred duty.

If the first three poles of the colonial lobby were political, military and religious, the fourth was the formation of a colonial bureaucracy, itself indicative of the extent to which the political class had quickly come to see the expansion and management of empire as an essential part of state activity. The ministry of colonies, therefore, was established in 1894 and although Algeria remained under the ministry of the interior and the protectorates under the ministry of foreign affairs, centralization of this nature brought the various strands of imperial policy together and gave it a clearer sense of direction. This process had already begun 5 years earlier with the creation of a bureaucracy which supplied about a fifth of all colonial officials. In this very precise manner colonialism now became a career structure where the development of an imperial *esprit de corps*, was paramount.

The final component of the colonial lobby was the settlers themselves. Benefiting from the plentiful supply of cheap labour, many had strong business interests to promote, something that was particularly significant in Algeria where the fact that settlers sent deputies to the National Assembly gave them added political clout. Together with the other groupings of the colonial lobby the settlers represented a coalition of interests convinced of the necessity of empire. Ten-thousand strong, the colonial lobby was determined to erode public indifference to empire. For them their mission was to make nation and empire synonymous in the minds of the French masses.

Arguments for empire

Broadly speaking the arguments advanced by colonial interests fell into three categories: economic, nationalist and religious. These were elevated into a kind of holy trinity.

The first argument was the economic one: capitalist expansion could not be divorced from colonialism. To ask whether this was true or not is to miss the point that many within the political élite believed this to be the case. For the likes of Ferry as the world moved away from the free-trading one of the mid-nineteenth century, securing raw materials and markets through colonization became an economic necessity. Recognizing the way in which not only key sectors of the economy, notably silk and sugar, but whole areas, most importantly Marseille and Bordeaux, were reliant on empire, annexing territories became crucial because it was seen to give national business a monopoly position in a period of widespread commercial uncertainty.

No less important was the notion that empire could not be separated from national prestige. Empire was the benchmark of great-power status and in the era of mass politics the Third Republic increasingly encouraged its citizens to identify themselves with the imperial state and nation. By taking for granted the right of French people to impose their will upon other cultures, the Third Republic mapped out a particular vision of the world with the metropole at the centre and the empire on the margins, and the simplicity of this appeal meant that imperialism came to be seen as a cement. In underlining the superiority of all French people it united the different social classes and warded off revolution.

For the left any nationalist justification for colonialism was intimately connected to the belief in colonialism's civilizing mission. Here colonialism was portrayed as an essentially humanitarian impulse, an act of deliverance liberating the colonies from superstition and ignorance. As the country of the rights of man, France was a universal model and in any description of French rule the image of light versus darkness became an all-pervading metaphor, summarizing colonialism as the battle of Enlightenment values against despotism and feudalism. On the right the preference was for a social-Darwinist line of thinking when discussing the nationalist motivations for colonialism. For the settler novelist Louis Bertrand, France in Algeria was taking up the Roman heritage which had fallen into abeyance during Muslim domination in Algeria. Practical, ruthless, virile, the settlers were, he claimed, creating a new Latin race whose ultimate aim was to regenerate France.

Although within the context of the metropole the Third Republic was avowedly secular, within the empire religion was an important ally. Anti-clericalism was not for export and in specific terms the safety of missionaries provided the pretext for French intervention in Indo-China and Tahiti, whilst on a wider scale the Third Republic's civilizing crusade was mirrored in the missionary zeal of the Catholic church. The most outspoken advocate of this expansionist doctrine was Cardinal Lavigerie who became archbishop of Algiers in 1866. For him Islam was the epitome of evil, a backward, retrograde religion which had to be cleansed from North Africa. With this end in mind he established the Society of African Missionaries, known as the white fathers because of their Arab dress, in 1868. The energy with which they set up schools and hospitals marked them out as the most militant of the missionary congregations and by 1875 they had spread from Algeria into Tunisia, setting up a religious protectorate that opened the way to formal annexation within 6 years. For the white fathers the Bible and colonialism went hand in hand.

In addition to the economic, nationalist and religious arguments the army emphasized the untapped potential of empire. For them native troops represented an answer to the demographic problem, a view encapsulated in Colonel Mangin's influential 1910 book, *La Force noire*, where he argued that the colonies would supply the troops necessary to match Germany's army. Mangin's writings reflected the widely held belief that colonial subjects were credulous children, lacking in rationality. The aim of colonialism, therefore, was to instil loyalty to the mother country.

Finally, the authorities saw the colonies as a safety valve for the metropole. After June 1848 thousands of workers were deported to Algeria, followed by thousands of communards to New Caledonia in 1871, whilst Devils Island off French Guyana became the site of a complex prison system for revolutionaries and criminals. In this way the colonies became a dumping ground for undesirables, saving the French mainland from social upheaval.

In the 25 years prior to the First World War these arguments made inroads into the popular imagination, making it possible to discern a growing colonial consciousness. Within the 1889 World's Fair 18 colonial pavilions complemented the Eiffel Tower, whilst 14 attracted the tourists in Paris in 1900. The way in which both represented submissive races dominated by the French undoubtedly touched a public nerve. In a similar fashion the stand-off at Fashoda in 1898, when a French expedition into the upper Nile backed down from conflict with British forces, was followed closely in the press, stirring up a widespread Anglophobia which nearly spilled into open warfare. Then 7 years later the Moroccan crises witnessed a further fusion of colonialism and nationalism, this time in an anti-German direction. In 1905 and then again in 1911 Kaiser Wilhelm II intervened to oppose French expansion into Morocco and the way in which he was forced to climb down, thereby paving the way for its annexation as a protectorate in 1912, went some way to restoring pride and self-confidence. The right-wing nationalist Maurice Barrès might have been initially sceptical about colonialism, but for him the acquisition of Morocco was a triumph because the colony would furnish the soldiers necessary to defeat Germany.

Fashoda and Morocco point towards the way in which, in a new era of naked power politics, the anti-colonialism of the 1880s had been effectively marginalized by the eve of the First World War. This process intensified between 1914 and 1918 when the contribution of the colonies to the war-effort – they supplied 500 000 soldiers and 200 000 industrial workers – transformed popular perceptions of empire. Even Clemenceau, who on returning as prime minister in November 1917 was instrumental in setting up the recruitment drive in the colonies, became a tireless defender of empire and the participation of these colonial troops on the battlefield, not only on the western front but also the Dardenelles and the Bulgarian front, had a profound impact on French perceptions. Suddenly empire took on a tangible form and in this concrete way the image of a close bond, uniting metropolitan and colonial France, began to take hold within the popular imagination.

In the wake of the First World War support for empire continued to extend itself across the political parties and in this context the most significant convert was the Socialist Party, Section Française de l'Internationale Ouvrière (SFIO). The attitudes of the SFIO leader, Léon Blum, talking in 1924, reveal how easily the universal beliefs at the heart of left-wing patriotism blended into notions of racial and cultural superiority:

> We are too imbued with love of our country to disavow the expansion of French thought and civilization ... We recognise the right and even the duty of superior races to draw unto them those who have not arrived at the same level of culture.[4]

That is not to say that Blum did not criticize certain colonial practices, but for him these now became right-wing abuses, open to reform through the application of left wing humanism. In political terms this meant that the only real opposition to colonialism came from the Communist Party (PCF), formed at Tours in 1920 by those within the French socialist movement who supported the Russian Revolution. In subscribing to the Third International the PCF sought to ally themselves with nationalist movements within the empire, with the result that when Abd el-Krim led a rebellion against the French and Spanish in the Rif mountains of northern Morocco in 1924 the party threw itself behind the uprising. The PCF, supported by surrealist intellectuals like André Breton and Louis Aragon, called on troops to desert. Even more provocatively the party deputy, Jacques Doriot, sent a telegram of support to the rebels, a move which stirred uproar in the National Assembly. But if thereafter anti-colonialism became a familiar rallying cry for communist activists it also needs to be underlined that the party during the 1920s represented a tiny minority, confined to the fringes of the political landscape.

Greater France: empire 1930–1945

It was to be the 1931 colonial exhibition that turned this language of the empire into common currency. Awesome, imposing, monumental, the exhibition projected the vision of a greater France where metropole and colonies were united as one. By stressing the vastness and diversity of these possessions the intention was to inculcate pride and commitment to the colonial project, producing a new national identity intimately connected to empire.

The exhibition was the outcome of 4 years of government planning and preparation under the meticulous direction of Marshal Louis-Hubert Lyautey, the hero of colonial expansion in Morocco. From the outset the ambition and exuberance of Lyautey's personality was firmly imprinted on the exhibition project, with the effect that, although there had been colonial sections within the World's Fairs of 1878, 1889 and 1900, and although Marseille had organized exhibitions about empire in 1906 and 1920, there was no doubt that the Paris exhibition would be the largest and most impressive expression of French imperial grandeur.

The opening ceremony of the exhibition on 6 May 1931 was a lavishly staged affair, attended by a host of dignitaries including the president and the prime minister, and within the official pronouncements Paul Reynaud, secretary of state for the colonies, outlined its ambitious purpose. The intention, he explained, was to make empire an integral part of the French consciousness; with this in mind the exhibition took the form of a tour

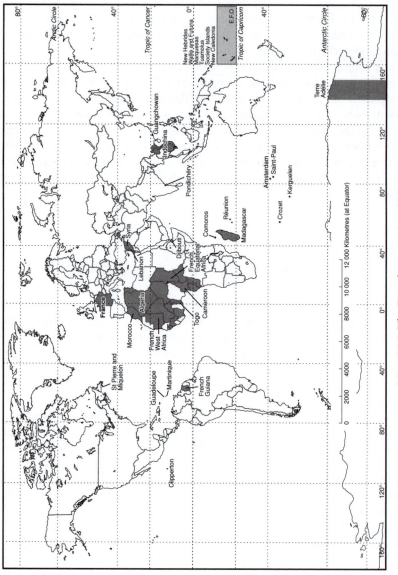

Map 16.1 The French empire in 1930

around the empire in miniature. Individual displays offered up glimpses of exotic other worlds, climaxing with the central attraction, a full-scale reconstruction of the Cambodian temple Angkor Wat. Food stalls sold produce from the colonies, whilst two pavilions looked at missionary work, thereby further reinforcing the overall image projected by the exhibition, that is of the empire as an ethnically diverse but politically unified entity, centralized under the guidance of the French. Without this modern framework, the exhibition explicitly stated, these traditional cultures would descend into anarchy and chaos.

For Lyautey the broader didactic aim was also reflected in the emphasis on information. All aspects of life in the colonies were thoroughly documented, ranging from tourism through to economic opportunities and agricultural practices, whilst figures of the colonial troops killed in the First World War provided a telling reminder of the empire's vital contribution to the French military machine. The organizers were mindful of the need to market the exhibition to the general public: to coincide with the opening a special collection of stamps, detailing scenes from the empire, was issued, which, along with the powerful new media of cinema and broadcasting, aimed to stimulate popular interest. Postcards, photographs and popular prints were also widely disseminated, whilst the monthly magazine, *L'Illustration*, produced a special catalogue edition.

At the same time within the exhibition it is possible to discern contradictory concepts of empire, reflecting the way in which, since its inception, the ministry of colonies had struggled with the twin concepts of assimilation and association. For assimilationists, whose supporters were largely found within the Republican Party, the guiding belief was that colonialism involved the exportation of the French model of government and learning. They wanted to turn the empire into an extension of the metropole. In contrast champions of association talked about unequal races with different rights and obligations. For those like Lyautey empire represented a protective shell within which separate and self-sufficient cultures could flourish. The purpose, therefore, was not to open up the colonies to new ideas but to return them to their historic traditions. Thus locked into the past, colonial subjects would be easier to control because they could have no claims on a modern future where French interests would predominate. Tensions between these two views straddled colonial policy right up until 1962, but if on many issues the camps were diametrically opposed on one thing they were united: the indissoluble link between France and empire.

When the exhibition began the PCF spoke out in protest. Likewise the surrealists, led by Breton, organized a counter-exhibition of 20 display panels of posters, photographs and maps which denounced colonialism as a sham. However, dissent was a minority phenomenon. Only a few thousand saw the surrealist exhibition whilst 8 million visited the colonial exhibition. Such success does not indicate an atmosphere of ignorance or indifference towards colonialism. Significantly it suggests that popular imperialism was something that happened *after* the scramble for colonies: the interest was in the defence of empire rather than its acquisition. Of course measuring popular attitudes is notoriously difficult and it would be true to say that the historical evidence, whether it be memoirs, diaries or oral testimony, points in several directions. Nonetheless what cannot be denied is the official importance now placed upon empire and the way that this discourse began to have a popular resonance, delineating notions of ownership in combination with a sense of the superiority of the 'civilized' over the 'primitive'. Such beliefs formed a framework of assumptions which permeated education, entertainment and the media. The French anti-colonialist intellectual Pierre Vidal-Naquet has a vivid memory of his primary-school education in Marseille during the 1930s. On the wall, he remembers, a large map marked out the empire in pink and each morning he and his fellow pupils were told to take pride in these colonies because they proved that France was a powerful country.

In a similar fashion Lyautey, who died in 1934, became the focus of a widespread personality cult. His image as the model colonial governor was assiduously cultivated through popular biographies and children's books, all of which stressed the manner in which he combined the qualities of athleticism and militarism with those of benevolence and good governance. Lyautey was the model colonial soldier and for Hélie de Saint-Marc, born into a bourgeois, Catholic family in the south-west of France, his example was a powerful inspiration. When recounting why he joined the French foreign legion in 1945 and why he subsequently become a hard-line supporter of colonial Algeria, he always underlines the formative influence of Lyautey's writings.

However, it needs to be emphasized that the impact of this colonialist discourse upon metropolitan society was not uniform. It was a disaggregated phenomenon which differed greatly according to class, gender and region. The importance of bourgeois businessmen and the dissident aristocracy in the expansion of empire has already been mentioned. On the face of it the peasantry and the working class were much less knowledgeable about the nature and extent of empire, much less sure of their role in the maintenance of colonies; and as the 1930s progressed, and the economic Depression intensified, it would be reasonable to assume that this indifference quickly deepened, turning the empire into a distant entity far divorced from the harsh realities of domestic affairs. Yet empire did have the potential to tap into the lived experience of the lower classes. Within working-class culture, for instance, the defence of empire could easily be equated with traditions of territorial rivalry and the assertion of masculinity. Likewise Robert Bonnaud is now a university lecturer in Paris and he clearly remembers how in the 1930s his father, a factory worker in Marseille, fantasized about beginning a new life in Indo-China. For his father, Bonnaud emphasizes, empire was a way of escaping his proletarian condition. This notion of escape was a powerful motivator for recruitment into the military, explaining why the poorer sections of Corsican society had a long tradition of supplying man-power for the colonial navy. Women, too, of whatever social class, could feel the pull of imperialist ideology. Again and again women were talked about as proud mothers of the empire whose duty was to bear and rear children – the next generation of the imperial race. Furthermore women had an important stabilizing influence, providing a secure domestic base for colonial expansion. Lastly, to variables of class and gender must be added the dimension of region. For the inhabitants of Marseille or Bordeaux empire was not an abstraction. For these cities the obvious economic importance of greater France meant that colonialism took on a tangible reality, making it an integral part of lived experience.

The complex interplay between official and popular becomes even more obvious in the late 1930s as the threat of war with Nazi Germany loomed large. Within government circles empire now became a familiar watchword because it transformed France from a puny 42 000 000 weakling into an imposing 100 000 000 giant, and such perceptions began to take root more widely, making the empire into a source of comfort and hope. Thus when fascist Italy called for the handover of Tunisia in November 1938 the popular response was belligerence. The empire was sacrosanct because it was going to save the Third Republic. It is no accident that it was the Senegalese regiments – whose fearsome military reputation was legendary – who received the loudest acclaim from the crowds lining the 1939 Bastille Day military parade in Paris.

On the left any belief in the reform of colonialism was also overshadowed by the gathering European crisis, with the effect that, although the 1936 Popular Front government did promise some limited changes, most famously the proposals by Maurice Viollette to extend voting rights to 25 000 Alger-ians, and although it did appoint a commission to investigate conditions in the colonies, such initiatives were soon sidelined by the confrontation with fascism. Indeed in 1937 the Popular Front government was instrumental in dissolving the leading party of Algerian nationalism, the North African Star, because in propagating independence it was seen as a threat to the Republic analagous to the fascist leagues. The international context also led to a reformulation of the PCF position in February 1939. Speaking in Algiers the party leader, Maurice Thorez, announced that henceforth the PCF would talk about Algeria as a nation in formation, meaning that for the time being at least it was impossible to envisage independence. According to this new schema the republic was playing a progressive role because in bringing together a melting pot of 20 races it was laying the foundations of future nationhood. Furthermore, given the threat of Hitler, Algeria needed France more than ever as protection against fascist aggression; in this respect the patriotic tone of the speech is very striking, a marked contrast to the militant anti-colonialism of a decade earlier.

During the Second World War both the Vichy regime and the Free French were wholeheartedly committed to empire. For Vichy in 1940 and 1941 as it strove to find a place within Hitler's New Order imperial possessions were vital bargaining counters, the basis of a collaborative partnership with Nazi Germany, whilst for the Free French the fact that the New Hebrides, French Oceania, the five cities of French India, New Caledonia and much of French Equatorial Africa rallied to de Gaulle gave Free France legitimacy and explains why empire remained so central to its ideology. Thereafter the empire, which was largely under Free French control by November 1942, made a capital contribution to the war-effort, supplying troops, financial and material resources as well as military bases, a role de Gaulle always recognized. Speaking in June 1942 de Gaulle underlined: 'There is one element which, in these terrible trials, has shown the nation that it is essential to her future and necessary for her greatness. That element is the empire'.[5] But if de Gaulle saw the empire as the basis for renewed greatness he was aware that the relationship had to evolve and with this aim in mind he convened a conference at Brazzaville in French Equatorial Africa in January 1944. Bringing together colonial governors and officials, though significantly not nationalist leaders, de Gaulle also wanted to send out a clear signal to the Americans, whose anti-colonialist sympathies were well documented. He wanted to demonstrate that the empire was a united bloc where, although the need for change was conceded, French authority was unchallenged. Reflecting this conservative tone, the concluding statement was emphatic in its opposition to independence. All possibility of self-government outside the French bloc of the empire was completely dismissed.

Impact of decolonization

Like the Franco-Prussian war, the defeat of 1940 was a traumatic experience. It seemed to signal that France was no longer a great power and this weakness was underlined by the way in which France was excluded from decision-making by Britain, America and the Soviet Union at the end of the Second World War. Non-participation wounded de Gaulle deeply, so much so that he became obsessed about the restoration of French status. From the outset empire was central to the recovery of lost greatness and for this reason the 1945–6 period witnessed a brutal reassertion of French sovereignty within the colonies. In Algeria independence demonstrations on 8 May 1945 were violently repressed, leading to anything up to 45 000 deaths. In Syria the French replied to a general strike by shelling Damascus on 29, 30 and 31 May 1945. In Indo-China the French military attempted to snuff out the nationalist movement with the bombardment of Haiphong on 23 November 1946. In Madagascar the March 1947 uprising brought a particularly fierce response. Extra troops were drafted in and slowly but surely the insurgents were isolated from the civilian population with the result that by December

1948 they had been starved into submission with the loss of 89 000 lives. Thus for the political élite, as well as the general populace, empire overcame doubts about rank and, as Jean-Pierre Rioux, a leading historian of the Fourth Republic, has noted, the imperial mystique was now carried to a level rarely equalled in modern French history.

It is important to stress that such views straddled all of the political spectrum. For the SFIO indigenous emancipation was to be achieved not by independence but through the development of even closer unity with a democratic and socialist France. The new Republic, based upon the anti-fascism of the Resistance, would, it was claimed, act as harbinger of modern progressive values, liberating the colonies not only from the abuses of traditional colonialism but also from the grip of feudal despotism. Thus it was not possible for the colonies to liberate themselves. Freedom emanated outwards from the metropole and not vice versa. Likewise the PCF, dropping its anti-colonial stance of the pre-1936 period, became a champion of empire. Stressing the twin themes of unity and assimilation, the PCF now argued that it was in the colonies' interests to remain attached to a socialist France as a bulwark against American imperialism. Exalting the vision of a fully democratic France of 100 million citizens, the PCF pointed towards the USSR, where the Russian empire had been transformed into a union of socialist republics, as a model to follow. Both the SFIO and PCF, therefore, accepted the fact that the link between France and the colonies would have to be reformulated and within the 1946 Fourth-Republic constitution this took the form of a new concept, the French union. In concrete terms this new arrangement was made up of two elements, the first of which was the indivisible republic, comprising the metropole, Algeria and other overseas departments, and the second the French union itself, which consisted of associated territories and states.

In commercial terms too the significance of empire dramatically expanded after the Second World War. This trend, as the economic historian Jacques Marseille has underlined, was already discernible during the interwar period, and for 15 years after 1945 the empire was France's most important trading partner, reaching a high point in 1952 when the colonies accounted for 42 per cent of French exports. Investment now took off in a big way, as did state funding of the general infrastructure – meaning that emotionally, politically and economically empire now became more important than ever. Yet ironically this was just the moment when nationalist movements began to assert themselves; the result was a bloody confrontation which explains why decolonization was such a protracted and painful affair.

The first major conflict was in Indo-China, where attempts by the French to recover their influence led to warfare with the Viet-Minh forces from December 1946 onwards. Humiliation in May 1954, when French forces were surrounded and defeated in a set-piece battle at Dien Bien Phu, was a major blow to national prestige and led to French withdrawal two months later. In patently underlining French weakness the Indo-China war gave encouragement to other anti-colonial movements in the empire and by the mid-1950s France was under pressure from all sides. Rebellions in Morocco and Tunisia led to independence for both countries in 1956 and in this sense the break-up of the French union cannot be separated from the wider international context. The end of empire was a dominant feature of the post-1945 world, a global process which happened suddenly and with extraordinary speed. Consequently when the Bandung conference in Indonesia in April 1955 brought together the newly independent countries of Africa and Asia, this was a major international event which gave decolonization a precise form and content. By making an explicit link between the racism of Nazism and the racism of colonialism the conference's final communiqué embodied the revolt of the Third World against European domination. Decolonization was now seen to possess an unstoppable dynamic and, as more and more independent countries acceded to the United Nations, anti-colonialism became an international idiom.

The spectre of decolonization led to hurried legislation in June 1956. Named after the minister for overseas France, Gaston Defferre, the Defferre law extended suffrage to all men and women in the empire. No less importantly, by accepting that territorial assemblies had the right to vote on local budgets, the law was quickly seen as a milestone by nationalists, particularly in black Africa, because it conceded greater autonomy to the colonies. Thus, although 2 years later de Gaulle tried to claw back some power with his concept of the community, in practice the way was now clear for a transition. The experience of self-government had whetted the appetite of nationalists and in September 1959 African leaders asked for complete authority to be transferred to them. By mid-1960 decolonization in sub-Saharan Africa was finished and the fact that in the main it had been a peaceful process was a marked contrast to parallel events in Algeria.

Nonetheless powerful elements within the French state were determined to hang onto the empire whatever the cost. The major force of resistance was the French army. For key parts of the army the retreat from empire was a painful humiliation. As the Fourth-Republic politicians caved in again and again in the face of successive colonial rebellions the sense of resentment began to run deep. Little wonder then that when the National Liberation Front (FLN) launched an armed struggle in Algeria in November 1954 this quickly became a war that the army had to win. Unlike the other colonies this was a sacred part of France, where a million settlers lived alongside 9 million natives, and by 1957 the army, bolstered by reservists, was fighting a dirty war.

Suspicious that the Fourth Republic was going to sell out French Algeria, army hard-liners in Algiers engineered a rebellion in May 1958 which toppled the regime and brought back de Gaulle. But if the rebels believed that de Gaulle was going to hang onto Algeria they were to be sadly deluded. De Gaulle might have been an erstwhile champion of colonialism, and he might have found the idea of losing to the FLN unpalatable, but he always had a wider perspective. For him Algeria was a burden, blocking all chance of renewal, meaning that eventually he saw no alternative but negotiation with the nationalists. Predictably de Gaulle's perceived betrayal led to a failed military coup in April 1961, as well as the formation of the Secret Army Organization (OAS), an underground movement of rebel officers and civilians, which in the final year of the war led a terror campaign in France and Algeria. The OAS only served to polarize French and Muslim still further, with the result that when independence was achieved in July 1962 there was an immediate exodus of the settlers to France.

For de Gaulle the OAS were lost soldiers who had not faced up to post-1945 realities. In this context after 1962 de Gaulle underlined the need to turn the page in a bold and assertive manner. In the new France, resolutely 'hexagonal' and clearly orientated towards the challenges of economic modernization, the conscripts, along with the million 'repatriated' settlers, now became embarrassing untidy reminders of outdated colonial values. Inasmuch as the government recognized any problem, it was hoped that the combination of consumerism and full employment would soon efface the trauma of decolonization. Henceforth the Algerian war became a taboo subject for the Gaullist regime.

Legacy of empire

De Gaulle might have eventually cast himself as the champion of the Third World, an image reinforced by French recognition of China in 1964 and his denunciation of the Vietnam war in 1966, but beneath the new language it was possible to discern continuities with the colonial epoch. Above all his policy of grandeur assumed that France was still a world power with global responsibilities, even if the yardstick of rank was now nuclear weapons rather than empire, and this has been the viewpoint of all successive presidents, whatever their political colouring. Instrumental in this approach has been the notion of Francophonie, a belief that the French language is the basis of a world culture which in international terms symbolizes a powerful counterweight to Anglo-Saxon domination. This explains why France has invested so much in maintaining links with the ex-colonies, particularly in black Africa. For the French they are vital spheres of influence. Not surprisingly, therefore, critics have found within the talk of partnership and understanding much baser motives. Francophonie, the argument runs, is little more than a neo-colonial façade, old wine in new bottles which, by propping up cooperative local élites, ensures that French interests are slavishly adhered to.

Elsewhere the last remnants of empire have continued to create problems. In New Caledonia, in the Pacific, tension between Melanesian Kanaks and

French settlers flared up into violence in 1988, forcing the government into a referendum which promised a further vote on independence in 10 years. In 1995 President Jacques Chirac's decision to use Mururoa atoll in French Polynesia for nuclear testing was widely greeted as a throwback to colonialism, replicating the way in which the outposts of empire were traditionally regarded as a dumping ground. In domestic terms too the legacy of empire has been no less apparent. One case in point is the plight of the Harkis, those Muslims who fought with the French in the Algerian war. Large numbers were abandoned by the French army and slaughtered as collaborators by the FLN in 1962. Those who escaped to the metropole were left to live in shanty towns in southern France, disowned by the government and shunned by the French populace. Not surprisingly this mistreatment generated huge resentment and in 1991 there were widespread protests by the Harki community, which by this time had grown to some 500000. Likewise bitterness is very obvious amongst the 1 million settlers who returned from Algeria. Like the Harkis, many have had difficulty in integrating into society. Even now many feel like outsiders, angry that they were sold out by de Gaulle.

The upshot of this is that large numbers of former settlers have voted for the extreme-right National Front. In the party leader, Jean-Marie Le Pen, who himself fought in Indo-China and Algeria, many see an expression of their estrangement from mainstream politics. Similarly, within his crude anti-immigrant platform Le Pen echoes their own nostalgia for the colonial order of things. Closed cultures, sovereign nations, self-sufficient and separate races, strong peoples – they warm to the way in which Le Pen's sense of French greatness is laced from end to end with its imperial legacy and past. For him immigration from former colonies is abhorrent because, in diluting the French race, it will produce a nation of misfits.

The success of the National Front, which since 1984 has consistently polled between 10 and 15 per cent of the vote, demonstrates the strength of anti-immigrant, and in particular anti-Algerian, racism. No part of society is immune to its pernicious effects and in this sense it is symptomatic of a colonial syndrome which will endure for many years to come. In formal terms empire might have ended in 1962 but the legacy of the imperial encounter is still painfully visible within contemporary France.

Acknowledgements

I should like to thank the British Academy, which financed the leave necessary for the completion of this chapter.

Notes

1 Quoted in A. Horne, *A Savage War of Peace: Algeria 1954–62* (London: Macmillan, 1977), p. 30.
2 Quoted in E. Said, *Orientalism* (London: Routledge & Kegan Paul, 1978), p. 219.
3 Quoted in R. Aldrich, *Greater France: A History of French Overseas Expansion* (London: Macmillan, 1996), p. 113.
4 Quoted in *ibid.*, p. 115.
5 Quoted in A. Shennan, *Rethinking France: Plans for Renewal 1940–1946* (Oxford: Clarendon Press, 1989), p. 67.

Further reading

Imperialism

Adamthwaite, A. *Grandeur and Misery: France's Bid for Power in Europe, 1914–1940* (London: Edward Arnold, 1995).
Aldrich, R. *Greater France: A History of French Overseas Expansion* (London: Macmillan, 1996).
Chafer, T. and Sackur, A. *The Popular Front and the French Empire* (London: Macmillan, 1999).
Chipman, J. *French Power in Africa* (Oxford: Blackwell, 1989).
Girardet, R. *L'Idée coloniale en France de 1871 à 1964* (Paris: La Table Ronde, 1972).
Hargreaves, A. and Heffernan, M. (eds.), *French and Algerian Identities from Colonial Times to the Present: A Century of Interaction* (Lampeter: Edwin Mellen, 1993).
Hobsbawm, E. *The Age of Empire* (London: Weidenfeld & Nicholson, 1987).
Kiernan, V. *European Empires from Conquest to Collapse* (London: Fontana, 1982).
——, *Imperialism and its Contradictions* (London: Routledge, 1995).
Lebovics, H. *True France: Wars over Cultural Identity 1900–1945* (Ithaca, NY: Cornell University Press, 1992).

Manning, P. *Francophone Sub-Saharan Africa, 1880–1995* (Cambridge: Cambridge University Press, 1988).
Said, E. *Orientalism* (London: Routledge & Kegan Paul, 1978).
——, *Culture and Imperialism* (London: Chatto & Windus, 1993).
Weber, E. *The Hollow Years: France in the 1930s* (London: Sinclair-Stevenson, 1995).

Decolonization

Ageron, C.-R. *La Décolonisation française* (Paris: Armand Colin, 1991).
Betts, R. *France and Decolonisation* (London: Macmillan, 1991).
Clayton, A. *The French Wars of Decolonization* (London: Longman, 1994).
Dalloz, J. *La Guerre d'Indochine* (Paris: Éditions du Seuil, 1987).
Kelly, G. *Lost Soldiers: The French Army and Empire in Crisis, 1947–1962* (Cambridge, MA: MIT Press, 1965).
Marseille, J. *Empire colonial et capitalisme français: histoire d'un divorce* (Paris: Albin Michel, 1986).
Marshall, B. D. *The French Colonial Myth and Constitution Making in the Fourth Republic* (New Haven: Yale University Press, 1973).
Shennan, A. *Rethinking France: Plans for Renewal 1940–1946* (Oxford: Clarendon Press, 1989).

Algerian war

Dine, P. *Images of the Algerian War: French Fiction and Film 1954–1992* (Oxford: Clarendon Press, 1994).
Evans, M. *The Memory of Resistance: French Opposition to the Algerian War 1954–62* (Oxford: Berg, 1997).
Harrison, A. *Challenging de Gaulle: The OAS and the Counter-Revolution in Algeria, 1954–1962* (New York: Praeger, 1989).
Horne, A. *A Savage War of Peace: Algeria, 1954–62* (London: Macmillan, 1977).
Kettle, M. *De Gaulle and Algeria, 1940–1960* (London: Quartet, 1993).
Maran, R. *Torture and the Role of Ideology: The French–Algerian War* (London: Greenwood Press, 1989).
Talbott, J. *The War Without a Name: France in Algeria, 1954–1962* (London: Faber & Faber, 1981).

Legacy of empire

Hargreaves, A. *Immigration in Post-War France: A Documentary Anthology* (London: Methuen, 1987).

——, *Immigration, 'Race' and Ethnicity in Contemporary France* (London: Routledge, 1995).

MacMaster, N. *Colonial Migrants and Racism: Algerians in France, 1900–62* (London: Macmillan, 1997).

Silverman, M. *Deconstructing the Nation: Immigration, Racism and Citizenship in Modern France* (London: Routledge, 1992).

Stora, B. *La Gangrène et l'oubli: la mémoire de la guerre d'Algérie* (Paris: La Découverte, 1992).

Index

Note: index covers pages 31–412 and is arranged in alphabetical order word by word. In French titles the article is ignored for alphabetization. Page numbers in italics refer to illustrations; those in bold refer to main sections on the topic.